Y0-DKM-065

FOR ALL
PALESTINIANS,
PAST, PRESENT,
AND FUTURE

**MAY THESE
VISUALS ONE DAY
BE ARTIFACTS FOR
FREE GENERATIONS
TO REMEMBER
THE JOURNEY
TO JUSTICE**

VISUALIZING**PALESTINE**

A CHRONICLE OF COLONIALISM & THE STRUGGLE FOR LIBERATION

Edited by Aline Batarseh, Jessica Anderson, and Yosra El Gazzar

Haymarket Books | Chicago, Illinois

Published in 2024 by
Haymarket Books
P.O. Box 180165
Chicago, IL 60618
www.haymarketbooks.org

ISBN: 979-8-88890-250-9

Distributed to the trade in the US through Consortium Book Sales and Distribution (www.cbsd.com) and internationally through Ingram Publisher Services International (www.ingramcontent.com).

This book was published with the generous support of Lannan Foundation, Wallace Action Fund, and Marguerite Casey Foundation.

Special discounts are available for bulk purchases by organizations and institutions. Please email info@haymarketbooks.org for more information.

Cover artwork by Yosra El Gazzar.

Printed in Canada by union labor.

Library of Congress Cataloging-in-Publication data is available.

10 9 8 7 6 5 4 3 2 1

MIX
Paper from
responsible sources
FSC® C103567
FSC
www.fsc.org

GCC/IBT

CONTENTS

INTRODUC

CTION

> **The English word "demonstration" has at least two meanings: one refers to the public act of protest—to march, rally, declare or express an opinion—and the other is to do with showing, with making something manifest or apparent in order to instruct or display. The Arabic *muthahara*, the Persian *tathaharat*, the French *manifestation*, the Italian *manifestazione* and the Spanish *manifestación*—all, regardless of their variant linguistic roots, agree that in a demonstration there are at least these two sides: one concerned with making something apparent and the other with objection. . . . This seems to make perfect sense: one could argue that in order to protest one needs to make something clear.**
>
> —*Hisham Matar,* A Month in Siena *(2019)*

This book spans more than a decade of work by Visualizing Palestine to demonstrate the urgency of the Palestinian struggle for freedom, justice, and equality. We focus on shifting narratives, recognizing that Palestine has been the subject of a century of colonial narratives designed to obscure, justify, and perpetuate oppression. The visuals in this book reflect the collaboration of dozens of people spanning continents and contributing different skill sets. Together, we create visual stories to nourish education, advocacy, organizing, and collective action for Palestinian liberation.

Visualizing Palestine debuted in 2012 with **Hunger Strikes** (pg. 198–99). We published this infographic as Palestinian political prisoner Khader Adnan, who was being held in an Israeli jail without charge or trial, was on his sixty-sixth day of hunger strike and reportedly near death.[1] Hunger Strikes uplifted Palestinian civil resistance as part of a resounding, universal human story of overcoming injustice. As an infographic distributed primarily online, it signified the nascent promise of social media to bring stories of Palestine directly to the masses, changing how people around the world engage with communities impacted by injustice.

Khader Adnan spent six years of his life in prison without charge and undertook five hunger strikes.[2] In May 2023, more than a decade after Hunger Strikes was published and just a few days before the seventy-fifth anniversary of the mass displacement of Palestinians known as the Nakba, he died as a result of medical neglect in an Israeli prison. His body had endured eighty-seven days without food.[3] With Khader Adnan's death, Hunger Strikes became part of the story of what the Palestinian collective body has endured while calling for freedom.

Today, Visualizing Palestine continues to specialize in deeply researched, visually compelling narrative interventions, with the goal of making Palestinian perspectives more accessible as part of wider anticolonial and antiracist narratives. We are determined to build on the significant progress the movement has made to mainstream understanding of settler colonialism and apartheid, key frameworks through which Palestinians understand their oppression. So far, people in seventy-six countries have self-reported accessing our resources via our website. Student groups are particularly active, using our visuals across more than a hundred college campuses. Educators use them to supplement curriculums at universities and high schools. Activists incorporate them into campaigns for boycott, divestment, and sanctions, movement education activities, and protests. People of multiple faiths use them to advance theologies centered on justice for the oppressed. Thanks to volunteers, the visuals exist in twenty-four languages beyond our two core languages of production, English and Arabic.

The movement for Palestinian liberation is growing more organized and impactful, but we also see conditions on the ground worsening for Palestinians. As we were curating this book in 2022, more Palestinians were killed by Israeli forces than in any prior year since 2005. Countless others endured escalating Israeli settler violence, home demolitions, poverty, and despair.[4] Amid these conditions, Israeli forces stormed the offices of seven Palestinian human rights organizations as part of a campaign of repression and intimidation against Palestinian civil society.[5]

In October 2023, we rewrote parts of this introduction as we witnessed the start of another Nakba-scale crisis in Palestine. In the first seven weeks of Israel's bombardment of Gaza, we saw Israeli forces kill more Palestinians than in the previous thirty-four years combined. In the months that followed, each morning brought

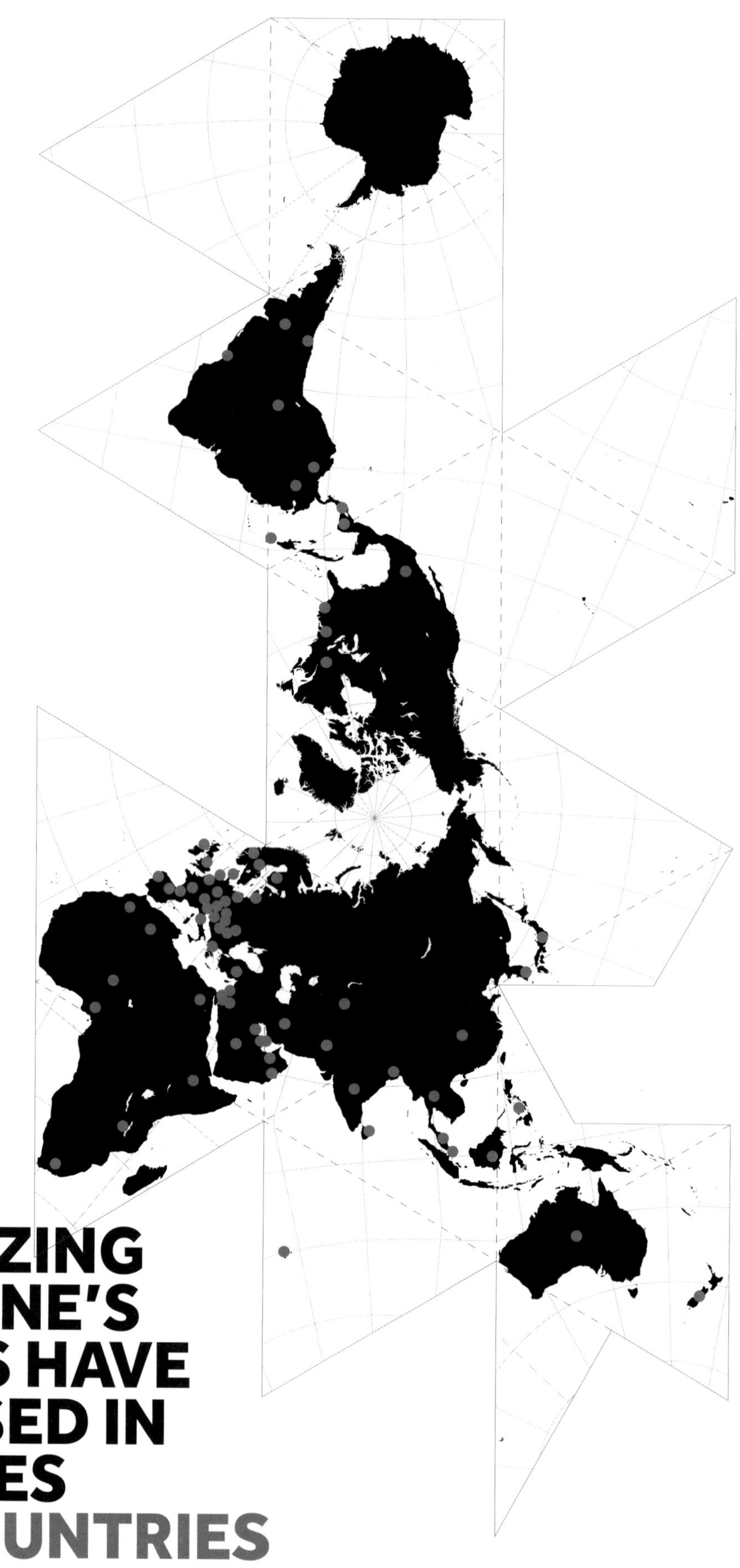

Since March 2015

VISUALIZING PALESTINE'S VISUALS HAVE BEEN USED IN 577 CITIES IN 76 COUNTRIES

SOURCE bit.ly/vp-global-movement

devastation as the numbers of Palestinians killed, missing in the rubble, injured, displaced, thirsty, starving, and sick climbed beyond comprehension and as governments failed in their duty to prevent "a textbook case of genocide."[6] Visuals we published became outdated almost instantly, and requests for updates poured in hourly.

In her essay "No Place for Self-Pity, No Room for Fear," novelist Toni Morrison recounts feeling too helpless to write amid the US war on Iraq and the reelection of George W. Bush. A friend tells her, "No! No, no, no! This is precisely the time when artists go to work—not when everything is fine, but in times of dread." These are times of dread indeed, but this is not unfamiliar terrain for any community that has struggled for freedom. It is widely understood that times of crisis open up possibilities for transformation. These are the possibilities we will keep pursuing relentlessly.

This book is a living reflection of the opportunities and challenges that come with using research and data to capture injustice and promote liberation. In English, the word "number" contains within it the word "numb." The human brain is not designed to comprehend mass atrocities, yet we seem to give numbers immense power to describe reality. What approaches render the scale of violations legible, while honoring the specificity of people's individual stories? What are the limits of our imagination and visual vocabulary in demonstrating systems of oppression that have been purposely designed to be invisible, fragmented, and opaque? How do we navigate gaps in data, and truths that cannot be measured or counted? And how can our knowledge effectively support transformative action?

We are working in a context where harmful narratives sustain systemic oppression against Palestinians, keeping people too confused, distracted, tired, helpless, or fearful to act. Since the Nakba in 1948, Israeli policies and practices have continuously sought to dispossess Palestinians not only of their territory, but also of their story as a people, treating dissenting narratives as an existential threat. Israeli authorities block access to historical archives, pass legislation to suppress commemoration of the Nakba, restrict Palestinians' right to protest, spend millions on public relations campaigns, run a government office dedicated to combating the boycott, divestment, and sanctions movement, ban Palestinian flags from public spaces, coordinate disinformation and smear attacks against outspoken people and organizations, and more. Despite the enormity of these tactics, our message for freedom and justice is breaking through.

Collaboration is a core feature of our process. Drawing on a brain trust of dedicated people, we are able to assemble the building blocks of facts, stories, and visuals into a justice-based narrative. Researchers, designers, lawyers, human rights defenders, organizers, artists, architects, entrepreneurs, communications specialists, outreach specialists, web developers, translators, project managers, and administrators are among those whose knowledge and skills have shaped the messages in this book and our overall strategy. Some of the earliest tools we created to facilitate collaboration, the Brief Template and Process Wheel, are included in the annex.

We are grateful to every person who makes this work possible, directly or indirectly: the dissenters and justice-seekers who came before us; the vision nurtured by our cofounders, Ramzi Jaber and Joumana al Jabri; the process established by early partners Ahmad Barclay, Hani Asfour, and Naji El Mir; the contributions of a growing network of current and former team members (see acknowledgments); the researchers and experts behind the hundreds of books, articles, reports, statistics, databases, maps, and analyses we reference in our visuals; the generosity of volunteers, partners, strategists, and friends; each person who has carried these visuals into spaces of education, advocacy, and action; and the many inspiring groups who strive every day toward freedom for all of us.

We hope that this book can be a source of inspiration and imagination as we work for a world in which these visuals are obsolete, not because they need to be updated with even more dire figures, but because the fundamental conditions of oppression have given way to justice.

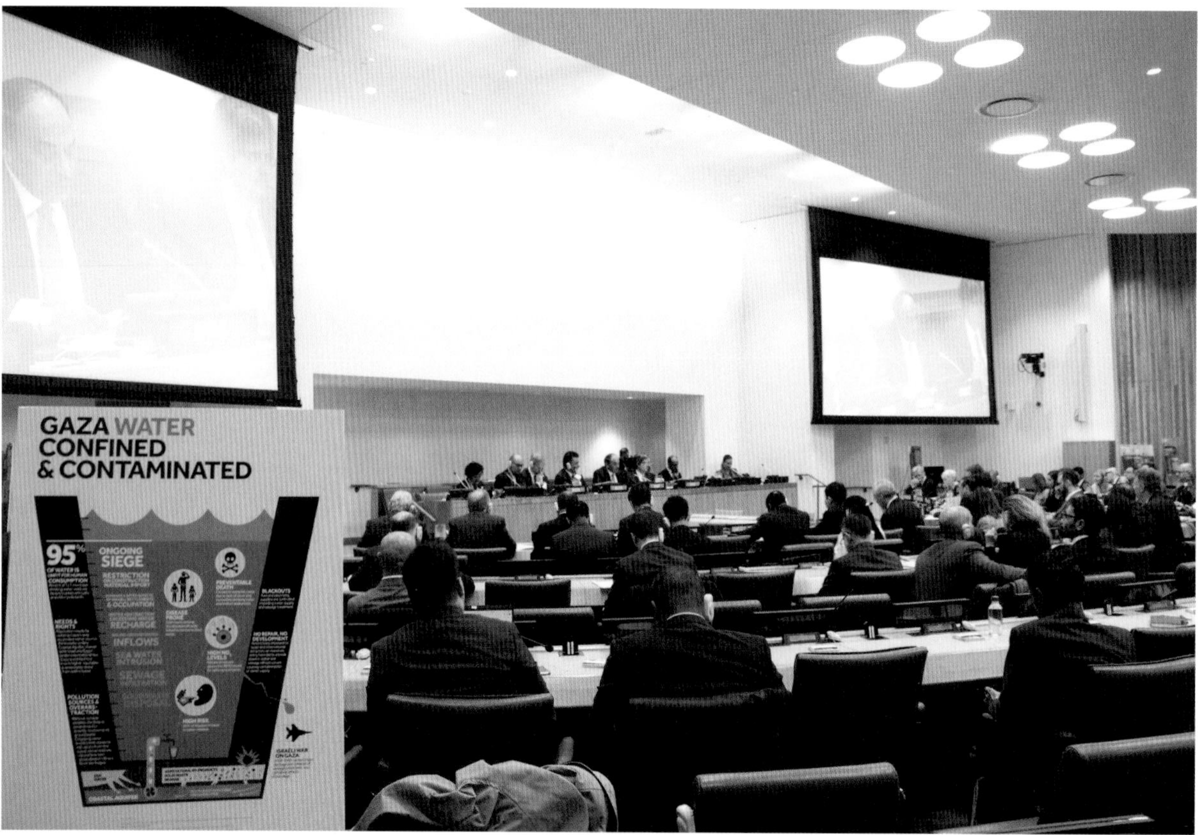
GAZA WATER
CONFINED
& CONTAMINATED
95%
ONGOING
SIEGE
INFLOWS

Exhibit posted by the Kuwait Mission to the United Nations at an informal meeting of members of the United Nations Security Council in New York, United States, 2018.

Visitors pick up Visualizing Palestine posters at the Palestinian Museum, Birzeit, Palestine, 2019.

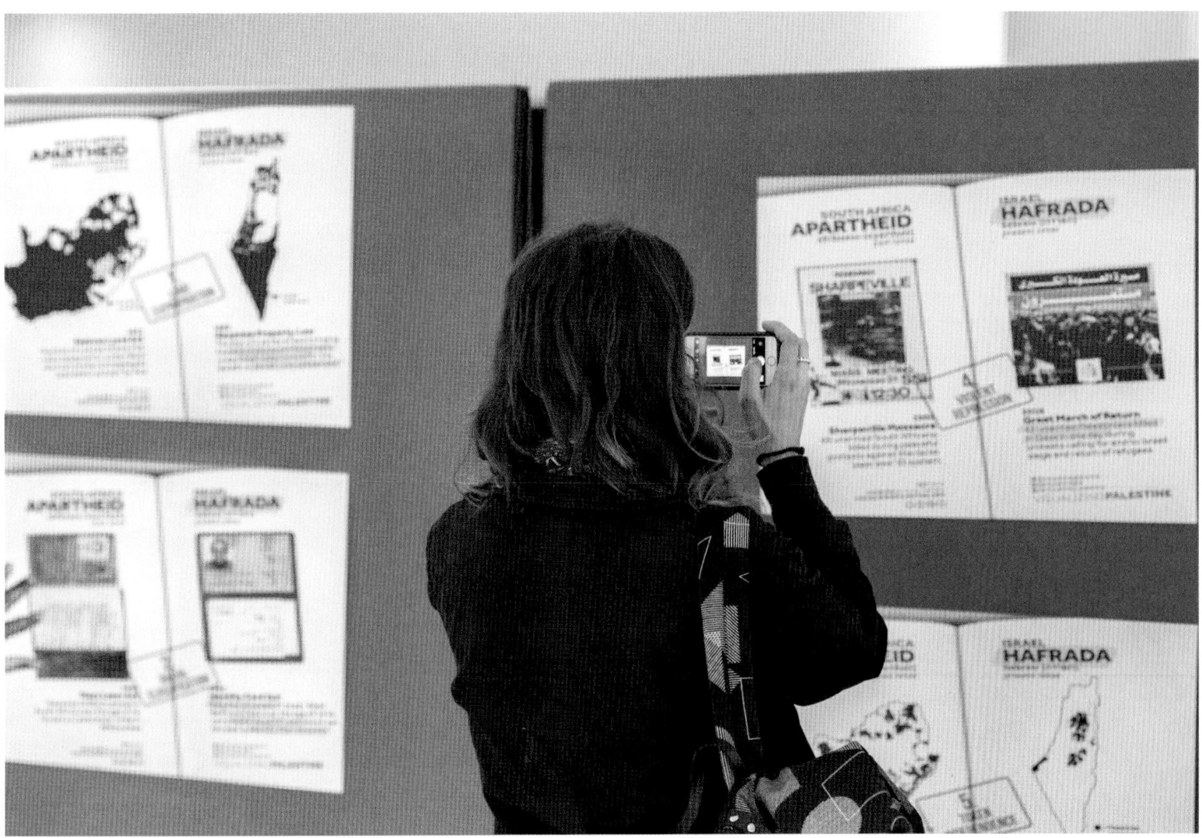
SOUTH AFRICA
APARTHEID
ISRAEL
HAFRADA
SHARPEVILLE
HAFRADA

Exhibition organized by the Palestine Solidarity Campaign, United Kingdom, 2018.

U.S. TAXPAYERS
FUNDED 670 MILLION
WEAPONS FOR ISRAEL
between 2000 and 2009
During these years
THE ISRAELI MILITARY
KILLED AT LEAST 2,960
UNARMED PALESTINIANS
END $30 BILLION OF MILITARY AID TO ISRAEL
END THE
OCCUPATION
VISUALIZINGPALESTINE
find out more at aidtoisrael.org
MT. VERNON
800
RAM 1500

Display during the American Israel Public Affairs Committee (AIPAC) conference in Washington, DC, United States, 2013.

MUSICIANS STAND FOR JUSTICE
Initiated by Palestinian civil society in 2005, the cultural boycott of Israel invites artists to stand in solidarity with human rights. This visual features a selection of musicians who have cancelled, or declined to schedule, appearances in Israel or at events sponsored by Israeli institutions that support the oppression of Palestinians.
DID NOT SCHEDULE EVENT
ENDORSED THE BOYCOTT
CANCELLED EVENT
RESPONDED TO CALL FOR BOYCOTT
UNSPECIFIED POSITION
SPOTIFY LISTENERS PER MONTH
1,000,000+
<1,000,000
<500,000
<150,000
<30,000
VISUALIZINGPALESTINE
PALESTINE
PALESTINE
PALESTINE
PALESTINE

Organizers in Amsterdam, Netherlands, call for a boycott of the Eurovision Song Contest, which was hosted in Israel in 2019. Photo: Nour Sadat

THE PEGASUS EFFECT

Human rights advocates from Al-Haq present at a session of the United Nations Human Rights Council in Geneva, Switzerland, 2022.

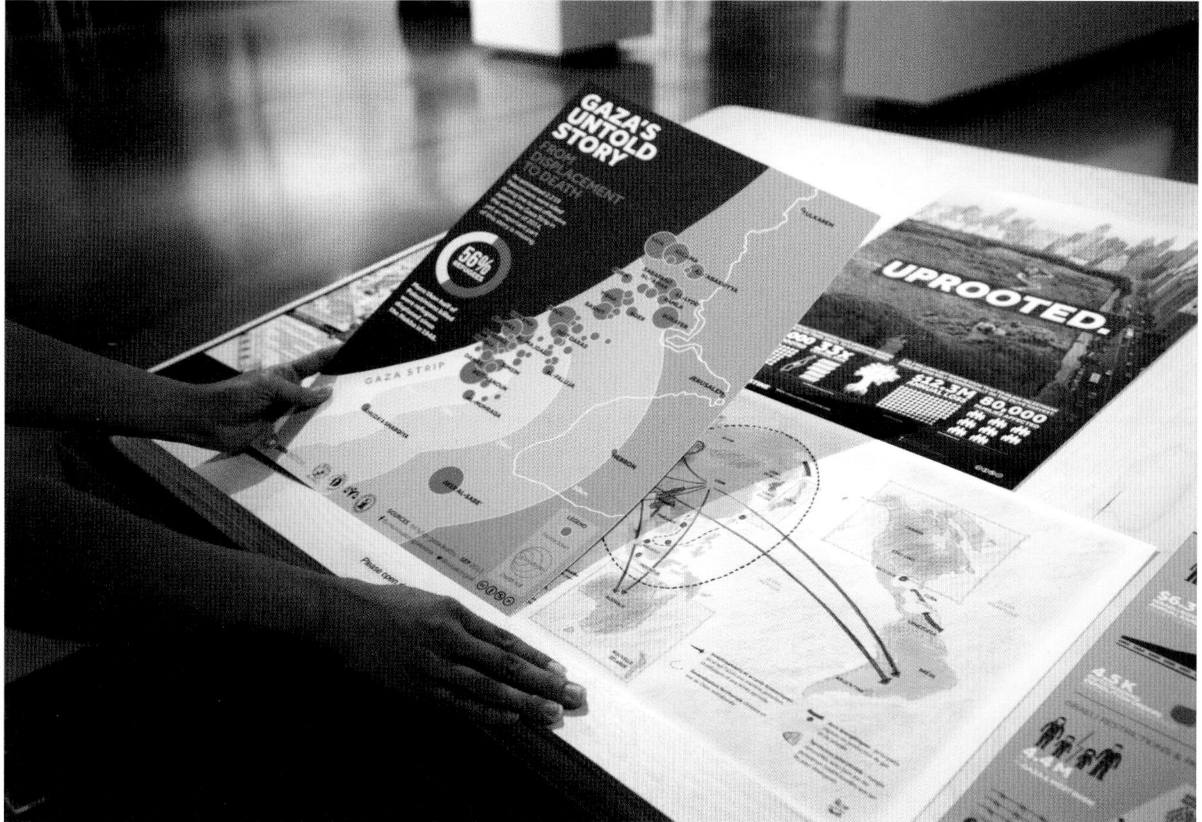
GAZA'S UNTOLD STORY
FROM DISPLACEMENT TO DEATH
56%
GAZA STRIP
JERUSALEM
HEBRON
UPROOTED.
80,000

Diagrams of Power exhibit at OCAD University, Toronto, Canada, 2018.

An exhibition at the Netherlands-Flemish Institute in Cairo, Egypt, 2019.

HOTEL
Stirling Sports
BOYCOTT PUMA
PROUD SPONSORS OF ISRAELI APARTHEID
PLAT
THE TEAM THAT COULD HAVE BEEN
FREE PALESTINE
FIGHT APARTHEID

Activists in Wellington, New Zealand, call for a boycott of Puma over its sponsorship of the Israeli Football Association, which includes teams and matches in illegal Israeli settlements, 2019.

A SYSTEM OF SILENCING
KILLING THE STORY

Visualizing Palestine exhibition at the Toronto Palestine Film Festival, Canada, 2023.

1. SETTLER COLONIAL

Visuals in this section: Palestine Shrinking, Expanding Israel | Settler Colonialism Is Still a Reality | The Zionist Colonization of Palestine | A History of Occupation | Palestinian and Israeli Deaths | Rising Israeli Settler Violence in the Occupied West Bank | Timeline of Violence since 1988 | Fatalities Data Statement | 20 Years of Mourning

ISM

To say "settler colonialism" is to name a distinctive phenomenon in which the settler arrives with the intent to stay and supplant native sovereignty—not merely to rule, but to replace through forced assimilation, geographical containment, juridical erasure, and killing.

—Noura Erakat and John Reynolds, "Understanding Apartheid" in Jewish Currents *(2022)*

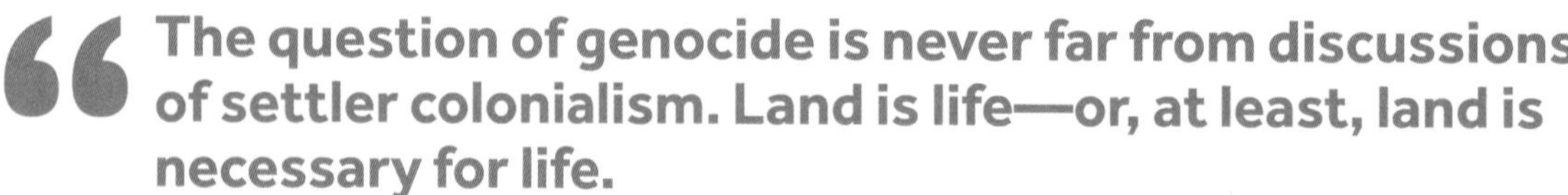

The question of genocide is never far from discussions of settler colonialism. Land is life—or, at least, land is necessary for life.

—Patrick Wolfe, "Settler Colonialism and the Elimination of the Native" in the Journal of Genocide Research *(2006)*

The Palestinian people's right to freedom is no more or less complicated than any other people's. We trace the roots of the Palestinian struggle to European colonialism, which is responsible for settler-colonial projects in Canada, the United States, Australia, New Zealand, South Africa, Palestine, and other territories.

We created two visuals to introduce settler colonialism: **Palestine Shrinking, Expanding Israel** and **Settler Colonialism Is Still a Reality**. We adapted Palestine Shrinking, Expanding Israel from a series of maps activists have used for decades to show how Israeli rule has confined Palestinians to ever-diminishing fragments of their land. These maps communicate that domination over land is at the heart of settler colonialism.[1] In much of our work, maps have been an important tool toward what Palestinian scholar Edward Said described as "reading Zionism from below," "from the standpoint of its victims."[2]

The first map in Palestine Shrinking, Expanding Israel dates to 1918, one year after British Foreign Secretary Arthur Balfour declared his government's support for a "national home for Jews" in Palestine. At that time, British rule extended over about a quarter of the world population, including Palestinians. Balfour supported the Zionist project because he felt it would "mitigate the age long miseries created for Western civilization by the presence in its midst of a Body which it too long regarded as alien, even hostile," referring to Jewish communities in Europe.[3] Balfour's antisemitic views also come across in a 1905 law he advanced to restrict Jewish immigration to Great Britain.[4] Of Palestinians, Balfour wrote, "We do not propose even to go through the form of consulting the wishes of the present inhabitants of the country."[5] These words mark the start of more than a century of erasure and dispossession for Palestinians.

Theodor Herzl, often called "the father of political Zionism," wrote in 1896 that Israel would be "a rampart of Europe against Asia, an outpost of civilization as opposed to barbarism."[6] His words reflect the ideological link between European white supremacy and Zionism, the political movement to form a Jewish ethnostate in Palestine at a time when more than 90 percent of its native population was not Jewish. Herzl and other early Zionist leaders understood that their project would involve the removal, or "transfer," of Palestinians. "If I wish to substitute a new building for an old one, I must demolish before I construct," he wrote.[7] In **The Zionist Colonization of Palestine**, we look at the history of Zionist settlement across historic Palestine. Importantly, this visual shows the settlement of Palestine as a continuous phenomenon, from the events leading up to the Nakba to the continuous expansion of illegal Israeli settlements today.

In the years after gaining control of 78 percent of historic Palestine in 1948, the Israeli regime pursued further territorial expansion. **A History of Occupation** shows the ever-shifting geography of Israeli military rule. As of this writing, Israel exercises de facto control over the entirety of historic Palestine and the Syrian Golan Heights.

In a system set up to ensure continued Israeli domination, Palestinians experience unrelenting violence. Paulo Freire tells us in his foundational work of critical pedagogy that violence begins with the relationship of oppression itself. In his view:

> Never in history has violence been initiated by the oppressed. . . . There would be no oppressed had there been no prior situation of violence to establish their subjugation. Violence is initiated by those who oppress, who exploit, who fail to recognize others as persons.[8]

While the human cost of colonialism cannot be measured by fatalities data alone (especially when that data is only documented back to 1988), **Palestinian and Israeli Deaths**; **Rising Israeli Settler Violence in the Occupied West Bank**; **Timeline of Violence since 1988**; **Fatalities Data Statement**; and **20 Years of Mourning** are all efforts to capture the vast asymmetry of violence enacted by settler states on colonized peoples. Sometimes, the systematized violence of settler colonialism unfolds incrementally, while other times it erupts into "genocidal moments" of mass killing and expulsion, as we are witnessing at the time of writing this book.[9]

PALESTINE **SHRINKING**

1918

UNDER OTTOMAN RULE, ZIONIST ORGANISATIONS, INCLUDING THE JEWISH NATIONAL FUND, BEGIN TO MAKE **LAND PURCHASES THROUGHOUT PALESTINE** FOR JEWISH SETTLEMENT.

1947

PRIVATISATION OF LAND UNDER THE BRITISH MANDATE **ACCELERATES ITS TRANSFER AND SALE TO ZIONIST ORGANISATIONS,** AND THE DISPLACEMENT OF PALESTINIAN INHABITANTS.

SOURCES

Text based on

BADIL, 2000. **Land Ownership In Palestine/Isra**
BADIL, 2012. **Living Land: Population Transfer**
B'Tselem, 2010. **By Hook And By Crook: Israeli**

VISUALIZING**PALESTINE**

WWW.VISUALIZINGPALES
SHARE AND DISTRIBUTE FR

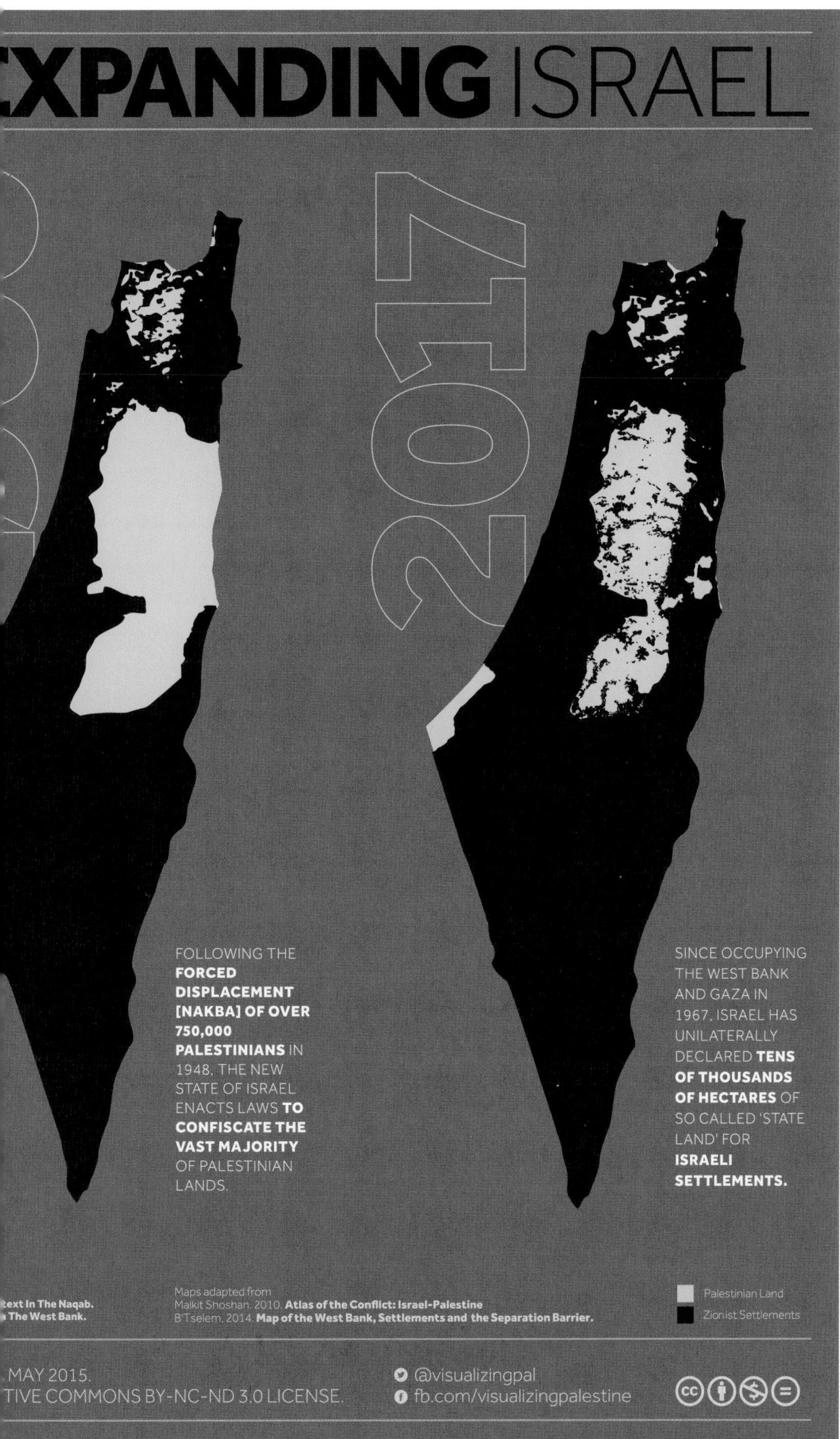
XPANDING ISRAEL
2017
FOLLOWING THE **FORCED DISPLACEMENT [NAKBA] OF OVER 750,000 PALESTINIANS** IN 1948, THE NEW STATE OF ISRAEL ENACTS LAWS **TO CONFISCATE THE VAST MAJORITY** OF PALESTINIAN LANDS.
SINCE OCCUPYING THE WEST BANK AND GAZA IN 1967, ISRAEL HAS UNILATERALLY DECLARED **TENS OF THOUSANDS OF HECTARES** OF SO CALLED 'STATE LAND' FOR **ISRAELI SETTLEMENTS.**
ext In The Naqab.
The West Bank.
Maps adapted from
Malkit Shoshan, 2010. **Atlas of the Conflict: Israel-Palestine**
B'Tselem, 2014. **Map of the West Bank, Settlements and the Separation Barrier.**
Palestinian Land
Zionist Settlements
MAY 2015.
TIVE COMMONS BY-NC-ND 3.0 LICENSE.
@visualizingpal
fb.com/visualizingpalestine

Year: 2015
Brief and copywriting: Joumana al Jabri, Ahmad Barclay, Ramzi Jaber
Design: Hani Asfour
Sources: bit.ly/vp-Sources-2012-2015

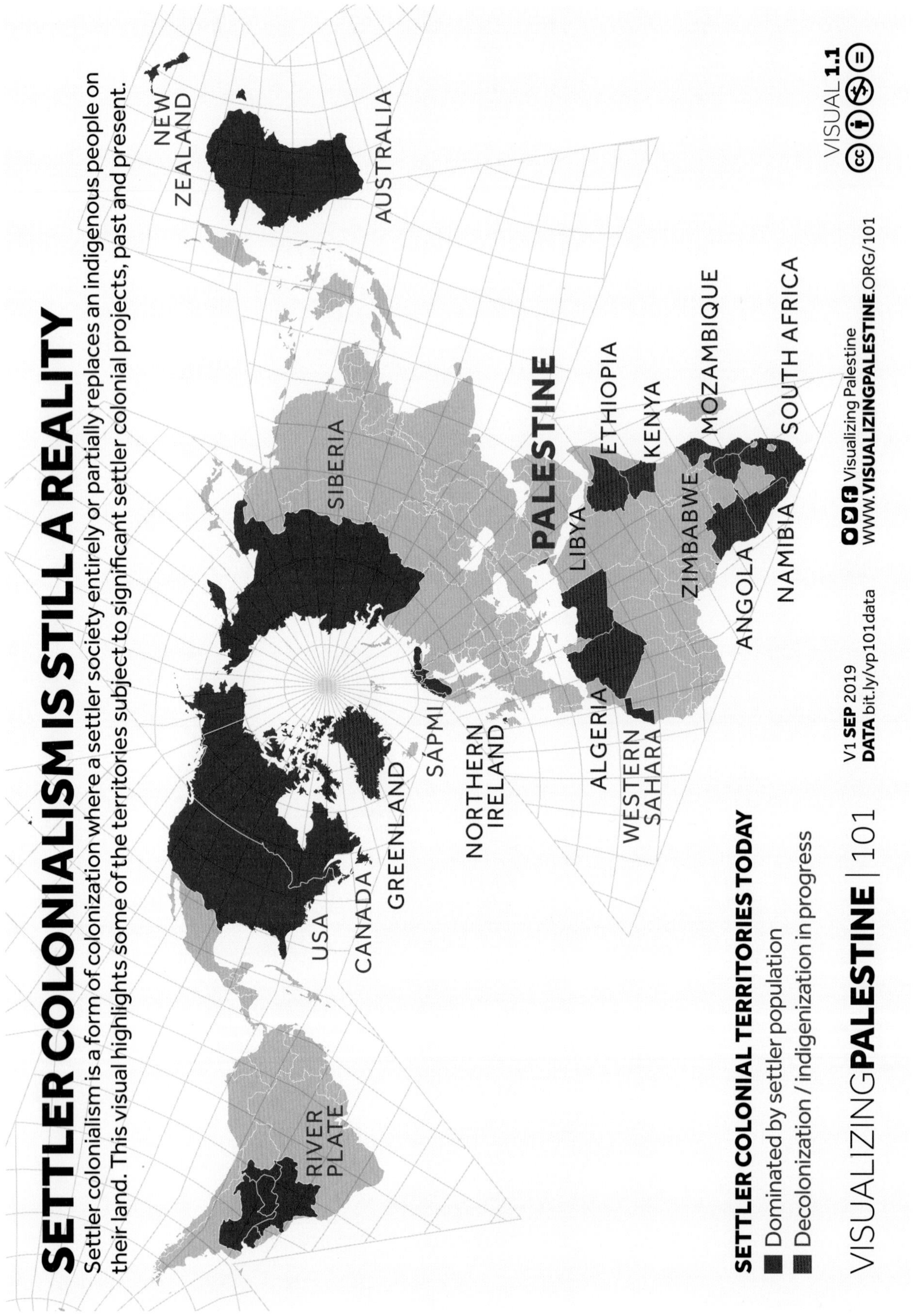

SETTLER COLONIALISM IS STILL A REALITY

Settler colonialism is a form of colonization where a settler society entirely or partially replaces an indigenous people on their land. This visual highlights some of the territories subject to significant settler colonial projects, past and present.

RIVER PLATE
USA
CANADA
GREENLAND
SÁPMI
NORTHERN IRELAND
ALGERIA
WESTERN SAHARA
LIBYA
PALESTINE
ETHIOPIA
KENYA
ZIMBABWE
ANGOLA
NAMIBIA
MOZAMBIQUE
SOUTH AFRICA
SIBERIA
NEW ZEALAND
AUSTRALIA

SETTLER COLONIAL TERRITORIES TODAY
- Dominated by settler population
- Decolonization / indigenization in progress

VISUALIZING**PALESTINE** | 101

V1 **SEP** 2019
DATA bit.ly/vp101data

Visualizing Palestine
WWW.**VISUALIZINGPALESTINE**.ORG/101

VISUAL **1.1**

Year: 2019 | **Brief and copywriting:** Ahmad Barclay | **Design:** Ahmad Barclay, Yosra El Gazzar | **Sources:** bit.ly/vp101data

THE ZIONIST COLONIZATION OF PALESTINE

● Zionist/Israeli locality ● Pre-existing/Palestinian locality

1882
First Zionist colony Rishon LeZion established under Ottoman rule

1947
Extent of Zionist colonization by end of British Mandate period

1966
Israeli colonization of lands expropriated from Palestinians in the Nakba

TODAY
Israeli colonization of occupied West Bank, Gaza and Golan Heights

VISUALIZING**PALESTINE** | 101

V1 **SEP** 2019
DATA bit.ly/vp101data

Visualizing Palestine
WWW.**VISUALIZINGPALESTINE**.ORG/101

VISUAL **1.3**

Year: 2019 | **Brief and copywriting:** Ahmad Barclay | **Design:** Ahmad Barclay, Yosra El Gazzar | **Sources:** bit.ly/vp101data

A HISTORY OF

ISRAELI TERRITORIAL CONTROL

In its short history, the State of Israel has not only occupied Palestinian land, but also the sovereign territory of 3 of its 4 neighboring countries. Today, Israel continues to occupy land in Syria, Lebanon, and Palestine.

South
Lebanon
1982–2000*
Golan
Syria
1967–present
Israel
1948–present**
West Bank
1967–present
Gaza
1967–present
Sinai
Egypt
1967–1982
80K km²
Land Area

*Israel continues to occupy the Shebaa Farms region of South Lebanon.

**The State of Israel was established on Palestinian land, displacing 700,000 indigenous people.

VP DATA SKETCH

SOURCES bit.ly/vp-occup

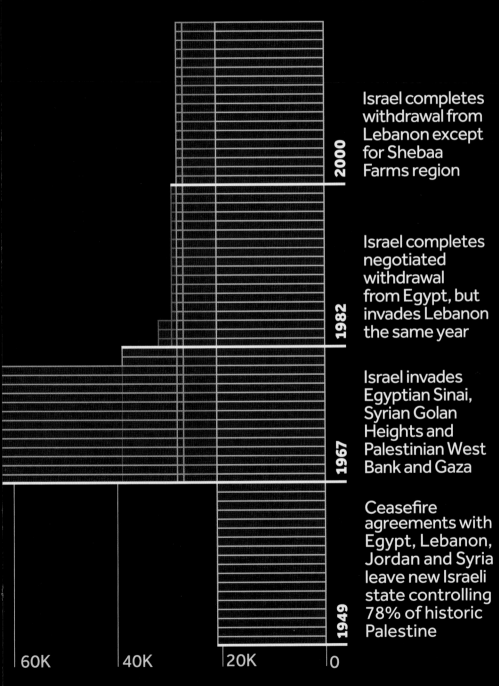

CCUPATION
2000
Israel completes withdrawal from Lebanon except for Shebaa Farms region
1982
Israel completes negotiated withdrawal from Egypt, but invades Lebanon the same year
1967
Israel invades Egyptian Sinai, Syrian Golan Heights and Palestinian West Bank and Gaza
1949
Ceasefire agreements with Egypt, Lebanon, Jordan and Syria leave new Israeli state controlling 78% of historic Palestine
60K
40K
20K
0
E 2017 • fb.me/visualizingpalestine • @visualizingpal

Year: 2017
Brief and copywriting: Ahmad Barclay, Reem Farah, Robin Jones
Design: Ahmad Barclay, Yosra El Gazzar
Sources: bit.ly/vp-occupied

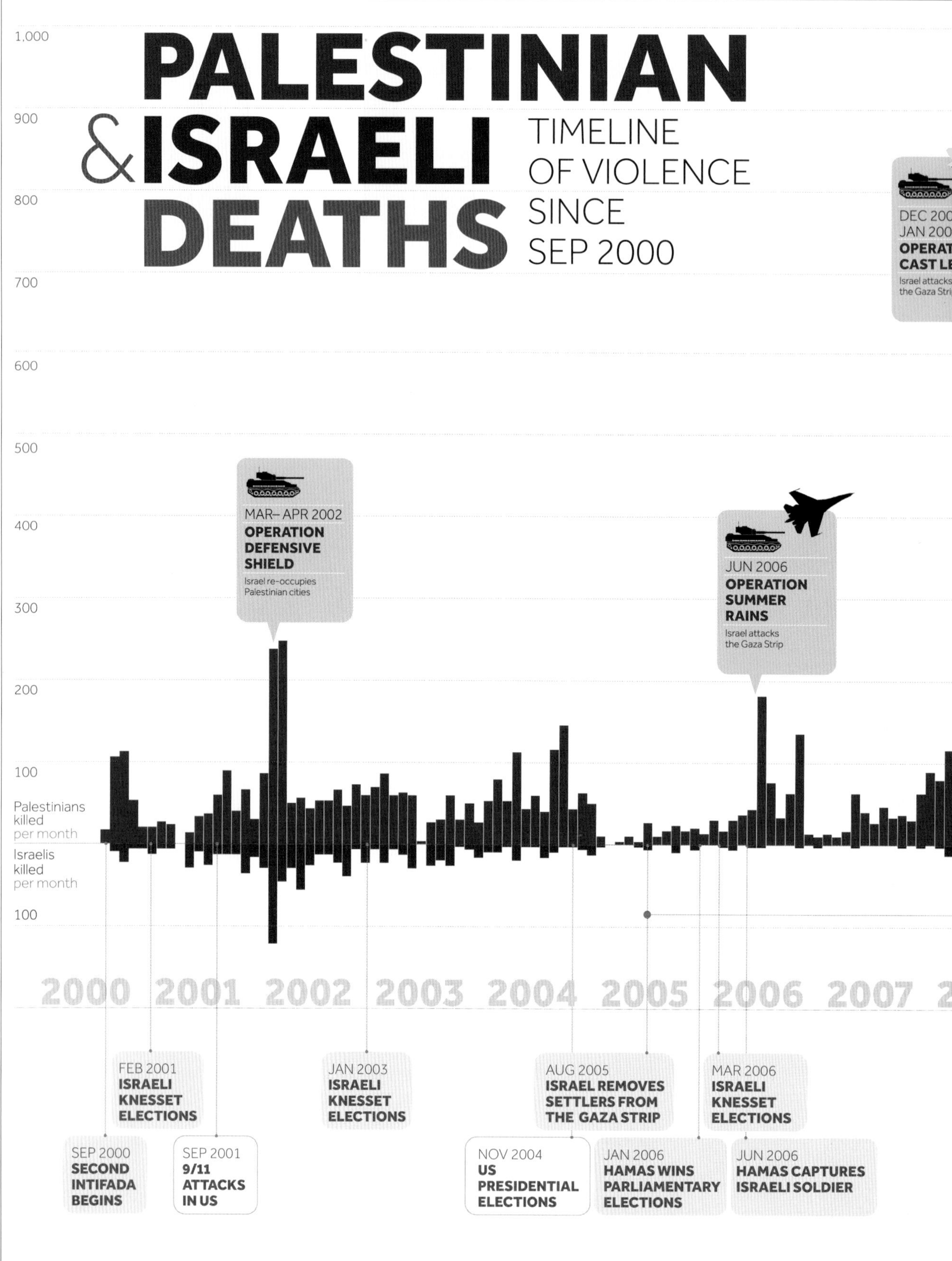
1,000
900
800
700
600
500
400
300
200
100
Palestinians killed per month
Israelis killed per month
100
PALESTINIAN &ISRAELI DEATHS
TIMELINE OF VIOLENCE SINCE SEP 2000
MAR–APR 2002
OPERATION DEFENSIVE SHIELD
Israel re-occupies Palestinian cities
JUN 2006
OPERATION SUMMER RAINS
Israel attacks the Gaza Strip
2000 2001 2002 2003 2004 2005 2006 2007
SEP 2000
SECOND INTIFADA BEGINS
FEB 2001
ISRAELI KNESSET ELECTIONS
SEP 2001
9/11 ATTACKS IN US
JAN 2003
ISRAELI KNESSET ELECTIONS
NOV 2004
US PRESIDENTIAL ELECTIONS
AUG 2005
ISRAEL REMOVES SETTLERS FROM THE GAZA STRIP
JAN 2006
HAMAS WINS PARLIAMENTARY ELECTIONS
MAR 2006
ISRAELI KNESSET ELECTIONS
JUN 2006
HAMAS CAPTURES ISRAELI SOLDIER
VISUALIZINGPALESTINE
WWW.VISUALIZINGPALESTINE.ORG. NOVEMBER 2012
SHARE AND DISTRIBUTE FREELY. CREATIVE COMMONS BY-NC-ND 3.0 LICENSE.
SOURCES
B'Tselem Statistics on Fatalities, http://www.btselem.org/statistics.
Palestinians. It does not include data on foreign nationals or 'friendly fire'
* Nancy Kanwisher et al, 2009, Reigniting Violence: How Do Ceasefires

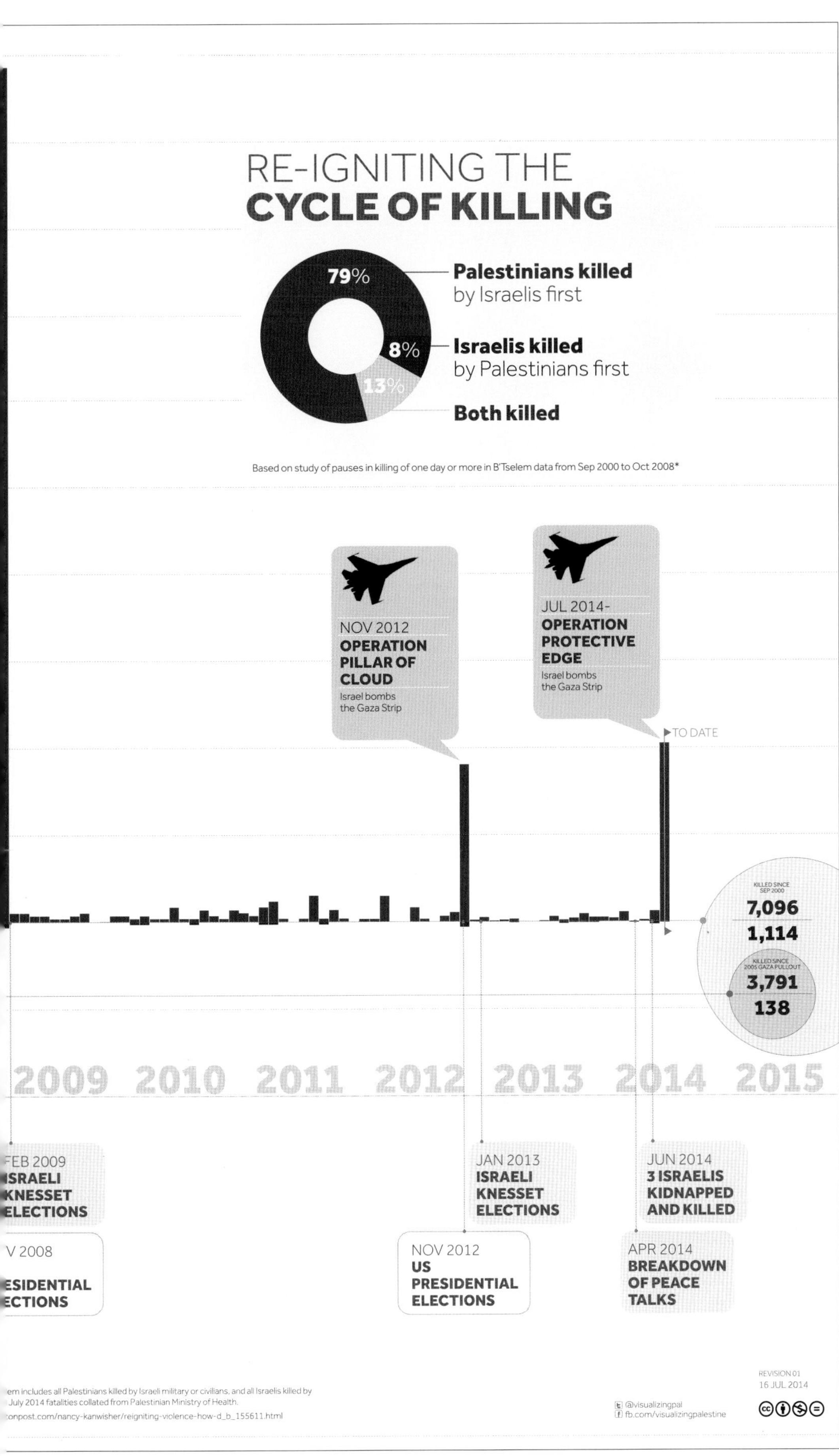
RE-IGNITING THE
CYCLE OF KILLING
79%
8%
13%
Palestinians killed by Israelis first
Israelis killed by Palestinians first
Both killed
Based on study of pauses in killing of one day or more in B'Tselem data from Sep 2000 to Oct 2008*
NOV 2012
OPERATION PILLAR OF CLOUD
Israel bombs the Gaza Strip
JUL 2014-
OPERATION PROTECTIVE EDGE
Israel bombs the Gaza Strip
TO DATE
KILLED SINCE SEP 2000
7,096
1,114
KILLED SINCE 2005 GAZA PULLOUT
3,791
138
2009
2010
2011
2012
2013
2014
2015
FEB 2009
ISRAELI KNESSET ELECTIONS
V 2008
ESIDENTIAL
ECTIONS
NOV 2012
US PRESIDENTIAL ELECTIONS
JAN 2013
ISRAELI KNESSET ELECTIONS
APR 2014
BREAKDOWN OF PEACE TALKS
JUN 2014
3 ISRAELIS KIDNAPPED AND KILLED
em includes all Palestinians killed by Israeli military or civilians, and all Israelis killed by
July 2014 fatalities collated from Palestinian Ministry of Health.
:onpost.com/nancy-kanwisher/reigniting-violence-how-d_b_155611.html
@visualizingpal
fb.com/visualizingpalestine
REVISION 01
16 JUL 2014

Year: 2014
Brief and copywriting: Joumana al Jabri, Ahmad Barclay, Christopher Fiorello, Ramzi Jaber
Design: Hani Asfour, Ahmad Barclay
Update: Patil Tchilinguirian
Sources: bit.ly/vp-Sources-2012-2015

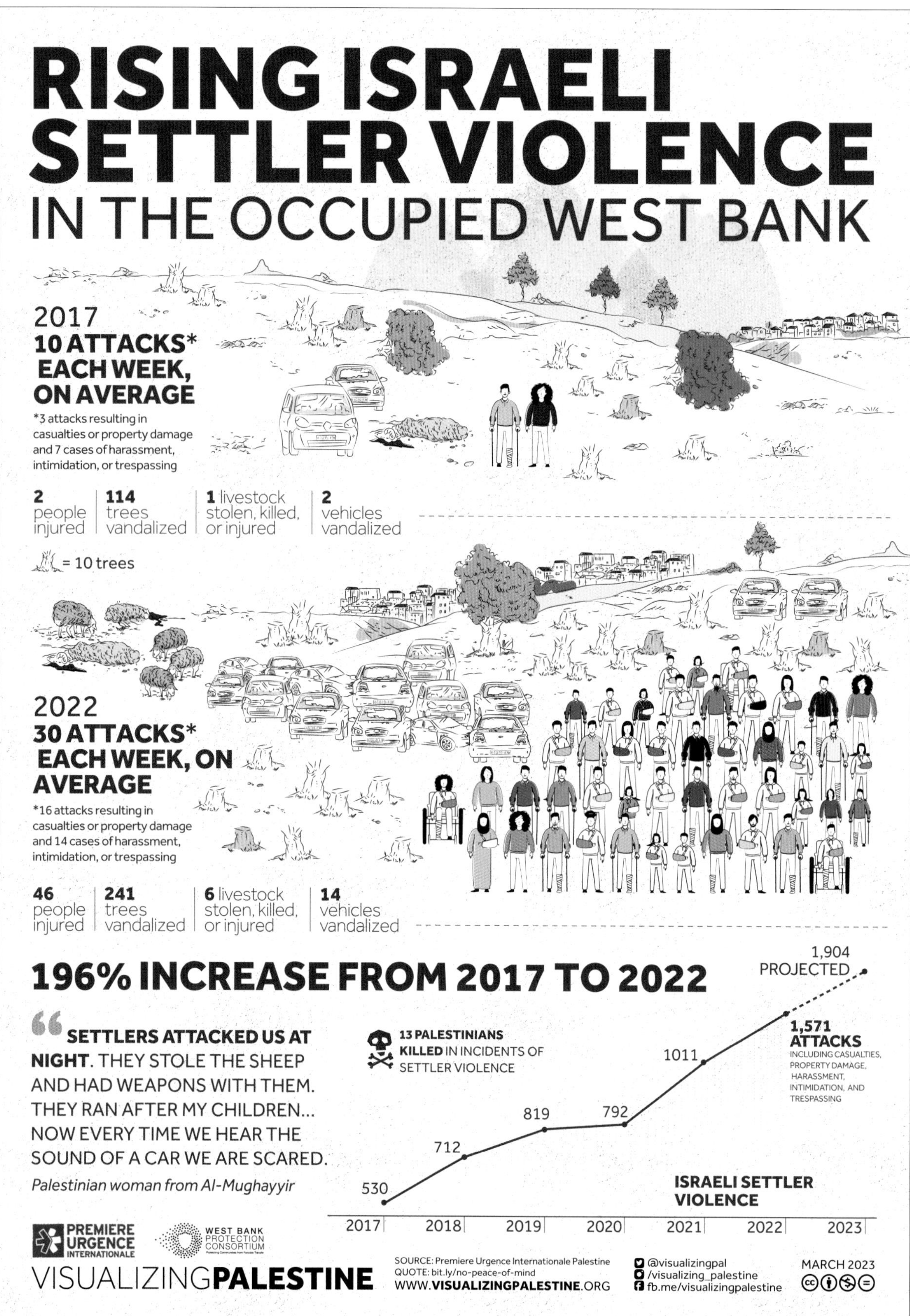
RISING ISRAELI SETTLER VIOLENCE
IN THE OCCUPIED WEST BANK
2017
10 ATTACKS* EACH WEEK, ON AVERAGE
*3 attacks resulting in casualties or property damage and 7 cases of harassment, intimidation, or trespassing
2 people injured
114 trees vandalized
1 livestock stolen, killed, or injured
2 vehicles vandalized
= 10 trees
2022
30 ATTACKS* EACH WEEK, ON AVERAGE
*16 attacks resulting in casualties or property damage and 14 cases of harassment, intimidation, or trespassing
46 people injured
241 trees vandalized
6 livestock stolen, killed, or injured
14 vehicles vandalized
196% INCREASE FROM 2017 TO 2022
SETTLERS ATTACKED US AT NIGHT. THEY STOLE THE SHEEP AND HAD WEAPONS WITH THEM. THEY RAN AFTER MY CHILDREN... NOW EVERY TIME WE HEAR THE SOUND OF A CAR WE ARE SCARED.
Palestinian woman from Al-Mughayyir
13 PALESTINIANS KILLED IN INCIDENTS OF SETTLER VIOLENCE
1,904
PROJECTED
1,571
ATTACKS
INCLUDING CASUALTIES, PROPERTY DAMAGE, HARASSMENT, INTIMIDATION, AND TRESPASSING
1011
819
792
712
530
ISRAELI SETTLER VIOLENCE
2017
2018
2019
2020
2021
2022
2023
PREMIERE URGENCE INTERNATIONALE
WEST BANK PROTECTION CONSORTIUM
VISUALIZINGPALESTINE
SOURCE: Premiere Urgence Internationale Palestine
QUOTE: bit.ly/no-peace-of-mind
WWW.VISUALIZINGPALESTINE.ORG
@visualizingpal
/visualizing_palestine
fb.me/visualizingpalestine
MARCH 2023

Year: 2023 | **Brief and copywriting:** Jessica Anderson, Lyne Jamin | **Design:** Yara Ramadan, Yosra El Gazzar | **Source:** Première Urgence Internationale Palestine

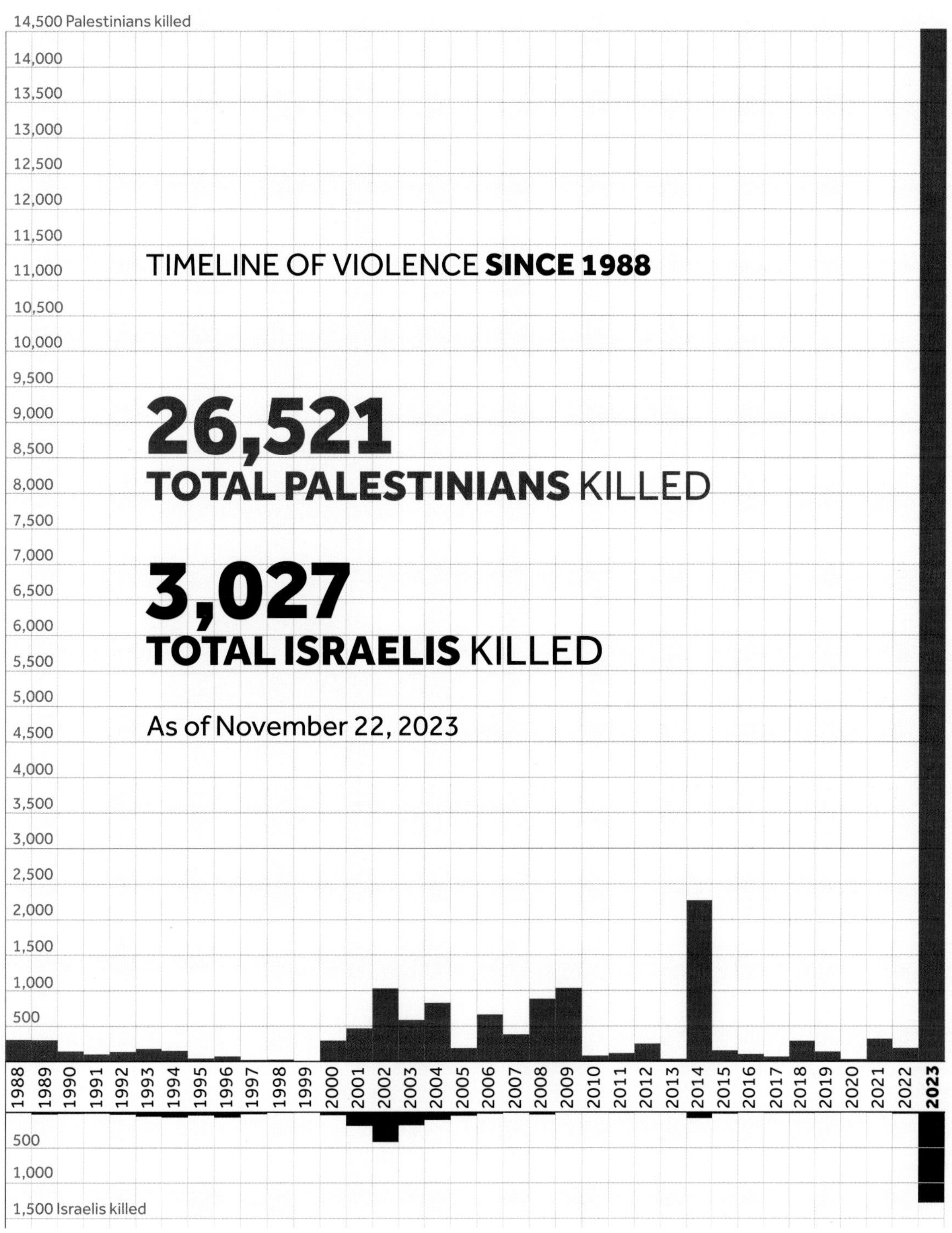
14,500 Palestinians killed
14,000
13,500
13,000
12,500
12,000
11,500
11,000
10,500
10,000
9,500
9,000
8,500
8,000
7,500
7,000
6,500
6,000
5,500
5,000
4,500
4,000
3,500
3,000
2,500
2,000
1,500
1,000
500
TIMELINE OF VIOLENCE **SINCE 1988**
26,521
TOTAL PALESTINIANS KILLED
3,027
TOTAL ISRAELIS KILLED
As of November 22, 2023
1988 1989 1990 1991 1992 1993 1994 1995 1996 1997 1998 1999 2000 2001 2002 2003 2004 2005 2006 2007 2008 2009 2010 2011 2012 2013 2014 2015 2016 2017 2018 2019 2020 2021 2022 **2023**
500
1,000
1,500 Israelis killed
VISUALIZING**PALESTINE** SOURCES bit.ly/vp-fatalities NOV2023

Year: 2023 | **Brief and copywriting:** Jessica Anderson | **Design:** Ahmad Barclay, Yosra El Gazzar | **Sources:** bit.ly/vp-fatalities

As of November 22, 2023

90%

OF TOTAL FATALITIES BETWEEN 1988 – 2023 WERE PALESTINIAN

3,027
TOTAL ISRAELIS KILLED (1988–2023)

26,521
TOTAL PALESTINIANS KILLED (1988–2023)

VISUALIZING**PALESTINE** SOURCES bit.ly/vp-fatalities NOV2023

Year: 2023 | **Brief and copywriting:** Jessica Anderson | **Design:** Yosra El Gazzar | **Sources:** bit.ly/vp-fatalities

20
YEARS OF
MOURNING

If we dedicated **1 day to mourn each person killed** between the Mediterranean Sea and the Jordan River from 2006–2022, we would be in mourning for **over 20 years**

>19 YEARS MOURNING **PALESTINIANS KILLED**
<1 YEAR MOURNING **ISRAELIS KILLED**

96% OF FATALITIES WERE PALESTINIAN (2006–2022)

VISUALIZING**PALESTINE** SOURCES bit.ly/vp-fatalities WWW.**VISUALIZINGPALESTINE**.ORG

@visualizingpal
/visualizing_palestine
fb.me/visualizingpalestine

OCT 2023

Year: 2023 | **Brief and copywriting:** Jessica Anderson | **Design:** Yosra El Gazzar | **Sources:** bit.ly/vp-fatalities

2. THE ONGOING NAKBA

Visuals in this section: An Ongoing Displacement | A Policy of Displacement | Where Palestinians Live Today | Back to School | Palestinian Labour Force in Lebanon | Return Is Possible (map) | Return Is Possible (list)

DING

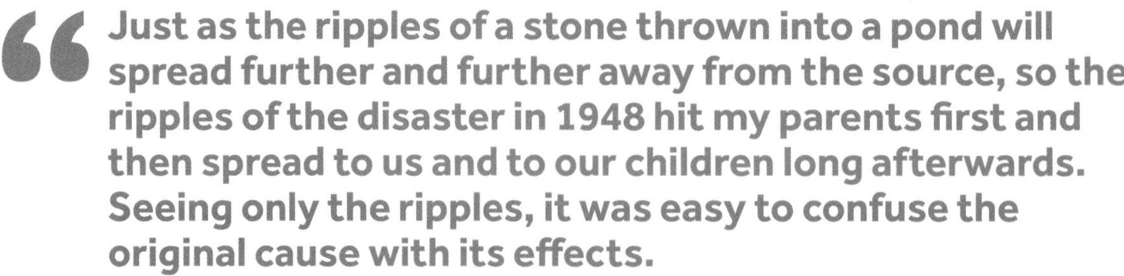

> **“Just as the ripples of a stone thrown into a pond will spread further and further away from the source, so the ripples of the disaster in 1948 hit my parents first and then spread to us and to our children long afterwards. Seeing only the ripples, it was easy to confuse the original cause with its effects.**
>
> —*Ghada Karmi,* Return: A Palestinian Memoir *(2015)*

> **“The Nakba is an extended present that promises to continue in the future. . . . For the Palestinians the meaning of this war consists in their being subjected to continual uprooting, in their transformation into refugees on their own land and beyond it, in the attempt, following the occupation of their land and history, to banish their existence, to turn their existence from an unequivocal entity in space and time to redundant shadows exiled from space and time.**
>
> —*Mahmoud Darwish,* Al-Ahram Weekly *(2001)*

In 1948, Zionist paramilitaries carried out the Nakba—the Arabic word for “catastrophe”—completely depopulating over 530 Palestinian localities and expelling around 750,000 Palestinians, or about three-quarters of the Indigenous population, in the areas that became part of the Israeli state. There is not a single Palestinian family who does not have a Nakba story, and every Palestinian has certainly experienced its ripple effects. **An Ongoing Displacement** shows how this formative period of ethnic cleansing was not a singular event. Instead, it marked the start of continuous displacement, dispossession, and erasure of Palestinian communities under Israeli rule.

A Policy of Displacement explores the ongoing Nakba through Israel’s policy of home demolitions and military bombardments, which have driven hundreds of thousands of Palestinians from their homes. To build a home in East Jerusalem and most of the West Bank, Palestinians must obtain a building permit from Israeli authorities. Israel either denies or delays the vast majority of requests to build in Palestinian areas, while approving scores of permits to expand housing in illegal Israeli settlements.[1] Since it is nearly impossible to build “legally,” thousands of Palestinians live under constant threat of having their home, the source of their safety and stability, demolished.

Where Palestinians Live Today illustrates that, despite decades of forced displacement, around half of the Palestinian people still live in their historic homeland. The majority of the other half is displaced in neighboring Arab countries, including in refugee camps administered by the United Nations Relief and Works Agency for Palestine Refugees in the Near East (UNRWA) in Jordan, Lebanon, and Syria, where they experience various layers of hardship. **Back to School** depicts the challenges faced by Palestinian refugee children in Syria in accessing the basic right to education. As of 2021, over half of the 438,000 Palestinian refugees in Syria had been displaced again within Syria, and 120,000 had fled to nearby countries, including Jordan and Lebanon.[2]

The **Palestinian Labour Force in Lebanon** series visualizes how, despite their valuable contributions to the Lebanese economy, Palestinian refugees in Lebanon continue to be disenfranchised three generations after the Nakba. Around 210,000 Palestinian refugees live in twelve official refugee camps in Lebanon, and 93 percent of them were living in poverty as of 2022. They face discriminatory policies that prevent them from accessing health care and limit their participation in thirty-nine professions.[3]

The right of return is central to the Palestinian struggle. In 1948, United Nations General Assembly Resolution 194 stated that Palestinian "refugees wishing to return to their homes and live at peace with their neighbours should be permitted to do so at the earliest practicable date."[4] Israeli policy systematically denies Palestinian refugees their right to return to their homes, or even to visit in many cases. Meanwhile, the Israeli Law of Return invites Jews from anywhere in the world not only to visit but to gain immediate citizenship. The two-part **Return Is Possible** series shows that the vast majority of destroyed Palestinian towns and villages in historic Palestine have not been built over. The visual reflects Palestinians' enduring connection to their cities, villages, and places of origin, and their collective imagination of what return would look like. Return Is Possible was partly inspired by the work of Palestinian researcher Salman Abu Sitta, who said, "We, all of us, must work actively for the return of the refugees. Only when they return, when they are rehabilitated in their own homes, assured of decent living and safety from racism and apartheid, can we say peace prevails."[5]

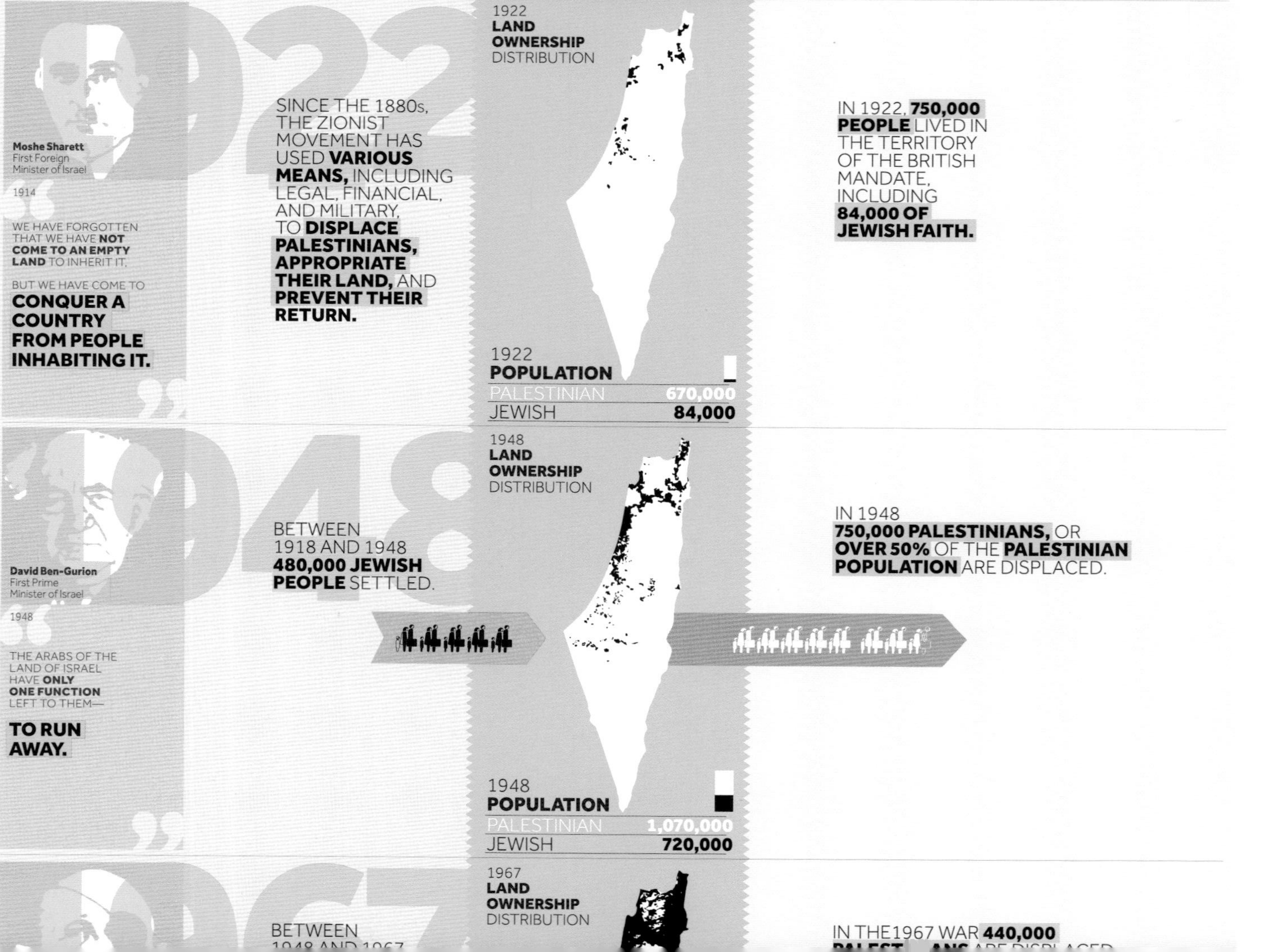
AN ONGOING DISPLACEMENT
THE FORCED EXILE OF THE PALESTINIANS
Moshe Sharett
First Foreign Minister of Israel
1914
WE HAVE FORGOTTEN THAT WE HAVE NOT COME TO AN EMPTY LAND TO INHERIT IT,
BUT WE HAVE COME TO CONQUER A COUNTRY FROM PEOPLE INHABITING IT.
1922
SINCE THE 1880s, THE ZIONIST MOVEMENT HAS USED VARIOUS MEANS, INCLUDING LEGAL, FINANCIAL, AND MILITARY, TO DISPLACE PALESTINIANS, APPROPRIATE THEIR LAND, AND PREVENT THEIR RETURN.
1922 LAND OWNERSHIP DISTRIBUTION
1922 POPULATION
PALESTINIAN 670,000
JEWISH 84,000
IN 1922, 750,000 PEOPLE LIVED IN THE TERRITORY OF THE BRITISH MANDATE, INCLUDING 84,000 OF JEWISH FAITH.
David Ben-Gurion
First Prime Minister of Israel
1948
THE ARABS OF THE LAND OF ISRAEL HAVE ONLY ONE FUNCTION LEFT TO THEM—
TO RUN AWAY.
1948
BETWEEN 1918 AND 1948 480,000 JEWISH PEOPLE SETTLED.
1948 LAND OWNERSHIP DISTRIBUTION
1948 POPULATION
PALESTINIAN 1,070,000
JEWISH 720,000
IN 1948 750,000 PALESTINIANS, OR OVER 50% OF THE PALESTINIAN POPULATION ARE DISPLACED.
1967 LAND OWNERSHIP DISTRIBUTION
BETWEEN
IN THE 1967 WAR 440,000

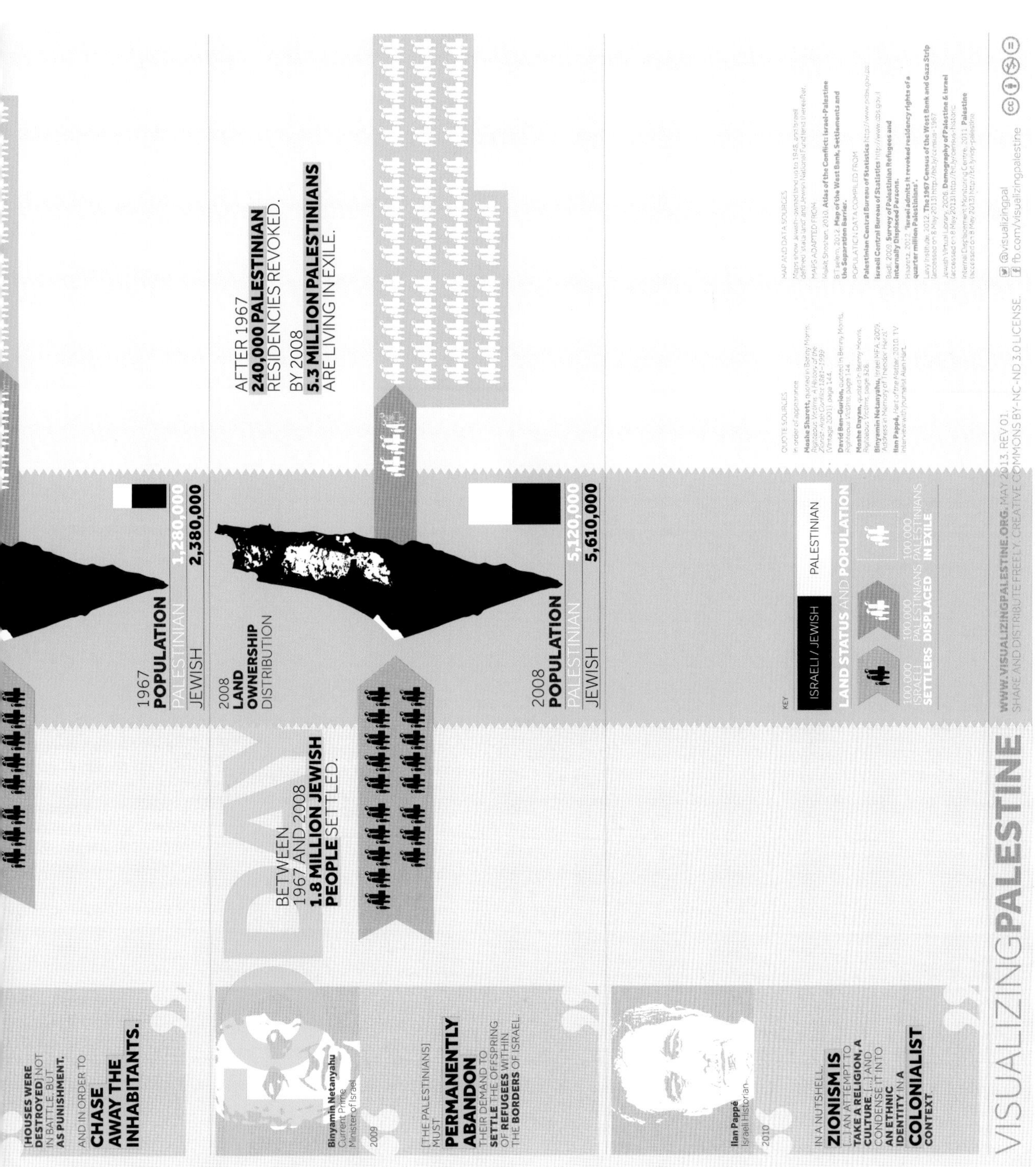
[HOUSES WERE DESTROYED] NOT IN BATTLE, BUT AS PUNISHMENT.
AND IN ORDER TO CHASE AWAY THE INHABITANTS.
1967 POPULATION
PALESTINIAN 1,280,000
JEWISH 2,380,000
Binyamin Netanyahu Current Prime Minister of Israel
2009
[THE PALESTINIANS] MUST PERMANENTLY ABANDON THEIR DEMAND TO SETTLE THE OFFSPRING OF REFUGEES WITHIN THE BORDERS OF ISRAEL.
BETWEEN 1967 AND 2008 1.8 MILLION JEWISH PEOPLE SETTLED.
2008 LAND OWNERSHIP DISTRIBUTION
AFTER 1967 240,000 PALESTINIAN RESIDENCIES REVOKED.
BY 2008 5.3 MILLION PALESTINIANS ARE LIVING IN EXILE.
2008 POPULATION
PALESTINIAN 5,120,000
JEWISH 5,610,000
Ilan Pappé Israeli Historian
2010
IN A NUTSHELL, ZIONISM IS [...] AN ATTEMPT TO TAKE A RELIGION, A CULTURE [...] AND CONDENSE IT INTO AN ETHNIC IDENTITY IN A COLONIALIST CONTEXT.
KEY
ISRAELI / JEWISH
PALESTINIAN
LAND STATUS AND POPULATION
100,000 ISRAELI SETTLERS
100,000 PALESTINIANS DISPLACED
100,000 PALESTINIANS IN EXILE
VISUALIZINGPALESTINE
WWW.VISUALIZINGPALESTINE.ORG, MAY 2013, REV 01.
SHARE AND DISTRIBUTE FREELY. CREATIVE COMMONS BY-NC-ND 3.0 LICENSE.
@visualizingpal
fb.com/visualizingpalestine

Year: 2013 | **Brief and copywriting:** Joumana al Jabri, Zaid Amr, Ahmad Barclay, Thoraya El-Rayyes, Christopher Fiorello, Nusayba Hammad, Institute for Middle East Understanding, Ramzi Jaber | **Design:** Hani Asfour, Ahmad Barclay, Sharmeen Inayat | **Icons:** Saeed Abu-Jaber | **Sources:** bit.ly/vp-Sources-2012-2015

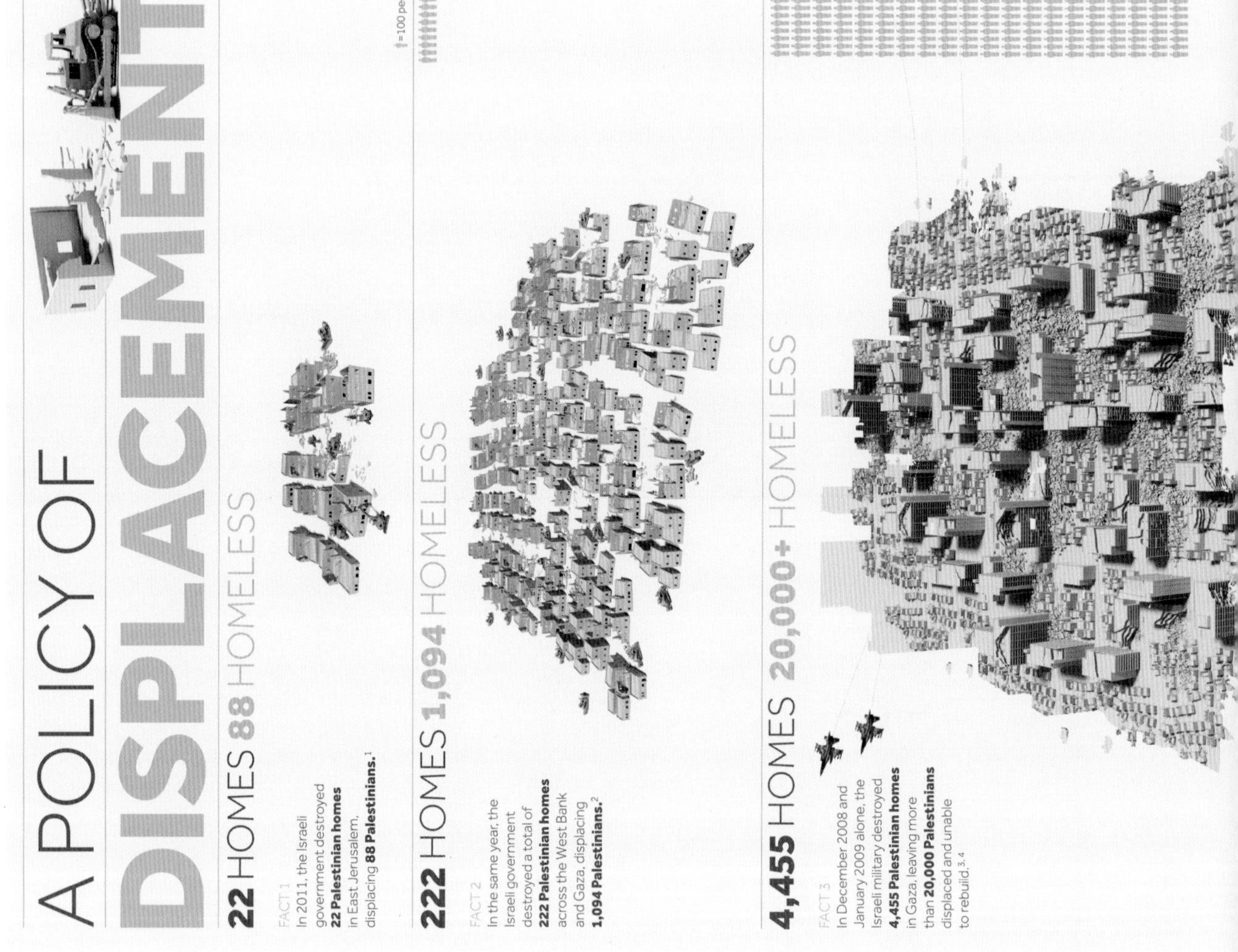
A POLICY OF
DISPLACEMENT
22 HOMES 88 HOMELESS
FACT 1
In 2011, the Israeli government destroyed 22 Palestinian homes in East Jerusalem, displacing 88 Palestinians.[1]
=100 people
222 HOMES 1,094 HOMELESS
FACT 2
In the same year, the Israeli government destroyed a total of 222 Palestinian homes across the West Bank and Gaza, displacing 1,094 Palestinians.[2]
4,455 HOMES 20,000+ HOMELESS
FACT 3
In December 2008 and January 2009 alone, the Israeli military destroyed 4,455 Palestinian homes in Gaza, leaving more than 20,000 Palestinians displaced and unable to rebuild.[3, 4]

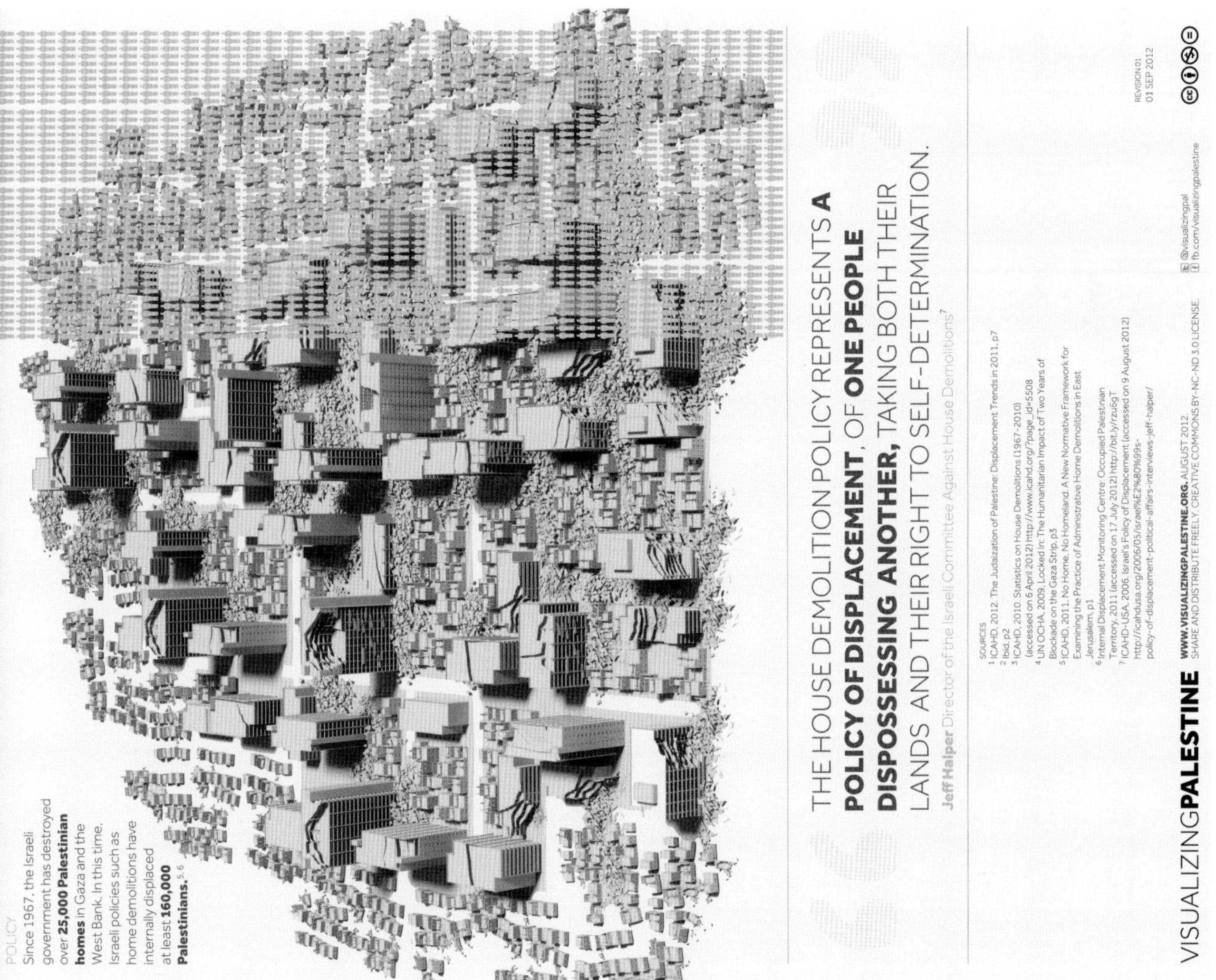
POLICY
Since 1967, the Israeli government has destroyed over **25,000 Palestinian homes** in Gaza and the West Bank. In this time, Israeli policies such as home demolitions have internally displaced at least **160,000 Palestinians.**[5, 6]
THE HOUSE DEMOLITION POLICY REPRESENTS **A POLICY OF DISPLACEMENT**, OF **ONE PEOPLE DISPOSSESSING ANOTHER,** TAKING BOTH THEIR LANDS AND THEIR RIGHT TO SELF-DETERMINATION.
Jeff Halper Director of the Israeli Committee Against House Demolitions[7]
VISUALIZING**PALESTINE**
WWW.VISUALIZINGPALESTINE.ORG, AUGUST 2012.
SHARE AND DISTRIBUTE FREELY. CREATIVE COMMONS BY-NC-ND 3.0 LICENSE.
REVISION 01
01 SEP 2012

Year: 2012 | **Brief and copywriting:** Joumana al Jabri, Zaid Amr, Ahmad Barclay, Ramzi Jaber | **Design:** Ahmad Barclay, Hani Asfour, Wade Fuh | **Sources:** bit.ly/vp-Sources-2012-2015

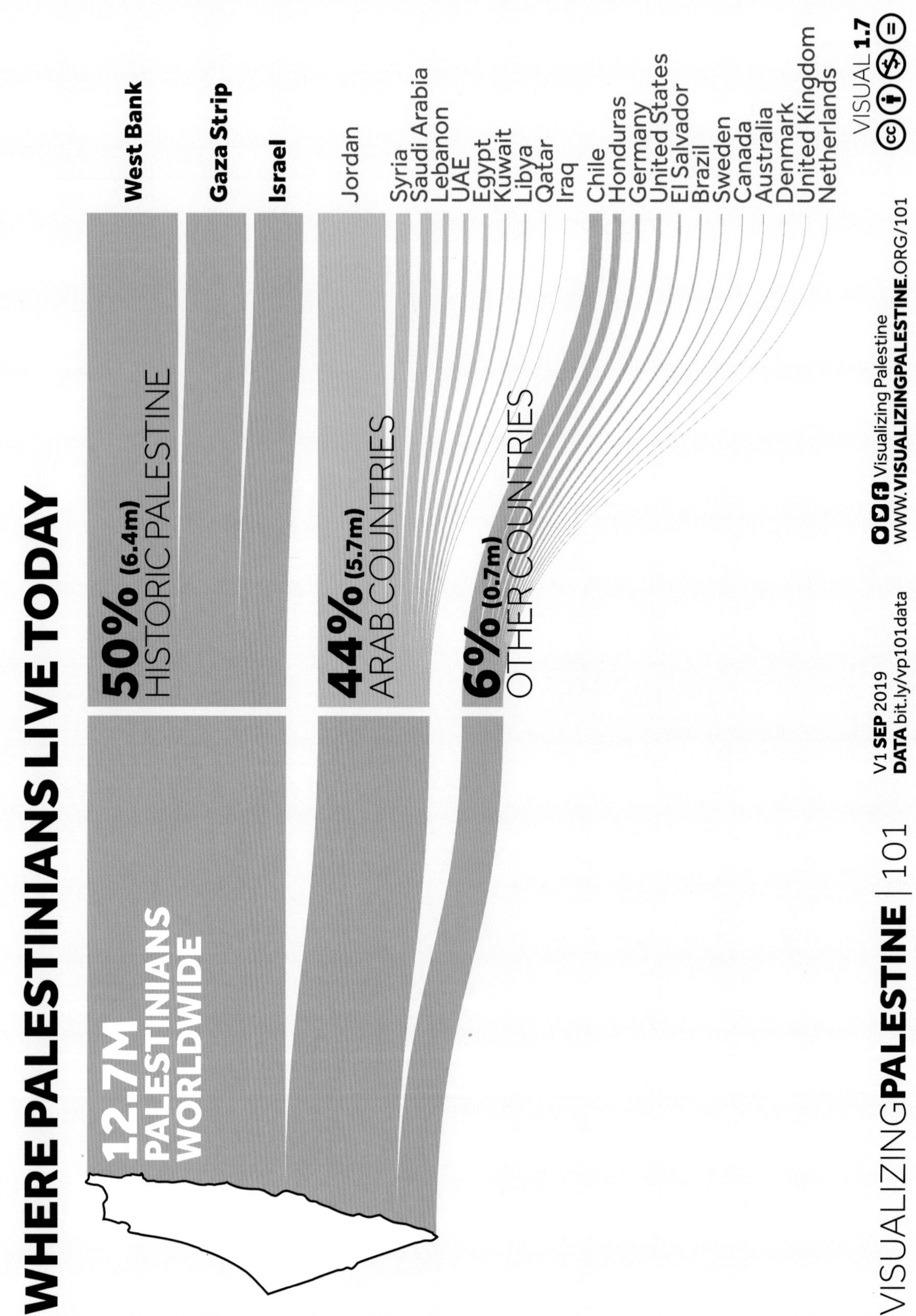
WHERE PALESTINIANS LIVE TODAY
12.7M
PALESTINIANS
WORLDWIDE
50% (6.4m)
HISTORIC PALESTINE
44% (5.7m)
ARAB COUNTRIES
6% (0.7m)
OTHER COUNTRIES
West Bank
Gaza Strip
Israel
Jordan
Syria
Saudi Arabia
Lebanon
UAE
Egypt
Kuwait
Libya
Qatar
Iraq
Chile
Honduras
Germany
United States
El Salvador
Brazil
Sweden
Canada
Australia
Denmark
United Kingdom
Netherlands
VISUALIZINGPALESTINE | 101
V1 SEP 2019
DATA bit.ly/vp101data
Visualizing Palestine
WWW.VISUALIZINGPALESTINE.ORG/101
VISUAL 1.7

Year: 2019 | **Brief and copywriting:** Ahmad Barclay | **Design:** Ahmad Barclay, Yosra El Gazzar | **Sources:** bit.ly/vp101data

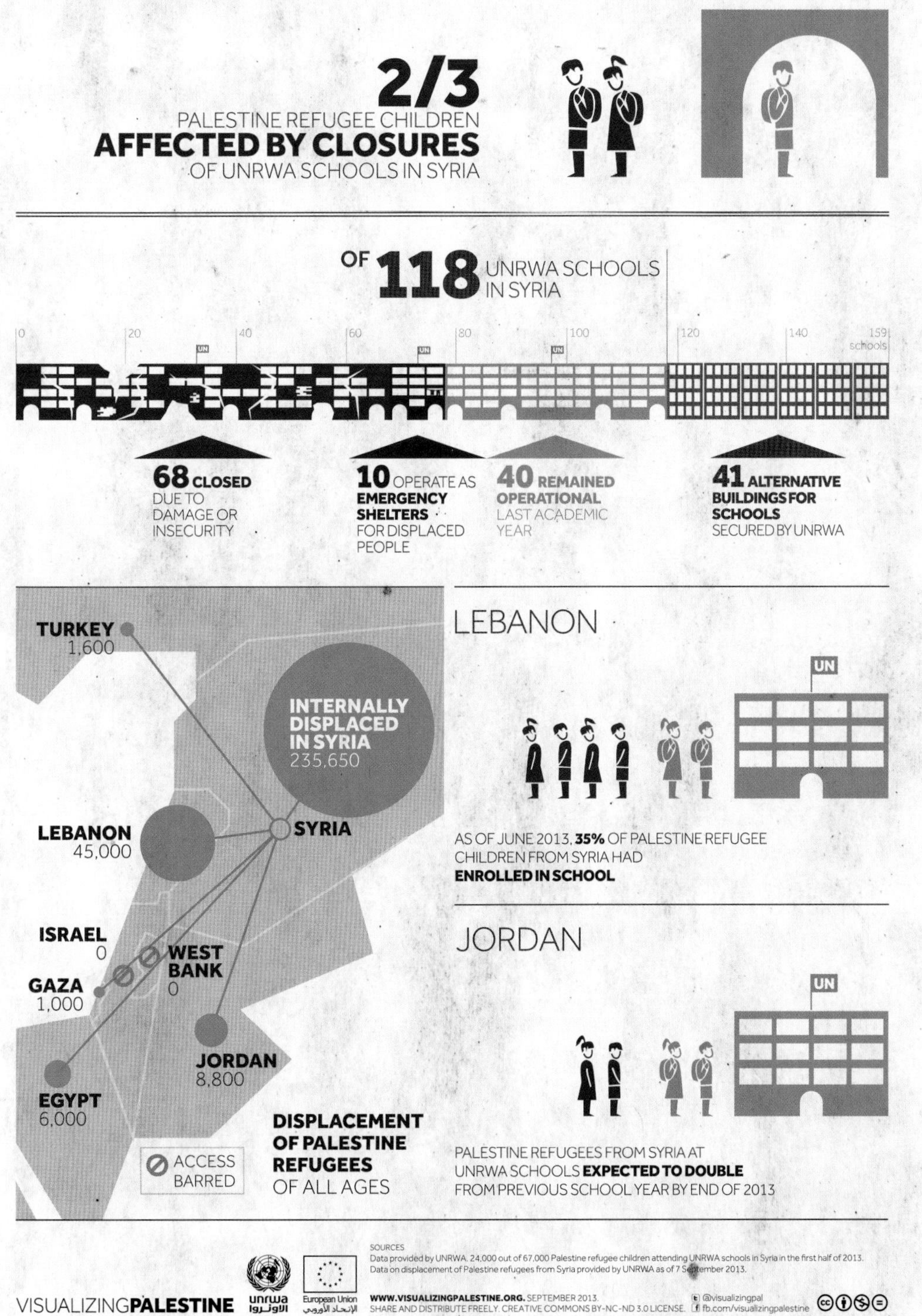
BACK TO SCHOOL
SYRIA EMERGENCY: PALESTINE REFUGEE CHILDREN
2/3
PALESTINE REFUGEE CHILDREN
AFFECTED BY CLOSURES
OF UNRWA SCHOOLS IN SYRIA
OF 118 UNRWA SCHOOLS IN SYRIA
0
20
40
60
80
100
120
140
159 schools
UN
68 CLOSED DUE TO DAMAGE OR INSECURITY
10 OPERATE AS EMERGENCY SHELTERS FOR DISPLACED PEOPLE
40 REMAINED OPERATIONAL LAST ACADEMIC YEAR
41 ALTERNATIVE BUILDINGS FOR SCHOOLS SECURED BY UNRWA
TURKEY 1,600
INTERNALLY DISPLACED IN SYRIA 235,650
LEBANON 45,000
SYRIA
ISRAEL 0
WEST BANK 0
GAZA 1,000
JORDAN 8,800
EGYPT 6,000
ACCESS BARRED
DISPLACEMENT OF PALESTINE REFUGEES OF ALL AGES
LEBANON
AS OF JUNE 2013, 35% OF PALESTINE REFUGEE CHILDREN FROM SYRIA HAD ENROLLED IN SCHOOL
JORDAN
PALESTINE REFUGEES FROM SYRIA AT UNRWA SCHOOLS EXPECTED TO DOUBLE FROM PREVIOUS SCHOOL YEAR BY END OF 2013
SOURCES
Data provided by UNRWA. 24,000 out of 67,000 Palestine refugee children attending UNRWA schools in Syria in the first half of 2013.
Data on displacement of Palestine refugees from Syria provided by UNRWA as of 7 September 2013.
VISUALIZINGPALESTINE
unrwa الاونروا
European Union الإتحاد الأوروبي
WWW.VISUALIZINGPALESTINE.ORG. SEPTEMBER 2013.
SHARE AND DISTRIBUTE FREELY. CREATIVE COMMONS BY-NC-ND 3.0 LICENSE.
@visualizingpal
fb.com/visualizingpalestine

Year: 2013 | **Brief and copywriting:** Joumana al Jabri, Ahmad Barclay, Ramzi Jaber, United Nations Relief and Works Agency for Palestine Refugees in the Near East | **Design:** Marwa Boukarim, Ahmad Barclay, Danny Khoury | **Sources:** bit.ly/vp-Sources-2012-2015

PALESTINIAN LABOUR FORCE IN LEBANON

THE PALESTINIAN CONTRIBUTION

ENTREPRENEURS

1 IN 4

PALESTINIAN REFUGEES

ARE EMPLOYERS OR SELF-EMPLOYED

EMPLOYERS

MANY ENTERPRISES, INCLUDING MAJOR BANKS, **ESTABLISHED BY LEBANESE OF PALESTINIAN ORIGIN** CREATING JOBS AND EXPANDING THE LEBANESE ECONOMY

VISUALIZINGPALESTINE

ILO

CEP

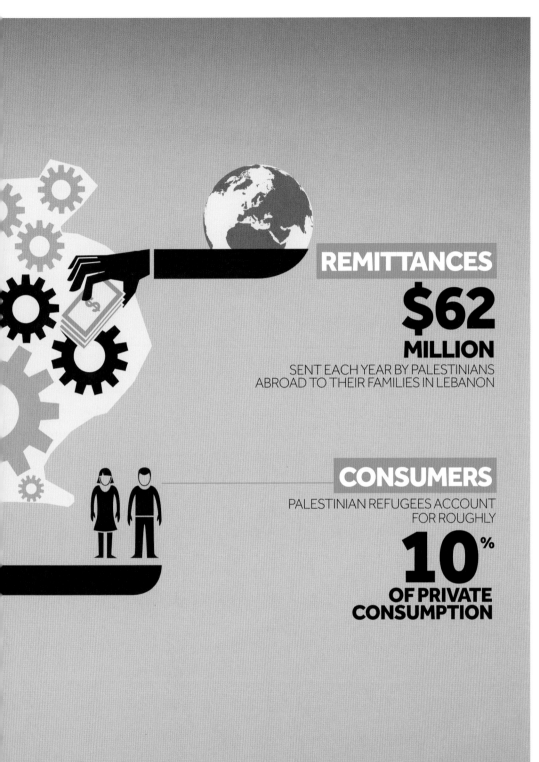

REMITTANCES

$62 MILLION

SENT EACH YEAR BY PALESTINIANS ABROAD TO THEIR FAMILIES IN LEBANON

CONSUMERS

PALESTINIAN REFUGEES ACCOUNT FOR ROUGHLY

10%

OF PRIVATE CONSUMPTION

ES
ıalidi & Riad Tabbarah. 2008. **Working Unprotected: Contributions of**
ıian Refugees to the Lebanese Economy
ian Human Rights Organization. 2007. **The Palestinians' Contributions to**
n's Economy

/ISUALIZINGPALESTINE.ORG. DECEMBER 2013.

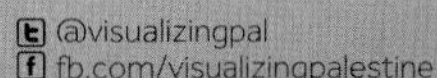
@visualizingpal
fb.com/visualizingpalestine

CREATIVE COMMONS
BY-NC-ND 3.0 LICENSE

Year: 2013
Brief and copywriting: Ahmad Barclay, Livia Bergmeijer, Christopher Fiorello, International Labour Organization, Fadi Shayya, Hana Sleiman
Design: Naji El Mir, Ahmad Barclay
Sources: bit.ly/vp-Sources-2012-2015

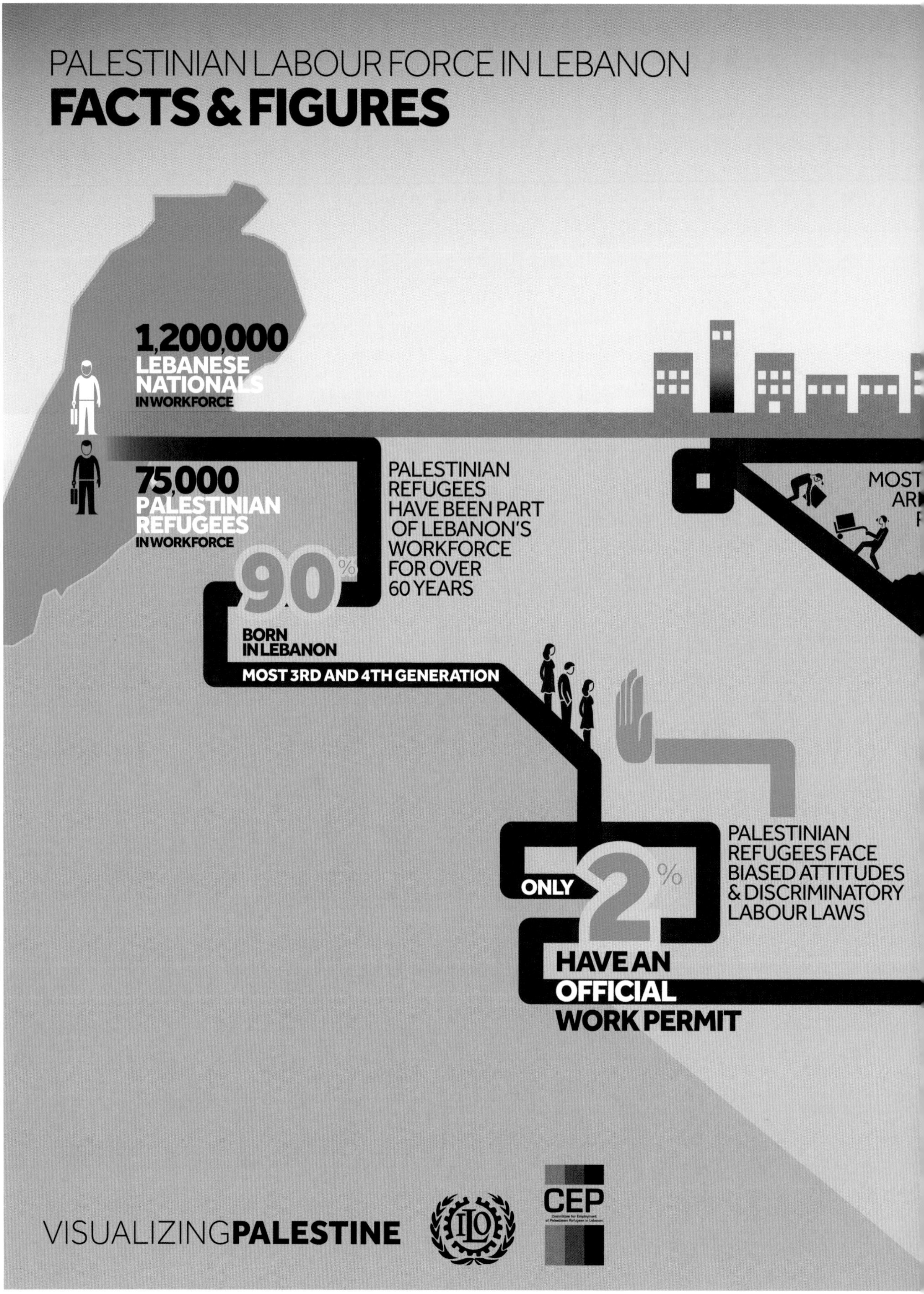

PALESTINIAN LABOUR FORCE IN LEBANON
FACTS & FIGURES

1,200,000
LEBANESE NATIONALS
IN WORKFORCE

75,000
PALESTINIAN REFUGEES
IN WORKFORCE

PALESTINIAN REFUGEES HAVE BEEN PART OF LEBANON'S WORKFORCE FOR OVER 60 YEARS

90%
BORN IN LEBANON
MOST 3RD AND 4TH GENERATION

MOST ... AR...

PALESTINIAN REFUGEES FACE BIASED ATTITUDES & DISCRIMINATORY LABOUR LAWS

ONLY 2%
HAVE AN OFFICIAL WORK PERMIT

VISUALIZINGPALESTINE

ILO

CEP

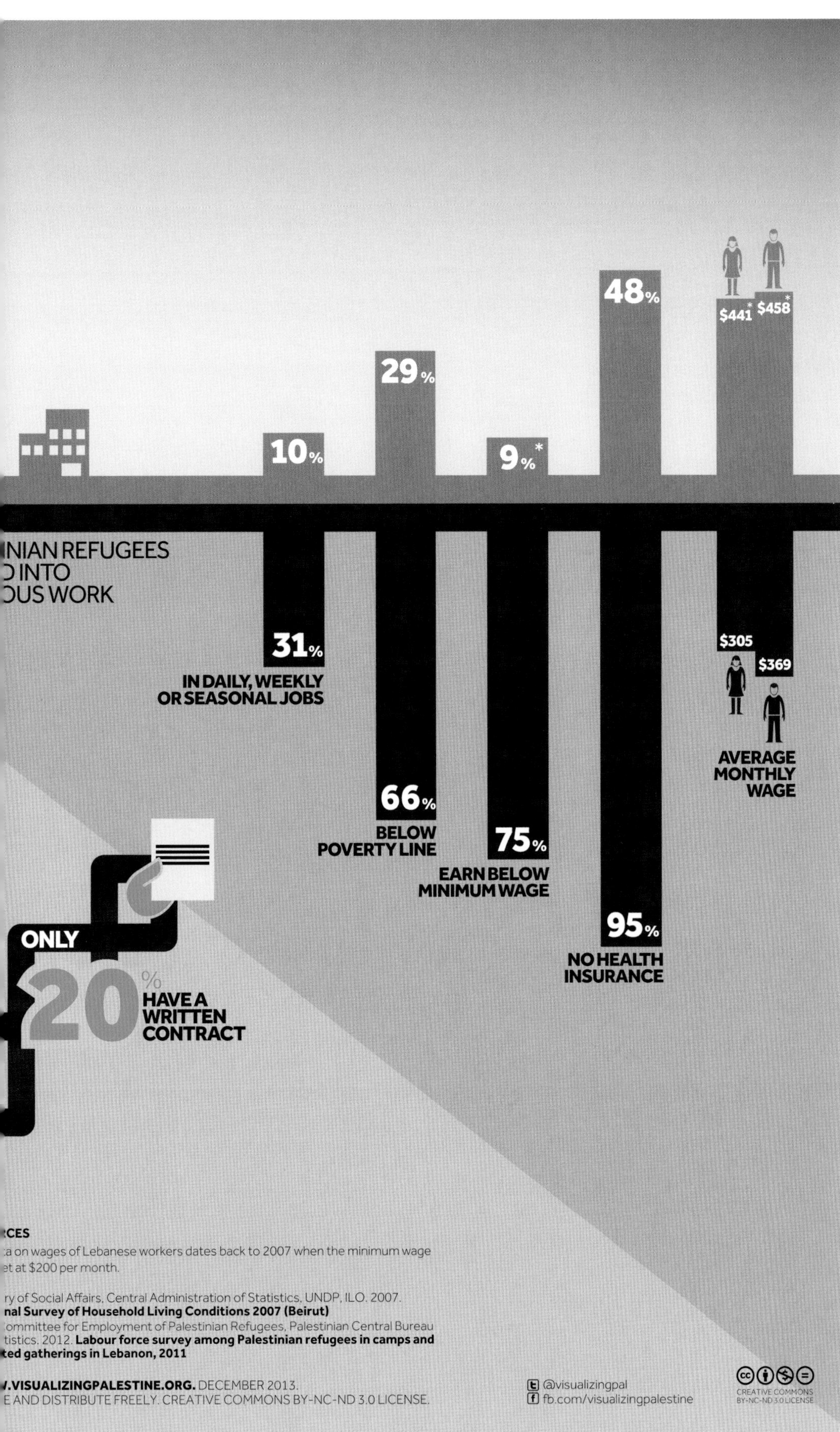
10%
29%
9%*
48%
$441*
$458*
NIAN REFUGEES
INTO
OUS WORK
31%
IN DAILY, WEEKLY
OR SEASONAL JOBS
66%
BELOW
POVERTY LINE
75%
EARN BELOW
MINIMUM WAGE
95%
NO HEALTH
INSURANCE
$305
$369
AVERAGE
MONTHLY
WAGE
ONLY
20%
HAVE A
WRITTEN
CONTRACT
CES
a on wages of Lebanese workers dates back to 2007 when the minimum wage
et at $200 per month.
ry of Social Affairs, Central Administration of Statistics, UNDP, ILO. 2007.
nal Survey of Household Living Conditions 2007 (Beirut)
ommittee for Employment of Palestinian Refugees, Palestinian Central Bureau
tistics. 2012. Labour force survey among Palestinian refugees in camps and
ted gatherings in Lebanon, 2011
.VISUALIZINGPALESTINE.ORG. DECEMBER 2013.
E AND DISTRIBUTE FREELY. CREATIVE COMMONS BY-NC-ND 3.0 LICENSE.
@visualizingpal
fb.com/visualizingpalestine
CREATIVE COMMONS
BY-NC-ND 3.0 LICENSE

Year: 2013
Brief and copywriting: Ahmad Barclay, Livia Bergmeijer, Christopher Fiorello, International Labour Organization, Fadi Shayya, Hana Sleiman
Design: Naji El Mir, Ahmad Barclay
Sources: bit.ly/vp-Sources-2012-2015

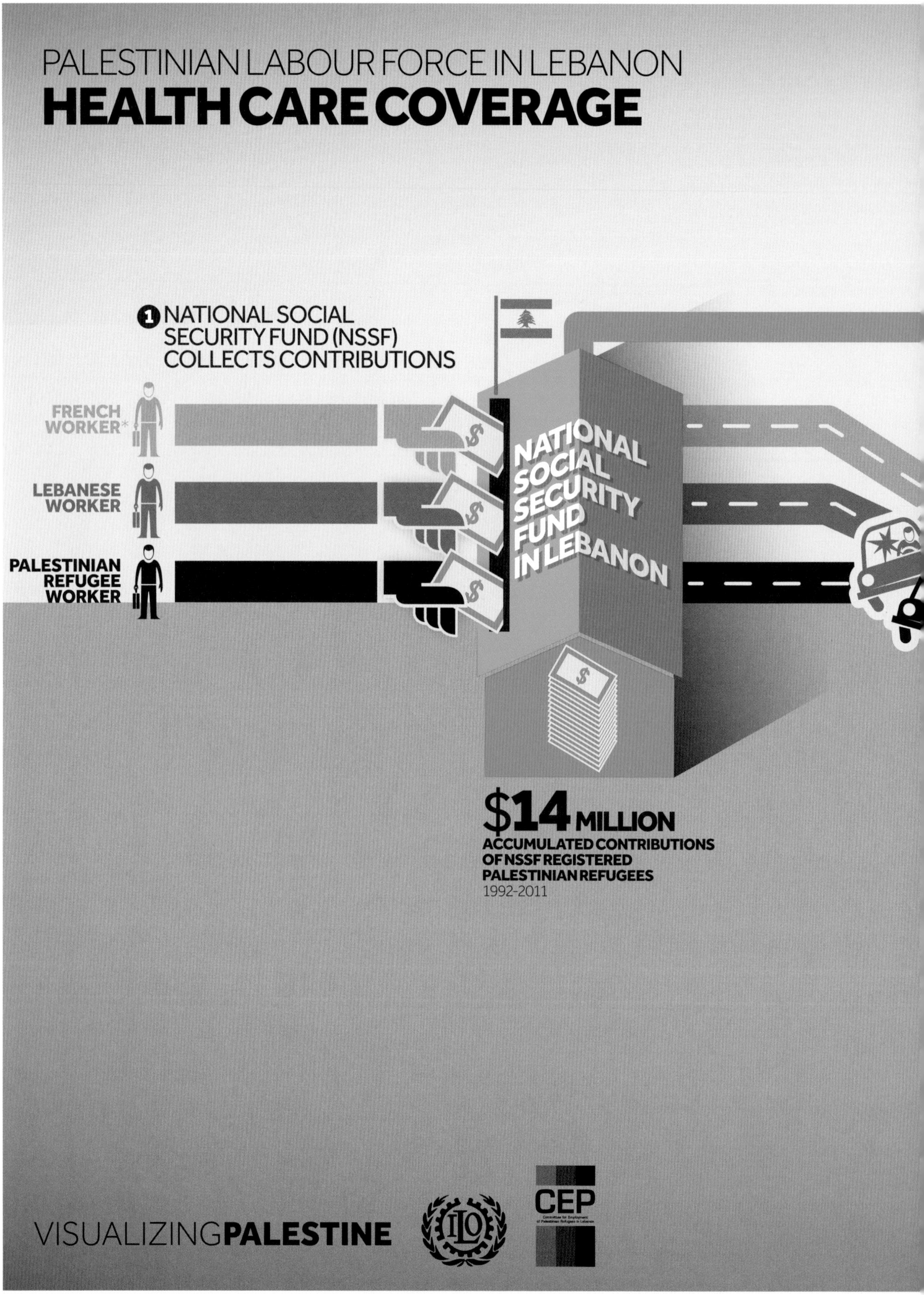

PALESTINIAN LABOUR FORCE IN LEBANON
HEALTH CARE COVERAGE

1 NATIONAL SOCIAL SECURITY FUND (NSSF) COLLECTS CONTRIBUTIONS

FRENCH WORKER*

LEBANESE WORKER

PALESTINIAN REFUGEE WORKER

NATIONAL SOCIAL SECURITY FUND IN LEBANON

$14 MILLION
ACCUMULATED CONTRIBUTIONS OF NSSF REGISTERED PALESTINIAN REFUGEES
1992-2011

VISUALIZING**PALESTINE**

CEP

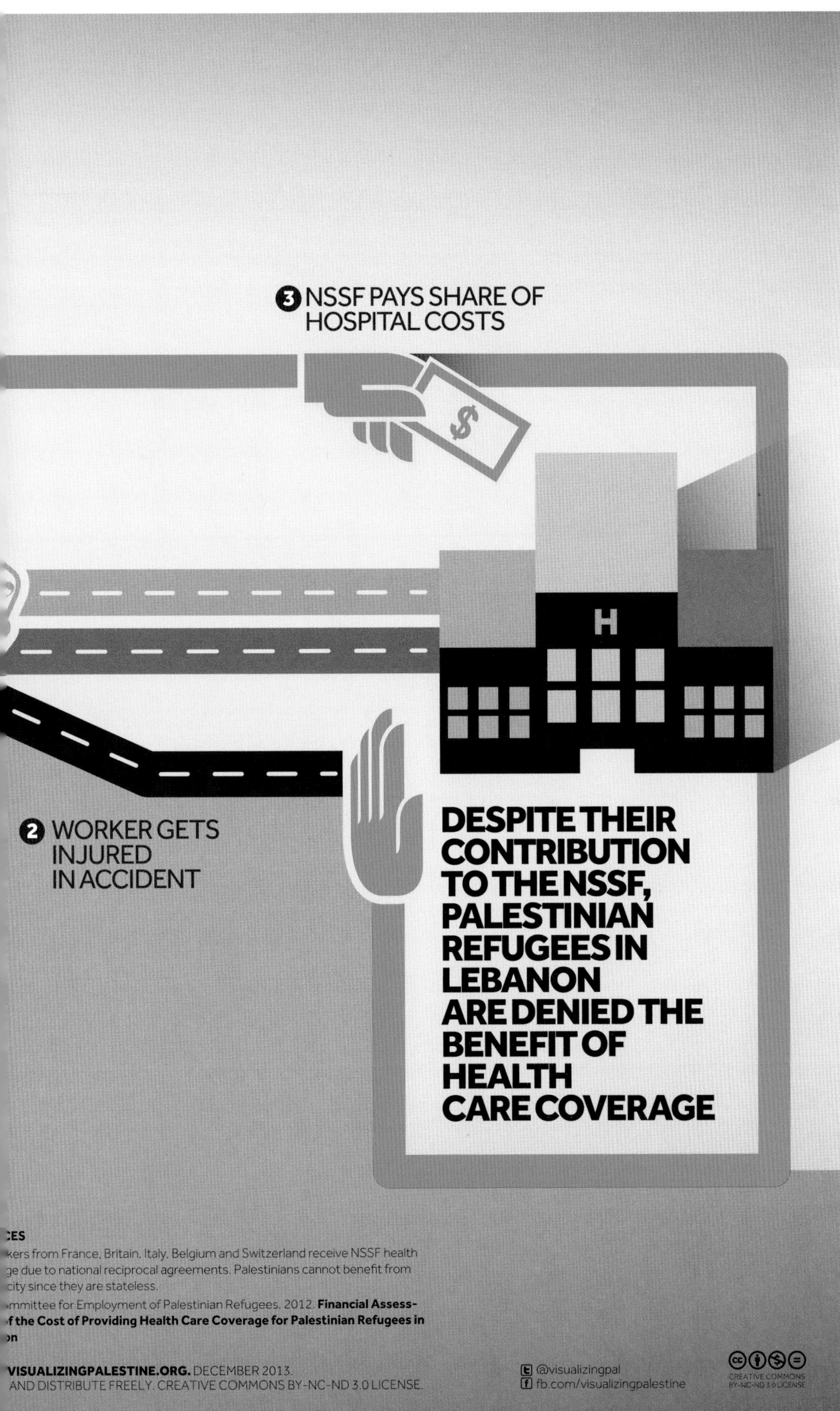
3 NSSF PAYS SHARE OF HOSPITAL COSTS
$
H
2 WORKER GETS INJURED IN ACCIDENT
DESPITE THEIR CONTRIBUTION TO THE NSSF, PALESTINIAN REFUGEES IN LEBANON ARE DENIED THE BENEFIT OF HEALTH CARE COVERAGE
ES
kers from France, Britain, Italy, Belgium and Switzerland receive NSSF health
ge due to national reciprocal agreements. Palestinians cannot benefit from
city since they are stateless.
mmittee for Employment of Palestinian Refugees. 2012. Financial Assess-
f the Cost of Providing Health Care Coverage for Palestinian Refugees in
on
VISUALIZINGPALESTINE.ORG. DECEMBER 2013.
AND DISTRIBUTE FREELY. CREATIVE COMMONS BY-NC-ND 3.0 LICENSE.
@visualizingpal
fb.com/visualizingpalestine
CREATIVE COMMONS BY-NC-ND 3.0 LICENSE

Year: 2013
Brief and copywriting: Ahmad Barclay, Livia Bergmeijer, Christopher Fiorello, International Labour Organization, Fadi Shayya, Hana Sleiman
Design: Naji El Mir, Ahmad Barclay
Sources: bit.ly/vp-Sources-2012-2015

PALESTINIAN LABOUR FORCE IN LEBANON
RESTRICTED PROFESSIONS

THE WORLD'S YOUNGEST DOCTOR

GUINNESS BOOK OF RECORDS

20 YEAR OLD **IQBAL ASSAD** WAS BORN AND RAISED IN **LEBANON**

VISUALIZING**PALESTINE**

ILO

CEP

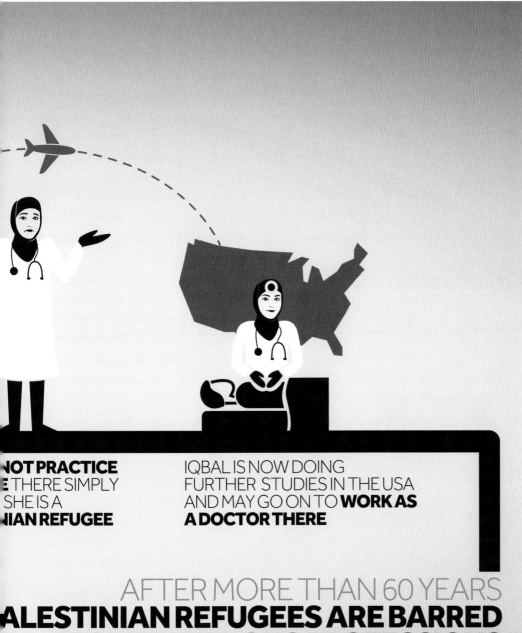

IOT PRACTICE
E THERE SIMPLY
SHE IS A
IIAN REFUGEE

IQBAL IS NOW DOING FURTHER STUDIES IN THE USA AND MAY GO ON TO **WORK AS A DOCTOR THERE**

AFTER MORE THAN 60 YEARS **ALESTINIAN REFUGEES ARE BARRED FROM NUMEROUS PROFESSIONS IN LEBANON, INCLUDING MEDICINE, LAW AND ENGINEERING, BECAUSE** THEY ARE DEFINED AS FOREIGNERS

ES

obrossi & Roger Chidiac. 2009. **Legal Texts Governing the Employment of ian Refugees in Lebanon**

ast Monitor. 2013. **Miracle Palestinian Refugee Doctor** (last accessed 12 er 2013)

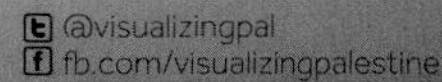
@visualizingpal
fb.com/visualizingpalestine

CREATIVE COMMONS
BY-NC-ND 3.0 LICENSE

Year: 2013
Brief and copywriting: Ahmad Barclay, Livia Bergmeijer, Christopher Fiorello, International Labour Organization, Fadi Shayya, Hana Sleiman
Design: Naji El Mir, Ahmad Barclay
Sources: bit.ly/vp-Sources-2012-2015

RETURN IS POSSIBLE

THE STATUS OF 536 PALESTINIAN VILLAGES DEPOPULATED BY ISRAEL

In 1948, the UN General Assembly declared that Palestinian "refugees wishing to return to their homes and live at peace with their neighbours should be permitted to do so at the earliest practicable date".

Today, Israel systematically denies Palestinians their right to return, yet the sites of their original homes remain largely empty. **77% of former Palestinian towns and villages in Israel have never been built over.**

77% NEVER BUILT OVER | 23% BUILT OVER

RAMLE: AL-LYDD, AL-RAMLE, ABU SHUSHA, AQIR, BASHSHIT, DAYR TARIF, MUZAYRI'A, QATRA, YIBNA, ZARNUQA, AL-QUBAYBA, AL-TIRA

BEERSHEBA: BEERSHEBA

GAZA: AL-MAJDAL, BARBARA, BAYT DARAS, IRAQ AL-MANSHIYYA, ISDUD, BAYT JIRJA, JULIS, AL-JURA, YASUR

SAFAD: SAFAD, ALMA, SA'SA', SALIHA, HUNIN, AL-KHALISA, AL-ZUQ AL-TAHTANI

TIBERIAS: TABARIYA

BEISAN

HEBRON: ZAKARIYYA, AL-DAWAYIMA, AL-QUBAYBA

TULKARM: QAQUN

JENIN

NAZARETH

HAIFA: HAIFA, BALAD AL-SHAYKH, IJZIM, AL-TANTURA, AL-TIRA

JAFFA: JAFFA, ABU KISHK, BAYT DAJAN, SALAMA, SAQIYA, YAZUR

ACRE: ACRE, DAYR AL-QASI, KHIRBAT JIDDIN, KUWAYKAT, AL-BASSA

JERUSALEM: JERUSALEM, AYN KARIM, LIFTA

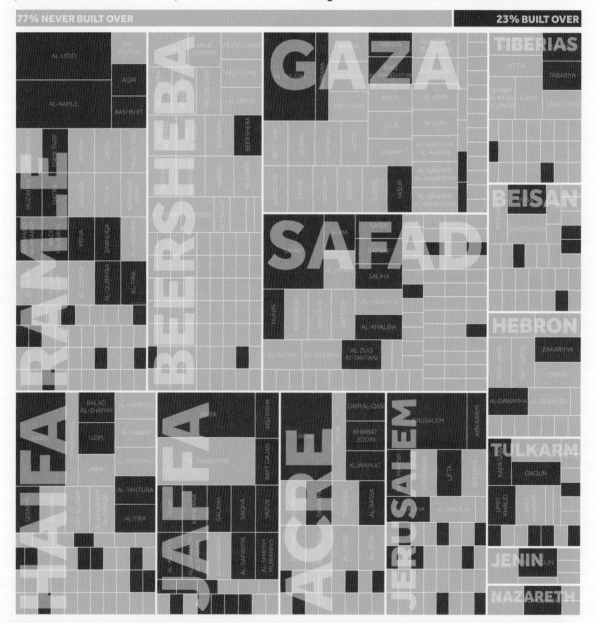

Depopulated towns/villages organised by British Mandate districts. The size of each is relative to population in 1948. 'Never built over' refers to the original built-up area of the village. Precise location of some communities in Beersheba district unknown, but assumed not to be built over as region is sparsely populated.

DATA SKETCH **SOURCES** bit.ly/vp-return • **V1** May 2017 • fb.me/visualizingpalestine • @visualizingpal

Year: 2017 | **Brief and copywriting:** Ahmad Barclay | **Design:** Ahmad Barclay | **Sources:** bit.ly/vp-return

RETURN IS POSSIBLE

THE STATUS OF 536 PALESTINIAN VILLAGES DEPOPULATED BY ISRAEL

In 1948, the UN General Assembly declared that Palestinian "refugees wishing to return to their homes and live at peace with their neighbours should be permitted to do so at the earliest practicable date".

Today, Israel systematically denies Palestinians their right to return, yet the sites of their original homes remain largely empty. **77% of former Palestinian towns and villages in Israel have never been built over.**

77% NOT BUILT OVER | 23% BUILT OVER

ACRE DISTRICT ACRE AL-BASSA AL-BIRWA AL-DAMUN AL-GHABISIYYA AL-KABRI AL-MANSHIYYA AL-MANSURA
AL-NABI RUBIN AL-NAHR AL-RUWAYS AL-SUMAYRIYYA AL-TALL AL-ZEEB AMQA ARAB AL-SAMNIYYA ARAB GHAWARINA
DAYR AL-QASI IQRIT KAFR 'INAN KHIRBAT 'IRIBBIN KHIRBAT JIDDIN KUWAYKAT MIAR SUHMATA SURUH TARBIKHA
TARSHIHA UMM AL-FARAJ BEERSHEBA DISTRICT ABU ABDOUN ABU AL UDOUS ABU AL-HUSSAIN ABU AMRAH ABU ATHERA
ABU BAKRAH ABU GHALION ABU GHALYUN ABU GRAINAT ABU JABER ABU JRAIBAN ABU JUGAIM ABU JUWAYED ABU KAFF
ABU KHATLEH ABU LIBBEH ABU MIDDAIN ABU MUAILIQ ABU RAWWAA ABU RBAIA ABU RQAYIQ ABU SHALHOUB
ABU SHUNNAR ABU SITTEH ABU SOUSAIN ABU SUAILIQ ABU SUHAIBAN ABU YEHYA AL ASAM AL BURAIQI AL FUKARA
AL-NUWAIRI AL OMOUR AL SANI AL SANI AL SOUFI AL ZRAIYE AL-ARAQIB AL-DIQS AL-HUZAIYIL AL-'IMARA AL-JAMMAMA
AL-KHALASA AL-KSARR AL-SAWAKHNEH AL-SMEERI AL-ZUWAIRA ARAB AL ASIYAT ARAB AL-QILAI ARAB SUBEIHAT
ARAB SUBHIYIN ARAB SUFIYIN ASLUJ ATAWNEH BDINAT BEERSHEBA BELI BENI OKBEH BIN AJLAN BIN RIFEE BIN SABBAH
FARAHEEN GALAZIN TAYAHA GATATWEH HKUK AL-ASSAD JANABIB KURNUB MASAMEREH MASOUDIYEEN MOHAMEDIYEEN
MUREIAT NABAAT NUSEIRAT RAWASHDEH SHEIKH NURAN SHLALYEEN SHO'OUR SUBAIHAT SUBHIYEEN THABET
UJA AL-HAFEER UMM AL-RASHRASH UROUR WUHAIDAT WUHAIDAT WULAYDEH ZARABEH ZARABEH BEISAN DISTRICT
AL-ASHRAFIYYA AL-BIRA AL-FATUR AL-GHAZZAWIYYA AL-HAMIDIYYA AL-HAMRA AL-KHUNAYZIR AL-MURASSAS
AL-SAKHINA AL-SAMIRIYYA AL-TIRA ARAB AL-ARIDA ARAB AL-BAWATI ARAB AL-SAFA ARAB ZARRA'A BASHATWI BEISAN
DANNA FARWANA JABBUL KAFRA KAWKAB AL-HAWA KHIRBAT AL-TAQA KHIRBAT AL-ZAWIYA MASIL AL-JIZL QUMYA
SHATTA SIRIN TALL AL-SHAWK UMM AJRA YUBLA ZABA GAZA DISTRICT AL-BATANI AL-GHARBI AL-BATANI AL-SHARQI
AL-FALUJA AL-JALADIYYA AL-JIYYA AL-JURA AL-MAJDAL AL-MASMIYYA AL-KABIRA AL-MASMIYYA AL-SAGHIRA
AL-MUHARRAQA AL-SAWAFIR AL-GHARBIYYA AL-SAWAFIR AL-SHAMALIYYA AL-SAWAFIR AL-SHARQIYYA ARAB SUQRIR
BARBARA BARQA BAYT AFFA BAYT DARAS BAYT JIRJA BAYT TIMA BI'LIN BURAYR DAYR SUNAYD DIMRA HAMAMA HATTA
HIRIBYA HUJ HULAYQAT IBDIS IRAQ AL-MANSHIYYA IRAQ SUWAYDAN ISDUD JULIS JUSAYR KARATIYYA KAWFAKHA
KAWKABA KHIRBET KHISAS NAJD NI'ILYA QASTINA SIMSIM SUMMIL TALL AL-TURMUS YASUR HAIFA DISTRICT ABU SHUSHA
ABU ZURAYQ AL-BUTAYMAT AL-GHUBAYYA AL-FAWQA AL-GHUBAYYA AL-TAHTA AL-JALAMA AL-KAFRAYN AL-KHUREIBA
AL-MANSI AL-MAZAR AL-NAGHNAGHIYYA AL-RIHANIYYA AL-SARAFAND AL-SAWAMIR AL-SHEIKH BUREIK AL-SINDIYANA
AL-TANTURA AL-TIRA AL-YAJUR ARAB AL-FUQARA' ARAB AL-NUFAYAT ARAB ZAHRAT AL-DUMAYRI ATLIT AYN GHAZAL
AYN HAWD BALAD AL-SHAYKH BARRAT QISARYA BURAYKA DALIYAT AL-RAWHA' HAIFA HAWSHA IJZIM JABA' KABARA
KAFR LAM KHIRBAT AL-BURJ KHIRBAT AL-DAMUN KHIRBAT AL-KASAIR KHIRBAT AL-MANARA KHIRBAT AL-MANSURA
KHIRBAT AL-SARKAS KHIRBAT QUMBAZA KHIRBAT SA'SA' KHIRBET LID KHUBBAYZA MAQURA QANNIR QIRA QISARYA
SABBARIN UMM AL-SHAWF UMM AL-ZINAT WA'ARAT AL-SARRIS WADI ARA HEBRON DISTRICT AJJUR AL-DAWAYIMA
AL-QUBAYBA BARQUSYA BAYT JIBRIN BAYT NATTIF DAYR AL-DUBBAN DAYR NAKHKHAS KHIRBAT UMM BURJ KUDNA
MUGHALLIS RA'NA TALL AL-SAFI ZAKARIYYA ZAYTA ZIKRIN JAFFA DISTRICT ABU KISHK AL-ABISIYYA AL-HARAM
AL-JAMMASIN AL-GHARBI AL-JAMMASIN AL-SHARQI AL-KHAYRIYYA AL-MANSHIYYA AL-MAS'UDIYYA AL-MIRR
AL-MUWAYLIH AL-SAFIRIYYA AL-SAWALIMA AL-SHAYKH MUWANNIS ARAB AWASSAT ARAB SHUBAKI BAYT DAJAN
BIYAR ADAS FAJJA MINTAQ'AT AL-SI'ADEEN IJLIL AL-QIBLIYYA IJLIL AL-SHAMALIYYA JAFFA JARISHA KAFR ANA RANTIYA
SALAMA SAQIYA SHEIKH SAEED AL QURANI YAZUR JENIN DISTRICT AL-LAJJUN AL-MAZAR AYN AL-MANSI
KHIRBAT AL-JAWFA NURIS ZIR'IN JERUSALEM DISTRICT AL-BURAYJ AL-JURA ALLAR AL-MALIHA AL-QABU AL-QASTAL
AL-WALAJA AQQUR ARTUF AYN KARIM BAYT 'ITAB BAYT MAHSIR BAYT NAQQUBA BAYT THUL BAYT UMM AL-MAYS
BEIT MAZMIL DAYR ABAN DAYR AL-HAWA DAYR AL-SHAYKH DAYR AMR DAYR RAFAT DAYR YASIN EIN JIDDI ISHWA' 'ISLIN
JARASH JERUSALEM KASLA KHIRBAT AL-LAWZ KHIRBAT AL-TANNUR KHIRBAT AL-'UMUR KHIRBAT ISM ALLAH LIFTA NITAF
QALUNYA RAS ABU AMMAR SARA SARIS SATAF SUBA SUFLA NAZARETH DISTRICT AL-MUJAYDAL INDUR MA'ALUL
SAFURIYYA RAMLA DISTRICT ABU AL-FADL ABU SHUSHA AJANJUL AL-BURJ AL-HADITHA AL-KHAYMA AL-KUNAYYISA
AL-LATRUN AL-LYDD AL-MAGHAR AL-MANSURA AL-MUKHAYZIN AL-NA'ANI AL-NABI RUBIN AL-QUBAB AL-QUBAYBA
AL-RAMLA AL-TINA AL-TIRA AQIR BARFILIYA BARRIYYA BASHSHIT BAYT JIZ BAYT NABALA BAYT NUBA BAYT SHANNA
BAYT SUSIN BIR MA'IN BIR SALIM DANIYAL DAYR ABU SALAMA DAYR AYYUB DAYR MUHAYSIN DAYR TARIF IDNIBBA IMWAS
INNABA JILYA JIMZU JINDAS KHARRUBA KHIRBAT BAYT FAR KHIRBAT BUWAYRA KHIRBAT ZAKARIYYA KHULDA MAJDAL
YABA MUZAYRIA NABI THARI QATRA QAZAZA QULA SAJAD SALBIT SARAFAND AL-KHARAB SARAFAND AMAR SAYDUN
SHAHMA SHILTA UMM KALKHA WADI HAUNAYN YALU YIBNA ZARNUQA SAFAD DISTRICT ABIL AL-QAMH AKBARA
AL-'URAYFIYYA AL-ABISIYYA AL-BUTAYHA AL-BUWAYZIYYA AL-DAWWARA AL-DIRBASHIYYA AL-DIRDARA
AL-FARRADIYYA AL-HAMRA AL-HUSAYNIYYA AL-JA'UNA AL-KHALISA AL-KHISAS ALMA AL-MALIKIYYA AL-MANSHIYYA
AL-MANSURA AL-MUFTAKHIRA AL-NABI YUSHA' AL-NA'IMA AL-QUDAYRIYYA AL-RAS AL-AHMAR AL-SALIHIYYA
AL-SAMMU'I AL-SANBARIYYA AL-SHAWKA AL-TAHTA AL-SHUNA AL-'ULMANIYYA AL-WAYZIYYA AL-ZAHIRIYYA AL-TAHTA
AL-ZANGHARIYYA AL-ZAWIYA AL-ZUQ AL-FAWQANI AL-ZUQ AT-TAHTANI AMMUQA ARAB AL-SHAMALINA
ARAB AL-ZUBAYD AYN AL-ZAYTUN BAYSAMUN BIRIYYA DALLATA DAYSHUM FARA FIR'IM GHABBATIYYA GHURABA
HARRAWI HUNIN JAHULA JUBB YUSUF KAFR BIR'IM KHAN AL-DUWAYR KHIRBAT AL-MUNTAR KHIRBAT KARRAZA KHIYAM
AL-WALID KIRAD AL-BAQQARA KIRAD AL-GHANNAMA LAZZAZA MADAHIL MALLAHA MANSURAT AL-KHAYT MARUS MIRUN
MUGHR AL-DRUZ MUGHR AL-KHAYT QABBA'A QADAS QADDITA QAYTIYYA SABALAN SAFAD SAFSAF SALIHA SA'SA'
TAYTABA TULAYL YARDA TIBERIAS DISTRICT AL-DALHAMIYYA AL-HAMMA AL-MAJDAL AL-MANARA AL-MANSURA
AL-NUQAYB AL-SAMAKIYYA AL-SAMRA AL-SHAJARA AL-TABIGHA AL-'UBAYDIYYA AWLAM EILABUN
GHUWAYR ABU SHUSHA HADATHA HITTIN KAFR SABT KHIRBAT AL-WA'ARA AL-SAWDA LUBYA MA'DHAR MANSHIYYAT
SAMAKH NASIR AL-DIN NIMRIN SAMAKH TABARIYA TALL AL-HUNUD WADI AL-HAMAM YAQUQ TULKARM DISTRICT
AL-JALAMA BASSAT AL-FALEK BAYYARAT HANNUN FARDISYA GHABAT ABABISHA GHABAT KAFR SUR KAFR SABA
KHIRBAT AL-BURJ KHIRBAT AL-MAJDAL KHIRBAT AL-ZABABIDA KHIRBAT BAYT LID KHIRBAT ZALAFA
KHIRBET AL-MANSHIYYA KHIRBET KHRESH MISKA QAQUN TABSUR UMM KHALID WADI AL-HAWARITH WADI QABBANI

Depopulated towns/villages organised alphabetically by British Mandate districts. 'Never built over' refers to the original built-up area of the village. Precise location of some communities in Beersheba district unknown, but assumed not to be built over as region is sparsely populated.

VP DATA SKETCH

SOURCES bit.ly/vp-return • **V1** May 2017 • fb.me/visualizingpalestine • @visualizingpal

Year: 2017 | **Brief and copywriting:** Ahmad Barclay | **Design:** Ahmad Barclay | **Sources:** bit.ly/vp-return

3.

RECOGNI APARTHE

Visuals in this section: Apartheid/Hafrada | The One State Reality | Identity Crisis | Divide and Dominate | Israeli Law Institutionalizes Discrimination | How the PA Aids Israel's Occupation | Jerusalem: A City for All? | Residency Revocation | Anatomy of Inequality | Living under Policies of Colonization in Jerusalem | Bethlehem Besieged | Heritage under

ZING

D

Threat | Shuhada St. | Politicians' Salaries and Income Inequality | The Crime of Apartheid | Born Unequal

Inhuman acts committed for the purpose of establishing and maintaining domination by one racial group of persons over any other racial group of persons and systematically oppressing them.

—Definition of the crime of apartheid, 1973 United Nations International Convention on the Suppression and Punishment of the Crime of Apartheid

[T]he available evidence establishes beyond a reasonable doubt that Israel is guilty of policies and practices that constitute the crime of apartheid.

—United Nations Economic and Social Commission for Western Asia (ESCWA), "Israeli Practices towards the Palestinian People and the Question of Apartheid" (withdrawn) (2017)

From 1945 to 1968, dozens of newly independent states in Africa and Asia entered the United Nations, where they formed a majority coalition. Together, they pushed for the 1973 Apartheid Convention, defining apartheid as a universal crime against humanity and making it illegal under international law. The crime of apartheid is now widely recognized as applicable to the system of Israeli rule over Palestinians.

Both the mass displacement of Palestinians by Israel and the formalization of apartheid in South Africa occurred in 1948. By the 1970s, the two apartheid regimes had formed a close military alliance.[1] Although apartheid looks different in every case, **Apartheid/Hafrada** introduces some of the parallels that leading anti-apartheid figures like Nelson Mandela and Archbishop Desmond Tutu recognized between the South African and Israeli regimes. In a 1997 address on the International Day of Solidarity with the Palestinian People, President Mandela said, "We know too well that our freedom is incomplete without the freedom of the Palestinians."[2] Seventeen years later, Archbishop Tutu called for sanctions against Israel, writing, "I know first-hand that Israel has created an apartheid reality within its borders and through its occupation. The parallels to my own beloved South Africa are painfully stark indeed."[3]

One of the ongoing goals of Visualizing Palestine's work has been to help people see beyond the disconnected and isolated events that put Palestinians in the headlines. Oppression in Palestine is "a structure, not an event,"[4] and apartheid is a system of control that permeates every aspect of Palestinians' daily life, from the mundane to the monumental. **The One State Reality** focuses on some of the more banal examples of this control. Its title speaks to the insistence by political elites, especially in the United States, that a two-state solution is the only formula for Palestinians to imagine their freedom, long after such a solution has been rendered obsolete by Israel's illegal settlement enterprise and apartheid policies.

In 2017, the United Nations Economic and Social Commission for Western Asia (ESCWA) became the first UN body to declare that Israel is committing the crime of apartheid. Under pressure from Israel and the United States, UN Secretary-General António Guterres withdrew ESCWA's groundbreaking report, titled "Israeli Practices towards the Palestinian People and the Question of Apartheid," claiming that the withdrawal was "not about content" but "process."[5]

The ESCWA report emphasizes the fragmentation of the Palestinian people as "the core method through which Israel enforces apartheid."[6] This fragmentation is administered by the Israeli identity card system, depicted in **Identity Crisis**. Since 1967, the Israeli government has issued an identity card to every person born between the Jordan River and the Mediterranean Sea. This system not only separates Jews from non-Jews, it also maintains control over Palestinians by fragmenting them into five different geographic and legal domains, shown again in **Divide and Dominate**. Color-coded identity cards uphold a hierarchy of rights, dictating who can and cannot move freely, live with the person they marry, access essential medical care, get a fair trial, and much more.

Apologists for Israeli apartheid often point out that Palestinian citizens of Israel can vote and hold political office, but **Israeli Law Institutionalizes Discrimination** shows that more than sixty Israeli laws make them second-class citizens. This includes the 2018 Nation-State Law, which explicitly states that only Jews have national rights under Israeli rule.

The Israeli-controlled Jerusalem Municipality adopted a city plan that aims to maintain a "demographic balance" of 60 percent Jews and 40 percent Palestinians in the city, in part through "spatial segregation of the various population groups."[7] **Jerusalem: A City for All?**, **Residency Revocation, Anatomy of Inequality,** and **Living under Policies of Colonization in Jerusalem** explore the layered, multifaceted ways that Israeli authorities pursue this goal in Jerusalem. Spatial segregation is visible across historic Palestine, and **Bethlehem Besieged**, **Heritage under Threat**, and **Shuhada St.** offer case studies from other cities.

The Palestinian Authority (PA) was established by the Oslo accords as a transitional body until the realization of an independent Palestinian state. Over the years, the PA has come to act as a subcontractor of Israeli military occupation. Palestinian scholar Alaa Tartir notes that the PA security establishment "has failed to protect Palestinians from the main source of their insecurity: the Israeli military occupation. Nor has it empowered Palestinians to resist that occupation."[8] **How the PA Aids Israel's Occupation** depicts the PA's lack of practical or moral authority in the struggle against apartheid. **Politicians' Salaries and Income Inequality** highlights the issue of corruption in Palestine and globally, based on data comparing the salaries of politicians to the national income per capita in their respective countries.

While the withdrawal of the ESCWA report in 2017 initially seemed like a setback for recognition of the apartheid framework, in retrospect it was an early indication of an impending shift in mainstream acknowledgment of the nature of Palestinian oppression. In April 2021, Human Rights Watch became the first international human rights organization to conclude that Israel is committing the crime of apartheid as defined in international law, in a report titled "A Threshold Crossed: Israeli Authorities and the Crimes of Apartheid and Persecution."[9] We partnered with them on two series of visuals for the report: **The Crime of Apartheid** and **Born Unequal**.

A few months before the Human Rights Watch report, B'Tselem, an Israeli human rights organization, issued a paper titled "A Regime of Jewish Supremacy from the Jordan River to the Mediterranean Sea: This Is Apartheid." The paper emphasizes that Israelis and Palestinians across historic Palestine live under a single regime that uses "laws, practices and state violence designed to cement the supremacy of one group."[10]

Amnesty International's report "Israel's Apartheid against Palestinians" followed one year later, in February 2022. It opens with a 2019 statement by Israeli Prime Minister Benjamin Netanyahu: "Israel is not a state of all its citizens . . . [but rather] the nation-state of the Jewish people and only them."[11] In March, the UN special rapporteur on human rights in the occupied Palestinian territories, Michael Lynk, submitted a report to the UN Human Rights Council stating that Israeli policy "has imposed upon Palestine an apartheid reality in a post-apartheid world."[12]

These reports mark a milestone in the international human rights community's approach to Israeli impunity. They are also a potent reminder that the world must listen to Palestinian activists and intellectuals, who have been ignored and punished for naming apartheid for generations. It is by uplifting Palestinian knowledge and histories of collective struggle that we will reach a more transformative vision of justice.

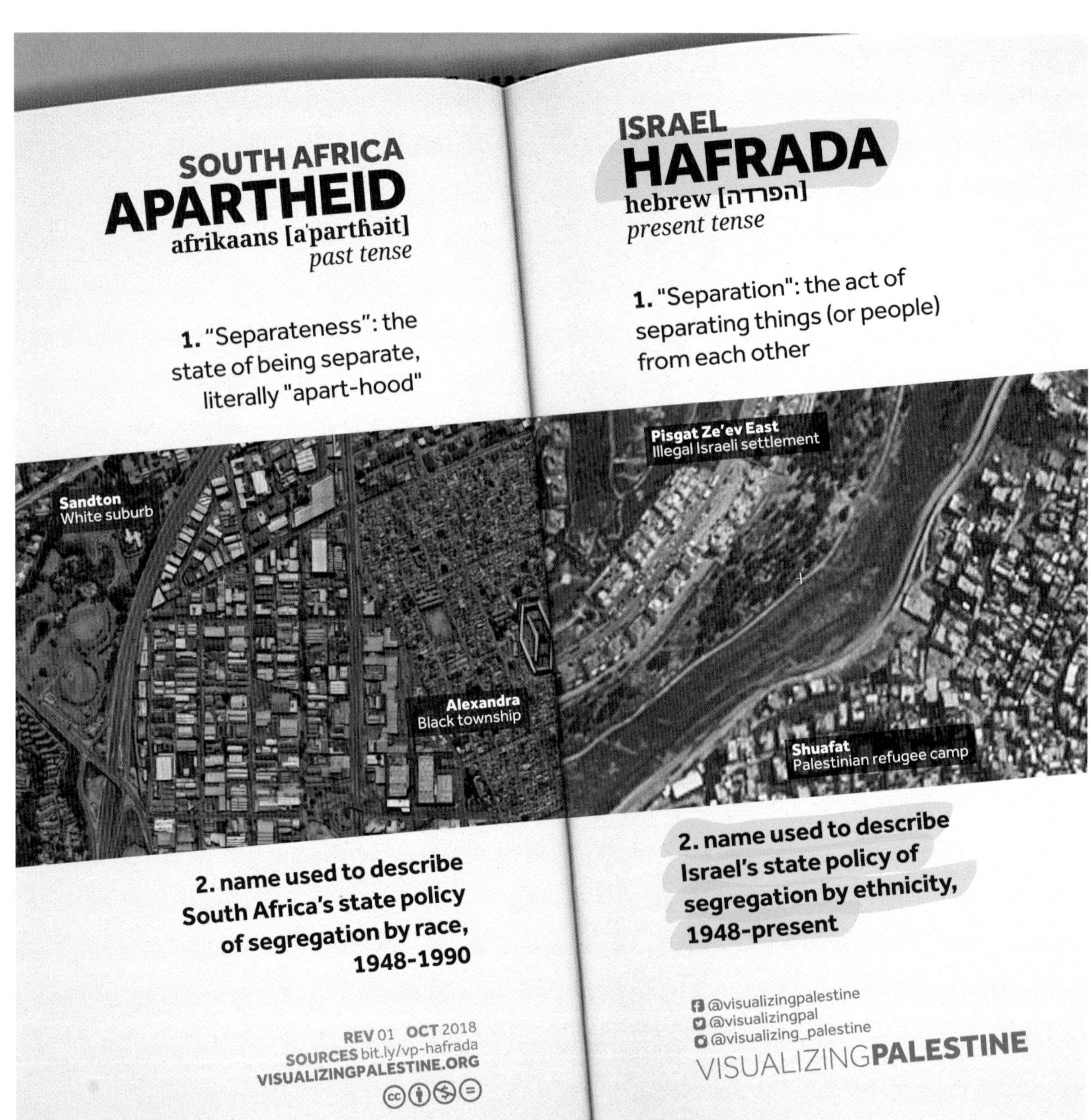
SOUTH AFRICA
APARTHEID
afrikaans [a'partɦəit]
past tense
1. "Separateness": the state of being separate, literally "apart-hood"
Sandton
White suburb
Alexandra
Black township
2. name used to describe South Africa's state policy of segregation by race, 1948-1990
REV 01 OCT 2018
SOURCES bit.ly/vp-hafrada
VISUALIZINGPALESTINE.ORG
ISRAEL
HAFRADA
hebrew [הפרדה]
present tense
1. "Separation": the act of separating things (or people) from each other
Pisgat Ze'ev East
Illegal Israeli settlement
Shuafat
Palestinian refugee camp
2. name used to describe Israel's state policy of segregation by ethnicity, 1948-present
@visualizingpalestine
@visualizingpal
@visualizing_palestine
VISUALIZINGPALESTINE

Year: 2018 | **Brief and copywriting:** Ahmad Barclay, Robin Jones | **Design:** Ahmad Barclay | **Sources:** bit.ly/vp-hafrada

SOUTH AFRICA
APARTHEID
afrikaans [a'partɦəit]
past tense
= No black ownership
1913
Natives Land Act
The first of a series of laws that were designed to outlaw Black land ownership and segregate 'population groups' by race
SEP 2018
SOURCES bit.ly/vp-hafrada
VISUALIZINGPALESTINE.ORG
1. LAND EXPROPRIATION
ISRAEL
HAFRADA
hebrew [הפרדה]
present tense
= Israeli 'state land'
1950
Absentee Property Law
The first of a series of laws bringing the land of displaced Palestinians under Israeli state control for the benefit of Jewish-only settlement
@visualizingpalestine
@visualizingpal
@visualizing_palestine
VISUALIZINGPALESTINE

SOUTH AFRICA
APARTHEID
afrikaans [a'partɦəit]
past tense

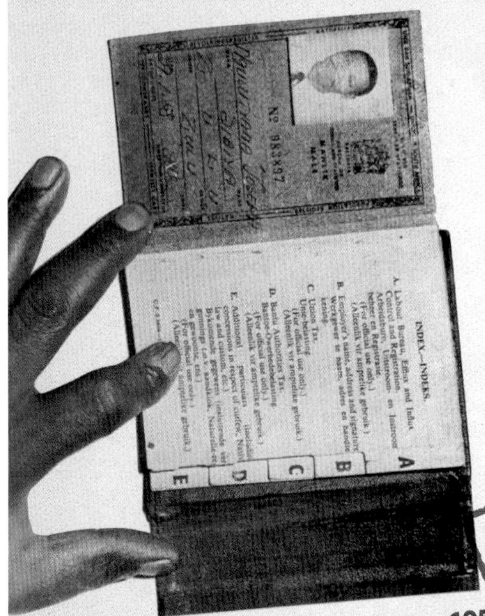

ISRAEL
HAFRADA
hebrew [הפרדה]
present tense
2.
RACIAL
CLASSIFICATION
1952
Pass Laws Act
Required all Black people in South Africa over the age of 16 to carry a 'pass book' while in White areas
1982
Identity Card Act
Requires all people in Israel, West Bank and Gaza over the age of 16 to carry Israeli issued ID card which can be used to identify their ethnicity
SEP 2018
SOURCES bit.ly/vp-hafrada
VISUALIZINGPALESTINE.ORG
@visualizingpalestine
@visualizingpal
@visualizing_palestine
VISUALIZINGPALESTINE

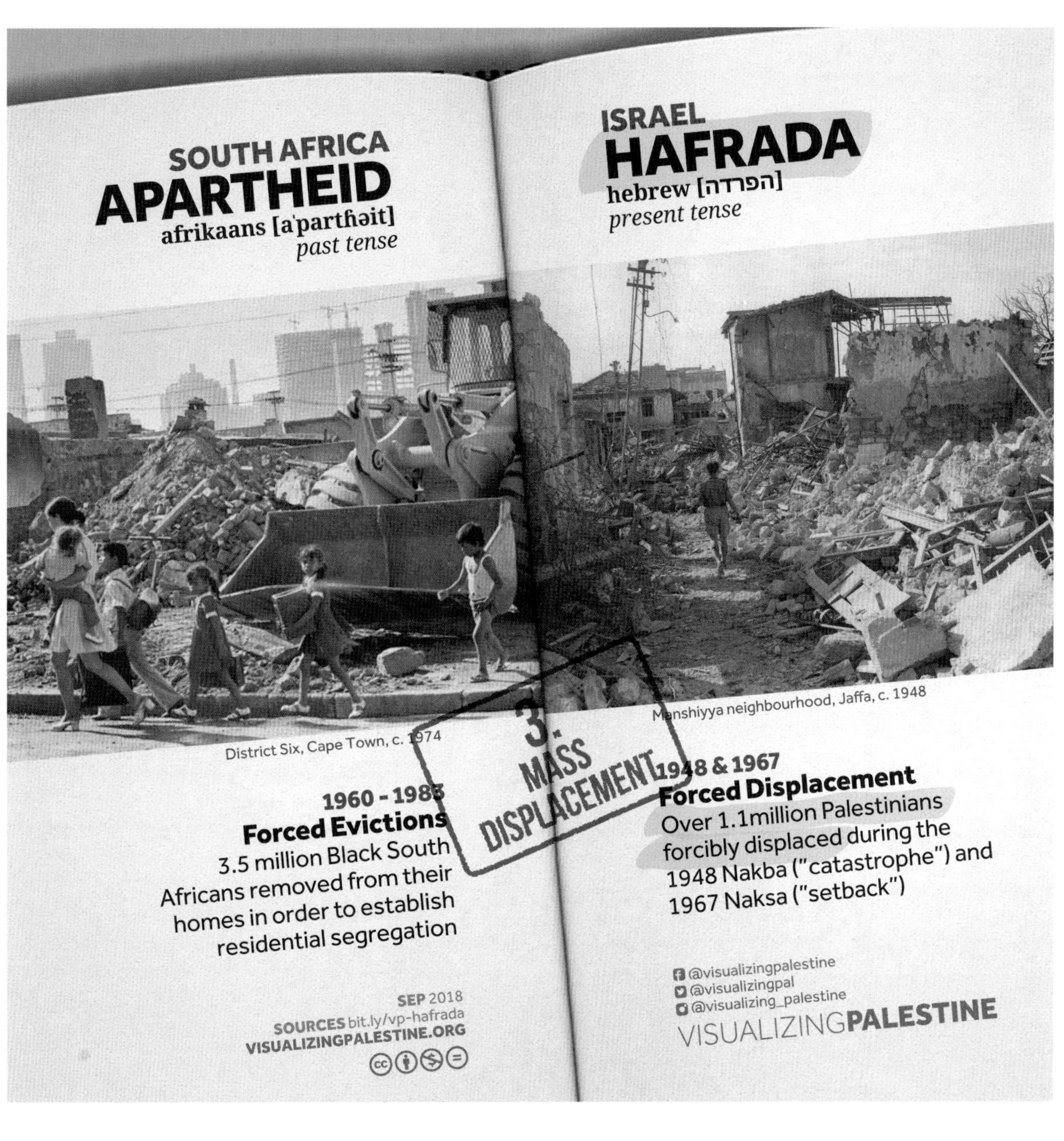
SOUTH AFRICA
APARTHEID
afrikaans [a'partɦəit]
past tense
District Six, Cape Town, c. 1974
1960 - 1983
Forced Evictions
3.5 million Black South Africans removed from their homes in order to establish residential segregation
SEP 2018
SOURCES bit.ly/vp-hafrada
VISUALIZINGPALESTINE.ORG
ISRAEL
HAFRADA
hebrew [הפרדה]
present tense
Manshiyya neighbourhood, Jaffa, c. 1948
3.
MASS
DISPLACEMENT
1948 & 1967
Forced Displacement
Over 1.1million Palestinians forcibly displaced during the 1948 Nakba ("catastrophe") and 1967 Naksa ("setback")
@visualizingpalestine
@visualizingpal
@visualizing_palestine
VISUALIZINGPALESTINE

SOUTH AFRICA
APARTHEID
afrikaans [a'partɦəit]
past tense

ISRAEL
HAFRADA
hebrew [הפרדה]
present tense

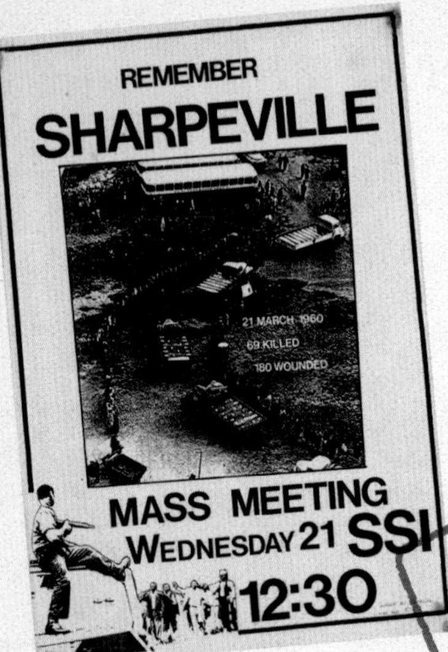
REMEMBER
SHARPEVILLE
21 MARCH 1960
69 KILLED
180 WOUNDED
MASS MEETING
WEDNESDAY 21
SSI
12:30

مسيرة العودة الكبرى
مستمرون

4.
VIOLENT
REPRESSION

1960
Sharpeville Massacre
69 unarmed South Africans killed during peaceful protests against the racist 'pass laws' ID system

2018
Great March of Return
42 unarmed Palestinians killed in Gaza in one day during protests calling for end to Israeli siege and return of refugees

SEP 2018
SOURCES bit.ly/vp-hafrada
VISUALIZINGPALESTINE.ORG

@visualizingpalestine
@visualizingpal
@visualizing_palestine
VISUALIZING**PALESTINE**

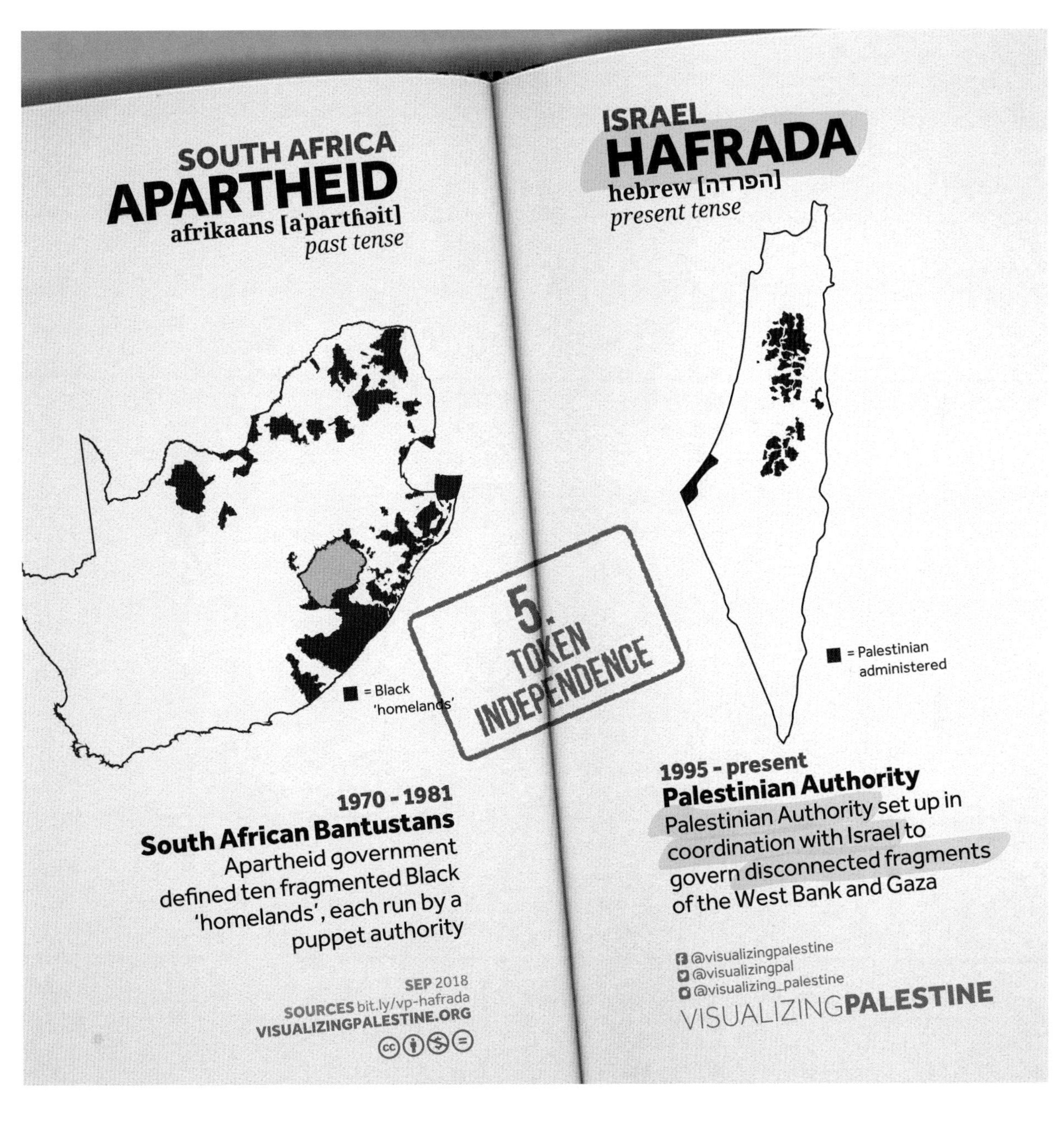
SOUTH AFRICA
APARTHEID
afrikaans [a'partheit]
past tense
= Black 'homelands'
1970 - 1981
South African Bantustans
Apartheid government defined ten fragmented Black 'homelands', each run by a puppet authority
SEP 2018
SOURCES bit.ly/vp-hafrada
VISUALIZINGPALESTINE.ORG
5. TOKEN INDEPENDENCE
ISRAEL
HAFRADA
hebrew [הפרדה]
present tense
= Palestinian administered
1995 - present
Palestinian Authority
Palestinian Authority set up in coordination with Israel to govern disconnected fragments of the West Bank and Gaza
@visualizingpalestine
@visualizingpal
@visualizing_palestine
VISUALIZINGPALESTINE

• THE ONE STA

ISRAELI CONTROL OF PA

To the international public, it often appears as thou
distinct entities with separate spheres of sovereignty.
Israel exercises control over every aspect of Pa

7:30 AM Take a shower

8:30 AM Drive to work, Bethlehem to Ramallah

1:30 PM Buy a sandwich

5:00 PM Fill your ca with gas

ISRAEL CONTROLS

WATER

Palestinians in the West Bank must buy water from Israel's national water company, Mekorot, which **appropriates 80% of the West Bank water supply.**

ACCESS

Israel maintains **over 98 fixed checkpoints** and hundreds of random "flying" checkpoints in the West Bank, choking Palestinian freedom of movement.

CURRENCY

Today, there is no Palestinian currency; **everybody uses the Israeli shekel.** Israel is capable of blocking any future attempts to create a Palestinian currency.

GASOLIN

Israel has **prevented Palestinians from accessin oil and gas reserves** on th own territory, making them dependent on Israel for energy needs.

VISUALIZING**PALESTINE**

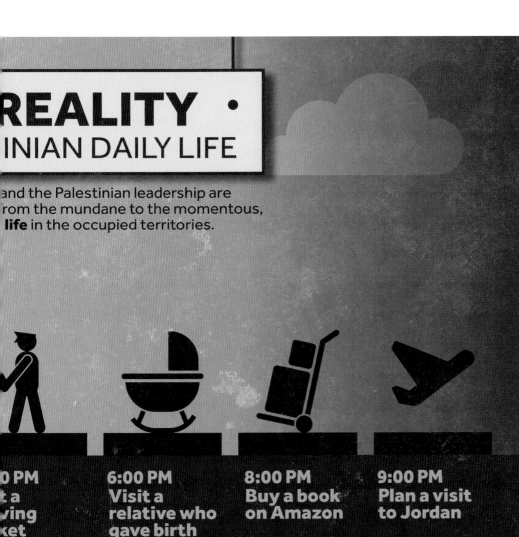

REALITY •

INIAN DAILY LIFE

and the Palestinian leadership are
rom the mundane to the momentous,
life in the occupied territories.

0 PM
t a
ving
ket

6:00 PM
Visit a relative who gave birth

8:00 PM
Buy a book on Amazon

9:00 PM
Plan a visit to Jordan

GAL
STEM

stinians
subject
raeli law
n in the
t Bank.
rea C,
el can issue
ng tickets
alestinians,
are subject
raeli military
ts in the
nt of non
ment.

POPULATION REGISTRY

Israel manages a single population registry. **All children must be registered with the Israeli registry** in order to receive an ID card and/or passport.

IMPORT & EXPORT

All Palestinian **imports go through the Israeli customs system.** Israeli authorities can block any import from reaching its recipient.

MOVEMENT

Any travel outside of Palestine/ Israel requires Israeli permission. There is no way of entering or leaving without crossing an Israeli-controlled border.

SOURCES B'tselem, hrw, bit.ly/vp-onestate
WWW.**VISUALIZINGPALESTINE**.ORG

@visualizingpal
/visualizing_palestine
fb.me/visualizingpalestine

NOV 2017

Year: 2017
Brief and copywriting: Iman Annab, Zaid Amr, Ramzi Jaber, Robin Jones
Design: Yosra El Gazzar
Sources: bit.ly/vp-onestate

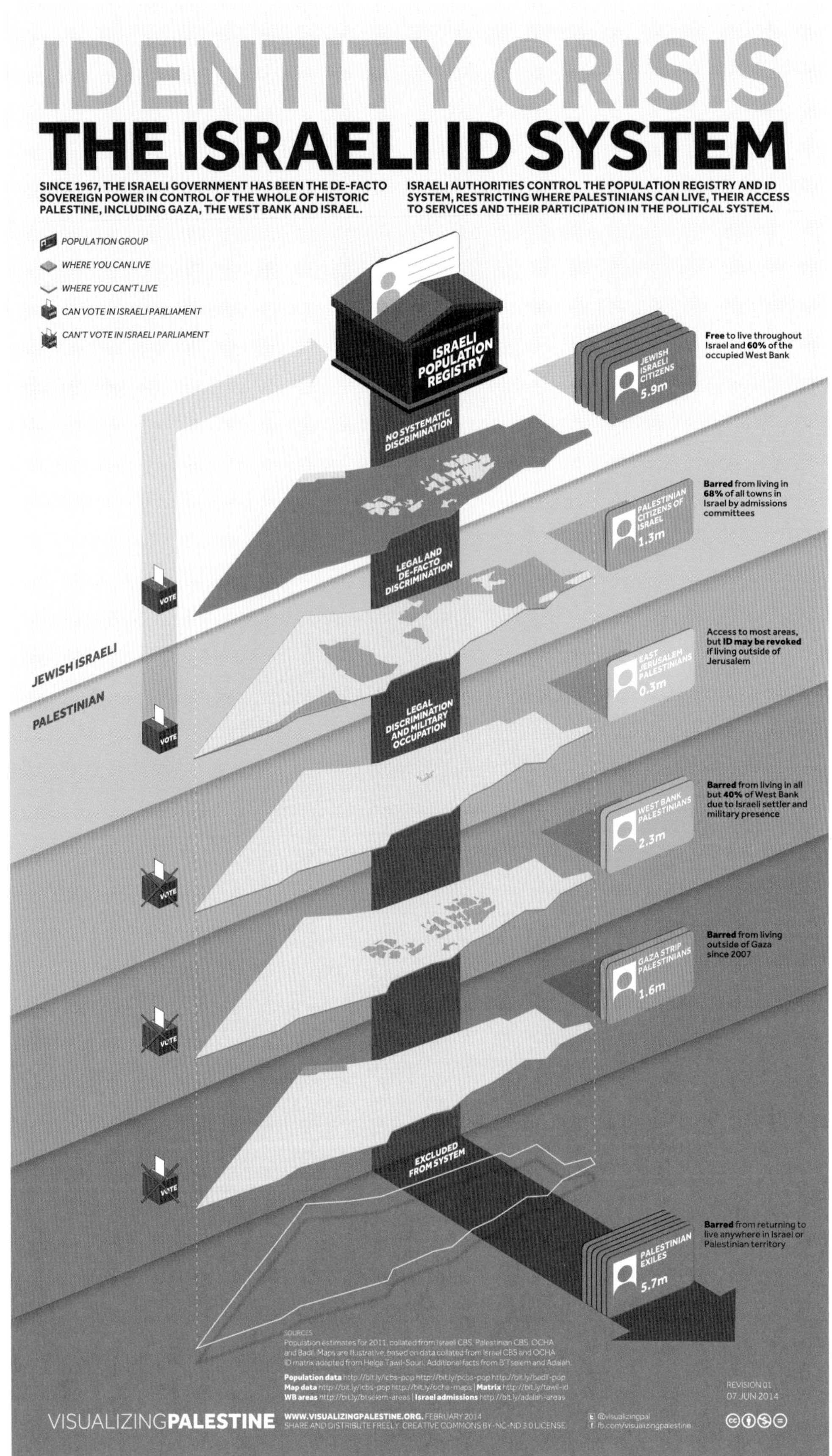
IDENTITY CRISIS
THE ISRAELI ID SYSTEM
SINCE 1967, THE ISRAELI GOVERNMENT HAS BEEN THE DE-FACTO SOVEREIGN POWER IN CONTROL OF THE WHOLE OF HISTORIC PALESTINE, INCLUDING GAZA, THE WEST BANK AND ISRAEL.
ISRAELI AUTHORITIES CONTROL THE POPULATION REGISTRY AND ID SYSTEM, RESTRICTING WHERE PALESTINIANS CAN LIVE, THEIR ACCESS TO SERVICES AND THEIR PARTICIPATION IN THE POLITICAL SYSTEM.
POPULATION GROUP
WHERE YOU CAN LIVE
WHERE YOU CAN'T LIVE
CAN VOTE IN ISRAELI PARLIAMENT
CAN'T VOTE IN ISRAELI PARLIAMENT
ISRAELI POPULATION REGISTRY
JEWISH ISRAELI CITIZENS 5.9m
Free to live throughout Israel and 60% of the occupied West Bank
NO SYSTEMATIC DISCRIMINATION
PALESTINIAN CITIZENS OF ISRAEL 1.3m
Barred from living in 68% of all towns in Israel by admissions committees
LEGAL AND DE-FACTO DISCRIMINATION
EAST JERUSALEM PALESTINIANS 0.3m
Access to most areas, but ID may be revoked if living outside of Jerusalem
JEWISH ISRAELI
PALESTINIAN
VOTE
LEGAL DISCRIMINATION AND MILITARY OCCUPATION
WEST BANK PALESTINIANS 2.3m
Barred from living in all but 40% of West Bank due to Israeli settler and military presence
GAZA STRIP PALESTINIANS 1.6m
Barred from living outside of Gaza since 2007
EXCLUDED FROM SYSTEM
PALESTINIAN EXILES 5.7m
Barred from returning to live anywhere in Israel or Palestinian territory
SOURCES
Population estimates for 2011, collated from Israeli CBS, Palestinian CBS, OCHA and Badil. Maps are illustrative, based on data collated from Israel CBS and OCHA. ID matrix adapted from Helga Tawil-Souri. Additional facts from B'Tselem and Adalah.
Population data http://bit.ly/icbs-pop http://bit.ly/pcbs-pop http://bit.ly/badil-pop
Map data http://bit.ly/icbs-pop http://bit.ly/ocha-maps | Matrix http://bit.ly/tawil-id
WB areas http://bit.ly/btselem-areas | Israel admissions http://bit.ly/adalah-areas
REVISION 01
07 JUN 2014
VISUALIZINGPALESTINE
WWW.VISUALIZINGPALESTINE.ORG. FEBRUARY 2014
SHARE AND DISTRIBUTE FREELY. CREATIVE COMMONS BY-NC-ND 3.0 LICENSE.
@visualizingpal
fb.com/visualizingpalestine

Year: 2014 | **Brief and copywriting:** Zaid Amro, Joumana al Jabri, Ahmad Barclay, Institute for Middle East Understanding, Ramzi Jaber, Fadi Shayya, Hana Sleiman | **Design:** Conor McNally, Hani Asfour, Ahmad Barclay, Danny Khoury | **Sources:** bit.ly/vp-Sources-2012-2015

Since 1948, Israeli laws, policies, and practices around nationality and land have institutionalized a regime of racial domination and oppression over the Palestinian people amounting to the crime of apartheid. Israel maintains its apartheid regime through the strategic fragmentation of the Palestinian people into at least four separate geographic, legal, and political domains
DIVIDE & DOMINATE
HOW ISRAEL MAINTAINS APARTHEID AND DENIES PALESTINIAN SELF-DETERMINATION
12% PALESTINIAN CITIZENS OF ISRAEL (1948 Palestine)
Citizenship status granted to Palestinians inferior to nationality status reserved for Jews only
35% PALESTINIANS LIVING UNDER MILITARY LAW
Prolonged Israeli military occupation, closure and blockade of the Gaza Strip, the annexation wall, & severe movement restrictions further entrench Israel's strategic fragmentation
As a result of strategic fragmentation, Palestinians cannot meet, group, or exercise collective rights, in particular the right to self determination
20% West Bank
15% Gaza
50%
PALESTINIAN REFUGEES & EXILES
Denied the right of return to their homes, land, and country. Note: an additional 760,000 Palestinians are internally displaced within historic Palestine
3%
PALESTINIANS IN JERUSALEM
Civil law institutionalizes a revocable residency status for Palestinians
Israel's apartheid laws, policies and practices are designed to ensure:
Denial of the right of return of Palestinian refugees
Continued population transfer
Dispossession of the Palestinian people
Entrenchment of Israeli settler colonialism
MAY 2022
@visualizingpal
/visualizing_palestine
fb.me/visualizingpalestine
SOURCES bit.ly/vp-apartheid
WWW.VISUALIZINGPALESTINE.ORG
مركز الميزان لحقوق الإنسان
Al Mezan Center for Human Rights
AL-HAQ
VISUALIZINGPALESTINE

Year: 2022 | **Brief and copywriting:** Wesam Ahmad, Jessica Anderson, Nada Awad, Elizabeth Rghebi | **Design:** Yosra El Gazzar | **Sources:** bit.ly/vp-apartheid

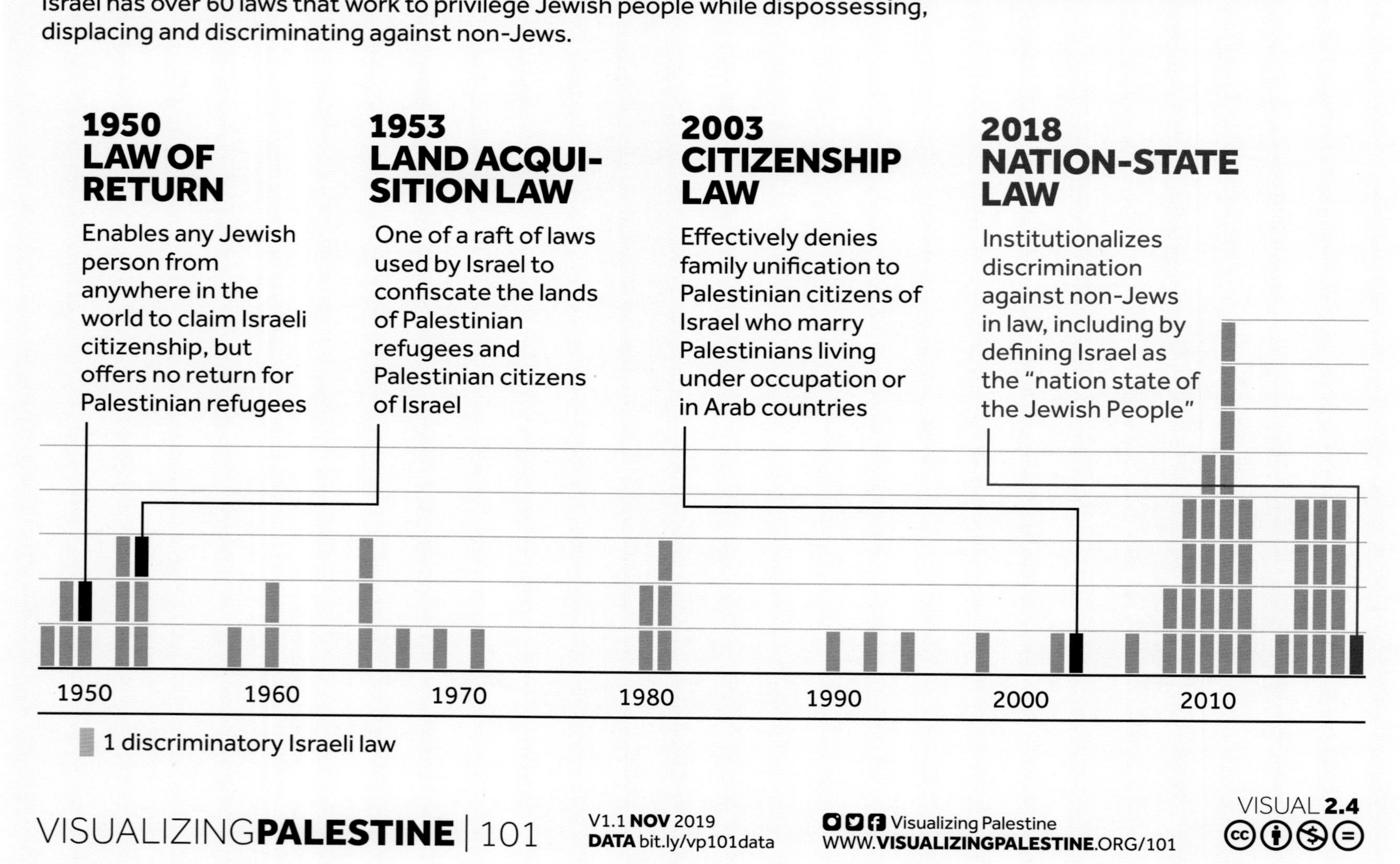
ISRAELI LAW INSTITUTIONALIZES DISCRIMINATION
Israel has over 60 laws that work to privilege Jewish people while dispossessing, displacing and discriminating against non-Jews.
1950 LAW OF RETURN
Enables any Jewish person from anywhere in the world to claim Israeli citizenship, but offers no return for Palestinian refugees
1953 LAND ACQUISITION LAW
One of a raft of laws used by Israel to confiscate the lands of Palestinian refugees and Palestinian citizens of Israel
2003 CITIZENSHIP LAW
Effectively denies family unification to Palestinian citizens of Israel who marry Palestinians living under occupation or in Arab countries
2018 NATION-STATE LAW
Institutionalizes discrimination against non-Jews in law, including by defining Israel as the "nation state of the Jewish People"
1950
1960
1970
1980
1990
2000
2010
1 discriminatory Israeli law
VISUALIZINGPALESTINE | 101
V1.1 NOV 2019
DATA bit.ly/vp101data
Visualizing Palestine
WWW.VISUALIZINGPALESTINE.ORG/101
VISUAL 2.4

Year: 2019 | **Brief and copywriting:** Ahmad Barclay | **Design:** Ahmad Barclay, Yosra El Gazzar | **Sources:** bit.ly/vp101data

HOW THE P.A. AIDS ISRAEL'S OCCUPATION
1 ISRAEL CONTROLS THE MAJORITY OF PALEST-INIAN AUTHORITY (PA) INCOME
55% Israeli controlled VAT & customs revenues
16% Foreign finance
26% PA direct revenue
2017 PA budget data
2 PA SPENDS HEAVILY ON ITS SECURITY FORCES, WHICH COORDINATE WITH ISRAEL
29% Security & public order
20% Education
19% Health & social services
31% All other spending
3 PA CRACKS DOWN ON PALESTINIAN POLITICAL DISSENT
68%
say that people cannot criticize the PA without fear
72%
support an end to security coordination with Israel
2018 polling data
VISUALIZINGPALESTINE | 101
V1 SEP 2019
DATA bit.ly/vp101data
Visualizing Palestine
WWW.VISUALIZINGPALESTINE.ORG/101
VISUAL 2.5

Year: 2019 | **Brief and copywriting:** Ahmad Barclay | **Design:** Ahmad Barclay, Yosra El Gazzar | **Sources:** bit.ly/vp101data

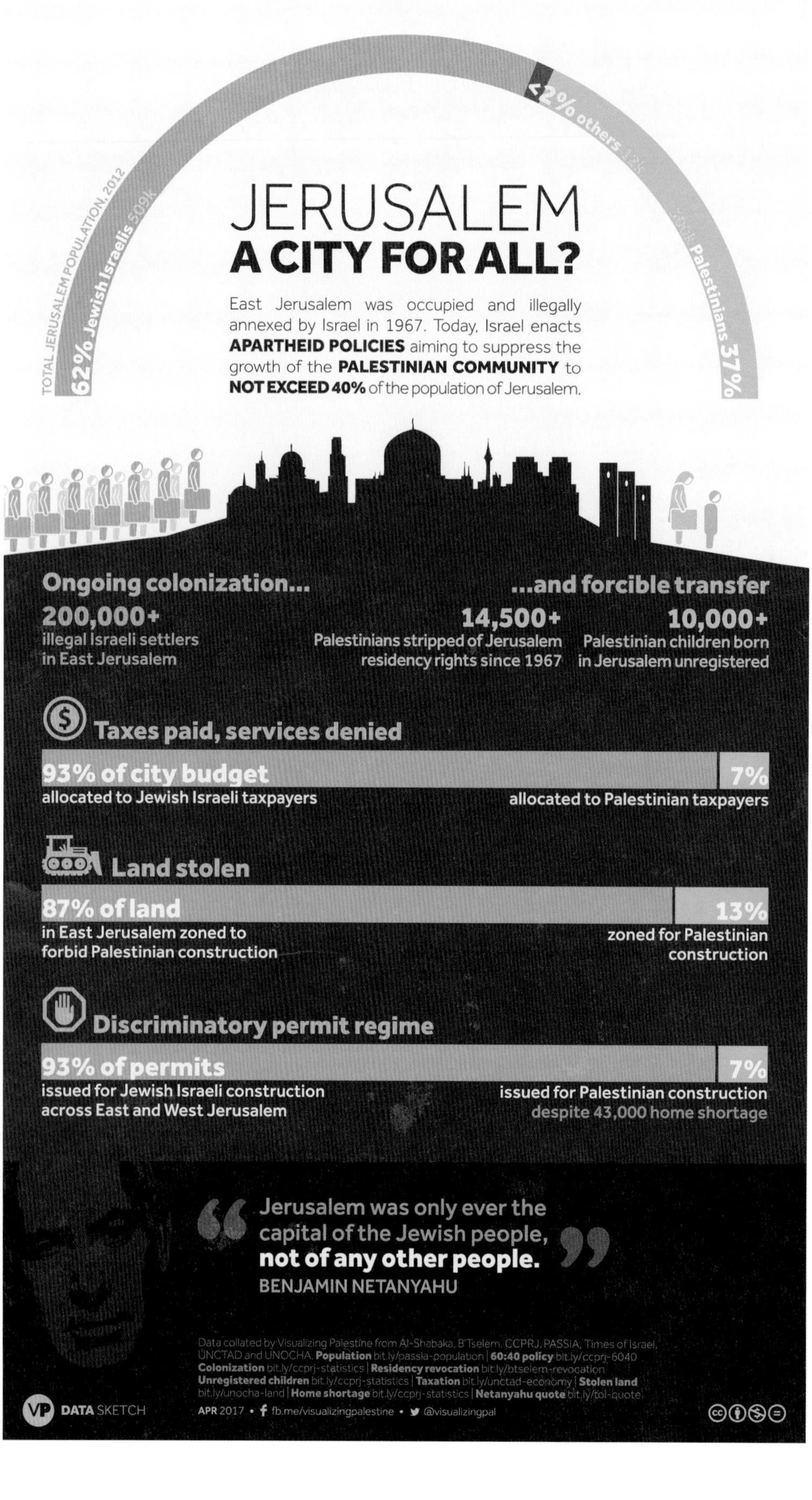

TOTAL JERUSALEM POPULATION, 2012
62% Jewish Israelis 509k
<2% others 13k
300k Palestinians 37%
JERUSALEM
A CITY FOR ALL?
East Jerusalem was occupied and illegally annexed by Israel in 1967. Today, Israel enacts APARTHEID POLICIES aiming to suppress the growth of the PALESTINIAN COMMUNITY to NOT EXCEED 40% of the population of Jerusalem.

Ongoing colonization...

200,000+
illegal Israeli settlers in East Jerusalem

...and forcible transfer

14,500+
Palestinians stripped of Jerusalem residency rights since 1967

10,000+
Palestinian children born in Jerusalem unregistered

Taxes paid, services denied

93% of city budget allocated to Jewish Israeli taxpayers

7% allocated to Palestinian taxpayers

Land stolen

87% of land in East Jerusalem zoned to forbid Palestinian construction

13% zoned for Palestinian construction

Discriminatory permit regime

93% of permits issued for Jewish Israeli construction across East and West Jerusalem

7% issued for Palestinian construction despite 43,000 home shortage

"Jerusalem was only ever the capital of the Jewish people, **not of any other people.**"
BENJAMIN NETANYAHU

Data collated by Visualizing Palestine from Al-Shabaka, B'Tselem, CCPRJ, PASSIA, Times of Israel, UNCTAD and UNOCHA. **Population** bit.ly/passia-population | **60:40 policy** bit.ly/ccprj-6040 **Colonization** bit.ly/ccprj-statistics | **Residency revocation** bit.ly/btselem-revocation **Unregistered children** bit.ly/ccprj-statistics | **Taxation** bit.ly/unctad-economy | **Stolen land** bit.ly/unocha-land | **Home shortage** bit.ly/ccprj-statistics | **Netanyahu quote** bit.ly/tol-quote

VP DATA SKETCH

APR 2017 • fb.me/visualizingpalestine • @visualizingpal

Year: 2017
Brief and copywriting: Iman Annab, Robin Jones
Design: Ahmad Barclay, Saeed Abu-Jaber
Sources: bit.ly/vp-Sources-2012-2015

JERUSALEM
A CITY FOR ALL?
90%
of Jerusalem's city budget is directed toward Jewish Israeli neighbourhoods
Only 10%
is directed toward Palestinian neighbourhoods,
home to 37% of the population
VISUALIZINGPALESTINE
SOURCES bit.ly/iramim-budget
WWW.VISUALIZINGPALESTINE.ORG
visualizingpal
visualizing_palestine
visualizingpalestine
OCT 2017

Year: 2017 | **Brief and copywriting:** Iman Annab, Robin Jones | **Design:** Ahmad Barclay, Saeed Abu-Jaber | **Sources:** bit.ly/iramim-budget

JERUSALEM
A CITY FOR ALL?

o = one Palestinian child

10,000
Palestinians born in Jerusalem have **no legal status because their parents hold different ID cards** and Israel will not register them

VISUALIZING**PALESTINE** SOURCES bit.ly/vp-civic-children
WWW.**VISUALIZINGPALESTINE**.ORG
visualizingpal
visualizing_palestine
visualizingpalestine
OCT 2017

Year: 2017 | **Brief and copywriting:** Iman Annab, Robin Jones | **Design:** Ahmad Barclay, Saeed Abu-Jaber | **Sources:** bit.ly/vp-civic-children

JERUSALEM
A CITY FOR ALL?

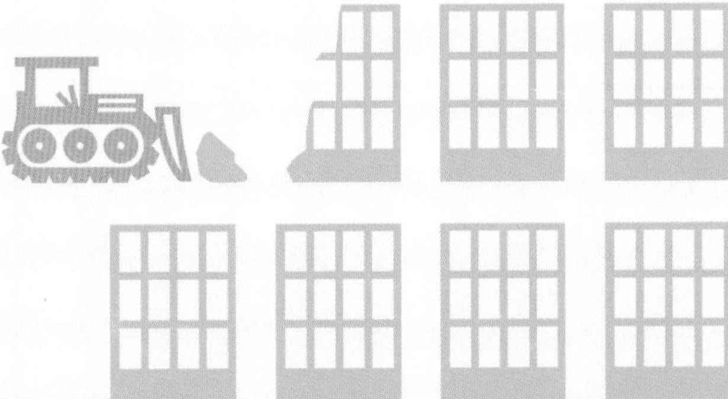

Israel demolished
685
Palestinian homes in Jerusalem
between 2004 and 2016.

2,513
people were made homeless.

VISUALIZING**PALESTINE** SOURCES bit.ly/BTselem-jrslm WWW.**VISUALIZINGPALESTINE**.ORG

visualizingpal
visualizing_palestine
visualizingpalestine

OCT 2017

Year: 2017 | **Brief and copywriting:** Iman Annab, Robin Jones | **Design:** Ahmad Barclay, Saeed Abu-Jaber | **Sources:** bit.ly/BTselem-jrslm

JERUSALEM
A CITY FOR ALL?
As of 2017, over
200,000
Israelis live in
illegal settlements
on Palestinian land
in East Jerusalem.
VISUALIZINGPALESTINE
SOURCES bit.ly/passia-jerusalem
WWW.VISUALIZINGPALESTINE.ORG
visualizingpal
visualizing_palestine
visualizingpalestine
OCT 2017

Year: 2017 | **Brief and copywriting:** Iman Annab, Robin Jones | **Design:** Ahmad Barclay, Saeed Abu-Jaber | **Sources:** bit.ly/passia-jerusalem

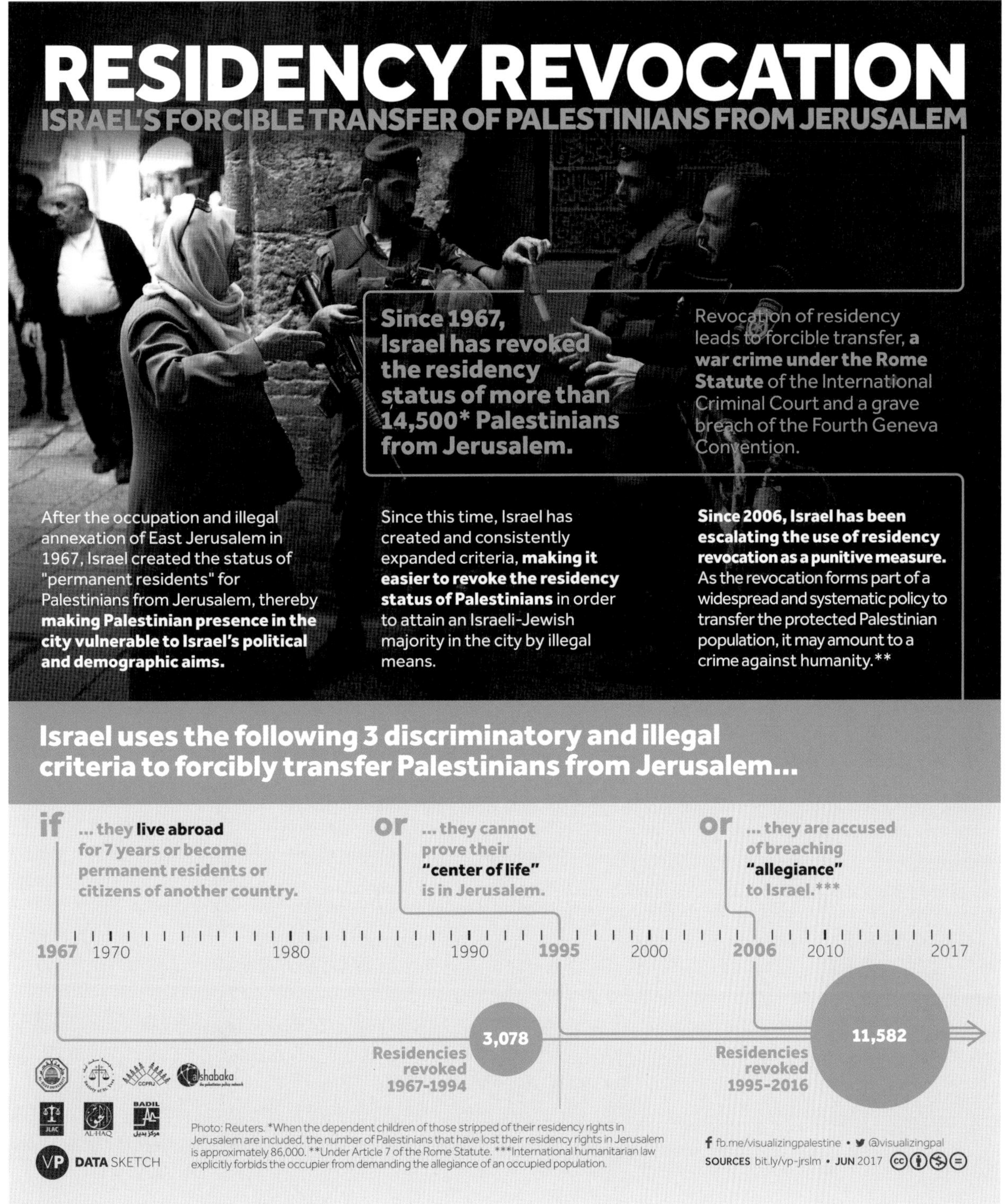
RESIDENCY REVOCATION
ISRAEL'S FORCIBLE TRANSFER OF PALESTINIANS FROM JERUSALEM
Since 1967, Israel has revoked the residency status of more than 14,500* Palestinians from Jerusalem.
Revocation of residency leads to forcible transfer, a war crime under the Rome Statute of the International Criminal Court and a grave breach of the Fourth Geneva Convention.
After the occupation and illegal annexation of East Jerusalem in 1967, Israel created the status of "permanent residents" for Palestinians from Jerusalem, thereby making Palestinian presence in the city vulnerable to Israel's political and demographic aims.
Since this time, Israel has created and consistently expanded criteria, making it easier to revoke the residency status of Palestinians in order to attain an Israeli-Jewish majority in the city by illegal means.
Since 2006, Israel has been escalating the use of residency revocation as a punitive measure. As the revocation forms part of a widespread and systematic policy to transfer the protected Palestinian population, it may amount to a crime against humanity.**
Israel uses the following 3 discriminatory and illegal criteria to forcibly transfer Palestinians from Jerusalem...
if ... they live abroad for 7 years or become permanent residents or citizens of another country.
or ... they cannot prove their "center of life" is in Jerusalem.
or ... they are accused of breaching "allegiance" to Israel.***
1967
1970
1980
1990
1995
2000
2006
2010
2017
3,078
Residencies revoked 1967-1994
11,582
Residencies revoked 1995-2016
alshabaka
CCPRJ
JLAC
AL-HAQ
BADIL
VP DATA SKETCH
Photo: Reuters. *When the dependent children of those stripped of their residency rights in Jerusalem are included, the number of Palestinians that have lost their residency rights in Jerusalem is approximately 86,000. **Under Article 7 of the Rome Statute. ***International humanitarian law explicitly forbids the occupier from demanding the allegiance of an occupied population.
fb.me/visualizingpalestine • @visualizingpal
SOURCES bit.ly/vp-jrslm • JUN 2017

Year: 2017 | **Brief and copywriting:** Iman Annab, Nada Awad | **Design:** Ahmad Barclay | **Photo:** Ronen Zvulun (Reuters) | **Sources:** bit.ly/vp-jrslm

JERUSALEM

ANATOMY OF INEQUALITY

West Jerusalem was ethnically cleansed of Palestinians in 1948. The rest of the city was annexed by Israel in 1967, along with most of its Palestinian inhabitants. Today, the Israeli controlled Jerusalem municipality enacts a system of apartheid policies and laws to aid Israeli settlement in the city while ensuring the Palestinian community does not exceed 40% of the population.

WESTERN JERUSALEM

OLD CITY

EASTERN JERUSALEM

HISTORIC DISPLACEMENT

50,000 FORCIBLY DISPLACED

Over 50,000 Palestinians were forcibly displaced from West Jerusalem in 1948. Today its population is almost exclusively Jewish Israeli.

LAND CONFISCATION

220,000 ILLEGAL SETTLERS

300,000 RESIDENTS LANDLESS

Since 1967, over 220,000 Jewish Israelis have settled illegally in East Jerusalem on land confiscated from its 300,000 Palestinian residents.

HOME

Israel's

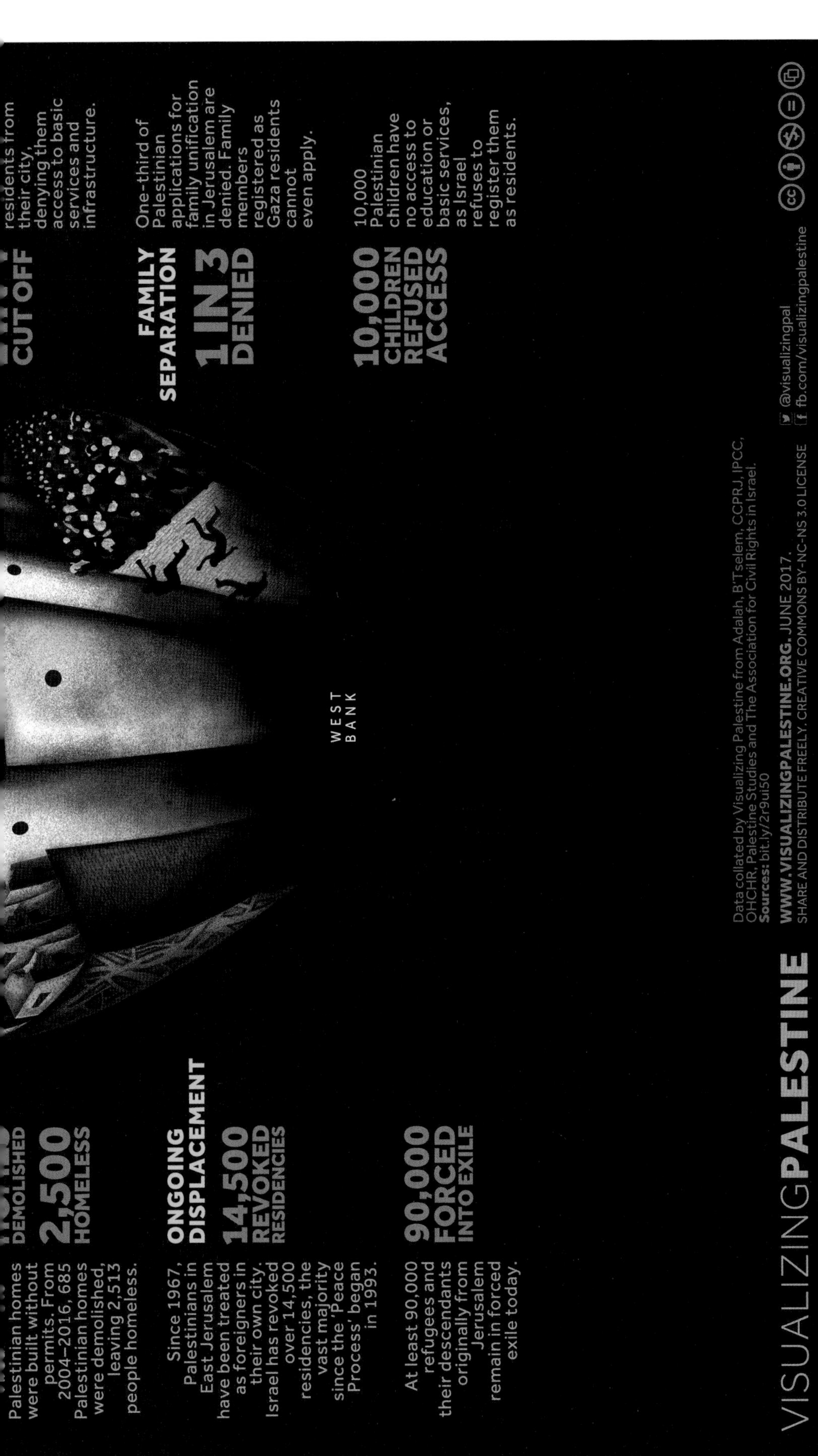
DEMOLISHED
2,500
HOMELESS
Palestinian homes were built without permits. From 2004–2016, 685 Palestinian homes were demolished, leaving 2,513 people homeless.
ONGOING DISPLACEMENT
14,500
REVOKED RESIDENCIES
Since 1967, Palestinians in East Jerusalem have been treated as foreigners in their own city; Israel has revoked over 14,500 residencies, the vast majority since the 'Peace Process' began in 1993.
90,000
FORCED INTO EXILE
At least 90,000 refugees and their descendants originally from Jerusalem remain in forced exile today.
WEST BANK
CUT OFF
residents from their city, denying them access to basic services and infrastructure.
FAMILY SEPARATION
1 IN 3
DENIED
One-third of Palestinian applications for family unification in Jerusalem are denied. Family members registered as Gaza residents cannot even apply.
10,000
CHILDREN REFUSED ACCESS
10,000 Palestinian children have no access to education or basic services, as Israel refuses to register them as residents.
VISUALIZINGPALESTINE
Data collated by Visualizing Palestine from Adalah, B'Tselem, CCPRJ, IPCC, OHCHR, Palestine Studies and The Association for Civil Rights in Israel.
Sources: bit.ly/2r9ui50
WWW.VISUALIZINGPALESTINE.ORG. JUNE 2017.
SHARE AND DISTRIBUTE FREELY. CREATIVE COMMONS BY-NC-NS 3.0 LICENSE
@visualizingpal
fb.com/visualizingpalestine

Year: 2017
Brief and copywriting: Iman Annab, Ramzi Jaber, Robin Jones
Design: Yosra El Gazzar, Hani Asfour
Sources: bit.ly/2r9ui50

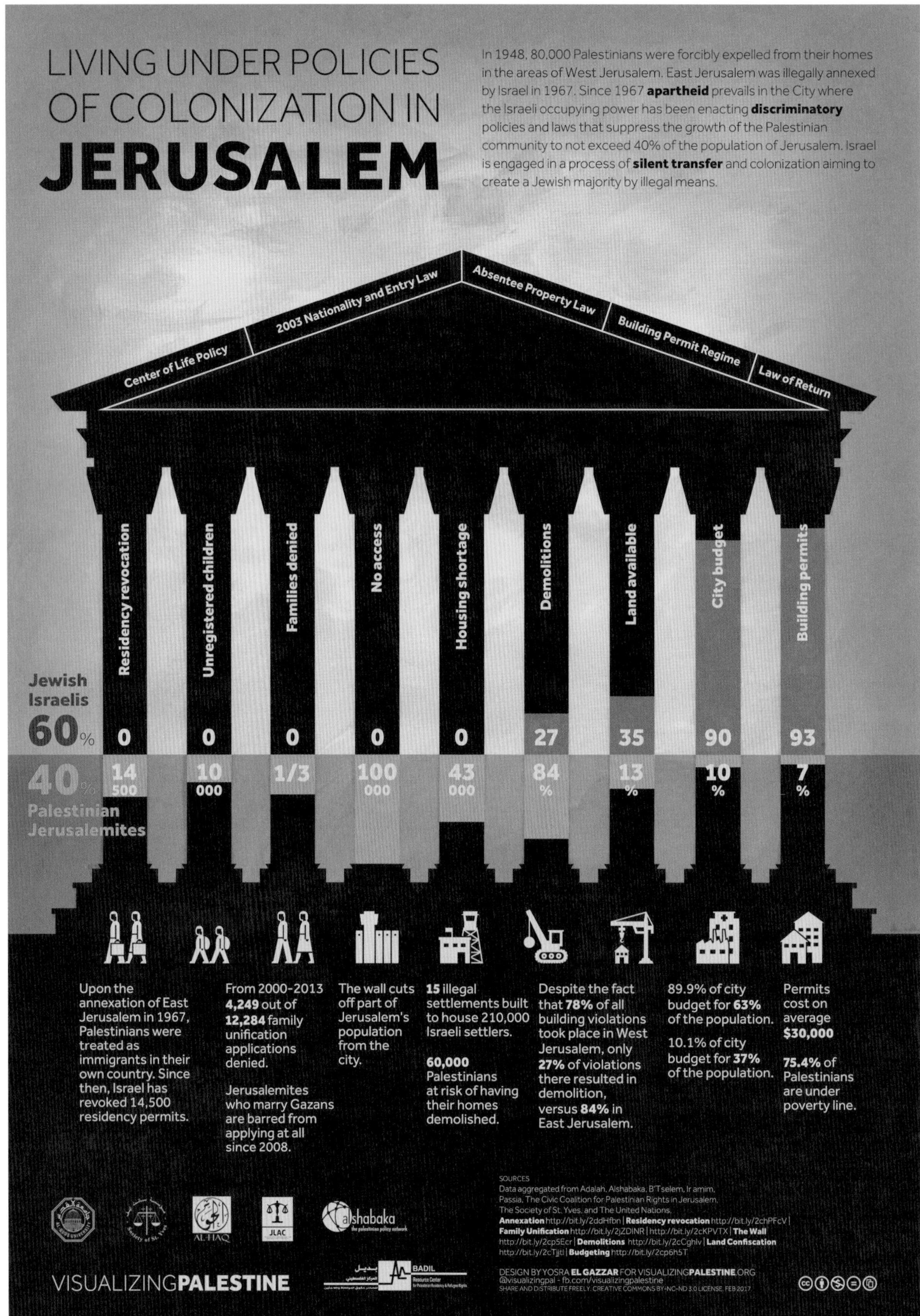
LIVING UNDER POLICIES OF COLONIZATION IN
JERUSALEM
In 1948, 80,000 Palestinians were forcibly expelled from their homes in the areas of West Jerusalem. East Jerusalem was illegally annexed by Israel in 1967. Since 1967 **apartheid** prevails in the City where the Israeli occupying power has been enacting **discriminatory** policies and laws that suppress the growth of the Palestinian community to not exceed 40% of the population of Jerusalem. Israel is engaged in a process of **silent transfer** and colonization aiming to create a Jewish majority by illegal means.
Center of Life Policy
2003 Nationality and Entry Law
Absentee Property Law
Building Permit Regime
Law of Return
Jewish Israelis
60%
40%
Palestinian Jerusalemites
Residency revocation 0 14 500
Unregistered children 0 10 000
Families denied 0 1/3
No access 0 100 000
Housing shortage 0 43 000
Demolitions 27 84 %
Land available 35 13 %
City budget 90 10 %
Building permits 93 7 %
Upon the annexation of East Jerusalem in 1967, Palestinians were treated as immigrants in their own country. Since then, Israel has revoked 14,500 residency permits.
From 2000-2013 **4,249** out of **12,284** family unification applications denied.
Jerusalemites who marry Gazans are barred from applying at all since 2008.
The wall cuts off part of Jerusalem's population from the city.
15 illegal settlements built to house 210,000 Israeli settlers.
60,000 Palestinians at risk of having their homes demolished.
Despite the fact that **78%** of all building violations took place in West Jerusalem, only **27%** of violations there resulted in demolition, versus **84%** in East Jerusalem.
89.9% of city budget for **63%** of the population.
10.1% of city budget for **37%** of the population.
Permits cost on average **$30,000**
75.4% of Palestinians are under poverty line.
SOURCES
Data aggregated from Adalah, Alshabaka, B'Tselem, Ir amim, Passia, The Civic Coalition for Palestinian Rights in Jerusalem, The Society of St. Yves, and The United Nations.
Annexation http://bit.ly/2ddHfbn | **Residency revocation** http://bit.ly/2chPFcV | **Family Unification** http://bit.ly/2jZDINR | http://bit.ly/2cKPVTX | **The Wall** http://bit.ly/2cp5Ecr | **Demolitions** http://bit.ly/2cCghlv | **Land Confiscation** http://bit.ly/2cTjjtl | **Budgeting** http://bit.ly/2cp6h5T
AL-HAQ
JLAC
al shabaka
BADIL
VISUALIZINGPALESTINE
DESIGN BY YOSRA **EL GAZZAR** FOR VISUALIZING**PALESTINE**.ORG
@visualizingpal - fb.com/visualizingpalestine
SHARE AND DISTRIBUTE FREELY. CREATIVE COMMONS BY-NC-ND 3.0 LICENSE. FEB 2017

Year: 2017 | **Brief and copywriting:** Iman Annab, Nada Awad, Robin Jones | **Design:** Yosra El Gazzar, Hani Asfour | **Sources:** bit.ly/vp-Sources-2012-2015

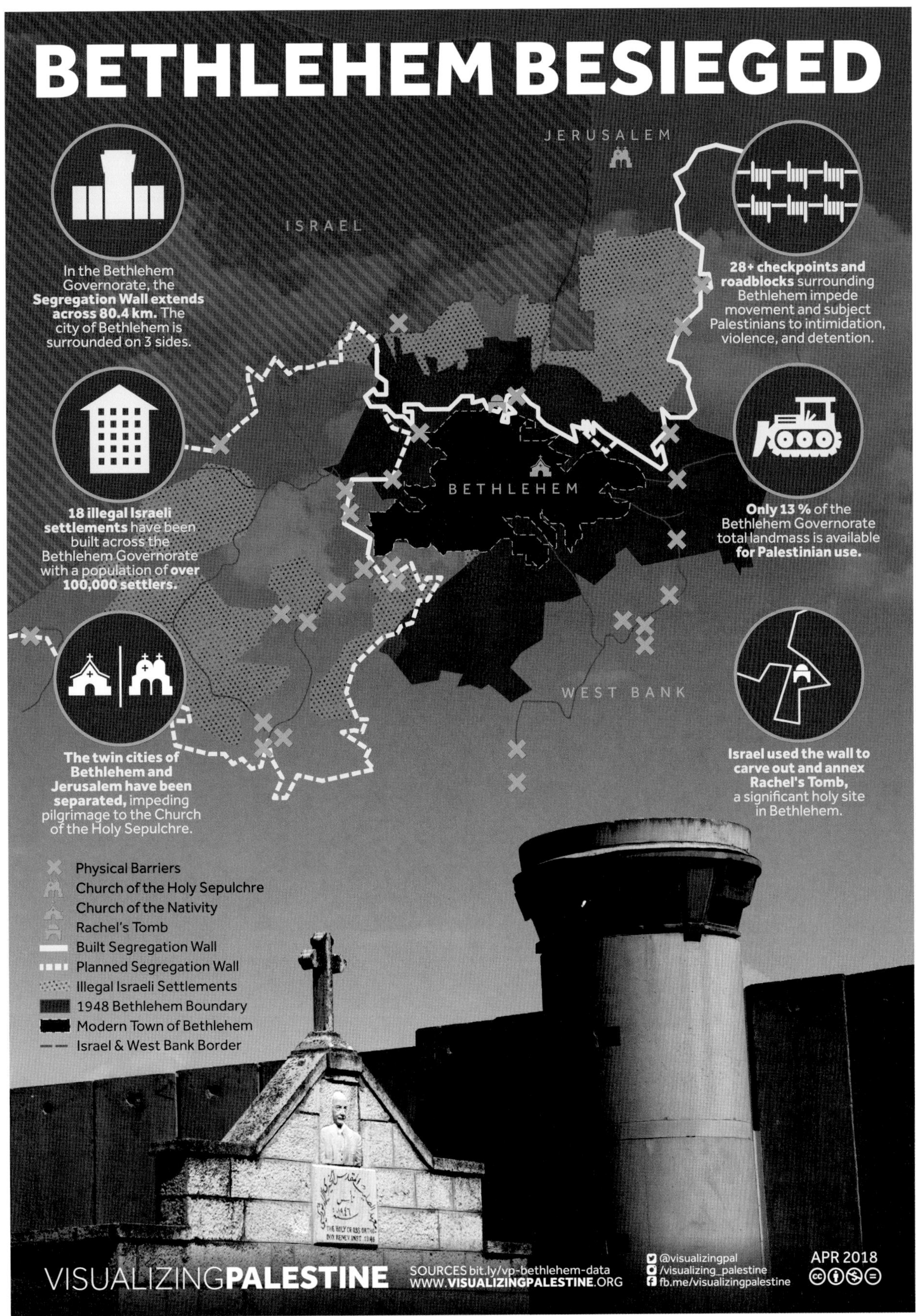
BETHLEHEM BESIEGED
JERUSALEM
ISRAEL
BETHLEHEM
WEST BANK
In the Bethlehem Governorate, the Segregation Wall extends across 80.4 km. The city of Bethlehem is surrounded on 3 sides.
28+ checkpoints and roadblocks surrounding Bethlehem impede movement and subject Palestinians to intimidation, violence, and detention.
18 illegal Israeli settlements have been built across the Bethlehem Governorate with a population of over 100,000 settlers.
Only 13 % of the Bethlehem Governorate total landmass is available for Palestinian use.
The twin cities of Bethlehem and Jerusalem have been separated, impeding pilgrimage to the Church of the Holy Sepulchre.
Israel used the wall to carve out and annex Rachel's Tomb, a significant holy site in Bethlehem.
Physical Barriers
Church of the Holy Sepulchre
Church of the Nativity
Rachel's Tomb
Built Segregation Wall
Planned Segregation Wall
Illegal Israeli Settlements
1948 Bethlehem Boundary
Modern Town of Bethlehem
Israel & West Bank Border
VISUALIZINGPALESTINE
SOURCES bit.ly/vp-bethlehem-data
WWW.VISUALIZINGPALESTINE.ORG
@visualizingpal
/visualizing_palestine
fb.me/visualizingpalestine
APR 2018

Year: 2018 | **Brief and copywriting:** Sharmeen Inayat | **Design:** Yosra El Gazzar, Ali Abbas Ahmadi | **Photo:** Ryan Rodrick Beiler (Activestills) | **Sources:** bit.ly/vp-bethlehem-data

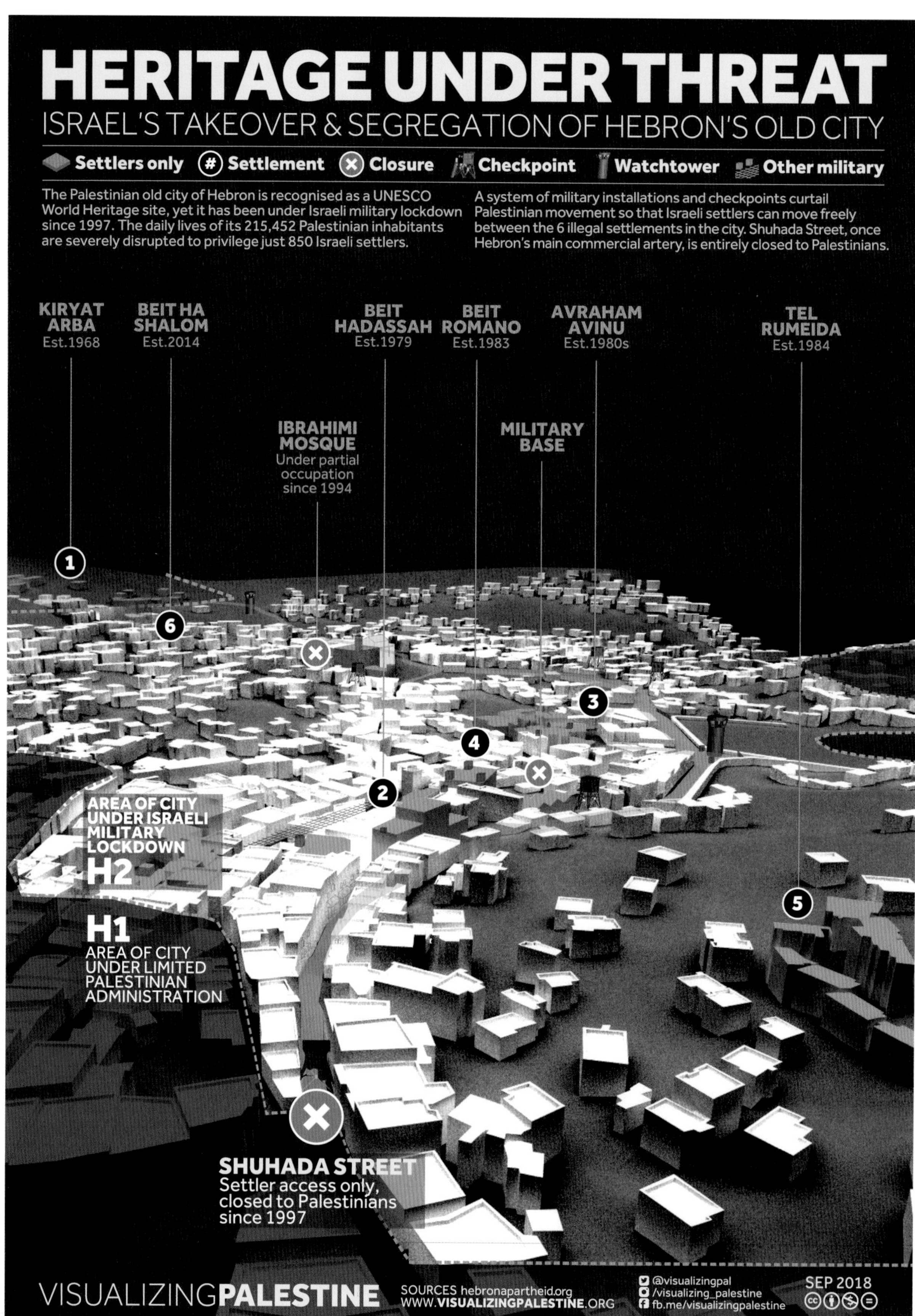
HERITAGE UNDER THREAT
ISRAEL'S TAKEOVER & SEGREGATION OF HEBRON'S OLD CITY
Settlers only
Settlement
Closure
Checkpoint
Watchtower
Other military
The Palestinian old city of Hebron is recognised as a UNESCO World Heritage site, yet it has been under Israeli military lockdown since 1997. The daily lives of its 215,452 Palestinian inhabitants are severely disrupted to privilege just 850 Israeli settlers.
A system of military installations and checkpoints curtail Palestinian movement so that Israeli settlers can move freely between the 6 illegal settlements in the city. Shuhada Street, once Hebron's main commercial artery, is entirely closed to Palestinians.
KIRYAT ARBA Est.1968
BEIT HA SHALOM Est.2014
BEIT HADASSAH Est.1979
BEIT ROMANO Est.1983
AVRAHAM AVINU Est.1980s
TEL RUMEIDA Est.1984
IBRAHIMI MOSQUE Under partial occupation since 1994
MILITARY BASE
1
6
3
4
2
5
AREA OF CITY UNDER ISRAELI MILITARY LOCKDOWN
H2
H1
AREA OF CITY UNDER LIMITED PALESTINIAN ADMINISTRATION
SHUHADA STREET
Settler access only, closed to Palestinians since 1997
VISUALIZINGPALESTINE
SOURCES hebronapartheid.org
WWW.VISUALIZINGPALESTINE.ORG
@visualizingpal
/visualizing_palestine
fb.me/visualizingpalestine
SEP 2018

Year: 2018 | **Brief and copywriting:** Marianna Castellari, Peige Desjarlais, Abeera Khan | **Design:** Ahmad Barclay, Yosra El Gazzar, Marianna Castellari | **Sources:** hebronapartheid.org

Hebron, the West Bank's largest city and traditional commercial center, has been on an Israeli military lockdown since 1997. Israel's policy of segregation in the city severely disrupts the daily lives of its 150,000 Palestinian inhabitants. An estimated 2000 Israeli soldiers work to provide privileged status to 850 illegal Israeli settlers living in the city center.
1997
DENIED ACCESS: ALL PALESTINIANS
ACCESS CONTINUES: ISRAELI SETTLERS
2000-2006
50%
DECLINE IN ATTENDANCE AT 3 CLOSEST SCHOOLS
2007
304
PALESTINIAN SHOPS AND WAREHOUSES CLOSED
By 2007
40%
OF HOMES FORCIBLY EMPTIED
SHUHADA ST
HOW ISRAEL TURNED HEBRON INTO A GHOST TOWN
VISUALIZINGPALESTINE
PHOTO: Human figures: B'Tselem
Street: Youth Against Settlements.
SOURCES bit.ly/vp-hebron
WWW.VISUALIZINGPALESTINE.ORG
@visualizingpal
/visualizing_palestine
fb.me/visualizingpalestine
OCT 2017

Year: 2017 | **Brief and copywriting:** Marianna Castellari, Peige Desjarlais, Abeera Khan | **Design:** Yosra El Gazzar | **Sources:** bit.ly/vp-hebron

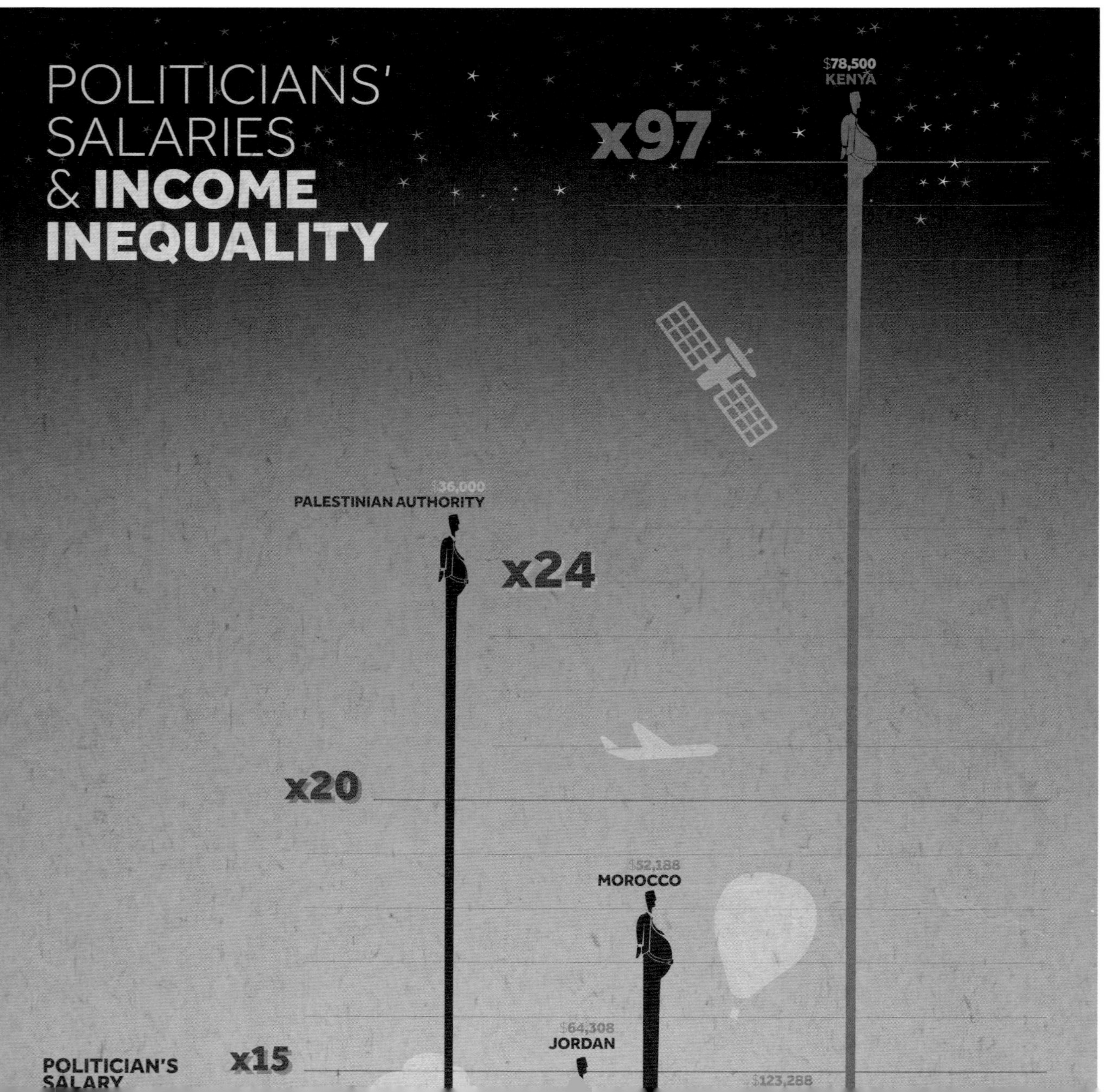
POLITICIANS'
SALARIES
& INCOME
INEQUALITY
x97
$78,500
KENYA
$36,000
PALESTINIAN AUTHORITY
x24
x20
$52,188
MOROCCO
$64,308
JORDAN
POLITICIAN'S
SALARY
x15
$123,288

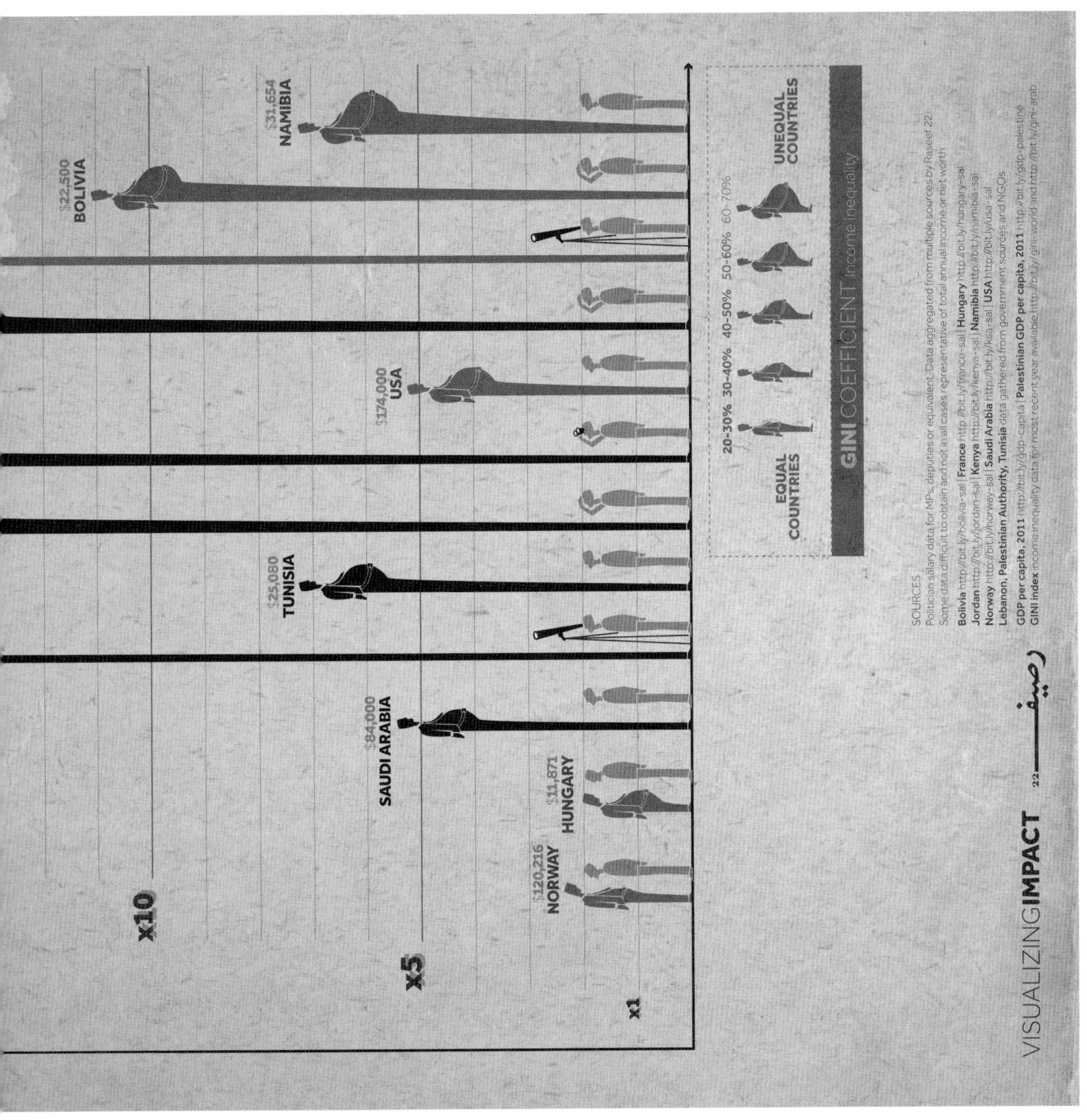
x10
x5
x1
$120,216
NORWAY
$11,871
HUNGARY
$84,000
SAUDI ARABIA
$25,080
TUNISIA
$174,000
USA
$22,500
BOLIVIA
$31,654
NAMIBIA
EQUAL COUNTRIES
20-30% 30-40% 40-50% 50-60% 60-70%
UNEQUAL COUNTRIES
GINI COEFFICIENT income inequality
SOURCES
VISUALIZINGIMPACT

Year: 2012 | **Brief and copywriting:** Joumana al Jabri, Zaid Amr, Ahmad Barclay, Christopher Fiorello, Ramzi Jaber, Raseef 22, Tamara Sawaya | **Design:** Naji El Mir, Ahmad Barclay | **Sources:** bit.ly/vp-Sources-2012-2015

THE CR
APART

The 1998 Rome Statute of the
and 1973 International Conven
Punishment of the Crime of Ap
crime against humanity consi
elements:

1 AN **INTENT TO MAIN**
BY ONE RACIAL GROU

2 A **CONTEXT OF SYST**
BY ONE RACIAL GRO

3 **INHUMANE ACTS**

HUMAN RIGHTS WATCH

VISUALIZING**PALESTINE** SOURC
WWW.

ME OF
EID

ıational Criminal Court
ɔn the Suppression and
id define apartheid as a
of three main

DOMINATION
/ER ANOTHER

TIC OPPRESSION
/ER ANOTHER

021). A Threshold Crossed
ZINGPALESTINE.ORG

@visualizingpal
/visualizing_palestine
fb.me/visualizingpalestine

APR 2021

Year: 2021
Brief and copywriting: Jessica Anderson, Omar Shakir, Grace Choi
Design: Nasreen Abd Elal, Yosra El Gazzar
Sources: HRW (2021), "A Threshold Crossed"

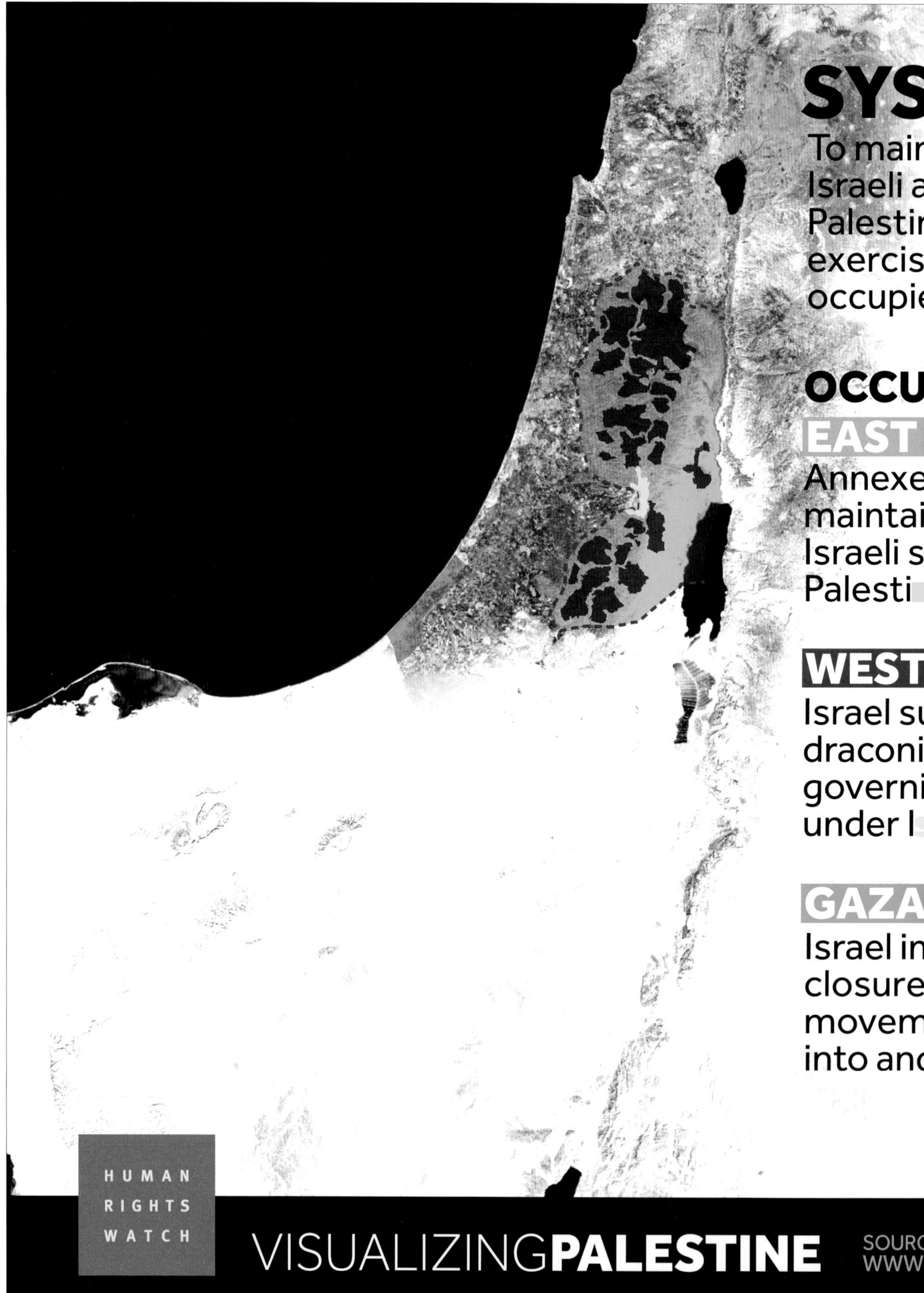
SYS
To mair
Israeli a
Palestir
exercis
occupie
OCCU
EAST
Annexe
maintai
Israeli s
Palesti
WEST
Israel su
draconi
governi
under I
GAZA
Israel in
closure
movem
into anc
HUMAN
RIGHTS
WATCH
VISUALIZINGPALESTINE
SOURC
WWW.

MATIC OPPRESSION

he domination of Jewish Israelis,
ities structurally discriminate against
hroughout the areas where Israel
ntrol. The severity of the repression in the
ritory amounts to systematic oppression

PALESTINIAN TERRITORY

JSALEM

srael, Israel effectively
e set of rules for Jewish
s and another for
n virtually all aspects of life

K

s Palestinians to
aeli military law, while
wish Israeli settlers
civil law

IP

s a generalized
rely restricting the
f people and goods
of the territory

2021). A Threshold Crossed
ZINGPALESTINE.ORG

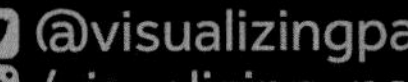
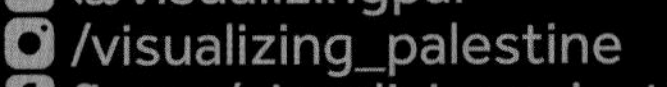

@visualizingpal
/visualizing_palestine
fb.me/visualizingpalestine

APR 2021

Year: 2021
Brief and copywriting: Jessica Anderson, Omar Shakir, Grace Choi
Design: Nasreen Abd Elal, Yosra El Gazzar
Sources: HRW (2021), "A Threshold Crossed"

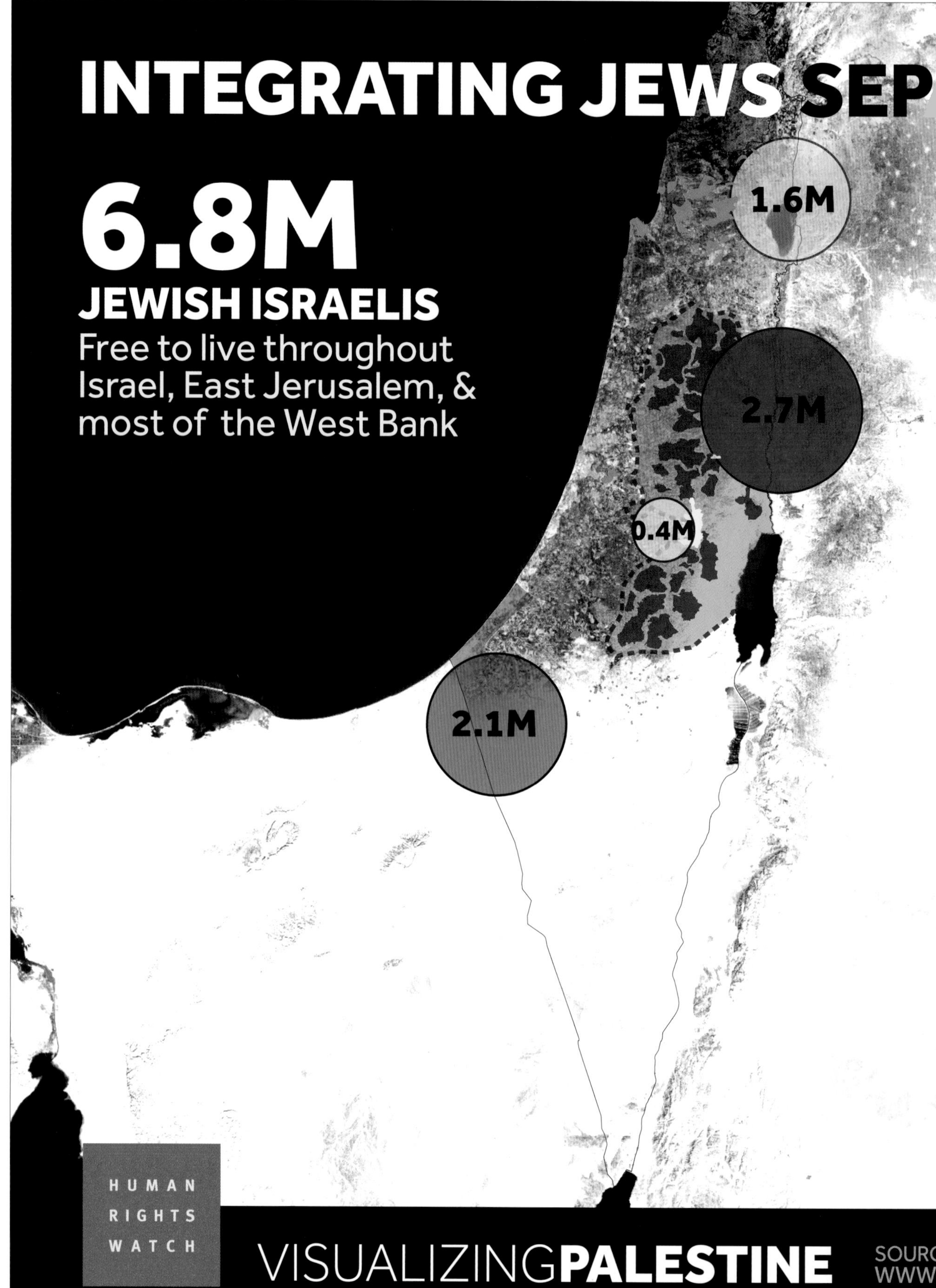
INTEGRATING JEWS SEP
6.8M
JEWISH ISRAELIS
Free to live throughout
Israel, East Jerusalem, &
most of the West Bank
1.6M
2.7M
0.4M
2.1M
HUMAN
RIGHTS
WATCH
VISUALIZINGPALESTINE
SOURC
WWW.

ATING PALESTINIANS

8M

STINIANS

STINIAN CITIZENS OF ISRAEL

d effectively from hundreds of Jewish towns in Israel & largely entrated on about 3% of the land

UPIED PALESTINIAN TERRITORY

JERUSALEM RESIDENTS

guarantees residency rights to h Israelis, but for Palestinians, ency is conditional and revocable

T BANK ID HOLDERS

d effectively from building in ajority of the West Bank or ing Israeli settlements

A ID HOLDERS

d with few exceptions from g Gaza or living in the other part e OPT (the West Bank, including Jerusalem)

021). A Threshold Crossed
ZINGPALESTINE.ORG

@visualizingpal
/visualizing_palestine
fb.me/visualizingpalestine

APR 2021

Year: 2021
Brief and copywriting: Jessica Anderson, Omar Shakir, Grace Choi
Design: Nasreen Abd Elal, Yosra El Gazzar
Sources: HRW (2021), "A Threshold Crossed"

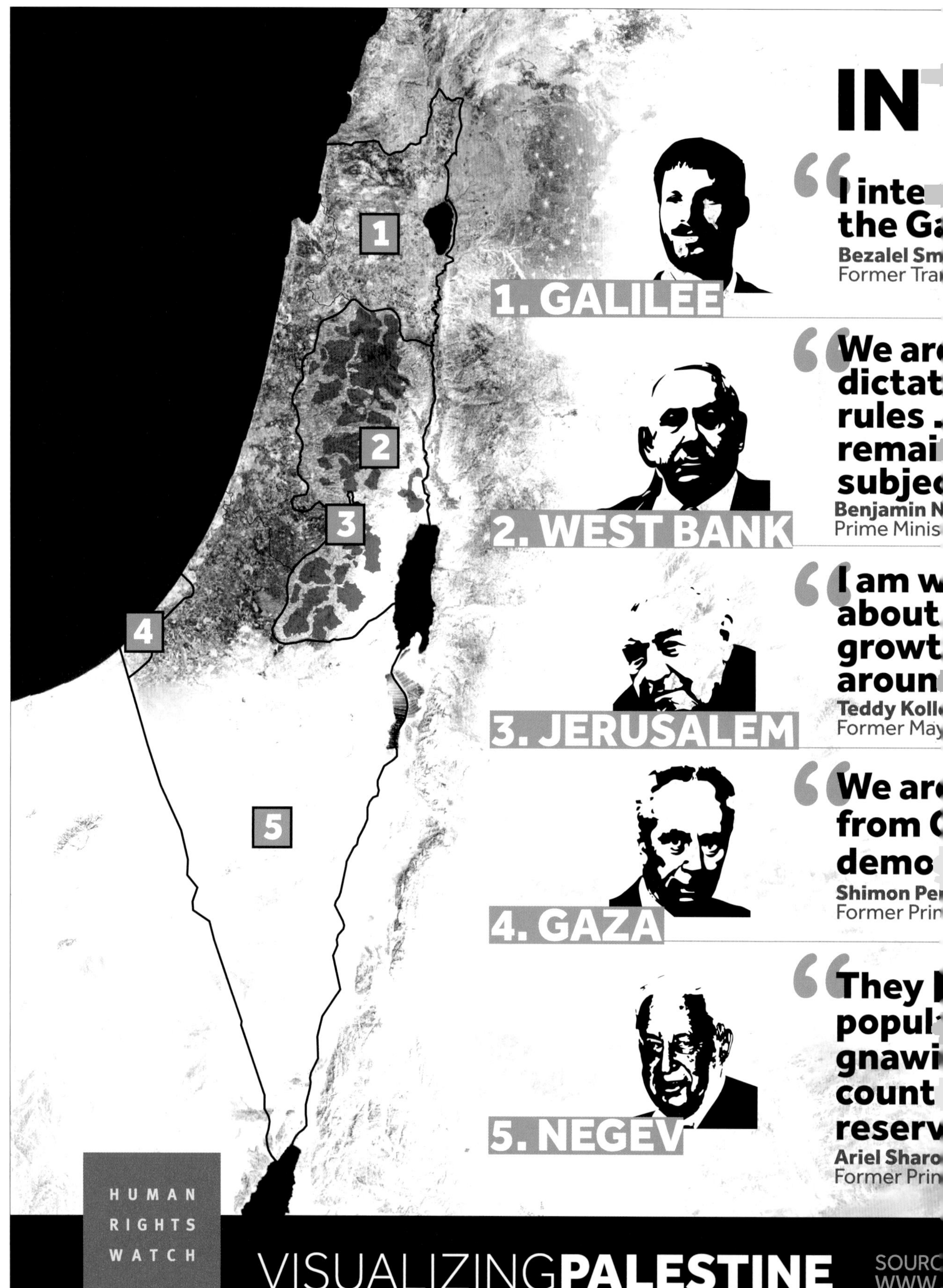
1
2
3
4
5
1. GALILEE
2. WEST BANK
3. JERUSALEM
4. GAZA
5. NEGEV
HUMAN
RIGHTS
WATCH
VISUALIZINGPALESTINE

NT TO DOMINATE

udaize **19** n Minister of Israel	Decades of land grabs and discriminatory planning hem in Palestinian local authorities, while nurturing the growth of neighboring Jewish communities
ones **curity** **y will** **stinian** **, 2020** el	Government plans for decades have sought to hold maximum territory for Jewish settlement and box Palestinians into dense enclaves
d **ab** **in and** **usalem** salem	Jerusalem Outline Plan 2000 sets a goal of "maintaining a solid Jewish majority in the city" and sets a target demographic ratio of 60% Jewish to 40% Palestinian
ngaging **due to** **y** r of Israel	Israeli policy seeks to isolate Gaza from the West Bank and effectively remove its 2+ million inhabitants from the demographic balance sheet, resulting in a Jewish majority across the rest of OPT and Israel
edouin **are** **the** **nd** r of Israel	Israel refuses to recognize 35 Palestinian Bedouin villages with 90,000 or so residents, and regularly demolishes Bedouin homes to make land available for Jewish settlement

2021). A Threshold Crossed
ZINGPALESTINE.ORG

@visualizingpal
/visualizing_palestine
fb.me/visualizingpalestine

APR 2021

Year: 2021
Brief and copywriting: Jessica Anderson, Omar Shakir, Grace Choi
Design: Nasreen Abd Elal, Yosra El Gazzar
Sources: HRW (2021), "A Threshold Crossed"

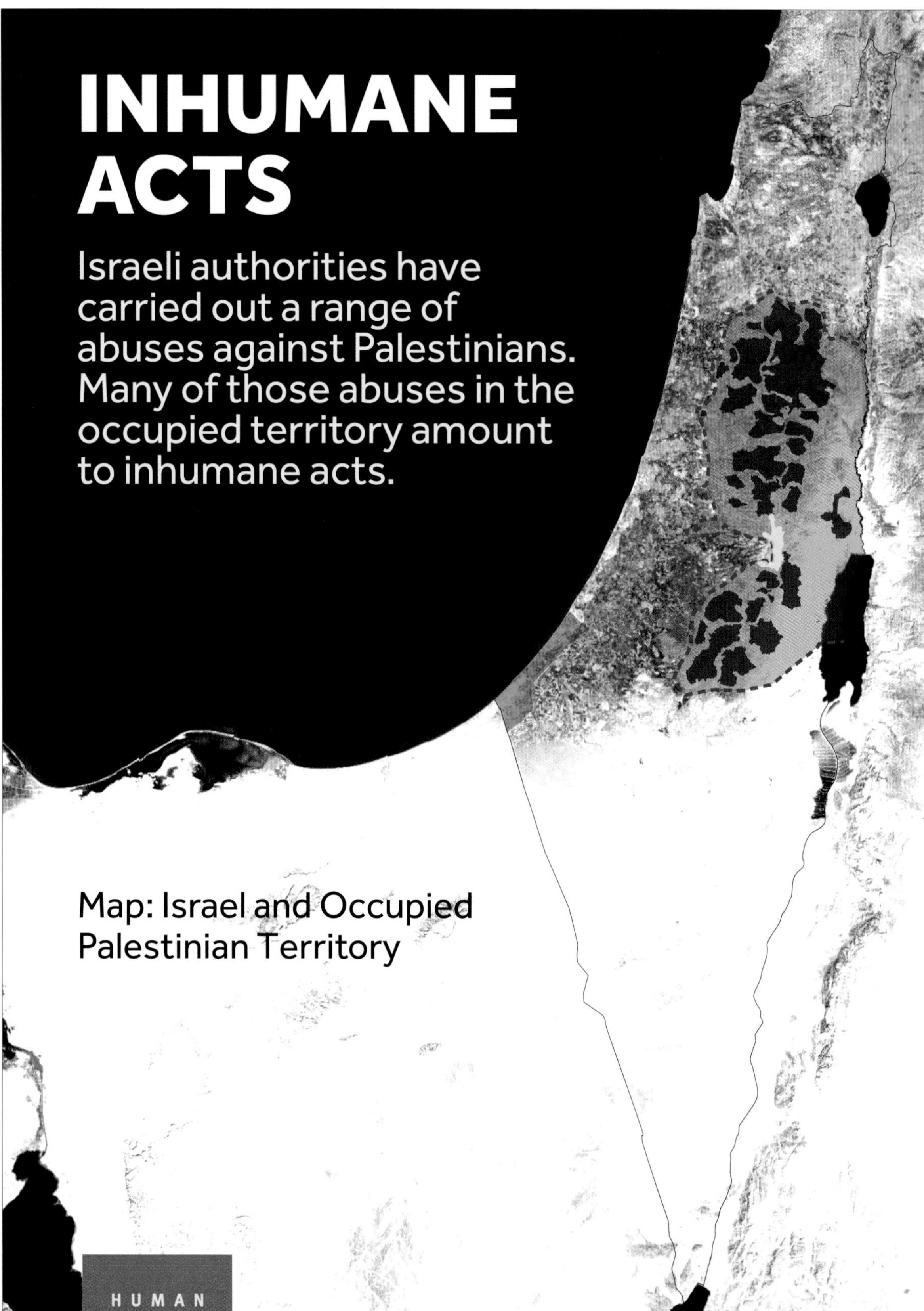
INHUMANE ACTS
Israeli authorities have carried out a range of abuses against Palestinians. Many of those abuses in the occupied territory amount to inhumane acts.
Map: Israel and Occupied Palestinian Territory
HUMAN RIGHTS WATCH
VISUALIZINGPALESTINE

NG MOVEMENT RESTRICTIONS

EST BANK

Gaza, imposition of permit regime, erection
on barrier in part on Palestinian land, and
checkpoints and other obstacles across the

ONFISCATION

NK EAST JERUSALEM

dunams of West Bank land confiscated (more
f its total land area), including in East Jerusalem

LE TRANSFER

NK EAST JERUSALEM

impossible for Palestinians to obtain building
most of the West Bank, including East
; thousands of homes demolished as a result

OF RESIDENCY RIGHTS

EST BANK EAST JERUSALEM

Palestinians across the occupied territory
f legal status since 1967

ISION OF CIVIL RIGHTS

EST BANK

Palestinians in the West Bank and Gaza have for
een denied basic civil rights, such as freedom of
d assembly or a say in the affairs that affect
t

2021). A Threshold Crossed
ZINGPALESTINE.ORG

@visualizingpal
/visualizing_palestine
fb.me/visualizingpalestine

APR 2021

Year: 2021
Brief and copywriting: Jessica Anderson, Omar Shakir, Grace Choi
Design: Nasreen Abd Elal, Yosra El Gazzar
Sources: HRW (2021), "A Threshold Crossed"

BORN UNEQUAL ABROAD

HANNAH

JEWISH AMERICAN
BORN IN THE U.S.

LEILA

PALESTINIAN REFUGEE
BORN IN LEBANON

CAN I VISIT ISRAEL & THE OCCUPIED PALESTINIAN TERRITORY?

YES

You can visit Israel and most of the West Bank, and you'll find programs that may help fund your trip

NO

You are barred from entry to Israel, the West Bank or Gaza

CAN I MOVE THERE?

YES

Because you're Jewish, the 1950 Law of Return guarantees your right to live in Israel. Plus, you'll get a free flight and a bunch of perks if you do so

NO

As a Palestinian refugee, you're barred from returning and denied residency rights, even if you have family living there

CAN I BECOME AN ISRAELI CITIZEN?

YES

The 1952 Citizenship Law entitles you to automatic citizenship, even if you've never set foot in Israel before

NO

You are ineligible if your family became refugees between 1947 and 1949, even if they had lived there for generations before

CAN I PASS ON MY LEGAL STATUS TO MY SPOUSE IN ISRAEL OR THE OPT?

YES

Upon becoming a citizen, you can pass along legal status and even citizenship to your spouse (except if they're Palestinian from the OPT or from several Arab countries)

NO

You have no legal status and cannot gain one, even by marrying a citizen or resident of Israel

HUMAN
RIGHTS
WATCH

VISUALIZING**PALESTINE**

The individuals depicted above are fictional representations for illustrative purposes only
SOURCES HRW (2021). A Threshold Crossed
WWW.**VISUALIZINGPALESTINE**.ORG

@visualizingpal
/visualizing_palestine
fb.me/visualizingpalestine

APR 2021

Year: 2021 | **Brief and copywriting:** Jessica Anderson, Omar Shakir, Grace Choi | **Design:** Yosra El Gazzar, Lamis Alsayed, Ahmad Barclay | **Sources:** HRW (2021), "A Threshold Crossed"

BORN UNEQUAL EAST JERUSALEM

NOA

ZEID

JEWISH CITIZEN OF ISRAEL BORN IN EAST JERUSALEM (SETTLEMENT)	**PALESTINIAN RESIDENT** BORN IN EAST JERUSALEM

IS MY LEGAL STATUS IN JERUSALEM SECURE?

YES	**NO**
You're an Israeli citizen and it's government policy to maintain a Jewish majority in the city	Just like foreigners who move to Israel, you're a resident, a conditional and revocable status. You can apply for citizenship, but you're unlikely to get it

CAN I MOVE ABROAD FOR A FEW YEARS AND COME BACK?

YES	**MAYBE NOT**
Whenever you decide to move back to Jerusalem, you'll be welcome	You can leave, but if you stay away too long, your residency could be revoked, leaving you without legal status

WILL I KEEP MY LEGAL STATUS IF I MOVE TO OTHER PARTS OF THE WEST BANK?

YES	**MAYBE NOT**
You can move to an Israeli settlement in the West Bank. Your legal status is secure, regardless of where you live	If Israeli authorities determine that you no longer "maintain a connection" to Jerusalem, you might lose your residency

CAN I EASILY MOVE TO A NEW HOME IN EAST JERUSALEM?

YES	**MAYBE NOT**
You should have no problem moving into a settlement	It's virtually impossible to obtain a building permit, and built-up Palestinian areas are already overcrowded

HUMAN RIGHTS WATCH

VISUALIZING**PALESTINE**

The individuals depicted above are fictional representations for illustrative purposes only
SOURCES HRW (2021). A Threshold Crossed
WWW.**VISUALIZINGPALESTINE**.ORG

@visualizingpal
/visualizing_palestine
fb.me/visualizingpalestine

APR 2021

Year: 2021 | **Brief and copywriting:** Jessica Anderson, Omar Shakir, Grace Choi | **Design:** Yosra El Gazzar, Lamis Alsayed, Ahmad Barclay | **Sources:** HRW (2021), "A Threshold Crossed"

BORN UNEQUAL WEST BANK

ILAN

MARIAM

JEWISH CITIZEN OF ISRAEL BORN IN AN ISRAELI SETTLEMENT	**PALESTINIAN ID HOLDER** BORN IN A PALESTINIAN VILLAGE (AREA C)

CAN I HOP IN MY CAR AND DRIVE TO JERUSALEM?

YES

You can do so on roads designed to bypass Palestinian communities and facilitate your commute

NO

You need a rarely issued Israeli permit that's generally time limited. Even with a permit, you'll face checkpoints where you're likely to experience delays and humiliation

IF I'M ARRESTED, WILL I GET A FAIR TRIAL?

YES

You'll be tried in Israeli civil courts with full due process rights

NO

You'll be tried in an Israeli military court with a near 100% conviction rate, or possibly even held in administrative detention without trial or charge, based on secret evidence

DO I HAVE THE RIGHT TO FREE SPEECH AND RIGHT TO PROTEST?

YES

Only speech with "near certainty" to "seriously jeopardize" vital security can be restricted. You can protest without fear of state repression

NO

Military orders restrict your right to free speech and right to protest. If you violate these vaguely worded orders, you could face up to 10 years in prison

CAN I BUILD A HOME?

YES

Israel has allocated large swaths of the West Bank to settlements, where plans have been approved to build thousands of homes

NO

Because you live in the 60% of the West Bank that is under exclusive Israeli control (Area C), it's virtually impossible. You may be more likely to have your home demolished than get a permit to build

HUMAN RIGHTS WATCH

VISUALIZING**PALESTINE**

The individuals depicted above are fictional representations for illustrative purposes only
SOURCES HRW (2021). A Threshold Crossed
WWW.**VISUALIZINGPALESTINE**.ORG

@visualizingpal
/visualizing_palestine
fb.me/visualizingpalestine

APR 2021

Year: 2021 | **Brief and copywriting:** Jessica Anderson, Omar Shakir, Grace Choi | **Design:** Yosra El Gazzar, Lamis Alsayed, Ahmad Barclay | **Sources:** HRW (2021), "A Threshold Crossed"

BORN UNEQUAL NEGEV

NIRIT

JEWISH CITIZEN OF ISRAEL
BORN IN AN ISRAELI TOWN

WISSAM

PALESTINIAN CITIZEN OF ISRAEL
BORN IN UNRECOGNIZED BEDOUIN VILLAGE

IS MY COMMUNITY RECOGNIZED BY THE GOVERNMENT?

YES

As part of a policy to "Judaize the Negev", Israel actively nurtures the development of Jewish communities in the Negev

NO

Israel does not recognize 35 Palestinian Bedouin communities, making it impossible for 90,000 or so residents to live lawfully in their homes

CAN I ACCESS BASIC SERVICES?

YES

Likely without any obstacles, thanks to billions of shekels Israel has invested in major infrastructure projects to attract Jewish residents to the area

NO

Israel refuses to connect your unrecognized village to national electricity or water grids or provide basic services like paved roads, sewage systems and schools

CAN I STAY HERE FOR YEARS TO COME?

YES

Israel continues to make more and more land available to Jewish communities to encourage you to stay and raise your family here

MAYBE NOT

Israel seeks to concentrate Bedouins in government-planned townships. As a resident of an unrecognized village, you live under constant threat of home demolition

IF I WANT TO MOVE, DO I HAVE A LOT OF OPTIONS?

YES

You can move to a big city or one of hundreds of other small Jewish towns across Israel

MAYBE NOT

Among other challenges, hundreds of small Jewish towns have admissions committees that have power by law to exclude Palestinian citizens from living there

HUMAN
RIGHTS
WATCH

VISUALIZING**PALESTINE**

The individuals depicted above are fictional representations for illustrative purposes only
SOURCES HRW (2021). A Threshold Crossed
WWW.VISUALIZINGPALESTINE.ORG

@visualizingpal
/visualizing_palestine
fb.me/visualizingpalestine

APR 2021

Year: 2021 | **Brief and copywriting:** Jessica Anderson, Omar Shakir, Grace Choi | **Design:** Yosra El Gazzar, Lamis Alsayed, Ahmad Barclay | **Sources:** HRW (2021), "A Threshold Crossed"

4.

NAVIGATI
APARTHE

Visuals in this section: Segregated Road System | Where Law Stands on the Wall | Across the Wall | Greater Israel Bus Connections | No Ticket to Ride | Freedom Is for Everyone | Born at Qalandia Checkpoint | Spot the Difference | Occupied Airwaves

NG

D

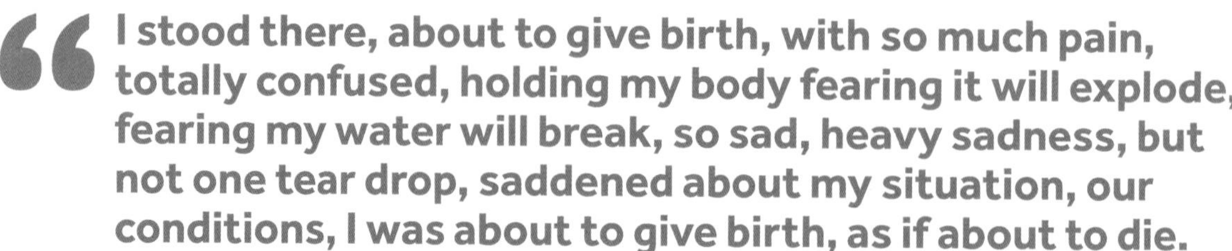

> **I stood there, about to give birth, with so much pain, totally confused, holding my body fearing it will explode, fearing my water will break, so sad, heavy sadness, but not one tear drop, saddened about my situation, our conditions, I was about to give birth, as if about to die.**
>
> *—Layal describes being in labor for three hours at an Israeli checkpoint in an interview with Nadera Shalhoub-Kevorkian, "The Politics of Birth and the Intimacies of Violence against Palestinian Women in Jerusalem," in the* British Journal of Criminology *(2015)*

> **We arrived in a Palestine Red Crescent Society ambulance at one of the checkpoints outside Jerusalem. The soldiers stopped us . . . I was lying in the ambulance, feeling totally helpless. . . . One and a half hours later, I was finally transferred to the ambulance that had come from Jerusalem to take me to the hospital.**
>
> *—Palestinian patient interviewed by Medical Aid for Palestinians, "Access to Healthcare" (2016)*

Imagine two people—one an Israeli citizen driving a yellow-plated car and one a Palestinian resident of the West Bank driving a white-plated car—commuting roughly the same distance over the same terrain. Why does it take the Palestinian driver much longer to cover the same ground?

Yitzhar and Itamar are two illegal Israeli settlements 6.4 kilometers apart in the occupied West Bank. To drive between them, Google Maps suggests a route of 9.7 kilometers with a drive time of twelve minutes.[1] Yitzhar sits on land confiscated from six Palestinian towns. One of these towns, Huwara, made headlines in February 2023 when hundreds of Israeli settlers rampaged through it, torching cars and setting homes on fire with people inside. To drive from Huwara to the Palestinian town of Kafr Qalil, a distance of 4.8 kilometers, Google Maps suggests a route of 43.5 kilometers, with a drive time of over an hour.

The app warns that both driving routes "may cross country borders," even though they fall entirely within the Palestinian West Bank. Google's inaccurate use of "country borders" refers to the infrastructure of Israeli apartheid and military occupation. The occupied West Bank is rife with such spatial absurdities by design, and we use design to expose them.

Segregated Road System—Visualizing Palestine's first exploration of apartheid infrastructure—shows roads that Palestinian residents of the West Bank are barred or restricted from using, based on documentation compiled by B'Tselem. Immediately after occupying the West Bank in 1967, Israel constructed two major north–south highways, the Allon Road and Route 90, which became the first corridor for illegal Israeli settlement activity. Then, they built a series of east–west highways and a network of bypass roads to enable settlers to reach their destinations without passing through Palestinian population centers. The roads accessible to Palestinians are often designed to disrupt the territorial contiguity of Palestinian towns, resulting in long detours and frequent stops at Israeli military checkpoints.

Starting in 2002, Israel's wall in the West Bank became one of the most visible manifestations of apartheid. It is over twice the height of the Berlin Wall, with a meandering route that deliberately reconfigures Palestinian space. Its path cuts deep into the West Bank, through the middle of Palestinian neighborhoods, separating Palestinian villages from their land and annexing the land without its population. **Where Law Stands on the Wall** captures the International Court of Justice's (ICJ) 2004 advisory ruling declaring the wall illegal based on its route and its role in violations of Palestinian rights.[2] ICJ judges ruled fourteen to one that Israel must dismantle the wall and pay reparations to Palestinians, but over twenty years later, construction continues.

We scraped an Israeli bus routes website to find routes that travel into the West Bank. **Across the Wall** and **Greater Israel Bus Connections** show bus routes that are almost exclusively used by Israeli settlers, running between Jerusalem and various illegal Israeli settlements on the opposite side of the wall. These transit maps illustrate the parallel realities of Palestinians and Israelis navigating a single space of apartheid. Across the Wall foregrounds obstructing structures, showing how Palestinians navigate a landscape marred by the wall, hundreds of Israeli military checkpoints, and infrastructure designed to disrupt rather than connect. The satirically titled Greater Israel Bus Connections does not show these barriers, which are typically excluded from official Israeli maps of the West Bank. Instead, it paints a picture of seamless connection. Israeli settlers are encouraged to see the West Bank as an extension of Israel, a suburb where they can find cheaper housing, lower taxes, convenient transportation, more space, and stunning views, all while rarely thinking about or interacting with Palestinians.

The end result of this system, depicted in **No Ticket to Ride**, is that numerous buses that operate in the West Bank do not serve the majority of people who live there. In 2011, a group of Palestinians boarded Israeli buses despite being West Bank ID holders. At a military checkpoint, they were arrested by Israeli soldiers.[3] **Freedom Is for Everyone** speaks to the significance of the US civil rights movement, particularly the Freedom Riders, as a source of inspiration for Palestinian civil disobedience.

As of 2020, there were some 593 Israeli military checkpoints and roadblocks throughout the occupied West Bank.[4] As a form of biopolitical surveillance and control, checkpoints are not just an inconvenience to Palestinians; they are often deadly. In 2015, for example, Ahmad Samih Bdeir did not survive his daily commute from the West Bank to an Israeli construction site. He was the second Palestinian commuter that year to be crushed to death by extreme overcrowding at al-Tayba checkpoint.[5]

Born at Qalandia Checkpoint is a glimpse into the less visible impacts of military occupation on Palestinian women, children, and family life. At Israeli checkpoints, Palestinian women experience what Nadera Shalhoub-Kevorkian describes as "pregnancy under the constraint of militarized space and time."[6] During the Second Intifada, from 2000 to 2005, at least sixty-seven babies were born to Palestinian mothers forced to wait at Israeli checkpoints on their way to the hospital. Many of the babies died.[7] These babies' accelerated journeys from womb to tomb unfold against a backdrop of years of Israeli debate about the "demographic time bomb" of Palestinian birth rates.

Israel's control over communications networks exacerbates the disruptions Palestinians experience in physical space. Israeli authorities barred Palestinian telecommunications companies in the West Bank from offering 3G services until 2018, four years after Israeli companies started offering 4G services to Israeli settlers living illegally in the same area, as we explore in **Spot the Difference** and **Occupied Airwaves**. These disruptions impact education, businesses, freedom of expression, and access to information. In late 2023, Israeli authorities imposed multiple complete communications blackouts on Gaza, preventing Palestinians from contacting each other or the outside world during periods of intense bombardment.[8]

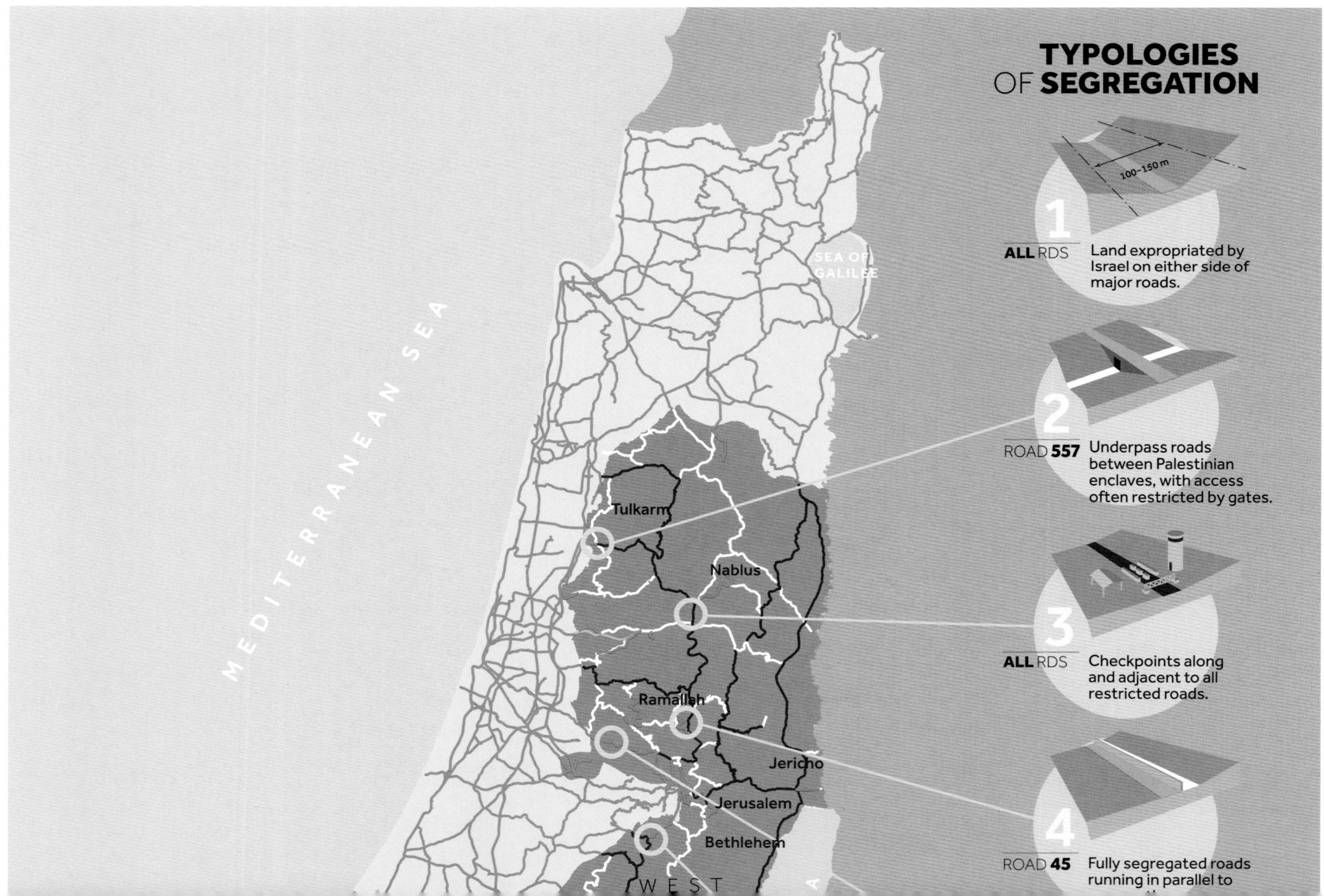
TYPOLOGIES OF SEGREGATION
1
ALL RDS
Land expropriated by Israel on either side of major roads.
100–150 m
2
ROAD 557
Underpass roads between Palestinian enclaves, with access often restricted by gates.
3
ALL RDS
Checkpoints along and adjacent to all restricted roads.
4
ROAD 45
Fully segregated roads running in parallel to
SEA OF GALILEE
Tulkarm
Nablus
Ramallah
Jericho
Jerusalem
Bethlehem
WEST
MEDITERRANEAN SEA

STRIP

ISRAEL

ROAD **443** Road blocks/trenches prevent access to main roads and travel between Palestinian enclaves.

ROAD **60** Israeli-only bridges and tunnels connecting Israeli settlements east of the separation wall.

IMAGINE A

SEGREGATED

ROAD SYSTEM

WHERE THE

COLOR

OF YOUR LICENSE PLATE

DICTATES

WHICH ROADS YOU

CAN **DRIVE** ON.

IL 29·521·65

Israeli license plate

- Accessible only to Israelis
- Accessible to Israelis
- Accessible to Israelis
  Except in Gaza

4·0039-43 ف P

Palestinian license plate

- Not accessible to Palestinians
- Restricted access to Palestinians
- Accessible to Palestinians

ROADS IN THE **WEST BANK**

Israeli-only **79** km

Restricted **155** km

SOURCES

'The Humanitarian Impact on Palestinians of Israeli Settlements and other Infrastructure in the West Bank', UN OCHA (Jerusalem, 2007)

'Forbidden Roads: Israel's Discriminatory Road Regime in the West Bank', B'Tselem (Jerusalem, 2004)

'Apartheid Roads: Promoting Settlements, Punishing Palestinians', Ma'an Development Center (Ramallah/Gaza, 2008)

openstreetmap.org

VISUALIZING**PALESTINE** **WWW.VISUALIZINGPALESTINE.ORG.** MARCH 2012.

@visualizingpal

fb.com/visualizingpalestine

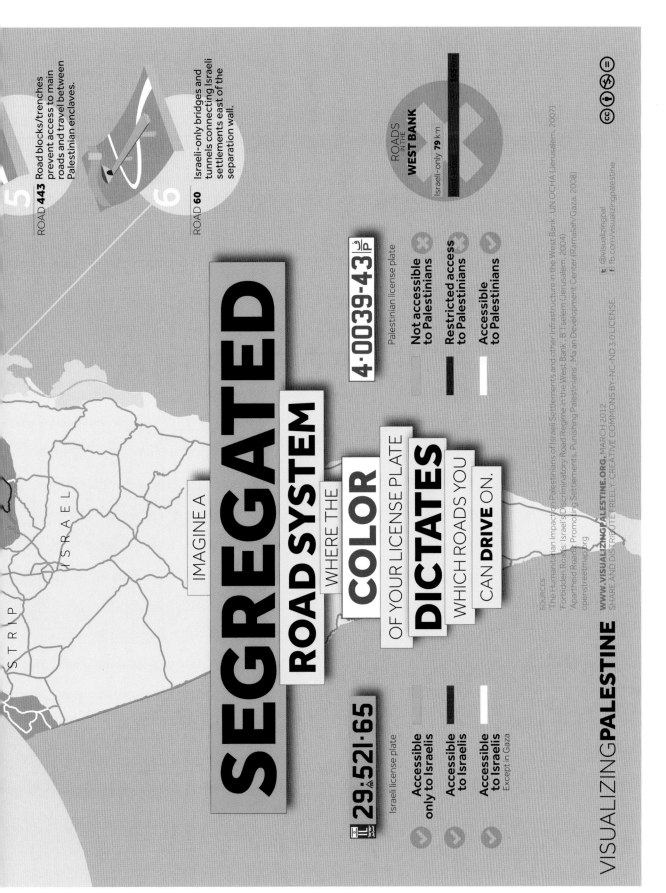

Year: 2012 | **Brief and copywriting:** Zaid Amr, Ahmad Barclay, Ramzi Jaber, Joumana al Jabri | **Design:** Ahmad Barclay, Hani Asfour | **Sources:** bit.ly/vp-Sources-2012-2015

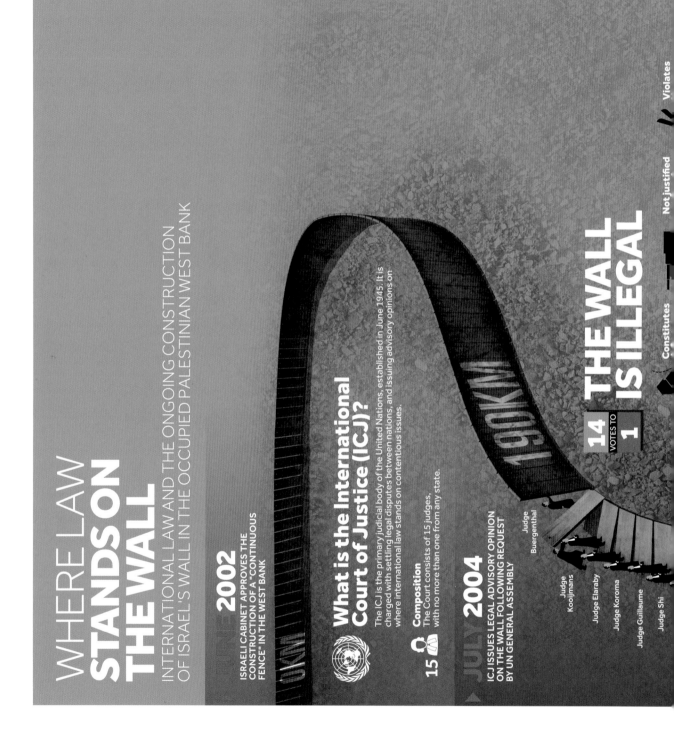

WHERE LAW STANDS ON THE WALL

INTERNATIONAL LAW AND THE ONGOING CONSTRUCTION OF ISRAEL'S WALL IN THE OCCUPIED PALESTINIAN WEST BANK

JUNE 2002

ISRAELI CABINET APPROVES THE CONSTRUCTION OF A "CONTINUOUS FENCE" IN THE WEST BANK

0KM

What is the International Court of Justice (ICJ)?

The ICJ is the primary judicial body of the United Nations, established in June 1945. It is charged with settling legal disputes between nations, and issuing advisory opinions on where international law stands on contentious issues.

Composition
15
The Court consists of 15 judges, with no more than one from any state.

JULY 2004

ICJ ISSUES LEGAL ADVISORY OPINION ON THE WALL FOLLOWING REQUEST BY UN GENERAL ASSEMBLY

190KM

Judge Buergenthal

Judge Kooijmans

Judge Elaraby

Judge Koroma

Judge Guillaume

Judge Shi

14 VOTES TO 1

THE WALL IS ILLEGAL

Constitutes

Not justified

Violates

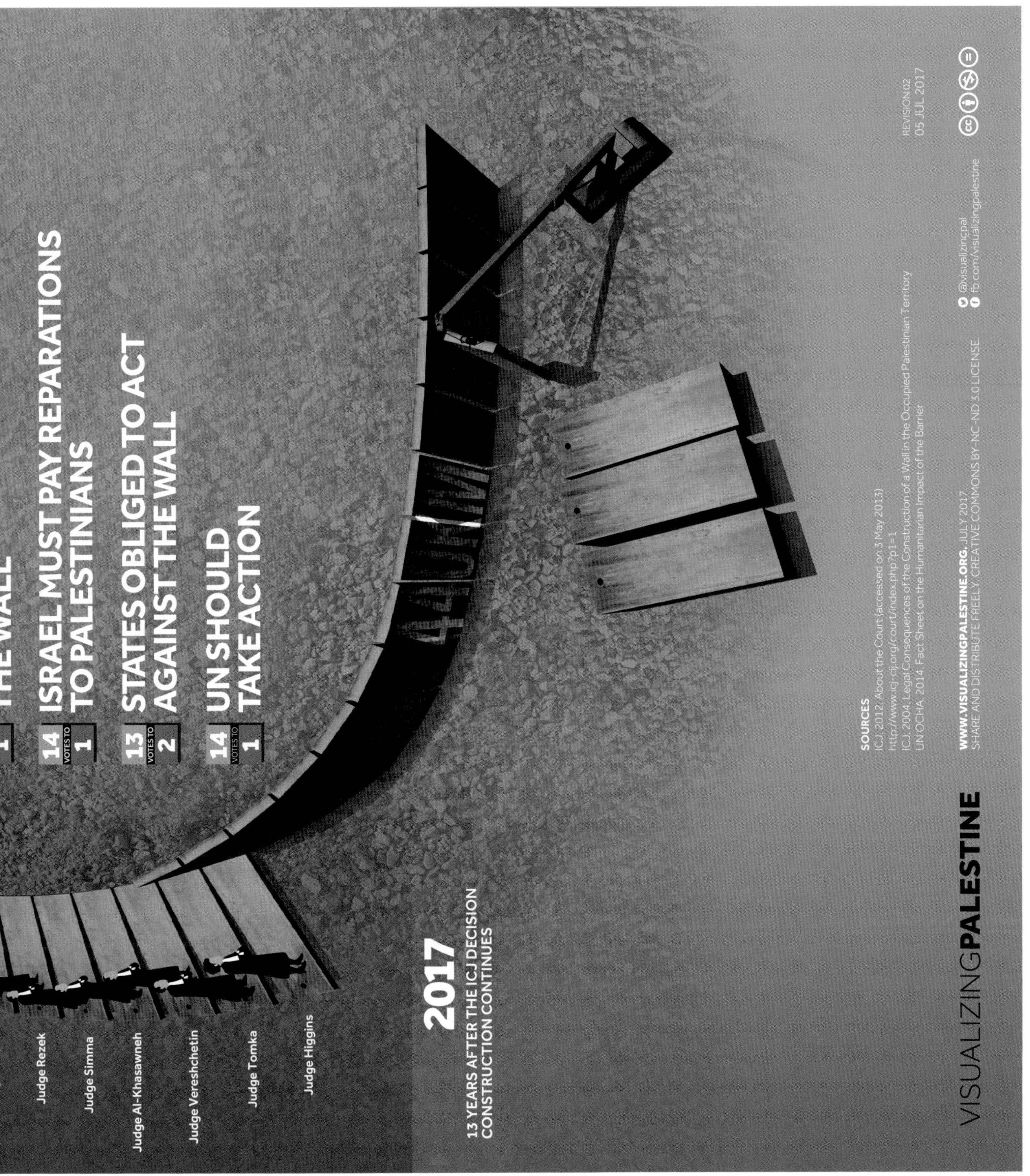
14 VOTES TO 1
ISRAEL MUST PAY REPARATIONS TO PALESTINIANS
13 VOTES TO 2
STATES OBLIGED TO ACT AGAINST THE WALL
14 VOTES TO 1
UN SHOULD TAKE ACTION
Judge Rezek
Judge Simma
Judge Al-Khasawneh
Judge Vereshchetin
Judge Tomka
Judge Higgins
2017
13 YEARS AFTER THE ICJ DECISION CONSTRUCTION CONTINUES
SOURCES
ICJ, 2012. About the Court (accessed on 3 May 2013)
http://www.icj-cij.org/court/index.php?p1=1
ICJ, 2004, Legal Consequences of the Construction of a Wall in the Occupied Palestinian Territory
UN OCHA, 2014. Fact Sheet on the Humanitarian Impact of the Barrier
REVISION 02
05 JUL 2017
VISUALIZINGPALESTINE
WWW.VISUALIZINGPALESTINE.ORG, JULY 2017.
SHARE AND DISTRIBUTE FREELY. CREATIVE COMMONS BY-NC-ND 3.0 LICENSE.
@visualizingpal
fb.com/visualizingpalestine

Year: 2017 | **Brief and copywriting:** Joumana al Jabri, Ahmad Barclay, Ramzi Jaber | **Design:** Naji El Mir | **Sources:** bit.ly/vp-Sources-2012-2015

Across the Wall

Israeli Settlement Bus Routes

Area Guide

Israeli bus companies operate a transport network connecting illegal Israeli-only settlements throughout the occupied Palestinian West Bank. Access to these services is barred to Palestinians living in the surrounding areas.

Separation Wall approved route
Green Line pre-1967 border
Palestinian areas **Limited Palestinian control**
Palestinian areas **Full Israeli control**
Palestinian areas **Annexed to Israel by Wall**

Travel Information

Israeli buses use an extensive network of roads built to seamlessly connect settlements on both sides of the Wall to cities within Israel. Many of these roads are prohibited to Palestinians or require them to apply for special permits from the Israeli military authority.

Bus line and stop
31 Route number
Gilo Israeli settlement
00:18 Journey time from West Jerusalem

Mediterranean Sea
THE WALL
ISRAEL
WEST BANK
Jordan River
Dead Sea
Tulkarm
Jenin
Qalqilya
Nablus
Salfit
Ramallah
Jericho
Bethlehem
Hebron
467 Imanu'el
477 Elon More 01:51
Ariel 251 01:12
Modi'in Illit 00:31 347
Beit El 00:48 170
147 Ofra 01:02
Ma'ale Efraim 01:10 949
Psagot 01:06 179
Tel Tsiyon 143 00:41
109 Mevo Horon 00:42
171 Givat Ze'ev 00:25
Ramat Shlomo 00:12 10
Ramot 00:18 31
142 Geva Binyamin 00:32
66 Pisgat Ze'ev 00:19
NEW E1 Planned
West Jerusalem
3 Old City 00:14
120 Ma'ale Adumim 00:24
173 Mishor Adumim 00:58
8 East Talpiot 00:10
31 Gilo 00:18
62 Har Gilo 00:15
Rachel's Tomb 00:32 163
298 Beitar Illit 00:25
167 Efrata 00:36
164 Bat Ayin 00:45
165 Asfar 01:14
160 Kiryat Arba 01:02
151 Shani Livne 02:02

Source:
http://bus.co.il/ last viewed on 6 July 2012
Journey times calculated from West Jerusalem Green Line crossing.

VISUALIZINGPALESTINE WWW.VISUALIZINGPALESTINE.ORG. JULY 2012

@visualizingpal
fb.com/visualizingpalestine

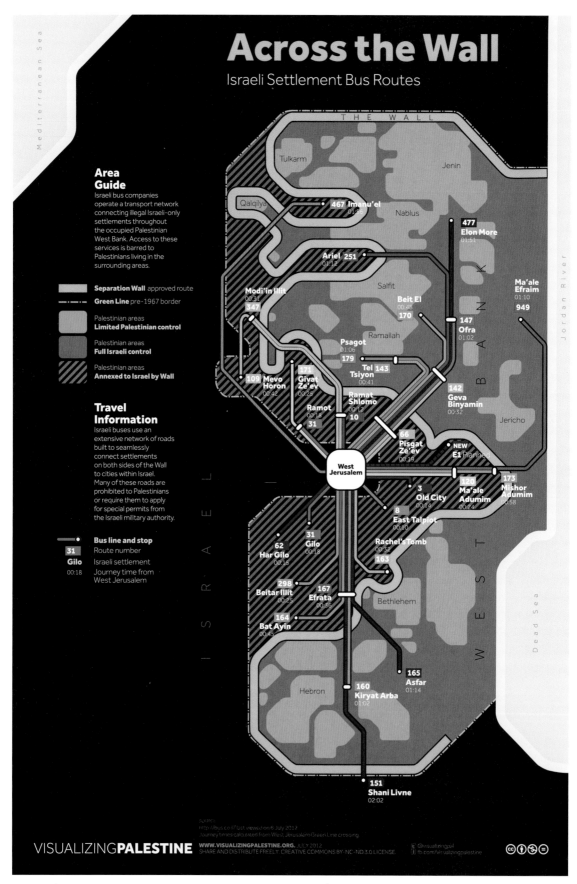

Year: 2012 | **Brief and copywriting:** Zaid Amr, Ahmad Barclay | **Design:** Ahmad Barclay, Hani Asfour | **Sources:** bit.ly/vp-Sources-2012-2015

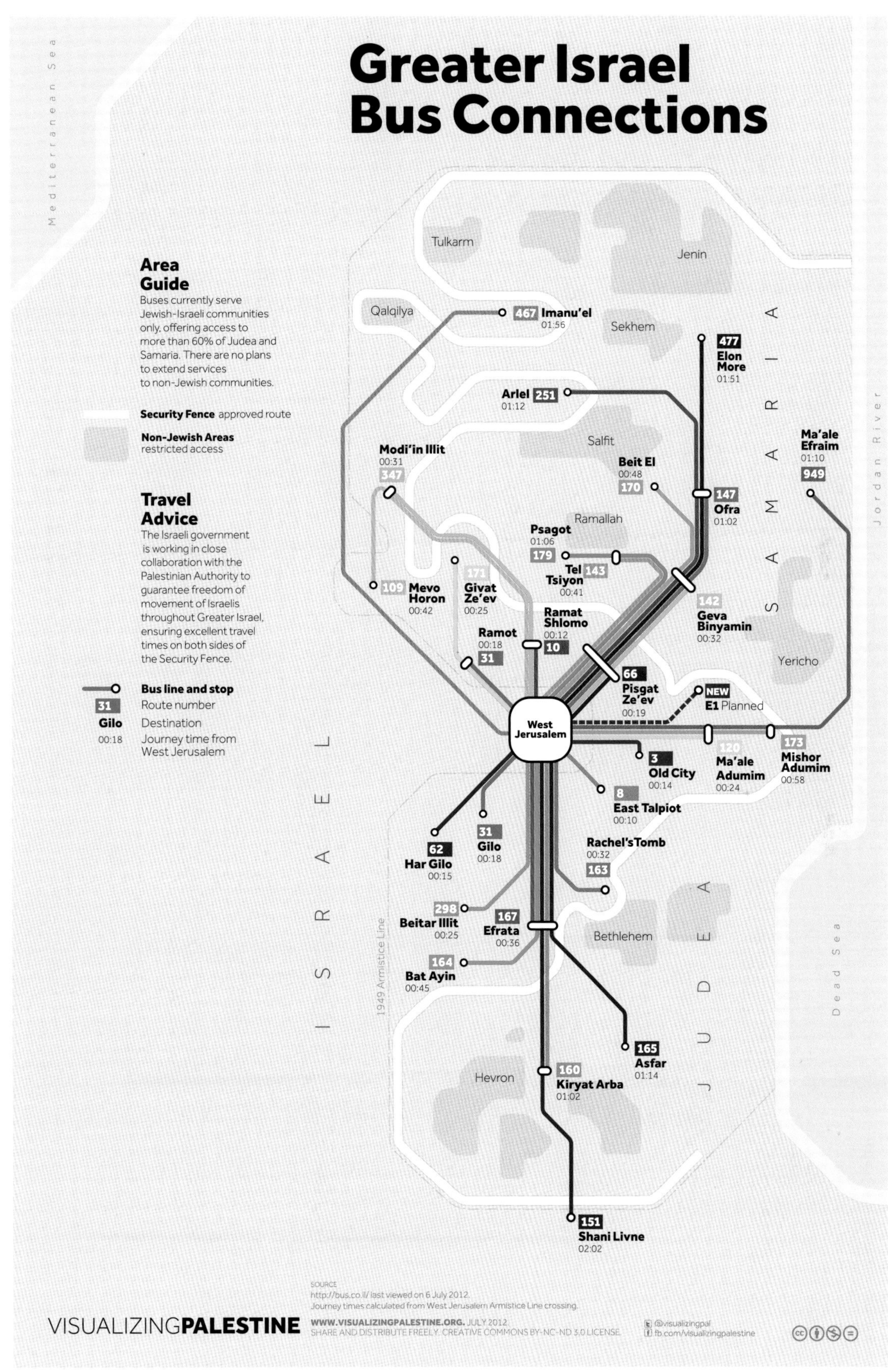
Greater Israel Bus Connections
Area Guide
Buses currently serve Jewish-Israeli communities only, offering access to more than 60% of Judea and Samaria. There are no plans to extend services to non-Jewish communities.
Security Fence approved route
Non-Jewish Areas restricted access
Travel Advice
The Israeli government is working in close collaboration with the Palestinian Authority to guarantee freedom of movement of Israelis throughout Greater Israel, ensuring excellent travel times on both sides of the Security Fence.
Bus line and stop
31 Route number
Gilo Destination
00:18 Journey time from West Jerusalem
Mediterranean Sea
Jordan River
Dead Sea
ISRAEL
SAMARIA
JUDEA
1949 Armistice Line
Tulkarm
Jenin
Qalqilya
Sekhem
Salfit
Ramallah
Yericho
Bethlehem
Hevron
467 Imanu'el 01:56
477 Elon More 01:51
Ariel 251 01:12
Ma'ale Efraim 01:10 949
Modi'in Illit 00:31 347
Beit El 00:48 170
147 Ofra 01:02
Psagot 01:06 179
Tel Tsiyon 143 00:41
109 Mevo Horon 00:42
171 Givat Ze'ev 00:25
Ramat Shlomo 00:12 10
142 Geva Binyamin 00:32
Ramot 00:18 31
66 Pisgat Ze'ev 00:19
NEW E1 Planned
West Jerusalem
3 Old City 00:14
120 Ma'ale Adumim 00:24
173 Mishor Adumim 00:58
8 East Talpiot 00:10
62 Har Gilo 00:15
31 Gilo 00:18
Rachel's Tomb 00:32 163
298 Beitar Illit 00:25
167 Efrata 00:36
164 Bat Ayin 00:45
165 Asfar 01:14
160 Kiryat Arba 01:02
151 Shani Livne 02:02
SOURCE
http://bus.co.il/ last viewed on 6 July 2012.
Journey times calculated from West Jerusalem Armistice Line crossing.
VISUALIZINGPALESTINE
WWW.VISUALIZINGPALESTINE.ORG. JULY 2012.
SHARE AND DISTRIBUTE FREELY. CREATIVE COMMONS BY-NC-ND 3.0 LICENSE.
@visualizingpal
fb.com/visualizingpalestine

Year: 2012 | **Brief and copywriting:** Zaid Amr, Ahmad Barclay | **Design:** Ahmad Barclay, Hani Asfour | **Sources:** bit.ly/vp-Sources-2012-2015

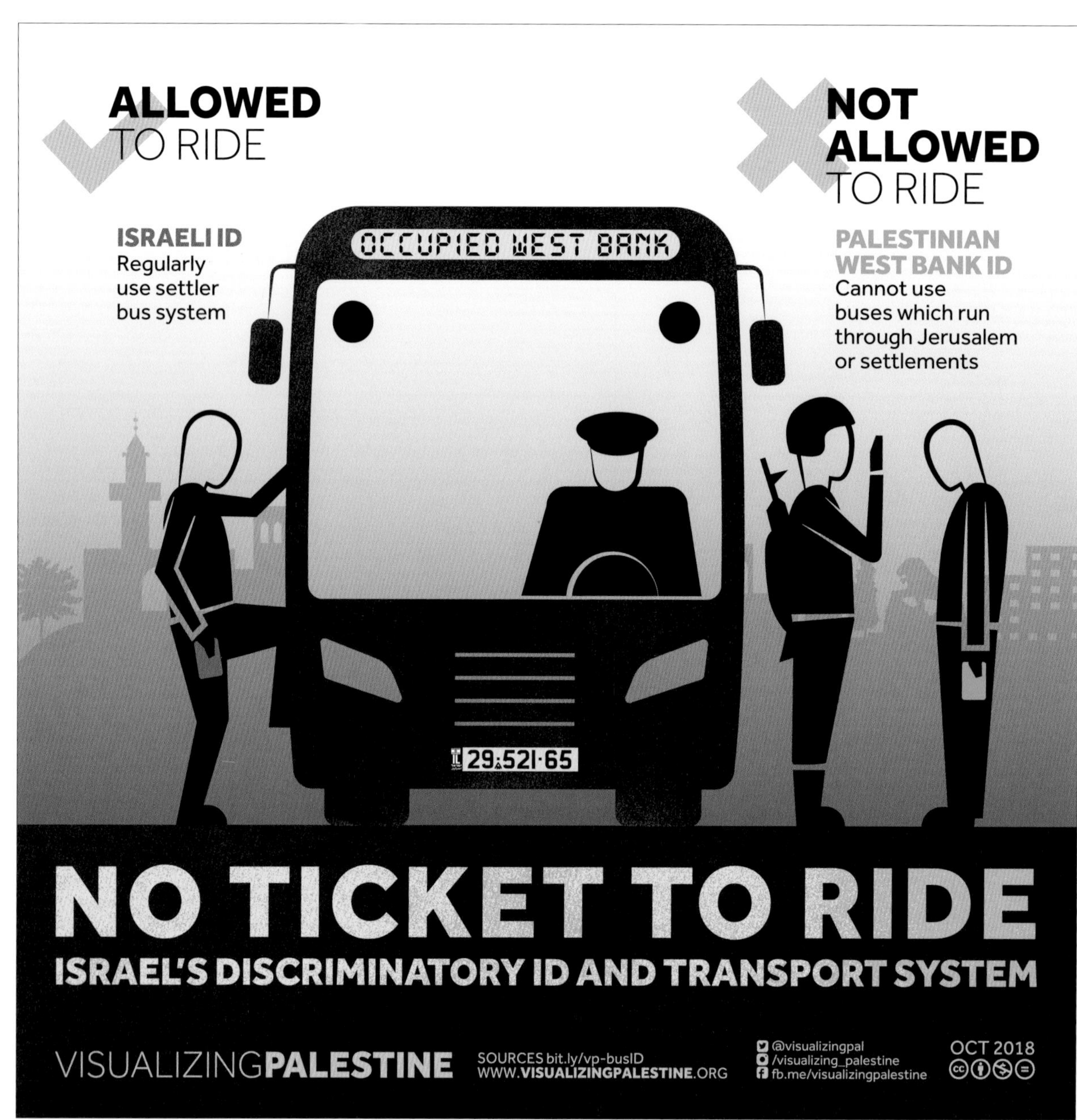
ALLOWED
TO RIDE
ISRAELI ID
Regularly use settler bus system
NOT ALLOWED
TO RIDE
PALESTINIAN WEST BANK ID
Cannot use buses which run through Jerusalem or settlements
OCCUPIED WEST BANK
29-521-65
NO TICKET TO RIDE
ISRAEL'S DISCRIMINATORY ID AND TRANSPORT SYSTEM
VISUALIZINGPALESTINE
SOURCES bit.ly/vp-busID
WWW.VISUALIZINGPALESTINE.ORG
@visualizingpal
/visualizing_palestine
fb.me/visualizingpalestine
OCT 2018

Year: 2018 | **Brief and copywriting:** Ramzi Jaber, Robin Jones | **Design:** Yosra El Gazzar | **Sources:** bit.ly/vp-busID

BLACKS BANNED
IN THE USA UNTIL 1960

PALESTINIANS BANNED
IN THE WEST BANK TODAY

FREEDOM IS FOR **EVERYONE** NO MATTER THEIR **COLOR** OR **ETHNICITY**

SOURCES
Arsenault, Raymond. 2006. *Freedom Riders: 1961 and the Struggle for Racial Justice*. Oxford University Press
Haim Levinson, *Haaretz*. 03 March 2013. 'Israel introduces 'Palestinian only' bus lines, following complaints from Jewish settlers.'
http://www.haaretz.com/news/national/israel-introduces-palestinian-only-bus-lines-following-complaints-from-jewish-settlers-1.506869

VISUALIZING**PALESTINE**

WWW.VISUALIZINGPALESTINE.ORG. MARCH 2013.

@visualizingpal
fb.com/visualizingpalestine

Year: 2013 | **Brief and copywriting:** Joumana al Jabri, Ahmad Barclay, Ramzi Jaber | **Design:** Hani Asfour | **Sources:** bit.ly/vp-Sources-2012-2015

Jason
I WAS
BORN AT
CLEVELAND
CLINIC
Camille
I WAS
BORN AT
ST VINCENT
DE PAUL HOSPITAL
Rami
I WAS
BORN AT
QALANDIA
CHECKPOINT

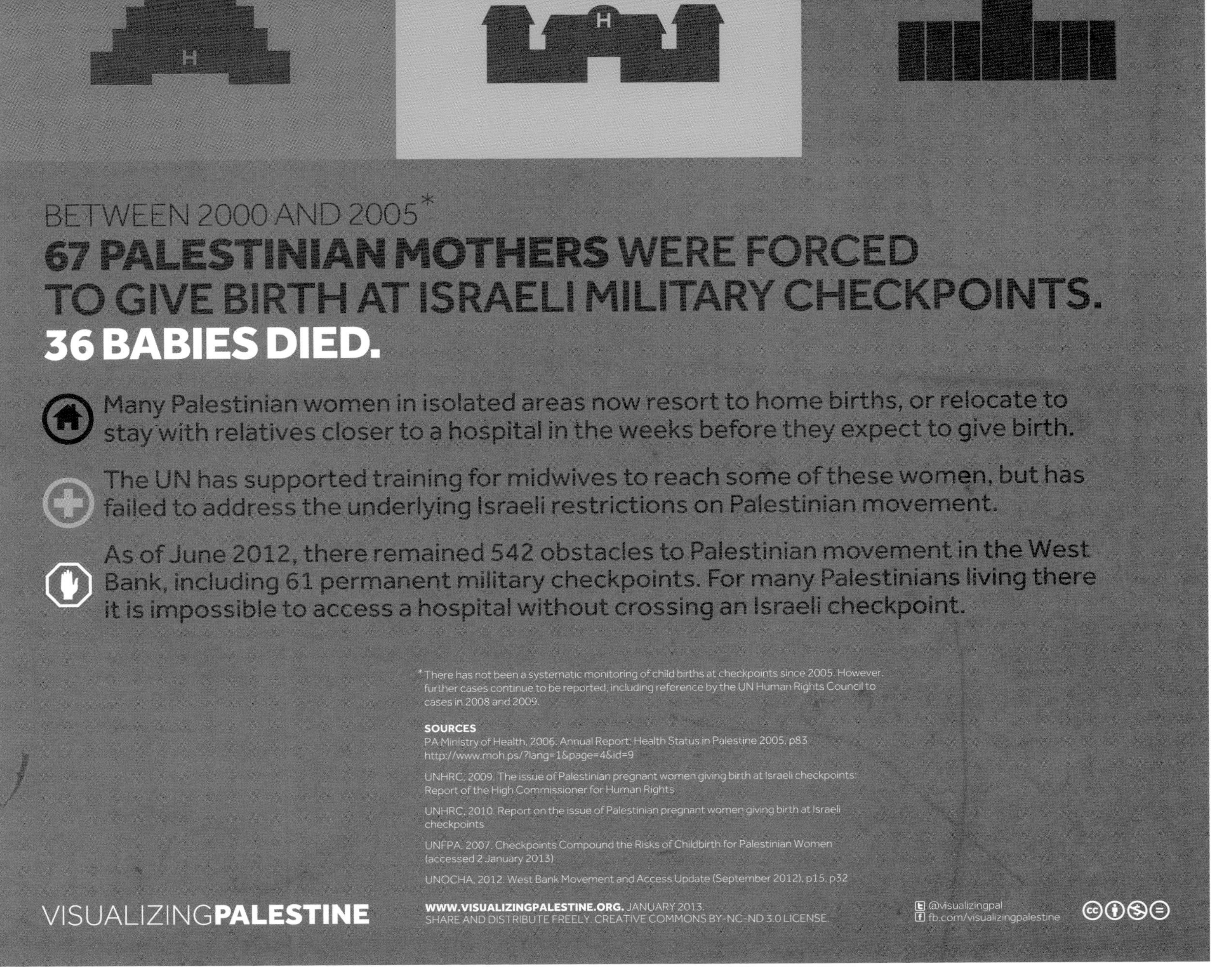
BETWEEN 2000 AND 2005*
67 PALESTINIAN MOTHERS WERE FORCED TO GIVE BIRTH AT ISRAELI MILITARY CHECKPOINTS.
36 BABIES DIED.
Many Palestinian women in isolated areas now resort to home births, or relocate to stay with relatives closer to a hospital in the weeks before they expect to give birth.
The UN has supported training for midwives to reach some of these women, but has failed to address the underlying Israeli restrictions on Palestinian movement.
As of June 2012, there remained 542 obstacles to Palestinian movement in the West Bank, including 61 permanent military checkpoints. For many Palestinians living there it is impossible to access a hospital without crossing an Israeli checkpoint.
* There has not been a systematic monitoring of child births at checkpoints since 2005. However, further cases continue to be reported, including reference by the UN Human Rights Council to cases in 2008 and 2009.
SOURCES
PA Ministry of Health. 2006. Annual Report: Health Status in Palestine 2005. p83 http://www.moh.ps/?lang=1&page=4&id=9
UNHRC. 2009. The issue of Palestinian pregnant women giving birth at Israeli checkpoints: Report of the High Commissioner for Human Rights
UNHRC. 2010. Report on the issue of Palestinian pregnant women giving birth at Israeli checkpoints
UNFPA. 2007. Checkpoints Compound the Risks of Childbirth for Palestinian Women (accessed 2 January 2013)
UNOCHA. 2012. West Bank Movement and Access Update (September 2012). p15, p32
VISUALIZINGPALESTINE
WWW.VISUALIZINGPALESTINE.ORG. JANUARY 2013.
SHARE AND DISTRIBUTE FREELY. CREATIVE COMMONS BY-NC-ND 3.0 LICENSE.
@visualizingpal
fb.com/visualizingpalestine

Year: 2013 | **Brief and copywriting:** Joumana al Jabri, Ahmad Barclay, Christopher Fiorello, Ramzi Jaber | **Design:** Naji El Mir | **Sources:** bit.ly/vp-Sources-2012-2015

SPOT THE DIFFEREN

ISRAELI VS PALESTINIAN CELLPHONE

Israeli authorities heavily restrict Palestinian access to the land, equipment and electromagnetic frequencies necessary to build modern cellphone infrastructure.

As a result, while Israeli settlers enjoy full 3G network coverage throughout the West Bank, Palestinians are presently limited to low capacity 2G networks.

WEST
BANK
ISRAELI
COVERAGE
GAZA
STRIP
ISRAEL

VP DATA SKETCH

SOURCE opensignal.cc

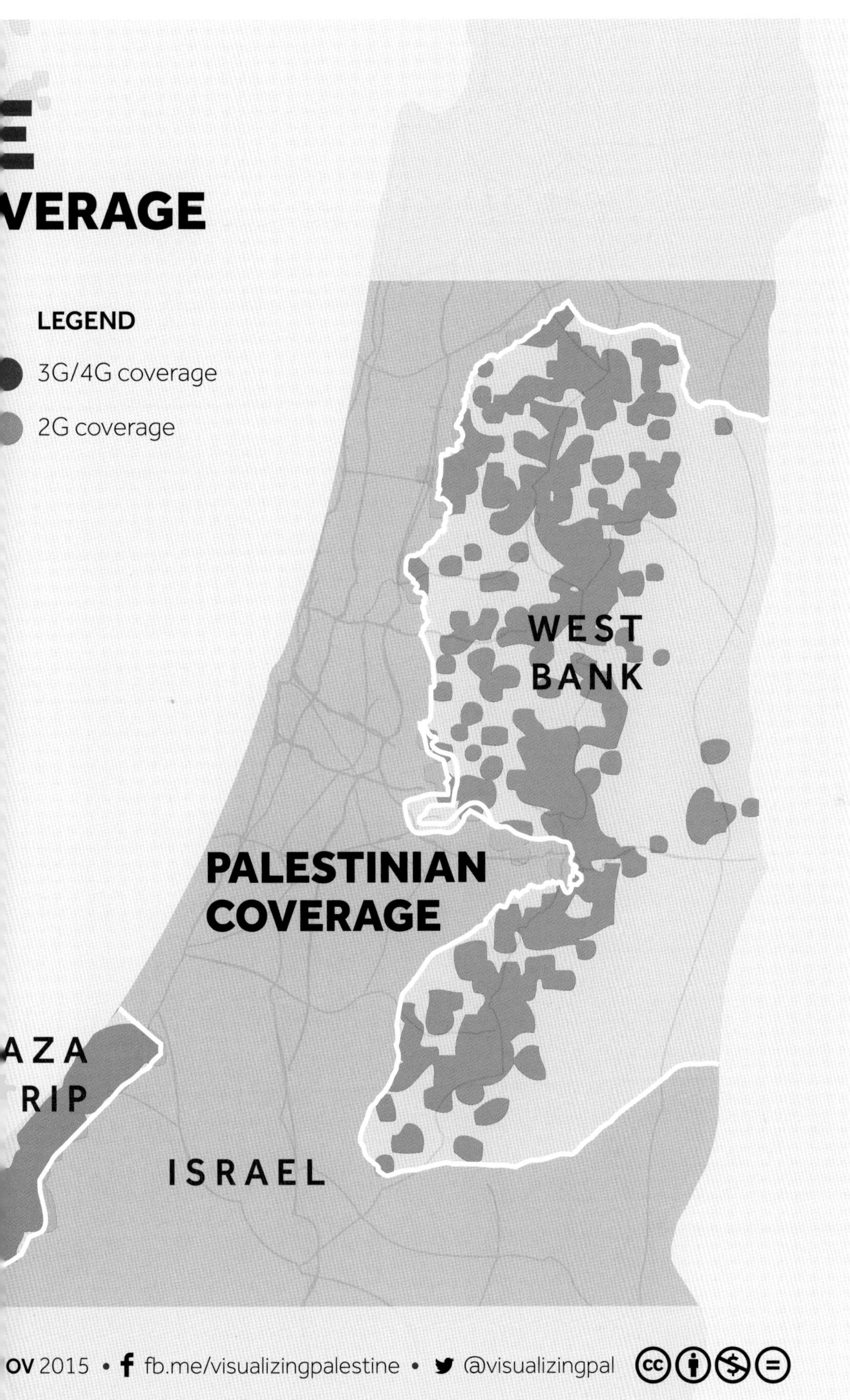
VERAGE
LEGEND
3G/4G coverage
2G coverage
WEST BANK
PALESTINIAN COVERAGE
AZA
RIP
ISRAEL
OV 2015 • fb.me/visualizingpalestine • @visualizingpal

Year: 2015
Brief and copywriting: Ahmad Barclay
Design: Ahmad Barclay
Sources: opensignal.com

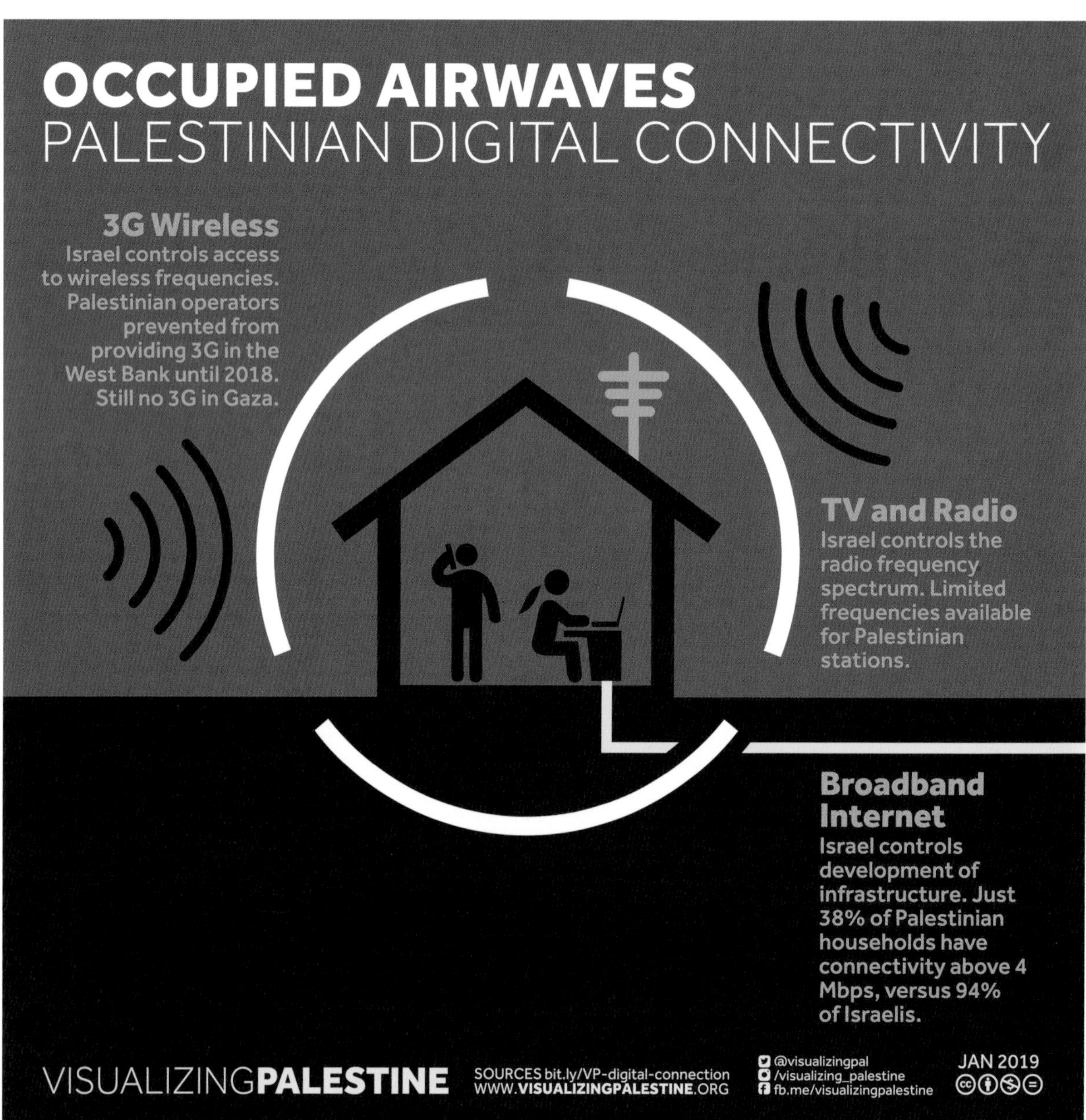
OCCUPIED AIRWAVES
PALESTINIAN DIGITAL CONNECTIVITY
3G Wireless
Israel controls access to wireless frequencies. Palestinian operators prevented from providing 3G in the West Bank until 2018. Still no 3G in Gaza.
TV and Radio
Israel controls the radio frequency spectrum. Limited frequencies available for Palestinian stations.
Broadband Internet
Israel controls development of infrastructure. Just 38% of Palestinian households have connectivity above 4 Mbps, versus 94% of Israelis.
VISUALIZINGPALESTINE
SOURCES bit.ly/VP-digital-connection
WWW.VISUALIZINGPALESTINE.ORG
@visualizingpal
/visualizing_palestine
fb.me/visualizingpalestine
JAN 2019

Year: 2019 | **Brief and copywriting:** Ahmad Barclay | **Design:** Ahmad Barclay | **Sources:** bit.ly/VP-digital-connection

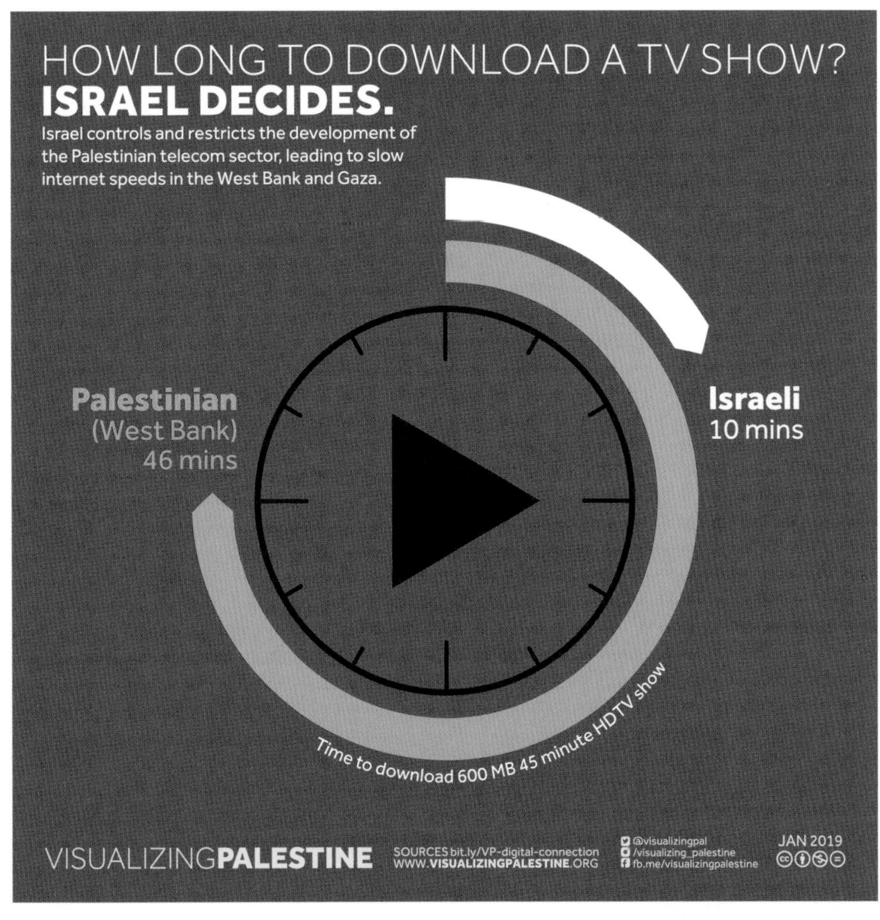
HOW LONG TO DOWNLOAD A TV SHOW?
ISRAEL DECIDES.
Israel controls and restricts the development of the Palestinian telecom sector, leading to slow internet speeds in the West Bank and Gaza.
Palestinian (West Bank) 46 mins
Israeli 10 mins
Time to download 600 MB 45 minute HDTV show
VISUALIZINGPALESTINE
SOURCES bit.ly/VP-digital-connection
WWW.VISUALIZINGPALESTINE.ORG
@visualizingpal
/visualizing_palestine
fb.me/visualizingpalestine
JAN 2019

PAYING MORE FOR LESS
BROADBAND PRICES FOR ISRAELIS AND PALESTINIANS
Israel's restrictions on the development of the Palestinian telecom sector result in Palestinians in the West Bank and Gaza paying higher prices for slower internet speeds.
$21 PER MONTH
less than 1% of per capita income
$37 PER MONTH
14% of per capita income
7.64 MEGABITS PER SECOND
Israeli
1.75 MEGABITS PER SECOND
Palestinian (West Bank)
VISUALIZINGPALESTINE
SOURCES bit.ly/VP-digital-connection
WWW.VISUALIZINGPALESTINE.ORG
@visualizingpal
/visualizing_palestine
fb.me/visualizingpalestine
JAN 2019

5. GAZA

Visuals in this section: Israel's Closure of Gaza Started Long Before the Blockade | Besieged | Gaza as 100 People | Gaza's Economic Collapse | Gaza's Untold Story | Short Walk Home, Long Walk to Freedom | Gaza Health Access | Treating Trauma under Israeli Fire (2023 update) | The Gaza Diet | Break the Siege | Four Wars Old | Six Wars Old |

Miscarriage of Justice | Palestinian Families with Multiple Fatalities | 74 Elders | Genocide Definition and Quotes | *New York Times* Ad | *Toronto Star* Ad | Justice Denied | The Israeli Guide to Obstructing Justice | Zero Accountability

> **Every second in Gaza under Israel's blockade—where water and medical care are luxuries—is tainted by tragedy. Every time a family cannot afford to put food on the table, every time a house fire claims yet another victim, every time a cancer patient cannot acquire life-saving treatment or another desperate person ends their life, the horror of the blockade comes into full view.**
>
> *—Jehad Abusalim, "Letter from Gaza: 'Alive Due to Lack of Death,'" Al Jazeera (2017)*

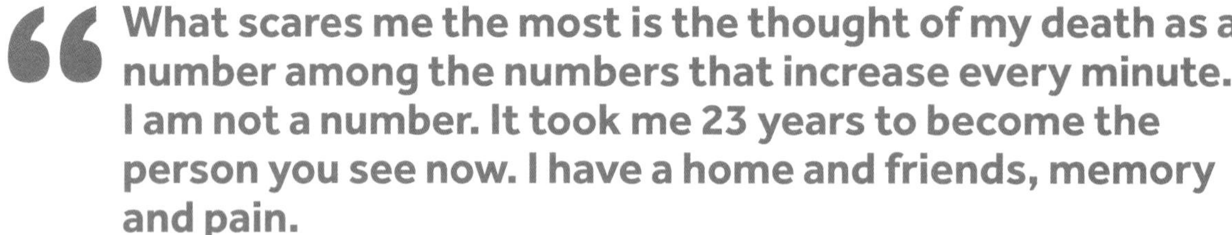

> **What scares me the most is the thought of my death as a number among the numbers that increase every minute. I am not a number. It took me 23 years to become the person you see now. I have a home and friends, memory and pain.**
>
> *—Shahrazad via X/Twitter (2023), quoted in Visualizing Palestine's We Had Dreams platform (see Special Projects)*

In 2023, 2.3 million Palestinians were living in the Gaza Strip, 47 percent of whom were children, 70 percent of whom were refugees,[1] and all of whom were held captive in 1 percent of their homeland. Exiting Gaza is extraordinarily difficult. Human rights experts and Palestinian residents of Gaza have described this tiny fragment of land as an "open-air prison."

In 2012, the United Nations projected that the Gaza Strip would be "unlivable" by 2020 as a result of the Israeli-imposed land, air, and sea blockade, implemented in 2007.[2] **Israel's Closure of Gaza Started Long Before the Blockade** depicts how this extreme measure is an intensification of decades of Israeli closures designed to strategically separate the population of Gaza from the rest of historic Palestine.

Israel's policy to isolate Gaza is directly related to its plans to annex the West Bank, maintaining control of as much of the land with as little of the Palestinian population as possible. Yisrael Katz, then Israel's minister of transport, explained this approach in 2016 when he said, "If we cut off from Gaza—we would be cut off from half of the Palestinian problem."[3] **Besieged** shows the suffocating conditions imposed on Gaza since the 2007 blockade. The intensity of this ongoing oppression created widespread desperation in Gaza, as the statistics in **Gaza as 100 People** demonstrate.

For thousands of years, Gaza was a bustling, prosperous gateway of international trade between Africa, Asia, and Europe. In **Gaza's Economic Collapse**, we show how Israel's control over the movement of people and goods in and out of Gaza decimated its main industries, creating deep poverty and one of the highest unemployment rates in the world, including a 64 percent unemployment rate among Gaza's youths (fifteen to twenty-four years old) as of 2021.[4]

During the Nakba in 1948, over 200,000 Palestinians from almost two hundred towns sought refuge in Gaza, which was inhabited by 100,000 residents at the time.[5] **Gaza's Untold Story** explores the accumulation of multiple forms of Israeli violence against those who were made refugees. A surreal and cruel geography emerges, where generations of Palestinian refugees live and die within walking distance of homes Israel prevents them from reaching.

During the Great March of Return in Gaza in March 2018, Palestinian protesters demanded an end to the Israeli blockade on Gaza, as well as the right to return to the homes from which their families were displaced in 1948. In response, Israeli snipers massacred 217 protesters, 147 of whom were refugees.[6] **Short Walk Home, Long Walk to Freedom**, a sister visual to Gaza's Untold Story, is a reflection on these events. The title of the visual references the title of Nelson Mandela's autobiography.[7]

Among the many devastating consequences of the Israeli blockade on Gaza are deteriorating health conditions and lack of access to healthcare services. As the COVID-19 pandemic set in globally in early 2020, it added a new burden to Gaza's health systems, which were already in severe crisis. To depict these compounding conditions, we worked during the early days of lockdown to create a series of five visuals on **Gaza Health Access**. These visuals are based on data from the World Health Organization (WHO) on Israel's failure to meet its legal obligation as an occupying power to guarantee Palestinians' right to health.

Three years later, in 2023, during Israel's sixth military bombardment of Gaza in sixteen years, Israeli forces targeted the health system in Gaza to the point of total collapse. In October and November 2023, our team updated **Treating Trauma under Israeli Fire** (one of the five visuals in the series) three times in fifty-four days to reflect violations that grew more dire each day. Health workers described being unable to offer pain relief to injured patients; treating patients on the floor in overflowing hospitals crowded with sick, injured, dead, and displaced people; performing surgeries lit by a cell phone flashlight; resorting to vinegar as a disinfectant; receiving impossible evacuation orders from the Israeli military; Israeli snipers firing through hospital windows; and other beyond-horrific conditions. At the end of November 2023, the WHO warned, "We will see more people dying from disease than we are even seeing from the bombardment if we are not able to put back (together) this health system."[8]

When Israeli officials announced on October 9, 2023, that they would not allow water, food, or fuel to enter Gaza, it echoed a history of using food as a weapon of war. In 2006, Dov Weisglas, a senior adviser to Prime Minister Ehud Olmert, described Israel's policy of restricting entry of food to Gaza as an effort to "put Palestinians on a diet, but not to make them die of hunger."[9] In 2012, an Israeli document titled "Food Consumption in the Gaza Strip–Red Lines" came to light, revealing collaboration between the Israeli military and the Israeli health ministry to make detailed calculations of the minimum calorie needs of Gaza's population, which it routinely failed to meet.[10] **The Gaza Diet** series captures the cruelty of these calculations. Although Israeli authorities supposedly stopped using the Red Lines policy in 2010, food insecurity in Gaza continued to rise.[11] This set the stage for the events of 2023, as depicted in **Break the Siege**, in which Israel used starvation as a weapon of genocide.

Gaza has one of the youngest populations in the world, and children are disproportionately impacted by Israel's repeated military bombardments.[12] In 2021, in the wake of Israel's fourth bombardment of Gaza in fourteen years, we created **Four Wars Old** to depict the trauma experienced by hundreds of thousands of Palestinian children who've only known life under Israeli siege.

In November 2023, we updated this visual to **Six Wars Old** at a moment when Israeli forces had killed six thousand Palestinian children in Gaza, with thousands missing under the rubble. The title of these visuals references a short poem by Sara Naim Khatib in which a child in Gaza, when asked about her age, replies "three wars, and still growing."[13] Refaat Alareer, a Palestinian professor, writer, and poet who was assassinated by Israeli forces in Gaza in December 2023, used the same expression to describe his daughter in a 2014 piece that inspired these visuals.[14]

No child should grow up in these conditions, and yet Palestinian children in Gaza (and throughout Palestine) experience what Nadera Shalhoub-Kevorkian refers to as the process of "unchilding," which is the "authorized eviction of children from childhood."[15] Palestinian children are treated as "*nobodies* who are unworthy of global children's rights" and are seen "as *dangerous* and *killable bodies* needing to be caged and dismembered, physically and mentally."[16] Palestinian children are considered a threat before they are born.

In chapter 4, "Navigating Apartheid," we reflected on the experiences of women giving birth under Israeli military occupation with our visual Born at Qalandia Checkpoint. In October 2023, the intersection of reproductive justice and Palestinian liberation came screaming to the forefront as thousands of pregnant women in Gaza had to bring life into the world amid a genocide. Behind the figures in **Miscarriage of Justice** are stories of countless women giving birth under the most dire circumstances imaginable, including a woman who gave birth one day after her five-year-old son was killed in an Israeli airstrike, a woman who took her last breaths as her child was delivered by C-section, a couple who was discharged from the hospital with their newborn to find their home reduced to rubble, and many more.

On October 15, 2023, over eight hundred scholars and practitioners of international law, conflict studies, and genocide studies signed a statement to emphasize "the existence of a serious risk of genocide being committed in the Gaza Strip."[17] In describing the severity of the situation, they note that "entire families across Gaza have been obliterated." Our visual on

Palestinian Families with Multiple Fatalities highlights the staggering number of Palestinian families who have lost multiple members. Since Palestinian families often live in multigenerational households, there are many cases of infants being killed with their siblings, parents, and grandparents. These atrocities echo the massacres of the 1948 Nakba, and many of the elders killed carried the memory of those events, as we highlight in **74 Elders**.

Genocide is defined in the Genocide Convention as any of five specific acts "committed with intent to destroy, in whole or in part, a national, ethnical, racial or religious group." Intent is an important part of the crime of genocide. In **Genocide Definition and Quotes**, we highlight statements by Israeli officials that clearly establish the intent of their actions. The international community, with North American and European governments at the helm, has not only failed in its duty to prevent the genocide, but it has enabled and abetted it.[18] US complicity has been especially evident in rhetoric, diplomatic measures, and material assistance in the form of weapons and equipment. The Center for Constitutional Rights notes: "There is a plausible and credible case to be made that the United States' actions to further the Israeli military operation, closure, and campaign against the Palestinian population in Gaza, rise to the level of complicity in the crime under international law."[19]

Throughout the excruciating weeks of fall 2023, we tied all of our work to one call to action: ceasefire now. We also highlighted this demand through partnered advertisements, including a ***New York Times* Ad** and ***Toronto Star* Ad**. The *New York Times* piece took a week to complete, and in that time, the death toll in Gaza had climbed from 3,620 on October 18 to 5,791 on October 24, highlighting the difficulty of communicating constantly evolving information during a genocide.

Decades of impunity for Israeli war crimes paved the way for the unfolding genocide in 2023. **The Israeli Guide to Obstructing Justice** and **Justice Denied** demonstrate how Israeli military courts do not meet the minimum international standard for investigating violations of international law, which requires investigations to be independent, impartial, effective, prompt, and transparent. Instead, Israeli military courts often make token convictions of soldiers for minor felonies, while Israeli military commanders and politicians are shielded from accountability. For example, no Israeli officials were held accountable for the 2014 indiscriminate bombings that left 142 Palestinian families burying three or more members,[20] including the Bakr family, whose four children between the ages of nine and eleven were killed by an Israeli missile strike as they played soccer on a beach in Gaza.[21]

As a "court of last resort," the International Criminal Court (ICC) takes up a case only when national courts have proven unwilling or unable to provide impartial and transparent proceedings to deal with serious international crimes. In 2021, the ICC launched an investigation into potential Israeli war crimes in the occupied Palestinian territory, including during Israel's brutal military attack on Gaza in 2014, summarized in two versions of the visual **Zero Accountability**. Since 2014, repeated Israeli bombardments of Gaza multiplied these figures many times over, forcing us to update this visual again and again.[22]

While European and North American governments have failed to hold Israel accountable for its cumulative crimes against humanity, in 2023 millions of people around the world protested for the Palestinian people's right to live in freedom and dignity, from Seoul to São Paulo to Johannesburg. In London, calls for a ceasefire in Gaza drew some of the largest crowds for a political protest in decades. In Berlin, people defied harsh protest bans to bring their demands to the streets. In the United States, commentators described the chorus of dissent as "the largest antiwar, anti-imperialist protests since the Iraq War in 2003."[23] At Freedom Plaza in Washington, DC, named in honor of Martin Luther King Jr., the Red Nation national chair Melanie Yazzie offered four words that summarize the struggle against settler colonialism, from Turtle Island to Palestine: "We are still here!"[24]

ISRAEL'S CLOSURE OF GAZA **STARTED LONG BEFORE THE BLOCKADE**

Israel's current military closure and blockade of the Gaza Strip represent an intensification of decades of escalating Israeli policies that made closure a way of life in Gaza.

During the 1948 Nakba, 200,000 Palestinian refugees fled to Gaza, tripling its population overnight. The Gaza Strip, a fraction of the pre-1948 Gaza District, was severed from the rest of historic Palestine, creating a densely populated, economically dependent territory. These events set the stage for Gaza to be subjected to some of the harshest Israeli policies of military closure and blockade.

مركز الميزان لحقوق الإنسان
AL Mezan Center for Human Rights

ADALAH
JUSTICE
PROJECT

VISUALIZING**PALESTINE**

2007 BLOCKADE IMPOSED
land, air, sea blockade represents most extreme closure to date

2006 CLOSURES INTENSIFY
amidst Palestinian elections

2005 UNILATERAL SEPARATION
Israel withdraws settlements in Gaza and continues military occupation from Gaza perimeter. PM Ariel Sharon states: **"Gaza cannot be held onto forever. Over one million Palestinians live there, and they double their numbers with every generation"**

2004

2003 FAMILY SEPARATION POLICY
Gaza residents living in the West Bank are forcibly expelled to Gaza, dividing families. A Palestinian resident of the West Bank can move to Gaza only if they permanently sign away their right to return to the West Bank.

2002

2001 ISRAELI FORCES BOMB GAZA AIRPORT
destroying only Palestinian airport

2000 ISRAELI FORCES BOMB GAZA SEAPORT
closures imposed during Second Intifada become permanent, including ban on students from Gaza studying in the West Bank. Israel adopts tight restrictions on imports into Gaza

1999

1998 WORK PERMITS AND PERMITS FOR FAMILY VISITS BECOME RARE

1997

1996 GAZA ECONOMY LARGELY SEVERED FROM WEST BANK
exports of goods from Gaza to West Bank decline dramatically; Israel restricts access to Palestinian territorial waters

1995

1994 ISRAEL BUILDS FENCE AROUND GAZA
deepening control over movement of people and goods

1993 FIRST SWEEPING CLOSURES
Israeli closure becomes permanent structural reality in Gaza

1992

1991 INTRODUCTION OF PERMIT SYSTEM
for the first time, no one can exit Gaza without an Israeli permit

SOURCES bit.ly/vp-gazaclosure
WWW.**VISUALIZINGPALESTINE**.ORG

@visualizingpal
/visualizing_palestine
fb.me/visualizingpalestine

JUNE 2022

Year: 2022
Brief and copywriting: Jessica Anderson
Design: Nasreen Abd Elal, Yosra El Gazzar
Special thanks: Jehad Abusalim, Sara Roy, Sandra Tamari
Sources: bit.ly/vp-gazaclosure

RESTRICTED GAS RESERVES

PALESTINIANS **BARRED FROM ACCESSING OFFSHORE GAS RESERVES** WORTH

$4BN

RESTRICTED FISHING

SINCE 2007, THE ISRAELI MILITARY HAS REPEATEDLY ATTACKED PALESTINIAN FISHERMEN, **KILLING 5 AND INJURING AT LEAST 25.** THE BLOCKADE BARS THEM FROM REACHING LARGER SHOALS OF FISH, FOUND AT A **MINIMUM OF 12-15 MILES OFF GAZA.**

ISRAELI MIL
PATROLS **REST**
PALESTIN
TO WITHIN 3
NAUTICAL MIL
THE CO
DENYING AC
TO GAZA'S
TERRITO
WATERS AND
WORLD BEY

◀ INTERNATIONAL WATERS

9

6

SOURCES
Data aggregated from Al Jazeera, ARIJ, B'Tselem, CS
Gaza population http://bit.ly/pcbs-pop2014 | **Unemp**
http://bit.ly/ocha-airport (p3) | **$4bn Gas reserves** ht
$375m Imports http://bit.ly/ynet-imports | **Restricte**

VISUALIZING**PALESTINE** WWW.VISUALIZINGPALESTINE.ORG. DECEMBER 2014.

BESIEGED
E ECONOMIC IMPACT OF THE ISRAELI SIEGE ON GAZA
DESTROYED PORTS
THE ISRAELI MILITARY DESTROYED GAZA'S UNCOMPLETED SEAPORT IN 2002 AND ITS AIRPORT IN 2001, PREVENTING PALESTINIANS FROM ENGAGING IN DIRECT TRADE WITH THE OUTSIDE WORLD.
RESTRICTED ELECTRICITY
GAZA'S ONLY POWER PLANT HAS FACED REPEATED ISRAELI ATTACKS AND BLOCKED FUEL DELIVERIES. ISRAELIS PROFIT $92M ANNUALLY SUPPLYING ELECTRICITY TO GAZA WHILE PALESTINIANS FACE
12-16HRS
OF POWER CUTS PER DAY.
RESTRICTED LAND
PALESTINIANS ARE BARRED FROM USING 17% OF GAZA'S LAND, INCLUDING
35%
OF FARMLAND, DUE TO AN ISRAELI-IMPOSED BUFFER ZONE
LAND BLOCKADE
SINCE 2007, PALESTINIAN IMPORTS HAVE BEEN HEAVILY RESTRICTED AND EXPORTS BARRED. ISRAELI COMPANIES PROFIT FROM A MONOPOLY ON SUPPLY OF GOODS TO GAZA, MAKING
$375M
IN 2012
SINCE 2007, ISRAELI AUTHORITIES HAVE IMPOSED A DEVASTATING LAND, AIR AND SEA BLOCKADE ON THE GAZA STRIP. THE 1.8 MILLION PALESTINIANS LIVING THERE ARE ISOLATED FROM THE OUTSIDE WORLD, DENIED ACCESS TO THEIR OWN RESOURCES, AND FACE A 45% UNEMPLOYMENT RATE.
0 NAUTICAL MILES
stinian CBS, World Bank and Ynet. Montage adapted from vector art by Natali Snailcat and Alexzel/Shutterstock
ly/wb-employment (p10) | 3-6nm Sea blockade http://bit.ly/gisha-blockade | Seaport http://bit.ly/aje-seaport | Airport
| $92m Electricity http://bit.ly/arij-cost | Fish shoals http://bit.ly/csm-fish | Fishermen attacks http://bit.ly/ocha-fishermen
otselem-nogo
@visualizingpal
fb.com/visualizingpalestine

Year: 2014 | **Brief and copywriting:** Ahmad Barclay, Diala Lteif, Shireen Tawil, Julia Tierney | **Design:** Hani Asfour, Ahmad Barclay | **Sources:** bit.ly/vp-Sources-2012-2015

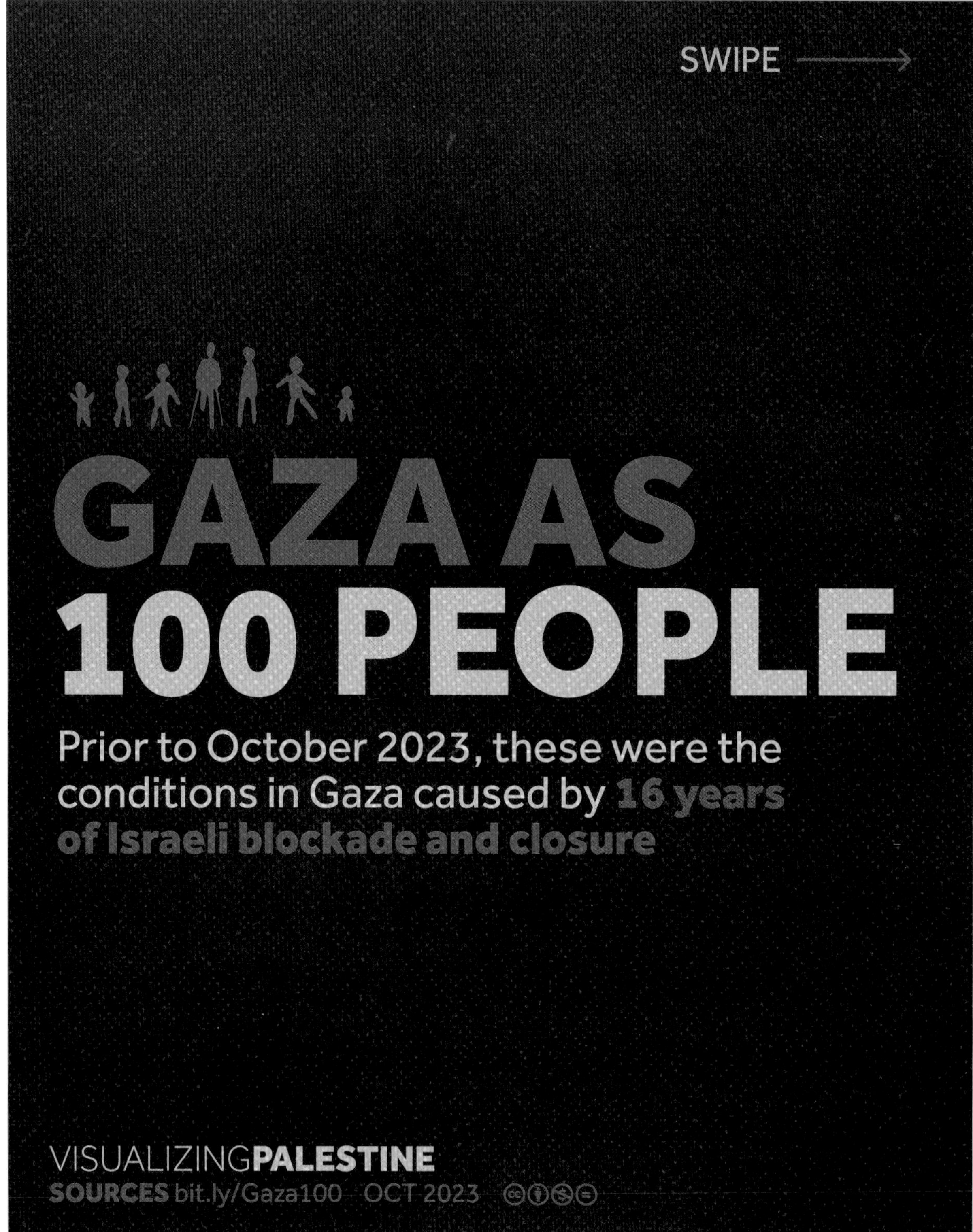
SWIPE
GAZA AS
100 PEOPLE
Prior to October 2023, these were the conditions in Gaza caused by 16 years of Israeli blockade and closure
VISUALIZINGPALESTINE
SOURCES bit.ly/Gaza100 OCT 2023

Year: 2023 | **Brief and copywriting:** Jessica Anderson | **Design:** Nasreen Abd Elal | **Sources:** bit.ly/Gaza100

GAZA AS 100 PEOPLE
47 are children
VISUALIZINGPALESTINE
SOURCES bit.ly/Gaza100 OCT 2023

GAZA AS 100 PEOPLE
45 of these children have trauma, depression, or anxiety
VISUALIZINGPALESTINE
SOURCES bit.ly/Gaza100 OCT 2023

GAZA AS 100 PEOPLE
53 are adults
VISUALIZINGPALESTINE
SOURCES bit.ly/Gaza100 OCT 2023

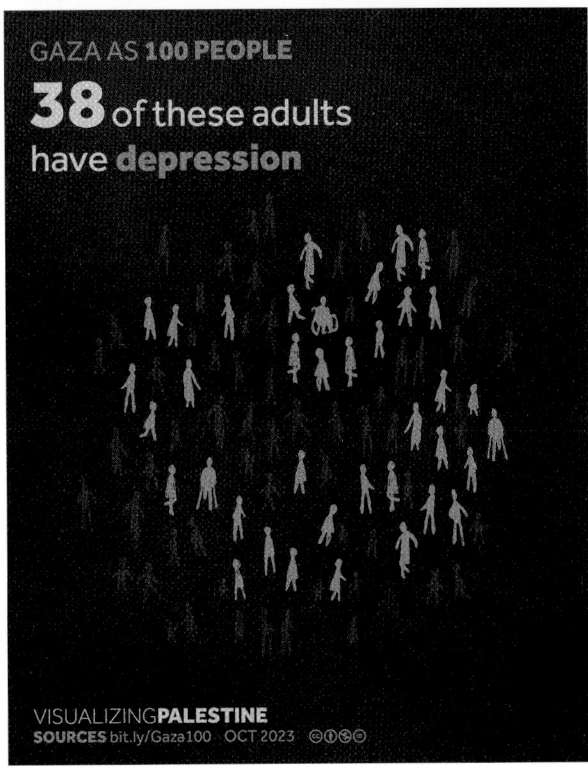
GAZA AS 100 PEOPLE
38 of these adults have depression
VISUALIZINGPALESTINE
SOURCES bit.ly/Gaza100 OCT 2023

GAZA AS 100 PEOPLE

70 are refugees

VISUALIZING**PALESTINE**

SOURCES bit.ly/Gaza100 OCT 2023

GAZA AS 100 PEOPLE
82 live in poverty
VISUALIZINGPALESTINE
SOURCES bit.ly/Gaza100 OCT 2023

GAZA AS 100 PEOPLE
63 are food insecure
VISUALIZINGPALESTINE
SOURCES bit.ly/Gaza100 OCT 2023

GAZA AS 100 PEOPLE
95 don't have direct access to clean water
VISUALIZINGPALESTINE
SOURCES bit.ly/Gaza100 OCT 2023

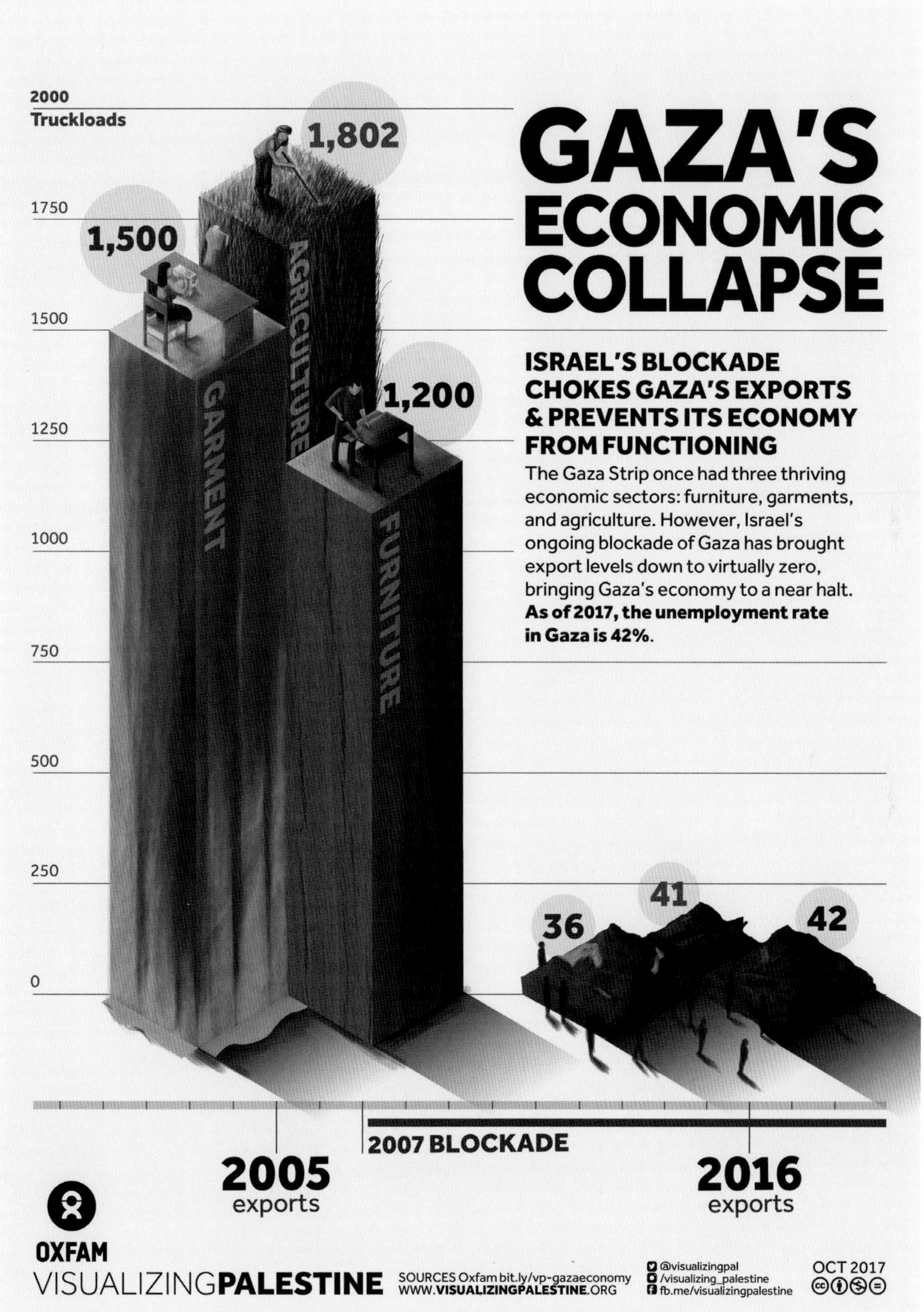
2000
Truckloads
1750
1500
1250
1000
750
500
250
0
1,802
1,500
1,200
AGRICULTURE
GARMENT
FURNITURE
GAZA'S ECONOMIC COLLAPSE
ISRAEL'S BLOCKADE CHOKES GAZA'S EXPORTS & PREVENTS ITS ECONOMY FROM FUNCTIONING
The Gaza Strip once had three thriving economic sectors: furniture, garments, and agriculture. However, Israel's ongoing blockade of Gaza has brought export levels down to virtually zero, bringing Gaza's economy to a near halt. As of 2017, the unemployment rate in Gaza is 42%.
36
41
42
2007 BLOCKADE
2005
exports
2016
exports
OXFAM
VISUALIZINGPALESTINE
SOURCES Oxfam bit.ly/vp-gazaeconomy
WWW.VISUALIZINGPALESTINE.ORG
@visualizingpal
/visualizing_palestine
fb.me/visualizingpalestine
OCT 2017

Year: 2017 | **Brief and copywriting:** Iman Annab, Roslyn Boatman, Reem Farah, Robin Jones | **Design:** Yosra El Gazzar | **Sources:** bit.ly/vp-gazaeconomy

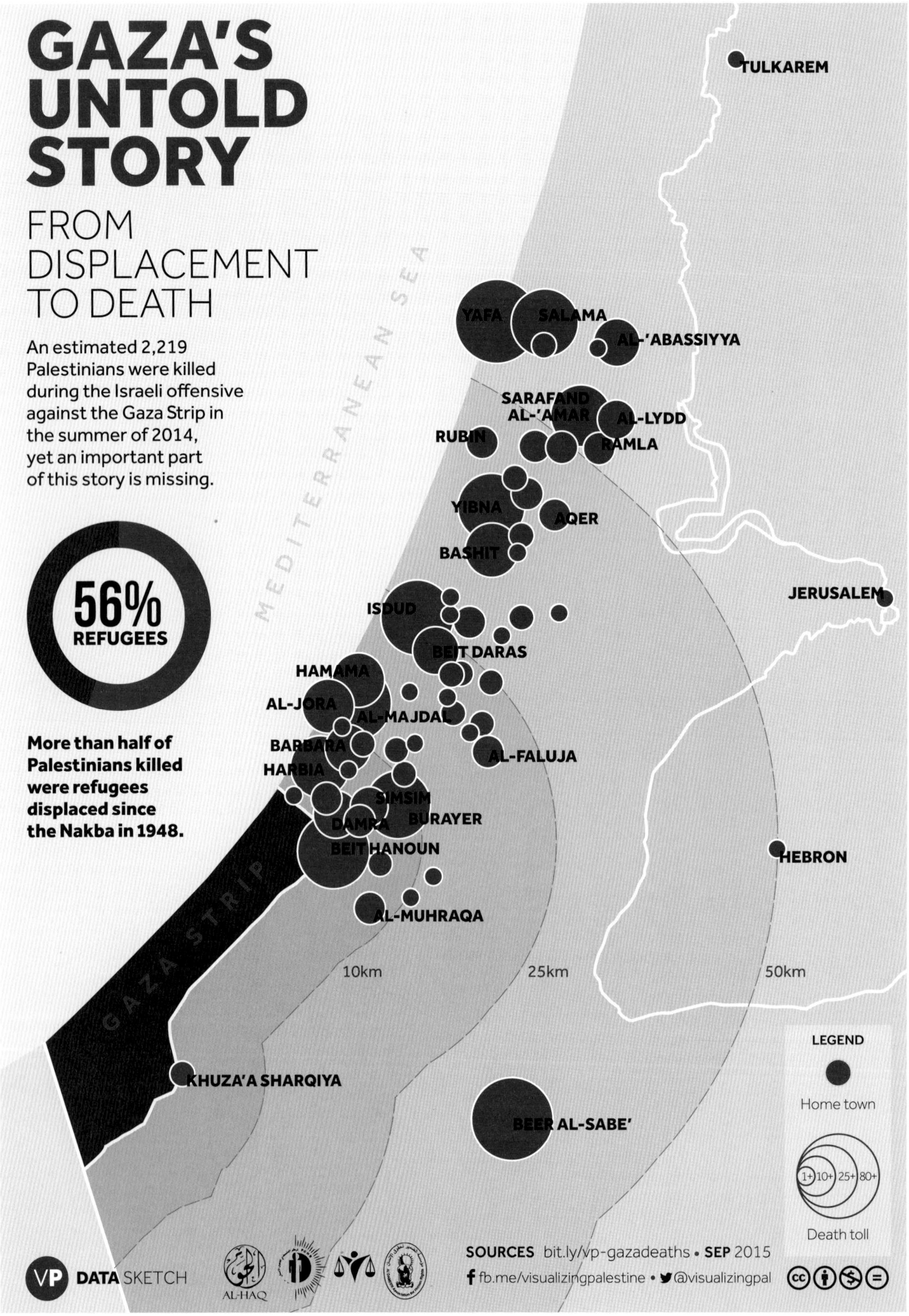

GAZA'S UNTOLD STORY

FROM DISPLACEMENT TO DEATH

An estimated 2,219 Palestinians were killed during the Israeli offensive against the Gaza Strip in the summer of 2014, yet an important part of this story is missing.

56%
REFUGEES

More than half of Palestinians killed were refugees displaced since the Nakba in 1948.

MEDITERRANEAN SEA
TULKAREM
YAFA
SALAMA
AL-'ABASSIYYA
SARAFAND AL-'AMAR
AL-LYDD
RUBIN
RAMLA
YIBNA
AQER
BASHIT
JERUSALEM
ISDUD
BEIT DARAS
HAMAMA
AL-JORA
AL-MAJDAL
BARBARA
AL-FALUJA
HARBIA
SIMSIM
DAMRA
BURAYER
BEIT HANOUN
HEBRON
AL-MUHRAQA
10km
25km
50km
GAZA STRIP
KHUZA'A SHARQIYA
BEER AL-SABE'

LEGEND
Home town
1+ 10+ 25+ 80+
Death toll

SOURCES bit.ly/vp-gazadeaths • SEP 2015
fb.me/visualizingpalestine • @visualizingpal

VP DATA SKETCH
AL-HAQ

Year: 2015 | **Brief and copywriting:** Wesam Ahmad, Ahmad Barclay | **Design:** Ahmad Barclay | **Sources:** bit.ly/vp-gazadeaths

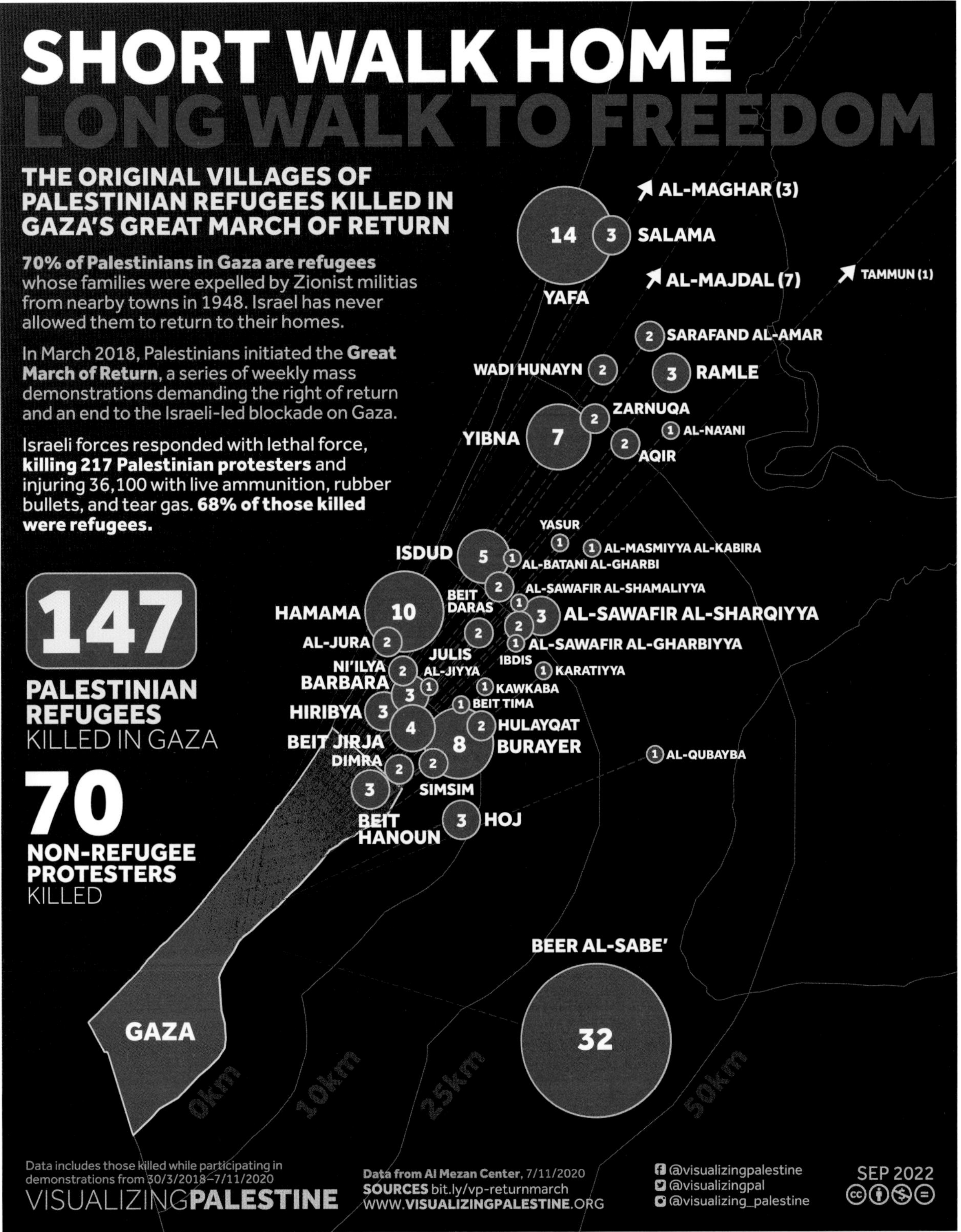
SHORT WALK HOME
LONG WALK TO FREEDOM
THE ORIGINAL VILLAGES OF PALESTINIAN REFUGEES KILLED IN GAZA'S GREAT MARCH OF RETURN
70% of Palestinians in Gaza are refugees whose families were expelled by Zionist militias from nearby towns in 1948. Israel has never allowed them to return to their homes.
In March 2018, Palestinians initiated the Great March of Return, a series of weekly mass demonstrations demanding the right of return and an end to the Israeli-led blockade on Gaza.
Israeli forces responded with lethal force, killing 217 Palestinian protesters and injuring 36,100 with live ammunition, rubber bullets, and tear gas. 68% of those killed were refugees.
147
PALESTINIAN REFUGEES KILLED IN GAZA
70
NON-REFUGEE PROTESTERS KILLED
AL-MAGHAR (3)
14 YAFA
3 SALAMA
AL-MAJDAL (7)
TAMMUN (1)
2 SARAFAND AL-AMAR
WADI HUNAYN 2
3 RAMLE
2 ZARNUQA
YIBNA 7
1 AL-NA'ANI
2 AQIR
YASUR 1
1 AL-MASMIYYA AL-KABIRA
ISDUD 5
1 AL-BATANI AL-GHARBI
2 AL-SAWAFIR AL-SHAMALIYYA
HAMAMA 10
BEIT DARAS 2
1
3 AL-SAWAFIR AL-SHARQIYYA
2
1 AL-SAWAFIR AL-GHARBIYYA
AL-JURA 2
JULIS
IBDIS
1 KARATIYYA
NI'ILYA 2
AL-JIYYA 1
BARBARA 3
1 KAWKABA
1 BEIT TIMA
HIRIBYA 3
4
2 HULAYQAT
8 BURAYER
BEIT JIRJA
DIMRA 2
2
1 AL-QUBAYBA
3
SIMSIM
BEIT HANOUN
3 HOJ
BEER AL-SABE'
32
GAZA
0km
10km
25km
50km
Data includes those killed while participating in demonstrations from 30/3/2018–7/11/2020
VISUALIZINGPALESTINE
Data from Al Mezan Center, 7/11/2020
SOURCES bit.ly/vp-returnmarch
WWW.VISUALIZINGPALESTINE.ORG
@visualizingpalestine
@visualizingpal
@visualizing_palestine
SEP 2022

Year: 2022 | **Brief and copywriting:** Jessica Anderson, Robin Jones | **Design:** Ahmad Barclay, Nasreen Abd Elal, Yosra El Gazzar | **Sources:** bit.ly/vp-returnmarch

GAZA HEALTH ACCESS UNDER ISRAELI SIEGE

2018
39%
OF PERMIT APPLICATIONS BY PATIENTS SEEKING MEDICAL CARE OUTSIDE GAZA **WERE DENIED/DELAYED BY ISRAEL**

2017
46%

2016
37%

2015
23.5%

2014
17.6%

2013
11.3%

2012
7.5%

54 PATIENTS IN GAZA DIED WAITING FOR A PERMIT IN 2017
Patients must submit a permit application **23 days** before their appointment

VISUALIZING**PALESTINE**
SOURCES bit.ly/vp-righttohealth
WWW.**VISUALIZINGPALESTINE**.ORG
@visualizingpal
/visualizing_palestine
fb.me/visualizingpalestine
MAR 2020

Year: 2020 | **Brief and copywriting:** Jessica Anderson | **Design:** Yosra El Gazzar | **Sources:** bit.ly/vp-righttohealth

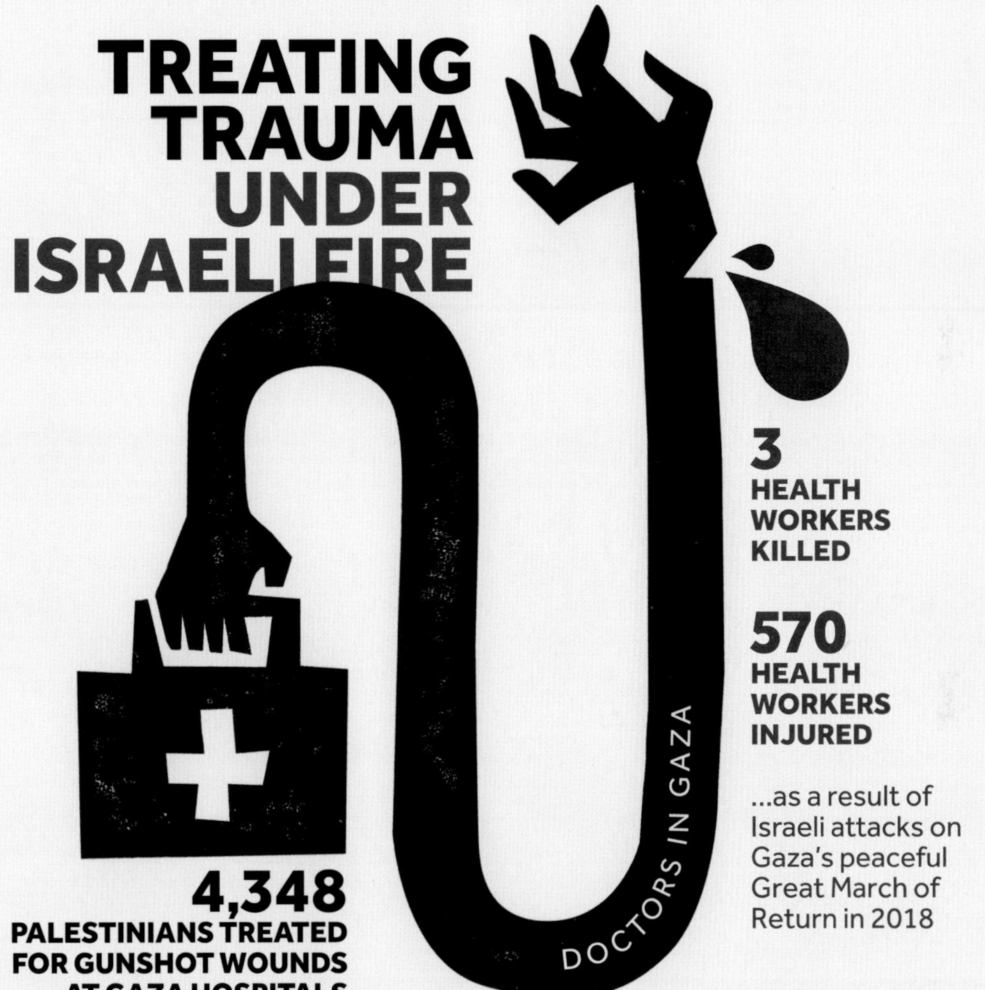
TREATING
TRAUMA
UNDER
ISRAELI FIRE
3
HEALTH
WORKERS
KILLED
570
HEALTH
WORKERS
INJURED
...as a result of
Israeli attacks on
Gaza's peaceful
Great March of
Return in 2018
DOCTORS IN GAZA
4,348
PALESTINIANS TREATED
FOR GUNSHOT WOUNDS
AT GAZA HOSPITALS

VISUALIZING**PALESTINE** SOURCES bit.ly/vp-righttohealth WWW.**VISUALIZINGPALESTINE**.ORG @visualizingpal /visualizing_palestine fb.me/visualizingpalestine MAR 2020

ISRAEL DENIES MEDICAL TRAINING

2% APPROVED

98%

RATE OF DENIAL/DELAY FOR PERMIT APPLICATIONS

by Palestinians to attend trainings, workshops, and conferences outside Gaza in 2018

68% PENDING

effectively denied because opportunities are usually time sensitive

VISUALIZINGPALESTINE

SOURCES bit.ly/vp-righttohealth
WWW.**VISUALIZINGPALESTINE**.ORG

@visualizingpal
/visualizing_palestine
fb.me/visualizingpalestine

MAR 2020

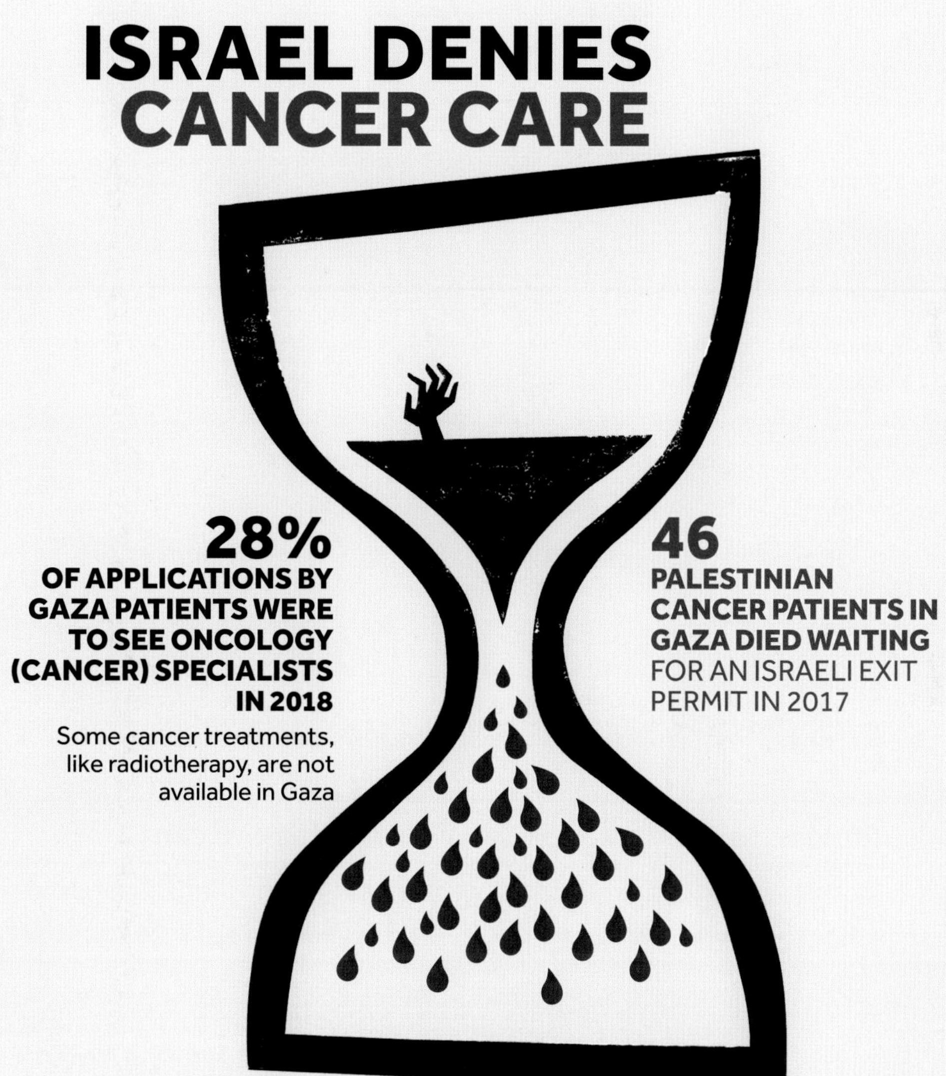
ISRAEL DENIES
CANCER CARE
28%
OF APPLICATIONS BY GAZA PATIENTS WERE TO SEE ONCOLOGY (CANCER) SPECIALISTS IN 2018
Some cancer treatments, like radiotherapy, are not available in Gaza
46
PALESTINIAN CANCER PATIENTS IN GAZA DIED WAITING FOR AN ISRAELI EXIT PERMIT IN 2017

VISUALIZING**PALESTINE** SOURCES bit.ly/vp-righttohealth WWW.**VISUALIZINGPALESTINE**.ORG

@visualizingpal
/visualizing_palestine
fb.me/visualizingpalestine

MAR 2020

CHILD
APPROVED
PARENT DENIED

1,821 kids approved without parent

59%
OF SICK KIDS APPLYING FOR AN ISRAELI PERMIT TO EXIT GAZA WERE APPROVED WITHOUT THEIR PARENT IN 2018

VISUALIZING**PALESTINE**

SOURCES bit.ly/vp-righttohealth
WWW.**VISUALIZINGPALESTINE**.ORG

@visualizingpal
/visualizing_palestine
fb.me/visualizingpalestine

MAR 2020

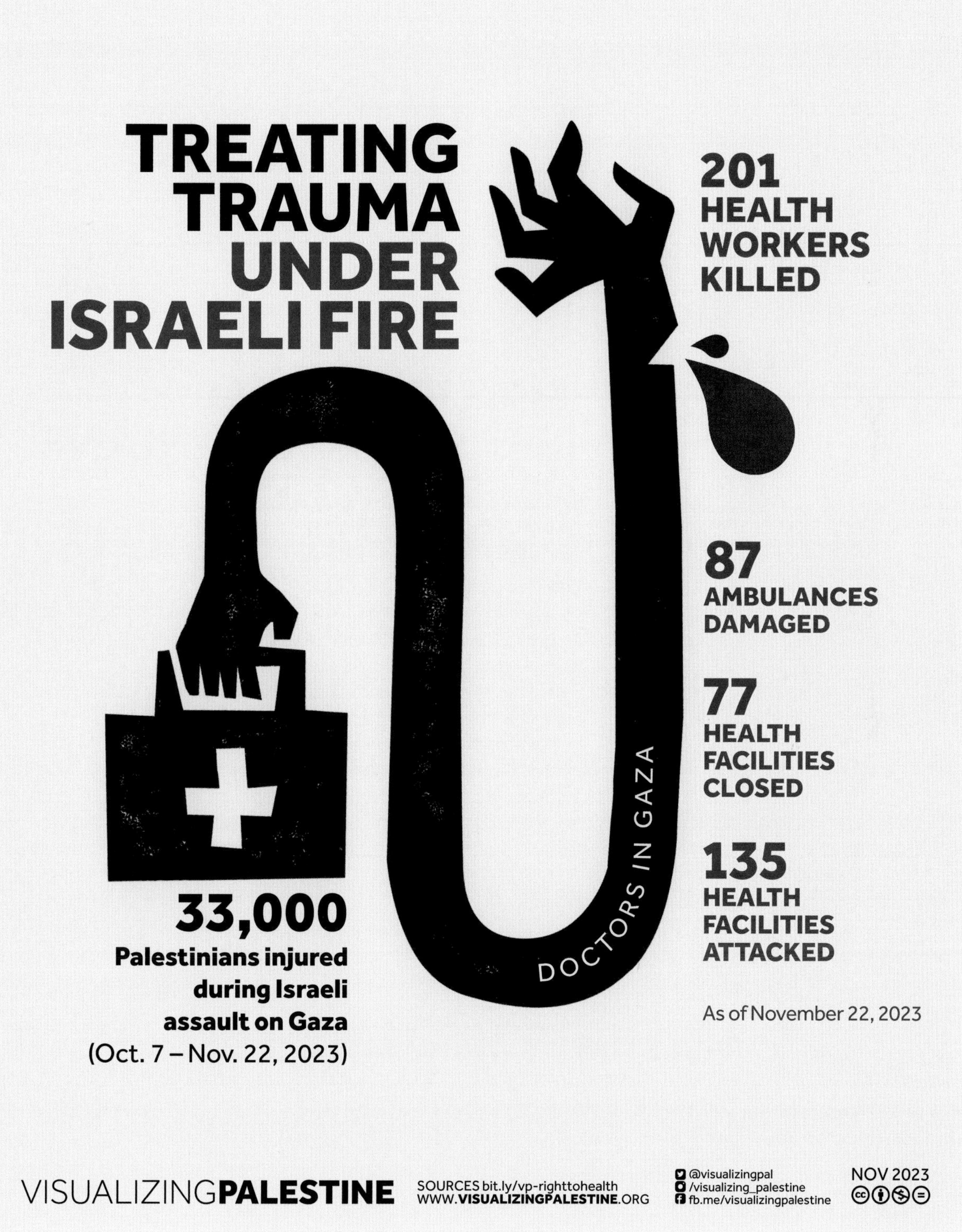
TREATING TRAUMA UNDER ISRAELI FIRE
201
HEALTH WORKERS KILLED
87
AMBULANCES DAMAGED
77
HEALTH FACILITIES CLOSED
135
HEALTH FACILITIES ATTACKED
As of November 22, 2023
DOCTORS IN GAZA
33,000
Palestinians injured during Israeli assault on Gaza
(Oct. 7 – Nov. 22, 2023)
VISUALIZINGPALESTINE
SOURCES bit.ly/vp-righttohealth
WWW.VISUALIZINGPALESTINE.ORG
@visualizingpal
/visualizing_palestine
fb.me/visualizingpalestine
NOV 2023

Year: 2023 | **Brief and copywriting:** Jessica Anderson | **Design:** Yosra El Gazar | **Sources:** bit.ly/vp-righttohealth

ACCORDING TO ISRAEL, PALESTINIANS NEED 43% LESS DAIRY THAN ISRAELIS.

The Red Lines Policy

Israel controls all food that enters the Gaza Strip. In 2007, Israeli authorities mandated that Palestinians in Gaza should receive a bare minimum of food to avoid malnutrition, featuring 43% less dairy than considered healthy for the average Israeli. Though Israel claims to have ended this policy, as of 2017 40% of Gaza's households suffered from severe food insecurity, largely as a result of Israel's blockade.

VISUALIZING**PALESTINE**

SOURCES COGAT, Gisha, Euro-Med Monitor, bit.ly/vp-gaza-food
WWW.**VISUALIZINGPALESTINE**.ORG

@visualizingpal
/visualizing_palestine
fb.me/visualizingpalestine

SEP 2018

Year: 2018 | **Brief and copywriting:** Reem Farah, Robin Jones, Ahmad Barclay | **Design:** Tucker McLachlan | **Sources:** bit.ly/vp-gaza-food

ACCORDING TO ISRAEL, PALESTINIANS NEED 19% LESS MEAT THAN ISRAELIS.

The Red Lines Policy

Israel controls all food that enters the Gaza Strip. In 2007, Israeli authorities mandated that Palestinians in Gaza should receive only the minimum of food to avoid malnutrition, featuring 19% less meat than the average Israeli. Though Israel claims to have ended this policy, as of 2017, 40% of Gaza's households suffered from severe food insecurity, largely as a result of Israel's blockade.

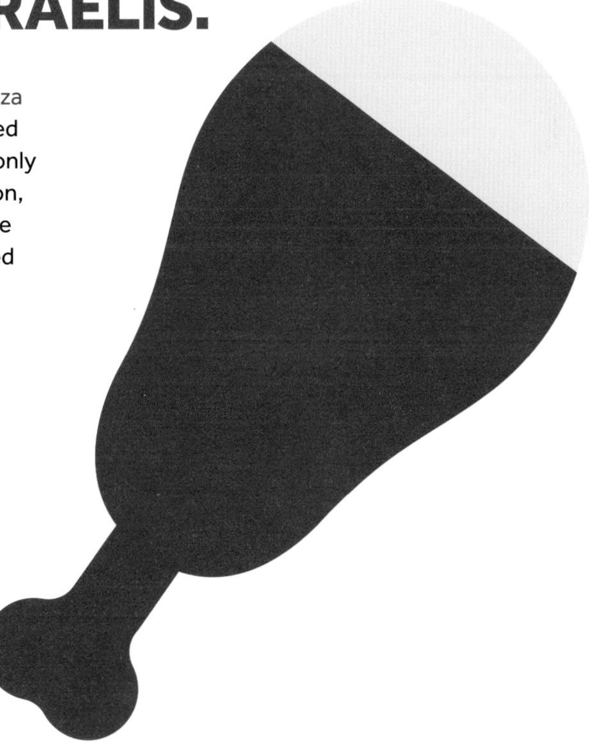

VISUALIZING**PALESTINE**

SOURCES COGAT, Gisha, bit.ly/vp-gazafood
WWW.**VISUALIZINGPALESTINE**.ORG

@visualizingpal
/visualizing_palestine
fb.me/visualizingpalestine

SEP 2018

ACCORDING TO ISRAEL, PALESTINIANS NEED 37% FEWER FRUITS AND VEGGIES THAN ISRAELIS.

The Red Lines Policy

Israel controls all food that enters the Gaza Strip. In 2007, Israeli authorities mandated that Palestinians in Gaza should receive only the minimum of food to avoid malnutrition, featuring 37% fewer fruits and veggies than the average Israeli. Though Israel claims to have ended this policy, as of 2017, 40% of Gaza's households suffered from severe food insecurity, largely as a result of Israel's blockade.

VISUALIZING**PALESTINE**

SOURCES COGAT, Gisha, bit.ly/vp-gazafood
WWW.**VISUALIZINGPALESTINE**.ORG

@visualizingpal
/visualizing_palestine
fb.me/visualizingpalestine

SEP 2018

Year: 2018 | **Research and copywriting:** Reem Farah, Robin Jones, Ahmad Barclay | **Design:** Tucker McLachlan | **Sources:** bit.ly/vp101data

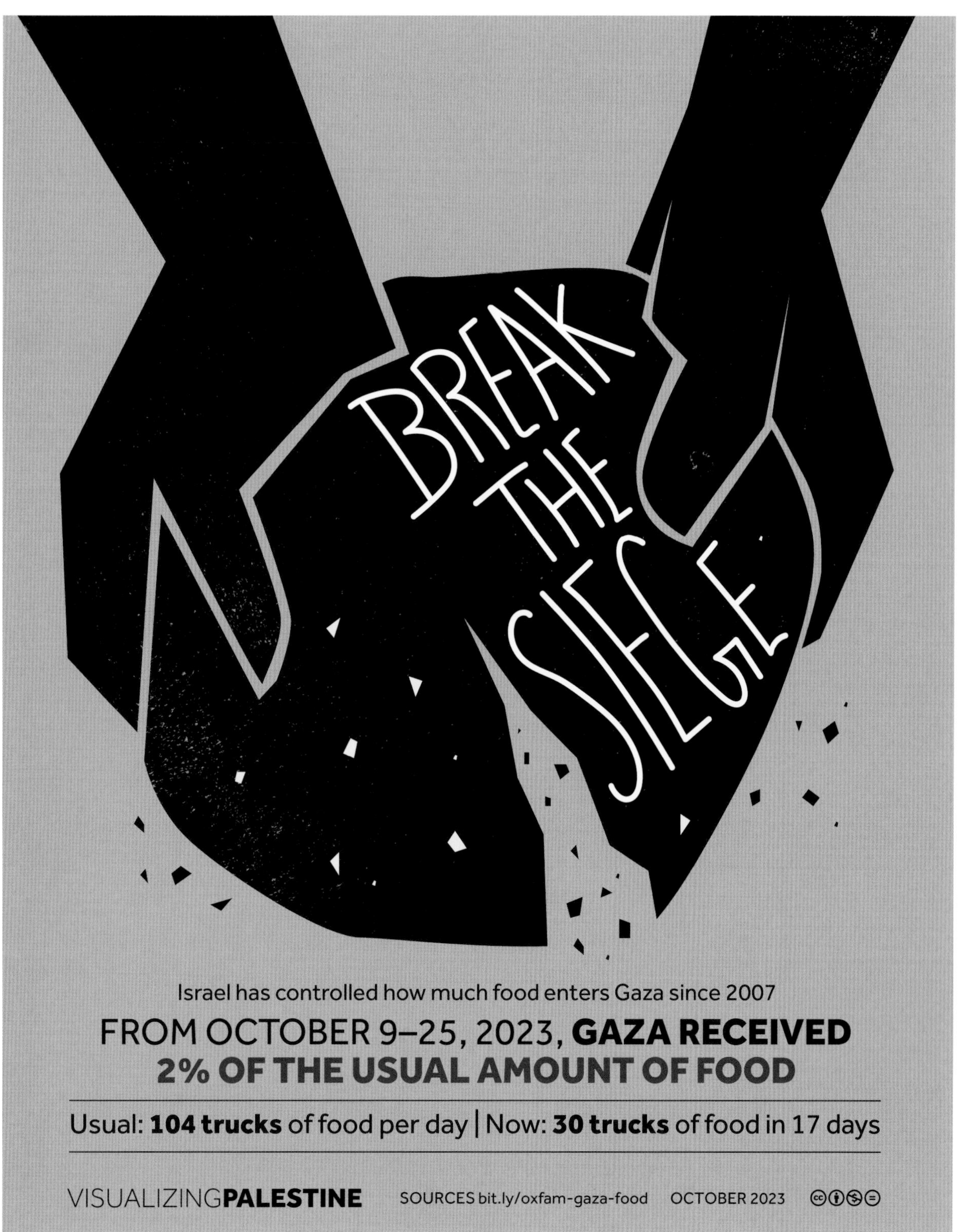
BREAK THE SIEGE
Israel has controlled how much food enters Gaza since 2007
FROM OCTOBER 9–25, 2023, GAZA RECEIVED 2% OF THE USUAL AMOUNT OF FOOD
Usual: 104 trucks of food per day | Now: 30 trucks of food in 17 days
VISUALIZINGPALESTINE SOURCES bit.ly/oxfam-gaza-food OCTOBER 2023

Year: 2023 | **Brief and copywriting:** Jessica Anderson | **Design:** Yosra El Gazzar | **Sources:** bit.ly/oxfam-gaza-food

FOUR WARS OLD

FOURTEEN YEARS OF CHILDHOOD IN GAZA

Of the
children
lived th
experie

LIFELONG CONDITIONS

WATER CRISIS

97% of fresh water contaminated. Lack of access to clean drinking water is a leading cause of illness and child mortality in Gaza

DEEP POVERTY

64% poverty rate / 69% food insecurity; 35% of Palestinian children under 5 at risk of not reaching their developmental potential due to chronic trauma

RIGHT TO EDUCATION

2/3 of schools in Gaza operate on double shifts due to classroom shortages

MENTAL HEALTH

88% of Gaza children participating in one study had experienced personal trauma; 54% meeting PTSD diagnostic criteria

2007

BORN A REFUGEE

I was born as one of the more than 70% of Palestinians in Gaza whose families were originally displaced during the Nakba in 1948

BLOCKADE

The year I was born, Israel imposed a blockade on Gaza (ongoing as of 2021) by land, air, and sea, intensifying earlier restrictions

DEC 2008-JAN 2009

FIRST WAR

I survived a 22 day attack on Gaza. Israeli forces killed 1,385 Palestinians, including 318 children

NOV 2012

SECOND WAR

I survived an eight day attack as Israeli forces killed 168 Palestinians in Gaza, including 33 children

JUL

TH WA

I survi
of ons
Israeli
2,251
in Gaz
556 c
1,500
orpha

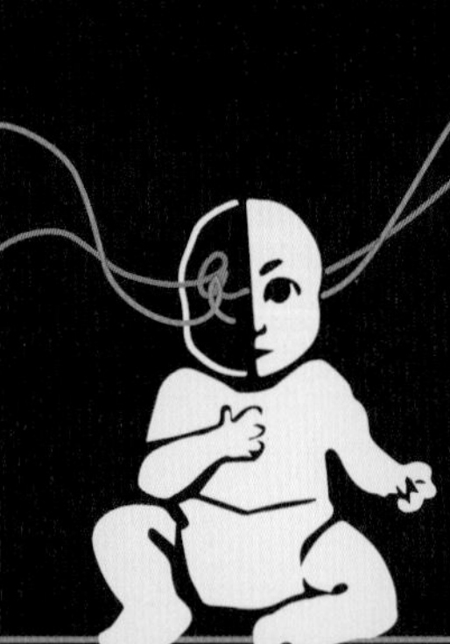

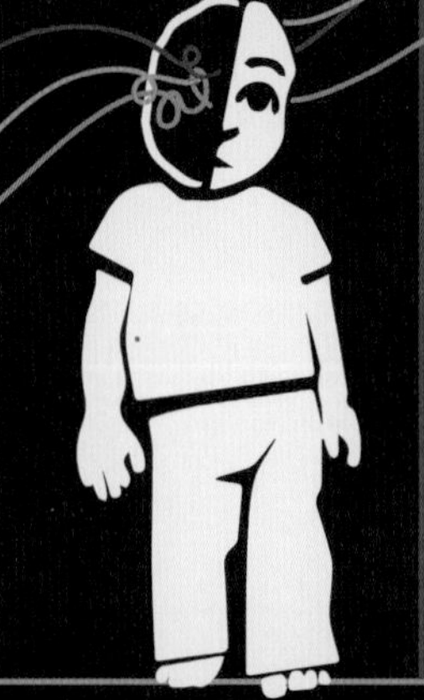

AGE 0

AGE 2

AGE 5

VISUALIZING**PALESTINE**

SOURCES bit.ly/vp-trauma
WWW.**VISUALIZINGPALESTINE.**

ı Palestinians in Gaza, 41% are
14 or under. These children have
re lives under Israeli blockade and
ıltiple types of trauma.

ıys
ed
ns
g
er
ere

MAR 2018-DEC 2019

GREAT RETURN MARCH

For two years, I saw my community turn out en masse to protest the blockade. Israeli forces killed 217 protesters, including 46 children, and injured 8,800 children with live ammunition, rubber bullets, and tear gas

MAY 2021

FOURTH WAR

I survived an eleven day attack as Israeli forces killed 230 Palestinians. Twelve of the 67 children killed were participating in a trauma recovery program

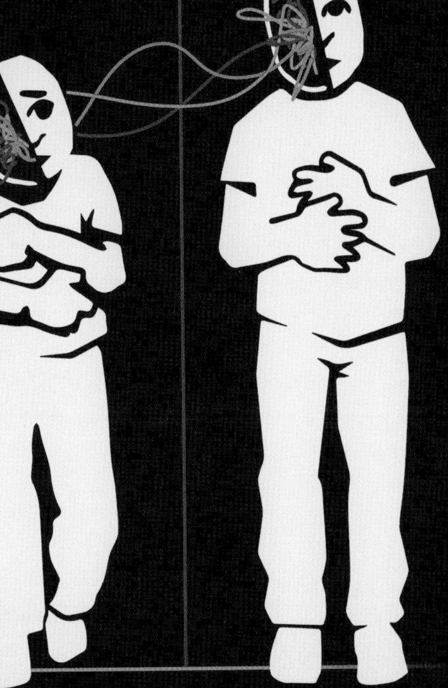

AGE 11 **AGE 14**

/visualizing_palestine
fb.me/visualizingpalestine
@visualizingpal

> **"In Gaza, there is no 'post' [traumatic] because the trauma is repetitive and ongoing and continuous.**
>
> **Samah Jabr**
> Chair of Mental Health Unit, Palestinian Ministry of Health

TYPES OF TRAUMA

CHRONIC TRAUMA

Prolonged, pervasive distressing events such as poverty or institutionalized discrimination

INTER-GENERATIONAL TRAUMA

Psychological trauma experienced by the descendants of a person who has survived a traumatic event

ACUTE TRAUMA

An extremely distressing individual event

JUNE 2021

Year: 2021
Brief and copywriting: Jessica Anderson
Design: Nasreen Abd Elal
Sources: bit.ly/vp-trauma

SIX WARS OLD

SIXTEEN YEARS OF CHILDHOO

LIFELONG CONDITIONS

WATER CRISIS

97% of fresh water contaminated. Lack of access to clean drinking water is a leading cause of illness and child mortality in Gaza

DEEP POVERTY

61% poverty rate / 63% food insecurity; 35% of Palestinian children under 5 at risk of not reaching their developmental potential due to chronic trauma

RIGHT TO EDUCATION

2/3 of schools in Gaza operate on double shifts due to classroom shortages

MENTAL HEALTH

95% of children in Gaza showed symptoms of anxiety, depression and trauma in one 2022 study

AGE 0

BORN A REFUGEE

I was born as one of the more than 70% of Palestinians in Gaza whose families were originally displaced during the Nakba in 1948

BLOCKADE

The year I was born, Israel imposed a blockade on Gaza (ongoing as of 2023) by land, air, and sea, intensifying earlier restrictions

2007

AGE 2

FIRST ASSAULT

I survived a 22 day attack on Gaza. Israeli forces killed 1,385 Palestinians, including 318 children

DEC 2008-JAN 2009

AGE 5

SECOND ASSAULT

I survived an eight day attack as Israeli forces killed 168 Palestinians in Gaza, including 33 children

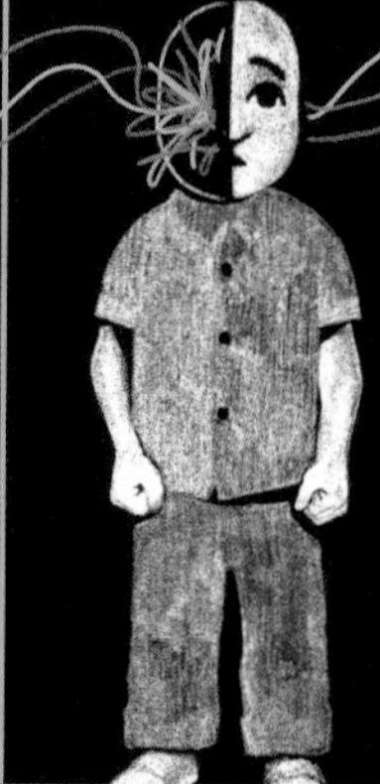

NOV 2012

AGE 7

THIRD ASSAULT

I survived fifty days of onslaught as Israeli forces killed 2,251 Palestinians in Gaza, including 556 children. Over 1,500 children were orphaned

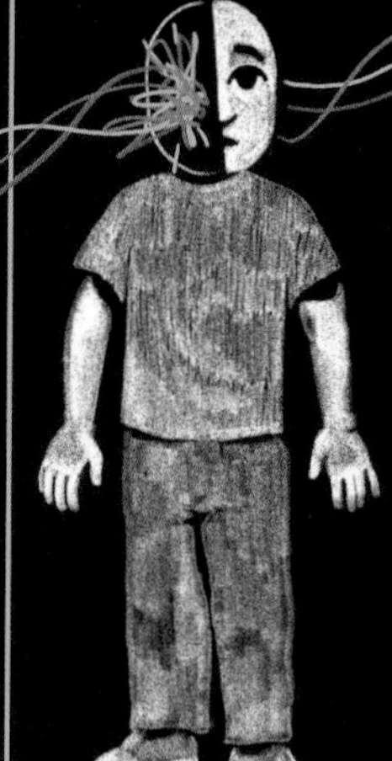

JULY 2014

M

VISUALIZINGPALESTINE

SOURCES bit.ly/vp-trauma
WWW.VISUALIZINGPALESTINE.ORG

@v
/vis

saw
turn
o
kade.
led
dren,
00
e
bber
r gas

GAZA

Of 2.3 million Palestinians in Gaza, **47% are children.** Most of these children have lived their entire life under Israeli blockade, **experiencing multiple types of trauma.**

AGE **14**

FOURTH ASSAULT

I survived an eleven day attack as Israeli forces killed 230 Palestinians. Twelve of the 67 children killed were participating in a trauma recovery program

MAY 2021

AGE **15**

FIFTH ASSAULT

I survived a three day attack on Gaza. Israeli forces killed 33 Palestinians, including 9 children

AUG 2022

AGE **16**

SIXTH ASSAULT

I am experiencing acts of genocide. In 46 days, Israeli forces killed 14,854 Palestinians, including 6,150 children. Thousands of children are missing in the rubble, and doctors are using the acronym WCNSF: wounded child no surviving family

OCT 2023-**ONGOING**

C 2019

> **In Gaza, there is no 'post' [traumatic] because the trauma is repetitive and ongoing and continuous.**
>
> **Samah Jabr**
> Chair of Mental Health Unit, Palestinian Ministry of Health

TYPES OF TRAUMA

CHRONIC TRAUMA
Prolonged, pervasive conditions such as poverty or institutionalized discrimination

INTER-GENERATIONAL TRAUMA
Psychological trauma experienced by the descendants of a person who has survived a traumatic event

ACUTE TRAUMA
An extremely distressing event

NOV 2023

Year: 2023 | **Brief and copywriting:** Jessica Anderson | **Design:** Nasreen Abd Elal | **Sources:** bit.ly/vp-trauma

MISCARRIAGE
OF JUSTICE
50000
PREGNANT
WOMEN
IN GAZA
10% are due in
the next month
VISUALIZINGPALESTINE SOURCES bit.ly/vp-pregnancy OCT 2023

Year: 2023 | **Brief and copywriting:** Jessica Anderson | **Design:** Nasreen Abd Elal | **Sources:** bit.ly/vp-pregnancy

MISCARRIAGE OF JUSTICE
Pregnancy under Israeli bombardment
No food
No clean water
No safe shelter
56 attacks on health services
Collapsing hospital system
Bombs overhead
VISUALIZINGPALESTINE SOURCES bit.ly/vp-pregnancy OCT 2023

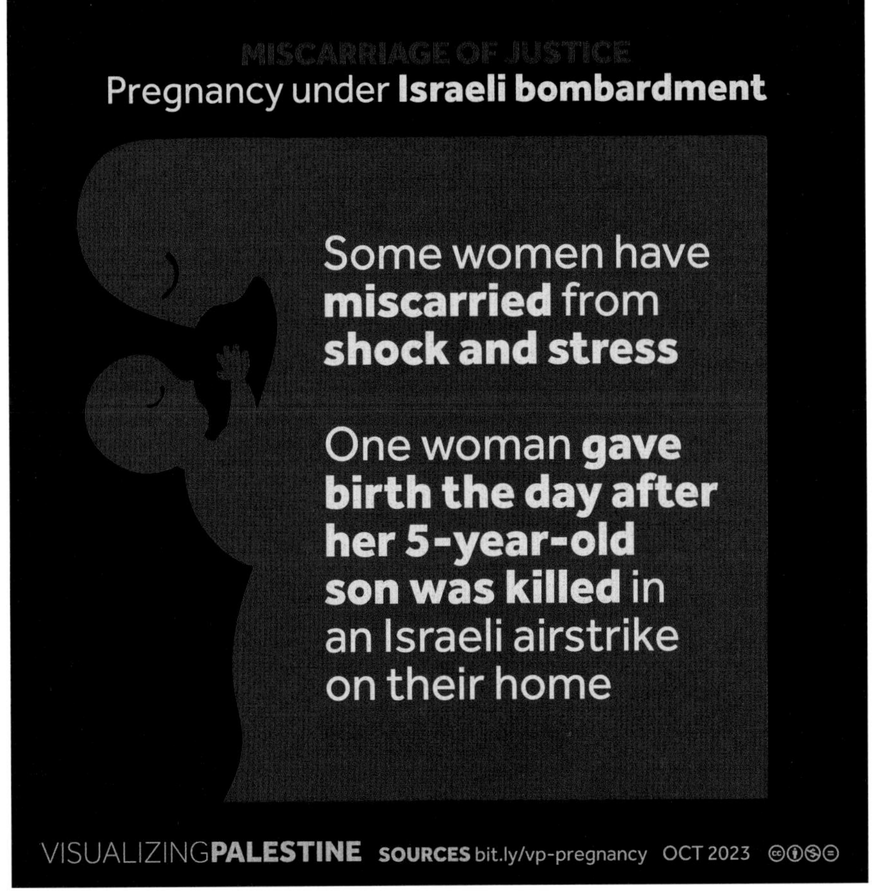
MISCARRIAGE OF JUSTICE
Pregnancy under Israeli bombardment
Some women have miscarried from shock and stress
One woman gave birth the day after her 5-year-old son was killed in an Israeli airstrike on their home
VISUALIZINGPALESTINE SOURCES bit.ly/vp-pregnancy OCT 2023

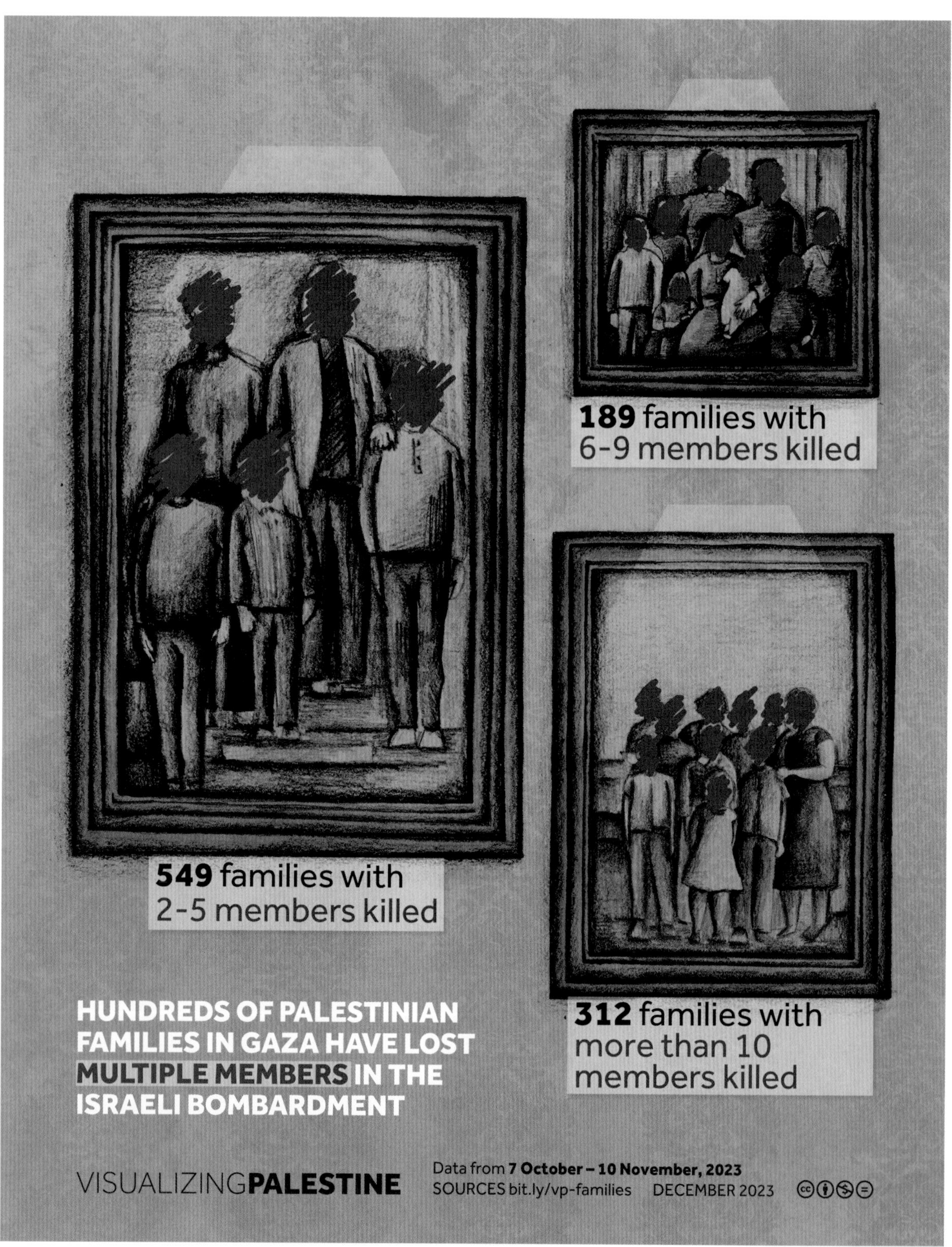
189 families with
6-9 members killed
549 families with
2-5 members killed
312 families with
more than 10
members killed
HUNDREDS OF PALESTINIAN
FAMILIES IN GAZA HAVE LOST
MULTIPLE MEMBERS IN THE
ISRAELI BOMBARDMENT
VISUALIZINGPALESTINE
Data from 7 October – 10 November, 2023
SOURCES bit.ly/vp-families DECEMBER 2023

Year: 2023 | **Brief and copywriting:** Jessica Anderson | **Design:** Yosra El Gazzar | **Sources:** bit.ly/vp-families

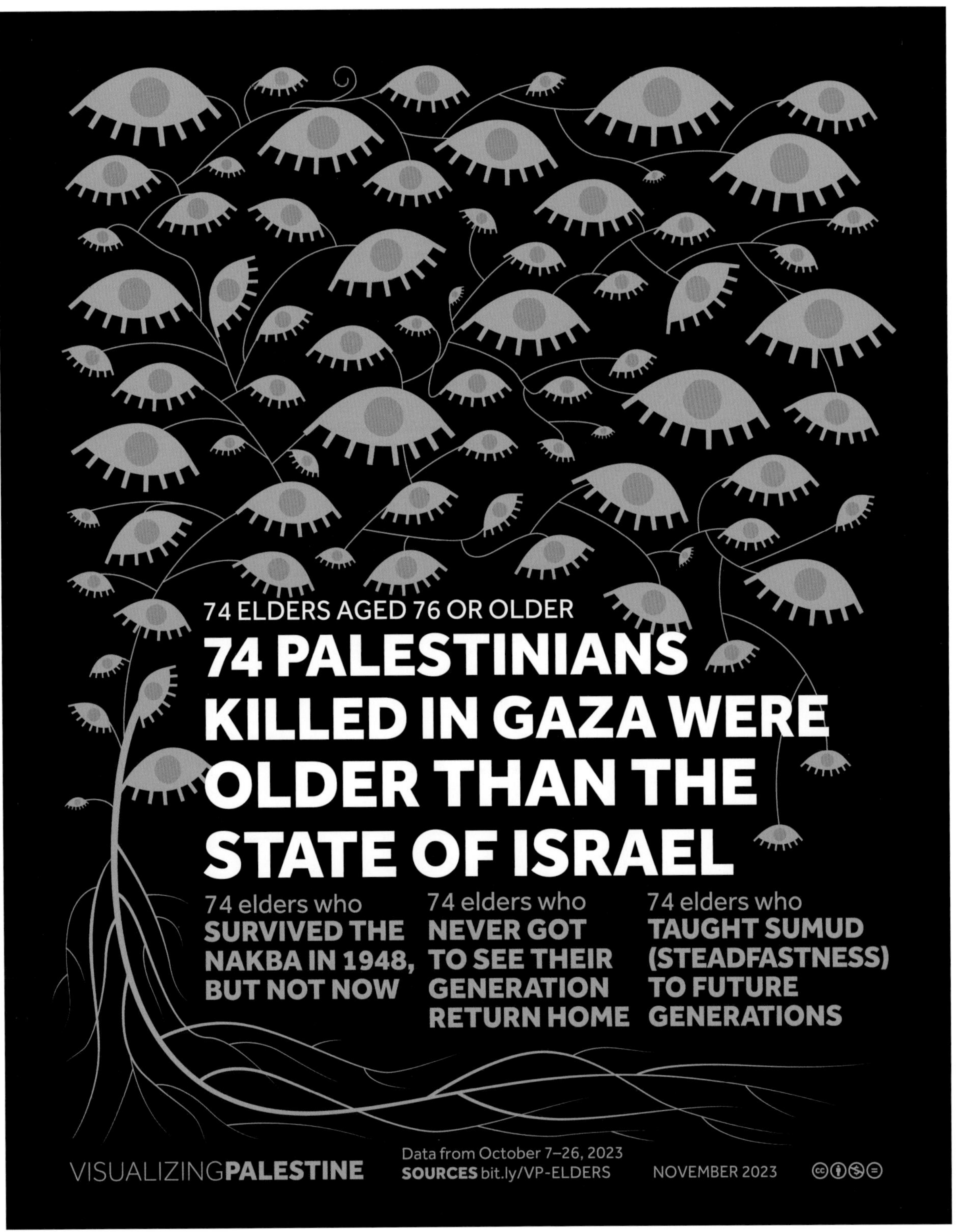
74 ELDERS AGED 76 OR OLDER
74 PALESTINIANS KILLED IN GAZA WERE OLDER THAN THE STATE OF ISRAEL
74 elders who SURVIVED THE NAKBA IN 1948, BUT NOT NOW
74 elders who NEVER GOT TO SEE THEIR GENERATION RETURN HOME
74 elders who TAUGHT SUMUD (STEADFASTNESS) TO FUTURE GENERATIONS
VISUALIZINGPALESTINE
Data from October 7–26, 2023
SOURCES bit.ly/VP-ELDERS
NOVEMBER 2023

Year: 2023 | **Brief and copywriting:** Jessica Anderson | **Design:** Yosra El Gazzar | **Sources:** bit.ly/VP-ELDERS

GENOCIDE
DEFINITION

The term "genocide" was defined in 1944 by Raphael Lemkin, a Jewish Polish legal scholar. Lemkin's definition became the basis of the **Genocide Convention**, adopted by the **General Assembly of the United Nations in 1948.**

SWIPE →

VISUALIZING**PALESTINE** SOURCES bit.ly/vp-genocide OCT 2023

Year: 2023 | **Brief and copywriting:** Jessica Anderson | **Design:** Yosra El Gazzar | **Sources:** bit.ly/vp-genocide

GENOCIDE DEFINITION

“More often **[genocide]** refers to a coordinated plan aimed at **destruction of the essential foundations of the life of national groups** so that these groups wither and die like plants that have suffered a blight. The end may be accomplished by the **forced disintegration of political and social institutions, of the culture of the people, of their language, their national feelings and their religion.** It may be accomplished by **wiping out all basis of personal security, liberty, health and dignity.** When these means fail **the machine gun can always be utilized as a last resort.** Genocide is directed against a national group as an entity and the attack on individuals is only secondary to the annihilation of the national group to which they belong.

VISUALIZING**PALESTINE** SOURCES bit.ly/vp-genocide OCT 2023

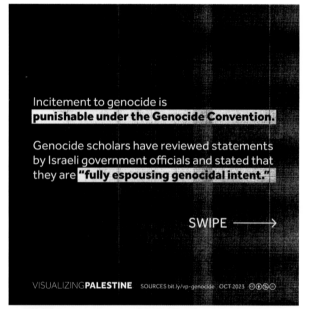

Incitement to genocide is **punishable under the Genocide Convention.**

Genocide scholars have reviewed statements by Israeli government officials and stated that they are **"fully espousing genocidal intent."**

SWIPE ⟶

VISUALIZING**PALESTINE** SOURCES bit.ly/vp-genocide OCT 2023

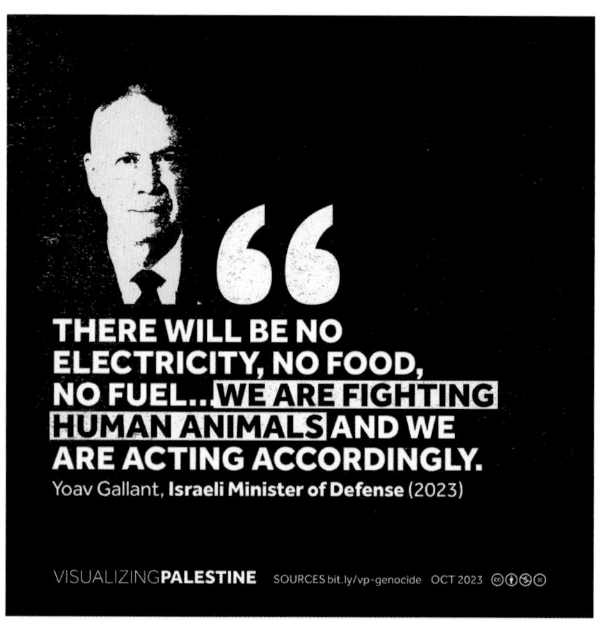
THERE WILL BE NO ELECTRICITY, NO FOOD, NO FUEL... WE ARE FIGHTING HUMAN ANIMALS AND WE ARE ACTING ACCORDINGLY.
Yoav Gallant, Israeli Minister of Defense (2023)
VISUALIZINGPALESTINE SOURCES bit.ly/vp-genocide OCT 2023

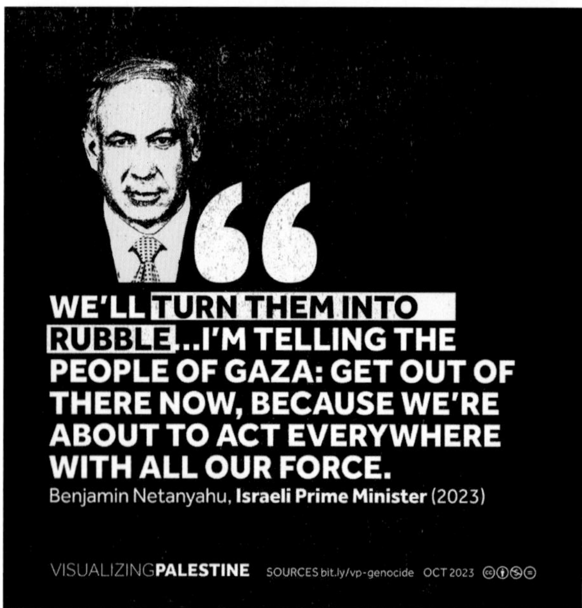
WE'LL TURN THEM INTO RUBBLE...I'M TELLING THE PEOPLE OF GAZA: GET OUT OF THERE NOW, BECAUSE WE'RE ABOUT TO ACT EVERYWHERE WITH ALL OUR FORCE.
Benjamin Netanyahu, Israeli Prime Minister (2023)
VISUALIZINGPALESTINE SOURCES bit.ly/vp-genocide OCT 2023

RIGHT NOW, ONE GOAL: NAKBA! A NAKBA THAT WILL OVERSHADOW THE NAKBA OF 48. NAKBA IN GAZA AND NAKBA TO ANYONE WHO DARES TO JOIN!
Ariel Kallner, Member of Israeli Knesset (2023)
VISUALIZINGPALESTINE SOURCES bit.ly/vp-genocide OCT 2023

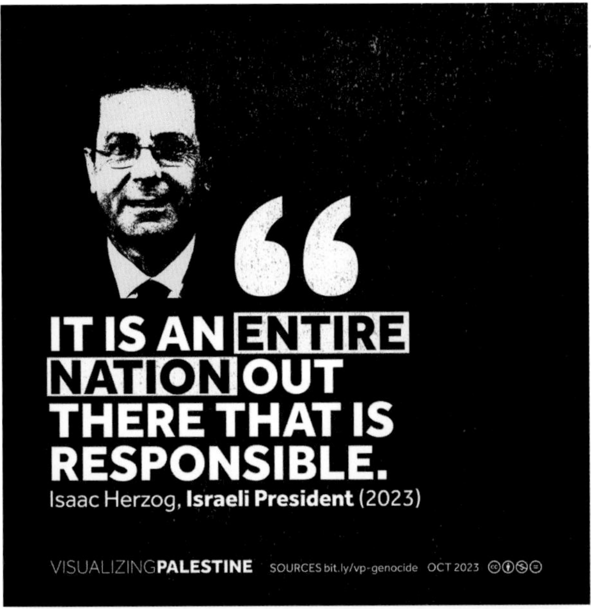
IT IS AN ENTIRE NATION OUT THERE THAT IS RESPONSIBLE.
Isaac Herzog, Israeli President (2023)
VISUALIZINGPALESTINE SOURCES bit.ly/vp-genocide OCT 2023

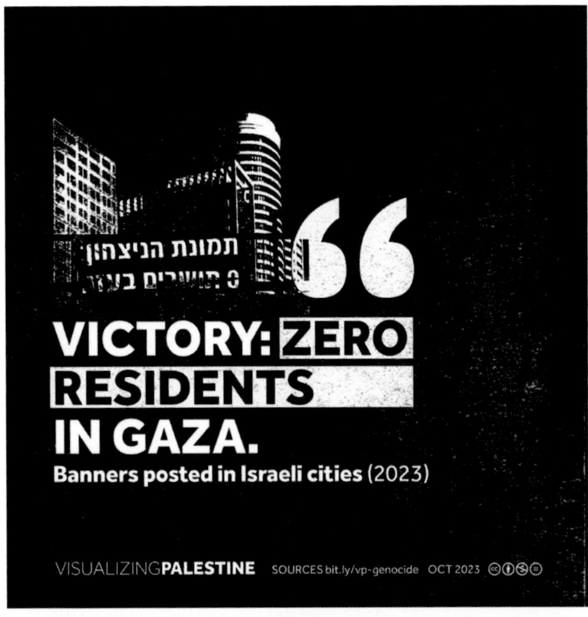
VICTORY: ZERO RESIDENTS IN GAZA.
Banners posted in Israeli cities (2023)
VISUALIZINGPALESTINE SOURCES bit.ly/vp-genocide OCT 2023

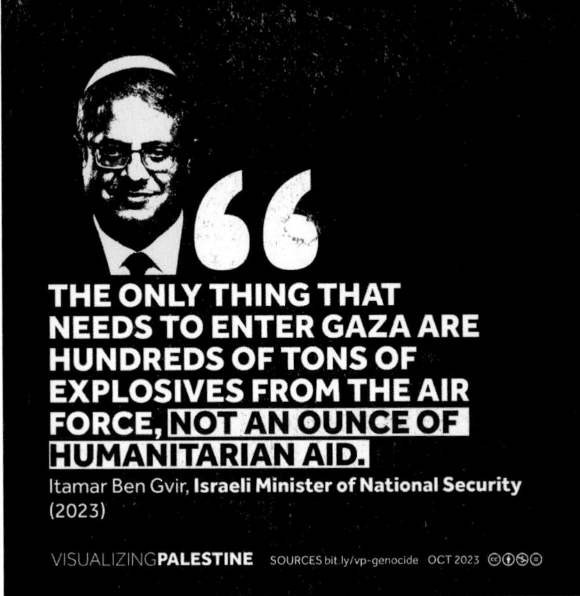
THE ONLY THING THAT NEEDS TO ENTER GAZA ARE HUNDREDS OF TONS OF EXPLOSIVES FROM THE AIR FORCE, NOT AN OUNCE OF HUMANITARIAN AID.
Itamar Ben Gvir, Israeli Minister of National Security (2023)
VISUALIZINGPALESTINE SOURCES bit.ly/vp-genocide OCT 2023

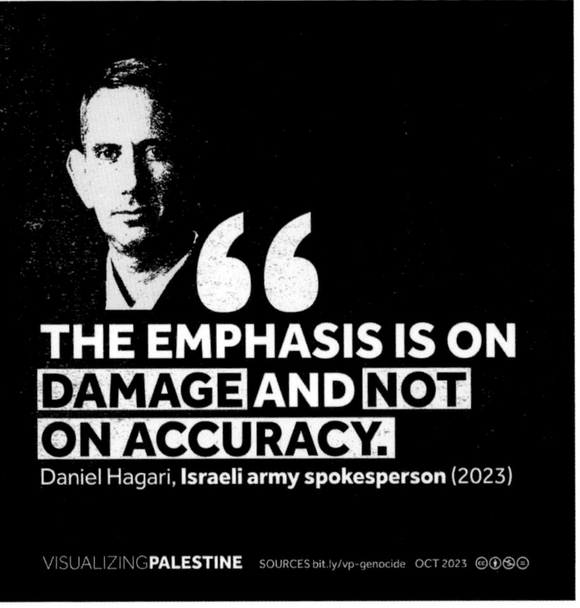
THE EMPHASIS IS ON DAMAGE AND NOT ON ACCURACY.
Daniel Hagari, Israeli army spokesperson (2023)
VISUALIZINGPALESTINE SOURCES bit.ly/vp-genocide OCT 2023

In memory of the 6,546* people killed during Israel's ongoing bombardment of Palestinians in Gaza. Over 2,700 were children.

MIDHAT SAIDAM
plastic and burn specialist at Al Shifa hospital, killed with 30 of his family members in an Israeli airstrike on their home
HALA ABU SA'DA
sign language interpreter, 13, killed with her family in an Israeli airstrike on their home in Jabalia refugee camp
KHALIL AL-SHARIF, YASSER AL-MASRI, AHMED DAHMAN
paramedics, killed in an Israeli airstrike on a Palestinian Red Crescent ambulance
AL-SHAIMA AKRAM SAIDAM
student, 18, killed in an Israeli airstrike on Al Nuseirat refugee camp after receiving the top mark in Palestine's high school exams
FALESTINE ABU ARAR
pregnant woman, 37, killed by shrapnel from an Israeli missile with her 14-month-old niece in her arms
"IF I DIE, REMEMBER THAT I, WE, WERE INDIVIDUALS, HUMANS,
WE HAD NAMES, DREAMS, AND ACHIEVEMENTS

THAT WE WERE
CLASSIFIED
AS INFERIOR."

BELAL ALDABBOUR
Palestinian neurologist, Gaza City via Twitter/X

OMAR SHAMALLAKH
2 months old, killed with his grandparents, parents, brother, and 4 uncles in an Israeli airstrike on their home

BESAN HELASA
medical student, 19, killed with her family in an Israeli airstrike 2 days after following Israeli orders to leave north Gaza

AHMAD SHEHAB
journalist, killed with his wife and 3 children in an Israeli airstrike on their home

HAIDI, QUSSAI, SIDRA, LINDA
siblings, 1, 3, 6, 7, killed with their mother, cousins, and aunt in an Israeli air strike on their home, survived by their father

YOUSEF ABU MOUSSA
6, brought to a local hospital where his identity was confirmed by his father, a doctor on duty, after an Israeli airstrike on their home

CEASEFIRE NOW
END THE SIEGE ON GAZA

*as of October 25, 2023. Source: Gaza Health Ministry
Paid for By The Arab American Association of New York

gazaispalestine.com

Year: 2023 | **Brief and copywriting:** Jessica Anderson, Aline Batarseh, Yasmin Hamidi, Linda Sarsour | **Design:** Nasreen Abd Elal | **Sources:** Gaza Ministry of Health

How many more children will be killed before Canada intervenes?
Over 4,237* Palestinian children have been killed by Israel, and over 1,350* are missing in the rubble (Oct. 7-Nov. 8).
This page only fits 973 of their names.

Rayan Abdullah Zakaria Al-Astal
Mian Yahya Yusuf Al-Astal
Salam Wael Ahmed Al-Astal
Zein al-Din Suleiman Moin al-Najjar
Yasmine Ramez Abdel Razzaq El Masry
Maria Nasser Kamel Abu Khatry
Aisha Jihad Jalal Shaheen
"Son of" Rahima Saadi Muhammad Shaheen
Muhammad Mamdouh Muhammad Abu Jazar
Tia Mamdouh Muhammad Abu Jazar
Bahaa Hani Jamal Musa
Rakan Hossam Hussein Musa
Musk Mahmoud Ibrahim Hegazy
Ahmed Mohamed Amin Nofal
Son of Nahla Nasr Muhammad Nofal
Moaz Hani Saadi Muhammad Al-Adi
Qais Ali Nabil Al-Adi
Nabil Bilal Nabil Al-Adi
Alma Moamen Muhammad Hamdan
Musk Muhammad Khalil Gouda
Bilal Muhammad Khalil Gouda
Abdel Rahim Ahmed Abdel Rahim Awad
Tahani Ezz El-Din Ahmed Zoroub
Muhammad Nidal Hisham Atallah
Mustafa Hani Essam Saqallah
Abdel Khaled Ibrahim Abdel Al-Farra
Muhammad Omar Mustafa Shehab
Sarah Fathi Abdel Karim Al-Farra
Bilal Khaled Muhammad Sobh
Obaida Bilal Youssef Abu Mualiq
Louay Mahmoud Saleh Al-Agami
Iyad Abdel Rahman Jihad Muheisen
Anisa Mahmoud Ahmed Ali
Hamza Muhammad Abdel Hamid Ashour
Salma Ibrahim Basem Shaaban
Muhammad Hussein Muhammad Abu Hamad
Aseed Hussein Muhammad Abu Hamad
Ahmed Moamen Ahmed Daloul
Muhammad Fadi Jihad Radwan
Aseel Muhammad Jumah Dhair
Nour Rifaat Omar Abu Yahya al-Akkad
Muhammad Hamed Nidal Aliwa
Eliana Muhammad Nabil Mekheimer
Abdel Rahman Samir Salama Saad
Omar Jihad Omar Al-Batrini
Watin Yahya Khaled Abu Hilal
Malak Abdul Salem Ali Abu Saif
Hoda Mustafa Hatem Abu Seif
Musk Abdul Hey Sami Al-Habibi
Omar Ahmed Abdel Nasser Shamlakh
Ibrahim Ammar Saad Al-Qara
Ahmed Shadi Talal Al-Haddad
Hoor Yassin Ahmed Sheikh Al-Eid
Mahmoud Saeed Nabil Al-Laham
Shaima Saeed Nabil Al-Lahham
Jihad Mohamad Jawad Al-Wadiya
Tim Samer Suleiman Jaarour
Ayla Uday Abdel Jawad Abu Ras
Amal Muhammad Ahmed Al-Bayouk
Layan Muhammad Youssef Hussein
Asaad Mher Aziz Lashin Iyam
Sham Muhammad Saleh Al-Sawalha
Muhammad Basil Mahmoud Al-Khayyat
Adam Majdy Jaber Al-Dahdouh
Adam Muhammad Samir Abu Ajwa
Jalal Nour al-Din Al-Astamond
Khaled Fadi Khaled Al Baba
Maha Fadi Khaled Al Baba
Ayat Abdul Aziz Omar Farwaneh
Firas Muhammad Abdel Aziz Tamraz
Essam Muhammad Essam Farag
Moatasem Billah Ahmed Muhammad Hammad
Khaled Bilal Mahmoud Abu Al-Amrain
Sarah Abdel Rahman Muhammad Hammad
Mahmoud Fadi Khaled Al-Baba
Abdel Khaled Fadi Khaled Al Baba
Reed Iter Nour al-Din Al-Astamond
George Sobhi George Al-Souri
Alia Abdel Nour Al-Souri
Ismail Ahmed Ismail Farhat
Rose Abdul Aziz Muhammad Al-Ghroul
Alyan Abdel Rahman Ali Al-Ashqar
Support Bilal Nabil Amara
Rima Muhammad Sabry Al-Buraim
Hassan Hamza Hassan Al-Amsi
Anas Tariq Muhammad Al-Hasanat
Zaid Khaled Juma Al-Abbasheri
Muhammad Ahmed Salih Al-Qanou

Rana Majd Ramzi Al-Moqyed
Abdul Rahman Abdul Aziz Yahya Al Balawi
Owais Amer Yahya Al-Balawi
Sawsan Mustafa Mahmoud Barbakh
Aiyan Muhammad Ali Al-Bayouk
Ghaith Muhammad Omar Al-Bahlool
Hour Mustafa Muhammad Al-Naqib
Mira Youssef Ibrahim Musleh
Anas Muhammad Mahmoud Al-Derawi
Sowar Mounir Harb Dawas
Samir Muhammad Fathi Abu Ajwa
Magd Muhammad Amin Al-Dahdouh
Mahmoud Basil Mahmoud Al-Khayyat
Amira Muhammad Samir Abu Ajwa
Malak Mahmoud Atef Halawa
Akram Mahmoud Moin Al-Harkali
Yara Muhammad Fayez Al-Hassani
Sila Dhafer Ahmed Abu Younis
Sowar Fouad Mahmoud Tabasi
Fayrouz Fadi Hameida Abu Salima
Sahad Ahmed Muhammad Abu Amran
Nourz Ahmed Shaaban Halasa
Mahmoud Muhammad Ahmed Abu Oreiban
Juliet Sobhi George Al-Souri
Anas Abdul Aziz Muhammad Zahir
Amna Khaled Ibrahim Rantisi
Maria Ahmed Salah Kurdieh
Mohamed Hossam Muhammad Hamad
Ahmed Thaer Sobhi Ghareeb
Sarah Rshaid Jihad Abu Jabbara
Muhammad Fathi Suleiman Al-Jawi
Alma Qais Abdul Karim Al-Zahrani
Jude Alaa Muhammad Al-Agha
Ayla Ahmed Abul Obaid
Ahmed Yasser Ahmed Abu Halhoul
Majid Ahmed Salem Al-Agami
Abdul Karim Kamel Zidane Al-Hawajri
Mustafa Musa Azmi Al-Jamal
Sham Ahmed Isbitan Abu Sido
Kenan Ibrahim Rami Al-Naji
Amir Rifaat Omar Al-Bayouk
Atef Mohamed Atef Muammar
Jude Salem Khamis Nasrallah
Sarah Musa Hamdi Akhil
Sham Muhammad Mustafa Othman
Amin Muhammad Mustafa Othman
Sila Ahmed Hussein Madi
Kenzi Fadi Salem Al Nabih
Saba Muhammad Imad Shabiq
Al-Baraa Muhammad Youssef Nasr
Diamond Muhammad Youssef Nasr
Quddus Majid Salem Al-Dali
Lama Mahmoud Yasser Dardouna
Ahmed Muhammad Yasser Dardouna
Asia Hassam Hamdi Al-Hinawi
Saeed Ziad Saeed Zaqoul
Zaher Adham Jamal Al-Garfud
Firas Adel Nabil Al-Qishawi
Dilla Jihad Hamada Al-Bakri
Uday Muhammad Fouad Hana
Sabreen Fahd Mahmoud Bashir
Mecca Ahmed Eid Abu Sharkh
Musa Ahmed Eid Abu Zneid
Ayman Muhammad Ayman Ismail
Masa Muhammad Adnan Al-Habashi
Taim Allah Muhammad Abdul Karim Jumah
Jumana Nabil Saeed Al-Qanou
Muhammad Mahmoud Dia'allah Al-Nadaiyat
Moaz Abdel Fattah Khaled Al-Zuhairi
Rima Hamed Kamal Abu Aoun
Hamza Alaa Ibrahim Abu Zuhair
Nima Abdullah Castro Abu Ashayba
Musk Ali Hassan Al-Rantisi
Maryam Muhammad Kamel Mohsen
Ghaith Iyad Muhammad Abu Draiaa
Tamim Nidal Ismail Abu Ajami
Asell Iyad Nabil Omran
Nour Ahmed Zakaria Al-Derini
Zuhair Ramadan Mahmoud Al-Dahouk
Adam Ezzat Muhammad Warsh Agha
Salah al-Din Osama Khalid Abu Laila
Iman Salem Mahmoud Abu Maarouf
Khamis Salem Mahmoud Abu Tahoun
Yaqin Badr Eid Abu Jabal
Mahmoud Mohieddin Mahmoud Al-Sebaei
Mian Muhammad Riad Abu Haddayd
Farah Suleiman Ra'ed Abu Shabab
Baraa Muhammad Raed Abu Shabab

Lynn Ghassan Mahmoud Al-Qanou
Anas Osama Nafez Al-Maghari
Wafa Karam Muhammad Baker
Khalil Ibrahim Fawzi Al-Nafar
Muhammad Hussein Al-Aal responded
Salma Nasser Kamel Abu Al-Azaib
Linda Musab Taher Al-Suwerki
Maria Zaid Nafer Al-Rahn
Abdel Rahman Abdel Nasser Daoud Al-Halisi
Islam Hashem Khalil Zaqout
Iman Arafat Jamal Qaddoumi
Ward Hamato Ahmed Al-Satri
Muhammad Talal Al-Gharabli
Sondos Ramez Nabil Shaqoura
Maryam Khaled Raed Rajab
Salim Youssef Nabil Abu Saif
Ahmed Mohammed Mohammed Khalifa
Adam Abdel Karim Kamel Abu Rahma
Amna Shawqi Rajeb Iqdih
Mustafa Islam Ali Abu Singer
Qusay Mahmoud Abham Al-Faloujj
Amer Salem Ali Al-Akin
Sham Tamer Hosni Azzam
Talal Osama Talal Al-Shaffi
Layan Muhammad Sayed Al-Aker
Batoul Osama Kamel Abu Al-Zebani
Al-Moataz Ahmed Muhammad Al-Ghaleed
Ahmed Fawzi Al-Qufadi responded
Hani Ahmed Rabhi Netil
Nabil Iyad Nabil Omar
Batoul Ismail Ibrahim Abu Zuhair
Sham Nidal Ibrahim Abu Zuhair
Navin Muhammad Rami Al-Saati
Nour Hamdan Muhammad Al-Buhaisi
Omar Ali Muhammad Qazi
Osama Abdel Aziz Ahmed Salem Daoud
Malak Muhammad Abu Shujar
Arya Ahmed Zakaria Barakat
Roaa Salim Yassin Al-Astal
Jihad Khaled Jihad Abu Amer
Saad Muhammad Ayman Lakiod
Watin Muhammad Salem Al-Hashash
Juri Muhammad Arif Shalayil
Kenan Tamer Khalil Ghariz
Fuun Ahmed Ramzi Attouh
Iyad Muhammad Saleh Abu Shariffa
Yamen Sami Saber Abu Wadi
Hamza Wael Ahmed Al-Astal
Ali Muhammad Zakaria Al-Astal
Sarah Bilal Muhammed Hessouna
Aisha Salah Al-Din Ismail Abu Shammala
Lara Ahmed Samir Abu Shammala
Dalal Majid Ismail Abu Shammala
Musab Mahmoud Nayef Abu Shammala
Beirut Muhammad Nayef Abu Shammala
Samia Muhammad Omar Hegazy
Roaa Salah al-Din Muhammad al-Masry
Yazan Ramez Muhammad Qeshta
Mirna Ali Mahmoud Qeshta
Souad Mohamed Mohamed Gouda
Muhammad Abdullah Ibrahim Gouda
Ahmed Mohammad Abdel Rahim al-Madhoun
Qusay Muhammad Alaa Al-Din Ahmed
Islam Sameh Hani Al-Madhoun
Omar Khamis Sidqi Al-Madhoun
Lynn Saeed Mahmoud Al-Madhoun
Bilal Amjad Majed Al-Agha
Ahmed Amjad Majed Al-Agha
Ibtisam Noman Suleiman Haboush
Muhammad Mohammed Youssef Al-Hassi
Gazal Jamel Moein Atallah
Riad Muhammad Riad Totah
Mahmoud Abdullah Al-Sheikh

Nour El-Din Hamada Ahmed Jarghoun
Eileen Jihad Hamada Al-Bakri
Amer Bilal Hassan Al Tatar
Bisan Osama Salama Hussein Ali
Khaled Abdullah Waheed Al-Tabash
Mahmoud Fahd Mahmoud Bashir
Malik Hisham Amin Al-Suwerki
Ibrahim Naeil Bashir Al-Rahn
Zaid Amer Akram Murtaja
Messk AL Khitam Ismail Awad Weishah
Reda Muawiyah Ahmed Khalia
Malak Ismail Rabih Habboub
Heya Alyousef Saleh Habboub
Abu Shammala
... Al-Mahloui
... Al Mahmoud Qeshta
Hour Hazem Kamal Hamdan
Karim Mahmoud Abdel Hamid Gouda
Maria Amjad Majed Abu Odeh
Sammamad Bilal Zahir Ahmed
Amir Abdullah Musa Zoroub
Muhammad Alaa El-Din Ahmed
Ibrahim Zoroub
... Hamdan Totah
Mazen Muhammad Maarouf
Muhammad Maarouf
Fifa has a beautiful Eid
Hassan Ahmed Hassan Al-Agami
Joen Yahya Youssef Daloul
Abdullah Muhammad Fathi Al-Fasih
Toulin Muhammad Rajab
Jude Suleiman Moin A...
Aya Salah Al-Din Hamida
Youssef Muhammed...
Ahmed Omar Ha...
Abdel Salam Ma...
Sila Hassan Jam...
Muhammad Abdu...
Youssef Hossam...
Muhammad Bah...
Adam Shaker Ma...
Muhammad Abdullah...
Adam Ayman Ismail ...
Zeina Ismail Sami A...
Suhad Hani Iyad Abu Shammala
Mahmoud Moamen Amin Nofal
Tamam Mustafa Amin Nofal
Ayoub Muhammad Suleiman Al-Nab
Tala Walid Salim Al-Asheleh
Muhammad Samed Muhammad Qasl
Rabab Mahmoud Nafez Al-Adi
Ahmed Ismail Fayez Abu Muailiq
Amir Jumah Rajeb Maarouf
Amin Mahmoud Abdul Hakim Al-Agrami
Tala Muhammad Mohieddin Sukayk
Marwan Mahmoud Ismail Abu Shammala
Hassan Ibrahim Abdullah Ashour
Nour El-Din Hamza Omar Abu Odeh
Randa Ibrahim Bassem Shaaban
Sarah Basil Ramadan, Al Shaer
Jad Hashem Muhammad Al-Bardawil
Juri Fadil Ziad Yassin
Musk Munther Saadallah Al-Helou
Sally Shehdeh Hassan Dhair
Abdul Aziz Radwan Naeem Al-Helou
Nada Essam Ahmed Salah
Muhammad Saqr Nasr Al-Sarhi
Magda Muhammad Shehdeh Khidr
Bisan Abdullah Munir Ghabayen
Amal Khalil Ibrahim Khadi
Retal Saeed Hussein Al-Ramlawi
Saeed Hisham Saeed Al-Ramlawi
Zain al-Din Muhammad Arafat al-Bahtini
Hadi Muhammad Riad Matar
Nada Essam Ahmed Salah
Muhammad Saqr Nasr Al-Sarhi
Hanan Mohamed Ismail Salam
Osama Imad Abdel Majeed Aslim
Zain Ali Muhammad Al-Qara
Sila Mahmoud Wajih Abu Zayed
Jamila Mahmoud Abdullah Abu Abu Zayed
Muhammad Bahaa Raffifan Tanboura
Bilal Muhammad Raffifan Tanboura
Yara Nouri Raffifan Tanboura
Farah Sammour Suleiman Jaarour
Sowar Muhammad Khader Abu Toba
Muhammad Salim Muhammad Abu Qouta
Abdul Rahman Muhammad Awni Al-Mahlawi
Maher Asaad Maher Abu Lashin
Anas Jihad Mahmoud Al-Akhras
Atwaf Hudhayfah Salah Abu Shakyan
Juri Abdullah Salah Abu Shakyan
Izz al-Din Hassan Fawzi al-Bawab
Rama Muhammad Bassam Abu Sharbin
Yamen Ahmed Omar Dababesh
Youmna Ahmed Omar Dababesh
Ahmed Shadi Walid Baroud
Salma Osama Hajjaj Al-Zarii
Rose Tamer Mahmoud Al-Khayyat

Gaza

—Amnesty International Canada

Demand that Canada call for a ceasefire now!

www.CJPME.org

*Source: Gaza Ministry of Health

Canadians for Justice and Peace in the Middle East | CJPME

Year: 2023 | **Brief and copywriting:** Jessica Anderson, Aline Batarseh, Thomas Woodley, Khaled Al Sabawi, Alex Paterson | **Design:** Hadeel Saalok | **Sources:** Gaza Ministry of Health

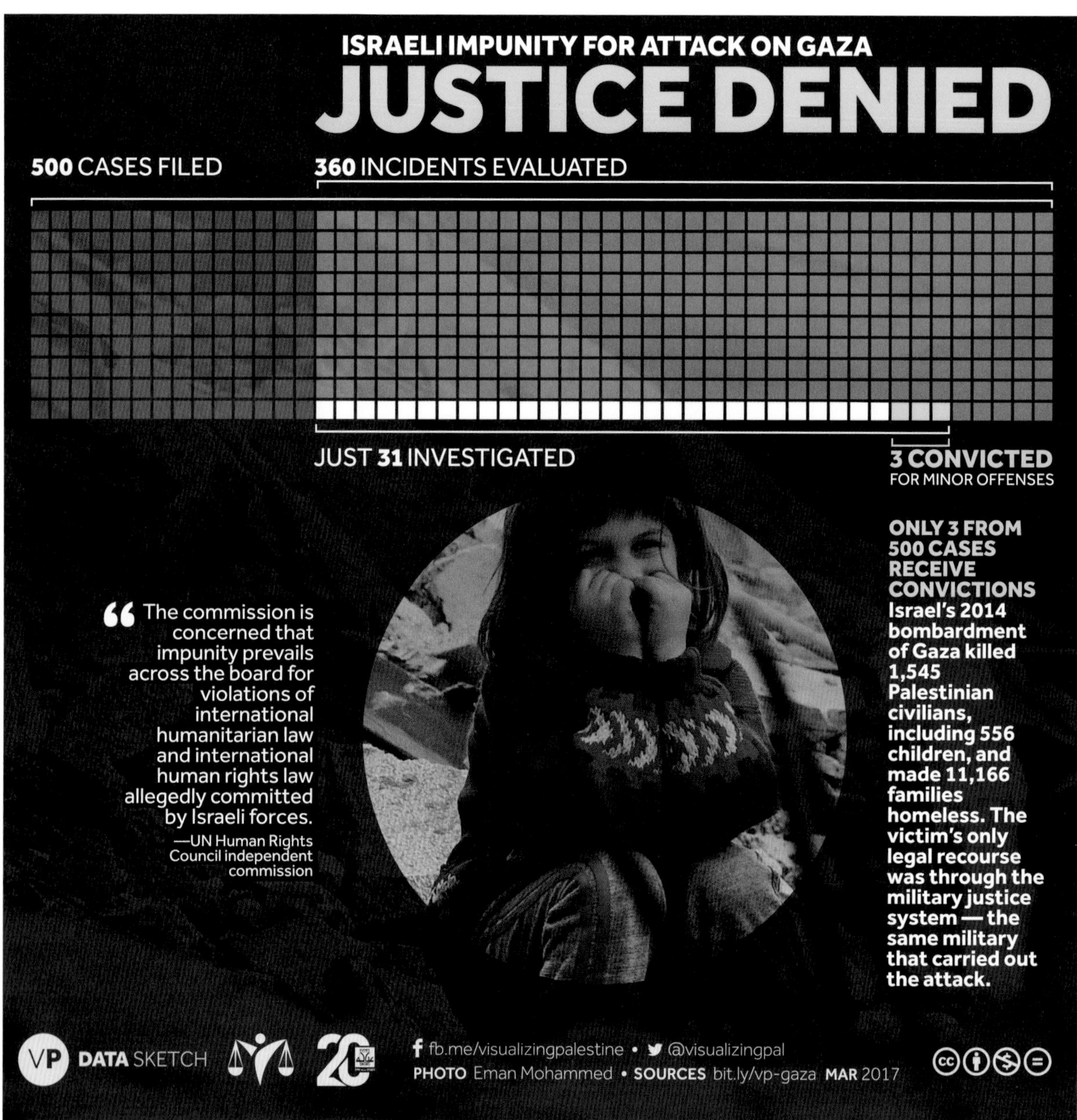

ISRAELI IMPUNITY FOR ATTACK ON GAZA
JUSTICE DENIED
500 CASES FILED
360 INCIDENTS EVALUATED
JUST 31 INVESTIGATED
3 CONVICTED
FOR MINOR OFFENSES
ONLY 3 FROM 500 CASES RECEIVE CONVICTIONS
Israel's 2014 bombardment of Gaza killed 1,545 Palestinian civilians, including 556 children, and made 11,166 families homeless. The victim's only legal recourse was through the military justice system — the same military that carried out the attack.
“The commission is concerned that impunity prevails across the board for violations of international humanitarian law and international human rights law allegedly committed by Israeli forces.
—UN Human Rights Council independent commission
VP DATA SKETCH
fb.me/visualizingpalestine • @visualizingpal
PHOTO Eman Mohammed • SOURCES bit.ly/vp-gaza MAR 2017

Year: 2017 | **Brief and copywriting:** Mahmoud Aburahma, Iman Annab, Nadia Ben-Youssef, Nuriya Oswald | **Design:** Ahmad Barclay, Hani Asfour | **Photo:** Eman Mohammed | **Sources:** bit.ly/vp-gaza

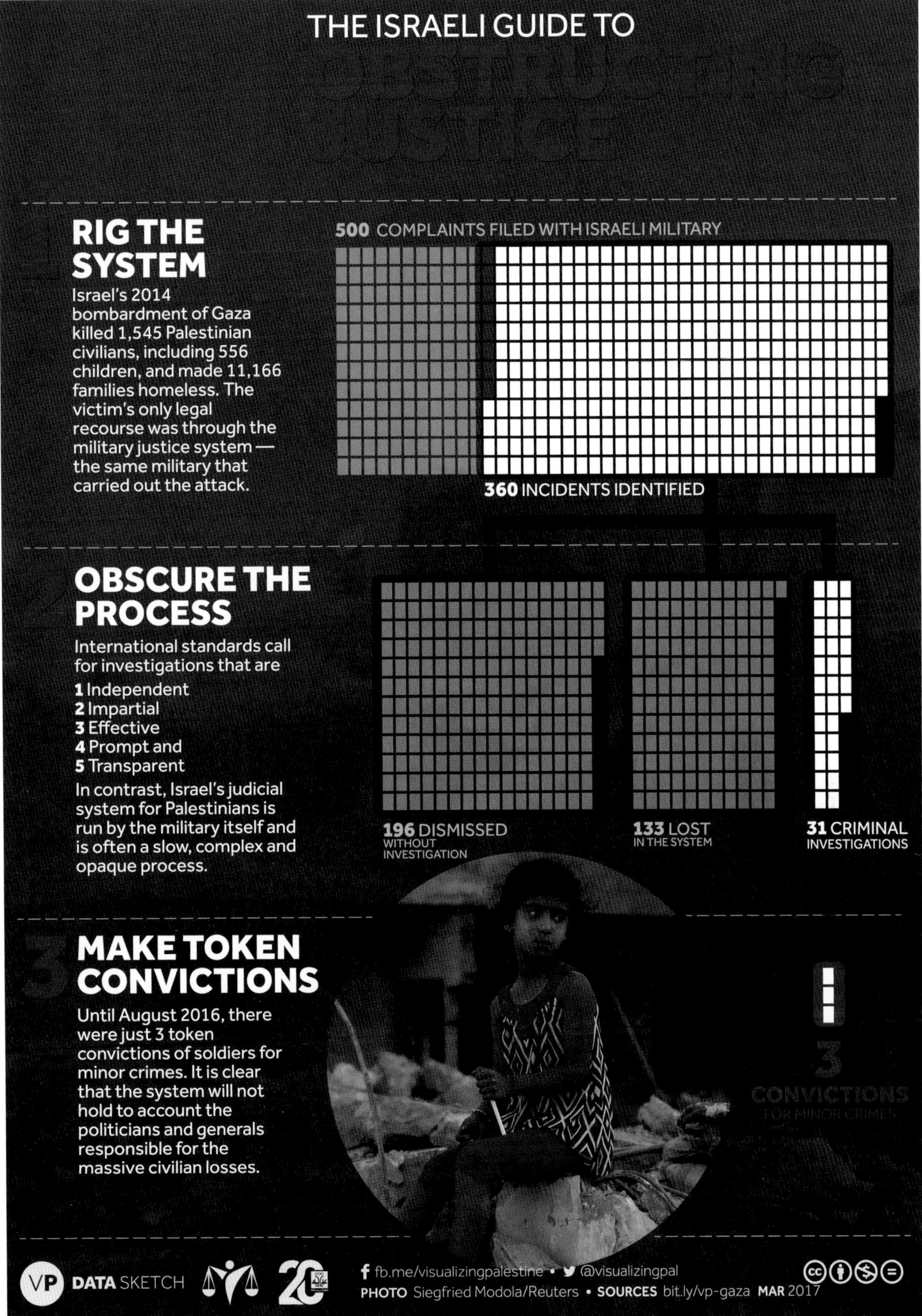
THE ISRAELI GUIDE TO
OBSTRUCTING JUSTICE
RIG THE SYSTEM
Israel's 2014 bombardment of Gaza killed 1,545 Palestinian civilians, including 556 children, and made 11,166 families homeless. The victim's only legal recourse was through the military justice system — the same military that carried out the attack.
500 COMPLAINTS FILED WITH ISRAELI MILITARY
360 INCIDENTS IDENTIFIED
OBSCURE THE PROCESS
International standards call for investigations that are
1 Independent
2 Impartial
3 Effective
4 Prompt and
5 Transparent
In contrast, Israel's judicial system for Palestinians is run by the military itself and is often a slow, complex and opaque process.
196 DISMISSED WITHOUT INVESTIGATION
133 LOST IN THE SYSTEM
31 CRIMINAL INVESTIGATIONS
MAKE TOKEN CONVICTIONS
Until August 2016, there were just 3 token convictions of soldiers for minor crimes. It is clear that the system will not hold to account the politicians and generals responsible for the massive civilian losses.
3 CONVICTIONS FOR MINOR CRIMES
VP DATA SKETCH
fb.me/visualizingpalestine • @visualizingpal
PHOTO Siegfried Modola/Reuters • SOURCES bit.ly/vp-gaza MAR 2017

Year: 2017 | **Brief and copywriting:** Mahmoud Aburahma, Iman Annab, Nadia Ben-Youssef, Nuriya Oswald | **Design:** Ahmad Barclay, Hani Asfour | **Photo:** Siegfried Modola (Reuters) | **Sources:** bit.ly/vp-gaza

“Israel's long-standing systematic impunity for international law violations has allowed for recurrence of grave violations without consequence.

UN Human Rights Council 2016

6,000+

ISRAELI RAIDS IN 50 DAYS

IN 2014 ATTACK ON GAZA

8,381
HOMES
COMPLETELY
DESTROYED

1,545
CIVILIANS
KILLED

132
PUBLIC
BUILDINGS
DESTROYED

556
CHILDREN
KILLED

FAMILIES
MADE
HOMELESS
ZERO
ISRAELI POLITICIANS
ZERO MILITARY
GENERALS HELD
ACCOUNTABLE.
PHOTO CREDIT: Unknown, SOURCES:
Data aggregated from Al Mezan, Israeli Ministry of Foreign Affairs
and UN Human Rights Council | 6000+ raids bit.ly/mfa-raid | Human
loss data bit.ly/mezan-loss | UN quote bit.ly/unhrc-accountable
fb.me/visualizingpalestine
@visualizingpal
/visualizing_palestine
WWW.VISUALIZINGPALESTINE.ORG. FEBRUARY 2017.
SHARE AND DISTRIBUTE FREELY.
مركز الميزان لحقوق الإنسان
AL Mezan Center for Human Rights
ADALAH
VISUALIZINGPALESTINE

Year: 2017 | **Brief and copywriting:** Mahmoud Aburahma, Iman Annab, Nadia Ben-Youssef, Nuriya Oswald | **Design:** Naji El Mir | **Sources:** bit.ly/vp-Sources-2012-2015

"Israel's long-standing systematic impunity for international law violations has allowed for recurrence of grave violations without consequence.

UN Human Rights Council 2016

MORE THAN **6,000** ISRAELI RAIDS IN 50 DAYS IN 2014 ATTACK ON GAZA

+ **8,381** HOMES COMPLETELY DESTROYED

+ **11,166** FAMILIES MADE HOMELESS

+ **132** PUBLIC BUILDINGS DESTROYED

+ **1,545** CIVILIANS KILLED

+ **556** CHILDREN KILLED

0

ZERO ISRAELI POLITICIANS ZERO MILITARY GENERALS HELD ACCOUNTABLE.

مركز الميزان لحقوق الإنسان
AL Mezan Center for Human Rights

ADALAH عدالة עדאלה

VISUALIZING**PALESTINE**

SOURCES
Data aggregated from **Al Mezan, Israeli Ministry of Foreign Affairs** and **UNHuman Rights Council** | **6000+ raids** http://bit.ly/mfa-raid | **Human loss data** http://bit.ly/-mezan-loss | **UN quote** http://bit.ly/unhrc-accountable

WWW.VISUALIZINGPALESTINE.ORG AUG 2017

@visualizingpalestine
@visualizingpal
@visualizing_palestine

Year: 2017 | **Brief and copywriting:** Mahmoud Aburahma, Iman Annab, Nadia Ben-Youssef, Nuriya Oswald | **Design:** Naji El Mir | **Sources:** bit.ly/vp-Sources-2012-2015

80 DAYS
OF BOMBING
ON GAZA
(Oct. 7–Dec. 26, 2023)
306,500
HOUSING UNITS
DAMAGED OR
DESTROYED
20,674
PALESTINIANS
KILLED
310
HEALTHCARE
WORKERS
KILLED
97
JOURNALISTS
KILLED
8,200
CHILDREN
KILLED
1,900,000
PEOPLE
INTERNALLY
DISPLACED
ZERO
ACCOUNTABILITY
FOR WAR CRIMES
VISUALIZINGPALESTINE
SOURCES bit.ly/vp-18-days
WWW.VISUALIZINGPALESTINE.ORG. DECEMBER 2023.
fb.me/visualizingpalestine
@visualizingpal
/visualizing_palestine

Year: 2023 | **Updated information:** Jessica Anderson | **Design:** Naji El Mir | **Updated design:** Yosra El Gazzar, Nasreen Abd Elal | **Sources:** bit.ly/vp-18-days

6. ECOLOGIC JUSTICE

Visuals in this section: Undrinkable | Gaza Water Confined and Contaminated | Gaza Water 2023 | Salinity | Not Enough Water in the West Bank? | Israeli Restrictions Affect Every Item on This Table | Uprooted | Between a Rising Tide and Apartheid | Green Colonialism | Toxic Occupation | Colonial Extraction | No War, No Warming

AL

> **The Israeli state has long coated its nation-building project in a green veneer . . . in this context trees, specifically, have been among the most potent weapons of land grabbing and occupation.**
>
> *—Naomi Klein, "Let Them Drown: The Violence of Othering in a Warming World" in* London Review of Books *(2016)*

> **[Z]a'atar and 'akkoub end up encompassing the Nakba, the Palestinian catastrophe. The plants tell the story of the Palestinian person who loses control over the smallest details of her life and connection to the land, who is suddenly subjected to the violence of the law and the criminalization of the Israeli legal system.**
>
> *—Rabea Eghbariah, "Jumana Manna and Rabea Eghbariah in Conversation," MoMA PS1 (2022)*

In January 2022, a new year in Palestine dawned with severe flooding in Gaza.[1] Scenes of submerged cars, evacuated homes, and children wading through rainwater mixed with sewage on their way to school added an extra layer of meaning to Naomi Klein's headline "Let Them Drown," an ecological justice piece that connects the climate crisis to colonialism and militarism around the world.[2] Climate change is impacting rainfall patterns in Palestine, making winter flash floods more frequent and severe every year. Gaza is just one of many places around the world where the poor and oppressed languish in flood zones while those in power stake out higher ground.

Some of the worst-affected neighborhoods of Gaza were those that had been repeatedly bombarded by Israeli forces, underscoring that events miscategorized as "natural" disasters might not be so disastrous if not for deliberate human actions—the choice to blockade millions of people in a tiny strip of land and pummel their civilian infrastructure every few years, for example. Ecological justice, and the related climate justice movement, are powerful frameworks for understanding that, although rain does not have an opinion on the value of Palestinian life, the government of Israel does.

While climate scientists calculate and recalculate humanity's ever-narrowing window to stop our planet from becoming unlivable, Gaza had already reached that point even before 2023, when the Israeli military launched its campaign of unprecedented destruction there.[3] A major reason for this, as we depict in **Undrinkable**, is contaminated drinking water. **Gaza Water Confined and Contaminated**, a visual we first published in 2012 and updated a decade later with even more dire figures, explains why 97 percent of water in Gaza is unfit for human consumption.[4] After Israeli authorities blocked all water, food, and fuel from entering Gaza on October 9, 2023, the water situation in Gaza became catastrophic, as we show in **Gaza Water 2023** and **Salinity**. Israel denies Palestinians the right to water not just in Gaza, but also in the West Bank. **Not Enough Water in the West Bank?** shows that Israeli settlers consume four times more water per capita than Palestinians.[5]

In 1921, a British census found that 80 percent of Palestinians depended on agriculture for their livelihoods.[6] Today, millions of Palestinians living under Israeli rule experience food insecurity, a product of being systematically severed from their land. **Israeli Restrictions Affect Every Item on This Table** tells the story of Israeli repression through the framework of food sovereignty, a call from the international peasants' movement for the transformation of food systems to address the root causes of food insecurity and prioritize life over profit.

About half of the cultivated land in the West Bank and Gaza is planted with olive trees, with tens of thousands of Palestinian families relying on the olive harvest.[7] Olive trees are frequently the target of destruction by the Israeli military or settlers. To put the scale of this destruction into perspective, we created **Uprooted**, which compares the number of olive trees uprooted in Palestine to the number of trees in New York City's Central Park. This visual has also prompted conversation about the widespread use of parks to uproot Indigenous peoples and other communities. Underneath Central Park lies the ruins of Seneca Village, the first free Black community in New York City, and underneath many Israeli parks lie the ruins of Palestinian villages.

At the same time that Gaza was underwater in January 2022, Palestinian Bedouin communities in the Naqab were protesting Israel's destruction of their villages to make way for the creation of a forest.[8] As this was unfolding, we released a series of visuals exploring how concepts from the ecological justice movement apply to the Palestinian context: **Between a Rising Tide and Apartheid**, **Green Colonialism**, **Toxic Occupation**, and **Colonial Extraction**. To protect the Earth and all its living systems, we must act in solidarity with the communities most impacted by the destructive forces of colonialism, militarism, and exploitative capitalism, including Palestinians.

In 1995, the United Nations hosted its first climate Conference of Parties (COP) in Berlin. As concern about climate change becomes more urgent, a growing spotlight has been fixed on the large platform COP provides for governments and corporations, which they often use to greenwash harms caused by their policies and champion false solutions to climate change. A record number of oil executives attended COP27 in Egypt in 2022, while outside the venue, climate justice activists wore white in solidarity with sixty thousand Egyptian political prisoners.[9] The Israeli delegation was one of the largest in attendance at COP27 and spent $1.4 million on a pavilion to market itself as a green country, despite it being a major military exporter and the top recipient of US military funding.[10] Inspired by grassroots groups' efforts to highlight militarism and military emissions—an issue long excluded from the COP agenda—we created **No War, No Warming** for COP27 and updated it for COP28, which coincided with the genocide in Gaza and took place in the oil state of the United Arab Emirates.

This body of work on ecological justice is an example of intersectionality—one of the core principles we thread through Visualizing Palestine's work. We believe that all forms of oppression are intertwined at the root and that reciprocal solidarity between communities widens the path toward collective liberation.

UNDRINKABLE.
97%
OF GAZA'S WATER
IS CONTAMINATED
DUE TO ISRAEL'S
BLOCKADE AND
MILITARY OCCUPATION
VISUALIZINGPALESTINE
SOURCE United Nations Environment Programme. State of Environment and Outlook Report for the oPt 2020. 2020.
WWW.VISUALIZINGPALESTINE.ORG
@visualizingpal
/visualizing_palestine
fb.me/visualizingpalestine
AUG 2022

Year: 2022 | **Brief and copywriting:** Nasreen Abd Elal, Ramzi Jaber | **Design:** Nasreen Abd Elal | **Sources:** United Nations Environment Programme, "State of Environment and Outlook Report for the OPT 2020"

GAZA WATER CONFINED & CONTAMINATED

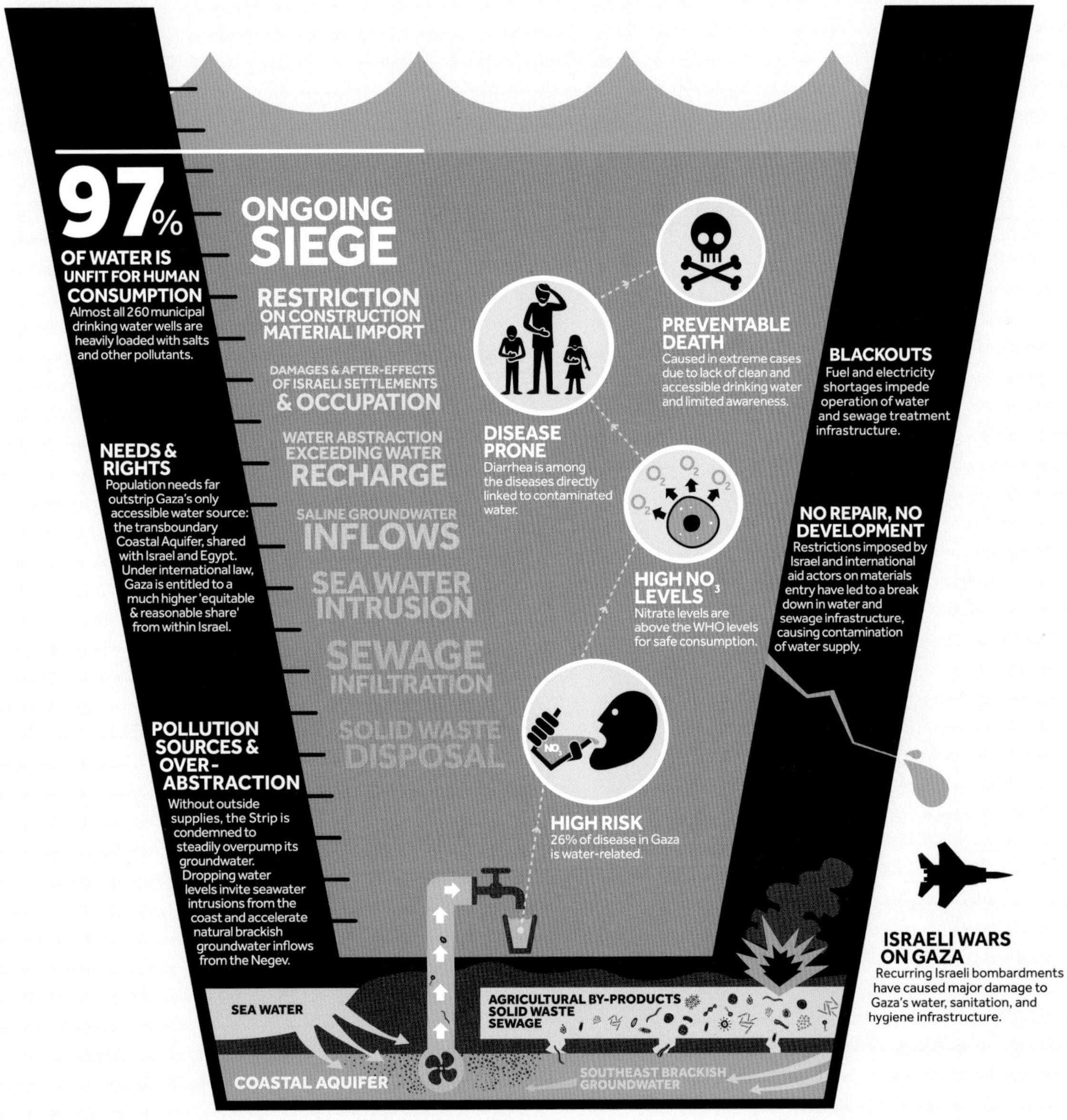
97%
OF WATER IS UNFIT FOR HUMAN CONSUMPTION
Almost all 260 municipal drinking water wells are heavily loaded with salts and other pollutants.
NEEDS & RIGHTS
Population needs far outstrip Gaza's only accessible water source: the transboundary Coastal Aquifer, shared with Israel and Egypt. Under international law, Gaza is entitled to a much higher 'equitable & reasonable share' from within Israel.
POLLUTION SOURCES & OVER-ABSTRACTION
Without outside supplies, the Strip is condemned to steadily overpump its groundwater. Dropping water levels invite seawater intrusions from the coast and accelerate natural brackish groundwater inflows from the Negev.
ONGOING SIEGE
RESTRICTION ON CONSTRUCTION MATERIAL IMPORT
DAMAGES & AFTER-EFFECTS OF ISRAELI SETTLEMENTS & OCCUPATION
WATER ABSTRACTION EXCEEDING WATER RECHARGE
SALINE GROUNDWATER INFLOWS
SEA WATER INTRUSION
SEWAGE INFILTRATION
SOLID WASTE DISPOSAL
DISEASE PRONE
Diarrhea is among the diseases directly linked to contaminated water.
PREVENTABLE DEATH
Caused in extreme cases due to lack of clean and accessible drinking water and limited awareness.
HIGH NO3 LEVELS
Nitrate levels are above the WHO levels for safe consumption.
HIGH RISK
26% of disease in Gaza is water-related.
BLACKOUTS
Fuel and electricity shortages impede operation of water and sewage treatment infrastructure.
NO REPAIR, NO DEVELOPMENT
Restrictions imposed by Israel and international aid actors on materials entry have led to a break down in water and sewage infrastructure, causing contamination of water supply.
ISRAELI WARS ON GAZA
Recurring Israeli bombardments have caused major damage to Gaza's water, sanitation, and hygiene infrastructure.
SEA WATER
AGRICULTURAL BY-PRODUCTS
SOLID WASTE
SEWAGE
COASTAL AQUIFER
SOUTHEAST BRACKISH GROUNDWATER

VISUALIZINGPALESTINE REVISION 03 SOURCES bit.ly/vp-gaza-water WWW.VISUALIZINGPALESTINE.ORG @visualizingpal /visualizing_palestine fb.me/visualizingpalestine SEP 2021

Year: 2021 | **Brief and copywriting:** Joumana al Jabri, Ahmad Barclay, Ramzi Jaber | **Design:** Naji El Mir, Hani Asfour | **Sources:** bit.ly/vp-gaza-water

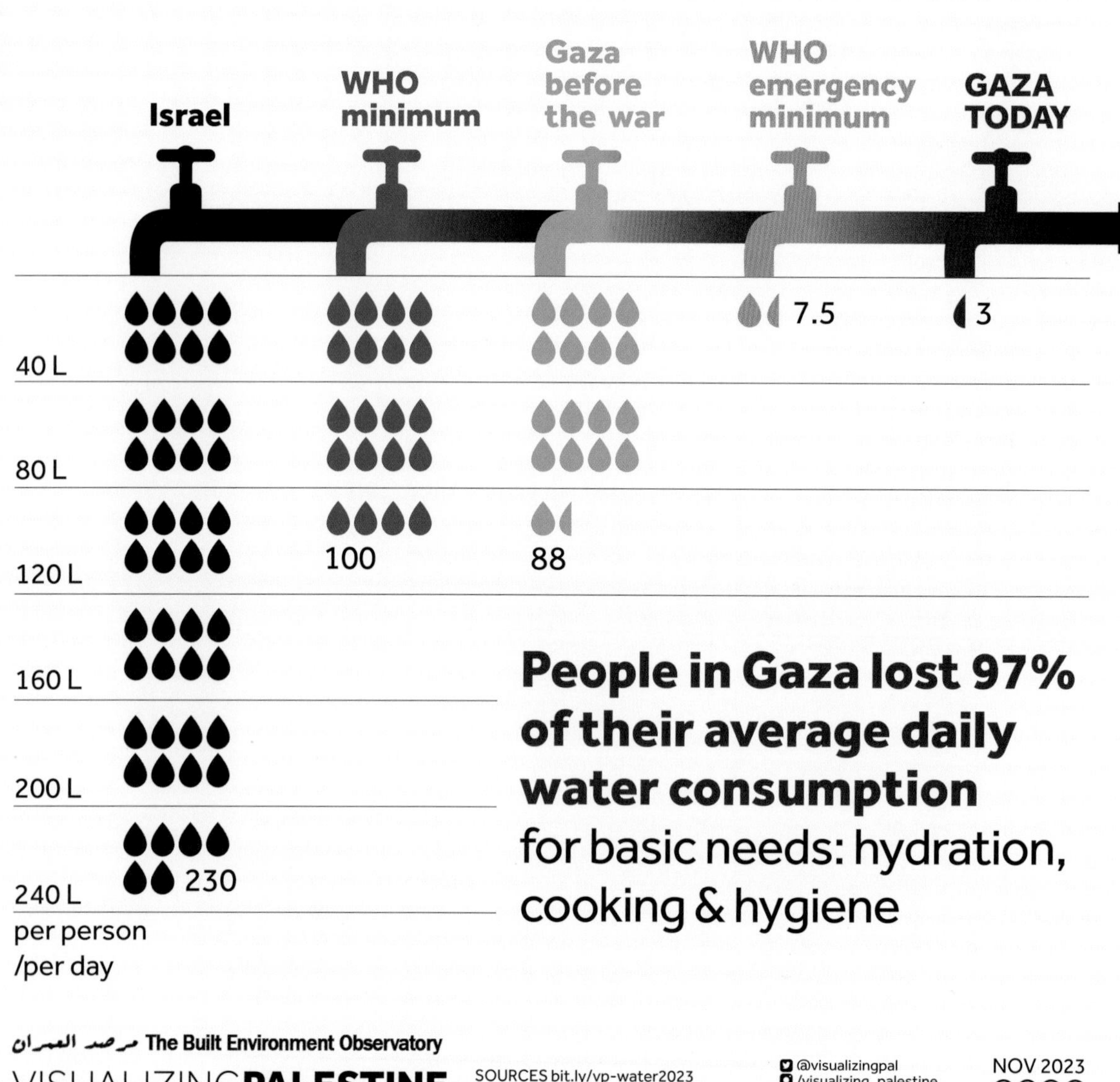
Israel
WHO minimum
Gaza before the war
WHO emergency minimum
GAZA TODAY
7.5
3
40 L
80 L
100
88
120 L
160 L
200 L
230
240 L
per person /per day
People in Gaza lost 97% of their average daily water consumption for basic needs: hydration, cooking & hygiene
مرصد العمران The Built Environment Observatory
VISUALIZINGPALESTINE
SOURCES bit.ly/vp-water2023
WWW.VISUALIZINGPALESTINE.ORG
@visualizingpal
/visualizing_palestine
fb.me/visualizingpalestine
NOV 2023

Year: 2023 | **Brief and copywriting:** Yahia Shawkat | **Design:** Yahia Shawkat, Dina ElMazzahi | **Sources:** bit.ly/vp-water2023

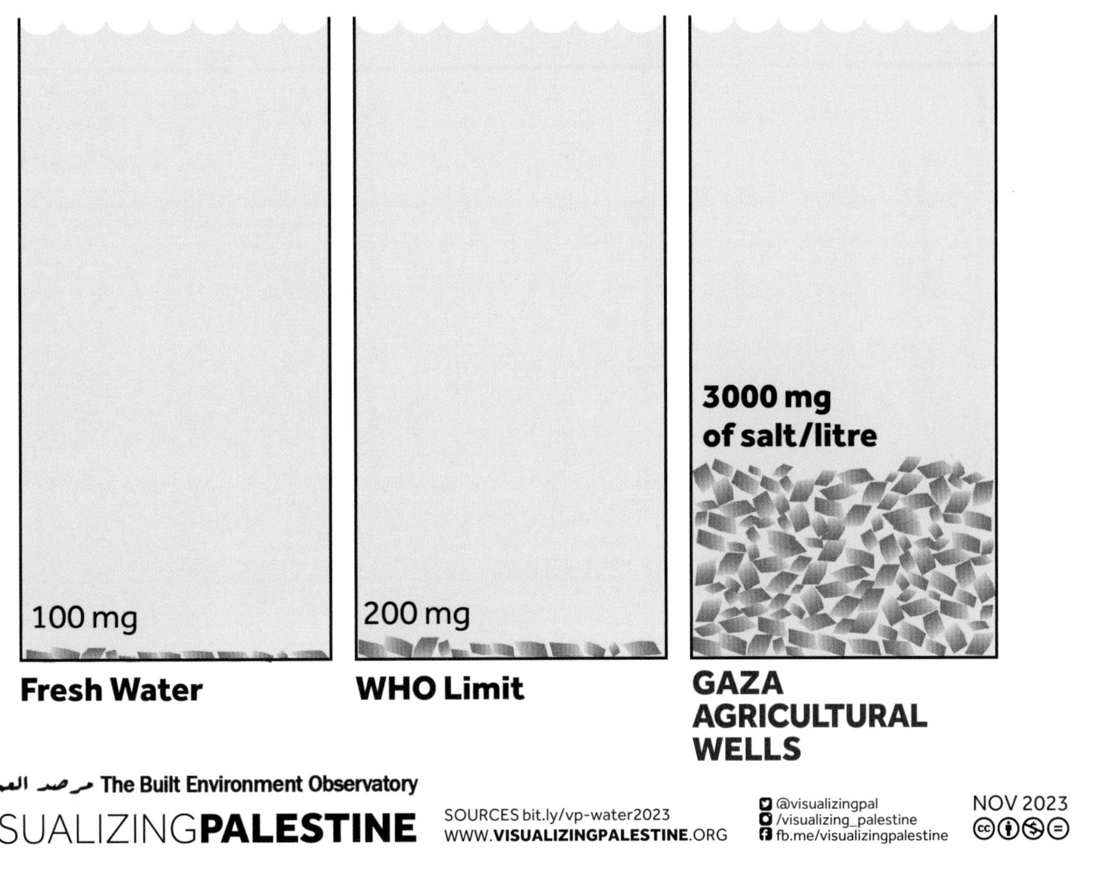
Most Palestinians in Gaza have resorted to drinking from agricultural wells that are 30x saltier than freshwater, posing an immediate health risk, especially to babies, pregnant women, and people with kidney disease.
100 mg
Fresh Water
200 mg
WHO Limit
3000 mg of salt/litre
GAZA AGRICULTURAL WELLS
مرصد العمران The Built Environment Observatory
VISUALIZINGPALESTINE
SOURCES bit.ly/vp-water2023
WWW.VISUALIZINGPALESTINE.ORG
@visualizingpal
/visualizing_palestine
fb.me/visualizingpalestine
NOV 2023

Year: 2023 | **Brief and copywriting:** Yahia Shawkat | **Design:** Yahia Shawkat, Dina ElMazzahi | **Sources:** bit.ly/vp-water2023

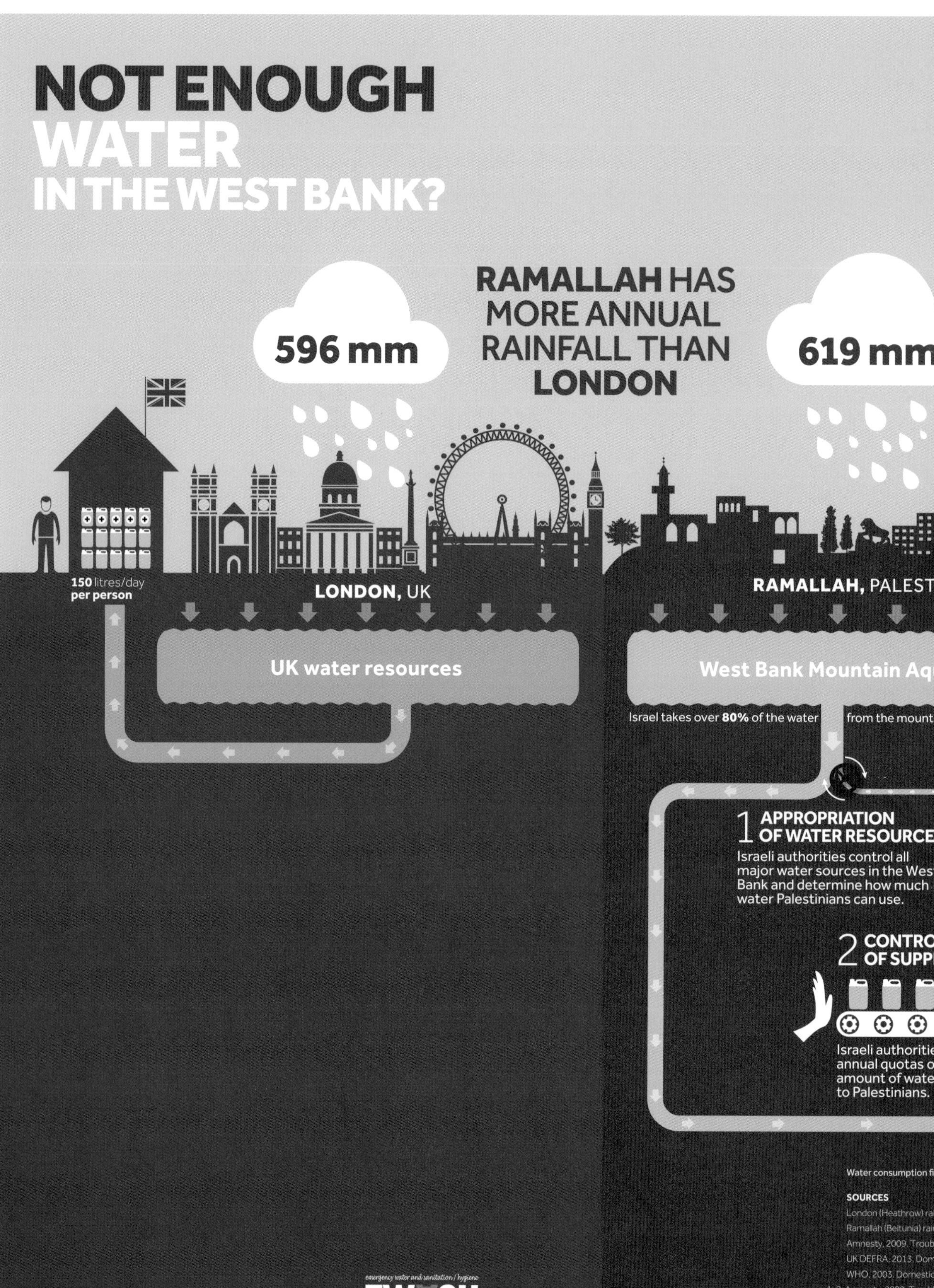
NOT ENOUGH
WATER
IN THE WEST BANK?
596 mm
RAMALLAH HAS MORE ANNUAL RAINFALL THAN LONDON
619 mm
150 litres/day per person
LONDON, UK
RAMALLAH,
UK water resources
West Bank Mountain
Israel takes over 80% of the water
from the
1 APPROPRIATION OF WATER RESOURCES
Israeli authorities control all major water sources in the West Bank and determine how much water Palestinians can use.
2 CONTROL OF SUPPLY
Israeli authorities
annual quotas on
amount of water
to Palestinians.
Water consumption
SOURCES
London (Heathrow) rainfall,
Ramallah (Beitunia) rainfall,
Amnesty, 2009. Troubled
UK DEFRA, 2013.
WHO, 2003. Domestic
1.,2. Amnesty, 2009. Troubled
3. C. Messerschmid, 2007.
4. EWASH, 2012. Israeli
VISUALIZINGPALESTINE
emergency water and sanitation / hygiene
EWASH OPT
WWW.EWASH.ORG
WWW.VISUALIZINGPALESTINE.ORG. FEBRUARY 2013.
SHARE AND DISTRIBUTE FREELY. CREATIVE COMMONS BY-NC-ND 3.0 LICENSE.

World Health Organization
70 litres/day per Palestinian in West Bank
300 litres/day per Israeli including settlers
WHO RECOMMENDS 100 litres/day per person
= 10 litres/day
= 10 litres/day above WHO recommendation
= 10 litres/day below WHO recommendation
ar
TRUCTION
DEVELOPMENT
alestinian wells
by Israeli authorities
st productive Western
ince 1967.
4 DESTRUCTION OF INFRASTRUCTURE
In 2011, the Israeli military demolished 89 water-related structures, including 21 wells and 34 rainwater cisterns essential for agriculture and herding.
Aquifers inside Israel, Jordan river basin & desalinated water
r use, excluding agricultural or industrial use.
K Met Office (2013). Historic Station Data metoffice.gov.uk/climate/uk/stationdata
VA (2003). Rainfall Variability and Change in the West Bank. SUSMAQ Project
denied fair access to water. p4
ssed on 7 February 2013) www.defra.gov.uk/environment/quality/water/conservation/domestic
Level and Health. p3
denied fair access to water. p15-16
ared Israeli, Palestinian groundwater resources. p14
sector in the Occupied Palestinian Territory and their impact on vulnerable communities. p16
@visualizingpal
fb.com/visualizingpalestine

Year: 2013
Brief and copywriting: Joumana al Jabri, Ahmad Barclay, Christopher Fiorello, Ramzi Jaber
Design: Naji El Mir, Hani Asfour
Sources: bit.ly/vp-Sources-2012-2015

ISRAELI RESTRICTIONS ON PALESTINIAN FOOD SOVEREIGNTY AFFECT EVERY ITEM ON THIS TABLE

WATER
Israel controls West Bank water and routinely demolishes water infrastructure; Gaza water 97% contaminated

BLACK GOATS
Banned, seized, and slaughtered, 1950-2017, decimating subsistence base of Bedouin communities

MILK, EGGS
Israeli quota system restricts market share of Palestinian farmers in Israel (1948 territory); Israeli products dominate market in West Bank & Gaza

FISH
2,265 attacks by the Israeli navy on fishers in Gaza's restricted fishing zone, 2007-2021

ZA'ATAR, SAGE, 'AKOUB
Foraging banned; fines or prison time imposed

GRAPES, EGGPLANTS, TOMATOES, ONIONS
In West Bank, subject to restrictive military orders since 1980s; discriminatory policies harm farmers' ability to compete with produce from illegal Israeli settlements

TOMATOES, STRAWBERRIES
Israel controls all imports and exports; restricts Gaza produce from reaching markets

VEGETABLES
35% of Gaza farmland is inaccessible; 13,000 dunums damaged by herbicides

OLIVES
Up to 1 million olive trees uprooted by Israeli military since 1967; in 2021 settlers vandalized or stole harvest from 1,600 trees

MUSHROOMS
By holding up essential imports and charging port storage fees, Israel shut down a Palestinian mushroom farm in 2016

WHEAT, MILLET, BARLEY
Israeli-controlled imports are overtaking locally adapted varieties and reducing biodiversity

THE COLONIZATION OF PALESTINIAN AGRICULTURE

Under Israel's system of apartheid, Palestinian food producers face **expropriation of their land, forced displacement, denial of the right to water, denial of freedom of movement, attacks by Israeli military forces and settlers, and restricted access to markets**, leading to food insecurity and the destruction of generations of Palestinian agricultural heritage in the Fertile Crescent.

WHAT IS FOOD SOVEREIGNTY?

Food sovereignty, a pillar of environmental justice, is the **right of peoples to healthy and culturally appropriate food produced through ecologically sound and sustainable methods, and their right to define their own food and agriculture systems**. Food sovereignty is key to ending hunger, food insecurity, poverty, and environmental harms perpetuated by colonialism and industrialized agriculture.

VISUALIZINGPALESTINE 

SOURCES bit.ly/VP-food
WWW.VISUALIZINGPALESTINE.ORG

@visualizingpal
/visualizing_palestine
fb.me/visualizingpalestine

MAY 2022

Year: 2022 | **Brief and copywriting:** Jessica Anderson, Aline Batarseh, Ida Audeh, Zeina Azzam, Nora Burgan, Taqwa Elhindi, Reem Farah | **Design:** Nasreen Abd Elal | **Sources:** bit.ly/VP-food

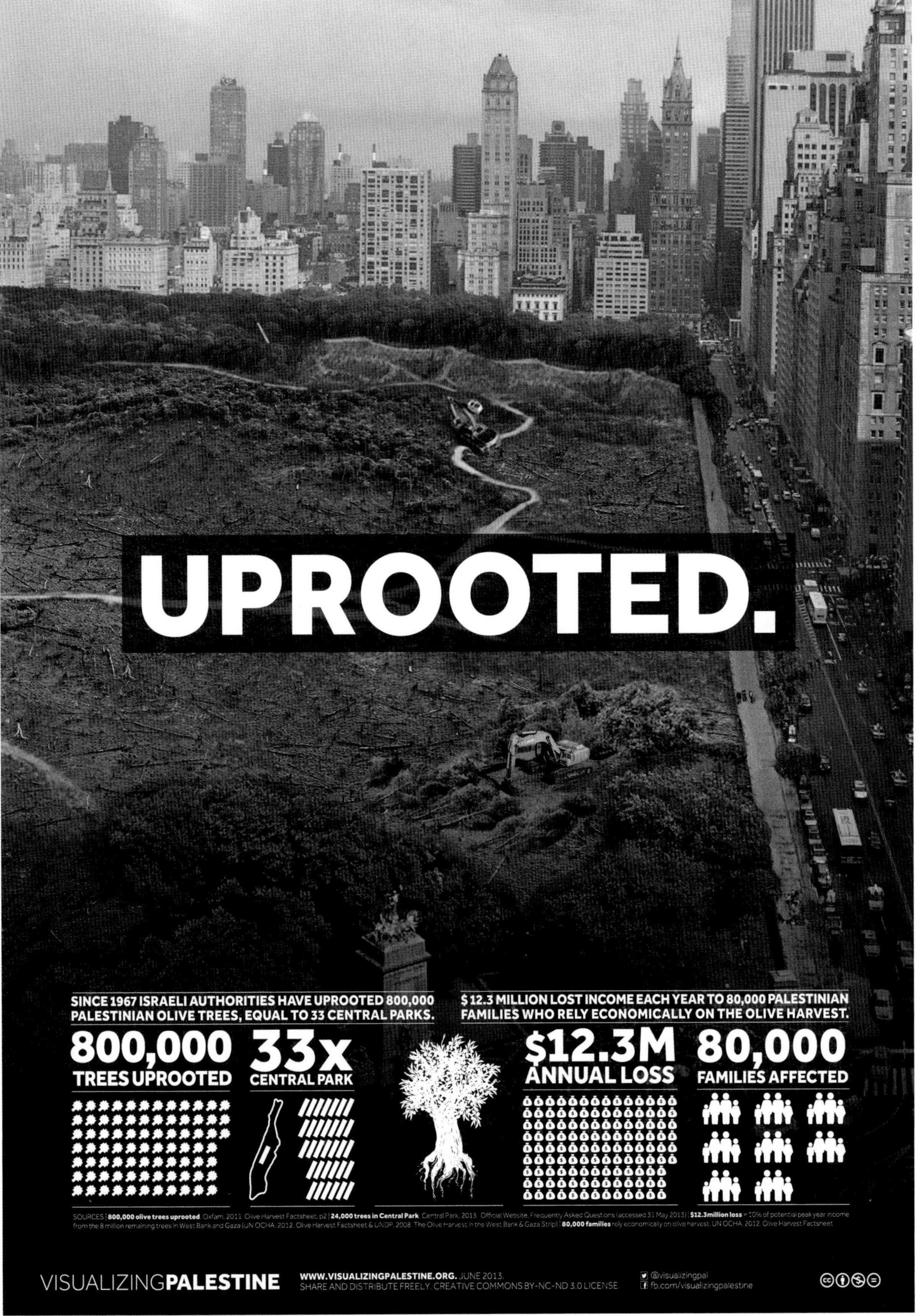
UPROOTED.
SINCE 1967 ISRAELI AUTHORITIES HAVE UPROOTED 800,000 PALESTINIAN OLIVE TREES, EQUAL TO 33 CENTRAL PARKS.
$12.3 MILLION LOST INCOME EACH YEAR TO 80,000 PALESTINIAN FAMILIES WHO RELY ECONOMICALLY ON THE OLIVE HARVEST.
800,000 TREES UPROOTED
33x CENTRAL PARK
$12.3M ANNUAL LOSS
80,000 FAMILIES AFFECTED
SOURCES | 800,000 olive trees uprooted. Oxfam, 2011. Olive Harvest Factsheet, p2 | 24,000 trees in Central Park. Central Park, 2013. Official Website, Frequently Asked Questions (accessed 31 May 2013) | $12.3million loss = 10% of potential peak year income from the 8 million remaining trees in West Bank and Gaza (UN OCHA, 2012. Olive Harvest Factsheet & UNDP, 2008. The Olive Harvest in the West Bank & Gaza Strip) | 80,000 families rely economically on olive harvest. UN OCHA, 2012. Olive Harvest Factsheet
VISUALIZINGPALESTINE
WWW.VISUALIZINGPALESTINE.ORG. JUNE 2013.
SHARE AND DISTRIBUTE FREELY. CREATIVE COMMONS BY-NC-ND 3.0 LICENSE.
@visualizingpal
fb.com/visualizingpalestine

Year: 2013 | **Brief and copywriting:** Joumana al Jabri, Ahmad Barclay, Christopher Fiorello, Ramzi Jaber | **Design:** Hani Asfour and Polypod | **Photomontage:** Philippe Ghabayen | **Sources:** bit.ly/vp-Sources-2012-2015

BETWEEN A RISING

PALESTINIAN CLIMAT

CLIMATE VULNERABILITY

is the susceptibility of people or systems to harm by climate hazards. Climate change impacts all of us, but communities experiencing systemic injustice bear a disproportionate burden and have less power to cope or adapt.

IN PALESTINE

Palestinians face increased exposure to climate-related hazards—such as water scarcity, food insecurity, and displacement—as a result of Israeli military occupation, according to the United Nations Development Programme.

THREAT

X

Palestinians are native to a region where temperatures are projected to continue rising faster than the global average.

CLIMATE PROJECTIONS BY 2100, IN THE OCCUPIED PALESTINIAN TERRITORIES:

- WARMING **+4.8°C** BY 2100
- SEA LEVEL RISE **38 CM–1 M**
- LESS RAINFALL **↓8-10 MM (↓22%)** AVG. MONTHLY PRECIPITATION

VU

Isra
dis
and

- AP
OC
SY
OP
PA
- **97**
UN
- **85**
RE
CO
- **69**
WE
AR

VISUALIZING**PALESTINE**

IDE & APARTHEID

ULNERABILITY

RABILITY

causes Palestinian
nt, fragmentation,
elopment.

D & MILITARY
ON:
TIC
ON OF
ANS BY ISRAEL

ZA WATER
ABLE

EST BANK WATER
ES ARE
LED BY ISRAEL

ZA & **33%** OF
K HOUSEHOLDS
INSECURE

=

RISK

Climate apartheid, or a future where the risks of climate change amplify existing injustices affecting millions of Palestinians.

PALESTINIANS FACE INCREASED RISKS OF:

FOOD & WATER INSECURITY

LAND & SOIL DEGRADATION

DESTRUCTION FROM EXTREME WEATHER EVENTS
I.E. FLOODING, FOREST FIRES, HEAT WAVES

SOURCES bit.ly/vp-EJ
WWW.**VISUALIZINGPALESTINE**.ORG

@visualizingpal
/visualizing_palestine
fb.me/visualizingpalestine

JAN 2022

Year: 2022
Brief and copywriting: Jessica Anderson, Reem Farah, Daleen Saah
Design: Daleen Saah, Nasreen Abd Elal
Special thanks: Zena Agha, Asmaa Abu Mezied, Muna Dajani
Sources: bit.ly/vp-EJ

GREEN CO

ISRAELI PARKS THAT ER

GREEN COLONIALISM describes how some organizations, policies, or programs harm the land and rights of Indigenous peoples in the name of environmental protection or climate change mitigation, reinforcing colonial legacies.

IN PALESTINE
Israel uses parks, nature reserves, and forests to conceal the ruins of depopulated Palestinian villages, appropriate land, and curtail Palestinian access and development.

NON-NATIVE FLORA
Only 11% of trees in Israeli forests are indigenous species due to Zionist groups planting vast areas of non-native trees

UNEQUAL ACCESS
The wall and Israeli policies restrict some Palestinians from access to nearby green spaces

ERASURE
182 Palestinian villages depopulated by Israel are concealed in Israeli parks & forests, preventing refugees from returning

VISUALIZINGPALESTINE

ONIALISM

AND DISPLACE

GREENWASHING

KKL-JNF
קק"ל

Some Israeli organizations use environmental projects to cultivate a positive global image, while displacing and discriminating against Palestinians

RESTRICTED DEVELOPMENT

Israeli-controlled parks block Palestinian development plans and marginalize the Palestinian tourism sector

Depopulated Palestinian villages within Israel Nature and Parks Authority reserves & parks

Depopulated Palestinian villages within Jewish National Fund forests & parks

Depopulated Palestinian villages within other tourist sites or hiking trails

SOURCES bit.ly/vp-EJ
WWW.**VISUALIZINGPALESTINE**.ORG

@visualizingpal
/visualizing_palestine
fb.me/visualizingpalestine

JAN 2022

Year: 2022
Brief and copywriting: Jessica Anderson, Reem Farah, Daleen Saah
Design: Daleen Saah, Nasreen Abd Elal
Special thanks: Ghada Sasa
Sources: bit.ly/vp-EJ

TOXIC OC

ISRAELI WASTE IN

ENVIRONMENTAL RACISM

We all produce waste, but not all of us have to live with it. Environmental racism describes how governments and corporations tend to dump environmental hazards—like waste—on communities that experience racial injustice, reflecting and reinforcing systemic racism.

IN PALESTINE

Israel exploits the West Bank to dump and process its waste. Under occupation, Palestinians are inundated in waste, which has become a symbol of how the Israeli system views Palestinians themselves: as disposable.

HAZARDOUS WASTE TRANSFER

15 Israeli waste facilities in the West Bank process waste—including hazardous waste—transported from Israel, in violation of international law

LACK OF REGULATORY SUPERVISION

Israel applies less rigorous environmental regulations to settlement industrial zones in the West Bank

Israeli Settlement Industrial Zones
Segregated Roads: Palestinians with West Bank IDs Prohibited
Israeli Settlements and Outposts
USED C
WASTE
COMPA

CUPATION
E WEST BANK

SEWAGE SLUDGE COMPANY
ELECTRONIC WASTE COMPANY
CHEMICAL SOLVENT WASTE COMPANY
CONSTRUCTION WASTE COMPANY

SOLID WASTE

647,800 Israeli settlers produce 2x more solid waste per capita than Palestinians, most of which is dumped in West Bank landfills

WASTEWATER

Illegal Israeli settlements discharge 40 million cubic meters (mcm) per year of untreated wastewater onto Palestinian land

POOR INFRASTRUCTURE

Israel's control over permits in Area C (60% of the West Bank) prevents Palestinians from developing adequate waste infrastructure

SOURCES bit.ly/vp-EJ
WWW.**VISUALIZINGPALESTINE**.ORG

@visualizingpal
/visualizing_palestine
fb.me/visualizingpalestine

JAN 2022

Year: 2022
Brief and copywriting: Jessica Anderson, Reem Farah, Daleen Saah
Design: Daleen Saah, Nasreen Abd Elal
Special thanks: Sophia Stamatopoulou-Robbins
Sources: bit.ly/vp-EJ

COLONIAL E

PILLAGING PALESTIN

COLONIAL EXTRACTION
describes how governments and corporations pillage colonized territories for raw material, denying local communities sovereignty over their own resources or a share in the benefits.

IN PALESTINE
Israel and multinational corporations extract millions of tons of non-renewable stone from occupied West Bank quarries, benefitting the Israeli economy while Palestinians experience de-development. International law prohibits an occupying power from depleting the resources of occupied territory for economic gain.

ISRAEL EXTRACTS PALESTINIAN RESOURCES

16 ISRAELI-ADMINISTERED STONE QUARRIES OPERATE IN AREA C OF THE WEST BANK

PALESTINIAN RESOURCES BUILD THE ISRAELI STATE

94% OF T
GOES T
ISRAELI
SUPPLYIN
ITS MINE
CONSU

VISUALIZING**PALESTINE**

TRACTION
O BUILD ISRAEL
ISRAEL'S PER CAPITA ECOLOGICAL FOOTPRINT IS 6.9X LARGER THAN THAT OF THE OCCUPIED PALESTINIAN TERRITORY

DEMAND FOR RESOURCES INCREASES

BY 2048,
UARRIES IN
EST BANK
A C WILL BE
KHAUSTED,
CORDING TO
OJECTIONS
MEANWHILE, ISRAELI RESTRICTIONS ON PALESTINIAN QUARRIES STRIP THE PALESTINIAN ECONOMY OF $3.4 BILLION PER YEAR
LD
T
OF
NE
N

ISRAEL ENJOYS ECONOMIC GROWTH & DEVELOPMENT
SOURCES bit.ly/vp-EJ
WWW.VISUALIZINGPALESTINE.ORG
@visualizingpal
/visualizing_palestine
fb.me/visualizingpalestine
JAN 2022

Year: 2022
Brief and copywriting: Jessica Anderson, Reem Farah, Daleen Saah
Design: Daleen Saah, Nasreen Abd Elal
Sources: bit.ly/vp-EJ

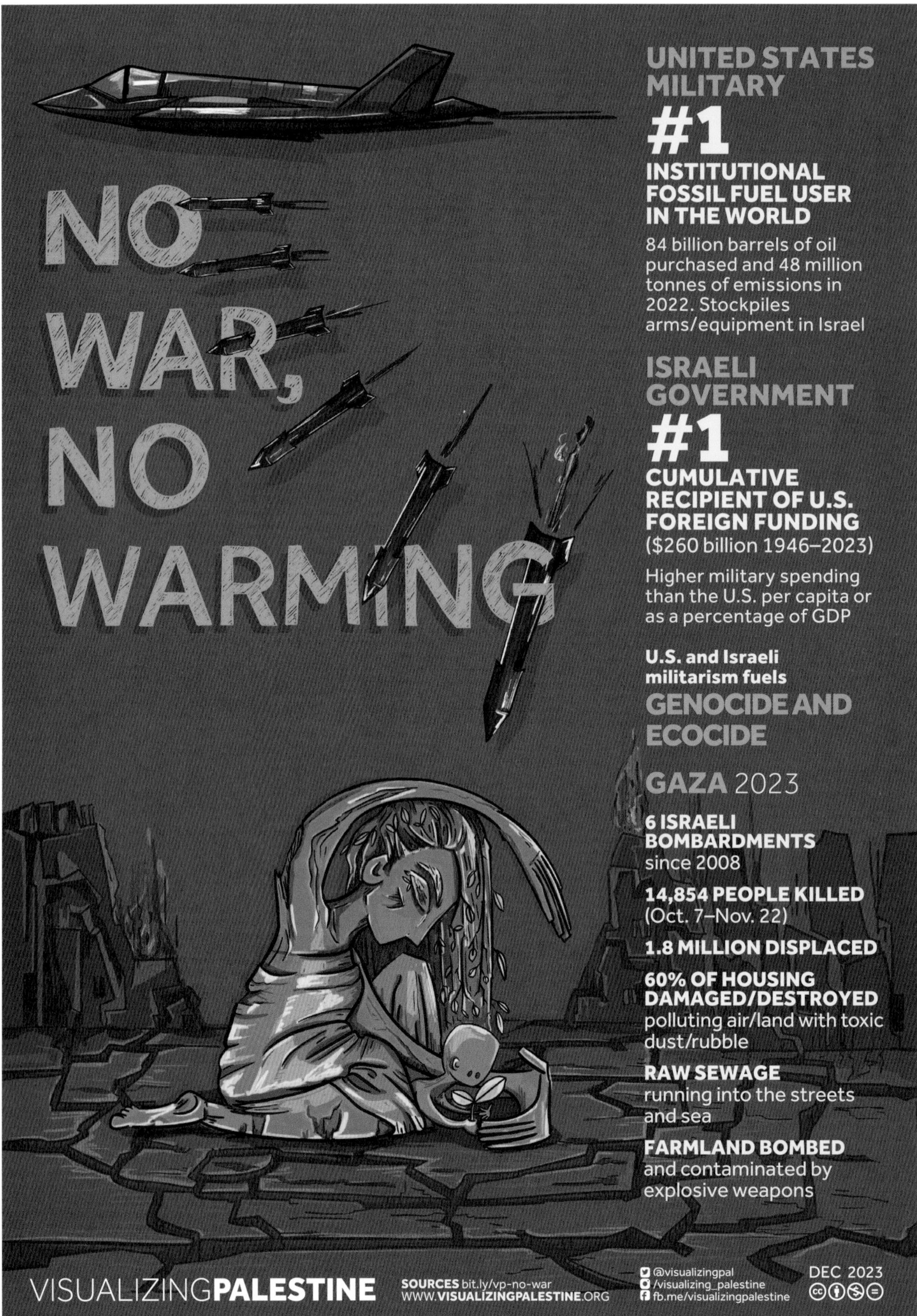
NO WAR, NO WARMING
UNITED STATES MILITARY
#1
INSTITUTIONAL FOSSIL FUEL USER IN THE WORLD
84 billion barrels of oil purchased and 48 million tonnes of emissions in 2022. Stockpiles arms/equipment in Israel
ISRAELI GOVERNMENT
#1
CUMULATIVE RECIPIENT OF U.S. FOREIGN FUNDING
($260 billion 1946–2023)
Higher military spending than the U.S. per capita or as a percentage of GDP
U.S. and Israeli militarism fuels
GENOCIDE AND ECOCIDE
GAZA 2023
6 ISRAELI BOMBARDMENTS since 2008
14,854 PEOPLE KILLED (Oct. 7–Nov. 22)
1.8 MILLION DISPLACED
60% OF HOUSING DAMAGED/DESTROYED polluting air/land with toxic dust/rubble
RAW SEWAGE running into the streets and sea
FARMLAND BOMBED and contaminated by explosive weapons
VISUALIZINGPALESTINE
SOURCES bit.ly/vp-no-war
WWW.VISUALIZINGPALESTINE.ORG
@visualizingpal
/visualizing_palestine
fb.me/visualizingpalestine
DEC 2023

Year: 2023 | **Brief and copywriting:** Jessica Anderson, Chloe Nielsen | **Design:** Haneen Nazzal, Nasreen Abd Elal | **Update:** Yara Ramadan | **Sources:** bit.ly/vp-no-war

7.

POLITICA PRISONE

Visuals in this section: A Guide to Administrative Detention | Hunger Strikes | History Repeats Itself | Child Prisoners | Ahed Tamimi

L

RS

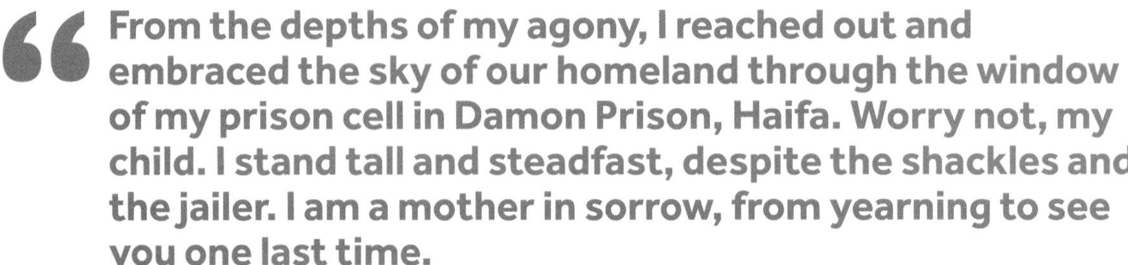

> **From the depths of my agony, I reached out and embraced the sky of our homeland through the window of my prison cell in Damon Prison, Haifa. Worry not, my child. I stand tall and steadfast, despite the shackles and the jailer. I am a mother in sorrow, from yearning to see you one last time.**
>
> *—Khalida Jarrar, letter from Damon Prison on the death of her daughter (2021)*

> **I hereby assert that I am confronting the occupiers not for my own sake as an individual, but for the sake of thousands of prisoners who are being deprived of their simplest human rights . . . I starve myself for you to remain. I die for you to live.**
>
> *—Khader Adnan, letter from his hospital bed (2012)*

After the mass arrests of the First and Second Intifadas, the Palestinian prisoner support group Addameer estimated that the equivalent of 40 percent of the Palestinian adult male population in the West Bank and Gaza had been imprisoned at some point since 1967.[1] The Israeli government uses administrative detention—meaning, incarceration without charge or trial— against Palestinians to try and subdue them and suppress resistance against settler colonialism and apartheid. At any given time, Israel holds hundreds or thousands of Palestinians under administrative detention for periods ranging from six months to several years. **A Guide to Administrative Detention** highlights some of the human rights violations detainees experience in Israeli prisons. **Hunger Strikes** is the first visual we published in 2012. It sheds light on the power of hunger strikes as a form of civil resistance frequently used by Palestinian political prisoners, who have no other means to protest Israel's unjust system of detention.

Much like the Israeli government, the apartheid regime in South Africa used administrative detention to try to break resistance. Almost twenty-three years before we released Hunger Strikes, hundreds of prisoners of the South African apartheid regime launched a hunger strike that is remembered as a pivotal event in the timeline of resistance to apartheid. In **History Repeats Itself**, we show how hunger strikes are a tactic of resistance that connects Palestinians and Black South Africans, informing an enduring politics of joint struggle.

The Israeli government operates two separate legal systems in the West Bank: civil law for Israelis and military law for Palestinians. In Israeli military courts, Palestinians are denied a fair trial and face a 99.7 percent conviction rate.[2] As **Child Prisoners** shows, this system also applies to children. Israel is the only country in the world that tries children in military courts, where between five hundred and seven hundred Palestinian children face trial annually.[3]

In 2018, Israel incarcerated sixteen-year-old **Ahed Tamimi**, who served eight months in prison after slapping an Israeli soldier who had trespassed into her family's yard.[4] One hour earlier, Ahed's fifteen-year-old cousin Mohammed Tamimi was shot in the face by an Israeli soldier, gravely injuring him. Ahed's story brought international attention to the extreme violence that Palestinian children endure at the hands of the Israeli government. Ahed's story is the story of millions of Palestinian children who experience the consequences of being born into life under Israeli military occupation. In a 2022 interview, Ahed describes her resistance as "a natural response to occupation—to reject it. Behind me are my mother and father who taught me to resist the occupier, and my grandmother . . . Behind me are the people all around me, the people I love, who I can lose in any minute. Behind me is an entire generation that I don't want to live through the same experience that I did."[5]

A GUIDE TO ADMINISTRATIVE DETENTION

WHY AM I HERE?

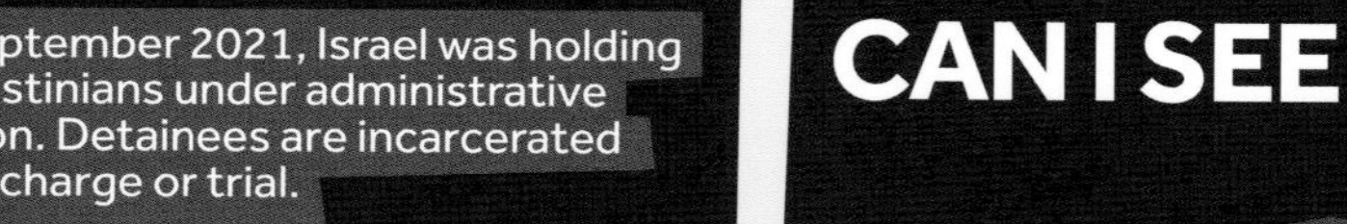

As of September 2021, Israel was holding 520 Palestinians under administrative detention. Detainees are incarcerated without charge or trial.

WHAT DID I DO?

TOP SECRET

Most detainees are held on the basis of 'secret evidence', meaning that they have no way to know what they're accused of.

CAN I GET A LAWYER?

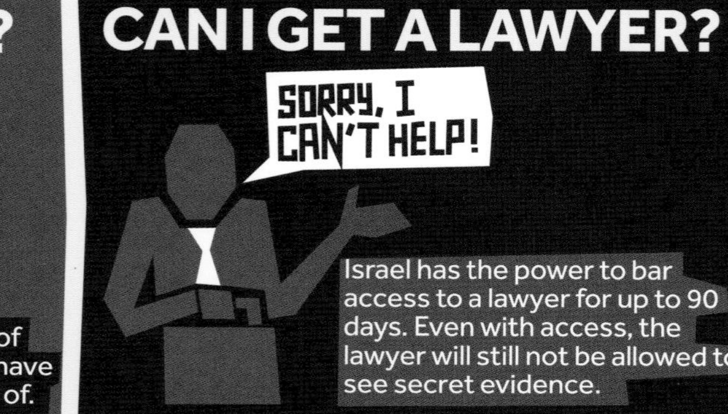
SORRY, I CAN'T HELP!

Israel has the power to bar access to a lawyer for up to 90 days. Even with access, the lawyer will still not be allowed to see secret evidence.

HOW LONG AM I HERE FOR?

Administrative detention orders last for a maximum of 6 months, but can be renewed indefinitely.

CAN I SEE MY FAMILY?

Israel often holds Palestinian detainees from the occupied territories in prisons inside Israel, which is illegal under international law. Family must obtain a special permit to visit, which Israeli authorities may deny without reason.

The Red Cross can visit, but will generally not publicly release information about your conditions.
I'M IN SOLITARY. MY HEALTH IS SUFFERING.
The duration of a Palestinian detainee's solitary confinement is approved by Israeli doctors. Physicians for Human Rights-Israel condemns this as complicity in human rights abuses.
Some women have been forced to give birth in Israeli prisons, where medical negligence is a systemic issue.
WHAT ABOUT DIPLOMATIC IMMUNITY?
Israel routinely holds Palestinian political leaders under administrative detention.
I WAS DUE FOR RELEASE THIS WEEK...
BUT THEY RENEWED MY DETENTION FOR ANOTHER 6 MONTHS
WHAT CAN I DO?
HUNGER STRIKE
Palestinian detainees have held mass hunger strikes to protest administrative detention, poor conditions, and ill treatment in Israeli prisons.
VISUALIZINGPALESTINE
REVISION 01
SOURCES bit.ly/vp-detention
WWW.VISUALIZINGPALESTINE.ORG
@visualizingpal
/visualizing_palestine
fb.me/visualizingpalestine
SEP 2021

Year: 2021 | **Brief and copywriting:** Joumana al Jabri, Ahmad Barclay, Christopher Fiorello, Ramzi Jaber | **Design:** Naji El Mir | **Sources:** bit.ly/vp-detention

HUNGER STRIKES

DAY 1 HUNGER PANGS & STOMACH CRAMPS DISAPPEAR AFTER THE 2ND - 3RD DAY

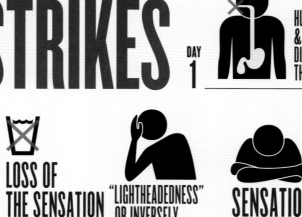

DAY 7 NELSON MANDELA PRISONERS STRIKE ENDS

DAY 14 "CATABOLYSIS" THE BODY STARTS TO BREAK DOWN MUSCLE TISSUE FOR SURVIVAL

DAY 15 LOSS OF THE SENSATION OF THIRST

"LIGHTHEADEDNESS" OR INVERSELY "MENTAL SLUGGISHNESS"

SENSATION OF COLD

DAY 18 STANDING UP MAY BECOME DIFFICULT TO IMPOSSIBLE

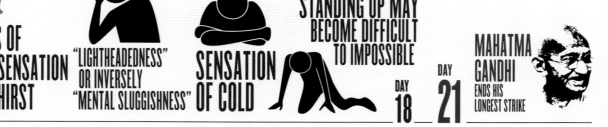

DAY 21 MAHATMA GANDHI ENDS HIS LONGEST STRIKE

DAY 22 LAILA SOUEIF ENDS HER STRIKE FOR HER SON ALAA

DAY 26 200+ GUANTANAMO DETAINEES 2005 COERCED TO END STRIKE

DAY 27 33 SOUTH AFRICAN DETAINEES END THEIR STRIKE 1989

DAY 28 18% WEIGHT LOSS

DAY 35 EXTREMELY UNPLEASANT SENSATIONS OF VERTIGO INCOERCIBLE VOMITING

OF THE EYES
“DIPLOPIA”
42
INCOHERENCE, CONCENTRATION
BECOMES DIFFICULT OR IMPOSSIBLE
HEARING
DAY
45
DEATH CAN OCCUR
AT ANY TIME DUE TO HEART FAILURE
“CARDIOVASCULAR COLLAPSE”
DAY
66
BOBBY SANDS
DIES IN PRISON
KHADER ADNAN
OVER 2 MONTHS ON STRIKE
NO CHARGE OR TRIAL
DAY
70
"WE ARE NOT IN SEARCH OF DEATH, WE ARE LOOKING FOR REAL LIFE."
June 1989, Tiananmen square hunger strike declaration
SOURCES
The information presented is based on a range of medical sources. Symptoms may vary from person to person.
Altuna, G et al, 2004. Deaths due to hunger strike: post-mortem findings. Forensic Science International. 146(1), pp35–38
Crosby, S et al, 2007. Hunger Strikes, Force-feeding, and Physicians' Responsibilities. The Journal of the Medical Association. 298(5), pp563–566
Peel, M, 1997. Hunger strikes: Understanding the underlying physiology will help doctors provide proper advice. British Medical Journal. 315, pp 829–830
VISUALIZINGPALESTINE
DESIGN BY NAJI EL MIR FOR VISUALIZINGPALESTINE.ORG
@visualizingpal - fb.com/visualizingpalestine
SHARE AND DISTRIBUTE FREELY. CREATIVE COMMONS BY-NC-ND 3.0 LICENSE. FEB 2012

Year: 2012 | **Brief and copywriting:** Joumana al Jabri, Ahmad Barclay, Ramzi Jaber | **Design:** Naji El Mir | **Sources:** bit.ly/vp-Sources-2012-2015

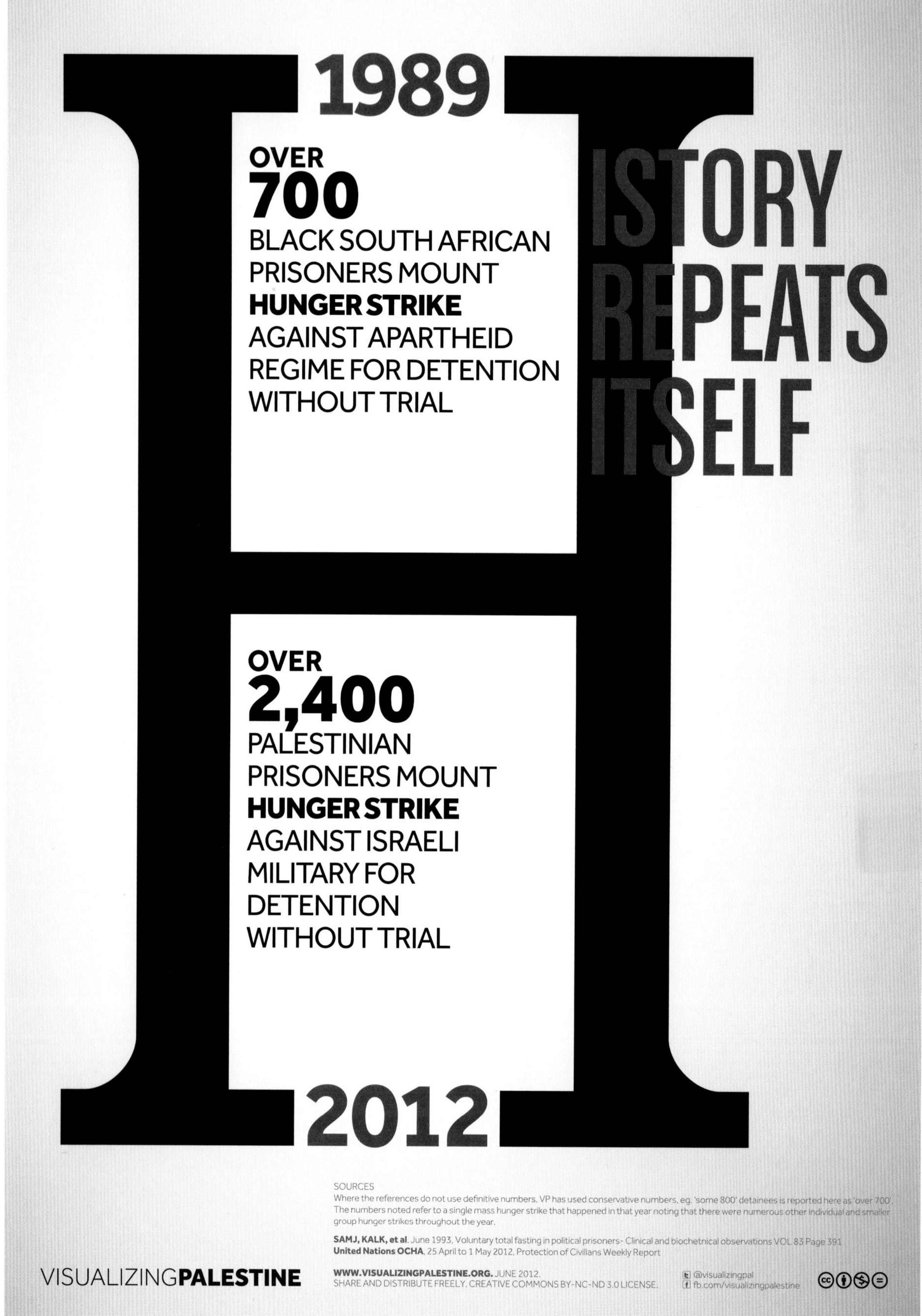
1989
OVER
700
BLACK SOUTH AFRICAN PRISONERS MOUNT
HUNGER STRIKE
AGAINST APARTHEID REGIME FOR DETENTION WITHOUT TRIAL
HISTORY REPEATS ITSELF
OVER
2,400
PALESTINIAN PRISONERS MOUNT
HUNGER STRIKE
AGAINST ISRAELI MILITARY FOR DETENTION WITHOUT TRIAL
2012
SOURCES
Where the references do not use definitive numbers, VP has used conservative numbers, eg. 'some 800' detainees is reported here as 'over 700'. The numbers noted refer to a single mass hunger strike that happened in that year noting that there were numerous other individual and smaller group hunger strikes throughout the year.
SAMJ, KALK, et al. June 1993, Voluntary total fasting in political prisoners- Clinical and biochetnical observations VOL 83 Page 391
United Nations OCHA, 25 April to 1 May 2012, Protection of Civilians Weekly Report
VISUALIZINGPALESTINE
WWW.VISUALIZINGPALESTINE.ORG. JUNE 2012.
SHARE AND DISTRIBUTE FREELY. CREATIVE COMMONS BY-NC-ND 3.0 LICENSE.
@visualizingpal
fb.com/visualizingpalestine

Year: 2012 | **Brief and copywriting:** Joumana al Jabri, Ahmad Barclay, Ramzi Jaber | **Design:** Naji El Mir | **Sources:** bit.ly/vp-Sources-2012-2015

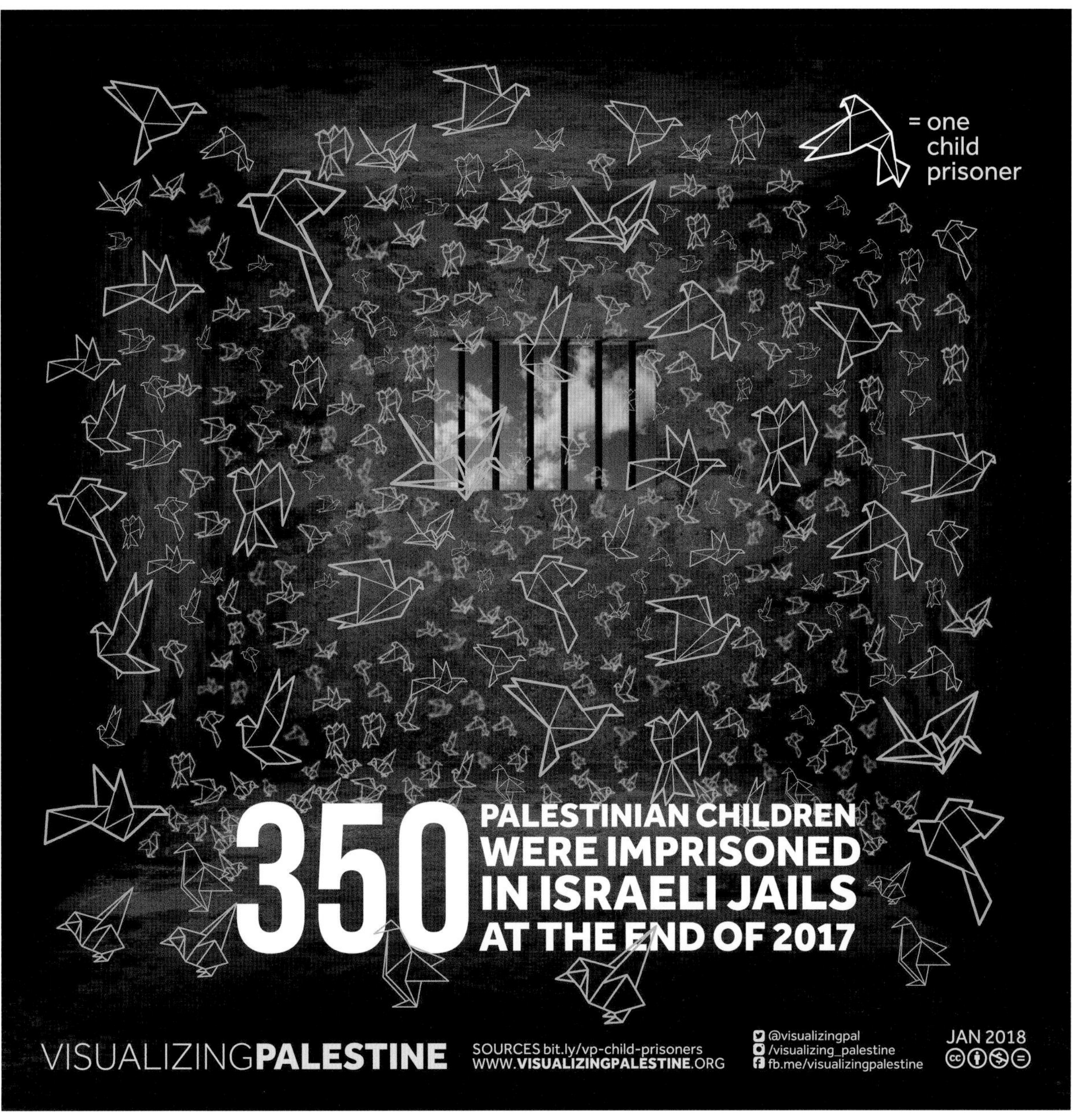
= one child prisoner
350 PALESTINIAN CHILDREN WERE IMPRISONED IN ISRAELI JAILS AT THE END OF 2017
VISUALIZINGPALESTINE
SOURCES bit.ly/vp-child-prisoners
WWW.VISUALIZINGPALESTINE.ORG
@visualizingpal
/visualizing_palestine
fb.me/visualizingpalestine
JAN 2018

Year: 2018 | **Brief and copywriting:** Robin Jones | **Design:** Yosra El Gazzar | **Sources:** bit.ly/vp-child-prisoners

שבס
OVER 8,000 PALESTINIAN CHILDREN HAVE BEEN ARRESTED AND PROSECUTED IN ISRAELI MILITARY COURTS SINCE 2000
"WE SHOULD EXTEND OUR STRUGGLES TO ONE ANOTHER IN ORDER TO END ALL OF THE WORLD'S INJUSTICES [...] I ENCOURAGE THOSE [WHO ARE OPPRESSED] TO CONTINUE THEIR RESISTANCE."
Ahed Tamimi
VISUALIZINGPALESTINE
SOURCES bit.ly/vp-ahed-data
WWW.VISUALIZINGPALESTINE.ORG
@visualizingpal
/visualizing_palestine
fb.me/visualizingpalestine
JAN 2018

Year: 2018 | **Brief and copywriting:** Robin Jones | **Design:** Yosra El Gazzar | **Sources:** bit.ly/vp-ahed-data

8.

A SYSTE OF SILEN

Visuals in this section: A System of Silencing | 5 Broken Cameras | The Use of Tear Gas on Protesters | Killing the Story | The Pegasus Effect | Inequity Offline, Censorship Online | Funder or Censor?

M

CING

> **For we have been socialized to respect fear more than our own needs for language and definition. And while we wait in silence for that final luxury of fearlessness, the weight of that silence will choke us.**
>
> *—Audre Lorde, "The Transformation of Silence into Language and Action" (1977)*

> **Why do we give the authority of narration to those who have murdered and displaced us, when the scarcity of their guilty consciences means honesty is never guaranteed? Why do we wait for those carrying the batons to speak when our bruised bodies told the whole truth?**
>
> *—Mohammed El-Kurd, "The Right to Speak for Ourselves" in the* Nation *(2023)*

Palestinians have documented and described their lived experiences under Israeli settler colonialism for generations, yet their history and existence continue to be questioned at best and subject to erasure at worst. Palestinian intellectual Edward Said wrote that Palestinians are denied "permission to narrate" their reality.[1] When Palestinians are allowed to speak, it is often conditioned on their ability to fulfill the "perfect victim" role, as Palestinian poet and writer Mohammed El-Kurd observes.[2]

In **A System of Silencing** we depict the wide range of tactics and actors involved in censoring, criminalizing, and demonizing speech on Palestine or speech that is critical of Israel and Zionism. These tactics contribute to the erasure of Palestinian narratives and attempt to undermine organizing and solidarity.

Under Israeli Military Order 101, issued in 1967, Palestinian participation in a gathering of more than ten people on an issue "that could be construed as political" requires a permit from the very Israeli military authorities that Palestinians gather to protest.[3] The order effectively constitutes a ban on protest, with violations punishable by a prison sentence of up to ten years. Israeli law also restricts Palestinian commemoration of the Nakba,[4] and in 2023, the Israeli minister of security Itamar Ben-Gvir instructed Israeli police to remove Palestinian flags from public places.[5]

Yet Palestinians refuse to be silenced, even when expression comes at a great cost. They continue to assert their right to exist, to pass down their history, to raise the Palestinian flag, to resist colonial oppression, and to tell their own stories. In **5 Broken Cameras**: Growing Up with the Bil'in Resistance, we chart the story of one Palestinian village's resistance against Israel's apartheid wall, based on a documentary film by the same name, which was nominated for an Academy Award in 2013.

Popular resistance is often met with a range of tactics that Israel uses to repress protest, including attacks by Israeli settlers (who are often accompanied by Israeli soldiers), indiscriminate military incursions, arrests, and the use of live ammunition, tear gas, and rubber-coated bullets on protesters. **The Use of Tear Gas on Protesters** offers a message of solidarity with all protesters of oppression around the world whose calls for justice are met with state violence and repression, including supposedly "less lethal" tactics such as tear gas. During Gaza's Great March of Return, at least seven Palestinian protesters were killed by tear gas canisters fired by Israeli forces directly into crowds of protesters.[6] No one has been held accountable for the murder of these protesters.

On May 11, 2022, a beloved Palestinian journalist for Al Jazeera, Shireen Abu Akleh, was shot dead by Israeli forces while covering their invasion of Jenin refugee camp.[7] She was clearly identifiable as a journalist by her press vest and helmet. One of the many images of Israeli brutality forever seared in the minds of Palestinians is that of Israeli police beating the pallbearers and mourners escorting Abu Akleh to her final resting place, events that were live streamed to the world by shocked Al Jazeera reporters. In **Killing the Story**, we point out that the lack of accountability for Abu Akleh's murder is not an anomaly, but part of a pattern of Israeli impunity for the systemic targeting of journalists, many of whose names are commemorated in this visual. In late 2023, Israeli forces killed more journalists in two months than in the previous twenty-two years. The Committee to Protect Journalists described this as the "deadliest period for journalists" in their history of documenting such killings.[8]

Israel's violence toward journalists has global ramifications. In 2018, Jamal Khashoggi, a journalist critical of the Saudi government, was murdered at the Saudi consulate in Turkey.[9] An investigation by the *Washington Post* later discovered that his wife's phone was infected with Pegasus, a spyware developed by an Israeli company in the context of Israel's mass surveillance of Palestinians.[10] In **The Pegasus Effect**, we depict how Israeli cyber technologies are tested on Palestinians and then exported to governments around the world to suppress human rights defenders, journalists, and political opponents.

In recent years, social media has been a critical tool for Palestinians to bring awareness to human rights violations and talk about the everyday reality of Israeli apartheid. But social media companies are not neutral platforms, and they have adopted content-moderation policies that cause further harm to communities trying to address oppression, or find reprieve from it, on these platforms. The **Inequity Offline, Censorship Online** series explores how oppressed communities—often faced with persecution and violence offline—also face censorship on social media platforms, significantly compromising the potential of social media to benefit social justice movements.

Silencing comes not only from obvious harmful actors, but often from those claiming to support Palestinian civil society. Palestinian nonprofit workers are very familiar with practices that prevent them from using terms like "apartheid," "the Nakba," or "Israeli military occupation," even as they deliver programs intended to "empower" Palestinians. In **Funder or Censor?** we illustrate how international funding bodies cave to pressure from the Israeli government and their own governments to impose politically motivated funding conditions that weaken the ability of Palestinian civil society to address the priorities of their communities, reinforcing the colonization of Palestinians.

As governments around the world share tactics to enforce silence and attack dissent, communities at the receiving end of state violence are making connections across struggles. As Martin Luther King Jr. wrote from jail in Birmingham, Alabama, "Injustice anywhere is a threat to justice everywhere. We are caught in an inescapable network of mutuality, tied in a single garment of destiny. Whatever affects one directly, affects all indirectly."[11]

A SYSTEM OF SILENCING

WHO'S SUPPRESSING SPEECH CRITICAL OF THE ISRAELI REGIME & ZIONISM?

The movement for Palestinian liberation is confronting a system of silencing designed to shield the Israeli regime and its partners from accountability. **Every voice for freedom helps dismantle this system and the oppressive reality it upholds.**

ISRAELI POLICY

POLITICAL VIOLENCE & ASSASSINATIONS

PROTEST REPRESSION

PROHIBITION OF BOYCOTTS

MASS SURVEILLANCE

Palestinian Authorities

INTERROGATIONS, ARRESTS, AND ASSASSINATIONS OF DISSIDENTS

RESTRICTIONS ON ONLINE EXPRESSION

Foreign Governments

DISCRIMINATORY APPLICATION OF BROAD COUNTER-TERRORISM LAWS

REPRESSION OF SOLIDARITY PROTESTS

ANTI-BOYCOTT LEGISLATION

Funders

RESTRICTIONS ON FUNDING FOR NGOS

Universities

SUPPRESSION OF ACADEMIC FREEDOM AND CAMPUS ORGANIZING

HUMAN RIGHTS DEFENDERS
DEFAMING POLITICAL SPEECH AS TERRORISM OR ANTISEMITISM
STRIPPING CITIZENSHIP FOR "DISLOYALTY"
BAN ON DISPLAY OF PALESTINIAN FLAG
SUPPRESSION OF NAKBA COMMEMORATION
CENSORSHIP OF ARCHIVAL RECORDS
DENIAL OF ENTRY AND TRAVEL BANS
RESTRICTIONS ON PALESTINIAN POLITICAL REPRESENTATION
Israel Lobby
LAWFARE AND LEGAL THREATS
DEFAMATION AND SMEAR CAMPAIGNS
CONFLATING CRITICISM OF ISRAEL WITH ANTISEMITISM
Media
EXCLUSION OF PALESTINIAN VOICES
CENSORSHIP BY SOCIAL MEDIA COMPANIES
FIRING CRITICAL REPORTERS
VISUALIZINGPALESTINE
SOURCES bit.ly/vp-silencing
WWW.VISUALIZINGPALESTINE.ORG
@visualizingpal
/visualizing_palestine
fb.me/visualizingpalestine
FEB 2023

Year: 2023
Brief and copywriting: Sarah Al-Yahya, Jessica Anderson
Design: Nasreen Abd Elal, Yosra El Gazzar
Sources: bit.ly/vp-silencing

5 BROKEN CAMERAS
GROWING UP WITH THE BIL'IN RESISTANCE

1
GIBREEL IS BORN
IDF SOLDIERS
OLIVE TREES
PALESTINIAN LAND
START OF BIL'IN NON-VIOLENT PROTESTS AGAINST ISRAELI LAND GRAB
EL-PHIL
HANDS OFF OUR OLIVES
51% OF BIL'IN'S LAND ANNEXED BY THE WALL

2005

GAS GRENADE BREAKS 1ST CAMERA
2
GIBREEL SPEAKS HIS FIRST WORDS
WALL ARMY
THE ICJ INTERNATIONAL COURT OF JUSTICE DECLARED THE WALL ILLEGAL 2004

2006

SETTLERS BURN OLIVE TREES
3,700 INCIDENTS OF VIOLENCE BY ISRAELI SETTLERS 2004 to 2011
TENS OF THOUSANDS OF OLIVE TREES UPROOTED TO MAKE WAY FOR WALL

EL-PHIL SHOWS GIBREEL ISRAELI SETTLEMENTS BEING BUILT ON PALESTINIAN LAND
25% INCREASE IN NUMBER OF ISRAELI SETTLERS 2005 to 2010
2ND CAMERA SMASHED BY ISRAELI SETTLER

3
GIBREEL INHALES TEAR GAS, TALKS ABOUT IT TO HIS MOTHER
SMELL ONIONS TO GET USED TO IT
OVER 595,000 TEAR GAS CANISTERS SENT FROM THE USA TO ISRAEL 2000 to 2009

2007

GIBREEL WATCHES HIS UNCLE KHALED ARRESTED FOR NON-VIOLENT RESISTANCE
COUNTLESS ARRESTS AT PROTESTS, 30 CONVICTED FOR NON-VIOLENT ACTS
GIBREEL JOINS CHILD PROTEST
WE WANT TO SLEEP
WE WANT PEACE

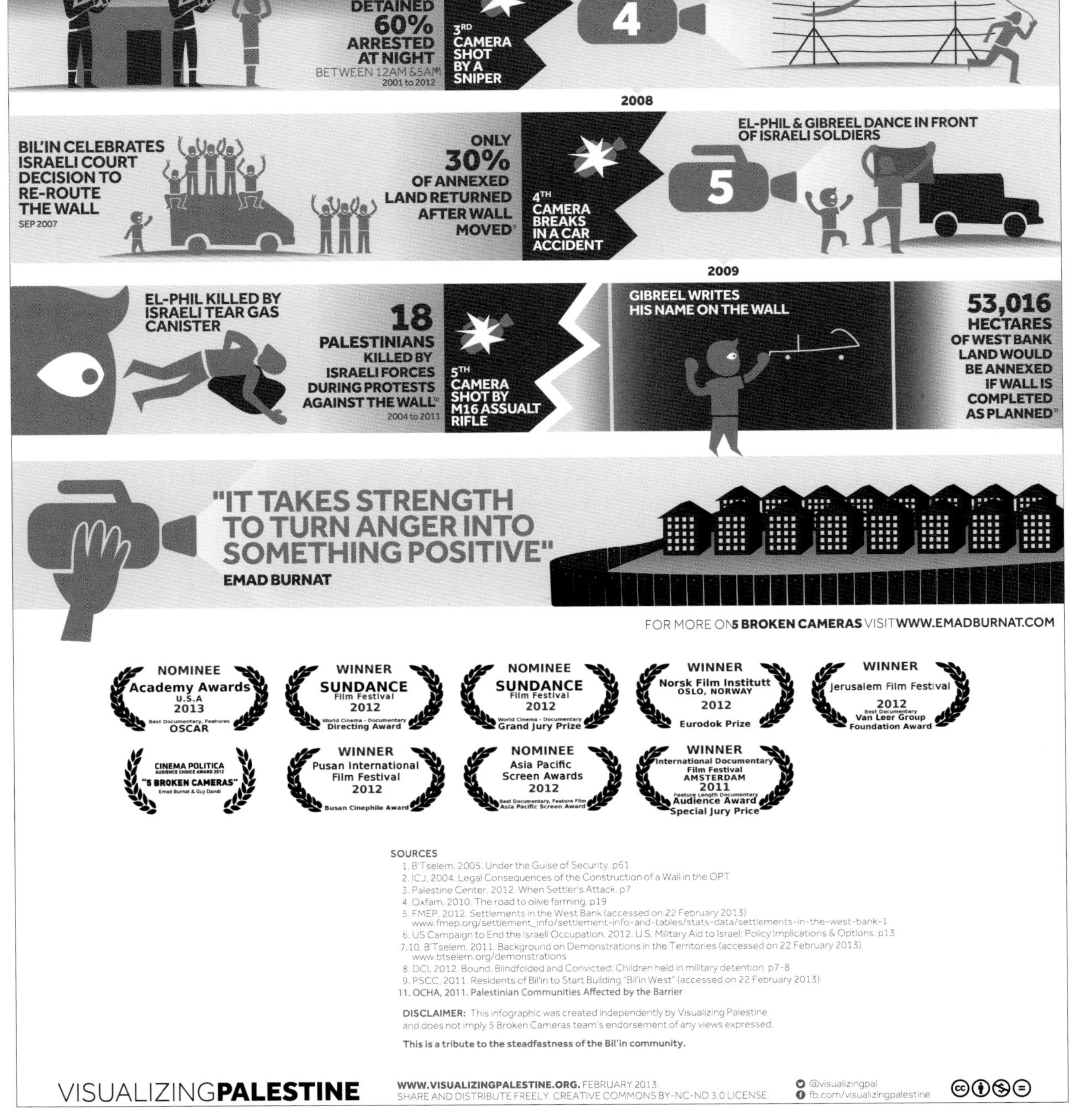
DETAINED
60%
ARRESTED
AT NIGHT
BETWEEN 12AM &5AM
2001 to 2012
3RD CAMERA SHOT BY A SNIPER
4
2008
BIL'IN CELEBRATES ISRAELI COURT DECISION TO RE-ROUTE THE WALL
SEP 2007
ONLY 30% OF ANNEXED LAND RETURNED AFTER WALL MOVED
4TH CAMERA BREAKS IN A CAR ACCIDENT
5
EL-PHIL & GIBREEL DANCE IN FRONT OF ISRAELI SOLDIERS
2009
EL-PHIL KILLED BY ISRAELI TEAR GAS CANISTER
18
PALESTINIANS KILLED BY ISRAELI FORCES DURING PROTESTS AGAINST THE WALL
2004 to 2011
5TH CAMERA SHOT BY M16 ASSUALT RIFLE
GIBREEL WRITES HIS NAME ON THE WALL
53,016 HECTARES OF WEST BANK LAND WOULD BE ANNEXED IF WALL IS COMPLETED AS PLANNED
"IT TAKES STRENGTH TO TURN ANGER INTO SOMETHING POSITIVE"
EMAD BURNAT
FOR MORE ON 5 BROKEN CAMERAS VISIT WWW.EMADBURNAT.COM
NOMINEE Academy Awards U.S.A 2013 Best Documentary, Features OSCAR
WINNER SUNDANCE Film Festival 2012 World Cinema - Documentary Directing Award
NOMINEE SUNDANCE Film Festival 2012 World Cinema - Documentary Grand Jury Prize
WINNER Norsk Film Institutt OSLO, NORWAY 2012 Eurodok Prize
WINNER Jerusalem Film Festival 2012 Best Documentary Van Leer Group Foundation Award
CINEMA POLITICA "5 BROKEN CAMERAS"
WINNER Pusan International Film Festival 2012 Busan Cinephile Award
NOMINEE Asia Pacific Screen Awards 2012 Best Documentary, Feature Film Asia Pacific Screen Award
WINNER International Documentary Film Festival AMSTERDAM 2011 Feature Length Documentary Audience Award Special Jury Price
SOURCES
1. B'Tselem, 2005. Under the Guise of Security. p61
2. ICJ, 2004. Legal Consequences of the Construction of a Wall in the OPT
3. Palestine Center, 2012. When Settler's Attack. p7
4. Oxfam, 2010. The road to olive farming. p19
5. FMEP, 2012. Settlements in the West Bank (accessed on 22 February 2013) www.fmep.org/settlement_info/settlement-info-and-tables/stats-data/settlements-in-the-west-bank-1
6. US Campaign to End the Israeli Occupation, 2012. U.S. Military Aid to Israel: Policy Implications & Options. p13
7.10. B'Tselem, 2011. Background on Demonstrations in the Territories (accessed on 22 February 2013) www.btselem.org/demonstrations
8. DCI, 2012. Bound, Blindfolded and Convicted: Children held in military detention. p7-8
9. PSCC, 2011. Residents of Bil'in to Start Building "Bil'in West" (accessed on 22 February 2013)
11. OCHA, 2011. Palestinian Communities Affected by the Barrier
DISCLAIMER: This infographic was created independently by Visualizing Palestine and does not imply 5 Broken Cameras team's endorsement of any views expressed.
This is a tribute to the steadfastness of the Bil'in community.
VISUALIZINGPALESTINE
WWW.VISUALIZINGPALESTINE.ORG. FEBRUARY 2013.
SHARE AND DISTRIBUTE FREELY. CREATIVE COMMONS BY-NC-ND 3.0 LICENSE
@visualizingpal
fb.com/visualizingpalestine

Year: 2013 | **Brief and copywriting:** Joumana al Jabri, Ahmad Barclay, Christopher Fiorello, Ramzi Jaber, Shireen Tawil | **Design:** Naji El Mir | **Sources:** bit.ly/vp-Sources-2012-2015

THE USE OF TEAR GAS ON PROTESTERS

Human rights groups respond, 2019-2020

EGYPT "full-throttle clampdown"
IRAQ "gruesome protester deaths"
SUDAN "without any restraint"
TURKEY "shocking unwarranted actions"
USA "dangerous & highly inappropriate"
LEBANON "violent crackdown"
COLOMBIA "excessive, disproportionate"
HONG KONG "police siege"
IRAN "scores injured"
PALESTINE "teargas canister... lodged in his face"

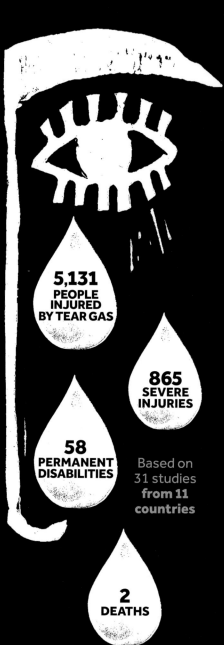

5,131 PEOPLE INJURED BY TEAR GAS

865 SEVERE INJURIES

58 PERMANENT DISABILITIES

Based on 31 studies **from 11 countries**

2 DEATHS

VISUALIZING**PALESTINE**

SOURCES bit.ly/VP-teargas
WWW.**VISUALIZINGPALESTINE**.ORG

@visualizingpal
/visualizing_palestine
fb.me/visualizingpalestine

JUN 2020

Year: 2020 | **Brief and copywriting:** Jessica Anderson | **Design:** Yosra El Gazzar | **Sources:** bit.ly/VP-teargas

KILLING THE STORY

AT LEAST **150 JOURNALISTS KILLED BY ISRAEL, 2000–2023**

TV

JAMES MILLER
Killed by the Israeli military with a single shot to the neck while filming a documentary in Gaza in 2003.

YASER MURTAJA
Killed by Israeli snipers with a shot to the abdomen while he was covering the Great March of Return in Gaza in 2018.

PRESS

SHIREEN ABU AKLEH
Killed by the Israeli military with a single shot below her ear while she was covering an Israeli invasion on the Jenin refugee camp in the West Bank in 2022.

NO ONE HAS BEEN HELD ACCOUNTABLE FOR THEIR MURDERS

JOURNALISTS KILLED BY ISRAEL

2000 • Aziz Yousef al-Tanh • **2001** • Mohammad Bishtawi • Othman Abd Elqader al-Qatnani • **2002** • Ahmad Nu'man . Amjad Bahjat al-Alami • Imad Subhi Abu Zahra • Issam Mithqal Hamza Al Tilawi • Jamil Abdullah al-Nawawreh • Raffaele Ciriello • **2003** • James Miller • Nazih Adel Darwazeh • Fadi Nashaat Alawneh • **2004** • Mohammed Abu Halima • **2008** • Fadel Shana'a • **2009** • Basil Ibrahim Faraj • Omar Abdel Hafidh Al Silawi • Alaa Hammad Mahmoud Murtaja • Ihab Jamal Hasan Al Wahidi • **2010** • Cevdet Kılıçlar • **2012** • Mohammad Mousa Abu Eisha • Husam Mohammad Salameh • Mahmood Ali Ahmad Al Koumi • **2014** • Abdulrahman Ziyad Abu Hin • Ahed Afif Zaqout • Bahaa al-Din al-Gharib • Ezzat Salama Duheir • Muhammad Majed Daher • Najla Mahmoud Al Haj • Shadi Hamdi Ayyad • Ali Shehda Abu Afash • Hamada Khaled Maqat • Hamid Abdallah Shihab • Khalid Riyadh Mohammad Hamad • Mohammad Al Deiri • Rami Fathi Hussein Rayan Samih Mohammad Al Aryan • Simone Camilli • **2015** • Ahmad Hirbawi • **2016** • Iyad Sajdia • **2018** • Ahmad Abu Hussein • Yaser Murtaja • **2021** • Yousef Abu Hussein • **2022** • Ghufran Warasneh • Shireen Abu Akleh • **2023** • Duaa Sharaf • Jamal Al-Faqaawi • Saed Al-Halabi • Ahmed Abu Mhadi • Salma Mkhaimer • Mohammed Imad Labad • Roshdi Sarraj • Mohammed Ali • Khalil Abu Aathra • Sameeh Al-Nady • Mohammad Balousha • Issam Bhar • Abdulhadi Habib • Yousef Maher Dawas • Salam Mema • Husam Mubarak • Issam Abdallah • Ahmed Shehab • Mohamed Fayez Abu Matar • Saeed al-Taweel • Mohammed Sobh • Hisham Nawajha • Assaad Shamlakh • Mohammad Al-Salhi • Mohammad Jarghoun • Ibrahim Lafi • Mohamad Al-Bayyari • Mohammed Abu Hatab • Majd Fadl Arandas • Iyad Matar • Imad Al-Wahidi • Majed Kashko • Nazmi Al-Nadim • Yasser Abu Namous • Mohamed Al Jaja • Mohamed Abu Hassira • Yahya Abu Manih • Ahmed Al-Qara • Yaacoub Al-Barsh (Mousa Al Barsh) • Ahmed Fatima • Mossab Ashour • Amro Salah Abu Hayah • Mostafa El Sawaf • Hassouneh Salim • Sari Mansour • Abdelhalim Awad • Bilal Jadallah • Ayat Khadoura • Rabih Al Maamari • Farah Omar • Mohamed Nabil Al-Zaq • Mohamed Mouin Ayyash • Mostafa Bakeer • Adham Hassouna • Montaser Al-Sawaf • Abdullah Darwish • Hassan Farajallah • Alaa Al-Sarraj • Nader Al-Nazli • Amal Zahed • Assem Al-Barsh (Moussa Al-Barash) • Mahmoud Matar • Zaher Al Afghani • Hani Madhoun • Shaima El-Gazzar • Ola Atallah • Duaa Jabbour • Samer Abu Daqqa • Haneen Kashtan • Assem Kamal Moussa • Abdallah Alwan • Adel Zorob • Mohamed Khalifeh (Mohammad Saidi) • Mohamed Naser Abu Huwaidi • Ahmad Jamal Al Madhoun • Mohamed Azzaytouniyah • Mohamad Al-Iff • Ahmed Khaireddine • Mohamed Khaireddine • Jabr Abu Hadrous • Huthaifa Lulu • Abdul Karim Odeh • Mohamed Abu Samra • Abd Al-Hamid Al-Qarinawi • Abdelraham Shihab • Ahmad Abu Absah • Alaa Al-Nimr • Anas Abu Shimalah • Hathifa Al-Najjar • A'id Al-Najjar • Hathim Hararah • Hamada Al-Yazji • Hanan Ayyad • Iman Al-Aqili • Jamal Haniah • Mahmoud Abu Tharifah • Marwan Al-Sawaf • Ahmad Farjallah (Mohammad Farjallah) • Rajab Al-Naqib • Mustafa Al-Naqib • Narmin Qawas • Ahmad Nahed Masoud • Khamis Salem Deab • Moussa Bursh • Salim Naffar • Mohammad Fayez Al Hassani •

VISUALIZING**PALESTINE**

SOURCES bit.ly/vp-journalists
WWW.**VISUALIZINGPALESTINE**.ORG

@visualizingpal
/visualizing_palestine
fb.me/visualizingpalestine

DEC 2023

Year: 2023 | **Brief and copywriting:** Sarah Al-Yahya, Jessica Anderson | **Design:** Nasreen Abd Elal, Yosra El Gazzar | **Sources:** bit.ly/vp-journalists

THE PEGASUS EFFECT

THE GLOBAL IMPACT OF ISRAELI SURVEILLANCE TECHNOLOGY

The Israeli military functions as an incubator for the country's private surveillance sector. This makes the NSO Group, the maker of Pegasus spyware, a case study in how repressive technologies piloted on Palestinians are deployed globally. Pegasus infections have been detected in at least 45 countries and counting.

ISRAELI CYBER

PALESTINE

TOGO
HUMAN RIGHTS DEFENDER
Targeted an anti-corruption activist fighting for constitutional and electoral reform

SPAIN
POLITICIAN
Targeted dozens of Catalan independence leaders. The Spanish Prime Minister & Defense Minister were also hacked

PALESTINE
HUMAN RIGHTS DEF
Targeted human righ
researchers at prom
organizations docun
Israeli war crimes

VISUALIZINGPALESTINE

AL-HAQ

MINDTHEGAP

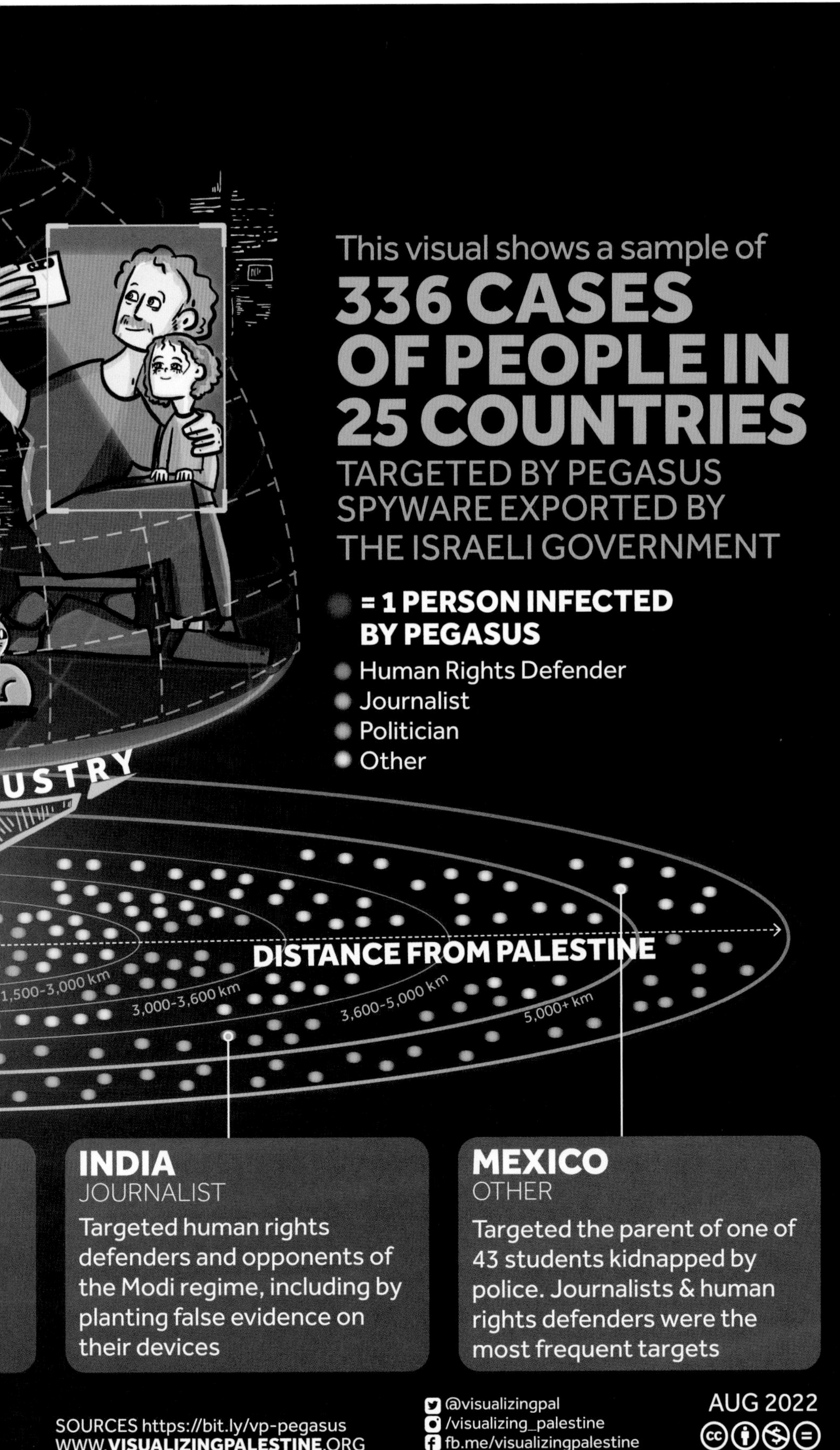

This visual shows a sample of
336 CASES OF PEOPLE IN 25 COUNTRIES
TARGETED BY PEGASUS SPYWARE EXPORTED BY THE ISRAELI GOVERNMENT
= 1 PERSON INFECTED BY PEGASUS
Human Rights Defender
Journalist
Politician
Other
USTRY
DISTANCE FROM PALESTINE
1,500-3,000 km
3,000-3,600 km
3,600-5,000 km
5,000+ km
INDIA
JOURNALIST
Targeted human rights defenders and opponents of the Modi regime, including by planting false evidence on their devices
MEXICO
OTHER
Targeted the parent of one of 43 students kidnapped by police. Journalists & human rights defenders were the most frequent targets
SOURCES https://bit.ly/vp-pegasus
WWW.VISUALIZINGPALESTINE.ORG
@visualizingpal
/visualizing_palestine
fb.me/visualizingpalestine
AUG 2022

Year: 2022
Brief and copywriting: Wesam Ahmad, Jessica Anderson, Daleen Saah
Design: Daleen Saah, Haneen Nazzal, Yosra El Gazzar
Sources: bit.ly/vp-pegasus

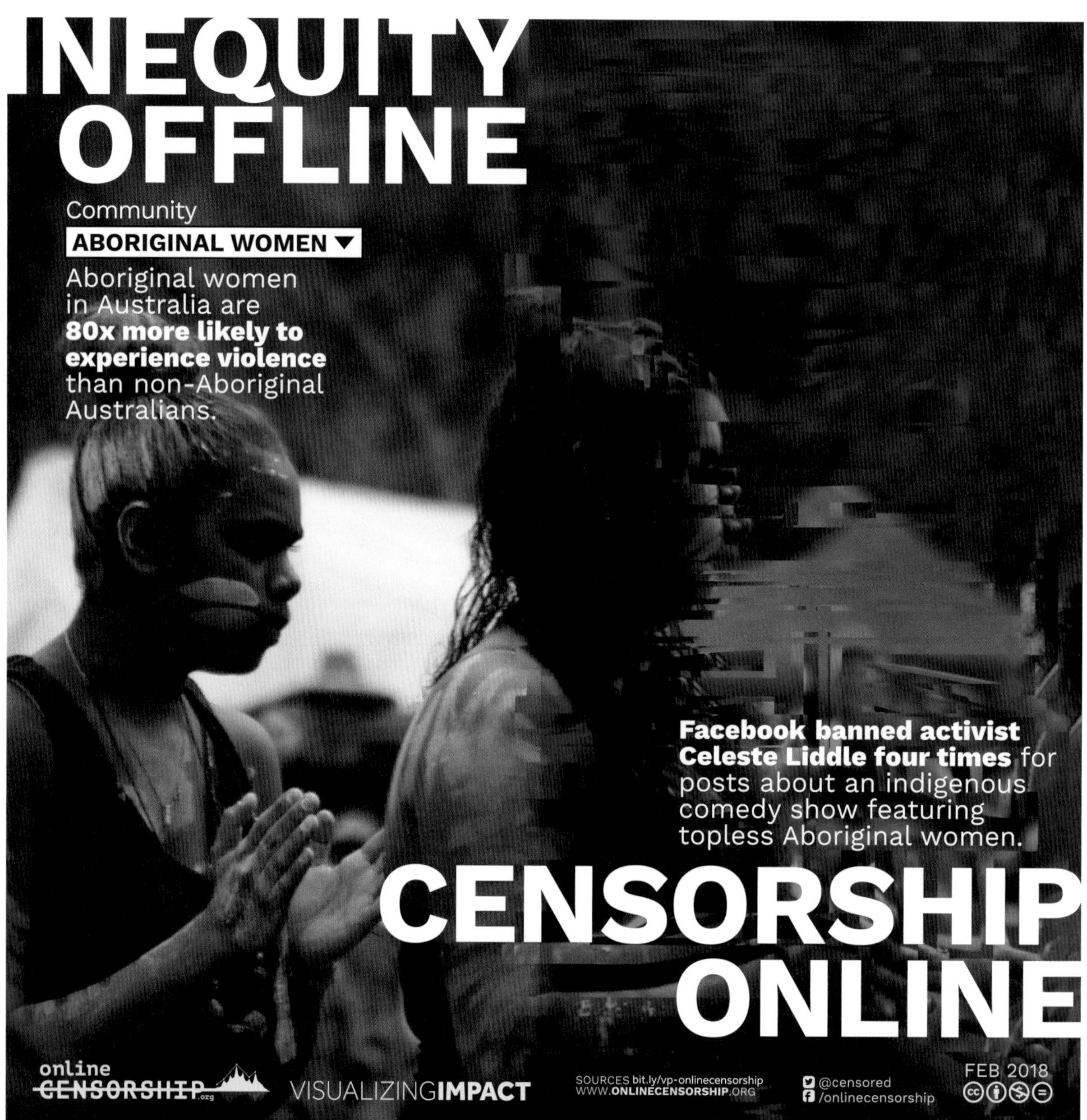
INEQUITY
OFFLINE
Community
ABORIGINAL WOMEN ▼
Aboriginal women in Australia are **80x more likely to experience violence** than non-Aboriginal Australians.
Facebook banned activist Celeste Liddle four times for posts about an indigenous comedy show featuring topless Aboriginal women.
CENSORSHIP
ONLINE
online CENSORSHIP.org
VISUALIZINGIMPACT
SOURCES bit.ly/vp-onlinecensorship
WWW.ONLINECENSORSHIP.ORG
@censored
/onlinecensorship
FEB 2018

Year: 2018 | **Brief and copywriting:** Jessica Anderson, Kimberly Carlson, Abeera Khan, Mathana, Sarah Myers West, Jillian C. York | **Design:** Yosra El Gazzar | **Photos:** Fibonacci Blue (Wikimedia), Malcolm Williams (Flickr), Jordi Bernabeu Farrús (Flickr), Benjamin A. Gifford, Middle East Monitor | **Sources:** bit.ly/vp-onlinecensorship

INEQUITY
OFFLINE
Community
BLACK AMERICANS ▼
Black Americans are
3x more likely to be killed by police than White Americans.
BLACK
MAT
LIVES
TER
In 2017, a coalition of 77 social and racial justice organizations wrote to Facebook about **censorship of Facebook users of color** and takedowns of images discussing racism.
CENSORSHIP
ONLINE
online CENSORSHIP.org
VISUALIZINGIMPACT
SOURCES https://eff.org/r.3tdz
WWW.ONLINECENSORSHIP.ORG
@censored
/onlinecensorship
FEB 2018

INEQUITY
OFFLINE
Community
DAKOTA PIPELINE PROTESTERS ▼
At least 739 protesters were arrested between August 2016 and February 2017.
STOP DA
P
Water is Life
#NoDAPL
Facebook censored a video of a mass arrest of 22 activists at a Dakota Access Pipeline protest.
CENSORSHIP
ONLINE
online CENSORSHIP.org
VISUALIZINGIMPACT
SOURCES https://eff.org/r.3tdz
WWW.ONLINECENSORSHIP.ORG
@censored
/onlinecensorship
FEB 2018

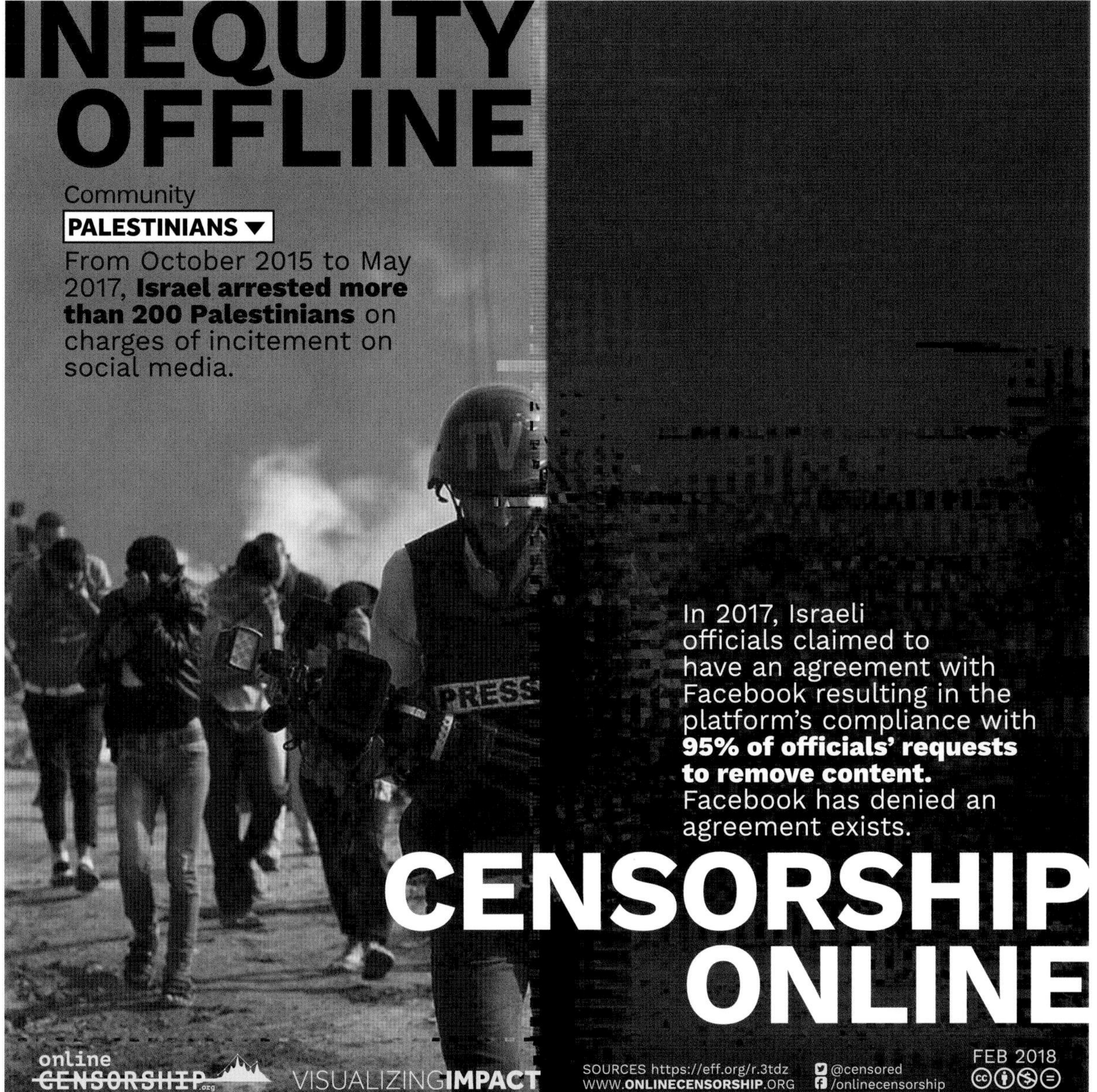
INEQUITY
OFFLINE
Community
PALESTINIANS
From October 2015 to May 2017, **Israel arrested more than 200 Palestinians** on charges of incitement on social media.
TV
PRESS
In 2017, Israeli officials claimed to have an agreement with Facebook resulting in the platform's compliance with **95% of officials' requests to remove content.** Facebook has denied an agreement exists.
CENSORSHIP
ONLINE
online CENSORSHIP.org
VISUALIZINGIMPACT
SOURCES https://eff.org/r.3tdz
WWW.ONLINECENSORSHIP.ORG
@censored
/onlinecensorship
FEB 2018

INEQUITY
OFFLINE

Community

NATIVE AMERICANS ▼

A generation of Native children **lost their cultural names due to the Dawes Act of 1887,** which passed out Christian names to Native peoples along with allotments of land.

Shane Creepingbear, a member of the Kiowa Tribe of Oklahoma, was **kicked off Facebook when the platform flagged his indigenous name as fake.**

CENSORSHIP ONLINE

online CENSORSHIP.org VISUALIZINGIMPACT

SOURCES https://eff.org/r.3tdz
WWW.ONLINECENSORSHIP.ORG

@censored
/onlinecensorship

FEB 2018

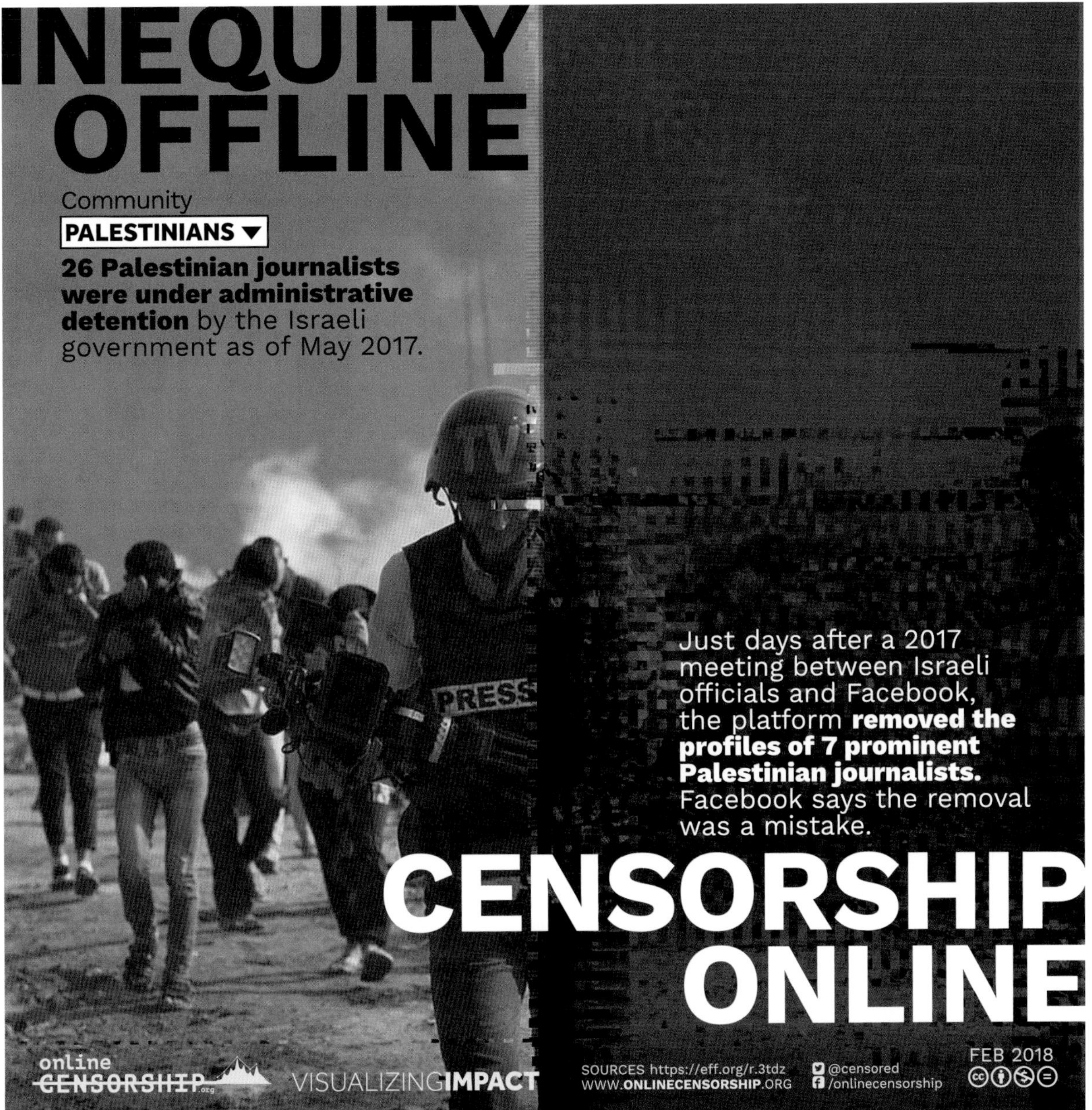
INEQUITY OFFLINE
Community
PALESTINIANS ▼
26 Palestinian journalists were under administrative detention by the Israeli government as of May 2017.
TV
PRESS
Just days after a 2017 meeting between Israeli officials and Facebook, the platform removed the profiles of 7 prominent Palestinian journalists. Facebook says the removal was a mistake.
CENSORSHIP ONLINE
online CENSORSHIP.org
VISUALIZINGIMPACT
SOURCES https://eff.org/r.3tdz
WWW.ONLINECENSORSHIP.ORG
@censored
/onlinecensorship
FEB 2018

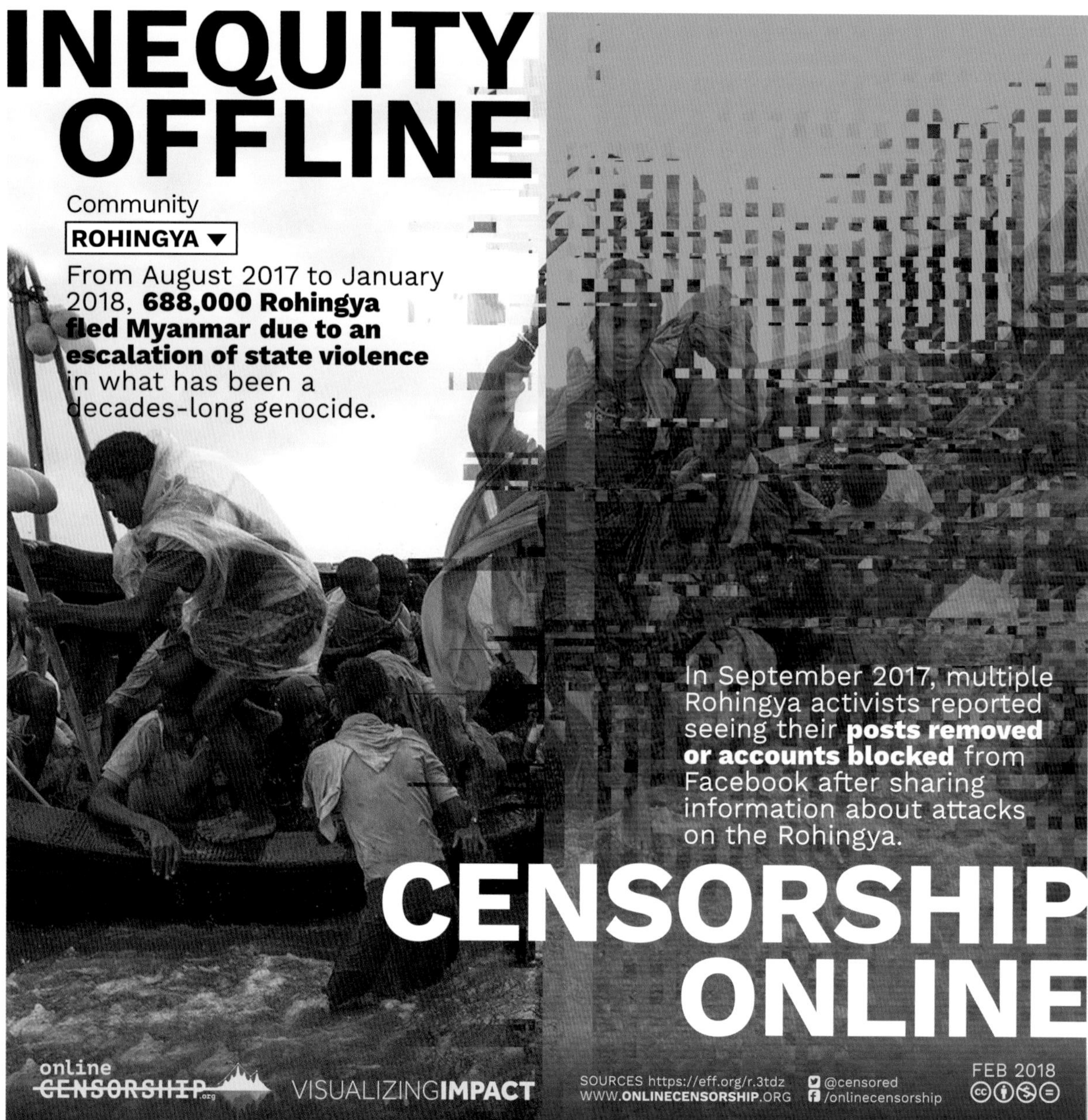
INEQUITY OFFLINE
Community
ROHINGYA ▼
From August 2017 to January 2018, 688,000 Rohingya fled Myanmar due to an escalation of state violence in what has been a decades-long genocide.
In September 2017, multiple Rohingya activists reported seeing their posts removed or accounts blocked from Facebook after sharing information about attacks on the Rohingya.
CENSORSHIP ONLINE
online CENSORSHIP.org
VISUALIZINGIMPACT
SOURCES https://eff.org/r.3tdz
WWW.ONLINECENSORSHIP.ORG
@censored
/onlinecensorship
FEB 2018

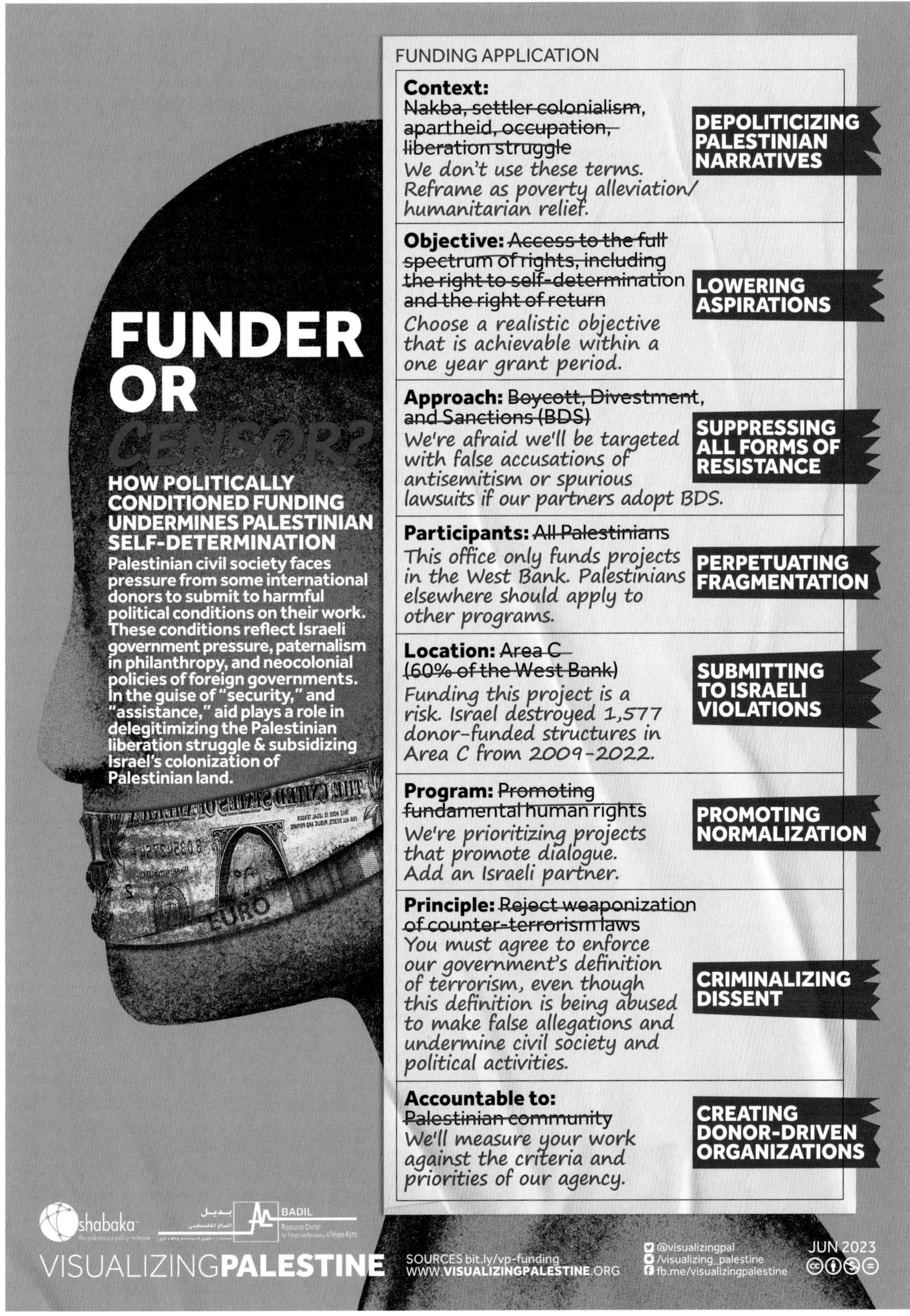
FUNDER OR CENSOR?
HOW POLITICALLY CONDITIONED FUNDING UNDERMINES PALESTINIAN SELF-DETERMINATION
Palestinian civil society faces pressure from some international donors to submit to harmful political conditions on their work. These conditions reflect Israeli government pressure, paternalism in philanthropy, and neocolonial policies of foreign governments. In the guise of "security," and "assistance," aid plays a role in delegitimizing the Palestinian liberation struggle & subsidizing Israel's colonization of Palestinian land.
FUNDING APPLICATION
Context: ~~Nakba, settler colonialism, apartheid, occupation, liberation struggle~~
We don't use these terms. Reframe as poverty alleviation/ humanitarian relief.
DEPOLITICIZING PALESTINIAN NARRATIVES
Objective: ~~Access to the full spectrum of rights, including the right to self-determination and the right of return~~
Choose a realistic objective that is achievable within a one year grant period.
LOWERING ASPIRATIONS
Approach: ~~Boycott, Divestment, and Sanctions (BDS)~~
We're afraid we'll be targeted with false accusations of antisemitism or spurious lawsuits if our partners adopt BDS.
SUPPRESSING ALL FORMS OF RESISTANCE
Participants: ~~All Palestinians~~
This office only funds projects in the West Bank. Palestinians elsewhere should apply to other programs.
PERPETUATING FRAGMENTATION
Location: ~~Area C (60% of the West Bank)~~
Funding this project is a risk. Israel destroyed 1,577 donor-funded structures in Area C from 2009-2022.
SUBMITTING TO ISRAELI VIOLATIONS
Program: ~~Promoting fundamental human rights~~
We're prioritizing projects that promote dialogue. Add an Israeli partner.
PROMOTING NORMALIZATION
Principle: ~~Reject weaponization of counter-terrorism laws~~
You must agree to enforce our government's definition of terrorism, even though this definition is being abused to make false allegations and undermine civil society and political activities.
CRIMINALIZING DISSENT
Accountable to: ~~Palestinian community~~
We'll measure your work against the criteria and priorities of our agency.
CREATING DONOR-DRIVEN ORGANIZATIONS
shabaka
BADIL
VISUALIZINGPALESTINE
SOURCES bit.ly/vp-funding
WWW.VISUALIZINGPALESTINE.ORG
@visualizingpal
/visualizing_palestine
fb.me/visualizingpalestine
JUN 2023

Year: 2023 | **Brief and copywriting:** Jessica Anderson, Aline Batarseh, Megan Driscoll, Yara Hawari, Saif Kassis, Alaa Tartir | **Design:** Yosra El Gazzar | **Special thanks:** Paul Carroll, Grassroots International, Nora Lester Murad, Rebecca Vilkomerson, Jeremy Wildeman | **Sources:** bit.ly/vp-funding

9. UNITED S

COMPLIC

Visuals in this section: Trump vs. International Law | Trump vs. A Global Consensus | US Military Aid to Israel | End Military Aid to Israel | Donating to Dispossession | "House by House, Lot by Lot" | In the Firing Zone | Not on Our Dime | Above the Law? | The Rise of US Anti-Boycott Legislation

TATES

TY

> **I am determined as ever to fight for a just future where everyone can live in peace, without fear and with true freedom, equal rights, and human dignity. . . . The failure to recognize the violent reality of living under siege, occupation, and apartheid makes no one safer. No person, no child anywhere should have to suffer or live in fear of violence. . . . As long as our country provides billions in unconditional funding to support the apartheid government, this heartbreaking cycle of violence will continue.**
>
> *—US Representative Rashida Tlaib (October 2023)*

> **[S]hared values compel us to reaffirm that our enduring friendship with the people of Israel and our unbreakable bonds with the state of Israel—that those bonds, that friendship cannot be broken. . . . Those values compel us to say that our commitment to Israel's security—and my commitment to Israel's security—is and always will be unshakeable.**
>
> *—President Barack Obama, remarks to Adas Israel Congregation (2015)*

The date of May 14, 2018, stands out as a day that symbolizes the state of US complicity with Israel and contempt for Palestinian life. On that day, Ivanka Trump and Jared Kushner were photographed smiling at the opening of the US embassy in Jerusalem while, a few dozen miles away, Israeli snipers were firing live ammunition at Palestinian protesters in Gaza, massacring sixty people and injuring thousands.[1] While successive US administrations have consistently referred to "shared values" with Israel, the opening of the embassy and the close relationship between US President Donald Trump and Israeli Prime Minister Benjamin Netanyahu laid bare what "shared values" really mean: support for both countries' colonization and domination of Indigenous peoples. **Trump vs. International Law** and **Trump vs. A Global Consensus** depict how Trump broke from previous administrations' policies when he recognized Israel's annexation of Jerusalem, in violation of international law.

Contempt for Palestinian life did not end when Trump left office. As Israel began carrying out acts of genocide in October 2023, the US State Department under Joe Biden's administration issued a memo instructing high-level officials not to use the phrases "de-escalation/ceasefire," "end to violence/bloodshed," and "restoring calm,"[2] while White House Press Secretary Karine Jean-Pierre called the demand for a ceasefire "disgraceful" and "repugnant."[3] President Biden engaged in genocide denial, saying he had "no notion that the Palestinians are telling the truth about how many people are killed" as the death toll in Gaza neared seven thousand and thousands were missing in the rubble.[4] Weeks later, a senior Biden administration official admitted that the numbers are "even higher than are being cited."[5] On October 28, three weeks into daily massacres, White House National Security Council Coordinator for Strategic Communications John Kirby said, "We're not drawing red lines for Israel."[6]

From 1946 to 2023, Israel received more than $124 billion in US military funding and missile systems.[7] The Congressional Research Service also notes that US military funding is "designed to maintain Israel's 'qualitative military edge' over neighboring militaries" and that the United States stockpiles weapons and military equipment in Israel, which the Israeli government can request to use.[8] In **US Military Aid to Israel**, we visualize how this blank check from the United States to Israel reflects the two countries' mutual investment in militarism and imperialism. This puts American taxpayers in the position of subsidizing the exploitation of Palestinians, and it also squanders resources that could be used to invest in justice and well-being for communities in the United States. The series **End Military Aid to Israel** appeared on billboards in Washington, DC, during the 2013 conference of the American Israel Public Affairs Committee (AIPAC), which spends millions of dollars every year to lobby Congress to implement policies favorable to Israel.

Military funding is one of many sources of US support for Israeli colonization. One investigation in 2015 found that, from 2009 to 2013, US organizations masquerading as charities funneled over $220 million to Israeli organizations involved in the expansion of illegal Israeli settlements.[9] In **Donating to Dispossession** we zoom in on one organization, the New York–registered Central Fund of Israel, and highlight the activities of several of its Israeli grantees. **"House by House, Lot by Lot"** and **In the Firing Zone** depict the role that Israeli settlement organizations play in a larger system that perpetuates the continued dispossession of the Palestinian people. We created these visuals in collaboration with a coalition of groups advancing the **Not on Our Dime** campaign, which is pushing for first-of-its-kind state legislation to stop New York charities from funding Israeli settler violence.

On top of its financial support, the United States facilitates impunity for Israel with its diplomatic power as a permanent member of the United Nations Security Council. **Above the Law?** visualizes how the United States routinely uses its veto power to block measures to hold Israel accountable for its violations of international law and Palestinian human rights. On October 18, 2023, the United States vetoed a resolution at the Security Council calling for Israel to allow humanitarian aid into Gaza at a time when Israel had cut off all water, food, fuel, and medicine.[10]

With the 2005 Palestinian call for Boycott, Divestment, and Sanctions (BDS) gaining momentum in the United States, a new repressive attack by US lawmakers emerged in the form of anti-boycott bills. **The Rise of US Anti-Boycott Legislation** visualizes 443 anti-boycott measures introduced by US lawmakers at the state and federal levels from 2014 to March 2023, threatening a constitutionally protected form of political expression and dissent. While these bills started as an attack on Palestinian solidarity, they have evolved into a broader attack on climate action, gun control, trans rights, abortion access, workplace equity, and more. Model legislation authored by the American Legislative Exchange Council, a right-wing corporate lobby group, is a driving force behind this all-out assault on the right to boycott. In addition to bringing attention to the criminalization of dissent, this visual highlights the interconnectedness of oppression and struggle across movements. In her book *Freedom Is a Constant Struggle*, Angela Davis wrote, "When we try to organize campaigns in solidarity with Palestine, when we try to challenge the Israeli state, it's not simply about focusing our struggles elsewhere, in another place. It also has to do with what happens in US communities."

TRUMP VS. INTERNATIO

Donald Trump's unilateral move to recognize Jerusalem as Israel's capital and the US embassy there directly violates international law and breaks with deca of consensus among US administrations, both Republican and Democrat.

"We continue to support [...] the international-ization of Jerusalem."

"[Relocating the embassy] would be inconsistent with the UN resolutions dealing with the international nature of Jerusalem."

"The United States considers [East Jerusalem] as occupied territory."

"We do not accept the new [Israeli basic law] as determining the status of Jerusalem."

TRUMAN 1945 **EISENHOWER** 1953 **KENNEDY** 1961 **JOHNSON** 1964 **NIXON** 1969 **FORD** 1975 **CARTER** 1977

1947 1948 1949 1967 1980 1981

NAKBA
Mass expulsion of Palestinians, including from West Jerusalem and surrounding villages.

UNGA RES. 181
States that Jerusalem should be "established as a corpus separatum" & "administered by the United Nations" - US is a signatory.

4TH GENEVA CONVENTION
Prohibits countries from moving populations into territories occupied in war - US is a signatory.

ANNEXATION
Israel's illegal annexation of East Jerusalem.

UNGA RES. 2253
States that all Israeli activities in East Jerusalem are illegal and should cease.

BASIC LAW
Israel passes new 'b claiming the whole Jerusalem as its ca

UNSC RES. 47
States that Israel's law" on Jerusalem violates internation Calls upon all states withdraw diplomati missions from Jeru

VISUALIZING**PALESTINE**

L LAW

DID NOT RECOGNIZE JERUSALEM AS ISRAEL'S CAPITAL
& did not move embassy to Jerusalem

RECOGNIZES JERUSALEM AS ISRAEL'S CAPITAL
& pledges to move embassy to Jerusalem

"It is unwise for the United States to take actions that could be interpreted as prejudicing sensitive matters, such as Jerusalem."

"Moving the embassy [...] would deepen the Israeli Palestinian crisis."

"I have determined that it is time to officially recognize Jerusalem as the capital of Israel"

AN HW BUSH CLINTON W BUSH OBAMA TRUMP

1993 1995 2001 2009 2016 2017

JERUSALEM EMBASSY ACT
Mandates for US Embassy in Israel to be moved to Jerusalem. President forced to sign a waiver every 6 months to prevent move.

UNSC RES. 2334
Reaffirms that Israel's settlement activity in East Jerusalem is illegal under international law.

As of 2017, over 200,000 Israeli settlers live in occupied East Jerusalem.

SOURCES bit.ly/vp-jerusalem-embassy
WWW.**VISUALIZINGPALESTINE**.ORG

@visualizingpal
/visualizing_palestine
fb.me/visualizingpalestine

DEC 2017

Year: 2017
Brief and copywriting: Ahmad Barclay, Robin Jones
Design: Yosra El Gazzar
Sources: bit.ly/vp-jerusalem-embassy

TRUMP VS. A GLOBAL CONSENSUS

In 1980, the UN Security Council passed a resolution calling upon all states to withdraw diplomatic missions from Jerusalem. There is a global consensus that hosting an embassy in Jerusalem legitimizes Israel's illegal annexation of territory in the city.

Today, no country in the world maintains an embassy in Jerusalem. In flagrant contravention of international law, Donald Trump announced that the US would recognize Jerusalem as the capital of Israel and pledged to move the US embassy there.

UNITED STATES

191
COUNTRIES
DO NOT HAVE EMBASSIES IN
JERUSALEM

1
COUNTRY
DECLARES THAT IT WILL MOVE ITS EMBASSY THERE

VISUALIZING**PALESTINE** SOURCES bit.ly/vp-jerusalem-embassy-2 WWW.**VISUALIZINGPALESTINE**.ORG
@visualizingpal
/visualizing_palestine
fb.me/visualizingpalestine
DEC 2017

Year: 2017 | **Brief and copywriting:** Ahmad Barclay, Robin Jones | **Design:** Yosra El Gazzar, Ahmad Barclay | **Sources:** bit.ly/vp-jerusalem-embassy-2

US MILITARY AID TO ISRAEL

INCREASING THE BILL TO US TAXPAYERS

On 14 September 2016, the Obama administration signed an agreement to increase foreign military financing to Israel by 27%.

Yet the US already gives more military aid to Israel than all other countries combined.

From 2019, US taxpayers will be giving $3.8 billion per year to Israel.

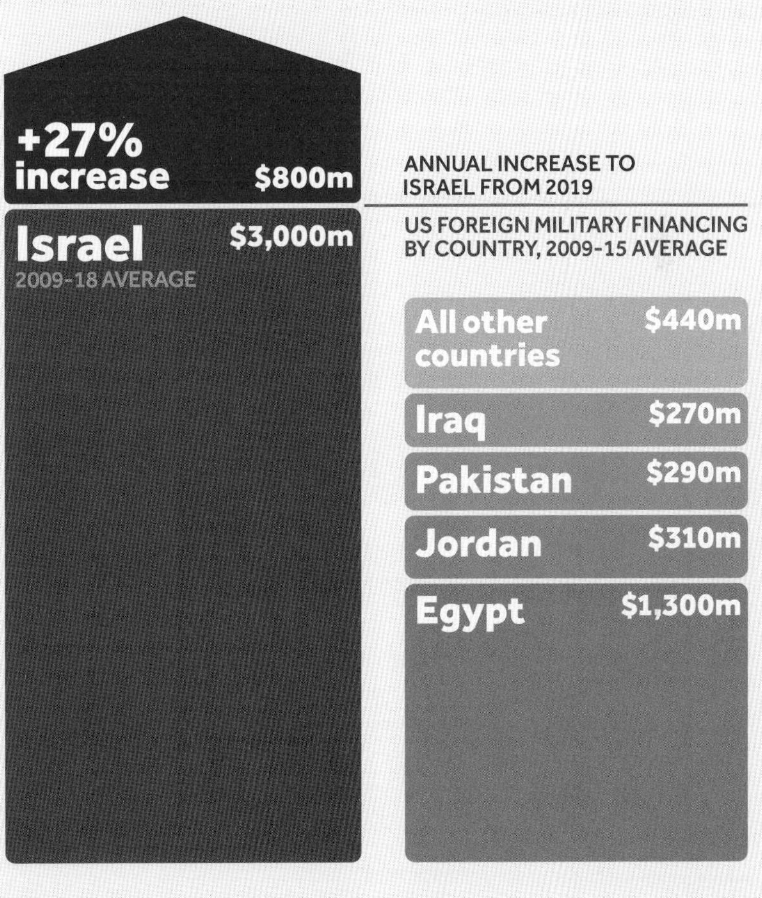
+27% increase
$800m
ANNUAL INCREASE TO ISRAEL FROM 2019
Israel
2009-18 AVERAGE
$3,000m
US FOREIGN MILITARY FINANCING BY COUNTRY, 2009-15 AVERAGE
All other countries
$440m
Iraq
$270m
Pakistan
$290m
Jordan
$310m
Egypt
$1,300m

fb.me/visualizingpalestine • @visualizingpal

DATA SKETCH

SOURCES bit.ly/4aOWgsw| bit.ly/wh-mou **SEP** 2016

Year: 2016 | **Brief and copywriting:** Reem Farah, Nusayba Hammad, Ramzi Jaber, Hasna Sami | **Design:** Ahmad Barclay, Zeina Jaber | **Sources:** bit.ly/4aOWgsw, bit.ly/wh-mou

40,000+

AFFORDABLE HOMES NEEDED FOR WORKING FAMILIES AROUND DC

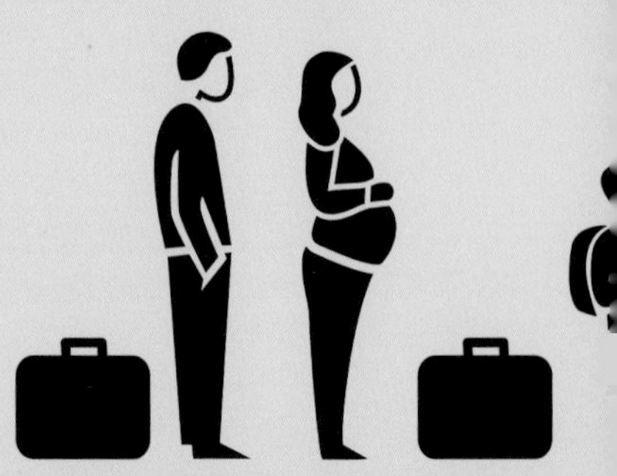

25,000+

PALESTINIAN HOMES DEMOLISHED FROM 1967 TO 2012

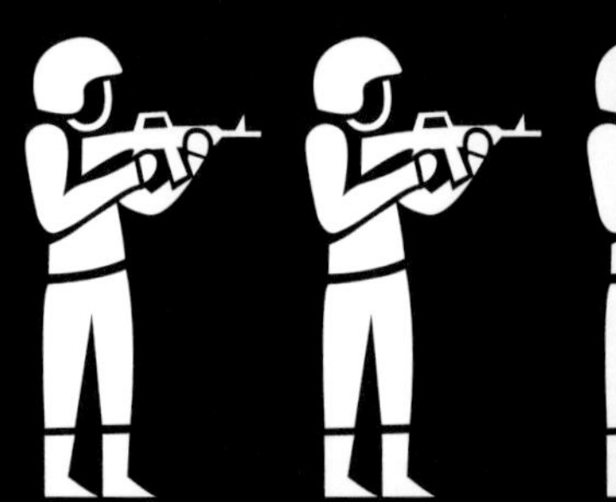

WEAPONS TO ISRAEL COME AT A PRICE

END $30 BILLION OF MIL

END THE
OCCUPATION
US CAMPAIGN TO END THE ISRAELI OCCUPATION

VISUALIZING**PALESTINE**

(1) $30billion total federal Foreign Military Financing to Israel, 2009-2018. bit.ly/
(2) Affordable housing shortage reported by Urban Land Institute, 2009. bit.ly/p
(3) Homes destroyed estimated by Israeli Committee Against House Demolition

ARY AID TO ISRAEL
find out more at **aidtoisrael.org**
This is a paid advertisement sponsored by the US Campaign to End the Israeli Occupation and Visualizing Palestine.
The advertising space is a designated public forum and does not imply WMATA's endorsement of any views expressed.
This design is published under a Creative Commons BY-NC-ND 3.0 license.

Year: 2013
Brief and copywriting: Joumana al Jabri, Ahmad Barclay, Christopher Fiorello, Nusayba Hammad, Ramzi Jaber
Design: Naji El Mir, Polypod
Sources: bit.ly/vp-Sources-2012-2015

INVEST IN OUR FUTURE

$30 billion could train nearly 5 million unemployed Americans for green jo

NOT IN ISRAEL'S OCCUPATI

Instead we're arming Israel with $30 billion of weapons over a decade

WEAPONS TO ISRAEL COME AT A PRICE

END $30 BILLION OF MI

END THE
OCCUPATION
US CAMPAIGN TO END THE ISRAELI OCCUPATION

VISUALIZING**PALESTINE**

(1) $30billion total federal Foreign Military Financing to Israel, 2009-2018. bit.ly/aid-me
(2) Jobs training estimated from budget for Green Jobs Innovation Fund, Dept. of Labor,
(3) Israeli weapons count based on data from Federation of American Scientists, 2011. bi

ARY AID TO ISRAEL

find out more at **aidtoisrael.org**

training

This is a paid advertisement sponsored by the US Campaign to End the Israeli Occupation and Visualizing Palestine.
The advertising space is a designated public forum and does not imply WMATA's endorsement of any views expressed.
This design is published under a Creative Commons BY-NC-ND 3.0 license.

Year: 2013
Brief and copywriting: Joumana al Jabri, Ahmad Barclay, Christopher Fiorello, Nusayba Hammad, Ramzi Jaber
Design: Naji El Mir, Polypod
Sources: bit.ly/vp-Sources-2012-2015

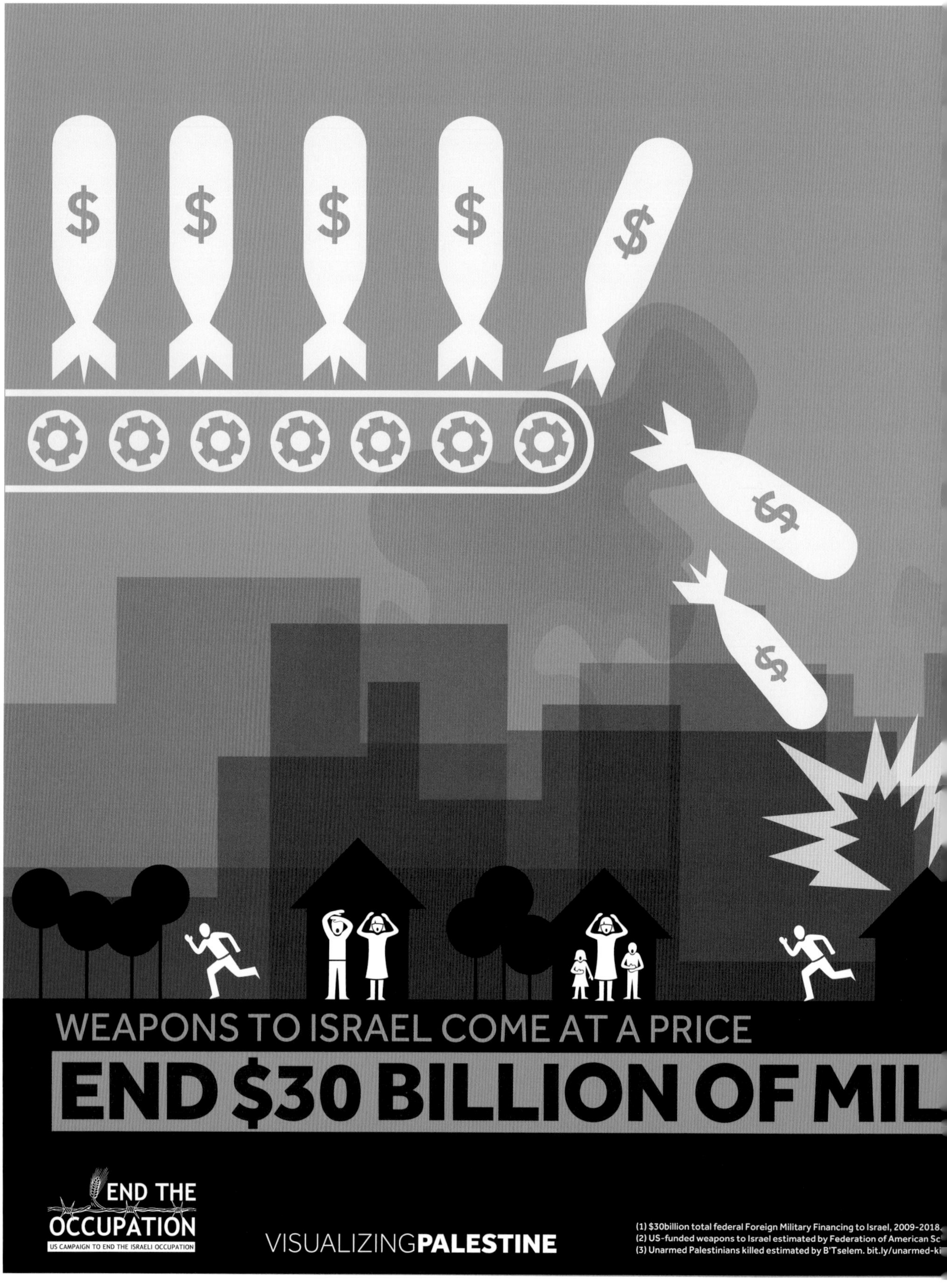

WEAPONS TO ISRAEL COME AT A PRICE

END $30 BILLION OF MIL

END THE OCCUPATION
US CAMPAIGN TO END THE ISRAELI OCCUPATION

VISUALIZING**PALESTINE**

(1) $30billion total federal Foreign Military Financing to Israel, 2009-2018.
(2) US-funded weapons to Israel estimated by Federation of American Sc
(3) Unarmed Palestinians killed estimated by B'Tselem. bit.ly/unarmed-ki

U.S. TAXPAYERS FUNDED 670 MILLION WEAPONS FOR ISRAEL
between 2000 and 2009

During these years
THE ISRAELI MILITARY KILLED AT LEAST 2,960 UNARMED PALESTINIANS

ARY AID TO ISRAEL

find out more at **aidtoisrael.org**

ndum
pons-data

This is a paid advertisement sponsored by the US Campaign to End the Israeli Occupation and Visualizing Palestine.
The advertising space is a designated public forum and does not imply WMATA's endorsement of any views expressed.
This design is published under a Creative Commons BY-NC-ND 3.0 license.

Year: 2013
Brief and copywriting: Joumana al Jabri, Ahmad Barclay, Christopher Fiorello, Nusayba Hammad, Ramzi Jaber
Design: Naji El Mir, Polypod
Sources: bit.ly/vp-Sources-2012-2015

DONATING TO DISPOS

HOW U.S. CHARITIES FUND ISRA

CENTRAL FUND OF ISRAEL (CFI)

The Central Fund of Israel is a New York-registered non-profit charity that funds Israeli settlement activity.

These are examples of the human rights abuses some of its grantees carry out in occupied Palestinian territory.

CFI GRANTEES

IN THEIR OWN WO

" Redeeming land " in Pale areas to create a **"greater Jewish presence"**
- Ateret Cohanim

Supporting agricultural pro to **"meet the critical daily of these Zionist pioneers**
- Efrat Development Founda

Upgrading settlement sec apparatus and roads **"to facilitate further constru**
- Efrat Development Founda

Marketing real estate as **" ideology property "** for buyers exclusively
- Israel Land Fund

Advocating with Israeli auth to **" drive the battle for Is sovereignty "** in Occupied Palestinian Territory
- Regavim

VISUALIZING**PALESTINE**

NOT ON OUR DIME

ESSION
LI SETTLEMENTS

ILLEGAL SETTLEMENT ACTIVITY
OCCUPIED PALESTINIAN TERRITORY

n

Expelling Palestinians

ds

Establishing Settlements

"

Expanding Settlement Infrastructure

n

Moving Settlers In

s

Legitimizing Illegal Settlements

SOURCES bit.ly/vp-cfi
WWW.**VISUALIZINGPALESTINE**.ORG

@visualizingpal
/visualizing_palestine
fb.me/visualizingpalestine

MAY 2023

Year: 2023
Brief and copywriting: Jessica Anderson, Center for Constitutional Rights, Daleen Saah
Design: Daleen Saah, Nasreen Abd Elal
Sources: bit.ly/vp-cfi

"HOUSE BY HOUSE, LO

THE ISRAELI SETTLEMENT ENT

Sheikh Jarrah is a neighborhood in occupied East Jerusalem where 72 Palestinian refugee families are resisting an Israeli system designed to forcibly displace them from their homes.

שייח' ג'ראח
الشيخ جراح
Sheikh Jarrah

DISCRIMI

ISRAELI MILITARY/POLICE

APARTHEID COURTS

SETT

ILLEGAL ISRA SETTLEMENT

THREATENED PALESTINIAN

CONSTRUCT

ISRAELI MILITARY & POLICE FORCES

Israeli police enforce displacement, provide security to settlers, and suppress Palestinian protest.

APARTHEID COURTS

Israeli courts use discriminatory laws to rule in favor of settlement organizations.

VISUALIZING**PALESTINE**

NOT ON OUR DIME

BY LOT"

PRISE IN SHEIKH JARRAH

ORY LAWS

ISRAELI POLITICIANS

MENT ORGANIZATIONS

LAN

DISCRIMINATORY LAWS

Legal & Administrative Matters Law (1970): Israel allows Jewish groups to pursue pre-1948 property claims, but not Palestinians.

ISRAELI POLITICIANS

Aryeh King, Deputy Mayor of Jerusalem, also founded the Israel Land Fund.

In 2009, the Ghawi family was forcibly displaced from their home in Sheikh Jarrah (pictured)

SETTLEMENT ORGANIZATIONS

The Israel Land Fund markets "ideology property" on its website for Jews only, and files lawsuits to forcibly turn over Palestinian homes to Israeli settlers.

SOURCES bit.ly/vp-cfi
WWW.**VISUALIZINGPALESTINE**.ORG

@visualizingpal
/visualizing_palestine
fb.me/visualizingpalestine

MAY 2023

Year: 2023
Brief and copywriting: Jessica Anderson, Center for Constitutional Rights, Daleen Saah, Elizabeth Eggert
Design: Daleen Saah
Photos: Oren Ziv (Activestills), Maria Zreik (Activestills)
Sources: bit.ly/vp-cfi

IN THE FIRING ZONE

THE ISRAELI SETTLEMENT ENT

Masafer Yatta is an area comprising more than a dozen Palestinian villages in the Israeli-occupied West Bank. Residents of these villages have been resisting mass displacement since the Israeli military declared their homes to be part of Firing Zone 918 in the 1980s and ordered them to leave.

Israeli military drill in Masafer Yatta, 2021

DISCRIMINA
ISRAELI MILITARY/POLICE
APARTHEID COURTS
SET
FIRING ZONE 9
APARTHEID WA
(PLANNED ROU
PALESTINIAN L
ISRAELI SETTL

ISRAELI MILITARY & POLICE FORCES

Israeli forces carry out demolition orders, ensure impunity for settler violence, and suppress Palestinian protest.

APARTHEID COURTS

In 2022, the Israeli Supreme Court approved the mass displacement of Palestinians from Masafer Yatta. One of the three justices on the case lives in an illegal Israeli settlement.

VISUALIZING**PALESTINE**

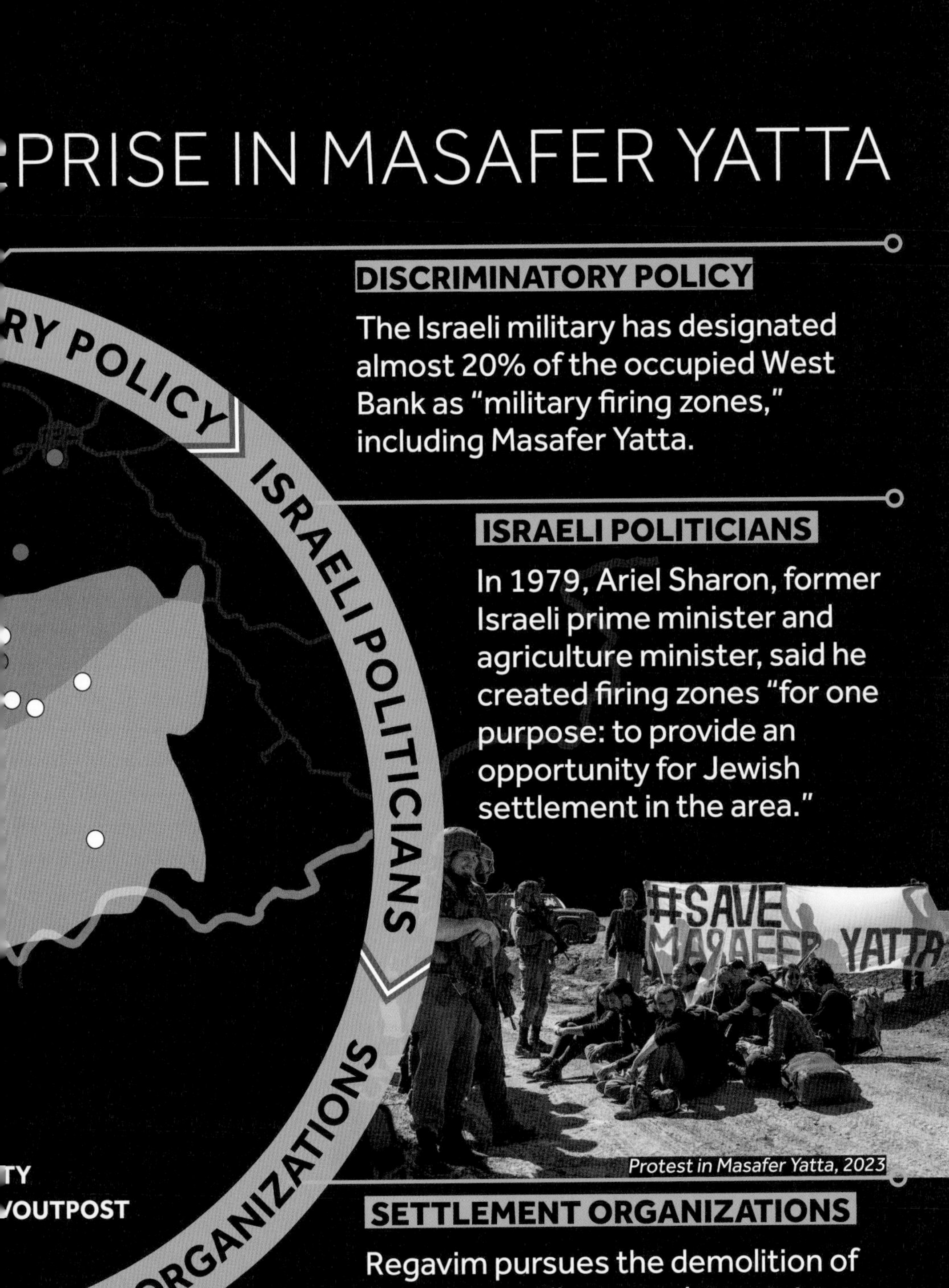

PRISE IN MASAFER YATTA
RY POLICY
ISRAELI POLITICIANS
MENT ORGANIZATIONS
DISCRIMINATORY POLICY
The Israeli military has designated almost 20% of the occupied West Bank as "military firing zones," including Masafer Yatta.
ISRAELI POLITICIANS
In 1979, Ariel Sharon, former Israeli prime minister and agriculture minister, said he created firing zones "for one purpose: to provide an opportunity for Jewish settlement in the area."
#SAVE MASAFER YATTA
Protest in Masafer Yatta, 2023
TY
OUTPOST
SETTLEMENT ORGANIZATIONS
Regavim pursues the demolition of Palestinian villages and property through Israeli courts and the military. HaShomer YOSH harasses Palestinian farmers and herders.
SOURCES bit.ly/vp-cfi
WWW.VISUALIZINGPALESTINE.ORG
@visualizingpal
/visualizing_palestine
fb.me/visualizingpalestine
MAY 2023

Year: 2023
Brief and copywriting: Jessica Anderson, Center for Constitutional Rights
Design: Daleen Saah
Photos: Keren Manor (Activestills), Heather Sharona Weiss (Activestills)
Sources: bit.ly/vp-cfi

NOT ON OUR DIME

END NEW YORK FUNDING OF IS

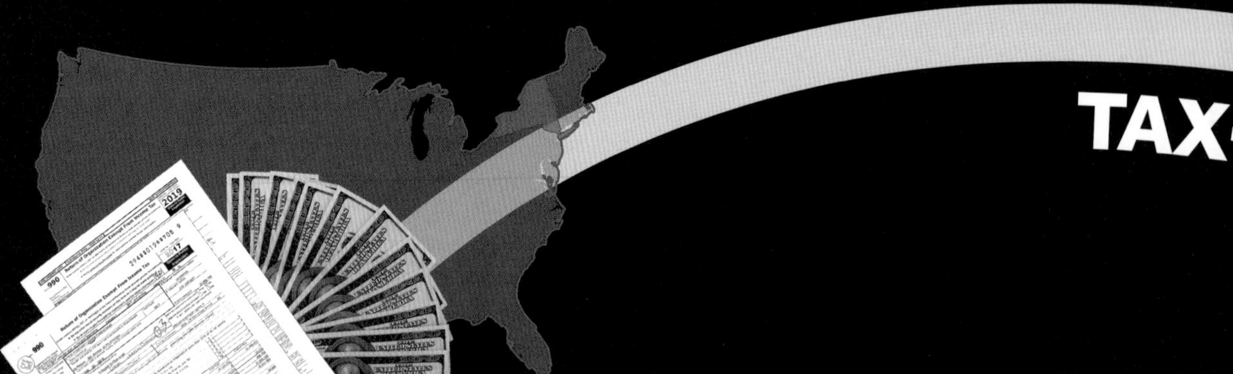
TAX-

NEW YORK SETTLEMENT FUNDERS

Organizations in New York State are funding the Israeli settlement enterprise in violation of international law. Masquerading as charities, these groups funnel hundreds of millions of dollars to war crimes while enjoying tax-breaks.

NEW YORK GOVERNME

Call on your New York State Re Not on Our Dime Act and end N violence

VISUALIZING**PALESTINE**

ELI SETTLER VIOLENCE

EE $$$
Sheikh Jarrah

HUMAN RIGHTS ABUSES

Israeli settlement organizations forcibly displace Palestinians and build illegal settlements within Occupied Palestinian Territory, in violation of international law.

TE
& IRS

esentatives to pass the
funding of Israeli settler

SOURCES bit.ly/vp-cfi
WWW.**VISUALIZINGPALESTINE**.ORG

@visualizingpal
/visualizing_palestine
fb.me/visualizingpalestine

MAY 2023

Year: 2023
Brief and copywriting: Jessica Anderson, Center for Constitutional Rights, Daleen Saah
Design: Daleen Saah
Photos: Oren Ziv (Activestills)
Sources: bit.ly/vp-cfi

ABOVE THE LAW?

UN SECURITY COUNCIL VETOES SINCE 1970

T
m
b
la
h
R
M
P

1970
1975
1980
1985
1990
1
VETOES BY YEAR

27%
42 U.S. vetoes for Israel

51%
79 total U.S. vetoes

VETOES BY COUNTRY

VP DATA SKETCH

SOURCES bit.ly/vp-vetoes **JUN 201**

ɔwer of veto allows permanent
ers of the UN Security Council to
·esolutions upholding international
d conventions. Since 1970, the US
ed its veto more than China, France,
/USSR and the UK combined.
.han half of US vetoes were to
·t Israel from accountability.

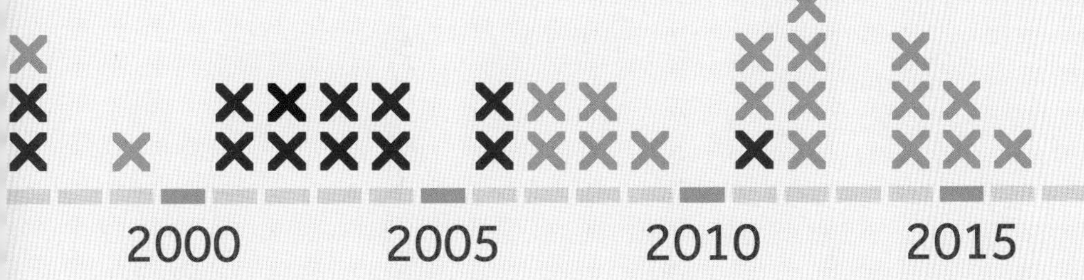
2000
2005
2010
2015

⁄o
tal vetoes by China,
e, Russia/USSR and UK

• f fb.me/visualizingpalestine
@visualizingpal • /visualizing_palestine

Year: 2017
Brief and copywriting: Ahmad Barclay, Livia Bergmeijer, Robin Jones
Design: Ahmad Barclay
Sources: bit.ly/vp-vetoes

THE RISE OF U.S. ANTI-BOYCOTT LEGISLATION

Th
fr
th
Bo
as
str
ag
ov
co

In 2014, both Democrat and Republican lawmakers began introducing **anti-boycott bills** to suppress **Palestinian rights activism**

In 2017, plaintiffs started suing their states, leading federal courts to strike down several anti-boycott laws as **unconstitutional**, but legislators keep revising and re-introducing them

In 2023, the U.S. Supreme Court **declined to review a challenge to a 2017 Arkansas anti-boycott law**, leaving it up to lower courts to decide whether or not to protect the right to boycott

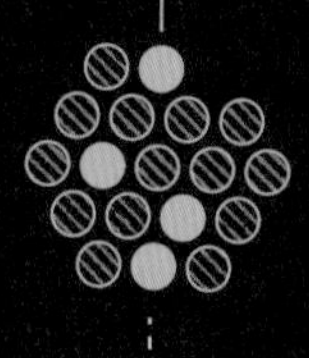
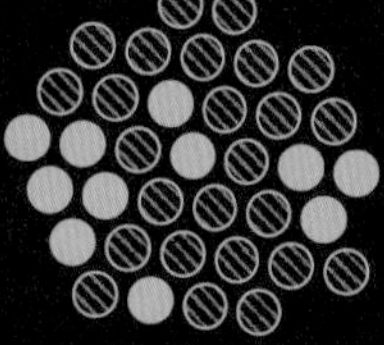
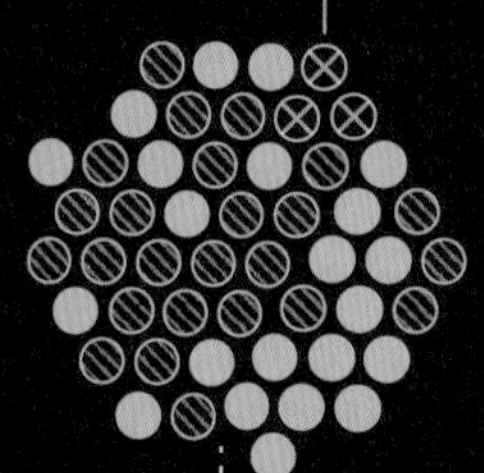
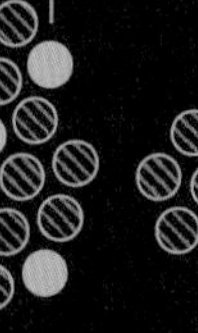
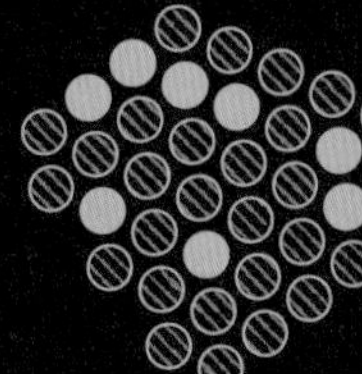

2014 **2015** **2016** **2017** **2018** **201**

Bills introduced per year

A TEMPLATE FOR REPRESSION

Texas's three anti-boycott laws share **almost identical language**

2019: TX SENATE BILL 793

"A governmental entity may not enter into a contract with a company [...] unless the contract contains a written verification from the company that it:

(1) does not **boycott Israel**

2021: TX SENATE BILL 13

"A governmental entity may not enter into a contract with a company [...] unless the contract contains a written verification from the company that it:

(1) does not **boycott energy companies**

2021: T

"A go may not contrac [...] unle contain. verificat compar

(1) doe **[discri a firear**

JUSTVISION PALESTINE LEGAL

VISUALIZING**PALESTINE**

he story of how a strategy designed to shield Israel countability paved the way for an all-out assault on t to boycott

are a time-honored tool of **political expression** in the U.S. In 2014, **t, Divestment, and Sanctions (BDS)** campaigns were growing in American lawmakers began introducing bills to **suppress boycotts** rael's regime of settler colonialism, military occupation, and apartheid alestinian people. In 2021, the same language started appearing in **egislation targeting other political protest movements.**

nwhile, el-focused boycott laws become nplate for cking other ements, such ycotts of **il fuels** and **rms industries**

Legislators have also **broadened attacks** on activism with bills to block public investments from considering **ESG (environmental, social, governance)** standards

In 2023, legislators introduced the **"Eliminate Economic Boycotts Act,"** a model bill drafted by a corporate lobbying group, to **expand the legislative assault** on trans rights, abortion access, and labor rights

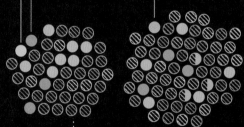

2020 2021 2022 2023 (JAN-MAR)

E BILL 19
al entity
o a
mpany
tract
the
against

TARGETS OF ANTI-BOYCOTT LEGISLATION

- Israel boycott (BDS)
- Fossil fuel boycott
- Gun lobby boycott
- Multiple types of boycotts and/or sustainable investment

STATUS OF LEGISLATION as of 2023

- In Effect
- Pending
- Dead
- Struck Down in Court

Timeline depicts bills by year of introduction, and the current status of each bill

SOURCES bit.ly/vp-boycott-laws
WWW.**VISUALIZINGPALESTINE**.ORG

@visualizingpal
/visualizing_palestine
fb.me/visualizingpalestine

APR 2023

Year: 2023
Brief and copywriting: Nasreen Abd Elal, Sarah Al-Yahya, Jessica Anderson, Guy Yadin Evron, Daniel Nerenberg, Meera Shah, Kate Schwartz
Design: Nasreen Abd Elal, Yosra El Gazzar
Sources: bit.ly/vp-boycott-laws

10.

CORPORA

COMPLIC

Visuals in this section: Airbnb Benefits from Israeli Rights Abuses | Bed and Breakfast on Stolen Land | From Savings to Settlements | Warning: Contains Human Rights Violations | Turning War Crimes into Wine | Field-Tested on Palestinians | Hope/Destruction | Watched | Light Rail, Heavy Losses

TE
ITY

> **Our struggle against death and suffering here in the Arizona borderlands is deeply implicated in the struggle against US-funded war and occupation in Palestine. . . . We continue to witness the same war-profiting industry that makes the assault on Gaza possible also contributing to the militarization of our communities in the US-Mexico borderlands.**
>
> *—No Más Muertes (No More Deaths), "Statement on Gaza" (2014)*

> **We cannot look the other way, as the products we build are used to deny Palestinians their basic rights, force Palestinians out of their homes and attack Palestinians in the Gaza Strip.**
>
> *—Over 1,000 anonymous Amazon and Google workers, "We Are Google and Amazon Workers. We Condemn Project Nimbus" (2021)*

In 2020, the United Nations Human Rights Office published a list of 112 companies involved in business activities in illegal Israeli settlements.[1] The list was significant not for its practical content, which was narrow in scope and had no immediate legal implications, but for its symbolic content. It overcame four years of attempts by US and Israeli officials to suppress its publication, and it implicitly acknowledged the role of economic pressure as a tool of accountability in the case of Israeli apartheid, a tactic that the UN enthusiastically endorsed during the period of apartheid in South Africa.[2]

The connection between colonialism and global capitalism is on full display in Palestine. An American company (Hewlett Packard Enterprise) built the database for Israel's population registry, the system that enforces segregation at checkpoints.[3] A British private security company (G4S) operated Israeli prisons that hold Palestinians without charge or trial.[4] A German company (HeidelbergCement) pays the Israeli military and an illegal Israeli settlement for mining rights in a Palestinian stone quarry in the occupied West Bank.[5] These are just a few of hundreds of examples.

Targeting apartheid profiteers—whether they are multinational companies operating in Palestine or Israeli companies marketing products to the global market as "field-tested" on Palestinians—is a strategy that has animated numerous inspiring and successful forms of transnational solidarity. We have supported several of these efforts with visual resources.

Airbnb, Booking.com, Expedia, and Tripadvisor were among the companies listed in the UN database of complicit corporations. By offering vacation rentals located in illegal Israeli settlements, they bolster the settlement economy, which is heavily involved in tourism. In 2018, we published **Airbnb Benefits from Israeli Rights Abuses** and **Bed and Breakfast on Stolen Land** for a Human Rights Watch report on this issue.[6] Amid growing pressure from a coalition of human rights groups, Airbnb announced that it would ban rental listings in settlements,[7] but it reversed its decision a few months later to settle a lawsuit by Israeli settlers.[8]

Nine Israeli banks are among the UN-listed complicit companies for their central role in financing every stage of illegal settlement construction. **From Savings to Settlements** emphasizes that, at the time we created the visual, multiple major European pension funds held investments in Israeli banks. Several have since divested or adopted investment screens to avoid complicity in violations of international law and Palestinian human rights.[9]

One of the glaring omissions from the UN's list of complicit companies was Israeli Chemicals Ltd. (ICL), which pumps millions of cubic meters of water out of the northern basin of the Dead Sea, located in the occupied Palestinian territory, to mine its abundant minerals: potash, bromine, and magnesium.[10] Dead Sea minerals have made ICL one of the largest fertilizer companies in the world.[11] In **Warning: Contains Human Rights Violations**, we look at the connection between military occupation and the exploitation of mineral-rich territories.

In 2019, Mike Pompeo, US secretary of state under Donald Trump, visited Psagot Winery, an Israeli settlement winery founded on land stolen from Palestinians. At the same time, the United States changed its trade policy to mandate that goods produced in Israeli settlements must be deceptively labeled "made in Israel."[12] Psagot Winery is owned by a Florida-based family of billionaires, the

Falic family. Members of the Falic family have made at least $5.6 million in "charitable" contributions to various Israeli settlement organizations and have been major contributors to both Israeli Prime Minister Benjamin Netanyahu and to US politicians who support the policies of the Israeli government.[13] At the time that we published **Turning War Crimes into Wine**, a European citizens' initiative was pushing for a ban on the trade of settlement goods in the European Union; the Canadian government had just ruled that illegal settlement goods cannot be marked as products of Israel;[14] and Florida activists were calling for a boycott of Duty Free Americas, a Falic family company that sells Psagot wine at North American airports and border crossings.

Israeli companies are prominent among the world's border profiteers. **Field-Tested on Palestinians** explores how Israel's military occupation of Palestine functions as a laboratory for these companies to develop and test methods of extreme violence and control (see also The Pegasus Effect in chapter 8). These technologies are then deployed to militarize border zones elsewhere. For example, drones made by Elbit Systems, Israel's largest military company, can be found patrolling the Mediterranean waters of the European Union, where thousands of migrants have drowned trying to reach safe shores.[15] In **Watched**, we follow Elbit Systems to the US border zone in Arizona, where Elbit surveillance towers oversee the deaths of migrants in the Sonoran Desert, subject Tohono O'odham reservation to round-the-clock surveillance, and have been turned against protesters. **Hope/Destruction** depicts the ongoing collective action against Elbit Systems, part of a broader call to impose a military embargo on Israel.

Several major corporations, such as Veolia, Orange, and G4S, have fully or partially ended their operations in Israel following long-term, high-profile campaigns highlighting how these companies contribute to human rights abuses against Palestinians. **Light Rail, Heavy Losses** tells the story of how Veolia, a French multinational company, lost billions of dollars in contracts over the course of a global, multiyear campaign regarding the company's involvement in building the Jerusalem Light Rail, an Israeli infrastructure project to connect and entrench illegal settlements. Veolia announced plans to withdraw from the Israeli market in 2014 and followed through in 2015.[16]

The successes of economic activism are hard won, and their impact is more significant than the dollar value attached to them. The next chapter looks more deeply at how the Boycott, Divestment, and Sanctions movement has mobilized broad campaigns for Palestinian freedom, justice, and equality, in the context of a global analysis of oppression in which communities trace the links between their respective experiences of injustice.

AIRBNB BENEFITS FROM ISRAELI RIGHTS ABUSES

Airbnb profits from rentals in Israeli settlements in the occupied Palestinian West Bank. **These rentals are inherently discriminatory since Palestinian ID holders are effectively barred from entering settlements,** while Israelis and foreigners are welcomed.

Human Rights Watch and Kerem Navot found at least **139 Airbnb property listings** in 61 Israeli settlements - excluding in East Jerusalem- from March to July 2018, including in 7 outposts illegal even under Israeli law.

- Palestinian community
- Israeli settlement
- Israeli outpost
  International law considers all settlements illegal. Some are also illegal under Israeli law.

1 4 16 **Number of property listings**

WEST BANK
Jenin
Tulkarm
❝ Studio house in Samiria
Nablus
❝ Vacation on Mount Kida
Ramallah
Jericho
Jerusalem
❝ Boutique guesthouse
Bethlehem
❝ Rustic caravan in Gush Etzion
Hebron
GAZA
ISRAEL

VISUALIZING**PALESTINE**

HUMAN RIGHTS WATCH

@visualizingpal
/visualizing_palestine
fb.me/visualizingpalestine
SOURCES bit.ly/vp-airbnb
WWW.**VISUALIZINGPALESTINE**.ORG

NOV 2018

Year: 2018 | **Brief and copywriting:** Robin Jones, Omar Shakir | **Design:** Ahmad Barclay, Yosra El Gazzar | **Sources:** bit.ly/vp-airbnb

BED & BREAKFAST ON STOLEN LAND

HOW AIRBNB BENEFITS FROM ISRAELI RIGHTS ABUSES

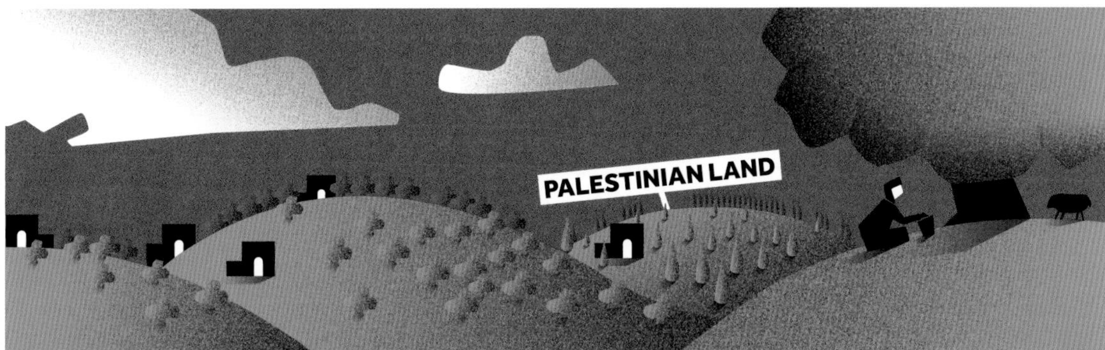
PALESTINIAN LAND

ISRAEL EXPROPRIATES PALESTINIAN LAND
Israel has seized more than 21% of the West Bank, excluding East Jerusalem, as 'state land'. It also enabled the takeover of thousands of hectares it acknowledges to be privately owned by Palestinians.

ISRAEL BUILDS ILLEGAL SETTLEMENTS
There are over 250 Israeli-only settlements in the West Bank including East Jerusalem, home to more than 628,000 settlers. All settlements are illegal under international law. Some are also illegal under Israeli law.

ISRAELI SETTLERS PROMOTE THEIR PROPERTIES ON AIRBNB
At least 139 Airbnb properties are listed in 61 Israeli settlements from March to July 2018, excluding in East Jerusalem. Airbnb does not disclose that these properties are located in settlements.

SETTLER PROPERTIES ARE LEASED TO EVERYONE EXCEPT PALESTINIANS
Palestinian ID holders are effectively barred from living in or visiting the settlements built on seized Palestinian land. Airbnb is facilitating rental of properties where hosts are mandated by law to discriminate against guests based on their national or ethnic origin.

AIRBNB CONTRIBUTES TO SERIOUS RIGHTS ABUSES
By doing business in settlements, on land unlawfully seized and under conditions of entrenched discrimination, Airbnb contributes to and benefits from serious violations of international law.

VISUALIZING**PALESTINE**

HUMAN
RIGHTS
WATCH

כרם נבות
KEREM NAVOT

@visualizingpal
/visualizing_palestine
fb.me/visualizingpalestine
SOURCES bit.ly/vp-airbnb
WWW.**VISUALIZINGPALESTINE**.ORG

NOV 2018

Year: 2018 | **Brief and copywriting:** Iman Annab, Robin Jones, Omar Shakir | **Design:** Yosra El Gazzar | **Sources:** bit.ly/vp-airbnb

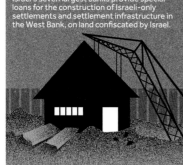

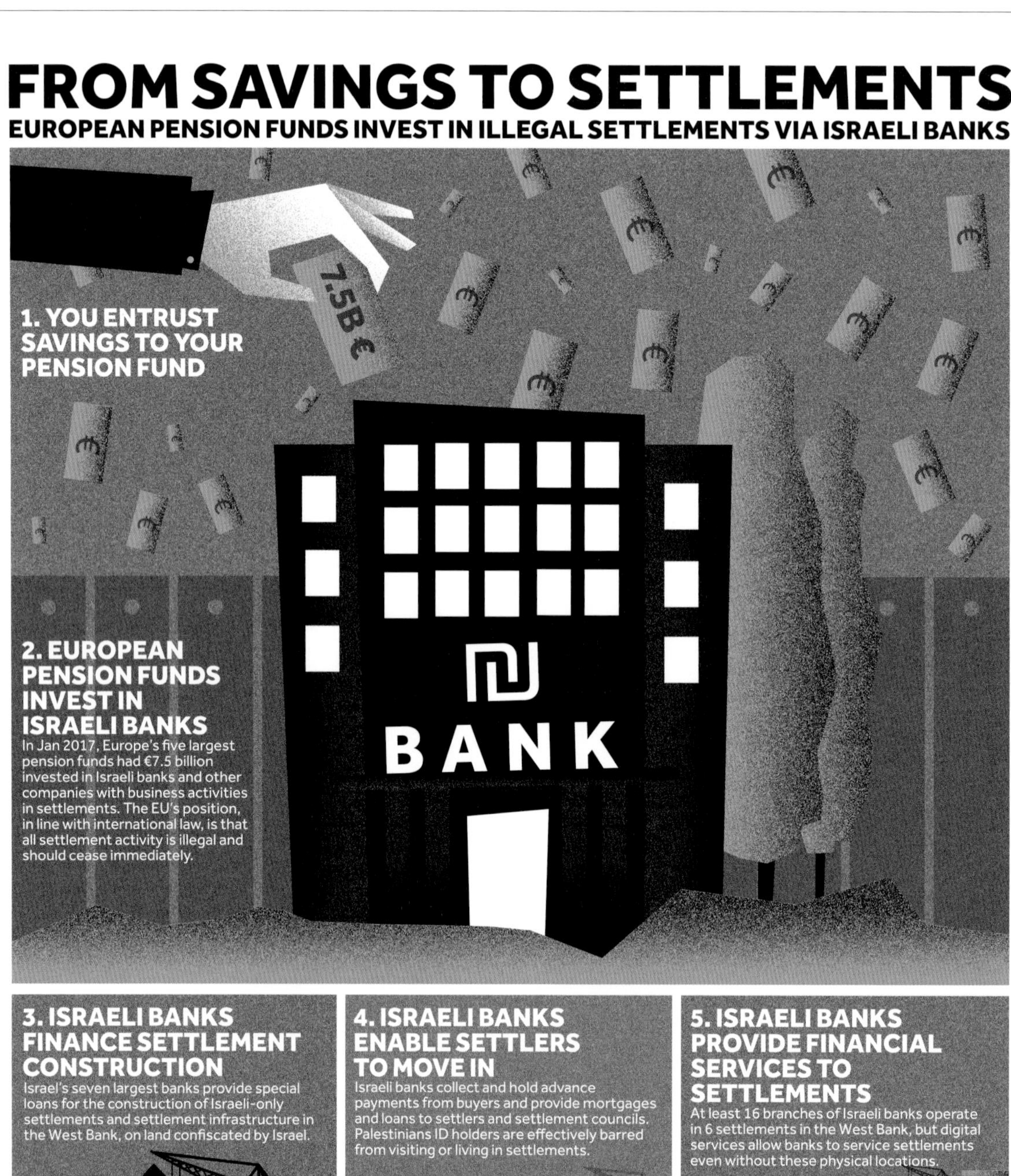
FROM SAVINGS TO SETTLEMENTS
EUROPEAN PENSION FUNDS INVEST IN ILLEGAL SETTLEMENTS VIA ISRAELI BANKS
7.5B €
1. YOU ENTRUST SAVINGS TO YOUR PENSION FUND
2. EUROPEAN PENSION FUNDS INVEST IN ISRAELI BANKS
In Jan 2017, Europe's five largest pension funds had €7.5 billion invested in Israeli banks and other companies with business activities in settlements. The EU's position, in line with international law, is that all settlement activity is illegal and should cease immediately.
BANK
3. ISRAELI BANKS FINANCE SETTLEMENT CONSTRUCTION
Israel's seven largest banks provide special loans for the construction of Israeli-only settlements and settlement infrastructure in the West Bank, on land confiscated by Israel.
4. ISRAELI BANKS ENABLE SETTLERS TO MOVE IN
Israeli banks collect and hold advance payments from buyers and provide mortgages and loans to settlers and settlement councils. Palestinians ID holders are effectively barred from visiting or living in settlements.
5. ISRAELI BANKS PROVIDE FINANCIAL SERVICES TO SETTLEMENTS
At least 16 branches of Israeli banks operate in 6 settlements in the West Bank, but digital services allow banks to service settlements even without these physical locations.
BANK
ISRAELI BANKS & THEIR INVESTORS BENEFIT FROM AND CONTRIBUTE TO GRAVE VIOLATIONS OF INTERNATIONAL LAW & PALESTINIAN HUMAN RIGHTS
VISUALIZINGPALESTINE
SOURCES bit.ly/vp-banks
WWW.VISUALIZINGPALESTINE.ORG
@visualizingpal
/visualizing_palestine
fb.me/visualizingpalestine
FEB 2020

Year: 2020 | **Brief and copywriting:** Jessica Anderson, Elizabeth Eggert | **Design:** Yosra El Gazzar | **Sources:** bit.ly/vp-banks

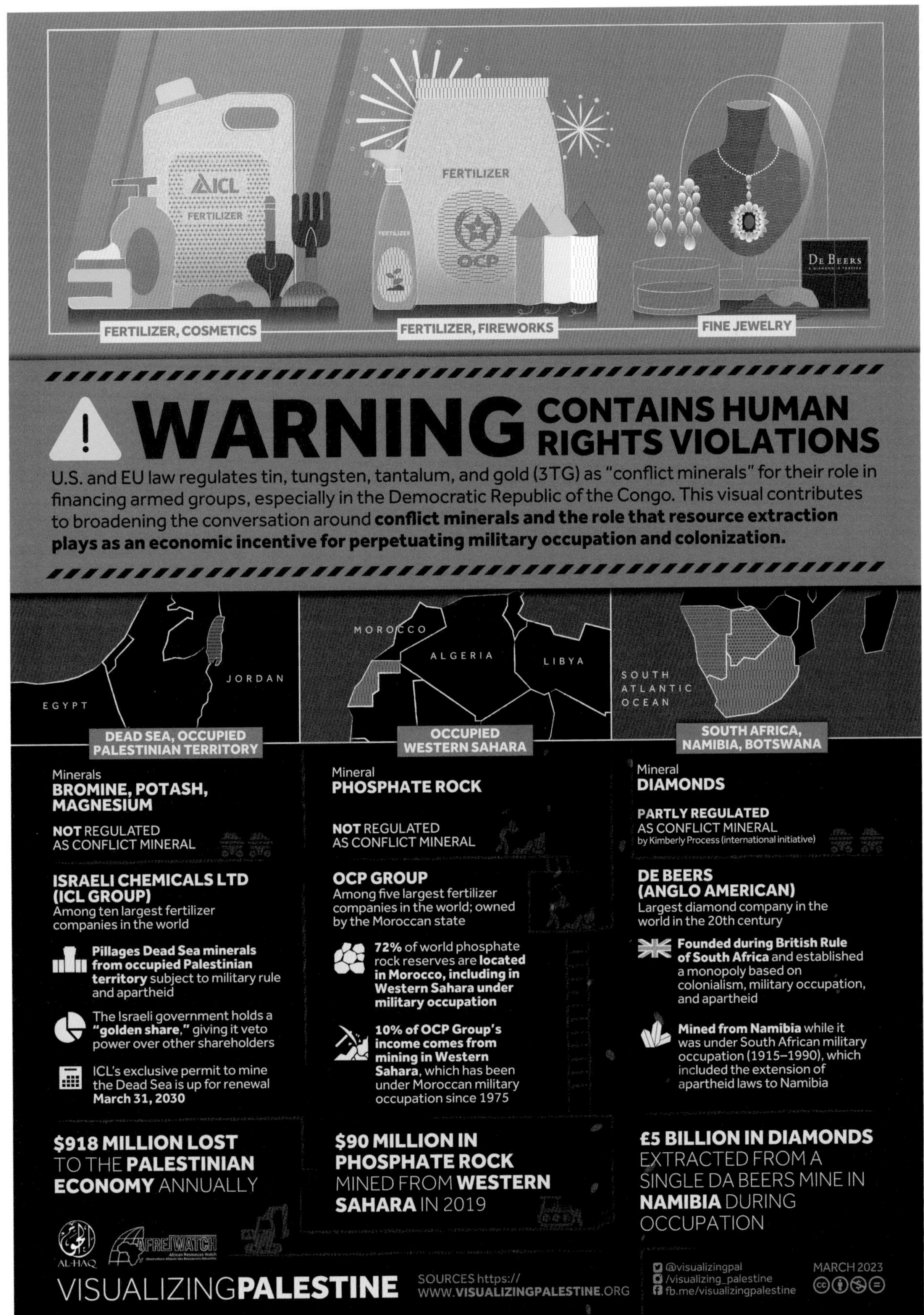

FERTILIZER, COSMETICS
FERTILIZER, FIREWORKS
FINE JEWELRY
WARNING CONTAINS HUMAN RIGHTS VIOLATIONS
U.S. and EU law regulates tin, tungsten, tantalum, and gold (3TG) as "conflict minerals" for their role in financing armed groups, especially in the Democratic Republic of the Congo. This visual contributes to broadening the conversation around conflict minerals and the role that resource extraction plays as an economic incentive for perpetuating military occupation and colonization.
EGYPT
JORDAN
MOROCCO
ALGERIA
LIBYA
SOUTH ATLANTIC OCEAN
DEAD SEA, OCCUPIED PALESTINIAN TERRITORY
OCCUPIED WESTERN SAHARA
SOUTH AFRICA, NAMIBIA, BOTSWANA
Minerals
BROMINE, POTASH, MAGNESIUM
NOT REGULATED AS CONFLICT MINERAL
ISRAELI CHEMICALS LTD (ICL GROUP)
Among ten largest fertilizer companies in the world
Pillages Dead Sea minerals from occupied Palestinian territory subject to military rule and apartheid
The Israeli government holds a "golden share," giving it veto power over other shareholders
ICL's exclusive permit to mine the Dead Sea is up for renewal March 31, 2030
$918 MILLION LOST TO THE PALESTINIAN ECONOMY ANNUALLY
Mineral
PHOSPHATE ROCK
NOT REGULATED AS CONFLICT MINERAL
OCP GROUP
Among five largest fertilizer companies in the world; owned by the Moroccan state
72% of world phosphate rock reserves are located in Morocco, including in Western Sahara under military occupation
10% of OCP Group's income comes from mining in Western Sahara, which has been under Moroccan military occupation since 1975
$90 MILLION IN PHOSPHATE ROCK MINED FROM WESTERN SAHARA IN 2019
Mineral
DIAMONDS
PARTLY REGULATED AS CONFLICT MINERAL
by Kimberly Process (international initiative)
DE BEERS (ANGLO AMERICAN)
Largest diamond company in the world in the 20th century
Founded during British Rule of South Africa and established a monopoly based on colonialism, military occupation, and apartheid
Mined from Namibia while it was under South African military occupation (1915–1990), which included the extension of apartheid laws to Namibia
£5 BILLION IN DIAMONDS EXTRACTED FROM A SINGLE DA BEERS MINE IN NAMIBIA DURING OCCUPATION
AL-HAQ
AFREWATCH
VISUALIZINGPALESTINE
SOURCES https:// WWW.VISUALIZINGPALESTINE.ORG
@visualizingpal
/visualizing_palestine
fb.me/visualizingpalestine
MARCH 2023

Year: 2023 | **Brief and copywriting:** Wesam Ahmad, Jessica Anderson | **Design:** Yara Ramadan, Yosra El Gazzar | **Sources:** bit.ly/vp-deadsea

THE CASE OF PSAGOT WINERY

Psagot Winery is one of 29 wineries operating in illegal Israeli settlements in the occupied West Bank. It was founded on 80 dunams of stolen Palestinian land in El Bireh, sources grapes from at least five other illegal settlement vineyards, and benefits from Israeli government subsidies. It offers a case study in the international incentive structure fueling the Israeli settlement enterprise, involving political contributions, non-transparent foreign investments and charitable donations, and trade policy.

THE WAR CRIMES

The Israeli settlement enterprise is associated with the following war crimes, defined by the Rome Statute of the International Criminal Court:

Transfer by an occupying power of parts of its own civilian population (Israeli settlers) into the territory it occupies

Forcible transfer of the population of the occupied territory (Palestinians) within or outside this territory

Pillage (theft) of Palestinian private property and natural resources

Extensive destruction and appropriation of property not justified by military necessity

UNITED STATES
TRADE POLICY
PRODUCT OF ISRAEL
DUTY FREE AMERICAS
70% OF
WINE IS
AND MA
DECEPT
LABELE
OF ISRA
FREE A
SHOPS
SALES
THE FALIC FAMILY
U.S. billionaire owners of
DUTY FREE AMERICAS,
chain of 180+ stores at
airports/borders
T
W
IN
NO TRANSPARENCY
IN 2007, THE FALICS INVESTED $1 M FOR 62% OWNERSHIP OF PSAGOT WINERY VIA A PANAMA SHELL COMPANY.
PSAGOT WINERY INC.
Falic family's shell company
based in Panama
PANAMA (TAX HAVEN)
CHARITABLE FU

JEWISH VOICE PEACE

AL-HAQ

VISUALIZINGPALESTINE

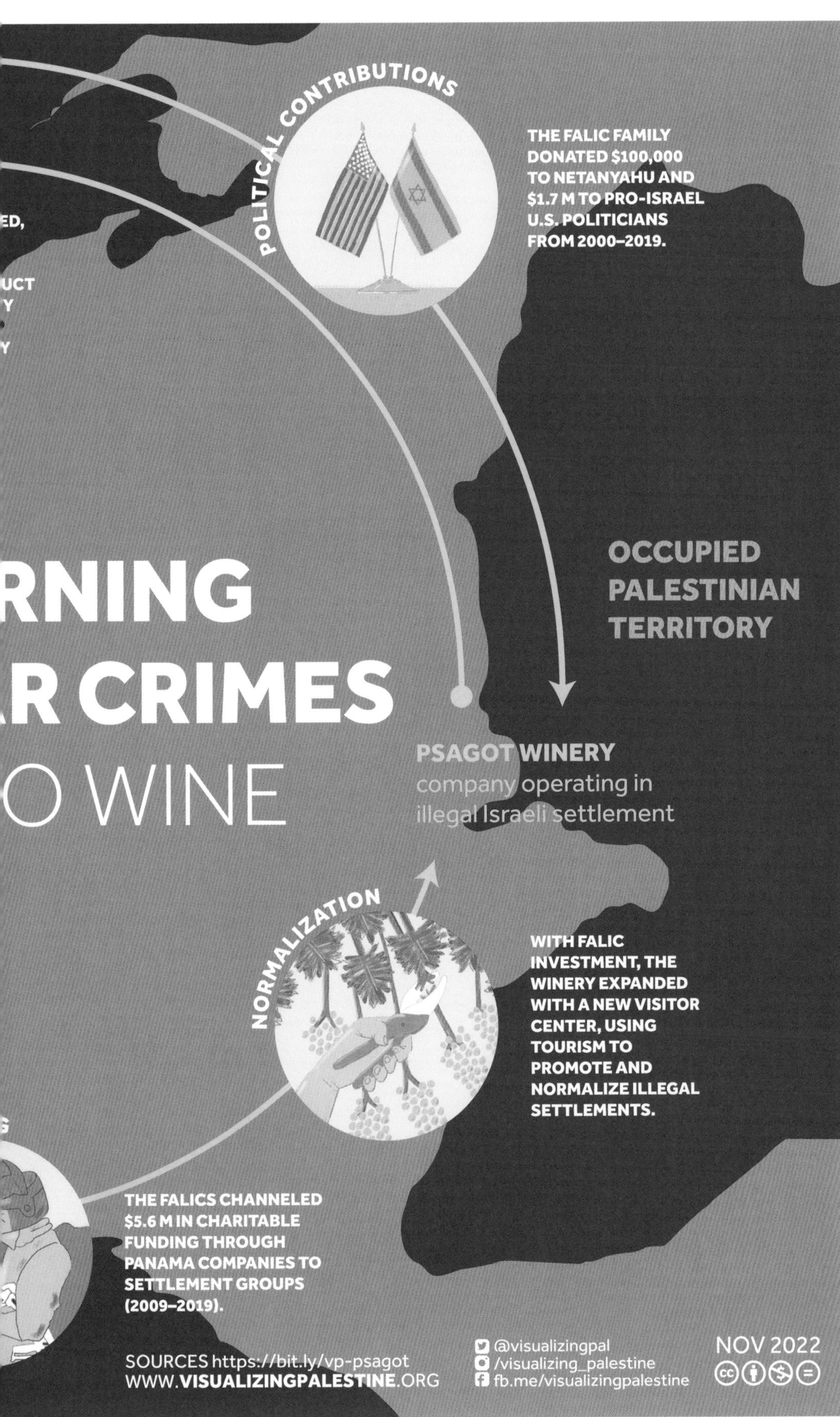
POLITICAL CONTRIBUTIONS
THE FALIC FAMILY DONATED $100,000 TO NETANYAHU AND $1.7 M TO PRO-ISRAEL U.S. POLITICIANS FROM 2000–2019.
RNING
R CRIMES
O WINE
OCCUPIED PALESTINIAN TERRITORY
PSAGOT WINERY
company operating in illegal Israeli settlement
NORMALIZATION
WITH FALIC INVESTMENT, THE WINERY EXPANDED WITH A NEW VISITOR CENTER, USING TOURISM TO PROMOTE AND NORMALIZE ILLEGAL SETTLEMENTS.
THE FALICS CHANNELED $5.6 M IN CHARITABLE FUNDING THROUGH PANAMA COMPANIES TO SETTLEMENT GROUPS (2009–2019).
SOURCES https://bit.ly/vp-psagot
WWW.VISUALIZINGPALESTINE.ORG
@visualizingpal
/visualizing_palestine
fb.me/visualizingpalestine
NOV 2022

Year: 2022
Brief and copywriting: Wesam Ahmad, Jessica Anderson
Design: Sara Sukhun
Sources: bit.ly/vp-psagot

ISRAEL'S LARGEST
ELBIT SYSTEMS
WEAPONS COMPANY

HERMES 900

FIELD-TESTED ON PALESTINIANS

The Hermes 900 is a lethal drone manufactured by Elbit Systems and first deployed during Israel's 2014 attack on the besieged Gaza Strip. Elbit supplies 85% of the drones used by the Israeli military for drone strikes and surveillance, resulting in grave human rights violations against Palestinians.

164
PALESTINIAN CHILDREN KILLED
by drone strikes during 2014 Israeli attack on the besieged Gaza Strip

20%
OF ELBIT'S 2018 PROFITS
came from supplying the Israeli military

FIELD-PROVEN
Elbit leverages its close relationship with the Israeli military to market its technology globally

VISUALIZING**PALESTINE** SOURCES bit.ly/vp-elbit WWW.**VISUALIZINGPALESTINE**.ORG

@visualizingpal
/visualizing_palestine
fb.me/visualizingpalestine

FEB 2020

Year: 2020 | **Brief and copywriting:** Jessica Anderson, Alys Samson Estapé, Stefanie Felsberger | **Design:** Yosra El Gazzar | **Sources:** bit.ly/vp-elbit

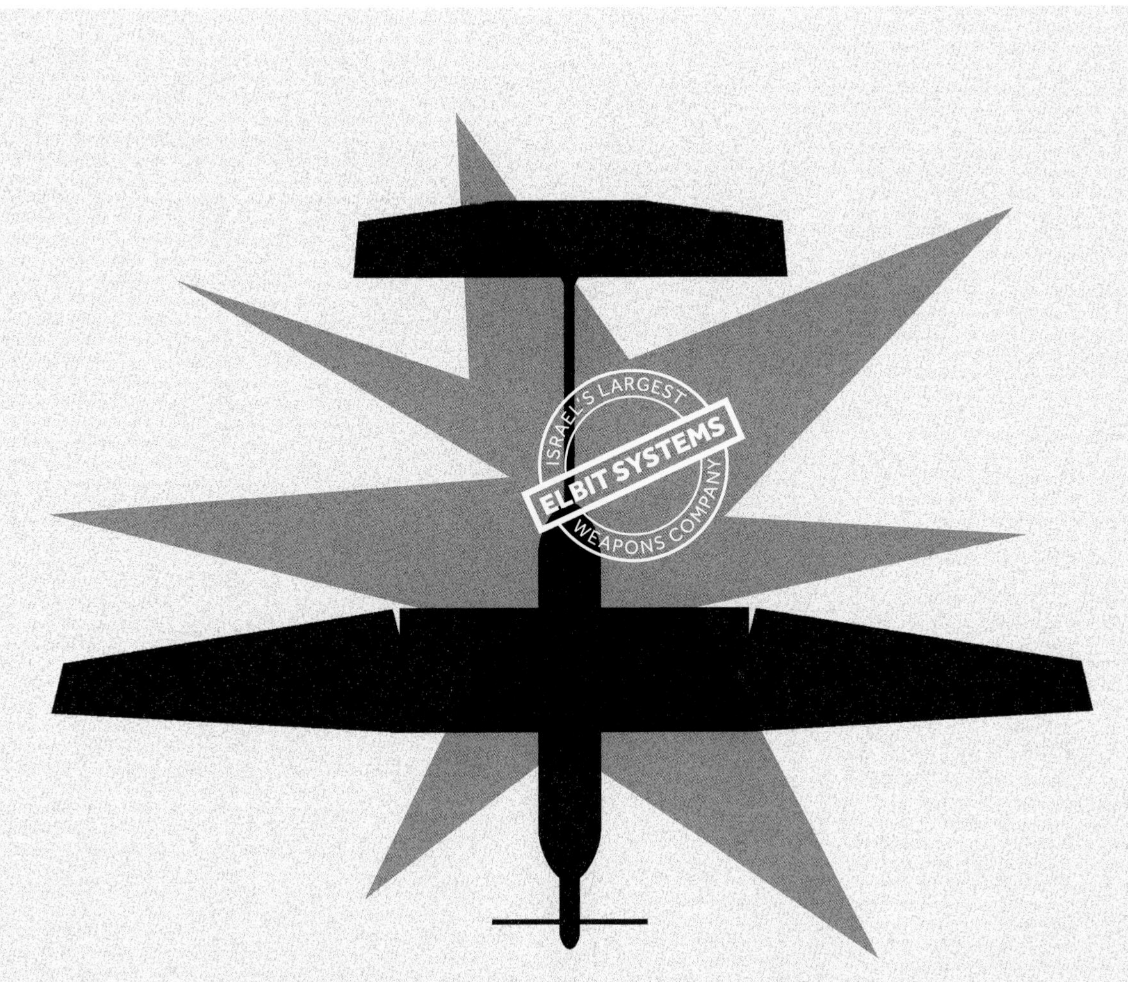
ISRAEL'S LARGEST
ELBIT SYSTEMS
WEAPONS COMPANY

SKYLARK SERIES

FIELD-TESTED ON PALESTINIANS

The Skylark is a miniature unmanned aerial vehicle used for surveillance and intelligence gathering, resulting in grave human rights violations against Palestinians. Elbit Systems supplies 85% of the drones used by the Israeli military.

350

PALESTINIANS ARRESTED
in Skylark-assisted Israeli night raids during 11-day period in the illegally occupied West Bank in 2014

20%

OF ELBIT'S 2018 PROFITS
came from supplying the Israeli military

14

GOVERNMENTS KNOWN TO HAVE PURCHASED ELBIT DRONES
Azerbaijan, Brazil, Chile, Colombia, the European Union, Georgia, India, Mexico, the Philippines, Singapore, Switzerland, Thailand, UK-NATO forces, U.S.

VISUALIZING**PALESTINE**

SOURCES bit.ly/vp-elbit
WWW.**VISUALIZINGPALESTINE**.ORG

@visualizingpal
/visualizing_palestine
fb.me/visualizingpalestine

FEB 2020

Year: 2020 | **Brief and copywriting:** Jessica Anderson, Alys Samson Estapé, Stefanie Felsberger | **Design:** Yosra El Gazzar | **Sources:** bit.ly/vp-elbit

ISRAEL'S LARGEST
ELBIT SYSTEMS
WEAPONS COMPANY

5.56MM BULLET
FIELD-TESTED ON PALESTINIANS

After acquiring Israeli state-owned IMI Systems in 2018, Elbit Systems became the exclusive supplier of small caliber ammunition to the Israeli military, police, and other forces. These munitions have been used to commit grave human rights violations against Palestinians.

6,106
PALESTINIANS STRUCK BY LIVE AMMUNITION
from Israeli sniper fire during Gaza Great March of Return protests in 2018—183 died

20%
OF ELBIT'S 2018 PROFITS
came from supplying the Israeli military

"LEADING LABORATORY FOR THE TESTING OF INFANTRY ASSAULT RIFLE WEAPON SYSTEMS & AMMUNITION"
IMI press release description of the Israeli military in 2018

VISUALIZINGPALESTINE

SOURCES bit.ly/vp-elbit
WWW.VISUALIZINGPALESTINE.ORG

@visualizingpal
/visualizing_palestine
fb.me/visualizingpalestine

FEB 2020

Year: 2020 | **Brief and copywriting:** Jessica Anderson, Alys Samson Estapé, Stefanie Felsberger | **Design:** Yosra El Gazzar | **Sources:** bit.ly/vp-elbit

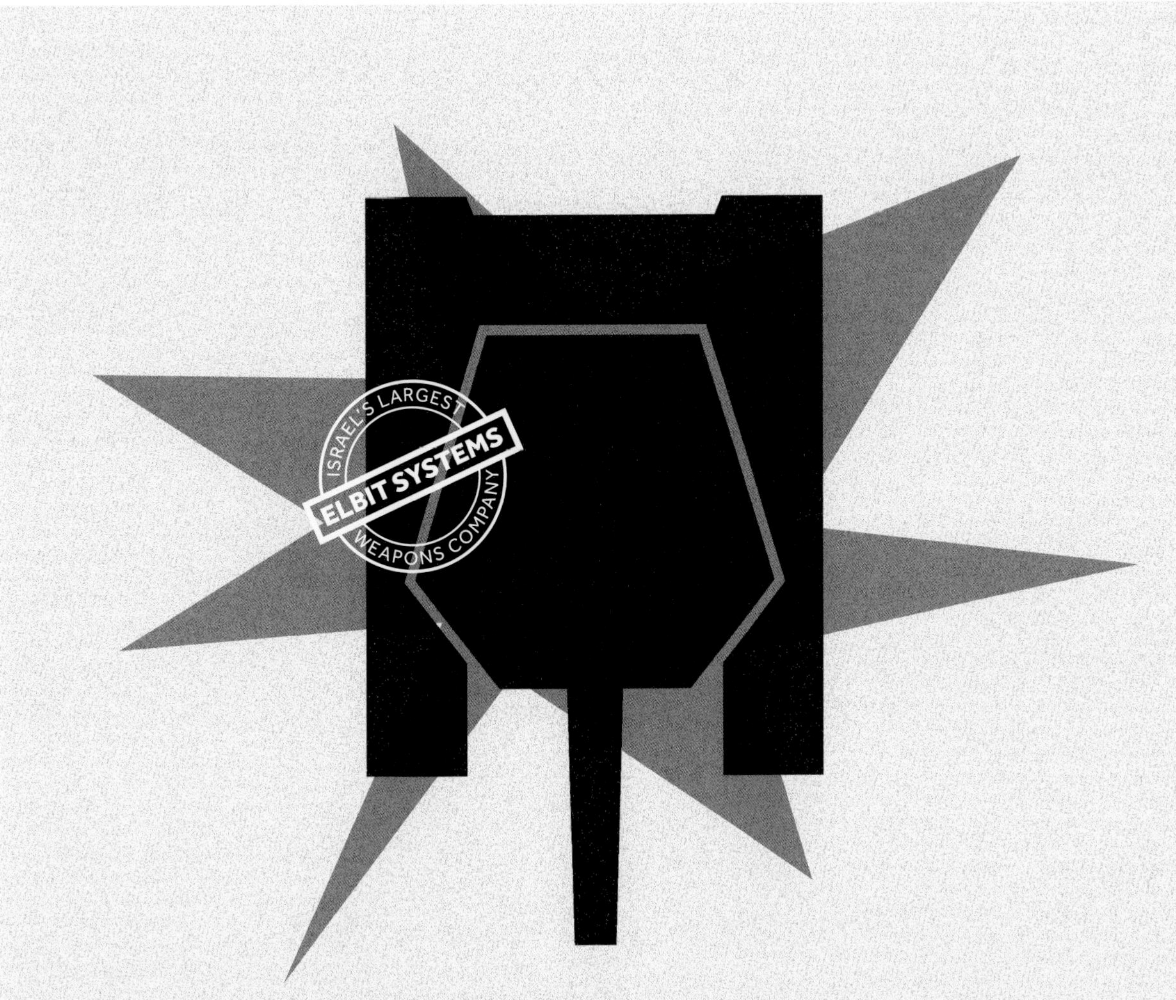
ISRAEL'S LARGEST
ELBIT SYSTEMS
WEAPONS COMPANY

MERKAVA TANK

FIELD-TESTED ON PALESTINIANS

Elbit Systems is responsible for outfitting Israel's tanks, attack aircraft, navy ships, and other weapons platforms. Israel has used these weapons in attacks on densely populated civilian areas, humanitarian delegations, medical facilities, farmers and fishers, and protests, leading to grave human rights violations against Palestinians.

81
CHILDREN KILLED
by Merkava tanks & artillery during 2014 Israeli attack on the besieged Gaza Strip

20%
OF ELBIT'S 2018 PROFITS
came from supplying the Israeli military

MYANMAR (BURMA) BOUGHT ISRAELI GUNBOATS
equipped with Elbit weapon systems during its 2017 genocidal campaign against the Rohingya community

VISUALIZING**PALESTINE**

SOURCES bit.ly/vp-elbit
WWW.**VISUALIZINGPALESTINE**.ORG

@visualizingpal
/visualizing_palestine
fb.me/visualizingpalestine

FEB 2020

Year: 2020 | **Brief and copywriting:** Jessica Anderson, Alys Samson Estapé, Stefanie Felsberger | **Design:** Yosra El Gazzar | **Sources:** bit.ly/vp-elbit

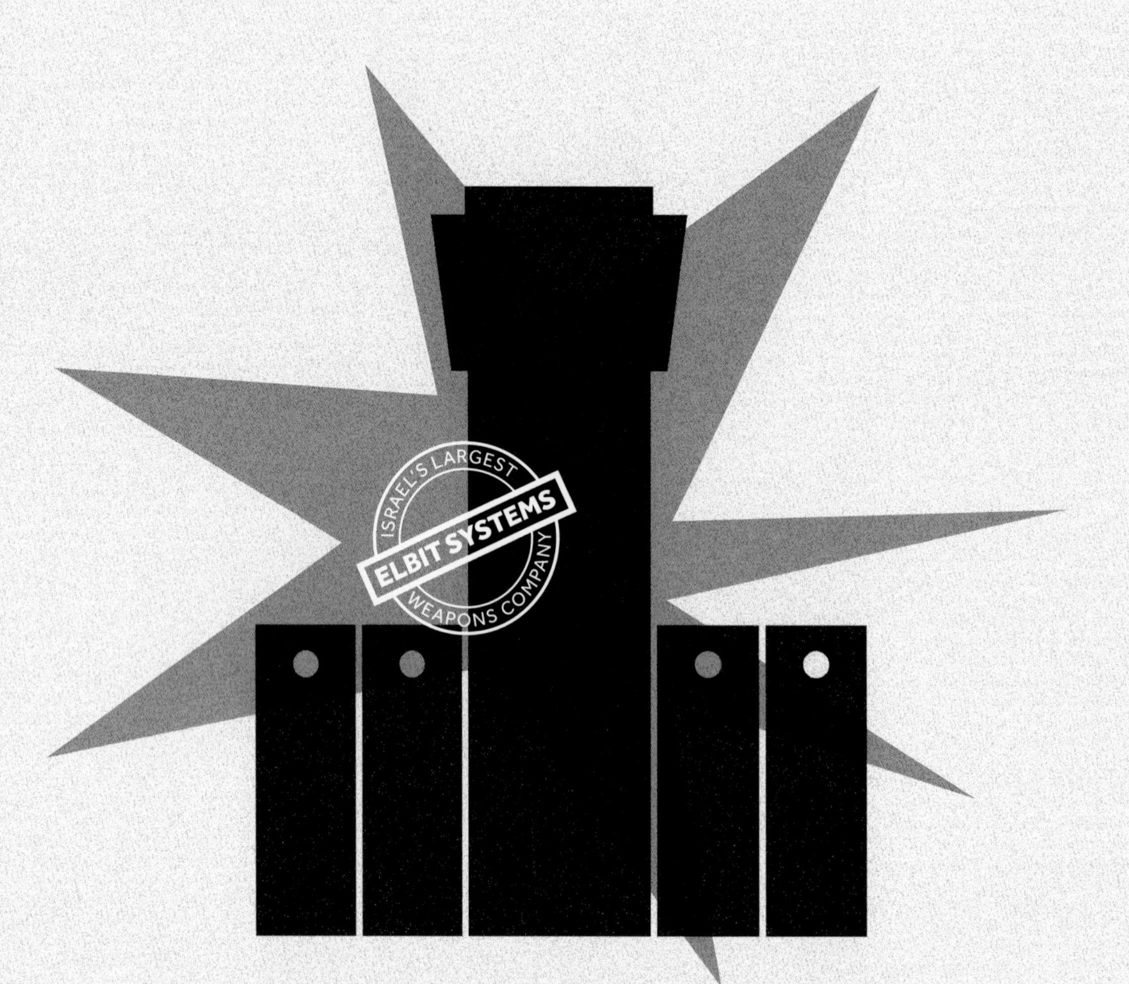
ISRAEL'S LARGEST
ELBIT SYSTEMS
WEAPONS COMPANY

BORDER SURVEILLANCE
FIELD-TESTED ON PALESTINIANS

Elbit Systems applies a web of surveillance technology to maintain Israel's system of spatial segregation and apartheid. Elbit surveillance systems are in place at Israel's illegal wall and military checkpoints in the West Bank, around besieged Gaza, in the illegally occupied Golan Heights, and at Ben Gurion airport.

$82m

COMBINED VALUE OF 3 ISRAELI CONTRACTS

Elbit and its subsidiaries received to install surve-illance systems in illegally occupied Jerusalem and the Golan Heights

$68m

VALUE OF THE EU CONTRACT

Elbit received in 2018 to monitor the Mediterranean coastline of "fortress Europe" against migrants

$171m

COMBINED VALUE OF 2 CONTRACTS ELBIT USA RECEIVED

in 2014 and 2019 to install a "virtual wall" of 24/7 survei-llance towers in the US border zone of Southern Arizona, including on Indigenous Tohono O'odham Nation land

VISUALIZINGPALESTINE SOURCES bit.ly/vp-elbit WWW.VISUALIZINGPALESTINE.ORG

@visualizingpal
/visualizing_palestine
fb.me/visualizingpalestine

FEB 2020

Year: 2020 | **Brief and copywriting:** Jessica Anderson, Alys Samson Estapé, Stefanie Felsberger | **Design:** Yosra El Gazzar | **Sources:** bit.ly/vp-elbit

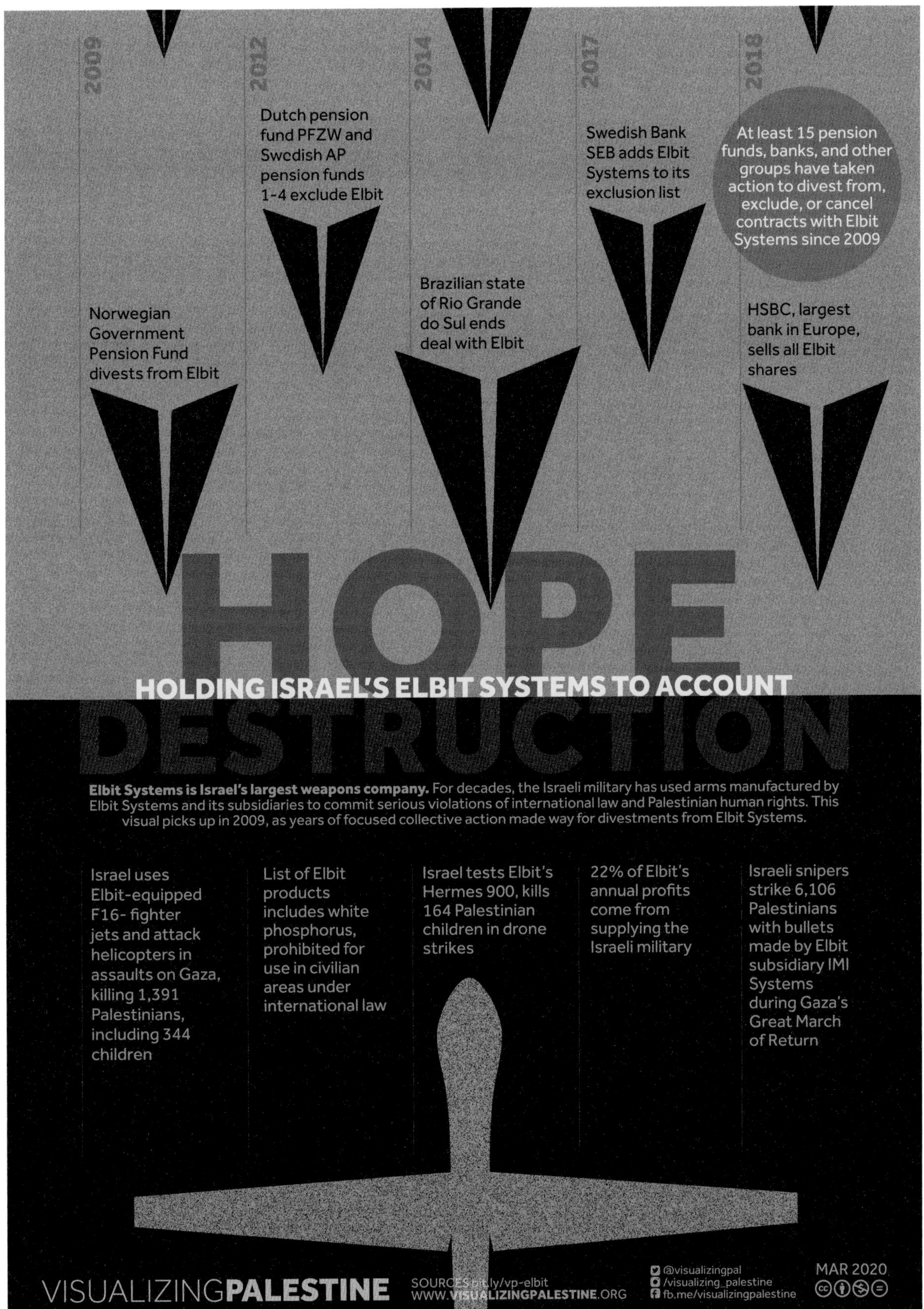
2009
2012
2014
2017
2018
Dutch pension fund PFZW and Swedish AP pension funds 1-4 exclude Elbit
Swedish Bank SEB adds Elbit Systems to its exclusion list
At least 15 pension funds, banks, and other groups have taken action to divest from, exclude, or cancel contracts with Elbit Systems since 2009
Brazilian state of Rio Grande do Sul ends deal with Elbit
Norwegian Government Pension Fund divests from Elbit
HSBC, largest bank in Europe, sells all Elbit shares
HOPE
HOLDING ISRAEL'S ELBIT SYSTEMS TO ACCOUNT
DESTRUCTION
Elbit Systems is Israel's largest weapons company. For decades, the Israeli military has used arms manufactured by Elbit Systems and its subsidiaries to commit serious violations of international law and Palestinian human rights. This visual picks up in 2009, as years of focused collective action made way for divestments from Elbit Systems.
Israel uses Elbit-equipped F16- fighter jets and attack helicopters in assaults on Gaza, killing 1,391 Palestinians, including 344 children
List of Elbit products includes white phosphorus, prohibited for use in civilian areas under international law
Israel tests Elbit's Hermes 900, kills 164 Palestinian children in drone strikes
22% of Elbit's annual profits come from supplying the Israeli military
Israeli snipers strike 6,106 Palestinians with bullets made by Elbit subsidiary IMI Systems during Gaza's Great March of Return
VISUALIZINGPALESTINE
SOURCES bit.ly/vp-elbit
WWW.VISUALIZINGPALESTINE.ORG
@visualizingpal
/visualizing_palestine
fb.me/visualizingpalestine
MAR 2020

Year: 2020 | **Brief and copywriting:** Jessica Anderson, Alys Samson Estapé, Stefanie Felsberger | **Design:** Yosra El Gazzar | **Sources:** bit.ly/vp-elbit

WATCHED

ISRAEL'S ELBIT SYSTEMS ON THE U.S. SOUTHERN BORDER

In Southern Arizona, since 2014, Israeli weapons giant Elbit Systems has installed a network of 53 surveillance towers up to 160 feet tall. These instruments of human control expand a layered system of U.S. border militarization made up of physical barriers, high-tech security, and armored patrols that lead to serious human rights violations.

KILLING MIGRANTS

3,186 recovered human remains in Arizona, 2000-2019. Most common cause of death: exposure

53 TOWERS in Southern Arizona

10 TOWERS on Tohono O'odham land

7/24 SURVEIL-LANCE

7.5 MI RADIUS CAMERA

13 MI RADIUS RADAR

VIOLATING INDIGENOUS TOHONO O'ODHAM & HIA CED O'ODHAM RIGHTS

Members and rights groups report restricted movement; disruption of cultural/religious practices; persistent surveillance; physical/verbal abuse by border agents

REPRESSING FREE EXPRESSION

Border surveillance tech appropriated to monitor "emerging threat of demonstrations" in San Diego and surveil protesters at Standing Rock

NO WALL

RECOGNIZE

Tohono O'odham Reservation

ARIZONA USA

Traditional Tohono O'odham lands

SONORA MEXICO

US/Mexico borderline
Border zone extends 100 miles into the US and as far south as Guatemala and Honduras

1,283 RECOVERED HUMAN REMAINS

of migrants found on Tohono O'odham Reservation, 2001-2019

• = one recovered human remain

• **Victoria** age: 20

• **David** age: 3

• **Jessica** age: 14

• **Jesus** age: 36

VISUALIZING**PALESTINE**

ARIZONA PALESTINE SOLIDARITY ALLIANCE

@visualizingpal
/visualizing_palestine
fb.me/visualizingpalestine
SOURCES bit.ly/vp-watched
WWW.**ARIZONAPALESTINE**.ORG
WWW.**VISUALIZINGPALESTINE**.ORG

MAR 2020

Year: 2020 | **Brief and copywriting:** Jessica Anderson, Gabbriel Schivone | **Design:** Yosra El Gazzar | **Photos:** Sarah Roberts, Laiken Jordahl, SLOWKING | **Sources:** bit.ly/vp-watched

LIGHT RAIL HEAVY LOSSES
HOW COLLECTIVE ACTION MADE APARTHEID UNPROFITABLE FOR VEOLIA
French multinational corporation Veolia had a stake in the Jerusalem Light Rail, a transit project built to service Israeli settlements, which are illegal under international law. Collective action, induced by the boycott, divestment, and sanctions movement, had a multibillion-dollar impact on Veolia, and in 2015, the company sold off all its operations in Israel.

At least..

$11.25B CONTRACTS NOT AWARDED

$10.10B CONTRACTS NOT RENEWED

$1.30M SHARES SOLD

42 ENTITIES TOOK ACTION

$21.35B TOTAL LOSS

2006	2008	2009	2010	2011	2012	2013	2014	2015
Dublin Tram	Dutch Triodos Bank	Sandwell City Council **$1.43b**	Dublin City Council	Tower Hamlets Council	East Sussex local authorities	Woodland-Davis Clean Water Authority **$0.33b**	Massachusetts commuter rail **$4.26b**	**VEOLIA SELLS OFF ALL OPERATIONS IN ISRAEL**
Dutch ASN Bank		Bordeaux local government **$1.00b**	Donegal County Council	Richmond Council	The Hague	Rennes City Council	University of New Mexico Grad Students	
		Galway City Council	Swansea City Council	South London Waste Partnership **$1.34b**	Quaker Friends Fiduciary Corporation **$0.14m**	Sussex University Union	Kuwaiti Ministry of Commerce & Industry **$0.75b**	
		Victorian State Government **$4.50b**	Cork City Council	East Hants/Winchester City	Board of Utrecht Regional	Sheffield University	Baltimore City Council **$0.50m**	
		Tehran City Council	Lille Public Transportation	Transport & Salaried Staff Association	Canterbury Council **$0.06b**	Queen Mary University Student Union		
		Stockholm City Council **$0.35b**	Caerphilly County Borough Council	Ealing Council **$0.49b**	North London Waste Authority **$6.21b**	St. Louis Water Division **$0.25m**		
			Edinburgh City Council	Cambridge University Students Union		TIAA-CREF Fund **$1.2m**		
				Portsmouth City Council				
				West London Waste Authority **$0.64b**				

VISUALIZING**PALESTINE** SOURCES bit.ly/vp-veolia WWW.**VISUALIZINGPALESTINE**.ORG

@visualizingpal /visualizing_palestine fb.me/visualizingpalestine

MAR 2019

Year: 2019 | **Brief and copywriting:** Reem Farah, Robin Jones | **Design:** Yosra El Gazzar | **Sources:** bit.ly/vp-veolia

11. BOYC DIVESTM & SANCT

Visuals in this section: Palestinians Want Freedom, Justice, and Equality | Boycott | Statesman/Terrorist | Resistance from a Distance | Divesting for Justice (with fossil fuels) | Divesting for Justice (timeline) | Divesting for Justice (Venn) | Academia Serving Apartheid | Love One Another | Musicians Stand for Justice | Musicians' Quotes |

OTT
ENT
ONS

Writers Stand for Justice (umbrella version) | Writers' Quotes | Writers Stand for Justice (newspaper version) | Moving the Goalposts | The Team That Could Have Been

> **"Power concedes nothing without a demand. . . . Find out just what any people will quietly submit to and you have found out the exact measure of injustice and wrong which will be imposed upon them, and these will continue till they are resisted.**
>
> —*Frederick Douglass, "If There Is No Struggle, There Is No Progress" (1857)*

> **"We, representatives of Palestinian civil society, call upon international civil society organizations and people of conscience all over the world to impose broad boycotts and implement divestment initiatives against Israel similar to those applied to South Africa in the apartheid era. We appeal to you to pressure your respective states to impose embargoes and sanctions against Israel. We also invite conscientious Israelis to support this Call, for the sake of justice and genuine peace.**
>
> —*"Palestinian Civil Society Call for BDS" (July 9, 2005)*

Palestinian resistance to imperial domination has deep roots. Before the Israeli regime took power, groups of Palestinians participated in popular action against Ottoman rule; Napoleon's French invasion in 1799; Egyptian rule in 1834; and British rule in 1936. Today, the chant "existence is resistance" is a frequent refrain at Palestine solidarity protests, capturing how Palestinians express *sumud* (steadfastness) simply by continuing to practice their culture and livelihoods in the face of erasure. The Palestinian story highlights the enduring will of all human beings to live freely and our collective refusal to accept systems of oppression, however entrenched they may be.

Organized resistance to Israeli settler colonialism and apartheid takes on numerous forms, including mass protests, Nakba commemorations, labor strikes, human rights advocacy, legal advocacy, and armed resistance. Israel's standard response to all expressions of Palestinian resistance on the ground is collective punishment of the entire population via repressive laws and policies or shows of military might. During the First Intifada, Israeli Minister of Defense Yitzhak Rabin (who became prime minister) ordered Israeli occupation forces to break the bones of protesters.[1] Israeli strategists use the macabre metaphor "mowing the grass" to describe how military operations that devastate Palestinian population centers are viewed as routine to the Israeli military establishment.[2]

Yet Palestinians continue to resist. In 2005, the Boycott, Divestment, and Sanctions (BDS) movement gained traction as a strategy for principled, transnational solidarity with Palestinians. More than 170 Palestinian civil society groups came together to call for BDS against Israel until it complies with international law.[3] The BDS movement has three demands, depicted in **Palestinians Want Freedom, Justice, and Equality**: full equality for Palestinian citizens of Israel, an end to Israel's military occupation, and the right of return for Palestinian refugees.

The BDS movement takes inspiration from the boycott of apartheid South Africa, an international movement that spanned more than thirty years. In the case of South Africa, diplomatic, economic, and cultural pressure tactics were embraced by the United Nations, the International Olympic Committee, university administrations, celebrities, and major corporations. In **Boycott**, we look back at this movement's major achievements. The South African anti-apartheid movement was not uncontroversial in its time. Nelson Mandela, for example, was on US terrorist watch lists until 2008 and was imprisoned by the South African apartheid regime for twenty-seven years, as the visual **Statesman/Terrorist** depicts.[4] Other activists, like Oliver Tambo, were forced to organize from exile, as we visualize in **Resistance from a Distance**.

BDS campaigns are not just symbolic; they also target the material conditions and technologies of oppression. Students, academics, labor unions, and faith-based collectives are some of the groups at the forefront of BDS grassroots activism. They are also core users of Visualizing Palestine's material. In the three-part series **Divesting for Justice**, we look at three student campaigns on North American college campuses: the campaign to divest from South African apartheid, the campaign to divest from Israeli apartheid, and the campaign to divest from fossil fuel companies. This visual is a tool students draw on to contextualize

Palestine solidarity actions on campus within the long tradition of student activism for civil and human rights and against war and militarism.

In **Academia Serving Apartheid**, we unpack how Israeli academic institutions play a role in the colonization of Palestine. A growing number of scholars and academic associations, including the American Studies Association, Association for Asian American Studies, Critical Ethnic Studies Association, Peace and Justice Studies Association, National Women's Studies Association, European Association of Social Anthropology, and Middle East Studies Association, have exercised their academic freedom by encouraging their members not to collaborate with or accept funding from these institutions.

In 2009, Palestinian Christians, members of some of the oldest Christian communities in the world, issued the Kairos Document, endorsing BDS and calling on Christians globally "not to offer theological cover-up for the injustice we suffer."[5] In response, faith communities began organizing divestment campaigns. **Love One Another** celebrates the millions of people who belong to a church or denominational group that has responded to Palestinian calls for BDS, practicing a faith oriented toward solidarity with the oppressed and marginalized.

Cultural workers, such as musicians, writers, and athletes, have also participated in BDS, refusing to offer their labor to bolster the image of an apartheid regime. **Musicians Stand for Justice** and **Writers Stand for Justice** celebrate artists who have refused to lend their words, voices, platforms, or talent to apartheid, a list that changes with artists' evolving political positions.

Sports have always been political, a fact recognized by athletes like Tommie Smith, John Carlos, and Muhammad Ali. The actions of international sports bodies in the wake of the 2022 Russian invasion of Ukraine further attest to this.[6] Palestinian athletes have called on the International Federation of Association Football (FIFA) to sanction the Israel Football Association, which hosts teams and matches in illegal Israeli settlements, mapped in **Moving the Goalposts**. BDS activists have used **The Team That Could**

Have Been to call for a boycott of PUMA until it withdraws its sponsorship of the Israel Football Association.

Even when BDS campaigns do not reach their goals, they force people in places of power to take a position on Palestine—in boardrooms, on college campuses, in city council meetings, and in the press. Many of these people would prefer to avoid or silence the issue, calling it "divisive," a word that BDS cofounder Omar Barghouti observes "tends to pop up all over the world whenever marginalized people fight for their rights."[7] But when oppression itself is not labeled divisive, BDS campaigns are a source of hope, an open window in a room of closed doors. And they embody a principled form of transnational solidarity that is transformative because it is rooted in strategies for mutual survival.

PALESTINIANS WANT FREEDOM, JUSTICE & EQUALITY

The vast majority of Palestinians support the three rights-based demands of the BDS movement, as founded in international law.

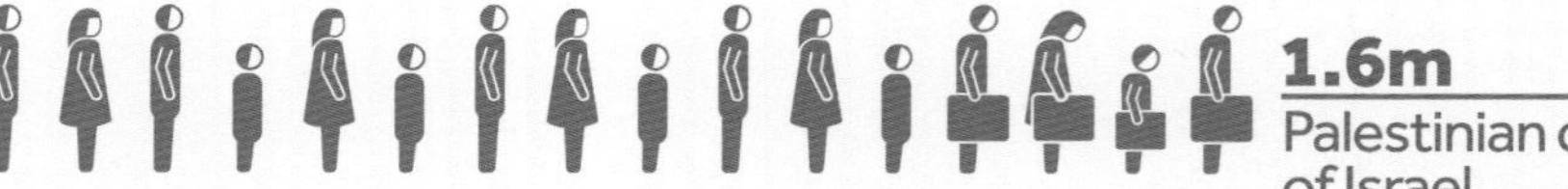

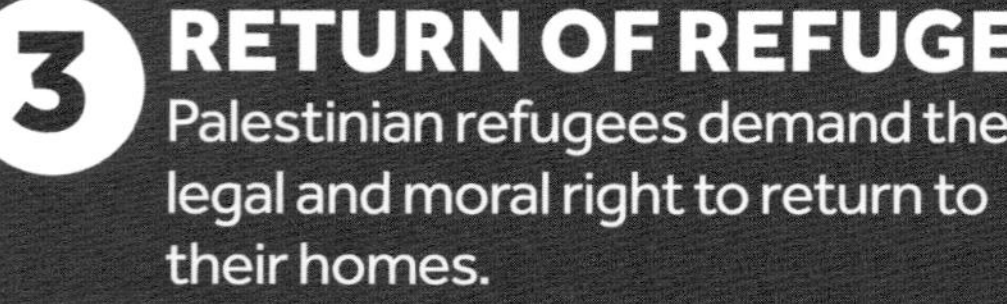

1.6m
Palestinian citizens of Israel
4.8m
Palestinians in West Bank & Gaza Strip
6.4m
Palestinians living in exile
100k displaced by Israel
100k never displaced

1 EQUAL RIGHTS
Palestinian citizens of Israel demand full equality with their fellow Jewish citizens.

2 AN END TO OCCUPATION
Palestinians under occupation demand a complete Israeli withdrawal from the West Bank, Gaza Strip and Golan Heights.

3 RETURN OF REFUGEES
Palestinian refugees demand their legal and moral right to return to their homes.

VISUALIZING**PALESTINE** | 101

V1 **SEP** 2019
DATA bit.ly/vp101data

Visualizing Palestine
WWW.**VISUALIZINGPALESTINE**.ORG/101

VISUAL **5.1**

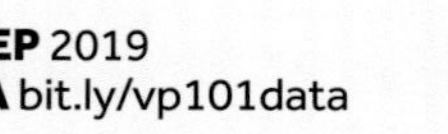

Year: 2019 | **Brief and copywriting:** Ahmad Barclay | **Design:** Ahmad Barclay, Yosra El Gazzar | **Sources:** bit.ly/vp101data

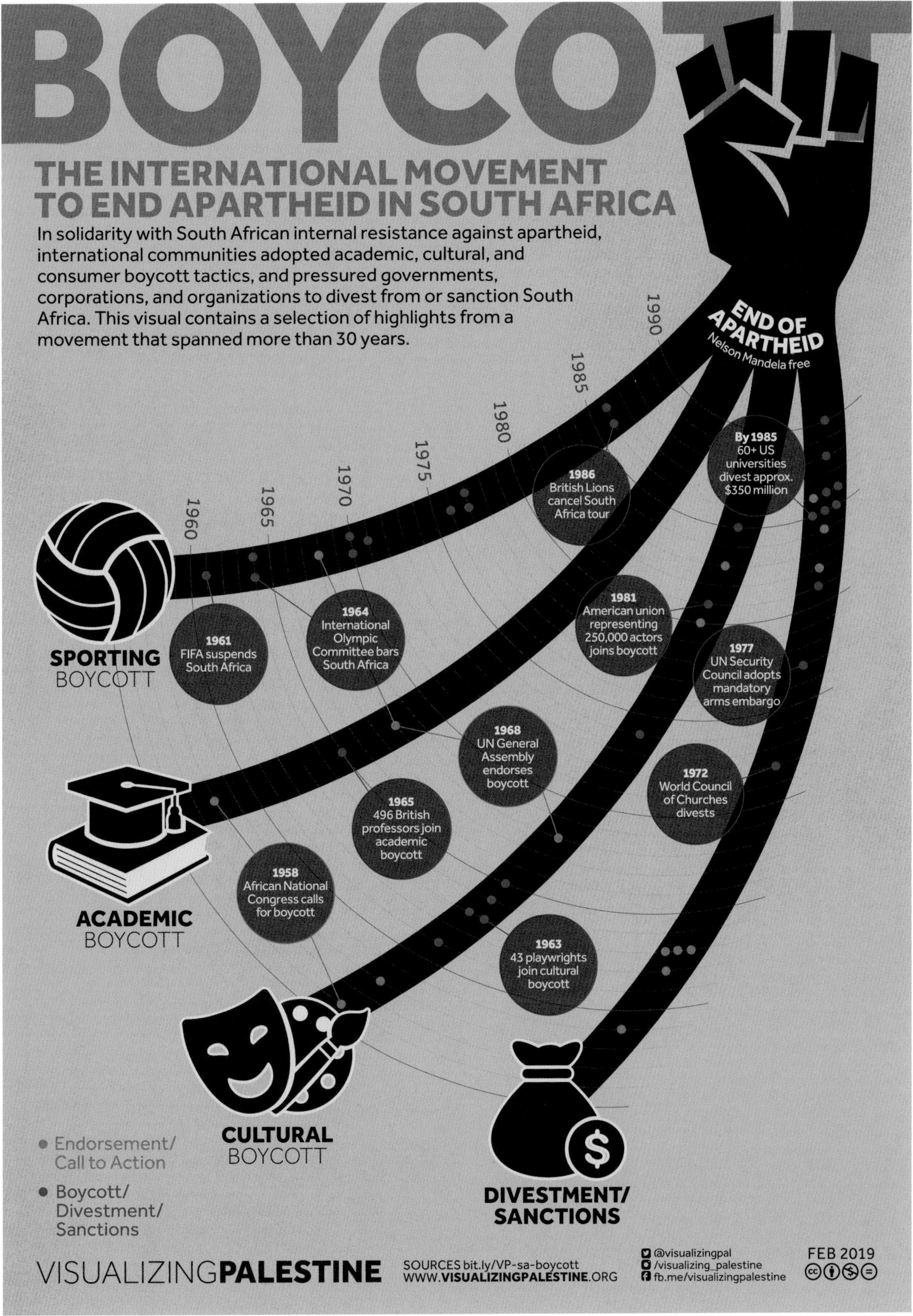
BOYCOTT
THE INTERNATIONAL MOVEMENT TO END APARTHEID IN SOUTH AFRICA
In solidarity with South African internal resistance against apartheid, international communities adopted academic, cultural, and consumer boycott tactics, and pressured governments, corporations, and organizations to divest from or sanction South Africa. This visual contains a selection of highlights from a movement that spanned more than 30 years.
1960
1965
1970
1975
1980
1985
1990
END OF APARTHEID
Nelson Mandela free
1986 British Lions cancel South Africa tour
By 1985 60+ US universities divest approx. $350 million
1981 American union representing 250,000 actors joins boycott
1977 UN Security Council adopts mandatory arms embargo
1972 World Council of Churches divests
1968 UN General Assembly endorses boycott
1964 International Olympic Committee bars South Africa
1961 FIFA suspends South Africa
1965 496 British professors join academic boycott
1958 African National Congress calls for boycott
1963 43 playwrights join cultural boycott
SPORTING BOYCOTT
ACADEMIC BOYCOTT
CULTURAL BOYCOTT
DIVESTMENT/ SANCTIONS
Endorsement/ Call to Action
Boycott/ Divestment/ Sanctions
VISUALIZINGPALESTINE
SOURCES bit.ly/VP-sa-boycott
WWW.VISUALIZINGPALESTINE.ORG
@visualizingpal
/visualizing_palestine
fb.me/visualizingpalestine
FEB 2019

Year: 2019 | **Brief and copywriting:** Jessica Anderson, Sharmeen Inayat, Robin Jones | **Design:** Yosra El Gazzar | **Sources:** bit.ly/VP-sa-boycott

1955
ACTIVIST
Organized series of non-violent ANC protests
1970s
ICON
Became key figure in global anti-apartheid struggle
1964
CRIMINAL
Life imprisonment for organizing acts of public violence
1961
MILITANT
SA government declares ANC 'terrorist organization'
STATESMAN | TERRORIST
1990
RESILIENT
Released from prison after 26 years
1980s
THREAT
Reagan and Thatcher call ANC 'terrorist organization'
1993
VISIONARY
Awarded Nobel Peace Prize
2008
ENDURING
Removed from US Terrorist Watch List
I WAS CALLED A TERRORIST YESTERDAY...TODAY I AM ADMIRED BY THE VERY PEOPLE WHO SAID I WAS ONE.
VISUALIZINGIMPACT

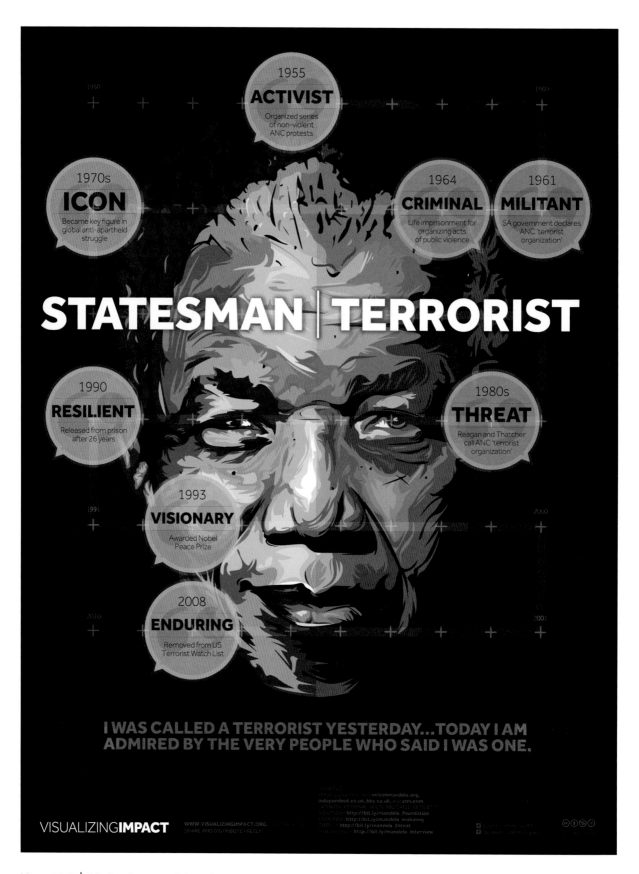

Year: 2013 | **Brief and copywriting:** Joumana al Jabri, Zaid Amr, Ahmad Barclay, Nusayba Hammad, Ramzi Jaber, Tamara Sawaya, Shireen Tawil | **Design:** Hani Asfour, Said Swayssi | **Sources:** bit.ly/vp-Sources-2012-2015

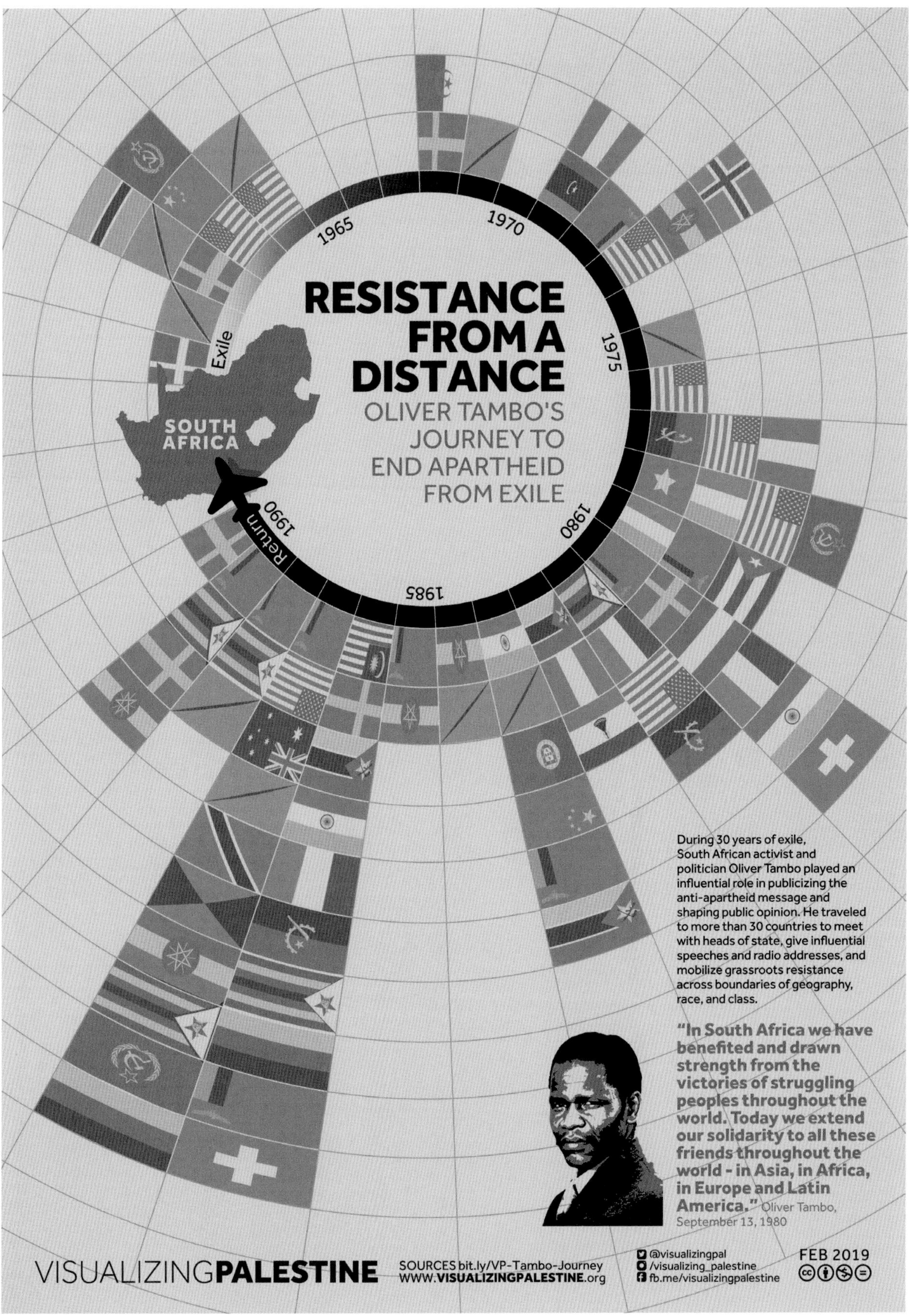
RESISTANCE FROM A DISTANCE
OLIVER TAMBO'S JOURNEY TO END APARTHEID FROM EXILE
1965
1970
1975
1980
1985
1990
Exile
Return
SOUTH AFRICA
During 30 years of exile, South African activist and politician Oliver Tambo played an influential role in publicizing the anti-apartheid message and shaping public opinion. He traveled to more than 30 countries to meet with heads of state, give influential speeches and radio addresses, and mobilize grassroots resistance across boundaries of geography, race, and class.
"In South Africa we have benefited and drawn strength from the victories of struggling peoples throughout the world. Today we extend our solidarity to all these friends throughout the world - in Asia, in Africa, in Europe and Latin America." Oliver Tambo, September 13, 1980
VISUALIZINGPALESTINE
SOURCES bit.ly/VP-Tambo-Journey
WWW.VISUALIZINGPALESTINE.org
@visualizingpal
/visualizing_palestine
fb.me/visualizingpalestine
FEB 2019

Year: 2019 | **Brief and copywriting:** Robin Jones | **Design:** Yosra El Gazzar | **Sources:** bit.ly/VP-Tambo-Journey

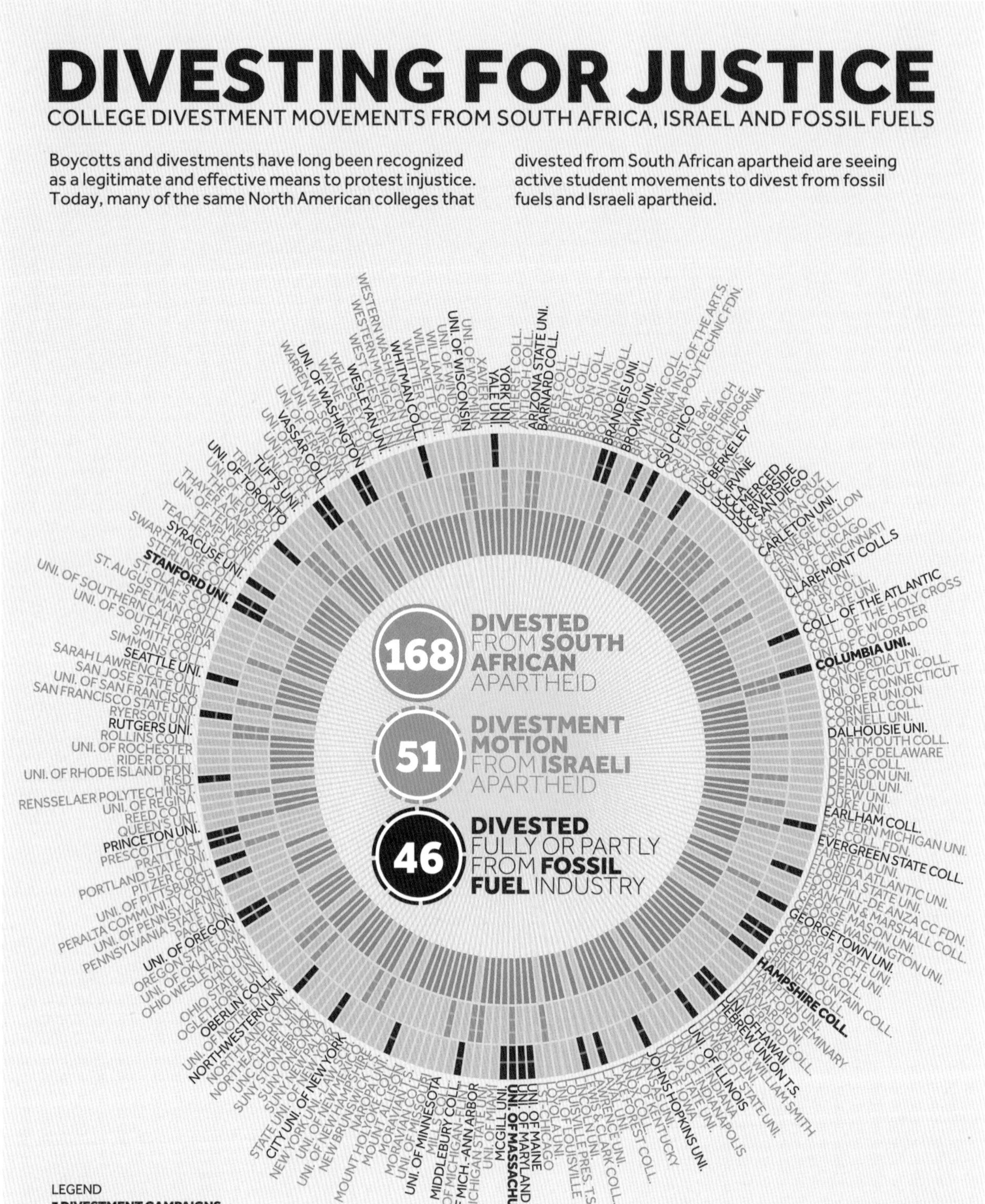

DIVESTING FOR JUSTICE

COLLEGE DIVESTMENT MOVEMENTS FROM SOUTH AFRICA, ISRAEL AND FOSSIL FUELS

Boycotts and divestments have long been recognized as a legitimate and effective means to protest injustice. Today, many of the same North American colleges that divested from South African apartheid are seeing active student movements to divest from fossil fuels and Israeli apartheid.

168 DIVESTED FROM SOUTH AFRICAN APARTHEID

51 DIVESTMENT MOTION FROM ISRAELI APARTHEID

46 DIVESTED FULLY OR PARTLY FROM FOSSIL FUEL INDUSTRY

LEGEND
3 DIVESTMENT CAMPAIGNS
2 DIVESTMENT CAMPAIGNS
1 DIVESTMENT CAMPAIGN

VISUALIZING**PALESTINE**

SOURCES bit.ly/vp-divest
WWW.**VISUALIZINGPALESTINE**.ORG

@visualizingpal
/visualizing_palestine
fb.me/visualizingpalestine

REV 1
MAY 2019

Year: 2019 | **Brief and copywriting:** Jessica Anderson, Ahmad Barclay, Reem Farah, Noura Moemen | **Design:** Ahmad Barclay, Hani Asfour | **Sources:** bit.ly/vp-divest

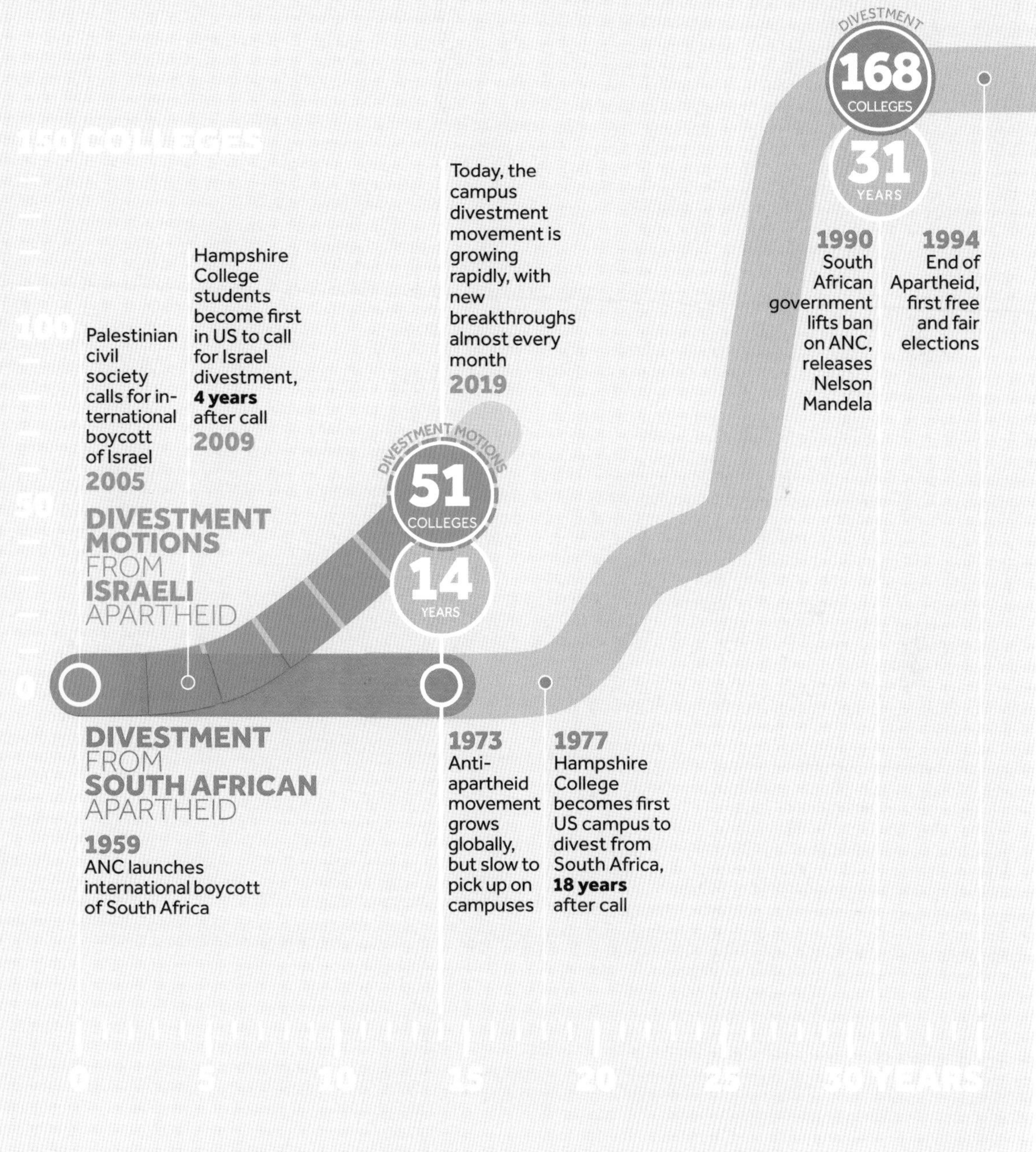
DIVESTING FOR JUSTICE
COLLEGE DIVESTMENTS AND DIVESTMENT MOTIONS FROM SOUTH AFRICA AND ISRAEL
Boycotts and divestments have long been recognized as a legitimate and effective means to protest injustice. This visual contrasts some of the major milestones in the history of North American campus divestment from South African apartheid with the growing movement to divest from Israeli Apartheid.
150 COLLEGES
100
50
0
DIVESTMENT
168
COLLEGES
31
YEARS
1990
South African government lifts ban on ANC, releases Nelson Mandela
1994
End of Apartheid, first free and fair elections
Today, the campus divestment movement is growing rapidly, with new breakthroughs almost every month
2019
Hampshire College students become first in US to call for Israel divestment, **4 years** after call
2009
Palestinian civil society calls for international boycott of Israel
2005
DIVESTMENT MOTIONS
51
COLLEGES
14
YEARS
DIVESTMENT MOTIONS FROM ISRAELI APARTHEID
DIVESTMENT FROM SOUTH AFRICAN APARTHEID
1959
ANC launches international boycott of South Africa
1973
Anti-apartheid movement grows globally, but slow to pick up on campuses
1977
Hampshire College becomes first US campus to divest from South Africa, **18 years** after call
0
5
10
15
20
25
30 YEARS
VISUALIZINGPALESTINE
SOURCES bit.ly/vp-divest
WWW.VISUALIZINGPALESTINE.ORG
@visualizingpal
/visualizing_palestine
fb.me/visualizingpalestine
REV 3
APR 2019

Year: 2019 | **Brief and copywriting:** Reem Farah | **Design:** Ahmad Barclay, Hani Asfour | **Sources:** bit.ly/vp-divest

DIVESTING FOR JUSTICE

COLLEGE DIVESTMENTS AND DIVESTMENT MOTIONS FROM SOUTH AFRICA AND ISRAEL

Boycotts and divestments have long been recognized as a legitimate and effective means to protest injustice. Today, many of the same North American colleges that boycotted South African apartheid have had official student bodies pass motions to divest from Israeli apartheid, highlighting the power of precedence.

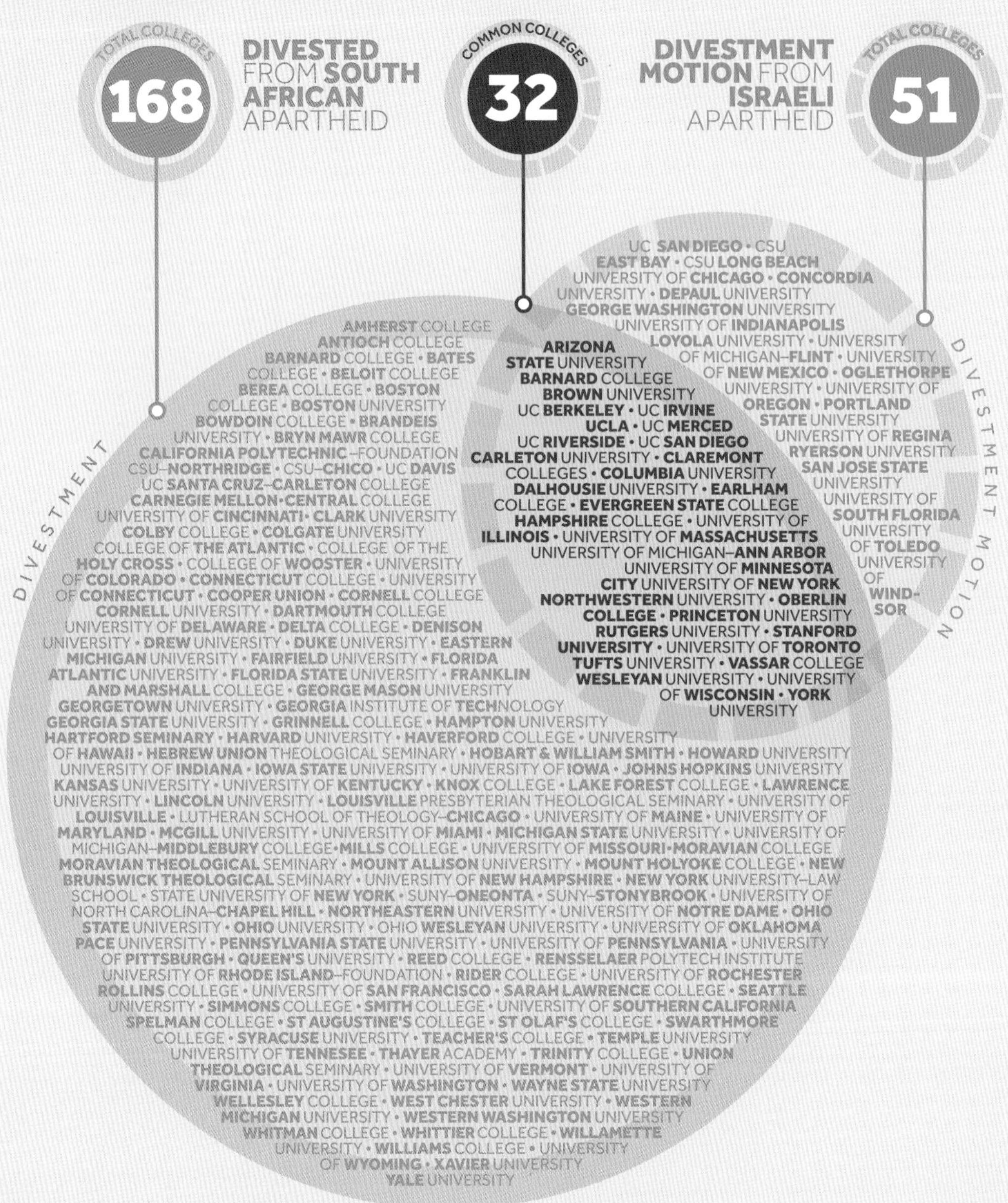

TOTAL COLLEGES
168
DIVESTED FROM SOUTH AFRICAN APARTHEID
COMMON COLLEGES
32
DIVESTMENT MOTION FROM ISRAELI APARTHEID
TOTAL COLLEGES
51
DIVESTMENT
DIVESTMENT MOTION
AMHERST COLLEGE
ANTIOCH COLLEGE
BARNARD COLLEGE • BATES
COLLEGE • BELOIT COLLEGE
BEREA COLLEGE • BOSTON
COLLEGE • BOSTON UNIVERSITY
BOWDOIN COLLEGE • BRANDEIS
UNIVERSITY • BRYN MAWR COLLEGE
CALIFORNIA POLYTECHNIC–FOUNDATION
CSU–NORTHRIDGE • CSU–CHICO • UC DAVIS
UC SANTA CRUZ–CARLETON COLLEGE
CARNEGIE MELLON•CENTRAL COLLEGE
UNIVERSITY OF CINCINNATI• CLARK UNIVERSITY
COLBY COLLEGE • COLGATE UNIVERSITY
COLLEGE OF THE ATLANTIC • COLLEGE OF THE
HOLY CROSS • COLLEGE OF WOOSTER • UNIVERSITY
OF COLORADO • CONNECTICUT COLLEGE • UNIVERSITY
OF CONNECTICUT • COOPER UNION • CORNELL COLLEGE
CORNELL UNIVERSITY • DARTMOUTH COLLEGE
UNIVERSITY OF DELAWARE • DELTA COLLEGE • DENISON
UNIVERSITY • DREW UNIVERSITY • DUKE UNIVERSITY • EASTERN
MICHIGAN UNIVERSITY • FAIRFIELD UNIVERSITY • FLORIDA
ATLANTIC UNIVERSITY • FLORIDA STATE UNIVERSITY • FRANKLIN
AND MARSHALL COLLEGE • GEORGE MASON UNIVERSITY
GEORGETOWN UNIVERSITY • GEORGIA INSTITUTE OF TECHNOLOGY
GEORGIA STATE UNIVERSITY • GRINNELL COLLEGE • HAMPTON UNIVERSITY
HARTFORD SEMINARY • HARVARD UNIVERSITY • HAVERFORD COLLEGE • UNIVERSITY
OF HAWAII • HEBREW UNION THEOLOGICAL SEMINARY • HOBART & WILLIAM SMITH • HOWARD UNIVERSITY
UNIVERSITY OF INDIANA • IOWA STATE UNIVERSITY • UNIVERSITY OF IOWA • JOHNS HOPKINS UNIVERSITY
KANSAS UNIVERSITY • UNIVERSITY OF KENTUCKY • KNOX COLLEGE • LAKE FOREST COLLEGE • LAWRENCE
UNIVERSITY • LINCOLN UNIVERSITY • LOUISVILLE PRESBYTERIAN THEOLOGICAL SEMINARY • UNIVERSITY OF
LOUISVILLE • LUTHERAN SCHOOL OF THEOLOGY–CHICAGO • UNIVERSITY OF MAINE • UNIVERSITY OF
MARYLAND • MCGILL UNIVERSITY • UNIVERSITY OF MIAMI • MICHIGAN STATE UNIVERSITY • UNIVERSITY OF
MICHIGAN–MIDDLEBURY COLLEGE•MILLS COLLEGE • UNIVERSITY OF MISSOURI•MORAVIAN COLLEGE
MORAVIAN THEOLOGICAL SEMINARY • MOUNT ALLISON UNIVERSITY • MOUNT HOLYOKE COLLEGE • NEW
BRUNSWICK THEOLOGICAL SEMINARY • UNIVERSITY OF NEW HAMPSHIRE • NEW YORK UNIVERSITY–LAW
SCHOOL • STATE UNIVERSITY OF NEW YORK • SUNY–ONEONTA • SUNY–STONYBROOK • UNIVERSITY OF
NORTH CAROLINA–CHAPEL HILL • NORTHEASTERN UNIVERSITY • UNIVERSITY OF NOTRE DAME • OHIO
STATE UNIVERSITY • OHIO UNIVERSITY • OHIO WESLEYAN UNIVERSITY • UNIVERSITY OF OKLAHOMA
PACE UNIVERSITY • PENNSYLVANIA STATE UNIVERSITY • UNIVERSITY OF PENNSYLVANIA • UNIVERSITY
OF PITTSBURGH • QUEEN'S UNIVERSITY • REED COLLEGE • RENSSELAER POLYTECH INSTITUTE
UNIVERSITY OF RHODE ISLAND–FOUNDATION • RIDER COLLEGE • UNIVERSITY OF ROCHESTER
ROLLINS COLLEGE • UNIVERSITY OF SAN FRANCISCO • SARAH LAWRENCE COLLEGE • SEATTLE
UNIVERSITY • SIMMONS COLLEGE • SMITH COLLEGE • UNIVERSITY OF SOUTHERN CALIFORNIA
SPELMAN COLLEGE • ST AUGUSTINE'S COLLEGE • ST OLAF'S COLLEGE • SWARTHMORE
COLLEGE • SYRACUSE UNIVERSITY • TEACHER'S COLLEGE • TEMPLE UNIVERSITY
UNIVERSITY OF TENNESSEE • THAYER ACADEMY • TRINITY COLLEGE • UNION
THEOLOGICAL SEMINARY • UNIVERSITY OF VERMONT • UNIVERSITY OF
VIRGINIA • UNIVERSITY OF WASHINGTON • WAYNE STATE UNIVERSITY
WELLESLEY COLLEGE • WEST CHESTER UNIVERSITY • WESTERN
MICHIGAN UNIVERSITY • WESTERN WASHINGTON UNIVERSITY
WHITMAN COLLEGE • WHITTIER COLLEGE • WILLAMETTE
UNIVERSITY • WILLIAMS COLLEGE • UNIVERSITY
OF WYOMING • XAVIER UNIVERSITY
YALE UNIVERSITY
ARIZONA
STATE UNIVERSITY
BARNARD COLLEGE
BROWN UNIVERSITY
UC BERKELEY • UC IRVINE
UCLA • UC MERCED
UC RIVERSIDE • UC SAN DIEGO
CARLETON UNIVERSITY • CLAREMONT
COLLEGES • COLUMBIA UNIVERSITY
DALHOUSIE UNIVERSITY • EARLHAM
COLLEGE • EVERGREEN STATE COLLEGE
HAMPSHIRE COLLEGE • UNIVERSITY OF
ILLINOIS • UNIVERSITY OF MASSACHUSETTS
UNIVERSITY OF MICHIGAN–ANN ARBOR
UNIVERSITY OF MINNESOTA
CITY UNIVERSITY OF NEW YORK
NORTHWESTERN UNIVERSITY • OBERLIN
COLLEGE • PRINCETON UNIVERSITY
RUTGERS UNIVERSITY • STANFORD
UNIVERSITY • UNIVERSITY OF TORONTO
TUFTS UNIVERSITY • VASSAR COLLEGE
WESLEYAN UNIVERSITY • UNIVERSITY
OF WISCONSIN • YORK
UNIVERSITY
UC SAN DIEGO • CSU
EAST BAY • CSU LONG BEACH
UNIVERSITY OF CHICAGO • CONCORDIA
UNIVERSITY • DEPAUL UNIVERSITY
GEORGE WASHINGTON UNIVERSITY
UNIVERSITY OF INDIANAPOLIS
LOYOLA UNIVERSITY • UNIVERSITY
OF MICHIGAN–FLINT • UNIVERSITY
OF NEW MEXICO • OGLETHORPE
UNIVERSITY • UNIVERSITY OF
OREGON • PORTLAND
STATE UNIVERSITY
UNIVERSITY OF REGINA
RYERSON UNIVERSITY
SAN JOSE STATE
UNIVERSITY
UNIVERSITY OF
SOUTH FLORIDA
UNIVERSITY
OF TOLEDO
UNIVERSITY
OF
WIND-
SOR

VISUALIZINGPALESTINE SOURCES bit.ly/vp-divest WWW.VISUALIZINGPALESTINE.ORG

@visualizingpal
/visualizing_palestine
fb.me/visualizingpalestine

REV 3
APR 2019

Year: 2019 | **Brief and copywriting:** Reem Farah | **Design:** Ahmad Barclay, Hani Asfour | **Sources:** bit.ly/vp-divest

ACADEMIA
SERVING
APARTHEID
Israeli universities maintain exceptionally close ties with the state's military establishment and corporate weapons manufacturers, and contribute to ongoing colonial violence and violations of Palestinian rights. This includes hosting military-sponsored programs, suppressing criticism of Israeli policies, and developing weapons technologies that are exported worldwide.
Palestinian activists are calling for a **boycott of complicit Israeli academic institutions**, as part of a broader movement to pressure Israel to comply with international law.
VISUALIZINGPALESTINE
SOURCES bit.ly/VP-israeliunis
WWW.VISUALIZINGPALESTINE.ORG
@visualizingpal
/visualizing_palestine
fb.me/visualizingpalestine
MAY 2022

Year: 2022 | **Brief and copywriting:** Jessica Anderson, Robin Jones, Nasreen Abd Elal | **Design:** Nasreen Abd Elal, Jana Elkhatib | **Sources:** bit.ly/VP-israeliunis

Israeli universities host propaganda initiatives and repress criticism of Israel

ACADEMIA SERVING APARTHEID

HAIFA UNIVERSITY

Revoked the degree of an MA student who researched the 1948 massacre of Palestinians in Tantura, emblematic of wider repression of critical research and expression at Israeli universities.

Hosts the Ambassadors Online program that trains students to become "digital advocates for Israel"

ASSOCIATION OF UNIVERSITY HEADS IN ISRAEL

Spearheads and coordinates intiatives against the Palestinian-led Boycott, Divestment, and Sanctions (BDS) movement for justice and equality

VISUALIZING**PALESTINE** **SOURCES** bit.ly/VP-israeliunis
WWW.**VISUALIZINGPALESTINE**.ORG

@visualizingpal
/visualizing_palestine
fb.me/visualizingpalestine

MAY 2022

Israeli universities develop military theory and promote the growth of Israeli surveillance and weapons industries

ACADEMIA SERVING APARTHEID

TEL AVIV UNIVERSITY

Develops military strategies such as the Dahiya Doctrine, which calls for disproportionate force and targeting civilian infrastructure to impose "long and expensive reconstruction processes"

TECHNION

Hosts a venture capital fund in partnership with the Israeli secret service (Shin Bet) to incubate start-up companies that specialize in surveillance technologies and artificial intelligence

Offers a program focused on branding and promoting the Israeli arms industry to international audiences

VISUALIZING**PALESTINE** **SOURCES** bit.ly/VP-israeliunis
WWW.**VISUALIZINGPALESTINE**.ORG

@visualizingpal
/visualizing_palestine
fb.me/visualizingpalestine

MAY 2022

Israeli universities benefit from close relationships with the military and multinational weapons companies

ACADEMIA SERVING APARTHEID

BAR-ILAN UNIVERSITY & TECHNION

Work with the Israeli military to develop unmanned combat vehicles and heavy machinery used to commit war crimes such as home demolitions

TECHNION, BAR-ILAN, & BEN GURION UNIVERSITIES

Participate in a robotics project funded by the Israeli Ministry of Defense and United States Department of Defense, an example of military priorities dictating academic research

TECHNION

Partners with arms developers such as Elbit and Rafael, whose weapons and surveillance technologies are tested on Palestinians and exported globally

VISUALIZING**PALESTINE** **SOURCES** bit.ly/VP-israeliunis WWW.**VISUALIZINGPALESTINE**.ORG

@visualizingpal
/visualizing_palestine
fb.me/visualizingpalestine

MAY 2022

Israeli universities cater to military recruitment and training

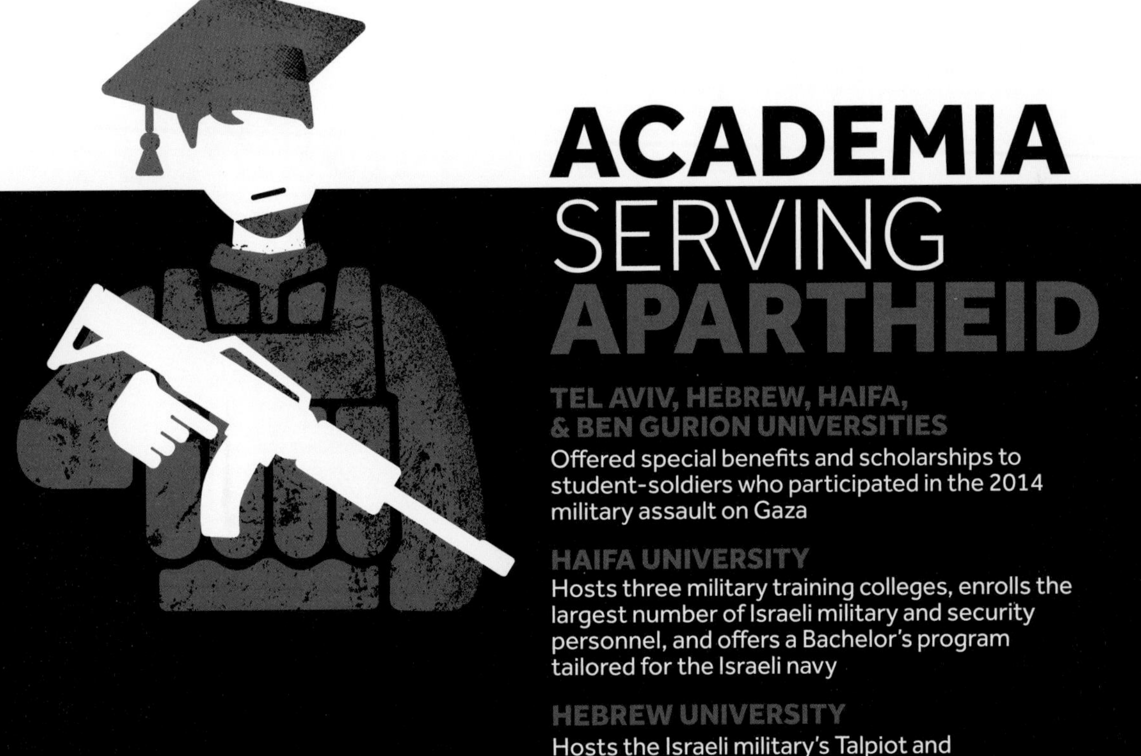
ACADEMIA
SERVING
APARTHEID
TEL AVIV, HEBREW, HAIFA, & BEN GURION UNIVERSITIES
Offered special benefits and scholarships to student-soldiers who participated in the 2014 military assault on Gaza
HAIFA UNIVERSITY
Hosts three military training colleges, enrolls the largest number of Israeli military and security personnel, and offers a Bachelor's program tailored for the Israeli navy
HEBREW UNIVERSITY
Hosts the Israeli military's Talpiot and Havatzalot programs, which recruit students into elite military units and the intelligence corps
VISUALIZINGPALESTINE
SOURCES bit.ly/VP-israeliunis
WWW.VISUALIZINGPALESTINE.ORG
@visualizingpal
/visualizing_palestine
fb.me/visualizingpalestine
MAY 2022

Israeli universities participate in colonization of Palestinian lands and forced displacement of Palestinian communities

ACADEMIA SERVING APARTHEID

TEL AVIV UNIVERSITY
Built on top of the depopulated Palestinian village of Sheikh Muwannis; suppresses commemoration of the ethnic cleansing of Palestinians in 1948

HEBREW UNIVERSITY
Situated in occupied East Jerusalem on confiscated land; collaborates with Israeli police in the surveillance and harrassment of the Palestinian neighborhood of Isawiyah

ARIEL UNIVERSITY
Located in Ariel, an illegal Israeli settlement in the occupied West Bank

VISUALIZINGPALESTINE **SOURCES** bit.ly/VP-israeliunis
WWW.**VISUALIZINGPALESTINE**.ORG

@visualizingpal
/visualizing_palestine
fb.me/visualizingpalestine

MAY 2022

Palestinian students, faculty, and staff at Israeli universities experience racism and discrimination

ACADEMIA SERVING APARTHEID

PALESTINIAN STUDENTS

In 2022, two Palestinian students at Hebrew University were arrested by off-duty police officers and suspended from campus for singing Arabic folk songs

40% of polled Palestinian students report experiencing racism from faculty; students have been denied access to scholarships or campus housing due to not serving in the Israeli military

PALESTINIAN FACULTY

20% of citizens of Israel are Palestinian, yet in 2020 Palestinians made up less than 4% of faculty at Israeli-accredited universities

PALESTINIAN STAFF

In 2016, Tel Aviv University banned staff at its tuition call center from speaking Arabic on calls

VISUALIZING**PALESTINE**

SOURCES bit.ly/VP-israeliunis
WWW.**VISUALIZINGPALESTINE**.ORG

@visualizingpal
/visualizing_palestine
fb.me/visualizingpalestine

MAY 2022

LOVE ONE ANOTHER

BOYCOTT AND DIVESTMENT ACTIONS BY AMERICAN CHURCHES

14.87 million Americans are a member of a church or denominational group that has divested from companies that profit off of Israel's human rights abuses, implemented a rights-conscious investment screen, or supported the strategic boycott of Israeli products as part of a faith-based commitment to stand with oppressed people.

2017
MENNONITE CHURCH USA
66,000

2018
EPISCOPAL CHURCH
1.87m members

2016
EVANGELICAL LUTHERAN CHURCH IN AMERICA
3.46m members

2016
UNITARIAN UNIVERSALIST ASSOCIATION
0.15m

Year of action: 2016
UNITED METHODIST CHURCH PENSION BOARD
6.95m members

2016
CATHOLIC CONFERENCE OF MAJOR SUPERIORS OF MEN
17,000

2015
UNITED CHURCH OF CHRIST
0.85m members

2016
ALLIANCE OF BAPTISTS
4,500

2014
THE PRESBYTERIAN CHURCH USA
1.42m members

2012
QUAKER FRIENDS FIDUCIARY CORPORATION
80,000

CHURCH OF THE NATIVITY, BETHLEHEM, PALESTINE

VISUALIZINGPALESTINE
SOURCES bit.ly/vp-churches
WWW.VISUALIZINGPALESTINE.ORG
@visualizingpal
/visualizing_palestine
fb.me/visualizingpalestine
APR 2019

Year: 2019 | **Brief and copywriting:** Jessica Anderson, Sharmeen Inayat | **Design:** Yosra El Gazzar, Ali Abbas Ahmadi | **Sources:** bit.ly/vp-churches

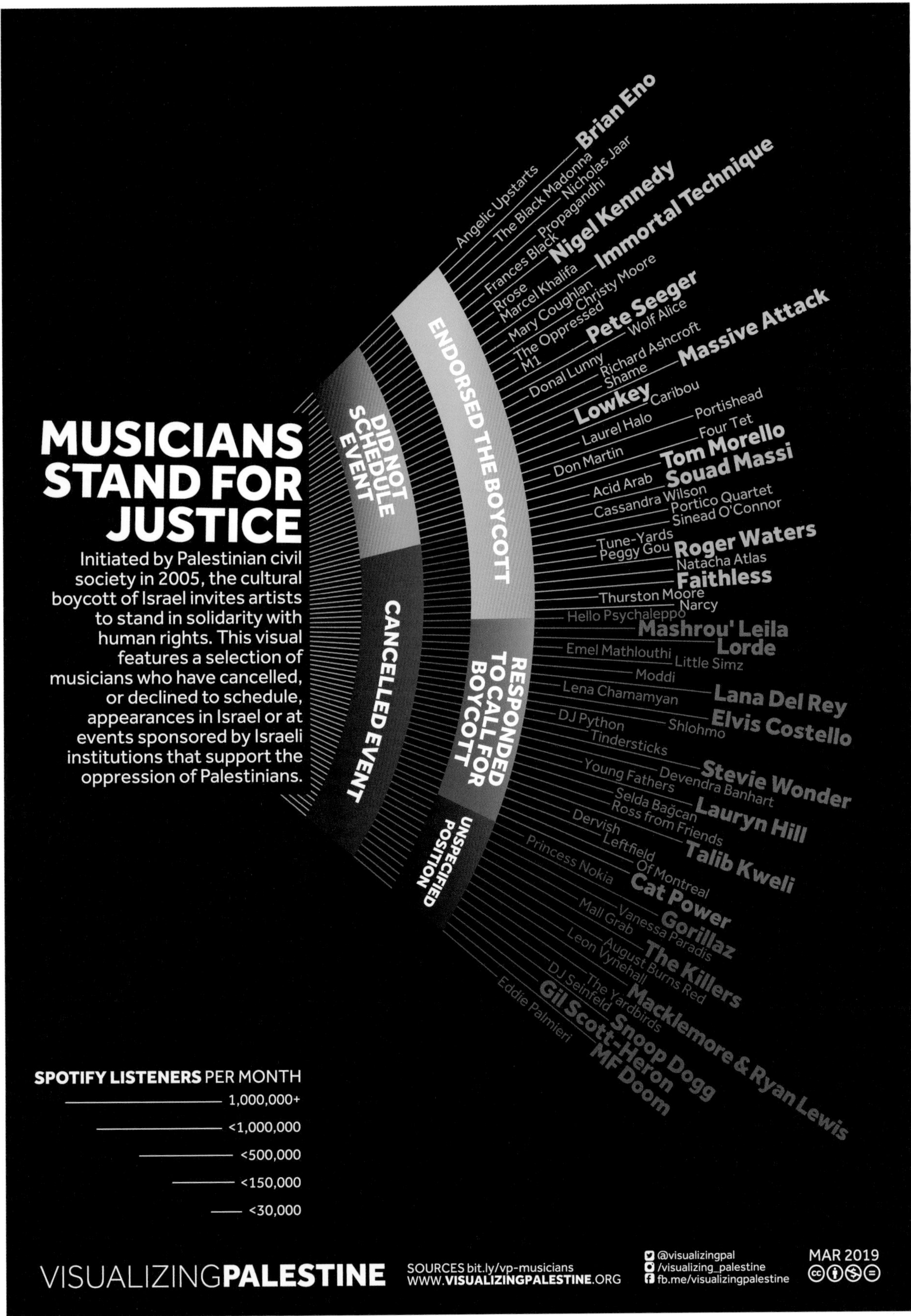
MUSICIANS STAND FOR JUSTICE
Initiated by Palestinian civil society in 2005, the cultural boycott of Israel invites artists to stand in solidarity with human rights. This visual features a selection of musicians who have cancelled, or declined to schedule, appearances in Israel or at events sponsored by Israeli institutions that support the oppression of Palestinians.
DID NOT SCHEDULE EVENT
CANCELLED EVENT
ENDORSED THE BOYCOTT
RESPONDED TO CALL FOR BOYCOTT
UNSPECIFIED POSITION
Angelic Upstarts
The Black Madonna
Brian Eno
Nicholas Jaar
Propagandhi
Frances Black
Nigel Kennedy
Rrose
Marcel Khalifa
Immortal Technique
Mary Coughlan
Christy Moore
The Oppressed
Pete Seeger
M1
Wolf Alice
Donal Lunny
Richard Ashcroft
Shame
Massive Attack
Lowkey
Caribou
Laurel Halo
Portishead
Four Tet
Don Martin
Tom Morello
Acid Arab
Souad Massi
Cassandra Wilson
Portico Quartet
Sinead O'Connor
Tune-Yards
Peggy Gou
Roger Waters
Natacha Atlas
Faithless
Thurston Moore
Narcy
Hello Psychaleppo
Mashrou' Leila
Lorde
Emel Mathlouthi
Little Simz
Moddi
Lena Chamamyan
Lana Del Rey
DJ Python
Shlohmo
Elvis Costello
Tindersticks
Young Fathers
Devendra Banhart
Stevie Wonder
Selda Bağcan
Ross from Friends
Lauryn Hill
Dervish
Leftfield
Talib Kweli
Princess Nokia
Of Montreal
Cat Power
Mall Grab
Vanessa Paradis
Gorillaz
Leon Vynehall
August Burns Red
The Killers
DJ Seinfeld
The Yardbirds
Macklemore & Ryan Lewis
Eddie Palmieri
Gil Scott-Heron
Snoop Dogg
MF Doom
SPOTIFY LISTENERS PER MONTH
1,000,000+
<1,000,000
<500,000
<150,000
<30,000
VISUALIZINGPALESTINE
SOURCES bit.ly/vp-musicians
WWW.VISUALIZINGPALESTINE.ORG
@visualizingpal
/visualizing_palestine
fb.me/visualizingpalestine
MAR 2019

Year: 2019 | **Brief and copywriting:** Robin Jones, Reem Farah | **Design:** Yosra El Gazzar | **Sources:** bit.ly/vp-musicians

WE ARE RIGHT TO
REFUSE TO
PLAY IN
ISRAEL
UNTIL THE
DAY COMES
-AND IT
SURELY WILL
COME-
WHEN THE WALL OF OCCUPATION FALLS
AND PALESTINIANS LIVE ALONGSIDE ISRAELIS IN THE
PEACE, FREEDOM,
JUSTICE AND DIGNITY
THAT THEY ALL DESERVE
-Roger Waters

In March 2011, Roger Waters publicly endorsed the BDS movement in an article for *the Guardian*.

VISUALIZINGPALESTINE SOURCES bit.ly/vp-musicians WWW.VISUALIZINGPALESTINE.ORG @visualizingpal /visualizing_palestine fb.me/visualizingpalestine MAR 2019

I NOW SEE THAT
IT WOULD BE MORE
EFFECTIVE
A STATEMENT TO
NOT GO
TO ISRAEL
UNTIL THIS
SYSTEMISED
APARTHEID
IS ABOLISHED
ONCE AND FOR ALL
- Natacha Atlas
In September 2011, Natacha Atlas canceled her performance in Israel and endorsed the BDS movement.
VISUALIZINGPALESTINE
SOURCES bit.ly/vp-musicians
WWW.VISUALIZINGPALESTINE.ORG
@visualizingpal
/visualizing_palestine
fb.me/visualizingpalestine
MAR 2019

I HAVE THE
RIGHT
NOT TO
PERFORM
IN A COUNTRY WHICH
MURDERS
SMALL CHILDREN
-Souad Massi
In August 2014, Souad Massi reiterated her support for the BDS movement and announced her refusal to play in Israel.
VISUALIZINGPALESTINE
SOURCES bit.ly/vp-musicians
WWW.VISUALIZINGPALESTINE.ORG
@visualizingpal
/visualizing_palestine
fb.me/visualizingpalestine
MAR 2019

WHILE HUMAN BEINGS
ARE BEING WILFULLY
DENIED
NOT JUST
THEIR RIGHTS
BUT THEIR NEEDS
FOR THEIR CHILDREN
AND GRANDPARENTS AND THEMSELVES
I FEEL DEEPLY THAT
I SHOULD NOT
BE SENDING EVEN TACIT SIGNALS
THAT THIS IS
'NORMAL'
OR 'OK'
-Maxi Jazz, Faithless
In August 2010, Faithless frontman Maxi Jazz cited Israel's denial of rights as the reason for his band's refusal to play in Israel.
VISUALIZINGPALESTINE
SOURCES bit.ly/vp-musicians
WWW.VISUALIZINGPALESTINE.ORG
@visualizingpal
/visualizing_palestine
fb.me/visualizingpalestine
MAR 2019

Year: 2019
Brief and copywriting: Robin Jones
Design: Yosra El Gazzar
Photos: Roger Waters: Roger Waters en el Palau Sant Jordi de Barcelona (The Wall Live) (Wikimedia), Natacha Atlas: Richard Kaby (Wikimedia), Souad Massi: Schorle (Wikimedia), Maxi Jazz: Exit Festival (Flickr)
Sources: bit.ly/vp-musicians

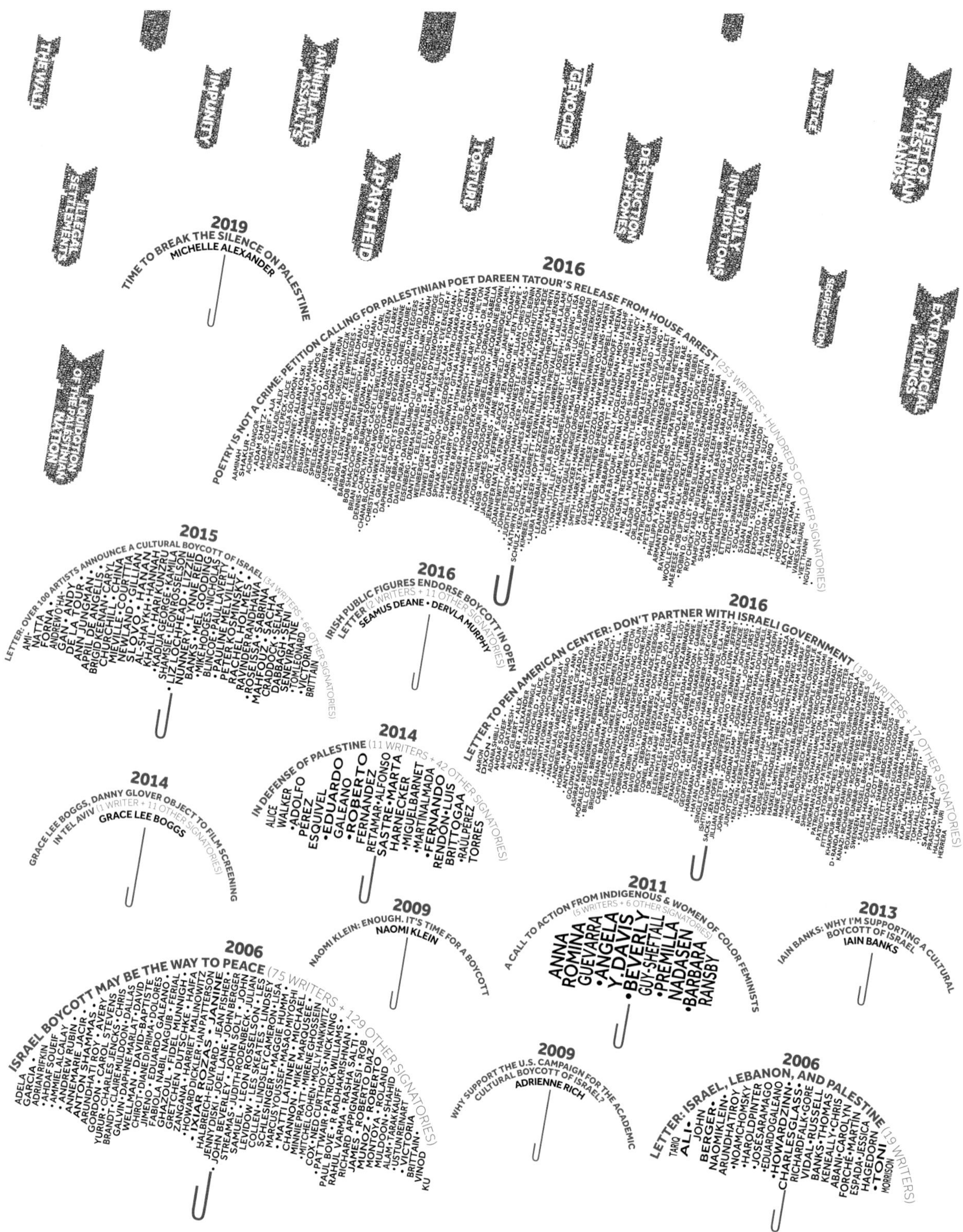
THE WALL
IMPUNITY
ANNIHILATIVE ASSAULTS
GENOCIDE
INJUSTICE
THEFT OF PALESTINIAN LANDS
ILLEGAL SETTLEMENTS
APARTHEID
TORTURE
DESTRUCTION OF HOMES
DAILY INTIMIDATIONS
EXTRAJUDICIAL KILLINGS
LIQUIDATION OF THE PALESTINIAN NATION
2019
TIME TO BREAK THE SILENCE ON PALESTINE
MICHELLE ALEXANDER
2016
POETRY IS NOT A CRIME: PETITION CALLING FOR PALESTINIAN POET DAREEN TATOUR'S RELEASE FROM HOUSE ARREST (253 WRITERS + HUNDREDS OF OTHER SIGNATORIES)
2015
LETTER: OVER 100 ARTISTS ANNOUNCE A CULTURAL BOYCOTT OF ISRAEL (34 WRITERS + 66 OTHER SIGNATORIES)
2016
IRISH PUBLIC FIGURES ENDORSE BOYCOTT IN OPEN LETTER (2 WRITERS + 11 OTHER SIGNATORIES)
SEAMUS DEANE • DERVLA MURPHY
2016
LETTER TO PEN AMERICAN CENTER: DON'T PARTNER WITH ISRAELI GOVERNMENT (199 WRITERS + 17 OTHER SIGNATORIES)
2014
GRACE LEE BOGGS, DANNY GLOVER OBJECT TO FILM SCREENING IN TEL AVIV (1 WRITER + 11 OTHER SIGNATORIES)
GRACE LEE BOGGS
2014
IN DEFENSE OF PALESTINE (11 WRITERS + 42 OTHER SIGNATORIES)
ALICE WALKER • ADOLFO PEREZ ESQUIVEL • EDUARDO GALEANO • ROBERTO FERNANDEZ RETAMAR • ALFONSO SASTRE • MARTA HARNECKER • MIGUEL BARNET • MARTIN ALMADA • FERNANDO RENDON • LUIS BRITTO GARCIA • RAUL PEREZ TORRES
2011
A CALL TO ACTION FROM INDIGENOUS & WOMEN OF COLOR FEMINISTS (5 WRITERS + 6 OTHER SIGNATORIES)
ANNA ROMINA GUEVARRA • ANGELA Y. DAVIS • BEVERLY GUY-SHEFTALL • PREMILLA NADASEN • BARBARA RANSBY
2013
IAIN BANKS: WHY I'M SUPPORTING A CULTURAL BOYCOTT OF ISRAEL
IAIN BANKS
2009
NAOMI KLEIN: ENOUGH. IT'S TIME FOR A BOYCOTT
NAOMI KLEIN
2006
ISRAEL BOYCOTT MAY BE THE WAY TO PEACE (75 WRITERS + 129 OTHER SIGNATORIES)
2009
WHY SUPPORT THE U.S. CAMPAIGN FOR THE ACADEMIC CULTURAL BOYCOTT OF ISRAEL?
ADRIENNE RICH
2006
LETTER: ISRAEL, LEBANON, AND PALESTINE (19 WRITERS)
TARIQ ALI • JOHN BERGER • NAOMI KLEIN • ARUNDHATI ROY • NOAM CHOMSKY • HAROLD PINTER • JOSE SARAMAGO • EDUARDO GALEANO • HOWARD ZINN • CHARLES GLASS • RICHARD FALK • GORE VIDAL • RUSSELL BANKS • THOMAS KENEALLY • CHRIS ABANI • CAROLYN FORCHÉ • MARTIN ESPADA • JESSICA HAGEDORN • TONI MORRISON

THIS VISUAL CONTAINS THE NAMES OF OVER 500 WRITERS WHO HAVE TAKEN A STAND FOR PALESTINIAN HUMAN RIGHTS

VISUALIZING**PALESTINE** SOURCES bit.ly/VP-Writers-Stand WWW.**VISUALIZINGPALESTINE**.ORG

@visualizingpal
/visualizing_palestine
fb.me/visualizingpalestine

FEB 2019

Year: 2019 | **Brief and copywriting:** Iman Annab, Sharmeen Inayat, Ahmed Hegazy, Robin Jones | **Design:** Naji El Mir | **Sources:** bit.ly/VP-Writers-Stand

"
THE BDS CAMPAIGN FOR JUSTICE FOR THE PALESTINIAN PEOPLE IS ONE I WOULD HOPE ANY DECENT, OPEN-MINDED PERSON WOULD SUPPORT ... THESE PEOPLE ARE OUR PEOPLE, AND COLLECTIVELY WE HAVE TURNED OUR BACKS ON THEIR SUFFERING FOR FAR TOO LONG.
IAIN BANKS
Science fiction writer, The Wasp Factory
VISUALIZINGPALESTINE
SOURCES bit.ly/VP-Writers-Stand
WWW.VISUALIZINGPALESTINE.ORG
@visualizingpal
/visualizing_palestine
fb.me/visualizingpalestine
MAR 2019

"

OVER THE DECADES THERE HAVE BEEN UPRISINGS, WARS, INTIFADAS. TENS OF THOUSANDS HAVE LOST THEIR LIVES. ACCORDS AND TREATIES HAVE BEEN SIGNED, CEASEFIRES DECLARED AND VIOLATED. BUT THE BLOODSHED DOESN'T END. PALESTINE STILL REMAINS ILLEGALLY OCCUPIED.

ARUNDHATI ROY
Author , *The God of Small Things*

VISUALIZING**PALESTINE** SOURCES bit.ly/VP-Writers-Stand WWW.**VISUALIZINGPALESTINE**.ORG @visualizingpal /visualizing_palestine fb.me/visualizingpalestine MAR 2019

Year: 2019
Brief and copywriting: Sharmeen Inayat
Design: Yosra El Gazzar
Photos: Iain Banks: Stuart Caie (Flickr), Arundhati Roy: jeanbaptisteparis (Flickr), Naomi Klein: Peoples' Social Forum (Flickr), Teju Cole: Michael Coghlan (Flickr), Ahdaf Soueif: Randa Ali (Flickr), Michelle Alexander: Miller Center (Flickr)
Sources: bit.ly/VP-Writers-Stand

"
IT'S TIME. LONG PAST TIME. THE BEST STRATEGY TO END THE INCREASINGLY BLOODY OCCUPATION IS FOR ISRAEL TO BECOME THE TARGET OF THE KIND OF GLOBAL MOVEMENT THAT PUT AN END TO APARTHEID IN SOUTH AFRICA.
NAOMI KLEIN
New York Times bestselling author, *No Logo*
VISUALIZINGPALESTINE
SOURCES bit.ly/VP-Writers-Stand
WWW.VISUALIZINGPALESTINE.ORG
@visualizingpal
/visualizing_palestine
fb.me/visualizingpalestine
MAR 2019

"
[PALESTINIANS] HAVE TO SPEND THEIR ENTIRE LIVES NEGOTIATING WHAT SHOULD NOT BE MATTERS FOR NEGOTIATION AT ALL: FREEDOM OF MOVEMENT, THE RIGHT TO SELF-DETERMINATION, EQUAL PROTECTION UNDER THE LAW.
TEJU COLE
Author, *Open City*
VISUALIZINGPALESTINE
SOURCES bit.ly/VP-Writers-Stand
WWW.VISUALIZINGPALESTINE.ORG
@visualizingpal
/visualizing_palestine
fb.me/visualizingpalestine
MAR 2019

"
TO TAKE THE ISRAELI GOVERNMENT'S MONEY, TO TREAT IT AS A CIVILISED SUPPORTER OF ART AND CULTURE, WHILE IT KILLS AND TORTURES AND SEGREGATES, IS TO AID AND ABET IT IN ITS CRIMES.
AHDAF SOUEIF
Author, *In the Eye of the Sun*
VISUALIZINGPALESTINE
SOURCES bit.ly/VP-Writers-Stand
WWW.VISUALIZINGPALESTINE.ORG
@visualizingpal
/visualizing_palestine
fb.me/visualizingpalestine
MAR 2019

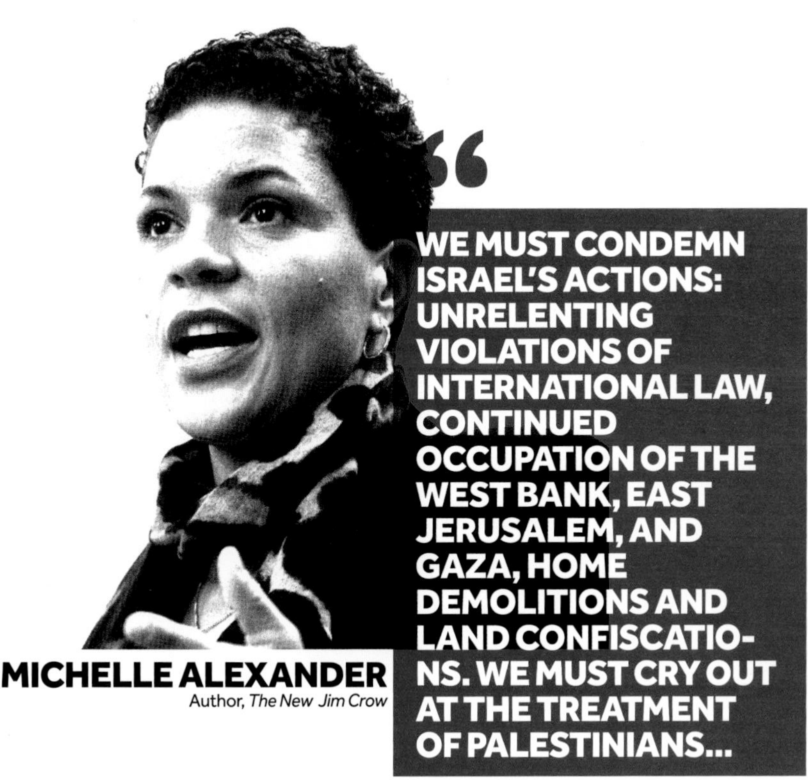
"
WE MUST CONDEMN ISRAEL'S ACTIONS: UNRELENTING VIOLATIONS OF INTERNATIONAL LAW, CONTINUED OCCUPATION OF THE WEST BANK, EAST JERUSALEM, AND GAZA, HOME DEMOLITIONS AND LAND CONFISCATIO-NS. WE MUST CRY OUT AT THE TREATMENT OF PALESTINIANS...
MICHELLE ALEXANDER
Author, *The New Jim Crow*
VISUALIZINGPALESTINE
SOURCES bit.ly/VP-Writers-Stand
WWW.VISUALIZINGPALESTINE.ORG
@visualizingpal
/visualizing_palestine
fb.me/visualizingpalestine
MAR 2019

Writers Stand for Justice

Feb. 2019

Over 500 Writers have taken a stand

This visual captures excerpts from 13 public letters or statements in solidarity with Palestinian freedom, justice, and equality, signed by over 500 writers of conscience.

2006

ISRAEL BOYCOTT MAY BE THE WAY TO PEACE

75 WRITERS

"The challenge of apartheid was fought better. The non-violent international response to apartheid was a campaign of boycott, divestment, and, finally UN imposed sanctions which enabled the regime to change without terrible bloodshed. Today Palestinians teachers, writers, film-makers and non-governmental organisations have called for a comparable academic and cultural boycott of Israel as offering another path to a just peace. This call has been endorsed internationally by university teachers in many European countries, by film-makers and architects, and by some brave Israeli dissidents. It is now time for others to join the campaign – as Primo Levi asked: If not now, when?"

LETTER: ISRAEL, LEBANON, & PALESTINE

Israeli Jewish dissidents arrested, Israeli youth imprisoned for conscientious refusal of military service. Academic institutions are surely only relative sites of power. But they are, in their funding and governance, implicated with state economic and military power."

NAOMI KLEIN: ENOUGH. IT'S TIME FOR A BOYCOTT

"It's time. Long past time. The best strategy to end the increasingly bloody occupation is for Israel to become the target of the kind of global movement that put an end to apartheid in South Africa. In July 2005 a huge coalition of Palestinian groups laid out plans to do just that. They called on "people of conscience all over the world to impose broad boycotts and implement divestment initiatives against Israel similar to those applied to South Africa in the apartheid era". The campaign Boycott, Divestment and Sanctions was born."

2011

A CALL TO ACTION FROM INDIGENOUS

Mandela: "We know too well that our freedom is incomplete without the freedom of the Palestinians." We affirm that Israel has morally and politically lost this battle in the face of the brave Palestinian people and the growing condemnation by the peoples of the world of a "criminal" state that violates international law. The unbreakable Palestinian resistance will be rewarded, sooner rather than later, with the smiles of their children in a free homeland."

GRACE LEE BOGGS, DANNY GLOVER OBJECT TO FILM SCREENING IN TEL AVIV

"We stand in solidarity with the people of Palestine, and support their call for cultural and academic boycott of Israel."

2015

LETTER: OVER 100 ARTISTS

of Palestinian lands and daily intimidation with tear gas and bullets."

LETTER TO PEN AMERICAN CENTER: DON'T PARTNER WITH ISRAELI GOVERNMENT

199 WRITERS

"Given PEN American Center's mission of supporting freedom of expression, it is deeply regrettable that the Festival has chosen to accept sponsorship from the Israeli government, even as it intensifies its decades-long denial of basic rights to the Palestinian people, including the frequent targeting of Palestinian writers and journalists."

POETRY IS NOT A CRIME: PETITION CALLING FOR PALESTINIAN POET DAREEN

subsequent arguments, accusations and vows, all serve as a distraction in order to divert world attention from a long-term military, economic and geographic practice whose political aim is nothing less than the liquidation of the Palestinian nation."

2009

ADRIENNE RICH: WHY SUPPORT THE U.S. CAMPAIGN FOR THE ACADEMIC & CULTURAL BOYCOTT OF ISRAEL?

"Until now, as a believer in boundary-crossings, I would not have endorsed a cultural and academic boycott. But Israel's continuing, annihilative assaults in Gaza and the one-sided rationalizations for them have driven me to re-examine my thoughts about cultural exchanges. Israel's blockading of information, compassionate aid, international witness and free cultural and scholarly expression has become extreme and morally stone-blind. Israeli Arab parties have been banned from the elections,

5 WRITERS

"We call upon all people of conscience to engage in serious dialogue about Palestine and to acknowledge connections between the Palestinian cause and other struggles for justice. Injustice anywhere is a threat to justice everywhere."

2013

IAIN BANKS: WHY I'M SUPPORTING A CULTURAL BOYCOTT OF ISRAEL

"I support the Boycott, Divestment and Sanctions (BDS) campaign because, especially in our instantly connected world, an injustice committed against one, or against one group of people, is an injustice against all, against every one of us; a collective injury."

2014

IN DEFENSE OF PALESTINE

11 WRITERS

"We adopt as our own the words of the revolutionary Nelson

ISRAEL

34 WRITERS

"We are announcing today that we will not engage in business-as-usual cultural relations with Israel. We will accept neither professional invitations to Israel, nor funding, from any institutions linked to its government. Since the summer war on Gaza, Palestinians have enjoyed no respite from Israel's unrelenting attack on their land, their livelihood, their right to political existence. '2014,' says the Israeli human rights organisation B'Tselem, was 'one of the cruellest and deadliest in the history of the occupation.' The Palestinian catastrophe goes on."

2016

IRISH PUBLIC FIGURES ENDORSE BOYCOTT IN OPEN LETTER

"The reasons to support BDS are systematically documented by organisations like Amnesty International, Defense for Children International, the United Nations and others which describe extrajudicial killings, imprisonment of children, destruction of people's homes and livelihoods, theft

ARREST

253 WRITERS

"We believe in the rights of artists and writers to openly express their artistic vision and share work freely. The Israeli government's actions reveal a desire to silence Tatour, part of a larger pattern of Israeli repression against all Palestinians."

2019

MICHELLE ALEXANDER: TIME TO BREAK THE SILENCE ON PALESTINE

"We must not tolerate Israel's refusal even to discuss the right of Palestinian refugees to return to their homes, as prescribed by United Nations resolutions, and we ought to question the U.S. government funds that have supported multiple hostilities and thousands of civilian casualties in Gaza, as well as the $38 billion the U.S. government has pledged in military support to Israel."

> **"It's time. Long past time. The best strategy to end the increasingly bloody occupation is for Israel to become the target of the kind of global movement that put an end to apartheid in South Africa."** - *Naomi Klein*

VISUALIZING**PALESTINE**

SOURCES bit.ly/VP-Writers-Stand
WWW.**VISUALIZINGPALESTINE**.ORG

@visualizingpal
/visualizing_palestine
fb.me/visualizingpalestine

FEB 2019

Year: 2019 | **Brief and copywriting:** Iman Annab, Sharmeen Inayat, Ahmed Hegazy, Robin Jones | **Design:** Naji El Mir | **Sources:** bit.ly/VP-Writers-Stand

MOVING THE GOALPOSTS
DELAYING PALESTINIAN FOOTBALL JUSTICE

ISRAELI ILLEGAL PITCHES

Under FIFA rules, national football associations are not allowed to host matches on another member's territory without permission. FIFA has repeatedly failed to enforce this law in the case of Israel, whose football association gives membership status to six clubs who play in illegal settlements built on stolen Palestinian land.

OCCUPIED WEST BANK

HAPO'EL ORANIT

MACCABI ARIEL INDOOR (FUTSAL) FOOTBALL CLUB

ARIEL MUNICIPAL FOOTBALL CLUB

HAPO'EL BIK'AT HAYARDEN TOMER

BEITAR GIVAT ZE'EV SHABI

BEITAR MA'ALEH ADOMIM

CRIMEA

RUSSIAN FOOTBALL UNION OUT OF CRIMEA

FIFA has taken action against other occupying powers, banning Russia from organizing matches in Crimea without the agreement of Ukraine.

DELAY 1 — **MAY 2015**
Instead of directly applying its rules against Israeli settlement teams, FIFA forms a committee to consider the issue.

DELAY 2 — **MAY 2016**
The committee receives an extension of its one-year mandate.

DELAY 3 — **OCT 2016**
The FIFA Council convenes and postpones a decision on settlement teams until the next meeting.

DELAY 4 — **JAN 2017**
FIFA again postpones decision at the Council meeting.

DELAY 5 — **MAY 2017**
At FIFA Congress, FIFA President blocks motion against settlement clubs and pushes through proposal delaying action again.

FIFA DELAY TACTICS

"... it's not clear why FIFA needs yet another year to decide whether or not to follow its own rules."
—Human Rights Watch

VISUALIZINGPALESTINE

SOURCES http://bit.ly/vp-fifa
WWW.VISUALIZINGPALESTINE.ORG

@visualizingpal
/visualizing_palestine
fb.me/visualizingpalestine

SEP 2017

Year: 2017 | **Brief and copywriting:** Iman Annab, Robin Jones, Fadi Quran | **Design:** Hani Asfour | **Sources:** bit.ly/vp-fifa

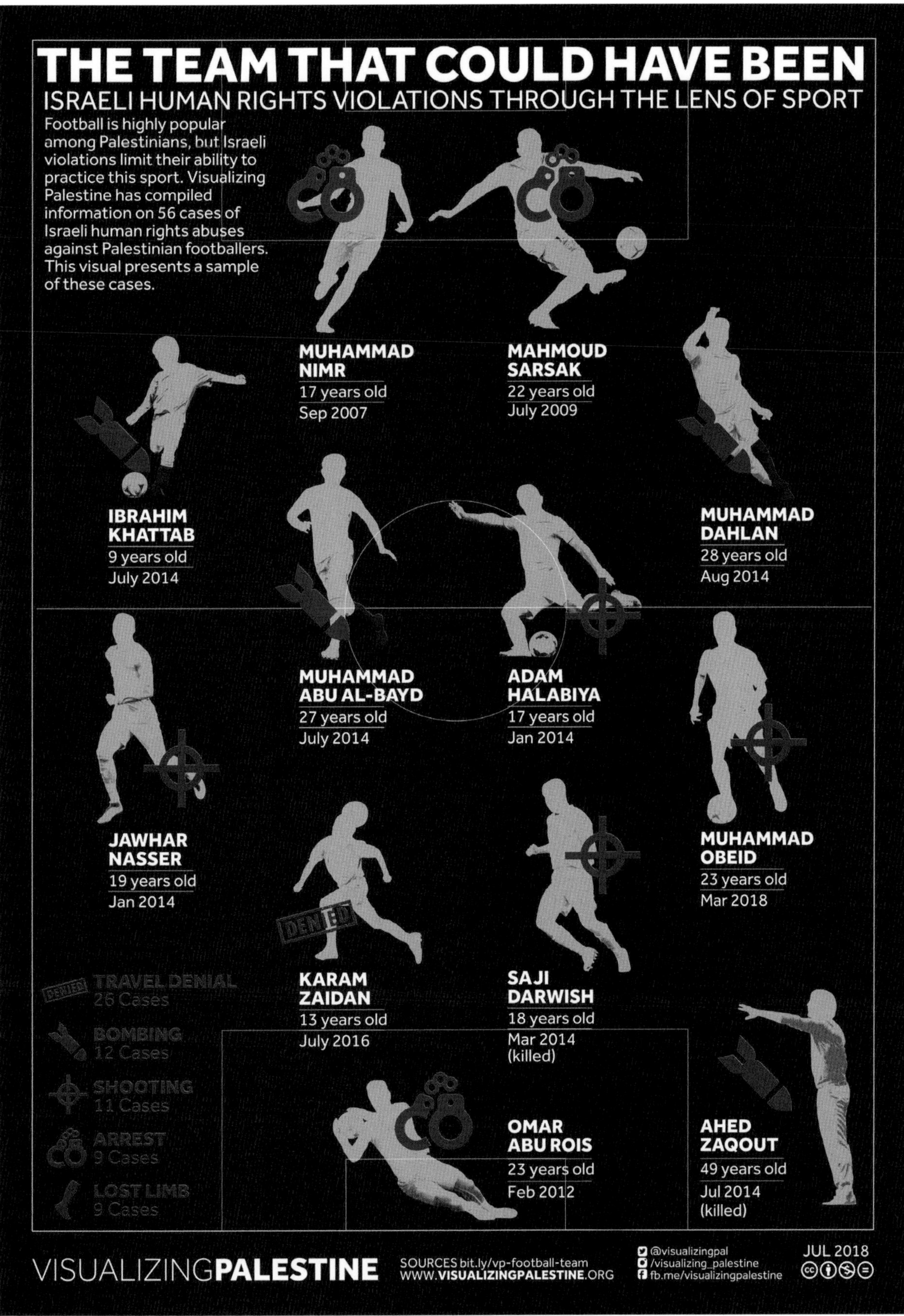
THE TEAM THAT COULD HAVE BEEN
ISRAELI HUMAN RIGHTS VIOLATIONS THROUGH THE LENS OF SPORT
Football is highly popular among Palestinians, but Israeli violations limit their ability to practice this sport. Visualizing Palestine has compiled information on 56 cases of Israeli human rights abuses against Palestinian footballers. This visual presents a sample of these cases.
MUHAMMAD NIMR
17 years old
Sep 2007
MAHMOUD SARSAK
22 years old
July 2009
IBRAHIM KHATTAB
9 years old
July 2014
MUHAMMAD DAHLAN
28 years old
Aug 2014
MUHAMMAD ABU AL-BAYD
27 years old
July 2014
ADAM HALABIYA
17 years old
Jan 2014
JAWHAR NASSER
19 years old
Jan 2014
MUHAMMAD OBEID
23 years old
Mar 2018
DENIED
KARAM ZAIDAN
13 years old
July 2016
SAJI DARWISH
18 years old
Mar 2014
(killed)
TRAVEL DENIAL
26 Cases
BOMBING
12 Cases
SHOOTING
11 Cases
ARREST
9 Cases
LOST LIMB
9 Cases
OMAR ABU ROIS
23 years old
Feb 2012
AHED ZAQOUT
49 years old
Jul 2014
(killed)
VISUALIZINGPALESTINE
SOURCES bit.ly/vp-football-team
WWW.VISUALIZINGPALESTINE.ORG
@visualizingpal
/visualizing_palestine
fb.me/visualizingpalestine
JUL 2018

Year: 2018 | **Brief and copywriting:** Ahmed Hegazy, Robin Jones | **Design:** Yosra El Gazzar, Ali Abbas Ahmadi | **Sources:** bit.ly/vp-football-team

12. SPECIAL PROJECT

Projects in this section: So Close Yet So Far | Growth of a Movement | Who's Complicit? | Palestine Open Maps | Palestine, Today | A National Monument | Visualizing Palestine 101 | We Had Dreams | Remember Their Names | A Place of Many Beginnings

The following pages introduce several of Visualizing Palestine's interactive projects or physical creations. We placed these projects in a dedicated section so that those interested in exploring them in more detail can seek them out, as well as to acknowledge the range of approaches we integrate in our storytelling.

SO CLOSE YET SO FAR

Series of Short Animations

In Palestine, distance is measured not just in kilometers, but in the insurmountable apartheid laws, bureaucracy, and infrastructure that keep so many Palestinians from having a sense of normalcy in their own homeland. In **So Close Yet So Far**, a series of short animations, we tell the stories of five Palestinian families separated by Israeli policy: Amani and Adnan, Ahmad and Rokaya, Samaher and Yasser, Hiba and her triplets, and Salma and Mousa.

Imagine a short drive to visit a relative causing a couple to be separated for years. This is what happened to Amani, Adnan, and their five children. Ahmad and Rokaya's children have to cross Israel's apartheid wall to see parents stuck on opposite sides of it. A Palestinian mother, Hiba, is sent back to Gaza just days after giving birth in Jerusalem, while her newborns stay at the hospital alone. Also in Jerusalem, Samaher refuses to leave her home for fear of being stopped by Israeli police and permanently separated from her spouse, Yasser. These families' circumstances may seem too absurd, bizarre, and surreal to be real, but they are all too common under Israeli apartheid.

A theme throughout So Close Yet So Far is the violence of bureaucracy, which puts Palestinian family life in the hands of a system that is brutal both in its most shocking displays of force and in the most intimate and mundane routines of life. We contextualized the distances in the story with reference to other geographies. One couple's struggle unfolds across 65 kilometers, roughly the distance from Amsterdam to the Hague. Another story spans 90 kilometers, roughly the distance from Manhattan to Long Island.

www.visualizingpalestine.org/visuals/so-close-yet-so-far
Year: 2020 | **Direction and animation:** Yosra El Gazzar | **Brief and copywriting:** Jessica Anderson, Reem Farah | **Narration:** Mohammad Al-Qaq, Dana Dajani, Sally Shalabi, Amir Shihadeh | **Sound studio:** Mohammed Hijazi (Obsolete Studios) and Tareq Mirza (dB-Pro) | **Sources:** bit.ly/VP-scysf

North
The family has owned land here for generations.

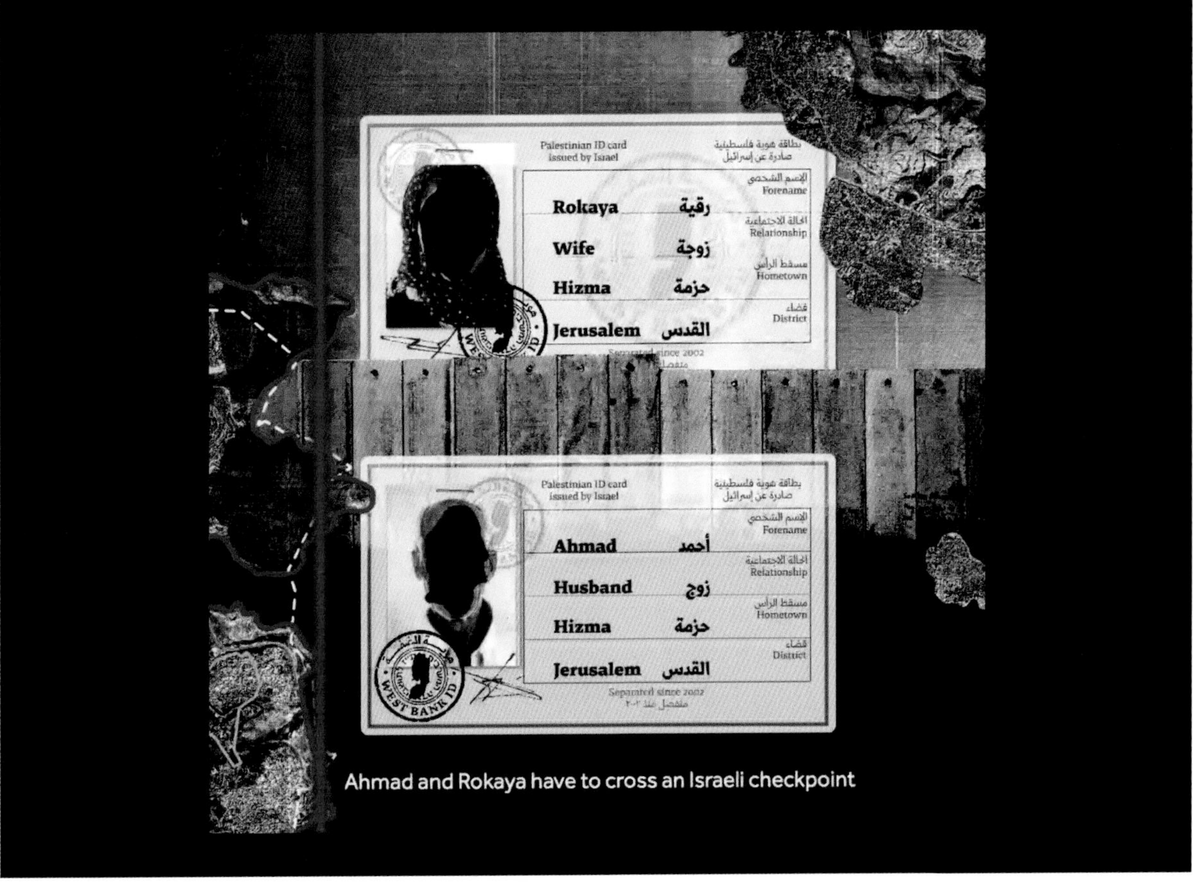
Palestinian ID card
issued by Israel
بطاقة هوية فلسطينية
صادرة عن إسرائيل
الإسم الشخصي
Forename
Rokaya رقية
الحالة الاجتماعية
Relationship
Wife زوجة
مسقط الرأس
Hometown
Hizma حزمة
قضاء
District
Jerusalem القدس
Palestinian ID card
issued by Israel
بطاقة هوية فلسطينية
صادرة عن إسرائيل
الإسم الشخصي
Forename
Ahmad أحمد
الحالة الاجتماعية
Relationship
Husband زوج
مسقط الرأس
Hometown
Hizma حزمة
قضاء
District
Jerusalem القدس
Separated since 2002
WEST BANK ID
Ahmad and Rokaya have to cross an Israeli checkpoint

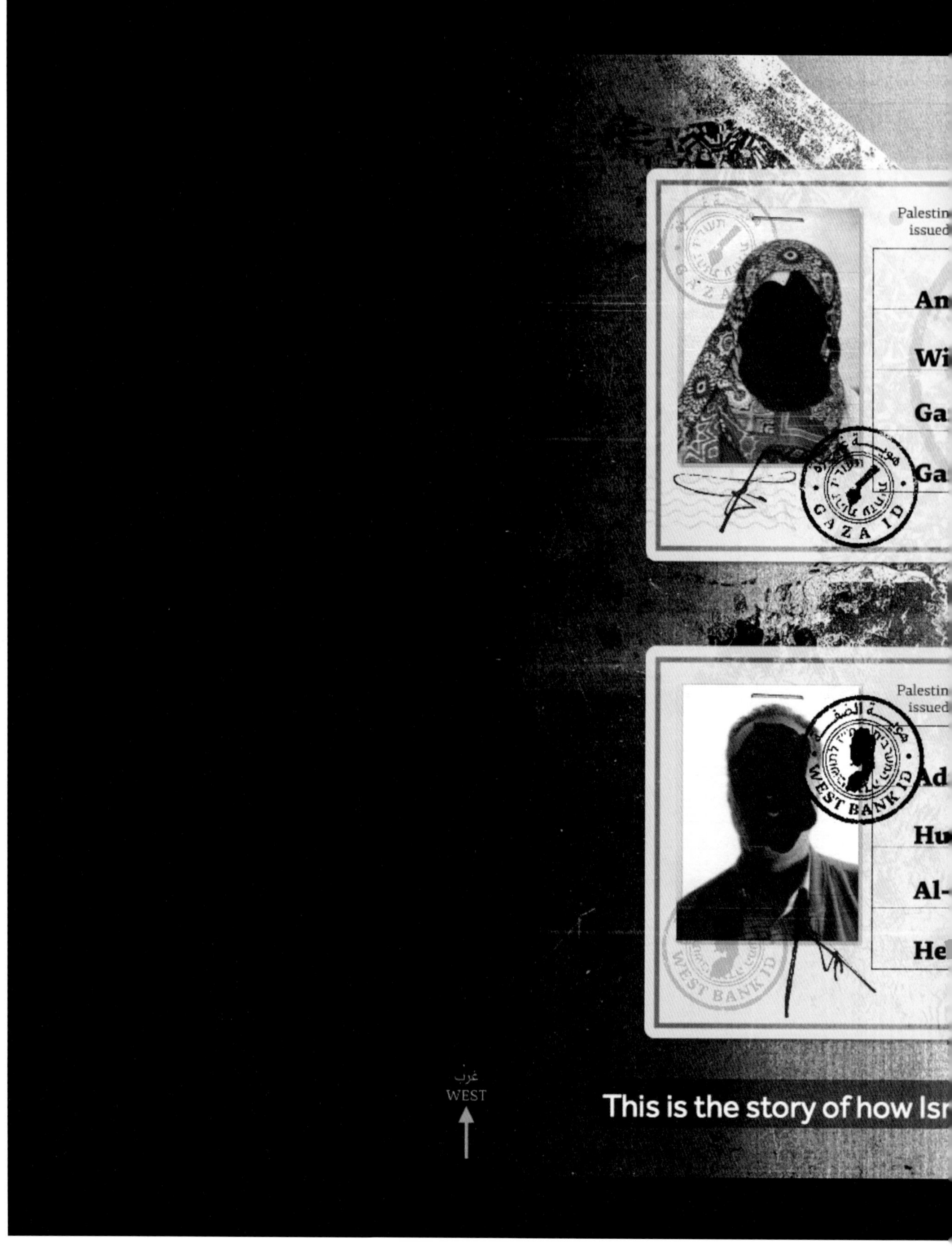
Palestin
issued
An
Wi
Ga
Ga
GAZA ID
Palestin
issued
Ad
Hu
Al-
He
WEST BANK ID
غرب
WEST
This is the story of how Isr

ard
l
بطاقة هوية فلسطينية
صادرة عن إسرائيل
الإسم الشخصي
Forename
أماني
الحالة الاجتماعية
Relationship
زوجة
مسقط الرأس
Hometown
غزة
قضاء
District
غزة
arated since 24/3/2013
منفصلة منذ ٢٠١٣/٣/٢٤
ard
l
بطاقة هوية فلسطينية
صادرة عن إسرائيل
الإسم الشخصي
Forename
عدنان
الحالة الاجتماعية
Relationship
nd
زوج
مسقط الرأس
Hometown
ub
العرّوب
قضاء
District
الخليل
arated since 24/3/2013
منفصل منذ ٢٠١٣/٣/٢٤
policy divided their family.

غـــزة
GAZA
البحر الابيض المتوسط
Mediterranean Sea
65 km كم
العـــرّوب
AL-'ARRUB
WEST
Just 65 km now stand between Amani and Adnan,

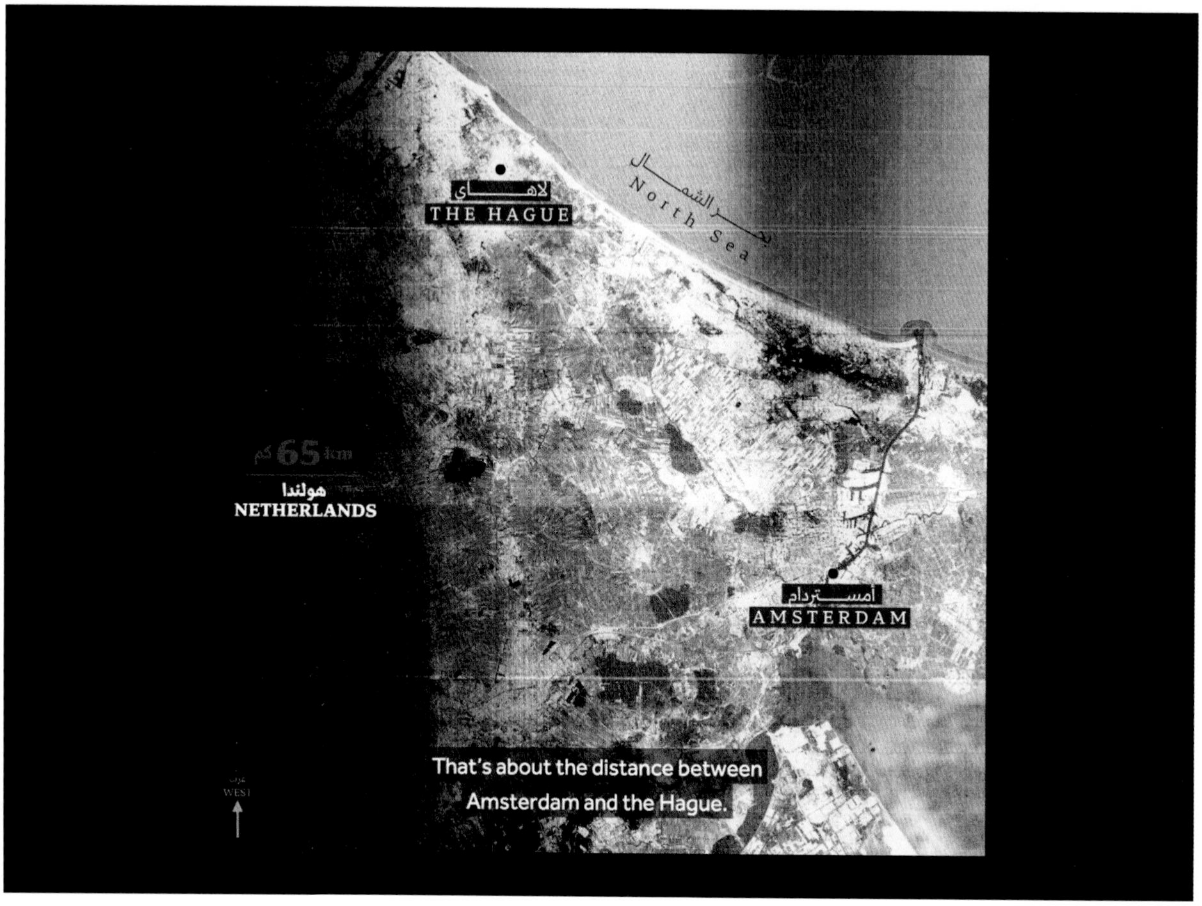

لاهـــاي
THE HAGUE
بحر الشمال
North Sea
65 km كم
هولندا
NETHERLANDS
أمستردام
AMSTERDAM
WEST
That's about the distance between
Amsterdam and the Hague.

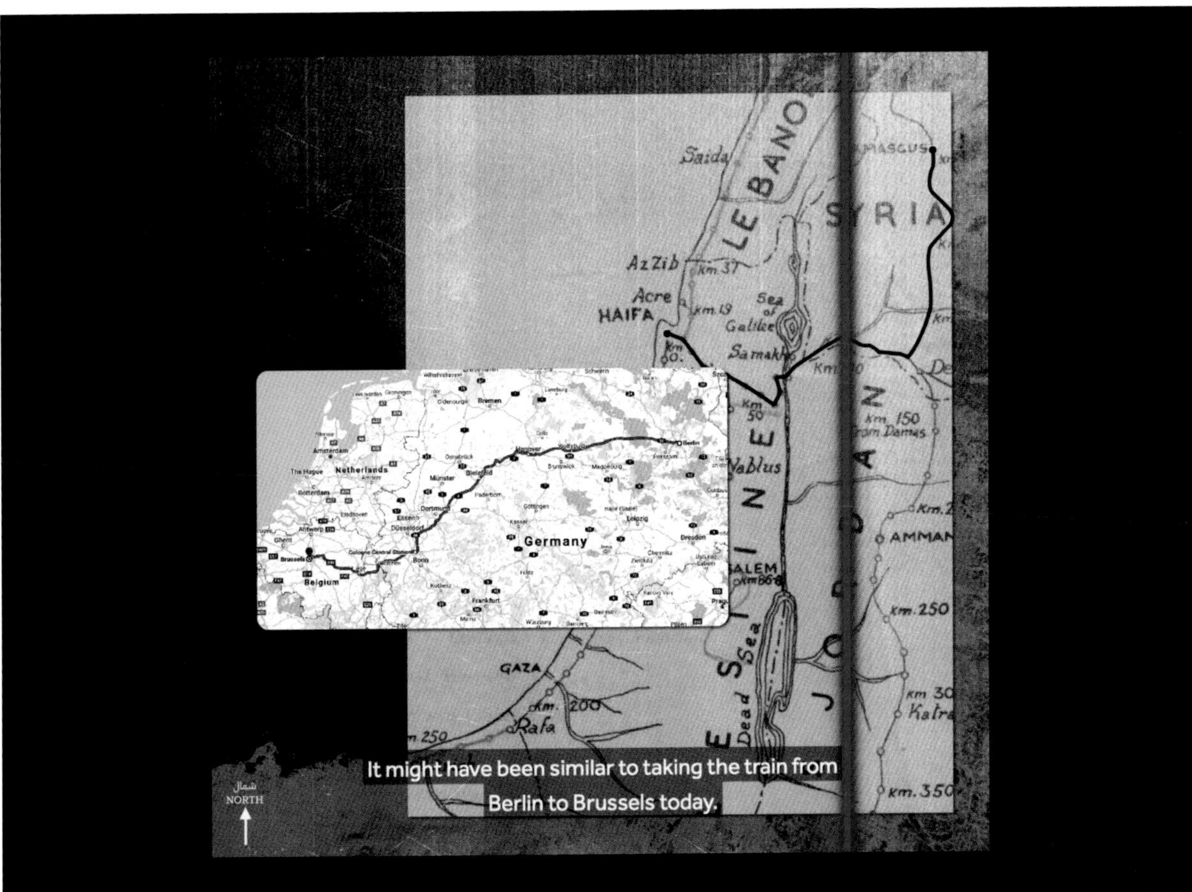
It might have been similar to taking the train from
Berlin to Brussels today.
شمال
NORTH
Saida
LEBANON
SYRIA
Az Zib
Acre
HAIFA
Sea of Galilee
Samakh
Nablus
AMMAN
GAZA
Rafa
Dead Sea
JORDAN
Netherlands
Germany
Belgium

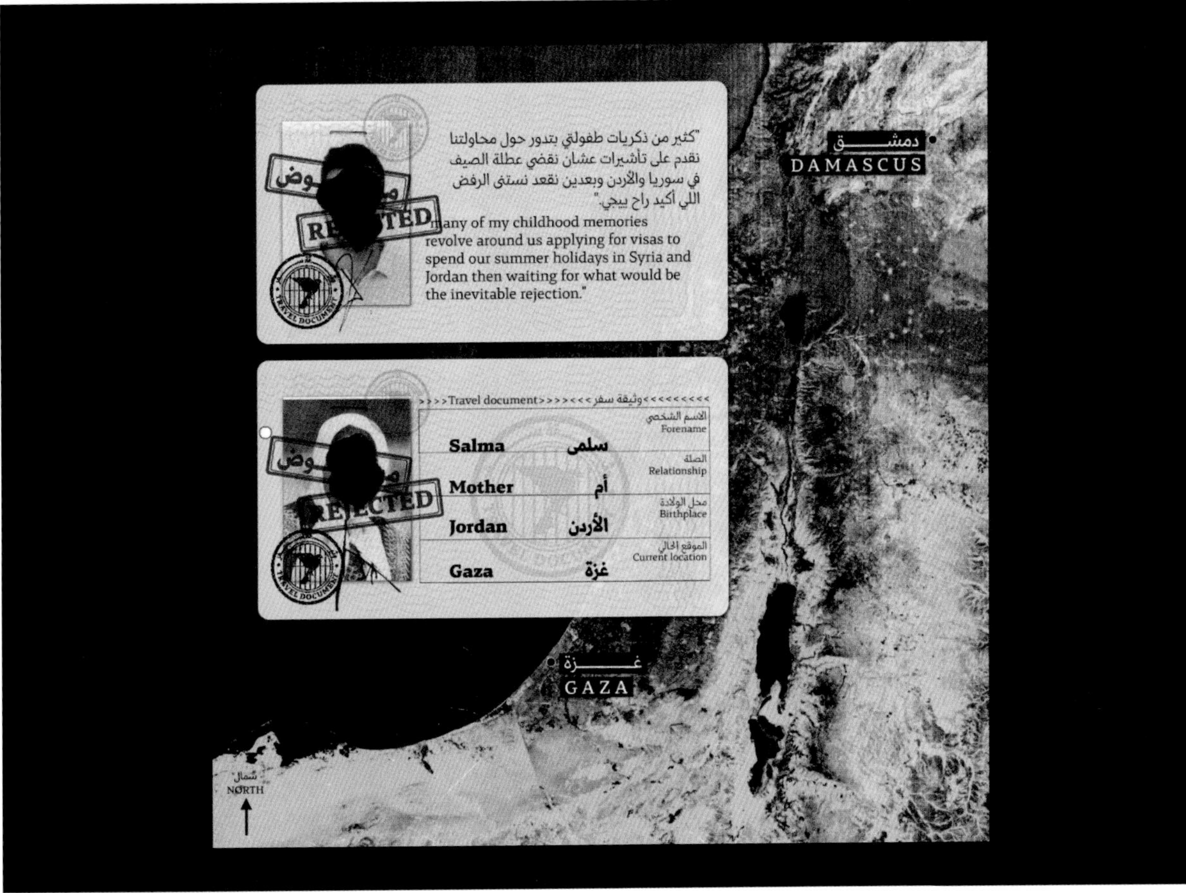
"كثير من ذكريات طفولتي بتدور حول محاولتنا
نقدم على تأشيرات عشان نقضي عطلة الصيف
في سوريا والأردن وبعدين نقعد نستنى الرفض
اللي أكيد راح ييجي."
"Many of my childhood memories revolve around us applying for visas to spend our summer holidays in Syria and Jordan then waiting for what would be the inevitable rejection."
REJECTED
>>>>Travel document>>>>>>>>وثيقة سفر>>>>>>>>>>
الاسم الشخصي Forename
Salma سلمى
الصلة Relationship
Mother أم
محل الولادة Birthplace
Jordan الأردن
الموقع الحالي Current location
Gaza غزة
دمشق
DAMASCUS
غزة
GAZA
شمال
NORTH

GROWTH OF A MOVEMENT
Interactive Timeline

Growth of a Movement documents key events that have shaped the Palestinian-led, global Boycott, Divestment, and Sanctions (BDS) movement for freedom, justice, and equality. As of 2023, the timeline includes 935 events from 2005 to 2022, which are searchable by campaign area, location, communities involved, and keywords. The Growth of a Movement timeline is hosted and edited by Visualizing Palestine, but it emerged in partnership and collaboration with the Boycott National Committee.

www.visualizingpalestine.org/collective-action-timeline
Brief and copywriting: Jessica Anderson, Ahmad Barclay, Boycott National Committee, Michael Deas, Reem Farah, Ramzi Jaber, Ziyaad Yousef, Shireen Tawil, Lylla Younes | **Development team:** Bassam Barham, Morad Taleeb | **Design:** Giorgio Uboldi (Calibro), Patil Tchilinguirian. Special thanks to dozens of volunteers who have participated in populating and updating the timeline.

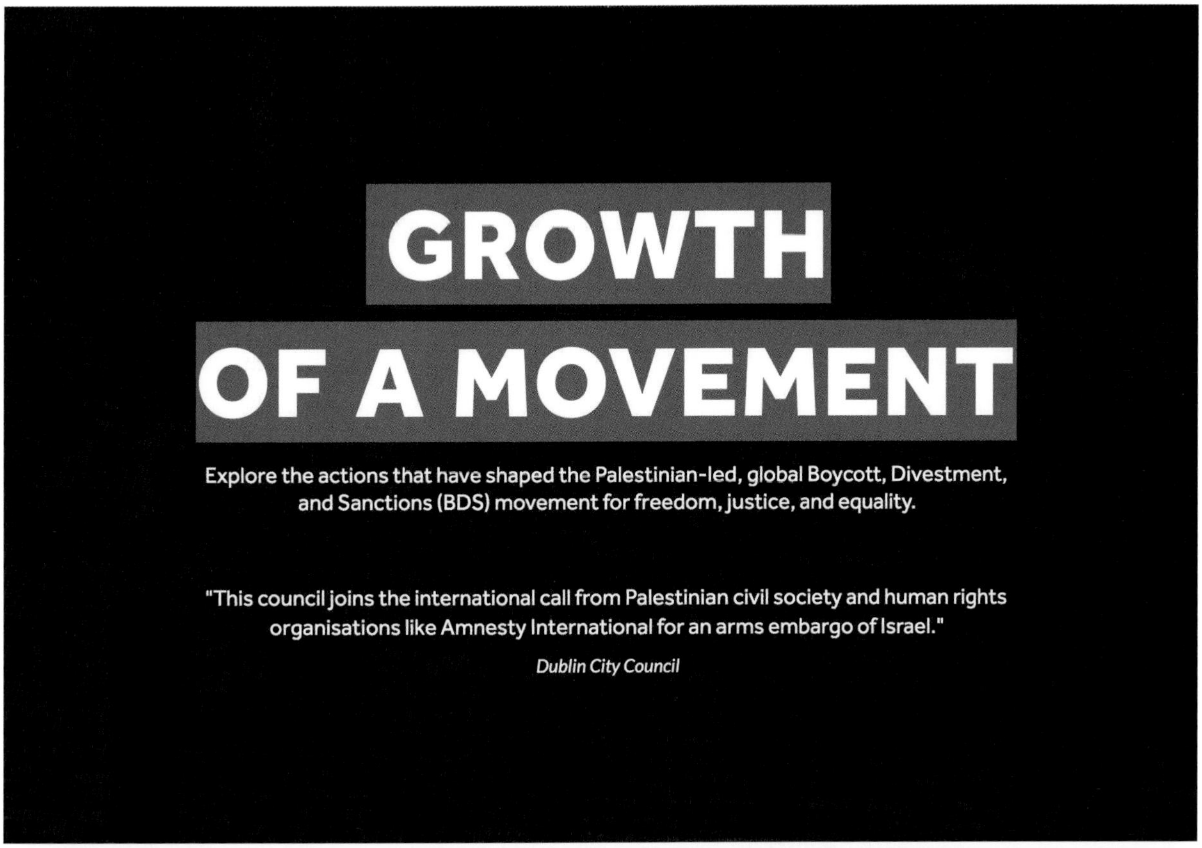

GROWTH OF A MOVEMENT

Explore the actions that have shaped the Palestinian-led, global Boycott, Divestment, and Sanctions (BDS) movement for freedom, justice, and equality.

"This council joins the international call from Palestinian civil society and human rights organisations like Amnesty International for an arms embargo of Israel."

Dublin City Council

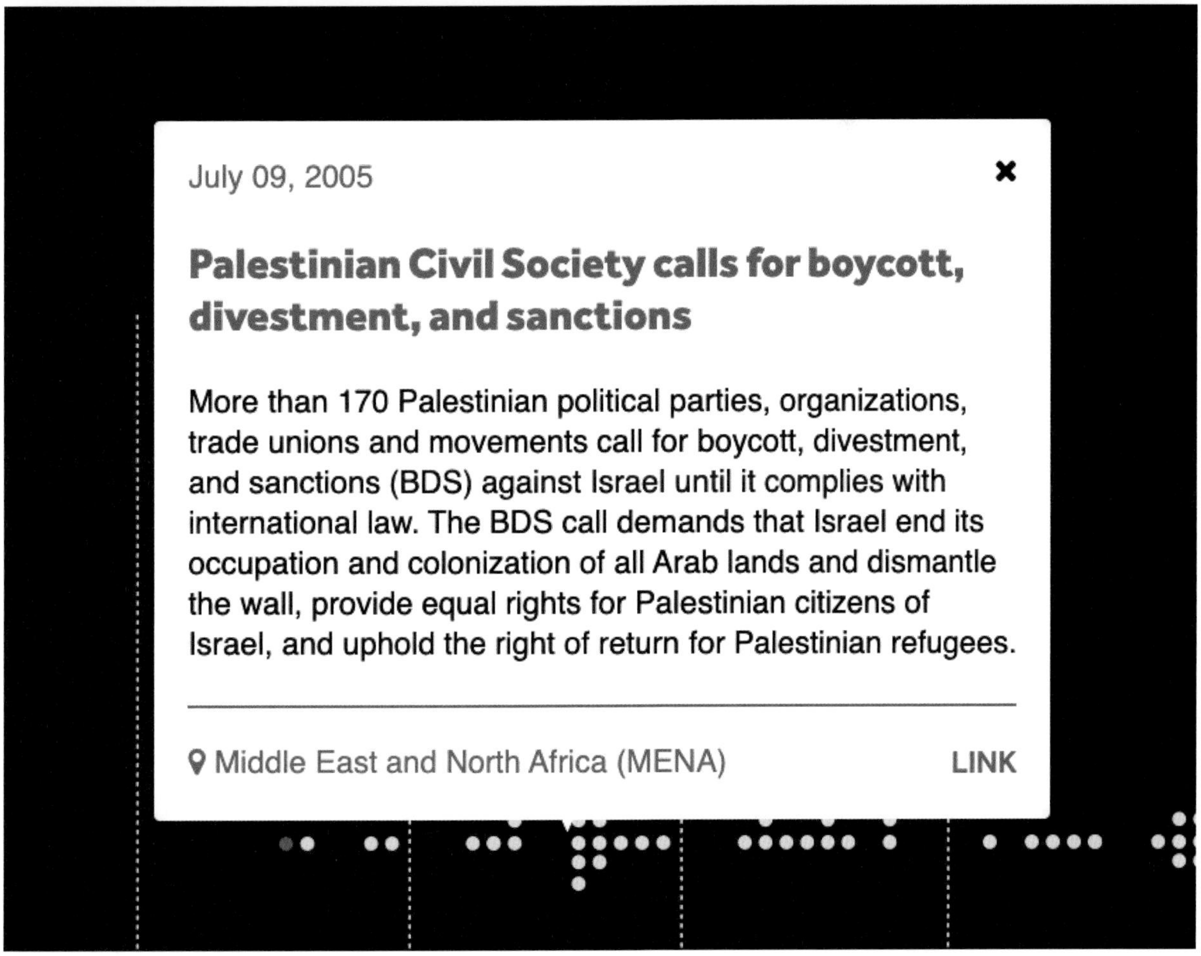

July 09, 2005

Palestinian Civil Society calls for boycott, divestment, and sanctions

More than 170 Palestinian political parties, organizations, trade unions and movements call for boycott, divestment, and sanctions (BDS) against Israel until it complies with international law. The BDS call demands that Israel end its occupation and colonization of all Arab lands and dismantle the wall, provide equal rights for Palestinian citizens of Israel, and uphold the right of return for Palestinian refugees.

Middle East and North Africa (MENA) LINK

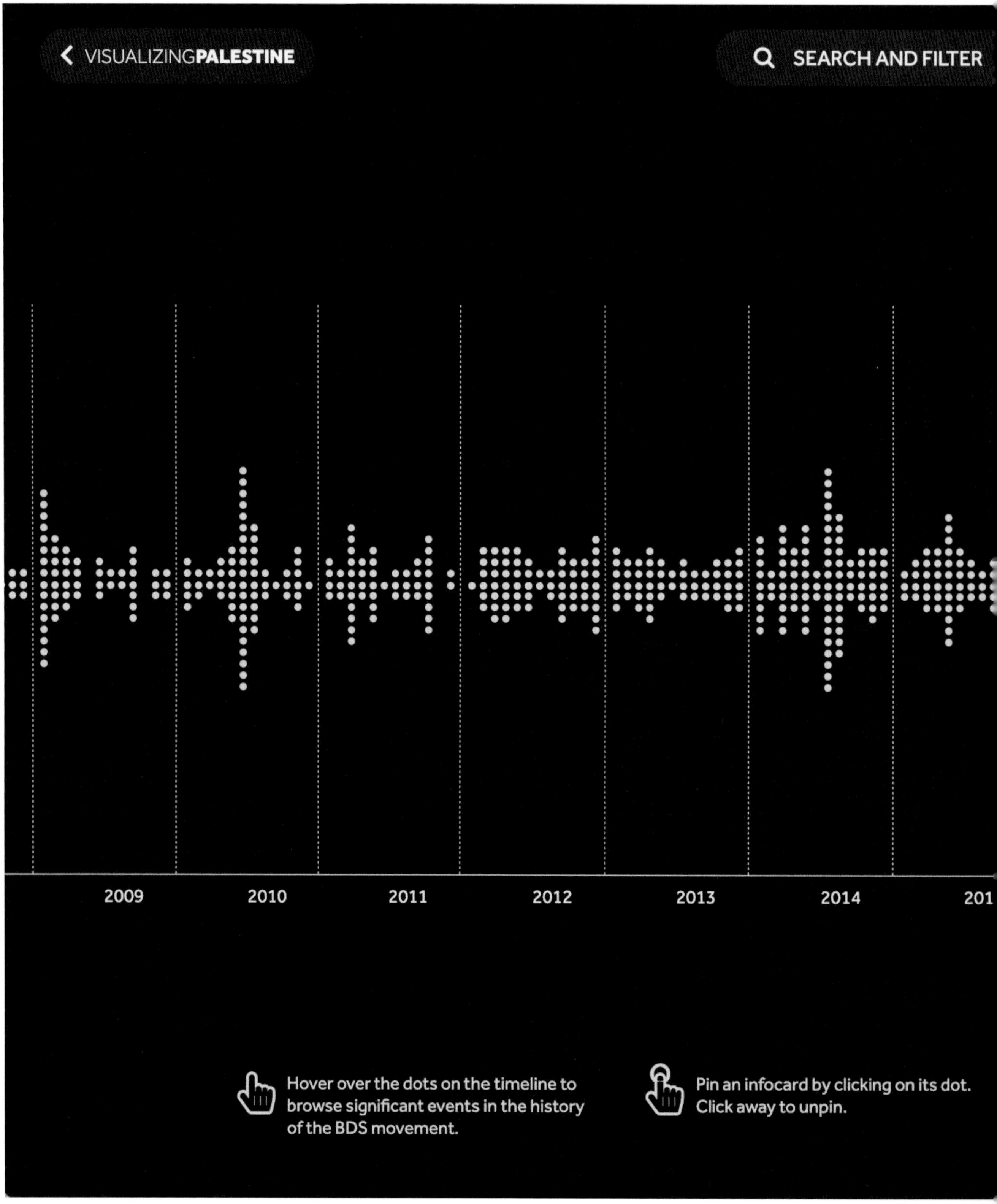

VISUALIZING**PALESTINE**

SEARCH AND FILTER

2009 2010 2011 2012 2013 2014 201

Hover over the dots on the timeline to browse significant events in the history of the BDS movement.

Pin an infocard by clicking on its dot. Click away to unpin.

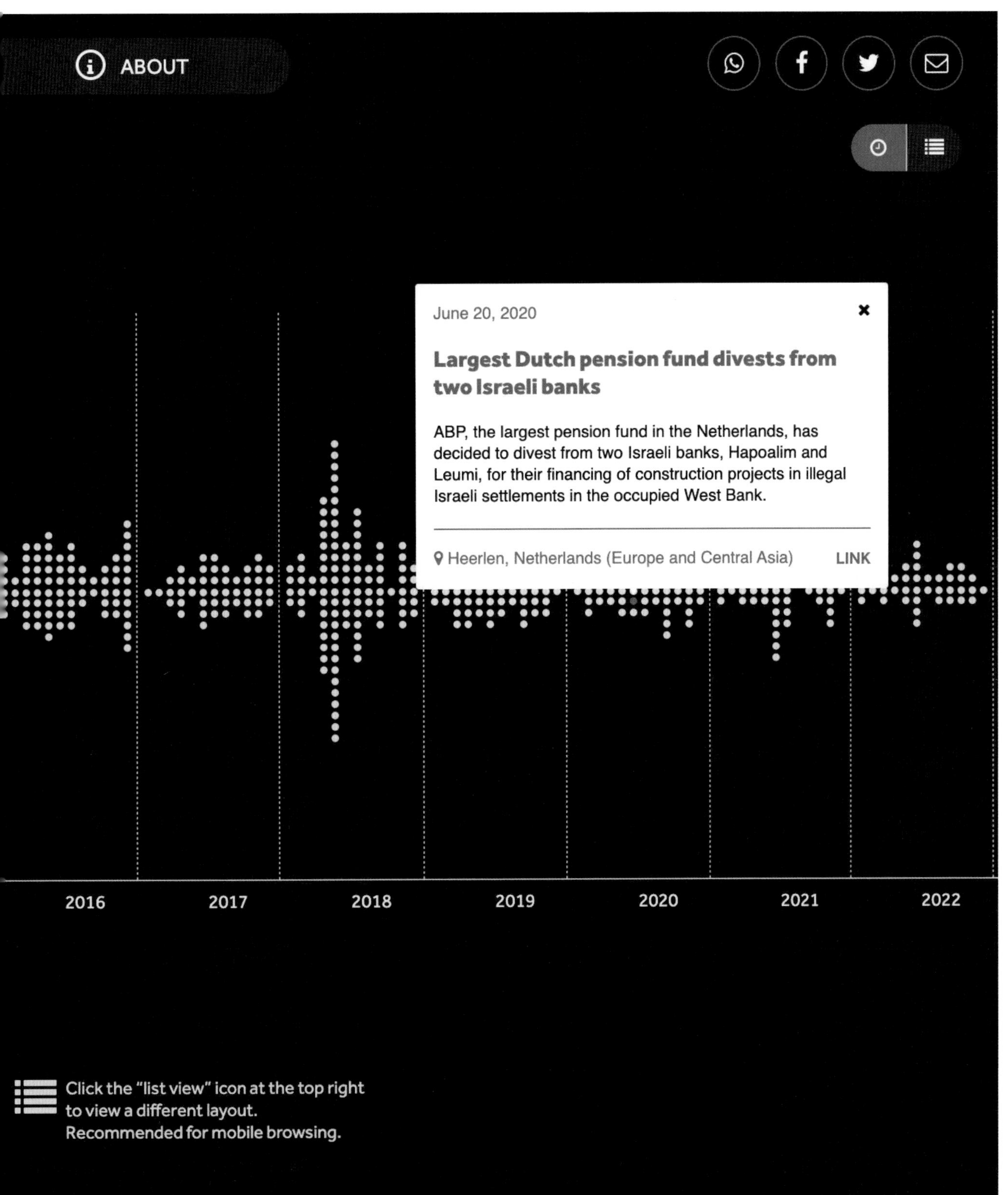
ABOUT
June 20, 2020
Largest Dutch pension fund divests from two Israeli banks
ABP, the largest pension fund in the Netherlands, has decided to divest from two Israeli banks, Hapoalim and Leumi, for their financing of construction projects in illegal Israeli settlements in the occupied West Bank.
Heerlen, Netherlands (Europe and Central Asia)
LINK
2016
2017
2018
2019
2020
2021
2022
Click the "list view" icon at the top right to view a different layout.
Recommended for mobile browsing.

WHO'S COMPLICIT?

Interactive Visual

In February 2020, following numerous delays, the United Nations Human Rights Council published a database of 112 companies complicit in business activities in illegal Israeli settlements. To help people better understand the scope of this step toward accountability, we created **Who's Complicit?** This interactive data visualization allows users to explore the companies listed by the nature of their violations and by the country in which they are based. Using a scaled bubble chart, we also integrated data on the total annual revenue of each company. In light of the narrow scope of the list, Who's Complicit? is a tool for pushing the UN to fulfill its mandate to continue updating and expanding on this list.

www.visualizingpalestine.org/un-database/index.html
Year: 2020 | **Brief and copywriting, design, and development:** Ahmad Barclay

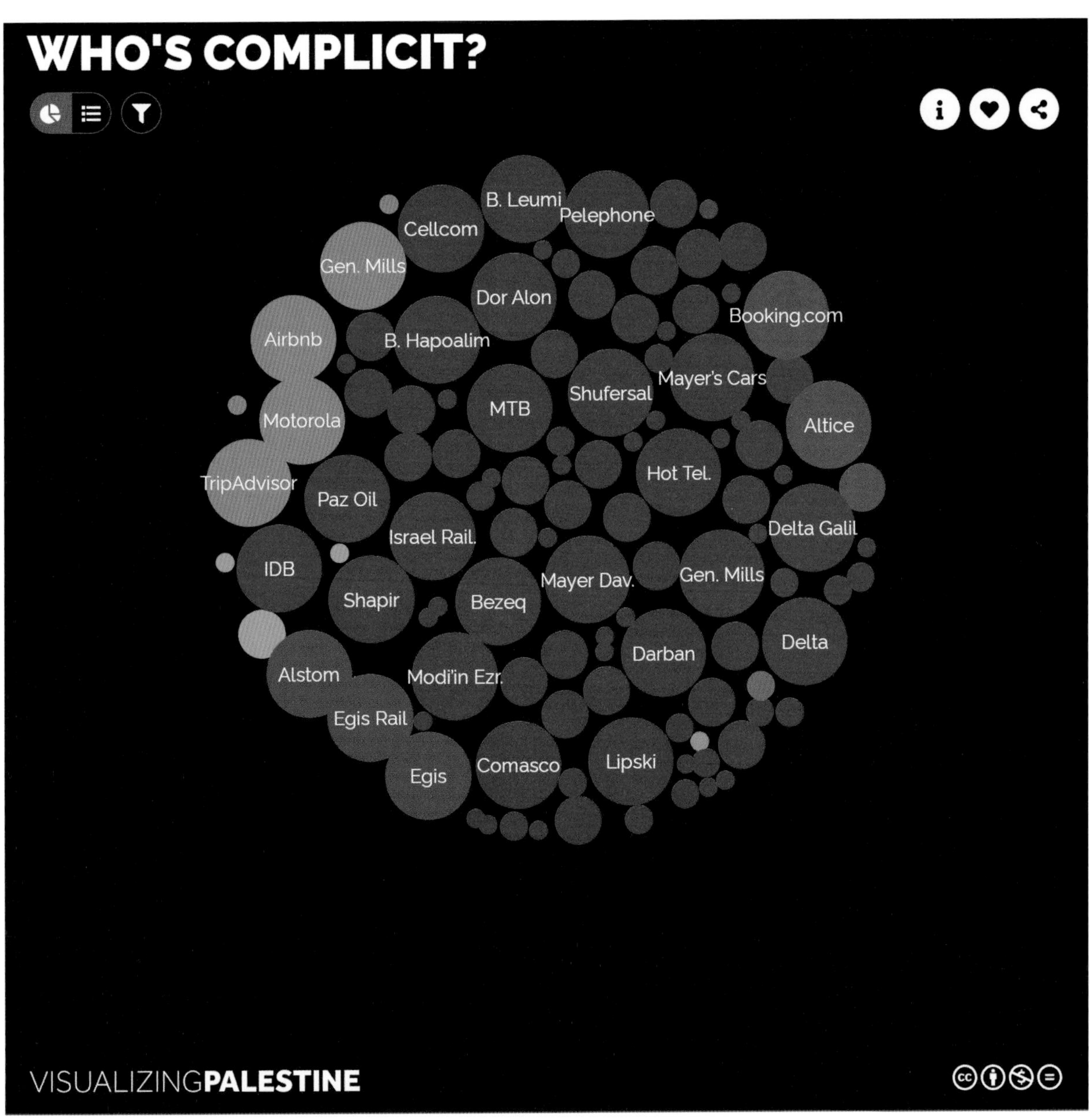
WHO'S COMPLICIT?
B. Leumi
Pelephone
Cellcom
Gen. Mills
Dor Alon
Booking.com
Airbnb
B. Hapoalim
Mayer's Cars
Shufersal
MTB
Motorola
Altice
Hot Tel.
TripAdvisor
Paz Oil
Israel Rail.
Delta Galil
IDB
Mayer Dav.
Gen. Mills
Shapir
Bezeq
Delta
Darban
Alstom
Modi'in Ezr.
Egis Rail
Comasco
Lipski
Egis
VISUALIZINGPALESTINE

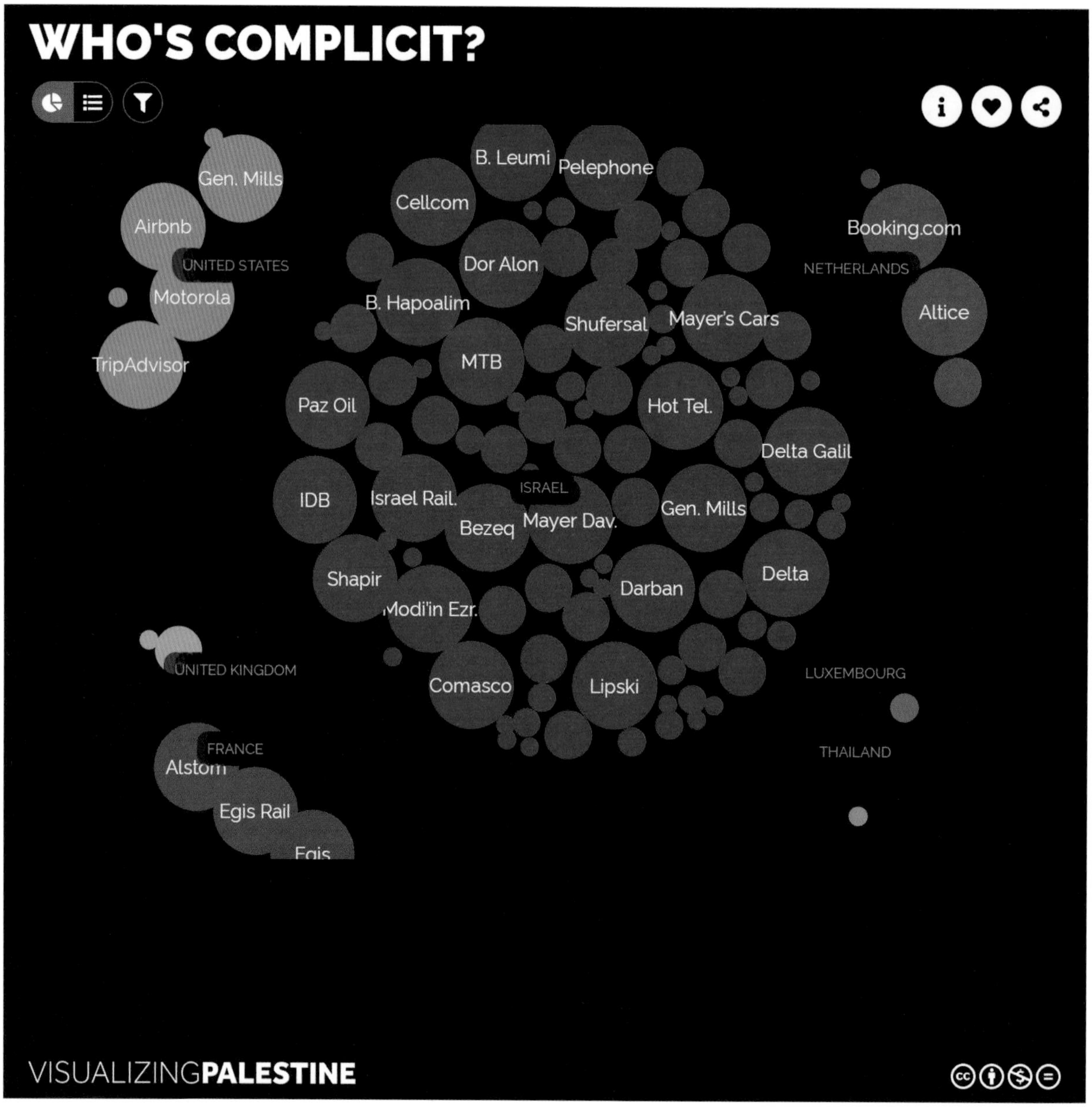

WHO'S COMPLICIT?
Gen. Mills
Airbnb
UNITED STATES
Motorola
TripAdvisor
B. Leumi
Pelephone
Cellcom
Dor Alon
B. Hapoalim
Shufersal
Mayer's Cars
MTB
Paz Oil
Hot Tel.
Delta Galil
IDB
Israel Rail.
ISRAEL
Bezeq
Mayer Dav.
Gen. Mills
Shapir
Modi'in Ezr.
Darban
Delta
Comasco
Lipski
Booking.com
NETHERLANDS
Altice
UNITED KINGDOM
FRANCE
Alstom
Egis Rail
Egis
LUXEMBOURG
THAILAND
VISUALIZINGPALESTINE

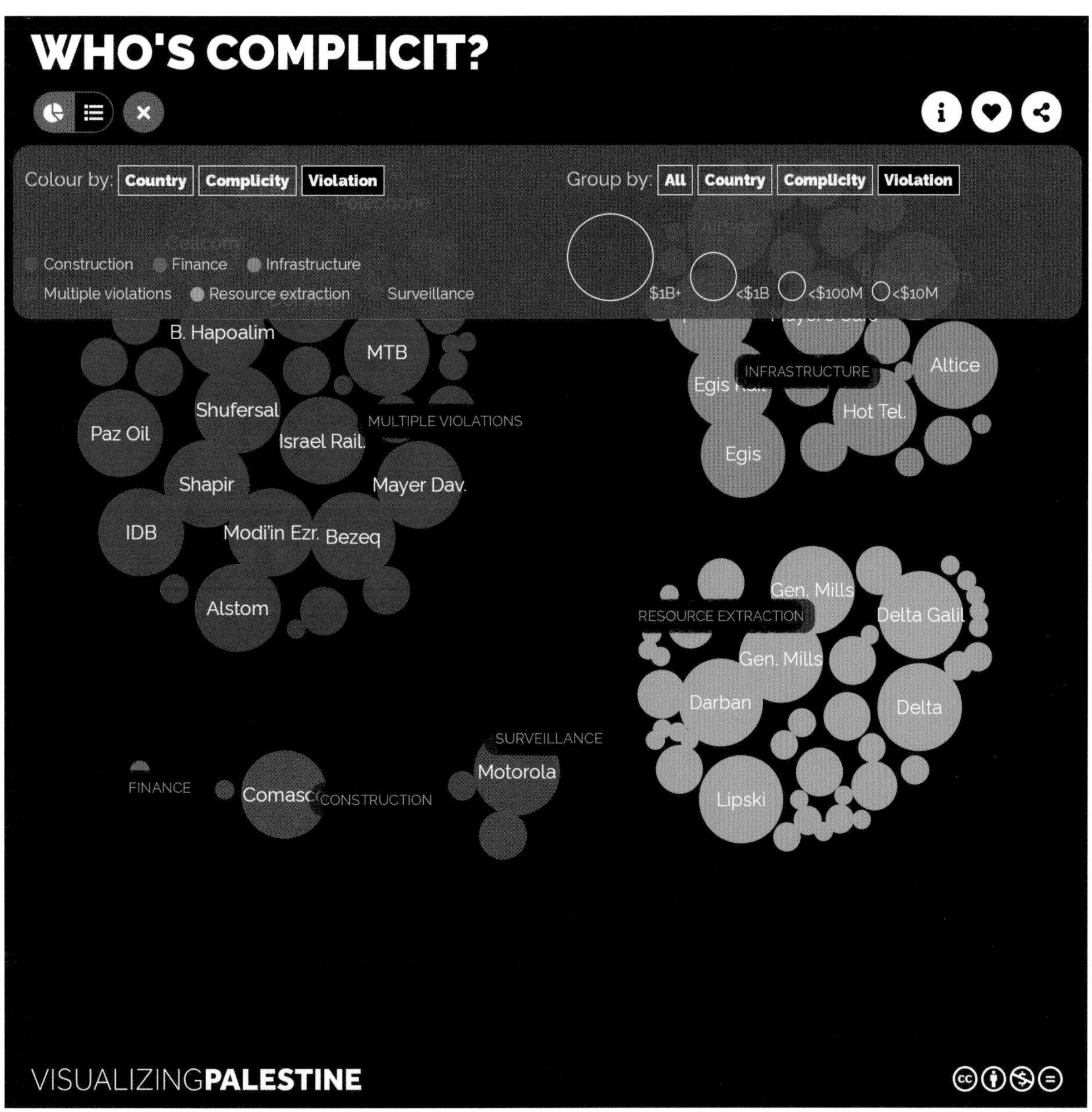
WHO'S COMPLICIT?
Colour by: Country Complicity Violation
Group by: All Country Complicity Violation
Construction
Finance
Infrastructure
Multiple violations
Resource extraction
Surveillance
$1B+
<$1B
<$100M
<$10M
B. Hapoalim
MTB
Shufersal
Paz Oil
Israel Rail.
MULTIPLE VIOLATIONS
Shapir
Mayer Dav.
IDB
Modi'in Ezr.
Bezeq
Alstom
INFRASTRUCTURE
Altice
Egis
Hot Tel.
Egis
Gen. Mills
RESOURCE EXTRACTION
Delta Galil
Gen. Mills
Darban
Delta
Lipski
SURVEILLANCE
Motorola
FINANCE
Comasco
CONSTRUCTION
VISUALIZINGPALESTINE

PALESTINE OPEN MAPS

Open Source Counter-Mapping Platform

Palestine Open Maps (POM) is a platform that allows users to explore, search, and download historical maps and spatial data on Palestine. Features of POM include:

- Detailed historical base-map layers from the 1870s to the 1950s
- Population data on over two thousand places, present and destroyed
- Aerial photography layers from the 1940s and today
- The ability to download hundreds of individual historical map sheets
- A split-screen mode to view past and present images side by side
- A 3D mode, showing the topography of Palestine
- The ability to overlay historical map features on present-day maps
- Links to the Palestinian Oral History Archive and other resources

The idea for this platform was inspired by a large collection of 1940s survey map sheets from the British Mandate of Palestine that became available digitally. These maps—all now in the public domain—cover the territory at scales of up to 1:20,000, offering a vivid snapshot of a human and natural geography immediately before the Nakba, with an unparalleled level of physical detail, including population centers, roads, topographic features, and property boundaries.

Although the maps were already in the public domain, their usefulness was limited since they comprise hundreds of separate sheets with no easy means to search, navigate, or otherwise comprehend. By combining these sheets into seamless layers that can be navigated online, and integrating them with other available data sources, such as the 1945 Village Statistics, historic aerial photography, oral histories, and present-day digital maps and data, this platform is a resource for mapping the transformation in the human geography of historic Palestine over the past seven and a half decades. POM is used widely by academics in both research and teaching and has served as an inspiration to other decolonial mapping projects around the world.

Palestine Open Maps

Welcome to Palestine Open Maps

Explore, search and download historical maps and spatial data on Palestine

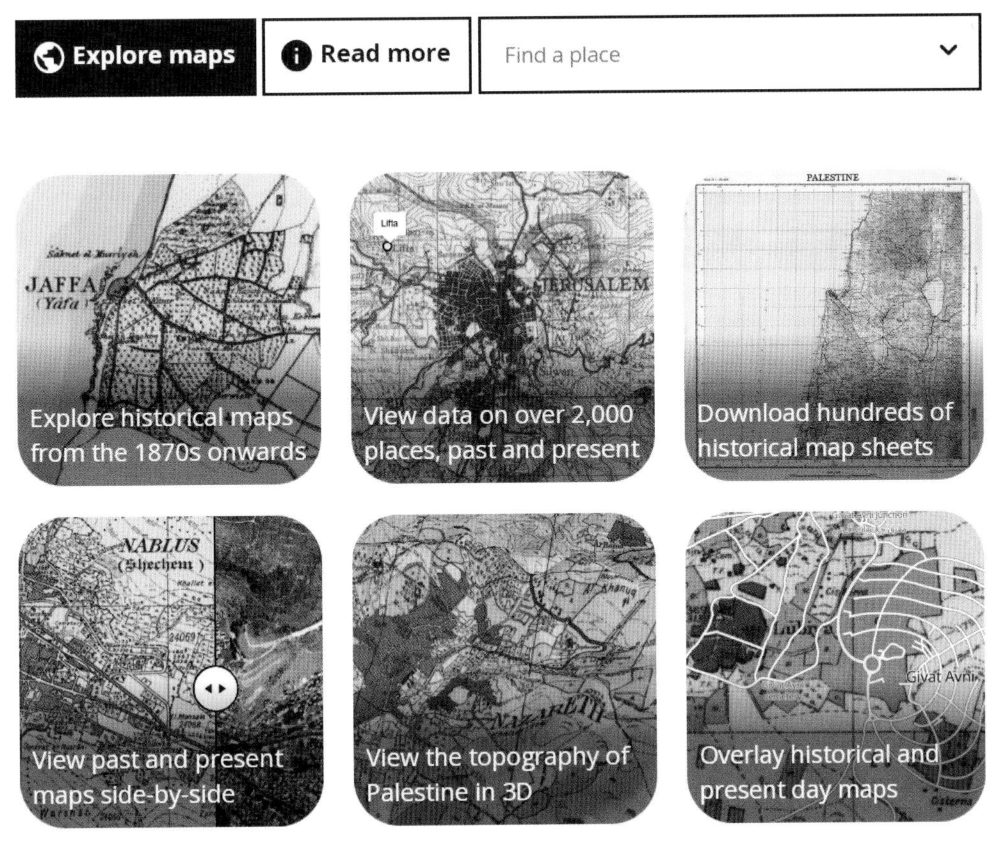
Explore maps
Read more
Find a place
JAFFA
(Yâfa)
Explore historical maps from the 1870s onwards
JERUSALEM
View data on over 2,000 places, past and present
PALESTINE
Download hundreds of historical map sheets
NABLUS
(Shechem)
View past and present maps side-by-side
NAZARETH
View the topography of Palestine in 3D
Givat Avni
Overlay historical and present day maps

Initiated and supported by VISUALIZING**PALESTINE**

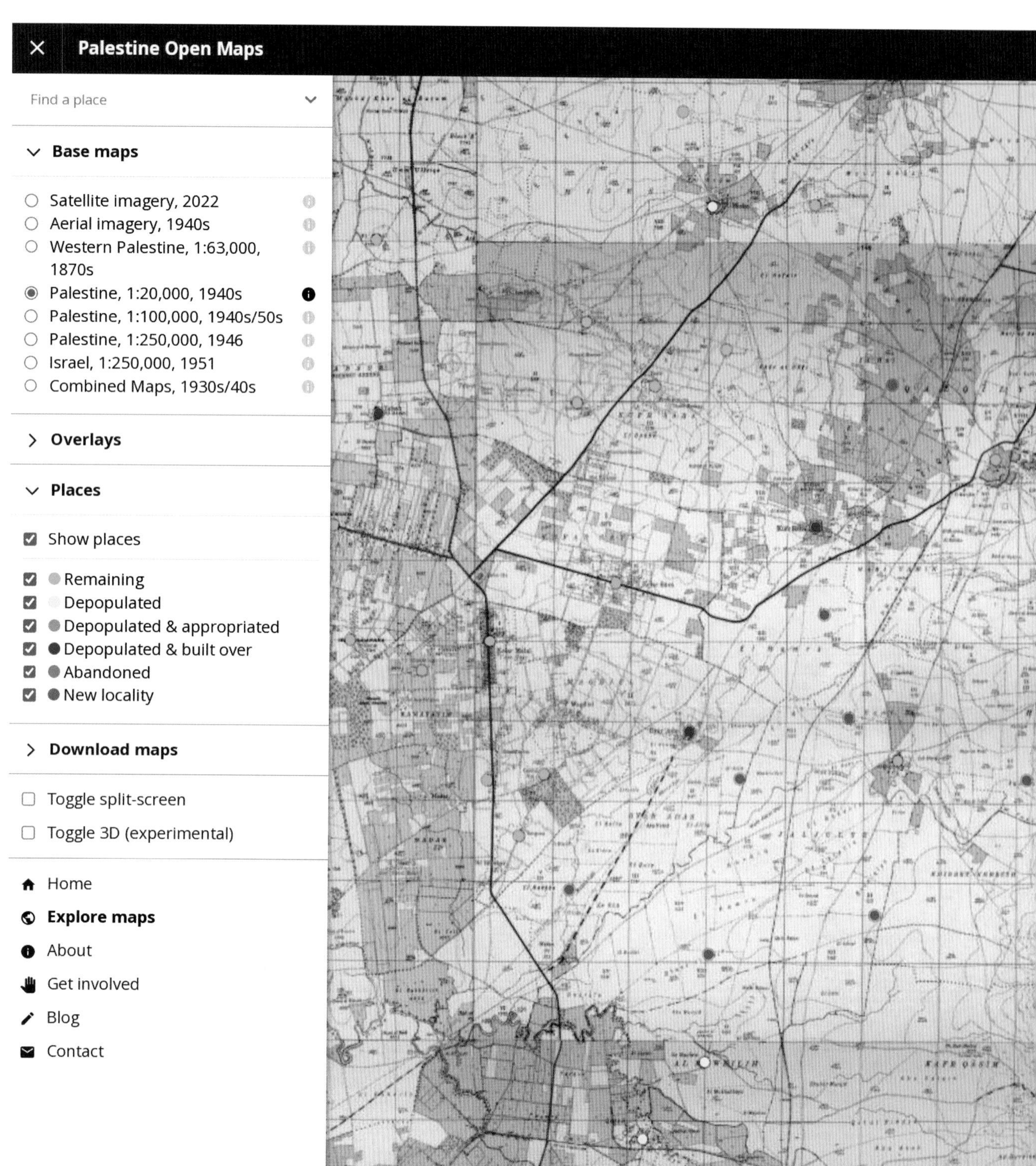
Palestine Open Maps
Find a place
Base maps
Satellite imagery, 2022
Aerial imagery, 1940s
Western Palestine, 1:63,000, 1870s
Palestine, 1:20,000, 1940s
Palestine, 1:100,000, 1940s/50s
Palestine, 1:250,000, 1946
Israel, 1:250,000, 1951
Combined Maps, 1930s/40s
Overlays
Places
Show places
Remaining
Depopulated
Depopulated & appropriated
Depopulated & built over
Abandoned
New locality
Download maps
Toggle split-screen
Toggle 3D (experimental)
Home
Explore maps
About
Get involved
Blog
Contact

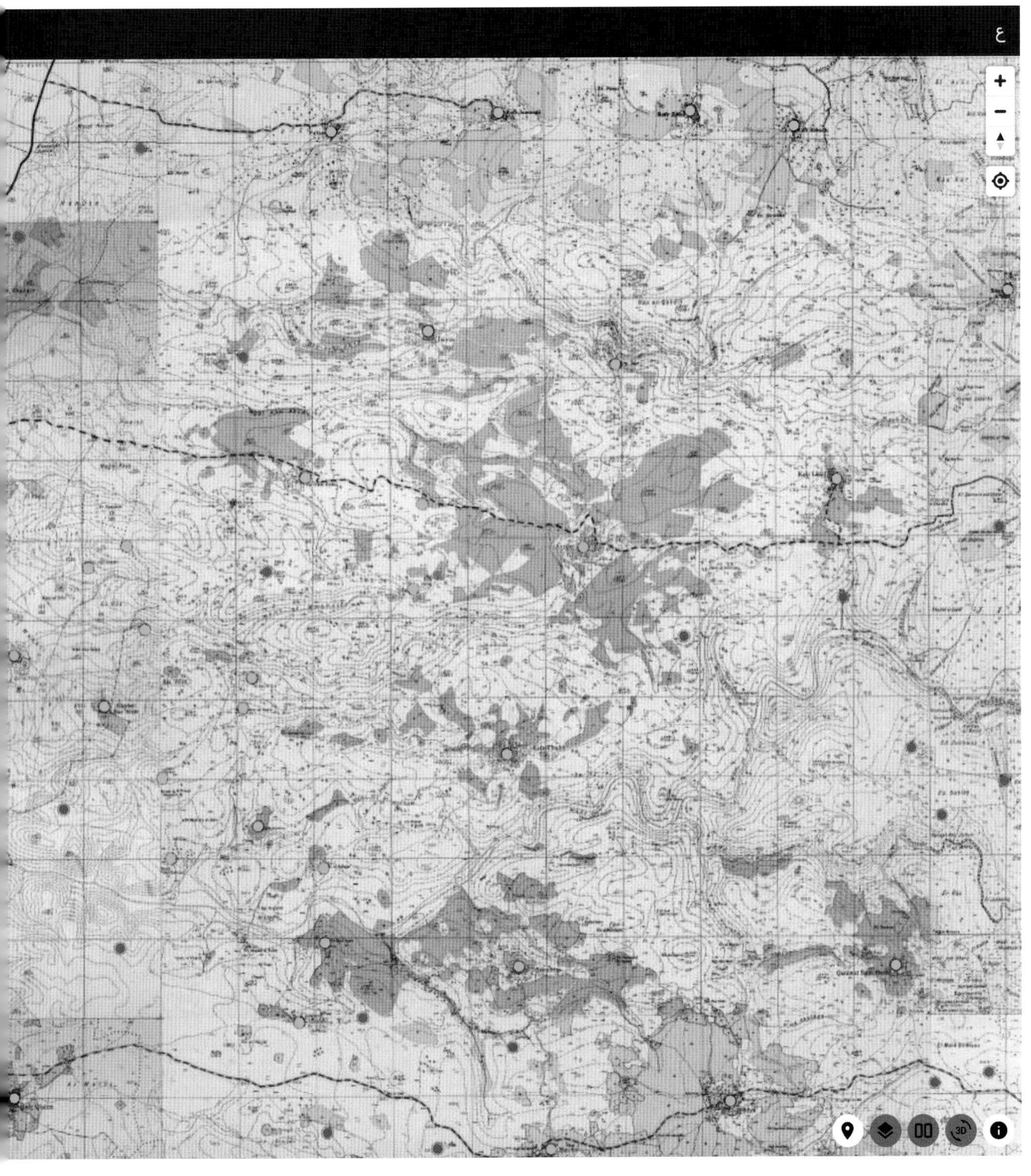
ع

Palestine Open Maps

Jerusalem

City in Jerusalem sub-district

CHANGE SINCE 1948

● Depopulated & appropriated

KEY DATES

Depopulated

1 May 1948

POPULATION

1945	2016
157,080	**882,700**

POPULATION BY GROUP

2016

1945

%	1945	2016
● Palestinian	38	38
● Jewish	62	61
● Other	N/A	2

JERUSALEM ON PALESTINIAN ORAL HISTORY ARCHIVE

Interview with Nicolas 'Abdū Ziyādah
Language: Arabic
Duration: 06:14:11

Interview with George Bāsil Farrāj
Language: Arabic
Duration: 00:41:34

Interview with Ḥasan Jamāl al-Ḥusaynī
Language: Arabic
Duration: 00:41:42

Interview with Bayān

Jerusalem

JERUSALEM

MOUNT OF OLIVES

Silwan

Wādī Qaddūm

El Harāyiq
Bāṭin el Jarmūh
Karm 'Abbās & Et Turbi'a
Umm er Rujūm
Habāyil Badī & Rās Hamdān
El Hinū
Rujūm es Suwwān & Ed Dureijāt
B I R M A I
Umm et 'Umdān
Khallat et Taban & Qismat Zāhir
Beit Shanna
Er Rās el Kabīr
Khallat Mūsā

Palestine Open Maps

Gaza

Base maps

Overlays

Show overlays

Vector overlay, 2020s
Vector overlay, 1940s

Buildings
Roads/rail
Place names

Places

Show places

Remaining
Depopulated
Depopulated & appropriated
Depopulated & built over
Abandoned
New locality

Download maps

Toggle split-screen
Toggle 3D (experimental)

Home
Explore maps
About
Get involved
Blog
Contact

2016
100
N/A

ASH SHATI REFUGEE CAMP
SHEIKH REDWAN
Gaza
غزة
Al-Qubbah
القبة
a-Zahra

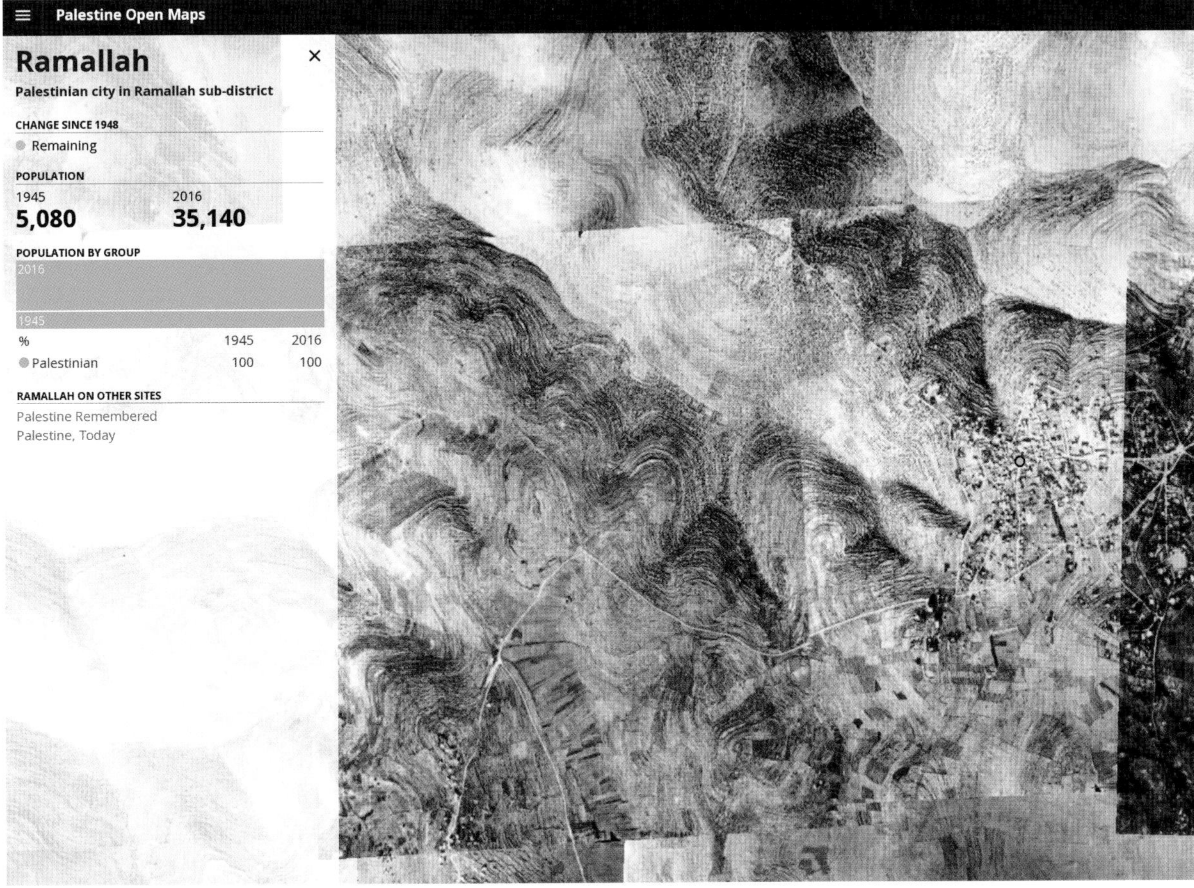
Palestine Open Maps
Ramallah
Palestinian city in Ramallah sub-district
CHANGE SINCE 1948
Remaining
POPULATION
1945
5,080
2016
35,140
POPULATION BY GROUP
2016
1945
% 1945 2016
Palestinian 100 100
RAMALLAH ON OTHER SITES
Palestine Remembered
Palestine, Today

Palestine Open Maps exhibited at Dar El Nimer for Arts and Culture in Beirut, Lebanon, 2019

www.palopenmaps.org/en

The project was initiated at Impact Data Lab, a workshop organized by Visualizing Palestine and Columbia University Studio-X Amman in March 2018. Majd Al-Shihabi's work on the project was partially supported by Creative Commons, Mozilla Foundation, and the Wikimedia Foundation via the Bassel Khartabil Fellowship.

Project leads: Ahmad Barclay, Majd Al-Shihabi | **Development team:** Ahmad Barclay, Majd Al-Shihabi, Hanan Yazigi, Morad Taleeb, Henry Zaccak, and Bassam Barham | **Special thanks:** Salman Abu Sitta, Zaki Boulos, Stella Ioannidou, Noor Lozi, Nora Akawi, and the Columbia Studio-X Amman team

PALESTINE, TODAY
Multimedia Interactive Platform

Palestine has been transformed dramatically over the decades since the Nakba of 1947–49, when over five hundred Palestinian towns and villages were depopulated and over 750,000 people were displaced during the creation of the State of Israel.

Palestine, Today tells the story of the many communities that were affected by the Nakba, including those that remained. Users can view the story of a random locality or select a site of special interest to them.

today.visualizingpalestine.org/
Design and development: Ahmad Barclay

PALESTINE, TODAY

EXPLORE HOW THE NAKBA TRANSFORMED PALESTINE

A project by Visualizing Palestine

START NOW SKIP TO END

The maps cover the most densely populated part of the country, from Rafah on the southwestern border with Egypt.

The colours of the markers represent the status of the community today.

● 102 communities were destroyed in the Nakba and built over by new settlements. ● 13 were depopulated in the Nakba and appropriated for Israeli habitation. ● 384 were depopulated in the Nakba, but have not been built over, and ● 693 communities remain standing today.

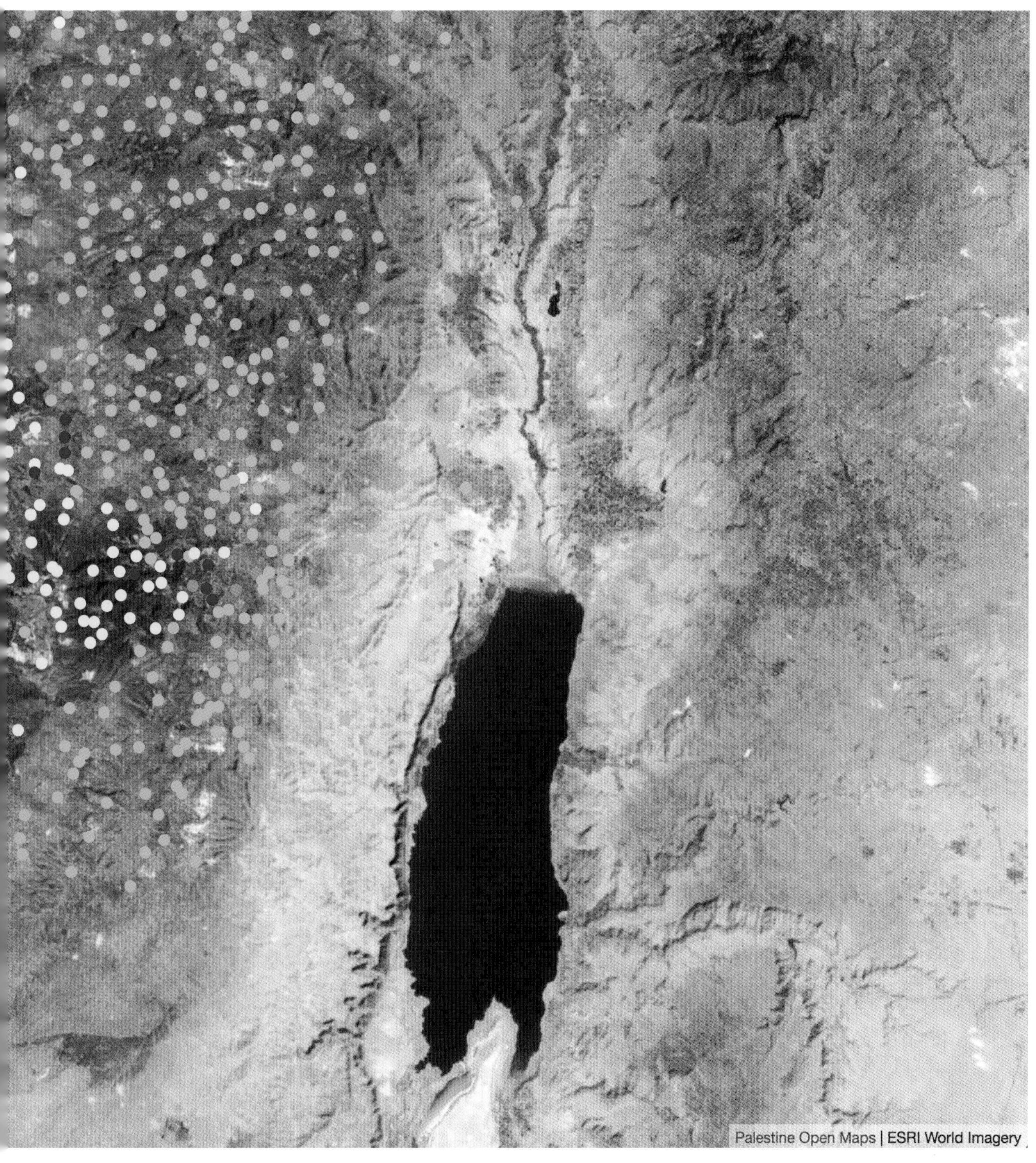
Palestine Open Maps | ESRI World Imagery

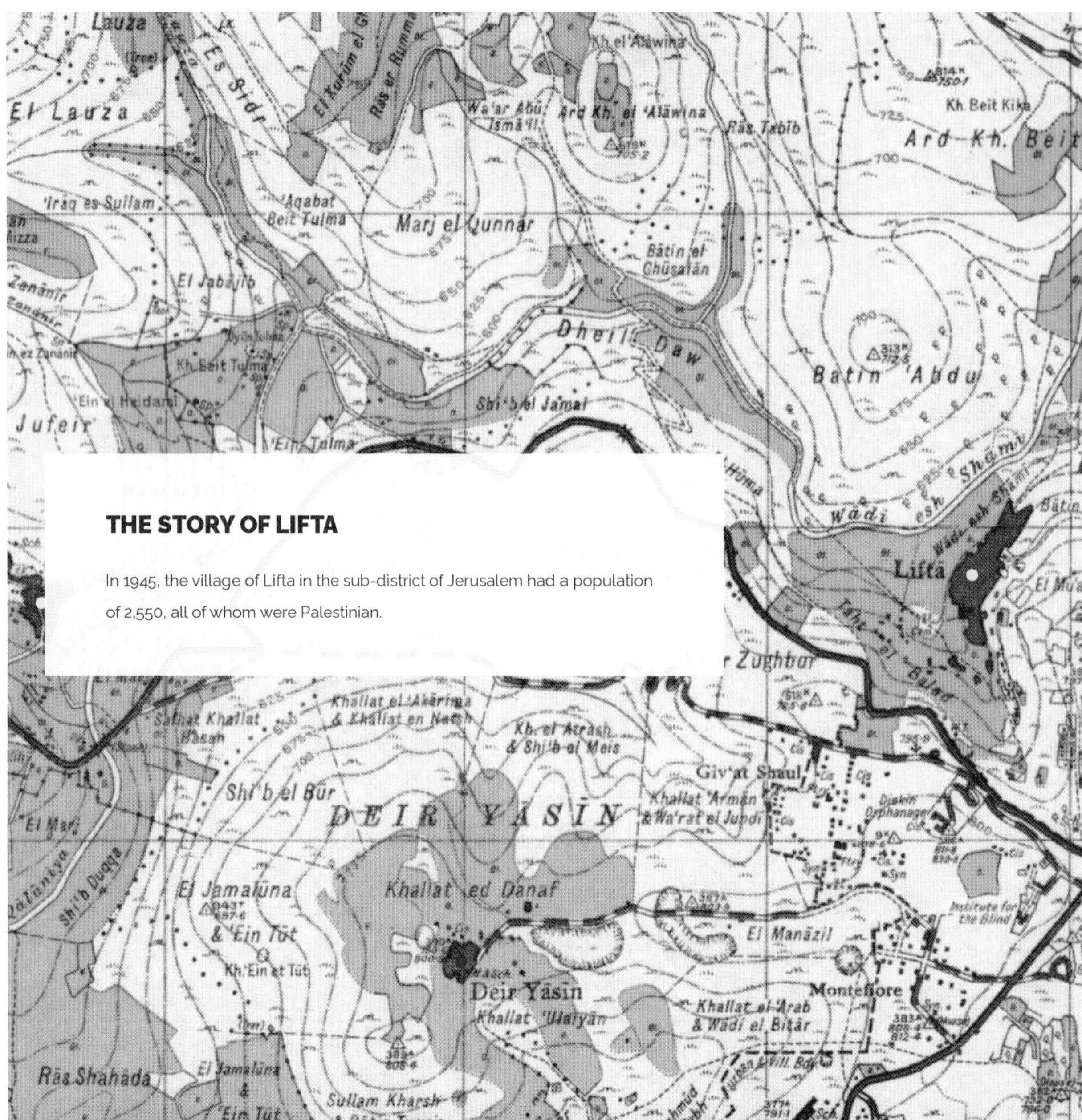
Lauza
El Lauza
Es Sidr
Kh. el 'Alawina
Wa'ar Abū Isma'il
Ard Kh. el 'Alawina
Rās Tabīb
Kh Beit Kika
Ard Kh. Beit
'Iraq es Sullam
'Aqabat Beit Tulma
Marj el Qunnar
Bātin el Ghūsalān
El Jabājib
Dheil Daw
Kh. Beit Tulma
Bātin 'Abdu
Shi'b el Jamal
Jufeir
Wādi esh Shāmi
Liftā
Tahl el Balad
Khallat el 'Akārima & Khallat en Natsh
Kh. el Atrash & Shi'b el Meis
Sāhat Khallat Hasan
Giv'at Shaul
Khallat 'Armān & Wa'rat el Jundi
Diskin Orphanage
Shi'b el Būr
DEIR YĀSĪN
El Marj
Shi'b Duqqa
El Jamalūna & 'Ein Tūt
Kh. 'Ein et Tūt
Khallat ed Danaf
El Manāzil
Institute for the Blind
Deir Yāsīn
Montefiore
Khallat 'Ulaiyān
Khallat el 'Arab & Wādi el Bitār
Rās Shahāda
Sullam Kharsh & Bātin Tuweis

THE STORY OF LIFTA

In 1945, the village of Lifta in the sub-district of Jerusalem had a population of 2,550, all of whom were Palestinian.

Today, the original built up area of Lifta remains empty, but its original inhabitants and their descendants are prevented from returning by Israel.

A NATIONAL MONUMENT
Art Piece

A National Monument is a limited-edition series of wooden topographic reliefs created by Visualizing Palestine in collaboration with artist Marwan Rechmaoui. Inspired by a series of highly detailed maps of Palestine from the British Mandate period, the works recreate a three-dimensional snapshot of major Palestinian cities and towns circa 1947, based on the final British surveys before the Nakba and digital elevation data from NASA. A National Monument was exhibited at Dar El Nimer for Arts and Culture in Beirut in 2019 and at Jameel Arts Center in Dubai in 2020. At both exhibits, the pieces were displayed alongside a large-scale installation of historic maps of Palestine from the Palestine Open Maps platform. Sales of A National Monument pieces support the ongoing work of Visualizing Palestine.

https://www.darelnimer.org/past-events/a-national-monument
Year: 2019 | **Researcher and curator:** Ahmad Barclay | **Artist:** Marwan Rechmaoui | **CNC machining:** Damj Design | **Strategy and sales:** Joumana al Jabri | **Coordination:** Sandy Nassif

Exhibition at Dar El Nimer for Arts and Culture in Beirut, Lebanon, 2019

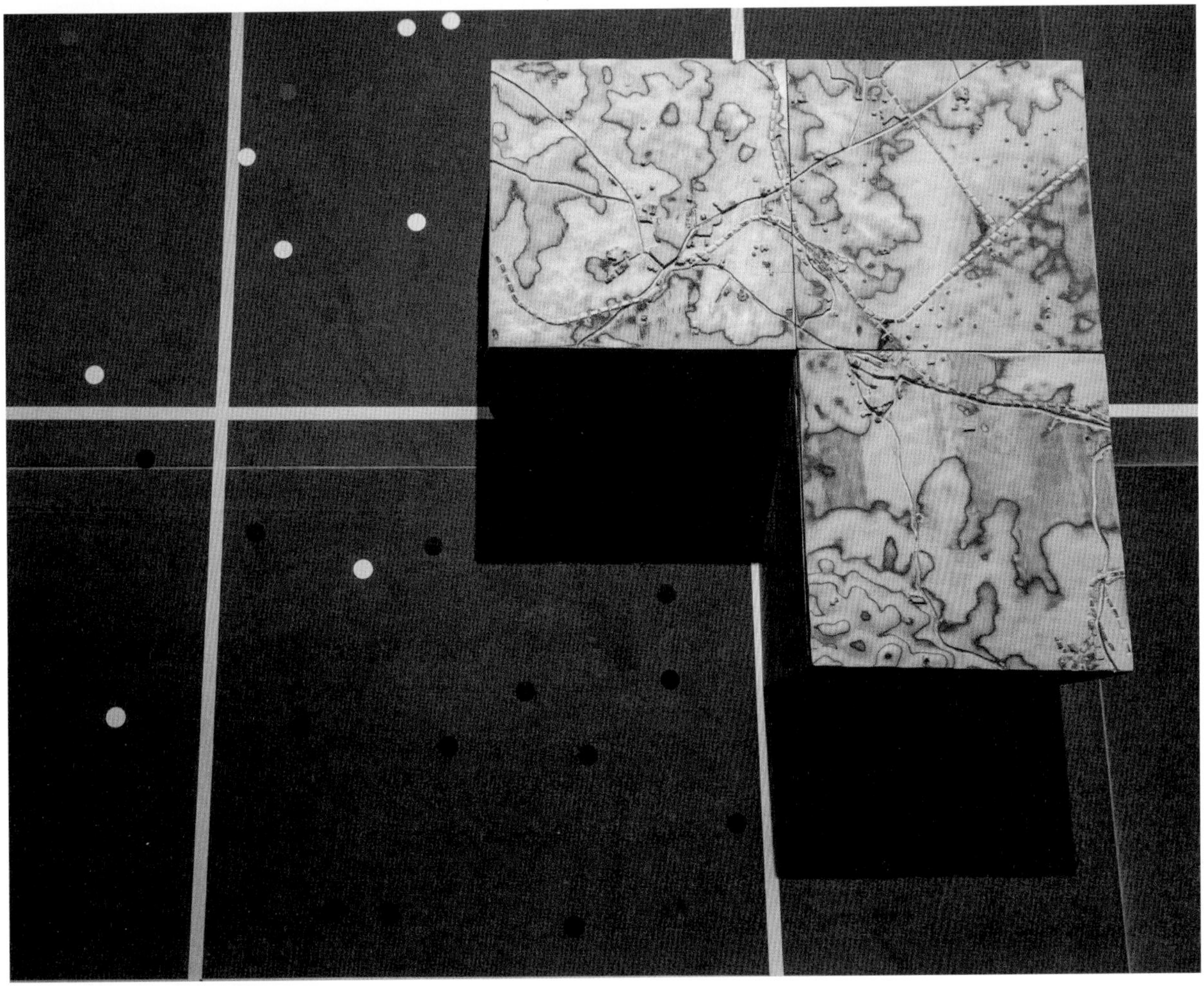

VISUALIZING PALESTINE 101
Educational Platform

Visualizing Palestine 101 (VP101) is a data-led visual resource and educational hub designed for people learning and teaching about Palestine. It includes twenty-five original infographics and related data sets, an index of glossary definitions, and a selection of other engaging audiovisual content from around the web. We interspersed several VP101 visuals throughout this book where they helped tell the story of a particular chapter, but they are best viewed as a cohesive collection.

101.visualizingpalestine.org
Year: 2019 | **Brief and copywriting:** Ahmad Barclay | **Design:** Ahmad Barclay, Yosra El Gazzar | **Microsite development:** Morad Taleeb | **Special thanks:** Ali Abunimah, Reem Abdul Majid, Zena Agha, Ramah Aleryan, Joumana al Jabri, Iman Annab, Zachariah Barghouti, Ronnie Barkan, Rabih Bashour, Cate Brown, Noura Erakat, Reem Farah, Stefanie Felsberger, Manal Hamzeh, Sami Hermez, Shir Hever, Ramzi Jaber, Ingrid Jaradat, Rania Masri, and Ben White | **Sources:** bit.ly/vp101data

VISUALIZINGPALESTINE | 101

VISUALS RESOURCES HOW TO  

Visualizing Palestine 101 is a data-led visual resource and educational hub for people learning and teaching about Palestine

Learn more...

SEE THE VISUALS

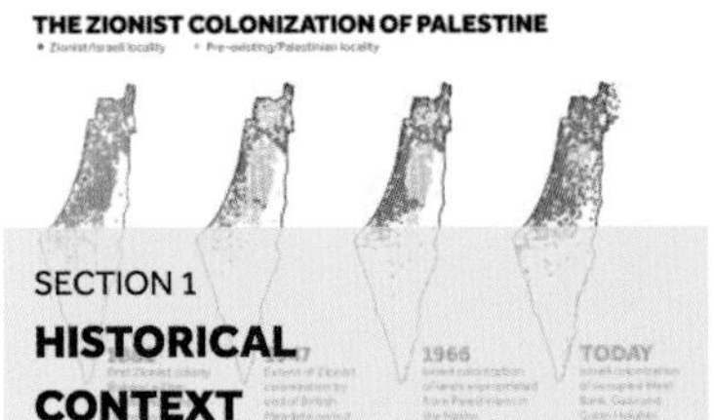
THE ZIONIST COLONIZATION OF PALESTINE
1966
TODAY

SECTION 1
HISTORICAL CONTEXT

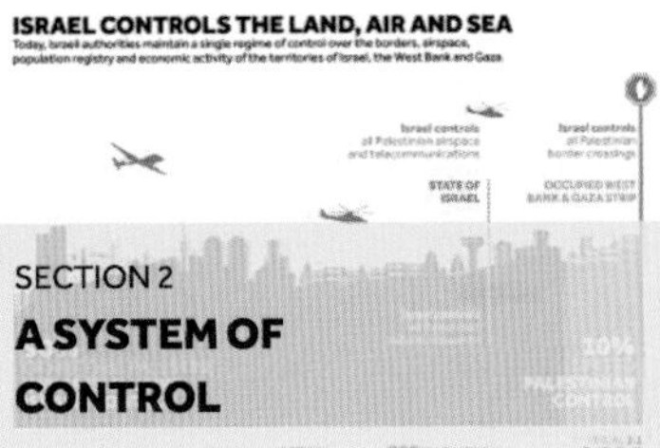
ISRAEL CONTROLS THE LAND, AIR AND SEA

SECTION 2
A SYSTEM OF CONTROL

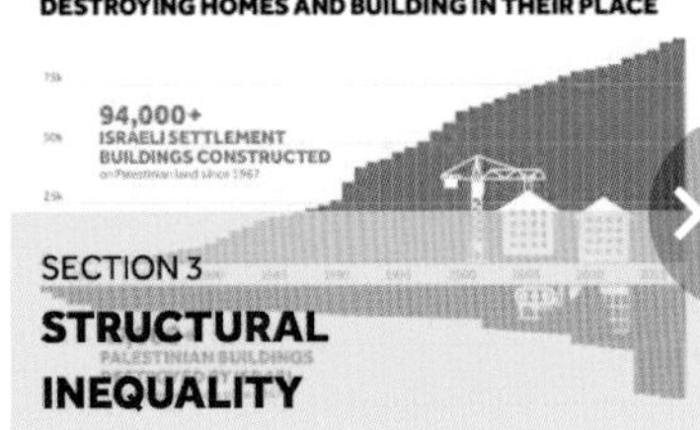
DESTROYING HOMES AND BUILDING IN THEIR PLACE
94,000+
ISRAELI SETTLEMENT BUILDINGS CONSTRUCTED

SECTION 3
STRUCTURAL INEQUALITY

"Israel and Palestine remains one of the most discussed, but least understood rights crises around ... Visualizing Palestine 101 stands out as among the most powerful resources to bolster the critical work of advocates for Palestinian rights."

OMAR SHAKIR
Israel & Palestine Director, Human Rights Watch

GLOSSARY
Definitions to help you to make sense of some key terms on the issue of Palestine.

AUDIOVISUALS
A selection of accessible and engaging explainer content from around the web.

GET THE DATA
Explore the raw data and sources behind the VP101 infographics.

A project of VISUALIZINGPALESTINE

ABOUT CONTACT BECOME A MEMBER SUBSCRIBE  

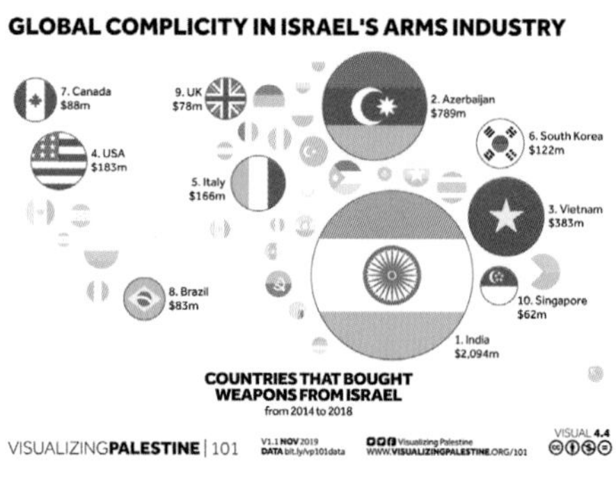
GLOBAL COMPLICITY IN ISRAEL'S ARMS INDUSTRY
7. Canada $88m
9. UK $78m
2. Azerbaijan $789m
6. South Korea $122m
4. USA $183m
5. Italy $166m
3. Vietnam $383m
8. Brazil $83m
10. Singapore $62m
1. India $2,094m
COUNTRIES THAT BOUGHT WEAPONS FROM ISRAEL from 2014 to 2018
VISUALIZINGPALESTINE | 101
VISUAL 4.4

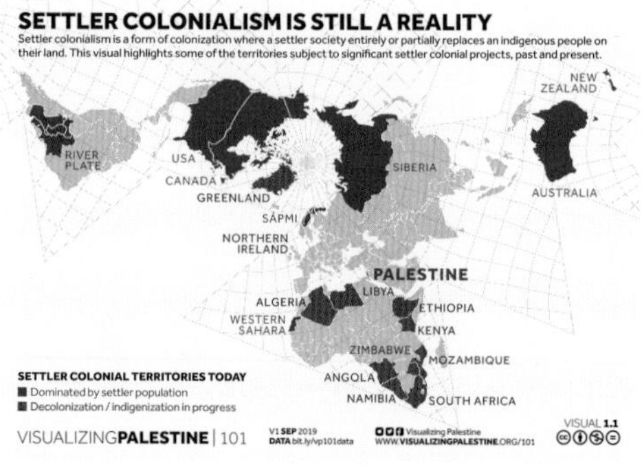
SETTLER COLONIALISM IS STILL A REALITY
Settler colonialism is a form of colonization where a settler society entirely or partially replaces an indigenous people on their land. This visual highlights some of the territories subject to significant settler colonial projects, past and present.
NEW ZEALAND
RIVER PLATE
USA
CANADA
GREENLAND
SIBERIA
AUSTRALIA
SÁPMI
NORTHERN IRELAND
PALESTINE
LIBYA
ALGERIA
WESTERN SAHARA
ETHIOPIA
KENYA
ZIMBABWE
MOZAMBIQUE
ANGOLA
NAMIBIA
SOUTH AFRICA
SETTLER COLONIAL TERRITORIES TODAY
Dominated by settler population
Decolonization / indigenization in progress
VISUALIZINGPALESTINE | 101
VISUAL 1.1

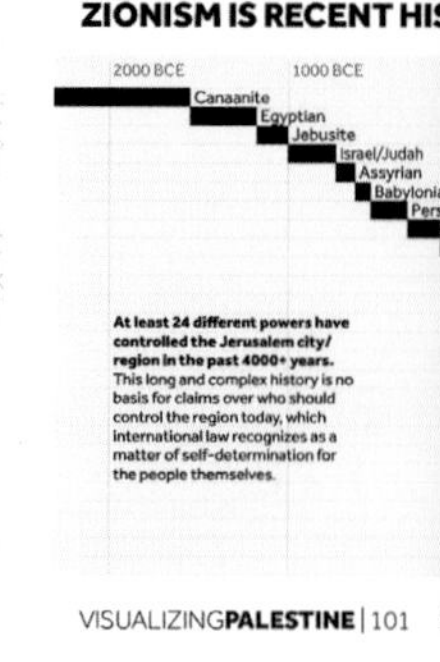
ZIONISM IS RECENT HIS
2000 BCE
1000 BCE
Canaanite
Egyptian
Jebusite
Israel/Judah
Assyrian
Babylonian
At least 24 different powers have controlled the Jerusalem city/ region in the past 4000+ years.
This long and complex history is no basis for claims over who should control the region today, which international law recognizes as a matter of self-determination for the people themselves.
VISUALIZINGPALESTINE | 101

PALESTINIANS WANT FREEDOM, JUSTICE & EQUALITY
The vast majority of Palestinians support the three rights-based demands of the BDS movement, as founded in international law.

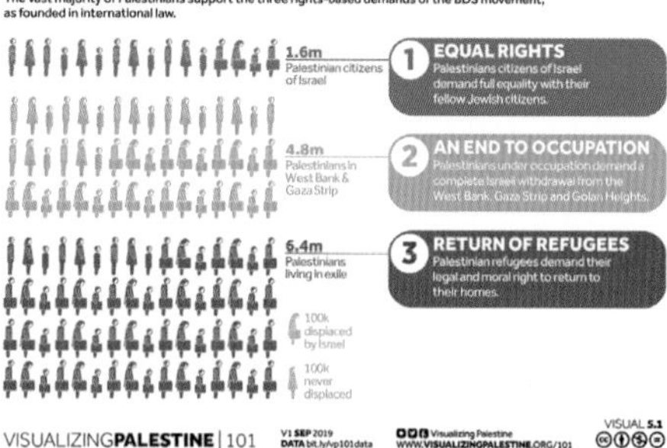
1.6m Palestinian citizens of Israel
1 EQUAL RIGHTS
Palestinians citizens of Israel demand full equality with their fellow Jewish citizens.
4.8m Palestinians in West Bank & Gaza Strip
2 AN END TO OCCUPATION
Palestinians under occupation demand a complete Israeli withdrawal from the West Bank, Gaza Strip and Golan Heights.
6.4m Palestinians living in exile
3 RETURN OF REFUGEES
Palestinian refugees demand their legal and moral right to return to their homes.
100k displaced by Israel
100k never displaced
VISUALIZINGPALESTINE | 101
VISUAL 5.1

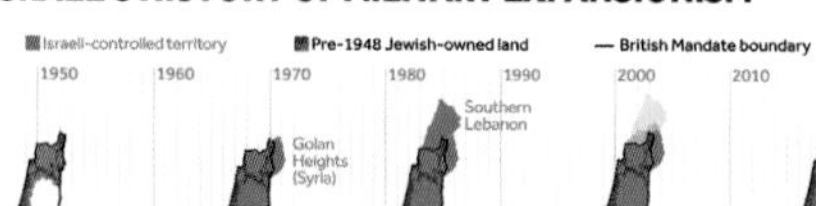
ISRAEL'S HISTORY OF MILITARY EXPANSIONISM
Israeli-controlled territory
Pre-1948 Jewish-owned land
British Mandate boundary
1950
1960
1970
1980
1990
2000
2010

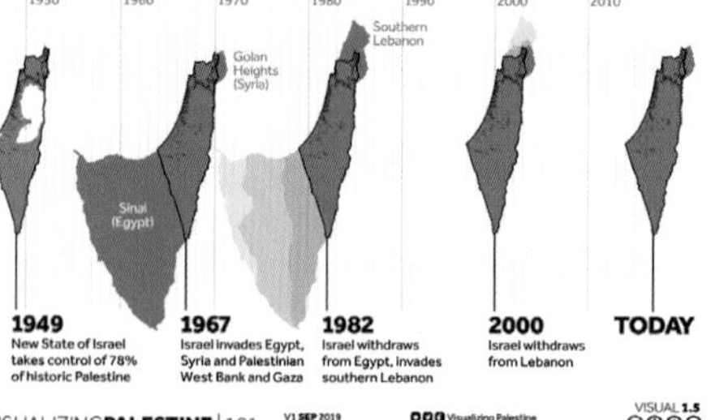
Golan Heights (Syria)
Southern Lebanon
Sinai (Egypt)
1949
New State of Israel takes control of 78% of historic Palestine
1967
Israel invades Egypt, Syria and Palestinian West Bank and Gaza
1982
Israel withdraws from Egypt, invades southern Lebanon
2000
Israel withdraws from Lebanon
TODAY
VISUALIZINGPALESTINE | 101
VISUAL 1.5

ONE POPULATION IS RE
1922-1947
British Mandate of Palestine
1948-1966
Nakba & Formation of Israeli State
1967-2018
Occupation of West Bank & Gaza
TOTAL JEWIS
VISUALIZINGPALESTINE | 101

WHAT FULL EQUAL RIGHTS SHOULD LOOK LIKE
In response to the State of Israel's institutionalized discrimination against its non-Jewish citizens, the NGO Adalah proposed an alternative "democratic, bilingual, multicultural" constitution.
RIGHT TO PARTICIPATION
Full participation in political decision making for Palestinian citizens of Israel
RIGHT TO JUSTICE
A criminal justice system run in accordance with rules of fairness, justice and equality
A STATE OF ALL ITS CITIZENS
Founded on the Universal Declaration of Human Rights and global democratic norms
LAND & PROPERTY RIGHTS
Equal access to land and property, including restitution of confiscated property
SOCIAL & ECONOMIC RIGHTS
Equal access to health, education, employment opportunities and social security
VISUALIZINGPALESTINE | 101
VISUAL 5.2

PALESTINIAN TERRITORY IS DIVIDED & FRAGMENTED
Territory under Israeli control since 1948/49
Internationally recognised Palestinian territory under Israeli occupation since 1967
STATE OF ISRAEL
WEST BANK
EAST JERU-SALEM
GAZA STRIP
78% of historic Palestine. Founded on lands of 500+ depopulated Palestinian villages
Divided into 166 separate enclaves. Colonized by 220+ Israeli settlements
Annexed from rest of West Bank and divided by Israel's separation wall
Cut off from West Bank and under Israeli-Egyptian siege since 2007
VISUALIZINGPALESTINE | 101
VISUAL 2.2

SOME PEOPLE ARE MOR
VISUALIZINGPALESTINE | 101

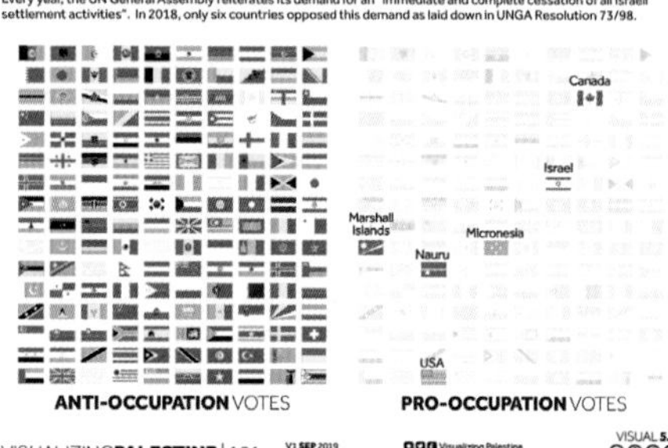
THE WORLD IS AGAINST THE OCCUPATION
Every year, the UN General Assembly reiterates its demand for an "immediate and complete cessation of all Israeli settlement activities". In 2018, only six countries opposed this demand as laid down in UNGA Resolution 73/98.
Canada
Israel
Marshall Islands
Micronesia
Nauru
USA
ANTI-OCCUPATION VOTES
PRO-OCCUPATION VOTES
VISUALIZINGPALESTINE | 101
VISUAL 5.3

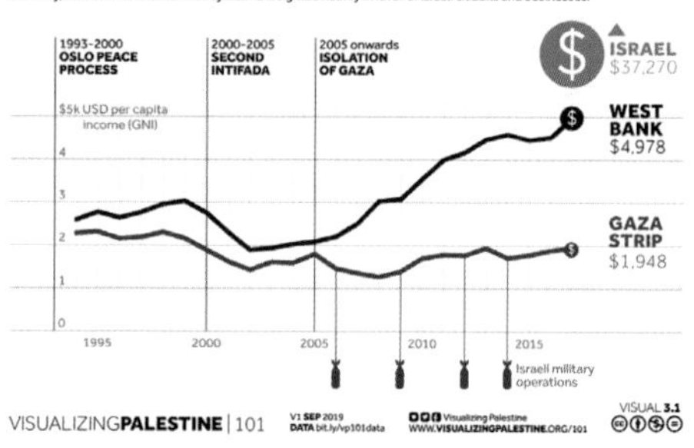
CAPTIVE TO AN UNEQUAL ECONOMIC SYSTEM
The Palestinian West Bank and Gaza are captive to the Israeli economic system, where Israel controls the currency, resources and trade. This system is weighted heavily in favor of Israeli citizens and businesses.
1993-2000 OSLO PEACE PROCESS
2000-2005 SECOND INTIFADA
2005 onwards ISOLATION OF GAZA
ISRAEL $37,270
$5k USD per capita income (GNI)
WEST BANK $4,978
GAZA STRIP $1,948
1995
2000
2005
2010
2015
Israeli military operations
VISUALIZINGPALESTINE | 101
VISUAL 3.1

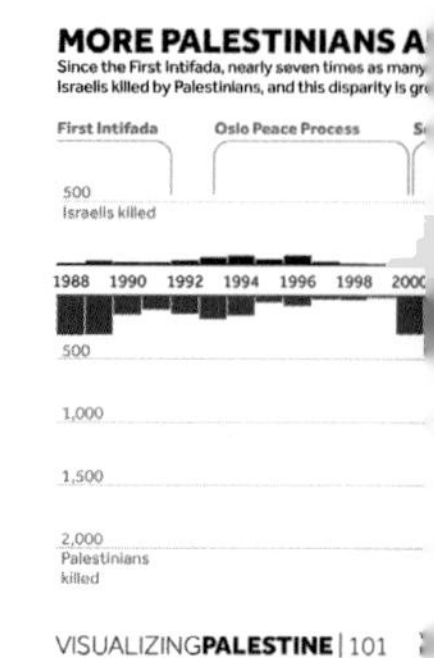
MORE PALESTINIANS A
First Intifada
Oslo Peace Process
500 Israelis killed
1988
1990
1992
1994
1996
1998
500
1,000
1,500
2,000 Palestinians killed
VISUALIZINGPALESTINE | 101

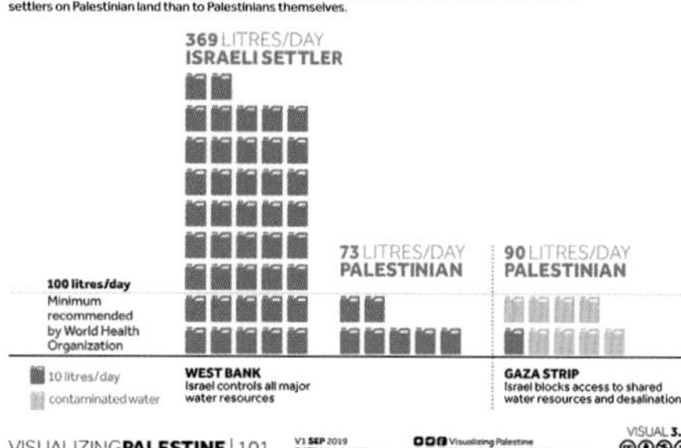
ISRAEL EXPLOITS PALESTINIAN NATURAL RESOURCES
Israel controls all major water resources and distributes more than four times as much water to Israeli settlers on Palestinian land than to Palestinians themselves.
369 LITRES/DAY ISRAELI SETTLER
73 LITRES/DAY PALESTINIAN
90 LITRES/DAY PALESTINIAN
100 litres/day Minimum recommended by World Health Organization
10 litres/day
contaminated water
WEST BANK Israel controls all major water resources
GAZA STRIP Israel blocks access to shared water resources and desalination
VISUALIZINGPALESTINE | 101
VISUAL 3.5

SOME COUNTRIES NEVER FACE SANCTIONS

Only apartheid-era South Africa has been condemned by more UN Security Council resolutions than Israel. However, unlike most countries on this list, Israel has never been subjected to UN sanctions.

Condemnations by UN (0–50)

	Rank
South Africa	1
Israel	2
Somalia	3
Lebanon	4
Angola	5
Sudan	6
DR Congo	7
South Sudan	7
Abkhazia (Georgia)	9
Iraq	9
Libya	11
Afghanistan	12
Zimbabwe	12
Eritrea	16
Haiti	16
North Korea	19
Liberia	21
C. African Rep.	26
Côte d'Ivoire	26
Guinea-Bissau	32
Iran	32
Mali	40
Rwanda	40
Sierra Leone	50

Top 10 countries condemned by UN Security Council

All other countries subjected to UN sanctions

CONDEMNED & SANCTIONED BY UN

CONDEMNED BUT NOT SANCTIONED BY UN

VISUALIZINGPALESTINE | 101 V1 SEP 2019 DATA bit.ly/vp101data Visualizing Palestine WWW.VISUALIZINGPALESTINE.ORG/101 VISUAL 4.1

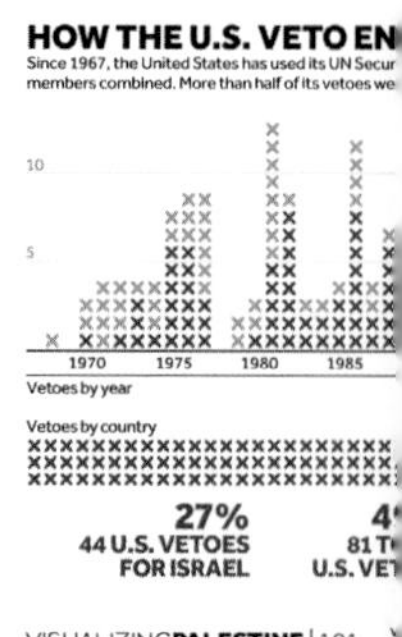
HOW THE U.S. VETO EN
Since 1967, the United States has used its UN Secur
1970
1975
1980
1985
Vetoes by year
Vetoes by country
27%
44 U.S. VETOES FOR ISRAEL
VISUALIZINGPALESTINE | 101

PALESTINE

1000 CE 2000 CE

zantine
ersian
yzantine
ashidun
Umayyad
Abbasid
Fatimid
Seljuk
Crusader
Ayyubid
Crusader
Mamluk
Ottoman
British
Israeli/Jordanian
Israeli

1882 FIRST ZIONIST COLONY FOUNDED

VISUAL 1.2

THE ZIONIST COLONIZATION OF PALESTINE

• Zionist/Israeli locality • Pre-existing/Palestinian locality

1882
First Zionist colony Rishon LeZion established under Ottoman rule
1947
Extent of Zionist colonization by end of British Mandate period
1966
Israeli colonization of lands expropriated from Palestinians in the Nakba
TODAY
Israeli colonization of occupied West Bank, Gaza and Golan Heights

VISUALIZINGPALESTINE | 101 V1 SEP 2019 DATA bit.ly/vp101data VISUAL 1.3

THE ETHNIC CLEANSING STARTED BEFORE THE WAR

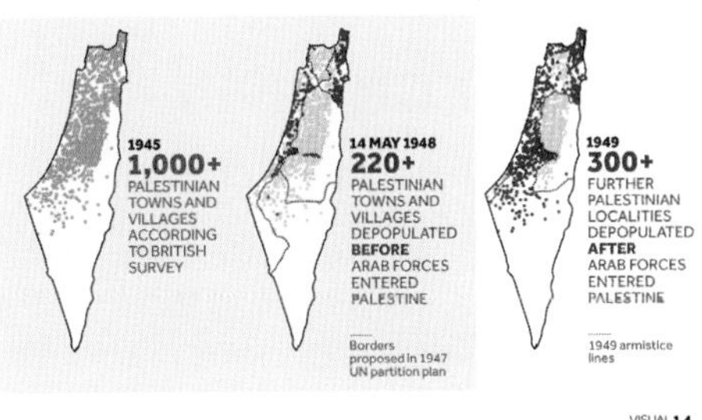

1945
1,000+
PALESTINIAN TOWNS AND VILLAGES ACCORDING TO BRITISH SURVEY
14 MAY 1948
220+
PALESTINIAN TOWNS AND VILLAGES DEPOPULATED BEFORE ARAB FORCES ENTERED PALESTINE
Borders proposed in 1947 UN partition plan
1949
300+
FURTHER PALESTINIAN LOCALITIES DEPOPULATED AFTER ARAB FORCES ENTERED PALESTINE
1949 armistice lines

VISUALIZINGPALESTINE | 101 V1 SEP 2019 DATA bit.ly/vp101data VISUAL 1.4

ANOTHER

100,000+
Palestinians expelled from Palestine or forced to leave homes
750,000+
Palestinians forcibly expelled in 1947–49 Nakba
35,000+
internally displaced within Israel
400,000+
Palestinians forcibly expelled in 1967 Naksa
240,000
residencies cancelled by Israel
200,000
internally displaced by Israel
1,725,000+
TOTAL PALESTINIANS DISPLACED

VISUAL 1.6

WHERE PALESTINIANS LIVE TODAY

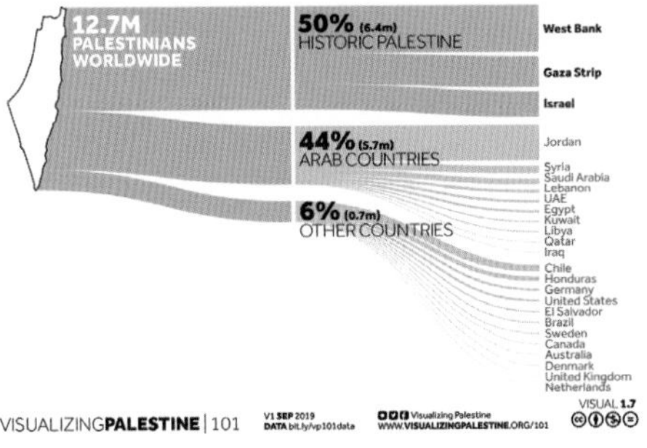

12.7M
PALESTINIANS WORLDWIDE
50% (6.4m)
HISTORIC PALESTINE
West Bank
Gaza Strip
Israel
44% (5.7m)
ARAB COUNTRIES
Jordan
Syria
Saudi Arabia
Lebanon
UAE
Egypt
Kuwait
Libya
Qatar
Iraq
6% (0.7m)
OTHER COUNTRIES
Chile
Honduras
Germany
United States
El Salvador
Brazil
Sweden
Canada
Australia
Denmark
United Kingdom
Netherlands

VISUALIZINGPALESTINE | 101 V1 SEP 2019 DATA bit.ly/vp101data VISUAL 1.7

ISRAEL CONTROLS THE LAND, AIR AND SEA

Today, Israeli authorities maintain a single regime of control over the borders, airspace, population registry and economic activity of the territories of Israel, the West Bank and Gaza.

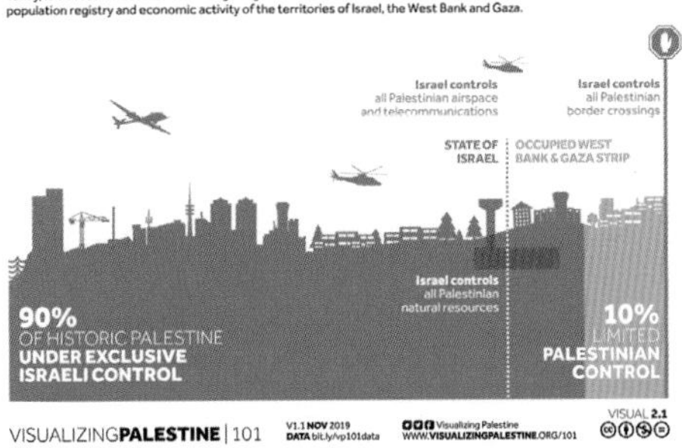

Israel controls all Palestinian airspace and telecommunications
Israel controls all Palestinian border crossings
STATE OF ISRAEL
OCCUPIED WEST BANK & GAZA STRIP
Israel controls all Palestinian natural resources
90%
OF HISTORIC PALESTINE UNDER EXCLUSIVE ISRAELI CONTROL
10%
LIMITED PALESTINIAN CONTROL

VISUALIZINGPALESTINE | 101 V1.1 NOV 2019 DATA bit.ly/vp101data VISUAL 2.1

THAN OTHERS

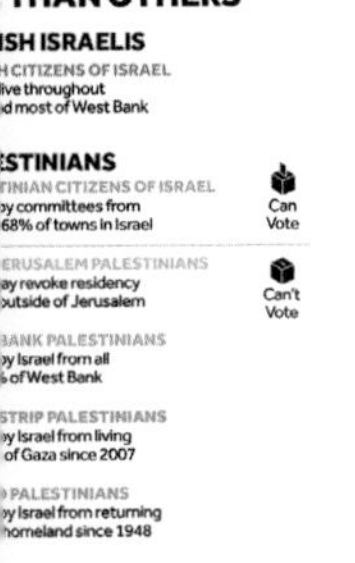

SH ISRAELIS
CITIZENS OF ISRAEL
live throughout
d most of West Bank
STINIANS
INIAN CITIZENS OF ISRAEL
by committees from
68% of towns in Israel
Can Vote
ERUSALEM PALESTINIANS
ay revoke residency
outside of Jerusalem
Can't Vote
ANK PALESTINIANS
by Israel from all
of West Bank
STRIP PALESTINIANS
by Israel from living
of Gaza since 2007
PALESTINIANS
by Israel from returning
homeland since 1948

VISUAL 2.3

ISRAELI LAW INSTITUTIONALIZES DISCRIMINATION

Israel has over 60 laws that work to privilege Jewish people while dispossessing, displacing and discriminating against non-Jews.

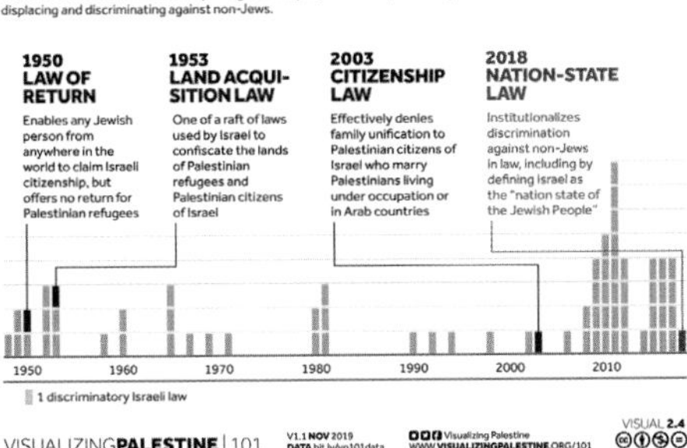

1950
LAW OF RETURN
Enables any Jewish person from anywhere in the world to claim Israeli citizenship, but offers no return for Palestinian refugees
1953
LAND ACQUISITION LAW
One of a raft of laws used by Israel to confiscate the lands of Palestinian refugees and Palestinian citizens of Israel
2003
CITIZENSHIP LAW
Effectively denies family unification to Palestinian citizens of Israel who marry Palestinians living under occupation or in Arab countries
2018
NATION-STATE LAW
Institutionalizes discrimination against non-Jews in law, including by defining Israel as the "nation state of the Jewish People"
1950
1960
1970
1980
1990
2000
2010
1 discriminatory Israeli law

VISUALIZINGPALESTINE | 101 V1.1 NOV 2019 DATA bit.ly/vp101data VISUAL 2.4

HOW THE P.A. AIDS ISRAEL'S OCCUPATION

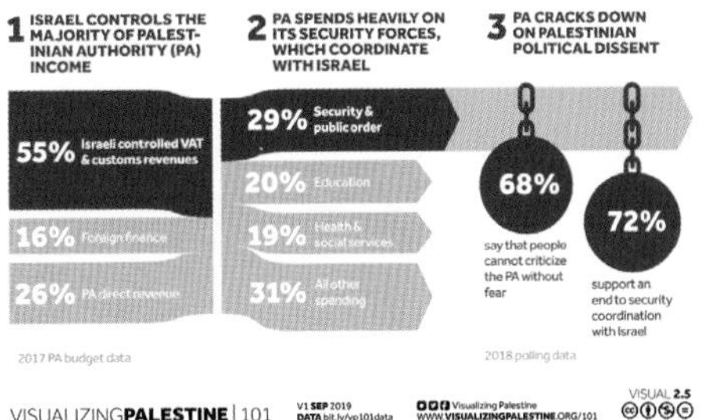

1 ISRAEL CONTROLS THE MAJORITY OF PALESTINIAN AUTHORITY (PA) INCOME
2 PA SPENDS HEAVILY ON ITS SECURITY FORCES, WHICH COORDINATE WITH ISRAEL
3 PA CRACKS DOWN ON PALESTINIAN POLITICAL DISSENT
55% Israeli controlled VAT & customs revenues
16% Foreign finance
26% PA direct revenue
29% Security & public order
20% Education
19% Health & social services
31% All other spending
68%
say that people cannot criticize the PA without fear
72%
support an end to security coordination with Israel
2017 PA budget data
2018 polling data

VISUALIZINGPALESTINE | 101 V1 SEP 2019 DATA bit.ly/vp101data VISUAL 2.5

NG KILLED

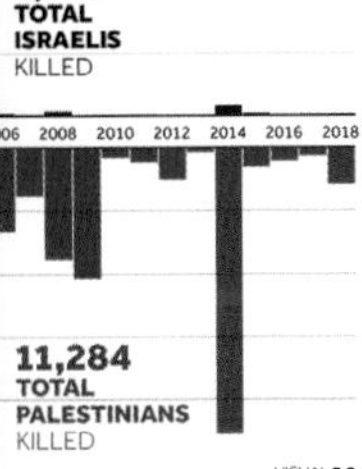

en killed by Israelis than
1,679
TOTAL ISRAELIS KILLED
2008 2010 2012 2014 2016 2018
11,284
TOTAL PALESTINIANS KILLED

VISUAL 3.2

ISRAEL INCARCERATES THOUSANDS OF PALESTINIANS

Palestinians in the West Bank and Gaza are subject to the Israeli military court system which has a near 100% conviction rate. Since 1967 over 800,000 Palestinians have been detained by Israeli authorities.

3,569 Serving sentence
232 CHILD PRISONERS
6,069
TOTAL PALESTINIANS IN ISRAELI DETENTION
ON 31 DEC 2018
2,006 Detained awaiting charge, trial or sentence
494 Administrative detainees held without charge
• 1 Palestinian prisoner

VISUALIZINGPALESTINE | 101 V1.1 NOV 2019 DATA bit.ly/vp101data VISUAL 3.3

DESTROYING HOMES AND BUILDING IN THEIR PLACE

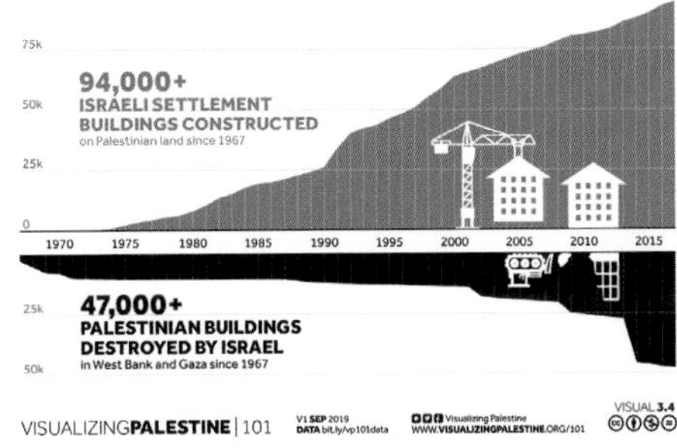

94,000+
ISRAELI SETTLEMENT BUILDINGS CONSTRUCTED
on Palestinian land since 1967
1970 1975 1980 1985 1990 1995 2000 2005 2010 2015
47,000+
PALESTINIAN BUILDINGS DESTROYED BY ISRAEL
in West Bank and Gaza since 1967

VISUALIZINGPALESTINE | 101 V1 SEP 2019 DATA bit.ly/vp101data VISUAL 3.4

RAELI IMPUNITY

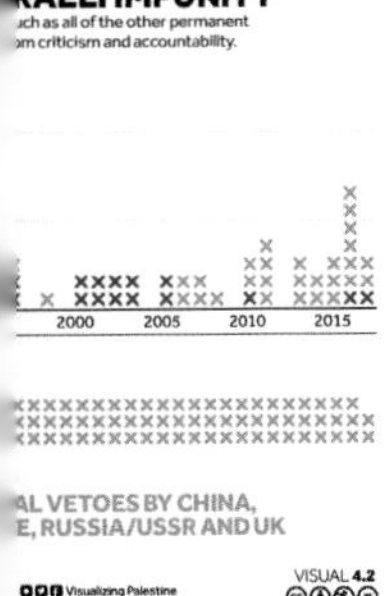

ch as all of the other permanent
m criticism and accountability.
2000 2005 2010 2015
AL VETOES BY CHINA,
E, RUSSIA/USSR AND UK

VISUAL 4.2

U.S. TAXPAYERS SUBSIDIZE ISRAEL'S MILITARY

The United States gives more in Foreign Military Financing to Israel each year than to all other countries in the world combined. On top of this, the U.S. also gives $500m each year to Israel's missile defence programme.
$3 billion per year US foreign military financing
ISRAEL
$3.3B
OTHER COUNTRIES
$0.44B
JORDAN
$0.35B
EGYPT
$1.3B

VISUALIZINGPALESTINE | 101 V1 SEP 2019 DATA bit.ly/vp101data VISUAL 4.3

THERE'S ENOUGH SPACE FOR EVERYONE

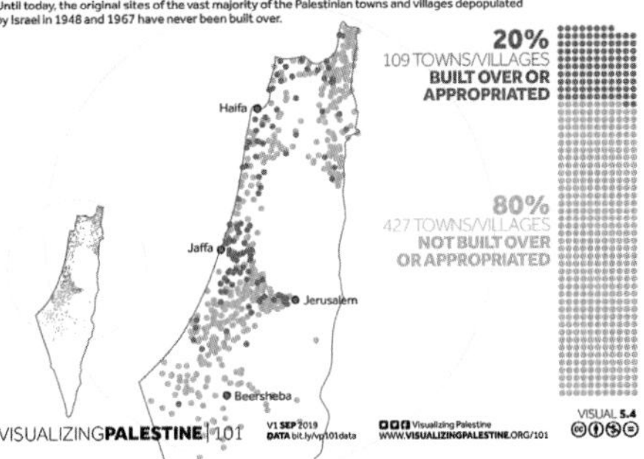

Until today, the original sites of the vast majority of the Palestinian towns and villages depopulated by Israel in 1948 and 1967 have never been built over.
20%
109 TOWNS/VILLAGES BUILT OVER OR APPROPRIATED
80%
427 TOWNS/VILLAGES NOT BUILT OVER OR APPROPRIATED
Haifa
Jaffa
Jerusalem
Beersheba
VISUALIZINGPALESTINE | 101 V1 SEP 2019 DATA bit.ly/vp101data

VISUAL 5.4

WE HAD DREAMS
Interactive Platform

We Had Dreams, a volunteer-led initiative, features testimonies of Palestinians in Gaza during the first week of the Israeli bombardment in 2023, during which Israeli forces dropped more than six thousand bombs on the tiny enclave.[1] We published this platform six days after Israeli officials announced that no water, food, or fuel would be allowed to enter Gaza.[2] Throughout the relentless Israeli bombardment, Palestinians in Gaza struggled to stay connected with the outside world, with no electricity, no fuel for generators, and periodic Israeli-imposed internet and telecommunications blackouts. But we heard and saw what they were experiencing loud and clear: "a textbook case of genocide."[3]

www.wehaddreams.com
Quote selection, design, and development: anonymous volunteer
Special thanks to volunteer translators who made the platform and quotes available in multiple languages and to Morad Taleeb for technical assistance.

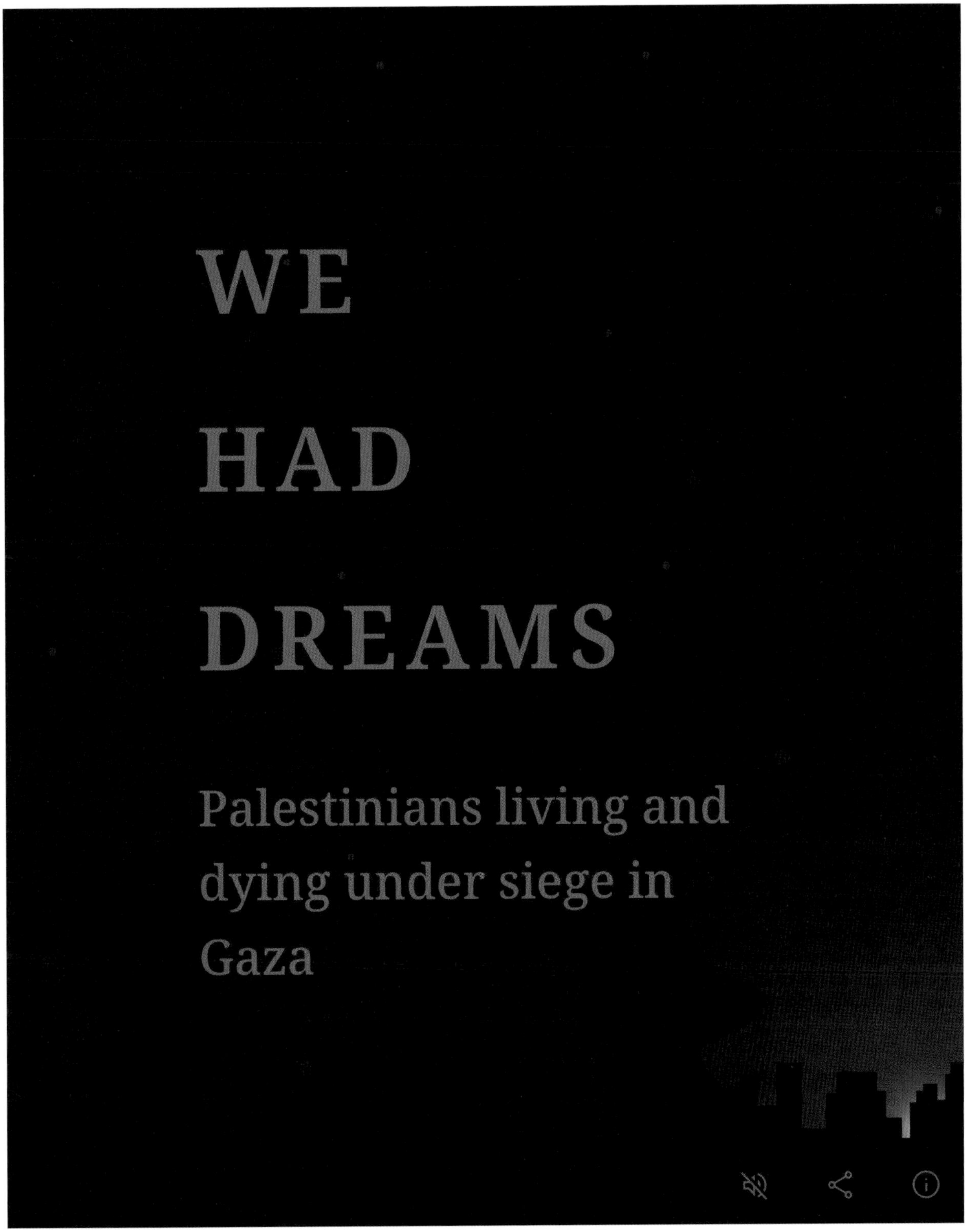

WE

HAD

DREAMS

Palestinians living and dying under siege in Gaza

If I die, remember that I, we, were individuals, humans, **we had names, dreams and achievements** and our only fault was that we were classified as inferior.

BELAL ALDABBOUR

My wish is that they drop the bombs on us while we are sleeping and that we all die together. This is why we are here together. So that **nobody is left alive** to mourn those who were killed.

AUNT MAY

There is no lonelier place in this universe than around the bed of a wounded child who has **no more family** to look after them.

GHASSAN ABU SITTA

What scares me the most is the thought of my death as a number among the numbers that increase every minute. **I am not a number.** It took me 23 years to become the person you see now. I have a home and friends, memory and pain.

SHAHARZAD

REMEMBER THEIR NAMES

Interactive Visual

Remember Their Names is a volunteer-led memorial initiative. Upon publication, it included the names of 6,767 Palestinians killed by Israeli forces in Gaza from October 7–26, 2023, based on information released by the Ministry of Health on October 27. The platform allows viewers to search for the details of specific individuals killed, filter by age range, and click an individual's name or silhouette to see their age. The Ministry of Health published these details one day after US President Joe Biden engaged in genocide denial, accusing Palestinians of exaggerating the number of people killed.[4] On November 6, a senior Biden administration official admitted that the numbers are "even higher than are being cited."[5]

www.visualizingpalestine.org/gaza-names/en.html
Year: 2023 | **Concept:** Rabi Siyam | **Design and development:** Ahmad Barclay
Child figures: Basant Elshimy | Special thanks to volunteers who reviewed the transliteration of names from Arabic to English, Rasha Sansur for volunteer coordination, and Morad Taleeb for technical assistance | **Source:** Ministry of Health in Gaza

REMEMBER THEIR NAMES

6,747 Palestinians killed in Gaza, 7 Oct - 26 Oct 2023

Type a name
Aged
0
to
93

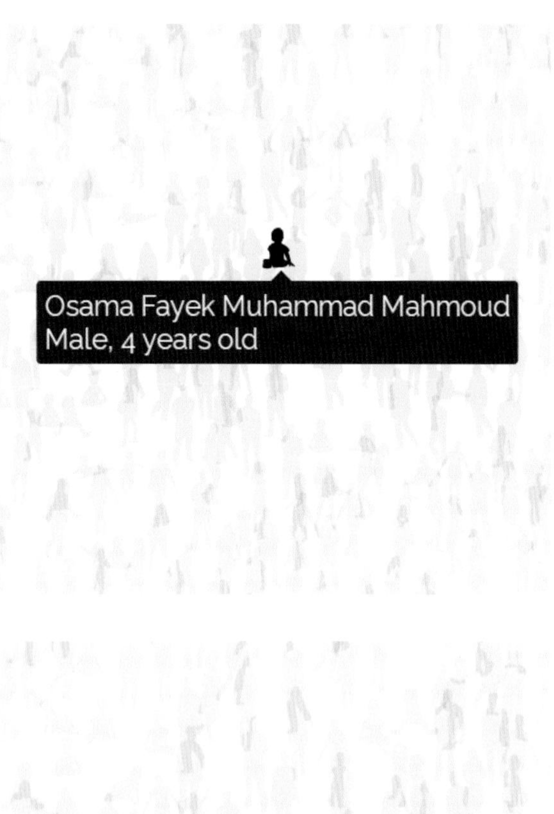
Osama Fayek Muhammad Mahmoud
Male, 4 years old

Amal Fawzi Khamis Al-Masoabi
Female, 36 years old

Amer Hussein Ibrahim Radwan
Male, 80 years old

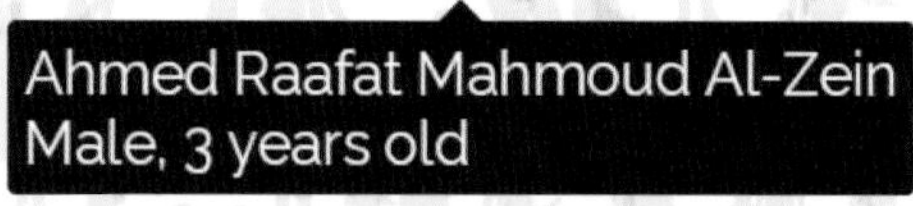
Ahmed Raafat Mahmoud Al-Zein
Male, 3 years old

Rahaf Jaafar Atiya Al-Nabahin
Female, 15 years old

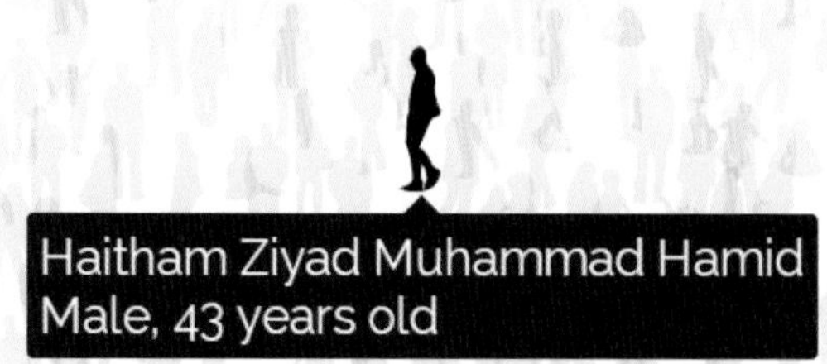
Haitham Ziyad Muhammad Hamid
Male, 43 years old

ABC
ع
Type a name
Aged
0
to
12

A PLACE OF MANY BEGINNINGS

Multimedia Interactive Platform

"The history of Palestine . . . has multiple 'beginnings' and the idea of Palestine has evolved over time from these multiple 'beginnings' into a geo-political concept and a distinct territorial polity."
—Nur Masalha, *Palestine: A Four Thousand Year History*

A Place of Many Beginnings: Three Paths into the History of Palestine explores key "beginnings" that have shaped Indigenous life in Palestine over the millennia, including agricultural revolution, cradles of civilization, international trade and transit, and multifaith histories. The project examines the extraordinary pluralism and blending of influences expressed in Palestinian material culture and place names and celebrates the work of scholars who are charting new paths to illuminate large swaths of Palestinian history that have been obscured by hundreds of years of colonial research agendas. The project launched at the Palestine Writes Literature Festival in September 2023.

https://palestinewrites.org/place-of-many-beginnings.php
Year: 2023 | **Brief and copywriting:** Nasreen Abd Elal, Susan Abulhawa, Majd Al-Rafie, Jessica Anderson, Aline Batarseh, Shuruq Josting, Alia Ragab | **Design:** Nasreen Abd Elal, Majd Al-Rafie | **Special thanks to** Nur Masalha, Salman Abu Sitta, and Bassam Abun Nadi for insights and feedback that strengthened this project. Friends and colleagues generously offered their time, knowledge, and encouragement at various phases. Morad Taleeb contributed technical assistance | **Sources:** bit.ly/vp-many-beginnings

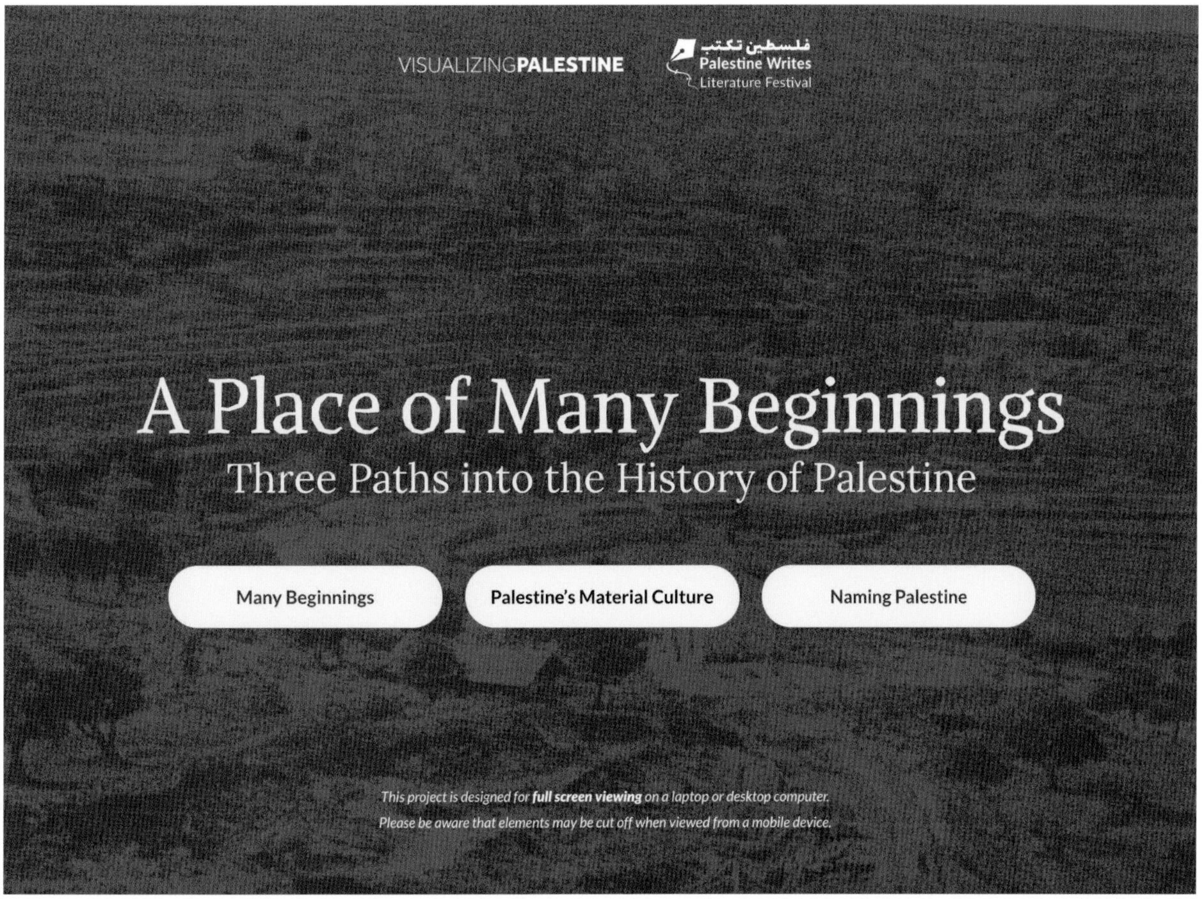

VISUALIZINGPALESTINE

فلسطين تكتب
Palestine Writes
Literature Festival

A Place of Many Beginnings

Three Paths into the History of Palestine

Many Beginnings

Palestine's Material Culture

Naming Palestine

*This project is designed for **full screen viewing** on a laptop or desktop computer.*
Please be aware that elements may be cut off when viewed from a mobile device.

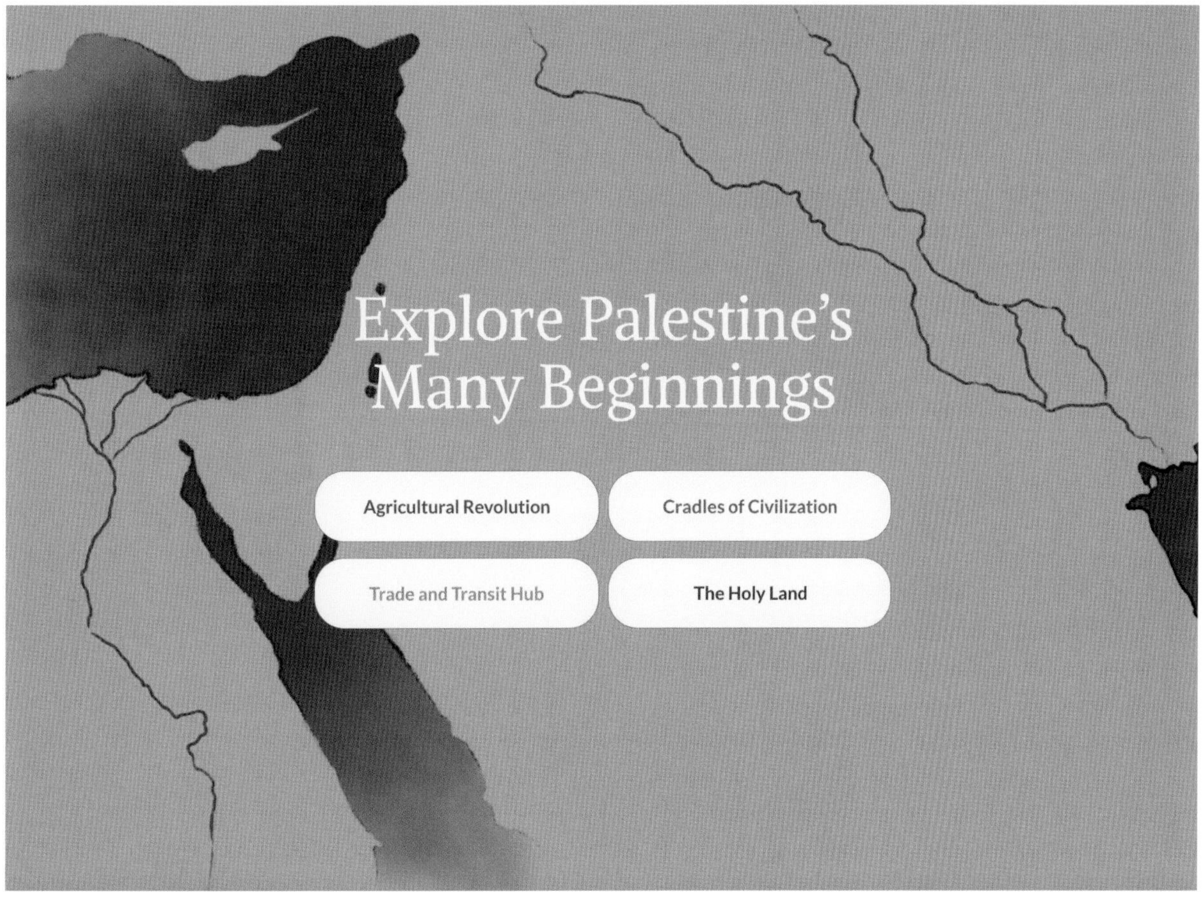
Explore Palestine's
Many Beginnings
Agricultural Revolution
Cradles of Civilization
Trade and Transit Hub
The Holy Land

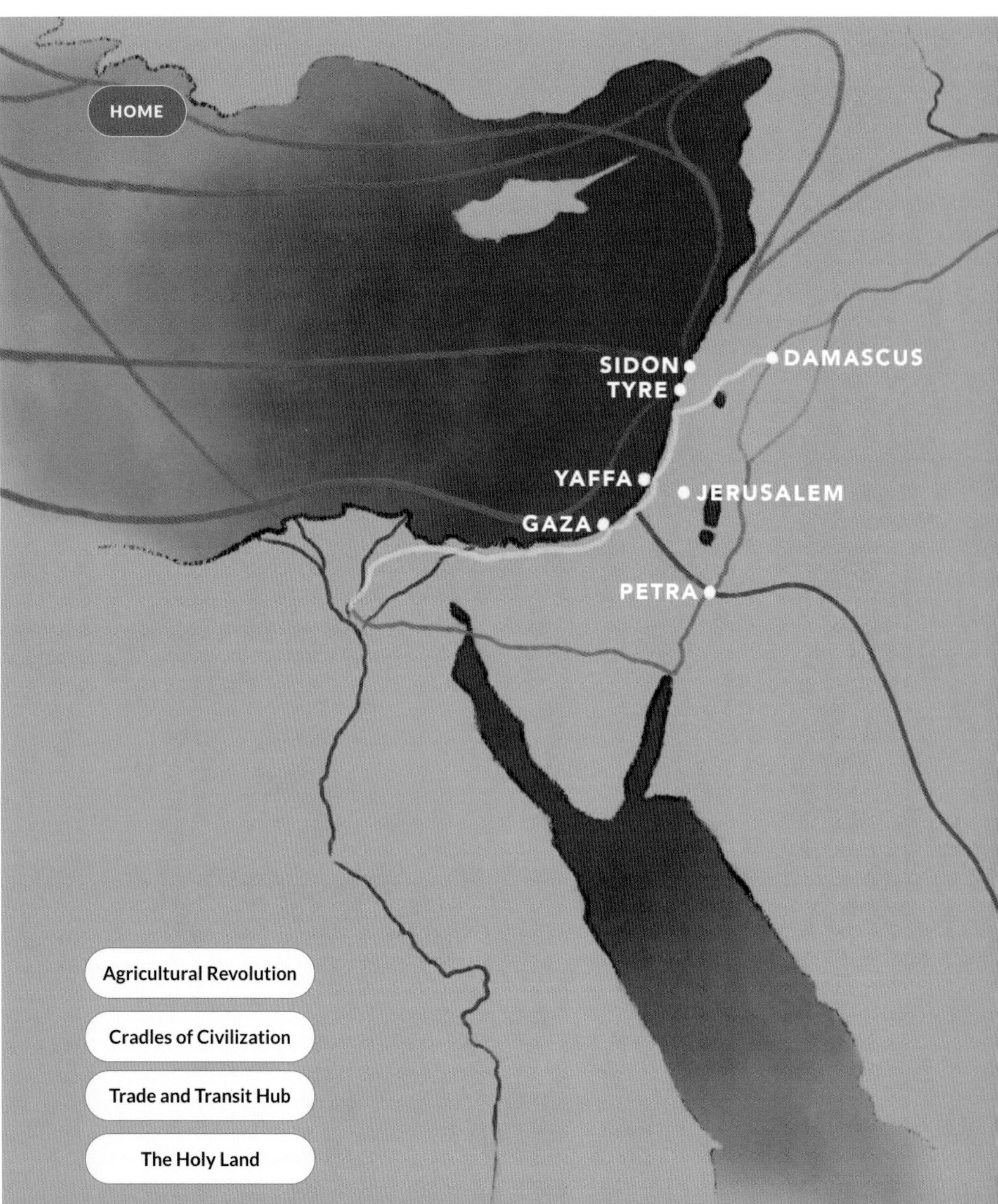
HOME
SIDON
TYRE
DAMASCUS
YAFFA
JERUSALEM
GAZA
PETRA
Agricultural Revolution
Cradles of Civilization
Trade and Transit Hub
The Holy Land

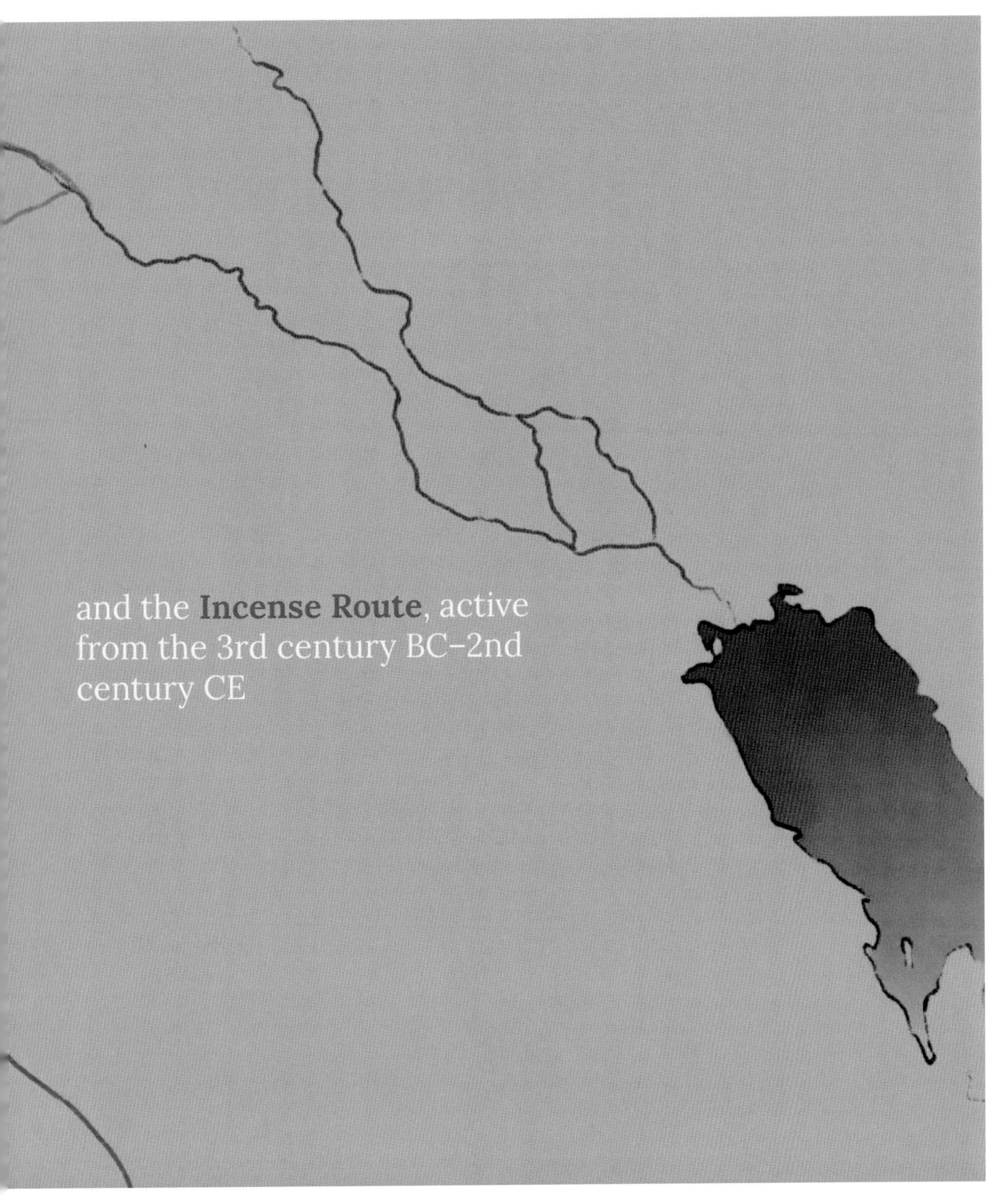
and the **Incense Route**, active from the 3rd century BC–2nd century CE

In 985 CE, the Jerusalem-born geographer and writer **Al-Maqdisi**—whose name means "person from Al-*Quds* (Jerusalem)"—recorded a conversation from his travels to **Shiraz** (now part of modern Iran):

> The master stonecutter asked me: Are you Egyptian?
>
> I said: No, I am Palestinian.
>
> He said: I heard that you carve stones like you would carve wood.
>
> I said: Yes.
>
> He said: Your stones are malleable and your craft gentle.
>
> Al-Maqdisi, *The Best Divisions for the Knowledge of the Regions*

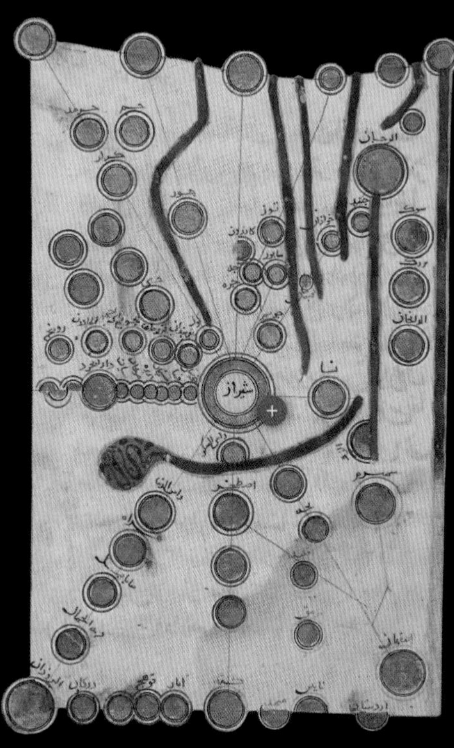
شيراز

Much of Palestinian Arabic toponymy has been erased as a result of the Nakba and the deliberate effort of Zionist projects to de-Palestinize the landscape.

This 1950 map captures the the Israeli renaming process, with purple Israeli amendments printed directly over British Mandate-era maps.

The Hebrew word הרוס, meaning 'destroyed,' marks the elimination of hundreds of Palestinian villages, with names of new settlements printed in their place.

Israel's Governmental Names Commission wrote in 1958, **"As long as the [Arabic] names did not appear in maps, they [Palestinians] cannot take possession in life,"** indicating that they understood maps and place names as tools of removal.

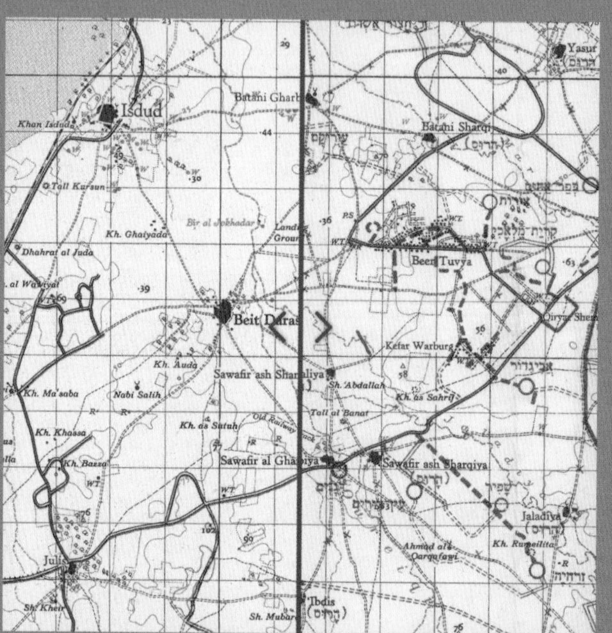
Isdud
Khan Isdud
Batani Gharbi
Batani Sharqi
Yasur
Toll Kursun
Kh. Ghaiyada
Dhahrat al Juda
Beer Tuvya
Beit Daras
Kefar Warburg
Kh. Auda
Nabi Salih
Kh. Ma'saba
Sawafir ash Shamaliya
Tall al Banat
Kh. Khasas
Sawafir al Gharbiya
Sawafir ash Sharqiya
Jaladiya
Julis
Ibdis

Use the slider bar to see the Israeli renaming effort in progress.

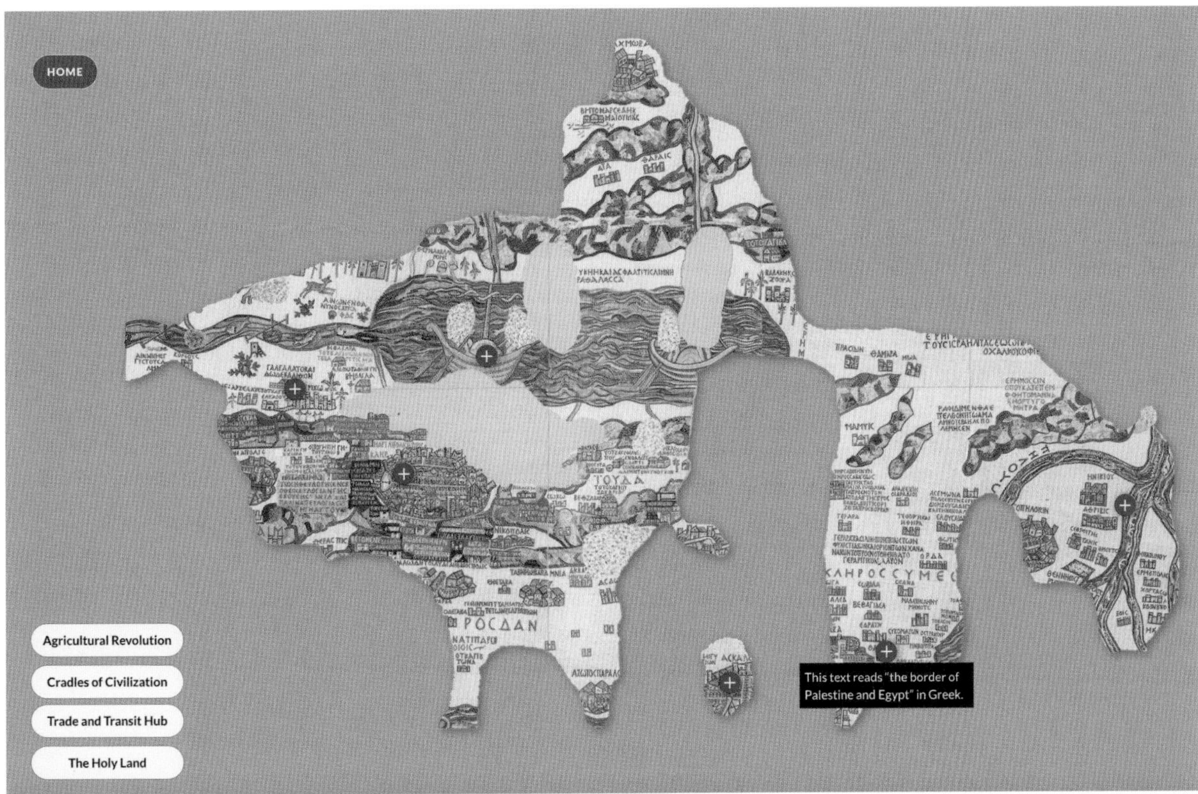
HOME
Agricultural Revolution
Cradles of Civilization
Trade and Transit Hub
The Holy Land
This text reads "the border of Palestine and Egypt" in Greek.

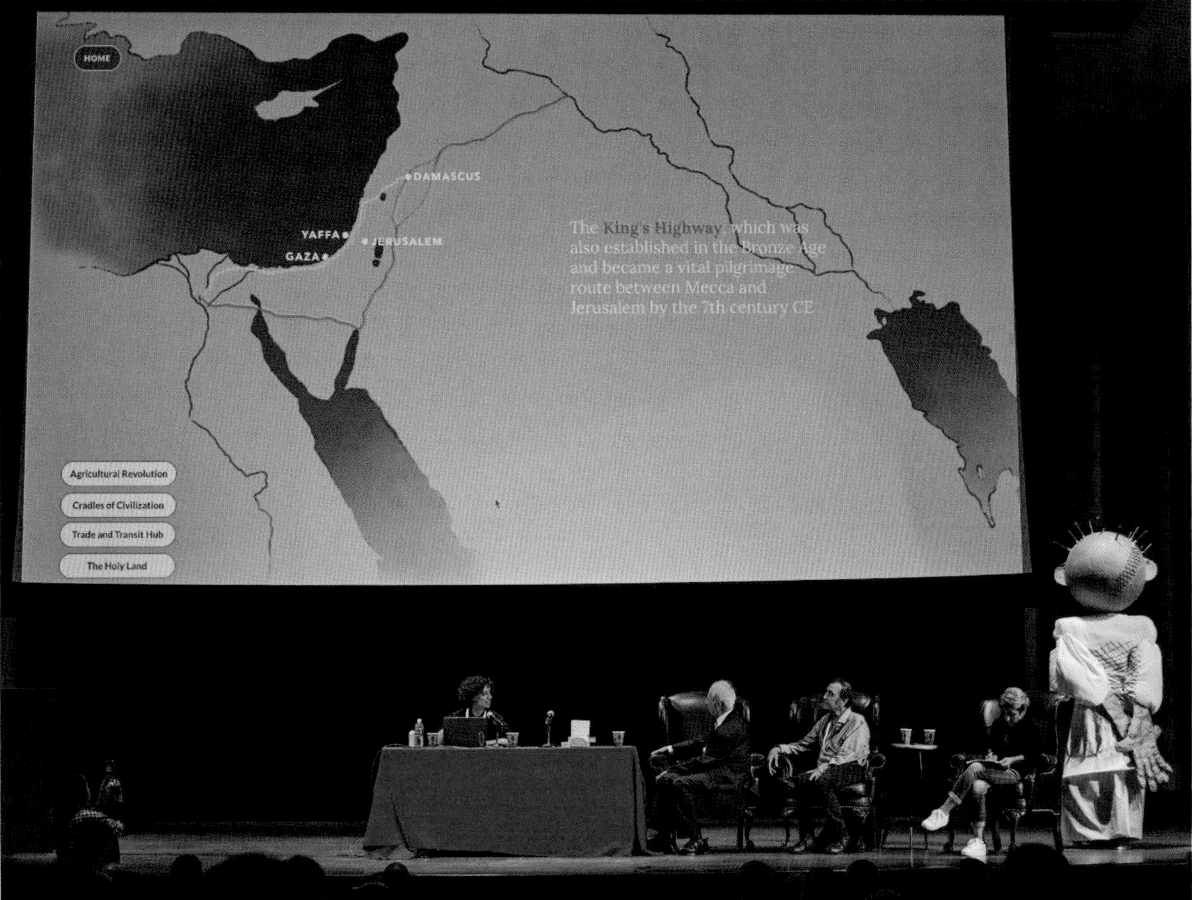
HOME
DAMASCUS
YAFFA
JERUSALEM
GAZA
The King's Highway, which was also established in the Bronze Age and became a vital pilgrimage route between Mecca and Jerusalem by the 7th century CE
Agricultural Revolution
Cradles of Civilization
Trade and Transit Hub
The Holy Land

Visualizing Palestine information designer Nasreen Abd Elal presenting "A Place of Many Beginnings" at the Palestine Writes Literature Festival in Philadelphia, United States, 2023.

ANNEX: VISUALIZING PALESTINE'S BRIEF TEMPLATE AND PROCESS WHEEL

Almost every visual in this book began with a research brief. Developed after the initial background research phase, we use the brief to help clarify the messaging, goals, and framing of a visual; distill key information; solicit feedback from partners and experts; and facilitate creative collaboration between researchers and designers. We also created a process wheel to document key stages of our collaborative process of data storytelling. The process wheel is a very early document in the history of Visualizing Palestine. The first draft existed before we released a single visual, and we published it on the first version of our website alongside a small handful of infographics.

BRIEF TEMPLATE

1. THEME

A single sentence describing the main topic or theme of the project.

2. AUDIENCE

Who is this project intended to influence or serve? Keep this brief, but also strive for specificity in naming key stakeholders.

3. PURPOSE

Is this project tied to a specific date, event, or strategy? How will it be used and disseminated?

4. KEY MESSAGES

What are the top two messages our audience should receive from this visual?

5. TITLE AND INTRODUCTION

List one or several possible title options (short titles are better) that will grab the audience's attention and frame the issue. Develop two to three introductory sentences as background context.

6. STORY

What's the story and how will it be told? (Comparative angle, single shocking statistic, case study. Consider use of photos, maps, charts, illustrations.)

7. KEY DATA AND INFORMATION

Include the exact data or information that should be featured in the visual, with detailed sources to facilitate final fact checking. This section should not be a data dump or summary of all research collected, but is a space to map out the information hierarchy, story, and clear, precise copy for the visual.

8. REFERENCE PROJECTS OR INSPIRATIONS

Include visuals from (and/or links to) other projects you find inspiring or relevant in terms of style, format or content, story framing, etc. Sketching ideas by hand is also helpful.

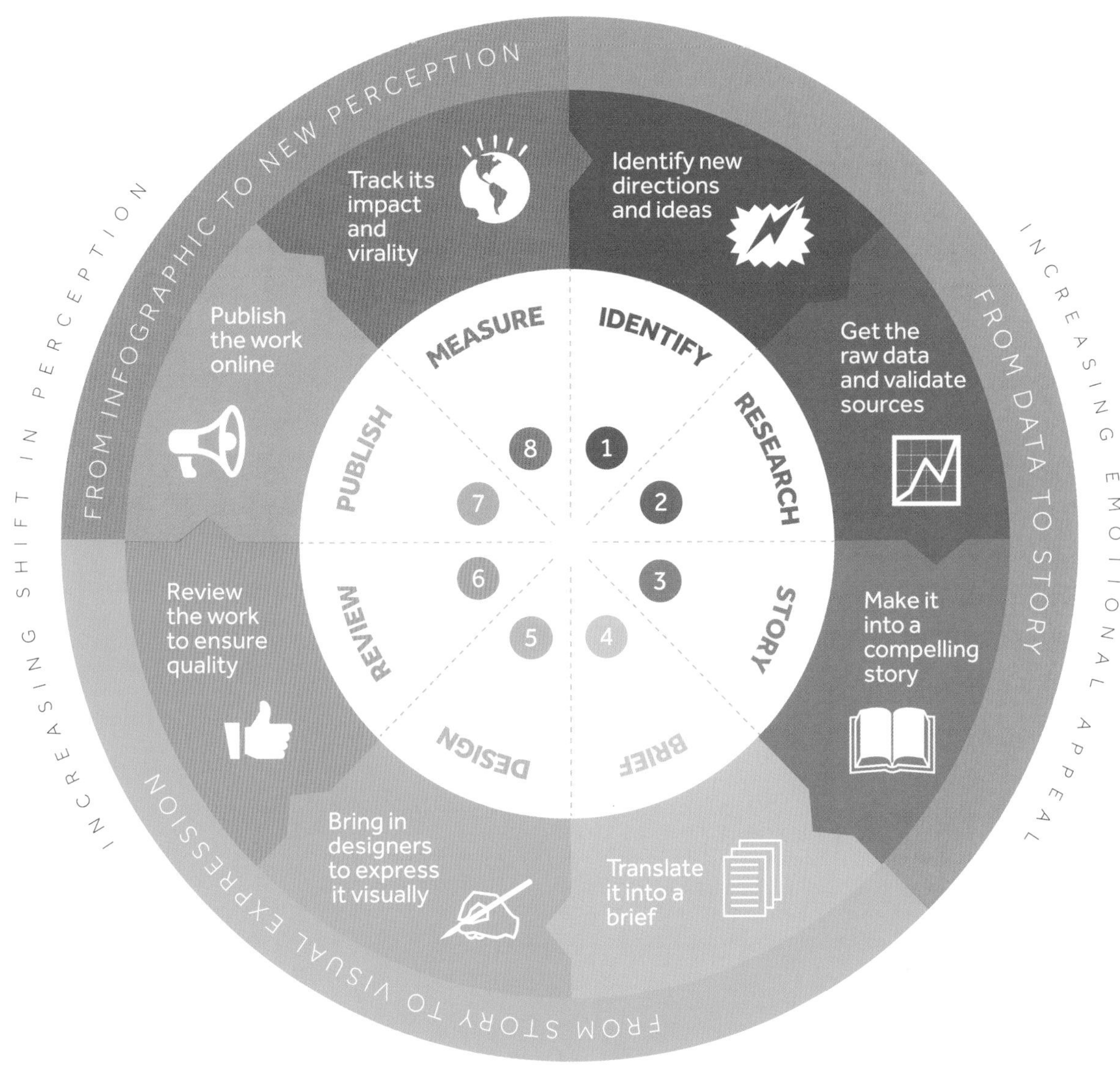
FROM INFOGRAPHIC TO NEW PERCEPTION
INCREASING SHIFT IN PERCEPTION
FROM DATA TO STORY
INCREASING EMOTIONAL APPEAL
FROM STORY TO VISUAL EXPRESSION
Identify new directions and ideas
Get the raw data and validate sources
Make it into a compelling story
Translate it into a brief
Bring in designers to express it visually
Review the work to ensure quality
Publish the work online
Track its impact and virality
IDENTIFY
RESEARCH
STORY
BRIEF
DESIGN
REVIEW
PUBLISH
MEASURE
1
2
3
4
5
6
7
8
CONCEPTION
PRODUCTION
RECEPTION

PROCESS WHEEL

Brief and copywriting: Joumana al Jabri, Hani Asfour, Ahmad Barclay, Ramzi Jaber
Design: Hani Asfour, Patil Tchilinguirian

SKETCHES

Exports
Farmers
AGRICULTURE
FURNITURE
GARMENT
2005
GAZA'S ECONOMIC COLLAPSE
Exports
2016
45% UNEMPLOYED
HOW AIRBNB
Paleslinian house
Israelis build settlements &
An Average Day in the "STATE OF PALESTINE"
ISRAEL CONTROLS
Water
Acess
Internet & Comm.
Currency
Gasoline
Legal System
Population Registry
Comm.
Import & export
Movement & immigration
PALESTINIAN Controls

ENIFITS FROM OCCUPATION
Israeli millitiants expels palestinians from land
Beautifull house with a view
Settlers list on AirBnB
HOW AIRBNB PROFITS FROM ISRAEL'S OCCUPATION
② No palestinians allowed
PAL
③ Built on a Stolen land
WATCHED!
160 ft tall
7.5 miles
border drawn by the US in 1854
xxxx citizens in Mexico
xxxx citizens in USA
O'odham community
Data point 1
Data Point 2
Data pt 3
THE CHRISTIAN POPULATION HAS FALLEN FROM 80-12% IN JUST 50 YEARS
1.
2.
3.
4.
5.
6.

RESISTANCE FROM A DISTANCE
Exile
South Africa
Years
1960
1961
1963
1964
JUN 2016
JUL 2015
UNITED METHODIST CHURCH
MAR 2016
CATHOLIC CONFERENCE OF MAJOR SUPERIORS & MEN
APR 2016
UNITARIAN UNIVERSALIST CHURCH
AUG 2016
ALLIANCE OF BAPTISTS
AUG 2016
EVANGELICAL LUTHERAN CHURCH
JULY 2017
MENONITE CHURCH.
CHRISTIANS UNITED AGAINST APARTHEID
DATA SKETCH SOURCES
Palestinian Doctors
52%
48%
Denial rate %
60%
50%
40%
30%
20%
2017
2013
NAME:
STATUS:
Distance from husband 65km
Status:

NAME AMANI
STATUS WIFE
Distance from husband: 65 km
Separated for: 4 years
WEST BANK ID
JERUSALEM RESIDENCY
Option 2-1 (Simpler version)
One linear story flow
Stop motion with papers
Audio
Collage
Atlas of Palestine
text only
kids growing without father
(kids depicted as flowers)

ACKNOWLEDGMENTS

The visuals in this book are a reflection of the efforts of countless people and the vision, ideas, spaces, processes, and possibilities we build together. Thank you.

Cofounders

Joumana al Jabri, *architect, codirector 2011–2020*
Ramzi Jaber, *engineer, codirector 2011–2020*

Early Partners

Several people played a foundational role in defining Visualizing Palestine's direction and strategy: Hani Asfour, *architect, information designer* | Ahmad Barclay, *architect, visual communicator* | Naji El Mir, *designer, visual artist*

Team (2023)

Aline Batarseh, *executive director* | Nasreen Abd Elal, *information designer* Jessica Anderson, *deputy director* | Yosra El Gazzar, *art director* | Maura James Dooley, *fundraising manager* | Sandy Nassif, *administrator* | Rasha Sansur, *outreach specialist*

Board of Directors (2023)

Fateh Azzam, *chair* | Lara Nasser, *treasurer* | Lena El-Malak, *secretary*
Nora Lester Murad, *member* | Rehab Nazzal, *member*

Various Visualizing Palestine team members and partners in Amman, Jordan, 2018

Former Team (2011–2022)
Saeed Abu-Jaber, *information designer* | Yazan Al-Saadi, *researcher* | Iman Annab, *project manager* | Zaid Amr, *researcher* | Leena Barakat, *head of development* | Bassam Barham, *web developer* | Tamara Ben-Halim, *communications and impact tracking* | Livia Caruso, *researcher* | Thoraya El-Rayyes, *project manager* | Reem Farah, *researcher* | Christopher Fiorello, *project manager* | Kelsey Gallagher, *researcher* | Shorouq Ghneim, *information designer* | Ahmad Ghunaim, *technology advisor* | Nussayba Hammad, *researcher* | Joanne Harik, *information designer* | Robin Jones, *researcher* | Diala Lteif, *project manager* | Mary Rizk, *creative community associate* | Nathalie Sabatier, *operations manager* | Abd El Samiea Talaat, *web developer* | Tamara Sawaya, *project manager* | Fadi Shayya, *operations strategist, project manager* | Luma Shihab-Eldin, *designer (logo/branding)* | Hana Sleiman, *researcher* | Mathana, *project manager* | Morad Taleeb, *web developer* | Shireen Tawil, *researcher* | Julia Tierney, *research fellow* | Patil Tchilinguirian, *information designer, visual communicator* | Tamara Qiblawi, *project manager* | Henry Zaccak, *technology advisor*

Extended network
An expansive community has accompanied various stages of Visualizing Palestine's work. While this book features a selection of visuals, it would take another book to fully capture all the people who have made some part of Visualizing Palestine possible, in ways large and small. Thank you for your

passion, expertise, encouragement, and generosity. Connecting with you has been a source of learning, growth, and meaning as we navigate how to work toward the just future we collectively imagine.

Researchers and knowledge creators
Each visual in this book includes a source link with detailed citations. We are grateful to every researcher, intellectual, writer, human rights expert, organization, academic, journalist, and analyst involved in building what Paulo Freire calls "knowledge in solidarity with action." Thanks to you, no one can claim ignorance for their role in the oppression of Palestinians.

Collaborators & partners
Numerous people have collaborated with the Visualizing Palestine team as consultants, partners, interns, or short-term contributors. Many are named in the credits throughout this book, while many others were active behind the scenes, enabling space for our work.

Arabic translation
Most VP resources are published in English and Arabic. Multiple translators have worked with us over the years to make this possible, with coordination support from Sandy Nassif, Rasha Sansur, and other team members.

Volunteers and pro bono contributors
Volunteers have participated in data entry, research, outreach, event planning, translations, information design, illustration, web development, fundraising, and more. Our visuals are available in twenty languages beyond English and Arabic, thanks entirely to volunteer translators. Many people have also opened their homes to various Visualizing Palestine team members or have helped connect us to collaborators. We're grateful for the skills and commitment each volunteer brings not only to our work, but to the broader movement.

Visualizing Palestine members and donors
Visualizing Palestine is in large part community-funded. At least 1,185 people have been active as Visualizing Palestine members at some point between 2017–2023, meaning they pledged a recurring monthly or annual contribution to support Visualizing Palestine. Including other types of donations (one-time, major donors), over 2,100 individuals have contributed financially so far, as well as several foundations. Thank you!

Visualizing Palestine advisors
Thirteen people have served on Visualizing Palestine's advisory committee over the years, contributing strategic feedback and insight through multiple chapters of our work and helping shape Visualizing Palestine into the organization it is today.

Book contributors
Thank you to those who offered encouragement, feedback, and support as

we compiled our first book. We want to particularly thank Elizabeth Eggert for proofreading visuals; Joumana al Jabri, Remi Kanazi, Ramzi Jaber, Racha Mourtada, Todd Reisz, Lana Shamma, and Lena El-Malak for sharing their insights and encouragement early on in our process; Fateh Azzam, Ahmad Barclay, Lena El-Malak, Reem Farah, Nora Lester Murad, Amir Naddaf, and Rehab Nazzal for feedback on the draft manuscript; and the entire team at Haymarket for their vision and patience as we brought this collection together.

A note on credits

Throughout this book, we have credited people closely involved in the brief and visual development of each visual, as well as citing sources for the information in the visuals (via source links). The editors of this volume were responsible for curating the credits, with reference to internal documentation kept by various team members over the years. Credits were reviewed by several current and former Visualizing Palestine team members and partners. We made efforts to contact every person credited to offer the opportunity to review. Since not all were reachable or available to review, these credits may be incomplete or contain oversights, which are unintentional. We are thankful to each person who has made a mark on these stories, either directly or from a distance.

ENDNOTES

Introduction

1. Harriet Sherwood, "Palestinian Hunger Striker Khader Adnan 'Near Death' in Israeli Detention," *Guardian*, February 16, 2012, https://www.theguardian.com/world/2012/feb/16/khader-adnan-palestinian-hunger-strike.
2. Amnesty International, "Israel/OPT: Death of Khader Adnan Highlights Israel's Cruel Treatment of Palestinian Prisoners," May 3, 2023, https://www.amnesty.org/en/latest/news/2023/05/israel-opt-death-of-khader-adnan-highlights-israels-cruel-treatment-of-palestinian-prisoners/.
3. Amnesty International, "Israel/OPT: Death of Khader Adnan."
4. UN Office of the High Commissioner for Human Rights, "Israel: UN Experts Condemn Record Year of Israeli Violence in the Occupied West Bank," December 15, 2023, https://www.ohchr.org/en/press-releases/2022/12/israel-un-experts-condemn-record-year-israeli-violence-occupied-west-bank.
5. Al-Haq, "The Raid on Al-Haq's Offices: 18 August 2022," September 18, 2022, https://www.alhaq.org/monitoring-documentation/20580.html.
6. Raz Segal, "A Textbook Case of Genocide," *Jewish Currents*, October 13, 2023, https://jewishcurrents.org/a-textbook-case-of-genocide.

1. Settler Colonialism

1. Patrick Wolfe, "Settler Colonialism and the Elimination of the Native," *Journal of Genocide Research* 8, no. 4 (December 2006): 387–409.
2. Edward W. Said, "Zionism from the Standpoint of Its Victims." *Social Text*, no. 1 (1979): 7–58.
3. Michael J. Cohen, *Britain's Moment in Palestine: Retrospect and Perspectives, 1917–1948* (Milton Park, UK: Routledge, 2015).
4. Yousef Munayyer "It's Time to Admit That Arthur Balfour Was a White Supremacist—and an Anti-Semite Too," Institute for Palestine Studies, November 1, 2017, https://www.palestine-studies.org/en/node/232119.
5. UN Information System on the Question of Palestine, "Origins and Evolution of the Palestine Problem: 1917–1947 (Part I)," https://www.un.org/unispal/history2/origins-and-evolution-of-the-palestine-problem/part-i-1917-1947.
6. Theodor Herzl, *The Jewish State* (New York: Dover, 1968), 85–96.
7. Herzl, *The Jewish State*.
8. Paulo Freire, *Pedagogy of the Oppressed* (New York: Continuum International Publishing Group, 2005).
9. Center for Constitutional Rights, "Israel's Unfolding Crime of Genocide of the Palestinian People & U.S. Failure to Prevent and Complicity in Genocide," October 18, 2023, https://ccrjustice.org/sites/default/files/attach/2023/10/Israels-Unfolding-Crime_ww.pdf.

2. The Ongoing Nakba

1. Peace Now, "Jerusalem Municipal Data Reveals Stark Israeli-Palestinian Discrepancy in Construction Permits in Jerusalem," December 9, 2019, https://peacenow.org.il/en/jerusalem-municipal-data-reveals-stark-israeli-palestinian-discrepancy-in-construction-permits-in-jerusalem.
2. UN Relief and Works Agency for Palestine Refugees in the Near East, "Syria: 10 Years of Multiple Hardships for Palestinian Refugees," March 15, 2021, https://www.unrwa.org/newsroom/press-releases/syria-10-years-multiple-hardships-palestine-refugees.
3. Philippe Lazzarini, "Hitting Rock Bottom: Palestine Refugees in Lebanon Risk Their Lives in Search of Dignity," October 21, 2022, https://www.un.org/unispal/document/hitting-rock-bottom-palestine-refugees-in-lebanon-risk-their-lives-in-search-of-dignity-unrwa-press-release.
4. UN General Assembly, "194 (III). Palestine - Progress Report of the United Nations Mediator," December 11, 1948, https://www.refworld.org/docid/4fe2e5672.html.
5. Salman Abu Sitta, "Palestine: Reversing Ethnic Cleansing," lecture at the American University of Beirut, January 14, 2010, https://www.aub.edu.lb/ifi/Documents/events/2010/20100114ifi_abu_sitta_transcript.pdf.

3. Recognizing Apartheid

1. Chris McGreal, "Brothers in Arms: Israel's Secret Pact with Pretoria," *Guardian*, February 7, 2006, https://www.theguardian.com/world/2006/feb/07/southafrica.israel.
2. Nelson Mandela, "Address by President Nelson Mandela at International Day of Solidarity with Palestinian People, Pretoria," December 4, 1997, https://web.archive.org/web/20230622032012/www.mandela.gov.za/mandela_speeches/1997/971204_palestinian.htm.
3. Chris McGreal, "When Desmond Tutu Stood Up for the Rights of Palestinians, He Could Not Be Ignored," *Guardian*, December 30, 2021, https://www.theguardian.com/commentisfree/2021/dec/30/desmond-tutu-palestinians-israel.
4. Patrick Wolfe, "Settler Colonialism and the Elimination of the Native," *Journal of Genocide Research* 8, no. 4 (December 2006): 387–409.
5. "Senior U.N. Official Quits after 'Apartheid' Israel Report Pulled," Reuters, March 17, 2017, https://www.reuters.com/article/us-un-israel-report-resignation-idUSKBN16O24X/.
6. UN Economic and Social Commission for Western Asia, "Israeli Practices towards the Palestinian People and the Question of Apartheid," 2017, https://electronicintifada.net/sites/default/files/2017-03/un_apartheid_report_15_march_english_final_.pdf.
7. Jerusalem Municipality, "Local Outline Plan Jerusalem 2000," August 2004, https://www.alhaq.org/cached_uploads/download/alhaq_files/en/wp-content/uploads/2018/03/LocalOutlinePlanJerusalem2000.pdf.
8. Alaa Tartir, "The Palestinian Authority Security Forces: Whose Security?" Al-Shabaka: The Palestinian Policy

Network, May 16, 2017, https://al-shabaka.org/summaries/palestinian-authority-security-forces-whose-security.
9. Human Rights Watch, "A Threshold Crossed: Israeli Authorities and the Crimes of Apartheid and Persecution," April 27, 2021, https://www.hrw.org/report/2021/04/27/threshold-crossed/israeli-authorities-and-crimes-apartheid-and-persecution.
10. B'Tselem, "A Regime of Jewish Supremacy from the Jordan River to the Mediterranean Sea: This Is Apartheid," January 12, 2021, https://www.btselem.org/publications/fulltext/202101_this_is_apartheid.
11. Amnesty International, "Israel's Apartheid against Palestinians: Cruel System of Domination and Crime against Humanity," February 1, 2022, https://www.amnesty.org/en/documents/mde15/5141/2022/en/.
12. UN Human Rights Council, "Special Rapporteur on the Situation of Human Rights in the Occupied Palestinian Territories: Israel Has Imposed upon Palestine an Apartheid Reality in a Post-Apartheid World," March 25, 2022, https://www.ohchr.org/en/press-releases/2022/03/special-rapporteur-situation-human-rights-occupied-palestinian-territories.

4. Navigating Apartheid

1. Routes from Yitzhar to Itamar and Huwara to Kaf Qalil were searched on August 4, 2023, on https://www.google.com/maps. Route suggestions often change over time.
2. International Court of Justice, "Legal Consequences of the Construction of a Wall in the Occupied Palestinian Territory," December 8, 2003, https://www.icj-cij.org/case/131.
3. "Palestinian 'Freedom Riders' Board Settlers' Bus," BBC, November 15, 2011, https://www.bbc.com/news/world-middle-east-15744576.
4. UN Office for the Coordination of Humanitarian Affairs, "Longstanding Access Restrictions Continue to Undermine the Living Conditions of West Bank Palestinians," June 8, 2020, https://ochaopt.org/content/longstanding-access-restrictions-continue-undermine-living-conditions-west-bank--palestinians.
5. Kate, "Palestinian Worker Is Crushed to Death at Overcrowded Checkpoint," *Mondoweiss*, January 3, 2015, https://mondoweiss.net/2015/01/palestinian-crushed-overcrowded-checkpoint.
6. Nadera Shalhoub-Kevorkian, "The Politics of Birth and the Intimacies of Violence against Palestinian Women in Jerusalem," *British Journal of Criminology* 55, no. 6 (May 2015): 1187–1206.
7. UN Human Rights Council, "Report of the United Nations High Commissioner for Human Rights on the Issue of Palestinian Pregnant Women Giving Birth at Israeli Checkpoints," March 17, 2010, https://www.refworld.org/docid/4bc57f562.html.
8. Access Now, "Gaza's Last Link Is Gone: Civil Society Urges Immediate Reversal of Total Communications Blackout Now Shrouding Human Rights Harms," October 27, 2023, https://www.accessnow.org/press-release/reverse-total-communications-blackout-gaza/.

5. Gaza

1. UN Relief and Works Agency for Palestine Refugees in the Near East, "Refugee Needs in the Gaza Strip," October 2018, https://www.ochaopt.org/sites/default/files/gaza_thematic_6_0.pdf.
2. UN Country Team in Palestine, "Gaza in 2020: A Liveable Place?," August 2012, https://www.unrwa.org/userfiles/file/publications/gaza/Gaza%20in%202020.pdf.
3. "Plans for Artificial Island off Gaza Coast in the Works," *Jerusalem Post*, May 22, 2016, https://www.jpost.com/annual-conference/plans-for-artificial-island-off-gaza-coast-in-the-works-says-intel-minister-katz-454721.
4. UN Relief and Works Agency for Palestine Refugees in the Near East, "Gaza—15 Years of Blockade," 2022, https://www.unrwa.org/gaza15-years-blockade.
5. Beryl Cheal, "Refugees in the Gaza Strip, December 1948–May 1950," *Journal of Palestine Studies* 18, no. 1 (1988): 138–57.
6. Al Mezan Center for Human Rights, "Attacks on Unarmed Protesters at the 'Great March of Return' Demonstrations," March 30, 2018, https://www.mezan.org/uploads/files/15952354571567.pdf.
7. Nelson Mandela, *Long Walk to Freedom: The Autobiography of Nelson Mandela* (New York: Back Bay Books, 1995).
8. Emma Farge, "Disease Could Be Bigger Killer than Bombs in Gaza - WHO," Reuters, November 28, 2023, https://www.reuters.com/world/middle-east/more-people-risk-death-disease-than-bombings-gaza-who-2023-11-28/.
9. Conal Urquhart, "Gaza on Brink of Implosion as Aid Cut-off Starts to Bite," *Guardian*, April 15, 2006, https://www.theguardian.com/world/2006/apr/16/israel.
10. "Israel Forced to Release Study on Gaza Blockade," BBC, October 17, 2012, https://www.bbc.com/news/world-middle-east-19975211.
11. UN Office for the Coordination of Humanitarian Affairs, "Movement in and out of Gaza in 2022," February 22, 2023, https://ochaopt.org/content/movement-and-out-gaza-2022.
12. Save the Children, "After 15 Years of Blockade, Four Out of Five Children in Gaza Say They Are Living with Depression, Grief, and Fear," June 15, 2022, https://www.savethechildren.net/news/after-15-years-blockade-four-out-five-children-gaza-say-they-are-living-depression-grief-and.
13. Yasmeen Khoudary, "Gaza Child: Three Wars Old," Al Jazeera, July 16, 2014, https://www.aljazeera.com/opinions/2014/7/16/gaza-child-three-wars-old.
14. Refaat Alareer, "My Child Asks, 'Can Israel Destroy Our Building if the Power Is Out?,'" *New York Times*, May 13, 2021, https://www.nytimes.com/2021/05/13/opinion/israel-gaza-rockets-airstrikes.html.
15. Heidi Morrison, "Shalhoub-Kevorkian, Incarcerated Childhood and the Politics of Unchilding," *Journal of Palestine Studies* 49, no. 3 (Spring 2020).
16. Morrison, "Shalhoub-Kevorkian."
17. "Public Statement: Scholars Warn of Potential Genocide in Gaza," *Third World Approaches to International Law Review*, October 17, 2023, https://

twailr.com/public-statement-scholars-warn-of-potential-genocide-in-gaza/.
18. Center for Constitutional Rights, "Emergency Legal Briefing Paper: Israel's Unfolding Crime of Genocide of the Palestinian People & U.S. Failure to Prevent and Complicity in Genocide," https://ccrjustice.org/sites/default/files/attach/2023/10/Israels-Unfolding-Crime_ww.pdf.
19. Center for Constitutional Rights, "Emergency Legal Briefing Paper."
20. Anne Paq and Ala Qandil, "Obliterated Families," 2016, https://obliteratedfamilies.com/en/.
21. Peter Beaumont, "Israel Exonerates Itself over Gaza Beach Killings of Four Children Last Year," *Guardian*, June 11, 2015, https://www.theguardian.com/world/2015/jun/11/israel-clears-military-gaza-beach-children.
22. International Criminal Court, "Statement of the ICC Prosecutor, Ms. Fatou Bensouda, on an Investigation into the Situation in Palestine," March 3, 2021, https://www.icc-cpi.int/fr/news/declaration-du-procureur-de-la-cpi-mme-fatou-bensouda-propos-dune-enquete-sur-la-situation-en.
23. Michael Arria, "We Are Witnessing the Largest U.S. Anti-War Protests in 20 Years," *Mondoweiss*, October 28, 2023, https://mondoweiss.net/2023/10/we-are-witnessing-the-largest-u-s-anti-war-protests-in-20-years/.
24. Melanie Yazzie, "March on Washington - The Red Nation Speech," November 4, 2023, https://www.youtube.com/watch?v=bi1l-fgB_xg.

6. Ecological Justice

1. American Near East Refugee Aid, "Gaza Situation Report," January 25, 2022, https://www.anera.org/wp-content/uploads/2022/02/Gaza-Flood-Situation-Report.pdf.
2. Naomi Klein, "Let Them Drown: The Violence of Othering in a Warming World," *London Review of Books* 38, no. 11 (2016), https://www.lrb.co.uk/the-paper/v38/n11/naomi-klein/let-them-drown.
3. UN Country Team in Palestine, "Gaza in 2020: A Liveable Place?," August 2012, https://www.unrwa.org/userfiles/file/publications/gaza/Gaza%20in%202020.pdf.
4. UN Environment Programme, "State of Environment and Outlook Report for the Occupied Palestinian Territory 2020," May 13, 2020, https://www.unep.org/resources/report/state-environment-and-outlook-report-occupied-palestinian-territory-2020.
5. Amnesty International, "Troubled Waters–Palestinians Denied Fair Access to Water," October 27, 2009, https://www.amnesty.org/en/latest/campaigns/2017/11/the-occupation-of-water.
6. Rosemary Sayigh, *The Palestinians: From Peasants to Revolutionaries* (London: Zed Books, 1979), xxiv.
7. MIFTAH, "Fact Sheet: Olive Trees–More Than Just a Tree in Palestine," November 21, 2012, https://reliefweb.int/report/occupied-palestinian-territory/fact-sheet-olive-trees-%E2%80%93-more-just-tree-palestine.
8. Zena Al Tahhan, "Israeli Forces Violently Suppress Palestinian Protest in Naqab," Al Jazeera, January 13, 2022, https://www.aljazeera.com/news/2022/1/13/israeli-forces-violently-suppress-palestinian-protest-in-naqab.
9. "'No Climate Justice without Human Rights': Groups Protest Inaction, Repression at U.N. Summit in Egypt," *Democracy Now!*, November 14, 2022, https://www.democracynow.org/2022/11/14/climate_justice_movement_human_rights_cop27.
10. Lee Yaron, "Israel's Herzog Arrives at COP27, Meets UAE President and King of Jordan," *Haaretz*, November 7, 2022, https://www.haaretz.com/science-and-health/climate-change/2022-11-07/ty-article/.premium/israels-herzog-arrives-at-cop27-meets-uae-president-and-king-of-jordan/00000184-51d8-d594-af9e-f7ff24b00000.

7. Political Prisoners

1. Addameer, "The Palestinian Prisoners of Israel," January 11, 2008, https://www.addameer.org/publications/palestinian-prisoners-israel.
2. Chaim Levinson, "Nearly 100% of All Military Court Cases in West Bank End in Conviction, *Haaretz* Learns," *Haaretz*, November 29, 2011, https://www.haaretz.com/2011-11-29/ty-article/nearly-100-of-all-military-court-cases-in-west-bank-end-in-conviction-haaretz-learns/0000017f-e7c4-da9b-a1ff-efef7ad70000.
3. No Way to Treat a Child, "Fact Sheet: Palestinian Children in Israeli Military Detention," May 5, 2023, https://nwttac.dci-palestine.org/fact_sheet_palestinian_children_in_israeli_military_detention.
4. David M. Halfinger, "Ahed Tamimi, Palestinian Teen, Gets 8 Months in Prison for Slapping Israeli Soldier," *New York Times*, March 21, 2018, https://www.nytimes.com/2018/03/21/world/middleeast/ahed-tamimi-palestinian-israel-soldier.html.
5. Nora Lester-Murad, "Interview with Ahed Tamimi, an Icon of the Palestinian Resistance," https://noralestermurad.com/interview-with-ahed-tamimi-an-icon-of-the-palestinian-resistance/.

8. A System of Silencing

1. Edward Said, "Permission to Narrate," *Journal of Palestine Studies* 13, no. 3 (1984): 27–48.
2. Mohammed El-Kurd, "The Right to Speak for Ourselves," *Nation*, November 27, 2023, https://www.thenation.com/article/world/palestinians-claim-the-right-to-narrate/.
3. Amnesty International, "50 Years of Israeli Occupation: Four Outrageous Facts about Military Order 101," August 25, 2017, https://www.amnesty.org/en/latest/campaigns/2017/08/50-years-of-israeli-occupation-four-outrageous-facts-about-military-order-101.
4. Adalah, "'Nakba Law' - Amendment No. 40 to the Budgets Foundations Law," https://www.adalah.org/en/law/view/496.
5. Amnesty International, "Israel/OPT: Flag Restrictions Are the Latest Attempt to Silence Palestinians and

Reduce Their Visibility," https://www.amnesty.org/en/latest/news/2023/01/israel-opt-flag-restrictions-are-the-latest-attempt-to-silence-palestinians-and-reduce-their-visibility/.

6. B'Tselem, "Lethal Use of Crowd Control Weapons: Seven Palestinians Killed in Great March of Return from Direct Teargas Canister Hits," August 6, 2019, https://www.btselem.org/press_releases/20190806_lethal_use_of_crowd_control_weapons_in_gaza.
7. Zena Al Tahhan, "Shireen Abu Akleh: Al Jazeera Reporter Killed by Israeli Forces," Al Jazeera, May 11, 2022, https://www.aljazeera.com/news/2022/5/11/shireen-abu-akleh-israeli-forces-kill-al-jazeera-journalist.
8. Committee to Protect Journalists, "Impunity for the Killers of Journalists at Nearly 80% on the International Day to End Impunity for Crimes against Journalists," November 2, 2023, https://cpj.org/thetorch/2023/11/impunity-for-the-killers-of-journalists-at-nearly-80-on-the-international-day-to-end-impunity-for-crimes-against-journalists/.
9. UN Human Rights, "Inquiry into the Killing of Mr. Jamal Khashoggi," https://www.ohchr.org/en/special-procedures/sr-executions/inquiry-killing-mr-jamal-kashoggi.
10. Dana Priest et al., "Jamal Khashoggi's Wife Targeted with Spyware before His Death," *Washington Post*, July 18, 2021, https://www.washingtonpost.com/investigations/interactive/2021/jamal-khashoggi-wife-fiancee-cellphone-hack.
11. Martin Luther King Jr., "Letter from a Birmingham Jail," April 16, 1963, https://www.africa.upenn.edu/Articles_Gen/Letter_Birmingham.html.

9. United States Complicity

1. Robert Mackey, "Ivanka Trump Opens U.S. Embassy in Jerusalem during Israeli Massacre of Palestinians in Gaza," *Intercept*, May 14, 2018, https://theintercept.com/2018/05/14/ivanka-trump-opens-u-s-embassy-jerusalem-israeli-massacre-palestinians.
2. Akbar Shahid Ahmed, "Stunning State Department Memo Warns Diplomats: No Gaza 'De-Escalation' Talk," *HuffPost*, October 13, 2023, https://www.yahoo.com/news/stunning-state-department-memo-warns-155722066.html.
3. Michael Arria, "The Shift: White House Press Secretary Calls Progressives Calling for Ceasefire 'Disgraceful' and 'Repugnant,'" *Mondoweiss*, October 13, 2023, https://mondoweiss.net/2023/10/the-shift-white-house-press-secretary-calls-progressives-calling-for-ceasefire-disgraceful-and-repugnant/.
4. White House, "Remarks by President Biden and Prime Minister Anthony Albanese of Australia in Joint Press Conference," October 25, 2023, https://www.whitehouse.gov/briefing-room/speeches-remarks/2023/10/25/remarks-by-president-biden-and-prime-minister-anthony-albanese-of-australia-in-joint-press-conference/.
5. Laura Kelly, "Death Toll in Gaza Likely 'Higher than Is Being Reported': US Official," *Hill*, November 9, 2023, https://thehill.com/policy/international/4301551-gaza-deaths-likely-higher-than-cited-us-official/?blm_aid=3599281153.
6. Associated Press, "White House Says 'Not Drawing Red Lines for Israel,'" October 27, 2023, https://www.timesofisrael.com/liveblog_entry/white-house-says-not-drawing-red-lines-for-israel/#:~:text=%E2%80%9CWe›re%20not%20drawing%20red,that%20they%20are%20doing%20this.%E2%80%9D.
7. Congressional Research Service, "U.S. Foreign Aid to Israel," March 1, 2023, https://sgp.fas.org/crs/mideast/RL33222.pdf.
8. Congressional Research Service, "U.S. Foreign Aid to Israel."
9. Uri Blau, "*Haaretz* Investigation: U.S. Donors Gave Settlements More than $220 Million in Tax-Exempt Funds over Five Years," *Haaretz*, December 7, 2015, https://www.haaretz.com/2015-12-07/ty-article/haaretz-investigates-u-s-donors-to-israeli-settlements/0000017f-f6bb-d460-afff-ffffd93e0000.
10. Patrick Wintour, "US Vetoes UN's Call for 'Humanitarian Pause' and Corridors into Gaza," *Guardian*, October 18, 2023, https://www.theguardian.com/world/2023/oct/18/us-vetoes-un-call-for-humanitarian-pause-and-corridors-into-gaza.

10. Corporate Complicity

1. UN Human Rights Office, "UN Rights Office Issues Report on Business Activities Related to Settlements in the Occupied Palestinian Territory," February 12, 2020, https://www.ohchr.org/en/press-releases/2020/02/un-rights-office-issues-report-business-activities-related-settlements.
2. UN, "The United Nations—Partner in the Struggle against Apartheid," https://www.un.org/en/events/mandeladay/un_against_apartheid.shtml.
3. Who Profits, "Technologies of Control: The Case of Hewlett Packard (HP)," December 2011, http://www.whoprofits.org/report/technologies-of-control-the-case-of-hewlett-packard-hp.
4. Who Profits, "The Case of G4S Private Security Companies and the Israeli Occupation," March 2011, https://whoprofits.org/report/the-case-of-g4s-private-security-companies-and-the-israeli-occupation.
5. Who Profits, "The Israeli Exploitation of Palestinian Natural Resources: Part II HeidelbergCement," November 2016, https://whoprofits.org/updates/the-israeli-exploitation-of-palestinian-natural-resources-part-ii-heidelberg-cement.
6. Human Rights Watch, "Bed and Breakfast on Stolen Land: Tourist Rental Listings in West Bank Settlements," November 20, 2018, https://www.hrw.org/report/2018/11/20/bed-and-breakfast-stolen-land/tourist-rental-listings-west-bank-settlements.
7. Airbnb, "Listings in Disputed Regions," November 19, 2018, https://news.airbnb.com/listings-in-disputed-regions.
8. Airbnb, "Update on Listings in Disputed Regions," April 9, 2019, https://news.airbnb.com/update-listings-disputed-regions.

9. "Norway: KLP Fund Divests from Firms Linked to Israeli Settlements," Al Jazeera, July 5, 2021, https://www.aljazeera.com/news/2021/7/5/norway-klp-fund-divests-from-firms-linked-to-israeli-settlements.
10. Israel Chemicals Ltd., "Release of Final Report Regarding the Israeli Governmental Actions Required in Preparation for the Expiration of the Dead Sea Concession Period," January 22, 2019, http://iclgroupv2.s3.amazonaws.com/corporate/wp-content/uploads/sites/1004/2019/01/Release-of-Final-Report-Regarding-the-Israeli-Governmental-Actions-Required-in-Preparation-for-the-Expiration-of-the-Dead-Sea-Concession-Period-January-22-2019.pdf
11. GRAIN, "The Fertiliser Trap: The Rising Cost of Farming's Addiction to Chemical Fertilisers," November 8, 2022, https://grain.org/en/article/6903-the-fertiliser-trap-the-rising-cost-of-farming-s-addiction-to-chemical-fertilisers.
12. "Pompeo Says U.S. to Mark Settlement Goods as 'Made in Israel,'" Reuters, November 19, 2020, https://www.reuters.com/article/uk-usa-pompeo-israel-settlements/pompeo-says-u-s-to-mark-settlement-goods-as-made-in-israel-idUKKBN27Z1O3.
13. Uri Blau and Josef Federman, "US Duty Free Magnates Fund Controversial Israeli Settlements," Associated Press, July 1, 2019, https://apnews.com/general-news-87e58e1f3779432fb353bb786794c6b7.
14. Canadians for Justice and Peace in the Middle East, "CJPME Welcomes Ruling That 'Product of Israel' Labels on Illegal Settlement Goods Are False and Unlawful," May 16, 2022, https://www.cjpme.org/pr_2022_05_16_settlement_wine.
15. Federica Martiny, "EU Signs €100m Drone Contract with Airbus and Israeli Arms Firms," October 22, 2020, https://www.euractiv.com/section/justice-home-affairs/news/eu-signs-contract-with-airbus-and-israeli-arms-companies-to-spot-migrant-boats-with-drones.
16. Palestinian BDS National Committee, "BDS Marks Another Victory as Veolia Sells Off All Israeli Operations," September 1, 2015, https://bdsmovement.net/news/bds-marks-another-victory-veolia-sells-all-israeli-operations.

11. Boycott, Divestment, and Sanctions

1. Shatha Hammad, "Stories from the First Intifada: 'They Broke My Bones,'" Al Jazeera, December 10, 2017, https://www.aljazeera.com/news/2017/12/10/stories-from-the-first-intifada-they-broke-my-bones.
2. Efraim Inbar and Eitan Shamir, "Mowing the Grass in Gaza," *Jerusalem Post*, July 22, 2014, https://www.jpost.com/opinion/columnists/mowing-the-grass-in-gaza-368516.
3. "Palestinian Civil Society Call for BDS," July 9, 2005, https://bdsmovement.net/call.
4. "Mandela Off U.S. Terrorism Watch List," CNN, July 1, 2008, https://www.cnn.com/2008/WORLD/africa/07/01/mandela.watch.
5. Kairos Palestine, "Kairos Document: A Moment of Truth, A Word of Faith, Hope and Love from the Heart of Palestinian Suffering," 2009, https://www.kairospalestine.ps/index.php/about-kairos/kairos-palestine-document.
6. "FIFA and UEFA Suspend Russia From International Football," Al Jazeera, February 28, 2022, https://www.aljazeera.com/news/2022/2/28/russia-expelled-from-world-cup-clubs-banned-from-competitions.
7. Omar Barghouti, "We Shouldn't Fear Being 'Divisive' in Pursuit of Justice," *Nation*, June 16, 2023, https://www.thenation.com/article/activism/bds-divisiveness-ethics.

12. Special Projects

1. "Israel Says 6,000 Bombs Dropped on Gaza as War with Hamas Nears a Week," Al Jazeera, October 12, 2023, https://www.aljazeera.com/news/2023/10/12/israel-says-6000-bombs-dropped-on-gaza-as-war-with-hamas-nears-a-week.
2. "Israel Announces 'Total' Blockade on Gaza," Al Jazeera, October 9, 2023, https://www.aljazeera.com/news/2023/10/9/israel-announces-total-blockade-on-gaza.
3. Raz Segal, "A Textbook Case of Genocide," *Jewish Currents*, October 13, 2023, https://jewishcurrents.org/a-textbook-case-of-genocide/
4. "Biden Says He Has 'No Confidence' in Palestinian Death Count," Reuters, October 25, 2023, https://www.reuters.com/world/middle-east/biden-says-he-has-no-confidence-palestinian-death-count-2023-10-26/.
5. Laura Kelly, "Death Toll in Gaza Likely 'Higher Than Is Being Reported': US Official," *Hill*, November 9, 2023, https://thehill.com/policy/international/4301551-gaza-deaths-likely-higher-than-cited-us-official.

INDEX

ABOUT THE EDITORS

Jessica Anderson is a human rights researcher based in Michigan. She was a first-year undergraduate during the 2008/2009 Israeli assault on Gaza, and a graduate student in refugee studies during Israel's 2012 bombardment, events that shaped her political consciousness and activism. She joined the Visualizing Palestine team in 2013, where she serves as deputy director.

Aline Batarseh is Palestinian, from Jerusalem. She has more than twenty years of experience working with several Palestinian and international nonprofits focused on advancing gender equality, reproductive justice, children's rights, mental health, social justice, and collective liberation. Aline joined the Visualizing Palestine team as executive director in 2021.

Yosra El Gazzar is a visual artist and graphic designer based in Cairo, Egypt. She joined the Visualizing Palestine team in 2016, where she is now the artistic director. Yosra holds a BA in applied sciences and arts from the German University in Cairo, and she was a part of Moutheqat/Women in Dox documentary program in Tunisia. Since then she has participated in various international exhibitions and art residencies.